TO BE CONTINUED . . .

To Be Continued . . . explores the world's most popular form of television drama, the soap opera. From Denver to Delhi, Moscow to Manchester, audiences eagerly await the next episode of *As the World Turns*, *The Rich Also Weep* or *EastEnders*. But the popularity of soap operas in Britain and the USA pales in comparison to the role that they play in media cultures in other parts of the world.

To Be Continued . . . investigates both the cultural specificity of television soap operas and their reception in other cultures, covering soap production and soap watching in the USA, Asia, Europe, Australia, and Latin America. The contributors consider the nature of soap as a media text, the history of the serial narrative as a form, and the role of the soap opera in the development of feminist media criticism.

To Be Continued . . . presents the first scholarly examination of soap opera as global media phenomenon.

The editor: Robert C. Allen is James Logan Godfrey Professor of American Studies, and Associate Dean of the College of Arts and Sciences at the University of North Carolina at Chapel Hill. He is the author of *Horrible Prettiness: Burlesque and American Culture* and *Speaking of Soap Operas*, co-author with Douglas Gomery of *Film History: Theory and Practice*, and editor of *Channels of Discourse* and *Channels of Discourse, Reassembled*.

TO BE CONTINUED . . .

Soap operas around the world

Edited by Robert C. Allen

London and New York

First published 1995
by Routledge
11 New Fetter Lane, London EC4P 4EE

Simultaneously published in the USA and Canada
by Routledge
29 West 35th Street, New York, NY 10001

Typeset in Times by
Ponting–Green Publishing Services, Chesham, Bucks
Printed in Great Britain by
TJ Press (Padstow) Ltd, Padstow, Cornwall

British Library Cataloguing in Publication Data
A catalogue record for this book is available from
the British Library

Library of Congress Cataloging in Publication Data
To be continued: soap operas around the world/edited by
Robert C. Allen.
p. cm.
Includes bibliographical references and index.
1. Soap operas–Social aspects
I. Allen, Robert Clyde.
PN1992.8.S4T6   1994
302.23'45–dc20   94–11394

ISBN 0–415–11006–8 (hbk)
ISBN 0–415–11007–6 (pbk)

Contents

List of contributors   vii
Acknowledgments   ix

Introduction   1
Robert C. Allen

1   Doubtless to be continued: A brief history of serial narrative   27
    Roger Hagedorn

2   The role of soap opera in the development of feminist television
    scholarship   49
    Charlotte Brunsdon

3   Social issues and realist soaps: A study of British soaps in
    the 1980s/1990s   66
    Christine Geraghty

4   National and cultural identity in a Welsh-language soap opera   81
    Alison Griffiths

5   Global *Neighbours*?   98
    Stephen Crofts

6   The end of civilization as we knew it: *Chances* and the postrealist
    soap opera   122
    Ien Ang and Jon Stratton

7   "I'm not a doctor, but I play one on TV": Characters, actors and
    acting in television soap opera   145
    Jeremy G. Butler

8   Plotting Paternity: Looking for dad on the daytime soaps   164
    Laura Stempel Mumford

9   "They killed off Marlena, but she's on another show now":
    Fantasy, reality, and pleasure in watching daytime soap operas 182
    Louise Spence

CONTENTS

10 "There's a queer in my soap!": The homophobia/AIDS story-line of *One Life to Live* 199
   Joy V. Fuqua

11 The consumption of soap opera: *The Young and the Restless* and mass consumption in Trinidad 213
   Daniel Miller

12 Not all "soaps" are created equal: Toward a cross-cultural criticism of television serials 234
   Gabriele Kreutzner and Ellen Seiter

13 Our welcomed guests: Telenovelas in Latin America 256
   Ana M. Lopez

14 Memory and form in the Latin American soap opera 276
   Jesús Martín-Barbero

15 Montezuma's revenge: Reading *Los Ricos También Lloran* in Russia 285
   Kate Baldwin

16 The melodrama of national identity in post-Tiananmen China 301
   Lisa Rofel

17 All in the (Raghu) family: A video epic in cultural context 321
   Philip Lutgendorf

18 Sacred serials, devotional viewing, and domestic worship: A case-study in the interpretation of two TV versions of *The Mahabharata* in a Hindu family in west London 354
   Marie Gillespie

   Select Bibliography 381
   Shari A. Novek

   Index 388

Contributors

Robert C. Allen teaches American studies and media studies at the University of North Carolina at Chapel Hill.

Ien Ang teaches media studies at Murdoch University in Australia.

Kate Baldwin is a Ph.D. candidate in Comparative Literature at Yale University.

Charlotte Brunsdon teaches film and media studies at the University of Warwick.

Jeremy G. Butler teaches film and media studies at the University of Alabama.

Stephen Crofts teaches film and media studies at Griffith University in Australia.

Joy V. Fuqua is a Ph.D. candidate in media studies at the University of Pittsburgh.

Christine Geraghty teaches media studies at Goldsmiths' College, University of London.

Marie Gillespie teaches media studies at the University of Cardiff.

Alison Griffiths is a Ph.D. candidate in Cinema Studies at New York University.

Roger Hagedorn teaches film and media studies at the University of South Dakota.

Gabriele Kreutzner is a freelance media scholar based in Germany.

Ana M. Lopez teaches film and media studies at Tulane University.

Philip Lutgendorf teaches in the Department of Asian Languages and Literature at the University of Iowa.

Jesús Martín-Barbero teaches media studies at the Universidád del Valle Cuidad Universitaria Meléndez in Cali, Colombia.

Daniel Miller teaches anthropology at University College London.

Shari A. Novek is a graduate student in communication studies at the University of North Carolina at Chapel Hill.

Lisa Rofel teaches anthropology at the University of California at Santa Cruz.

Ellen Seiter teaches film and media studies at the University of Indiana.

Louise Spence teaches film and media studies at Sacred Heart College, Fairfield, Connecticut.

Laura Stempel Mumford is an independent scholar based in Madison, Wisconsin.

Jon Stratton teaches media studies at Edith Cowan University in Perth, Australia.

Acknowledgments

The editor wishes to thank Aaron Hoffman and Sarah Doig for their help with this project.

Permission to reprint copyright material from the following sources is gratefully acknowledged:
An earlier version of Chapter 3 appeared in Dominic Strinati and Stephen Wagg (eds) *Come on Down: Popular Media Culture in Post-War Britain*, London, Routledge: 1992. Chapter 4 was originally presented at ITSC 91 and was first published in Phillip Drummond, Richard Paterson and Janet Willis (eds), *National Identity and Europe: The Television Revolution*, BFI: 1993. A shorter version of Chapter 5 has appeared in *Tomorrow Never Knows: Soap on Australian Television, Moving Image* no. 3, Melbourne, Australian Film Institute: 1994. A shorter version of Chapter 6 was first published in *Metro*, Winter 1993, pp. 8–16. Chapter 7 was first published in *Cinema Journal*, Vol. 30: 4 (Summer 1991), pp. 75–91, University of Texas Press, copyright © 1991. By permission of the University of Texas Press. Chapter 8 was first published in *Genders*, Vol. 12 (Winter 1991), pp. 45–61, University of Texas press, copyright © 1991. By permission of the University of Texas Press. Chapter 12 was first published in *Screen*, Vol. 32, no. 2. Chapter 14 is a re-writing of the first chapters of *Televisión y Melodrama*, Jesús Martín-Barbero, Bogota, Tercer Mundo Editores: 1992. Chapter 16 is a version, with substantial changes, of an article first printed in *American Ethnologist*, Vol. 21, no. 4 (1994). By kind permission of the American Anthropological Association. Chapter 17 was originally written for a conference on "Religion and Media in South Asia" sponsored by the Social Science Research Council and held in Carmel, California in 1989. A longer version of it appeared under the title "Ramayan: the Video!" in *The Drama Review*, Vol. 34, no. 2 (summer 1990). The present version also appears in the volume which grew out of the Carmel conference, Lawrence A. Babb and Susan S. Wadley (eds) *New Modulations: South Asian Religions and Modern Communications Media*, Philadelphia, University of Pennsylvania Press: in press, and is reprinted here by kind permission of the editors of that volume.

Introduction

Robert C. Allen

This is a collection of essays about a form of television drama being watched (quite literally) at this very moment by tens of millions of people around the world. Whether called soap operas, soaps, telenovelas, *teleromans*, or, as my mother calls them, simply "my stories," television serials together constitute one of the most popular and resilient forms of storytelling ever devised. In some television cultures (Russia, China, Italy, Germany), serials are relatively new phenomena. In others (the US, Great Britain, Australia, and several countries of Latin America), they have been staples of broadcast programming since the early days of radio. Some serials eventually end (if only after hundreds of episodes). Others, even after a half-century of continuous unfolding, are no closer to their characters living "happily ever after" than when the first episode was broadcast.

Whether set in a middle-class American suburb, a Welsh village, nineteenth-century Rio, or the sacred time and place of Hindu myth, television serials are linked – in the way they are constructed, broadcast and watched – by their distinctive serial narrational structure. A serial narrative is not merely a narrative that has been segmented, but one whose segmentation produces an interruption in the reading, listening, or viewing process. Furthermore, that interruption is controlled by the producer or distributor of the narrative, not by the reader. In other words, the producer of the narrative determines not only how and when the narration of the story stops and starts, but also how and when the reader's engagement with the text stops and starts.

As Roger Hagedorn points out in his chapter, the serialization of narrative long predates the broadcast soap opera. Indeed, the rise of the literary serial narrative in the eighteenth century marks a crucial turning-point in the development of both literature and publishing. By the 1850s serialization had become a standard means of publishing novels in Europe and America. Most of Dickens's readers during his lifetime read his works as magazine serials not published books. One of the key institutional roles of the serial form has been to exploit new technologies of narrative production and distribution. Serialized novels in the nineteenth century helped build consumer demand for mass circulation newspapers and magazines, which had themselves been

1

made possible by the development of high-speed presses. Serial comic strips facilitated the exploitation of high-speed color printing around the turn of the century. Movie serials helped to build a regular audience for the cinema in the 1910s.

Serial narrative was also crucial to the development of national broadcasting systems in a number of countries, and no more so than in the US. Devised around 1930 as one of a number of programming strategies to lure women to daytime radio and advertisers to program sponsorship, within only a few years soap operas proved to be one of the most effective broadcasting advertising vehicles ever devised. By 1940, the sixty-four serials broadcast on network radio constituted 92 percent of all sponsored programs during daytime hours. The ten highest-rated daytime programs were all serials. In 1948, of the thirty top-rated daytime radio programs, all but five were serials.[1] Serials have dominated daytime television schedules in the US since the 1950s. Several serials have run continuously for twenty-five years, and one, *Guiding Light*, has been seen or heard (with a short gap in the 1940s) since 1937, making it the longest story ever told.

Although the fashion for prime-time serials in the US has waxed and waned since the astonishing success of *Peyton Place* in the mid-1960s and the global popularity of *Dallas* and *Dynasty* in the 1980s, daytime serials are no less important to broadcasters today than they were half a century ago and are certainly no less popular. It is estimated that over half of all US women living in homes with television sets "keep up" with at least one soap opera. Such sustained and loyal viewership among women between the ages of 18 and 35 provides the basis for soap opera's enormous profitability for US network broadcasters.

The contemporary popularity of serials in the US is overshadowed by what popular journalists have taken to describing as outbreaks of "soapmania" in other parts of the world. As Lisa Rofel discusses in her chapter, the most popular and talked about television program in China in 1991 was *Kewang* (*Yearnings* or *Expectations*), which was, according to the *Washington Post*, "the biggest hit on television in Chinese history." Telenovelas constitute half of the total output of Televisa, Mexico's largest communications company, and in 1991 one Televisa serial was watched by 70 percent of the population with access to television. Most Latin American television systems broadcast a dozen or more telenovelas each weekday, and they consistently produce higher viewership than any other form of programming – domestic or imported. In Brazil, choice prime-time slots are reserved for serials, which can be expected to attract an audience of up to 40 million viewers.[2]

Philip Lutgendorf examines what is perhaps the most striking demonstration of the popularity of serial television: the seventy-two part weekly serialization of the Hindu religious epic *Ramayan* broadcast in India in 1987–1988 and regularly watched by an audience of 80 to 100 million people. Broadcast on Sunday mornings, the popularity of the *Ramayan* prompted students at a number of schools to demonstrate against the scheduling of examinations on Sunday mornings and provoked the destruction of an electrical substation when a power failure interrupted a *Ramayan* broadcast. Three thousand sanitation workers in Amritsar responded to the news of the serial's imminent end by going out on strike. As the city braced for a cholera epidemic, business leaders threatened to close their doors unless agreement could be reached with the Ministry of Information and Broadcasting for the serial to be extended. It was.

Although American serials are distributed widely around the world, they are eclipsed by the astounding global circulation of serials made in other cultures. Mexico's Televisa exports its serials to fifty-nine countries, including the US. A Televisa serial was the most popular program in Korea in 1991, and, as Kate Baldwin discusses in her chapter, in 1992 another became the most popular dramatic series in the history of Russian television. Serials are one of Australia's most important media exports, and British serials have been sold to nearly twenty countries. But the prize for the world's most successful exporter of serial drama goes to Brazil's TV-Globo, the world's fourth largest television corporation. TV-Globo serials have been seen in more than 100 countries.

Why do they say such terrible things about soap operas?

No other form of television fiction has attracted more viewers in more countries more regularly over a longer period of time than has the serial. Given this fact, it is ironic that, until very recently, serials largely have been ignored in the "serious" literature on television and typically have been regarded with dismissive disdain in the popular press. Elsewhere I have argued that in the United States, this paradox is primarily a function of the status of soap operas as a gendered form of narrative and its resistance to being read according to the protocols of more closed narrative forms. Especially when compared to high-brow forms of fiction or drama, the soap opera seemed to critics to be the very epitome of the low. As early as 1940, one American commentator called radio soap operas "serialized drool."[3]

Kate Baldwin will use the metaphors of feces and toilet training in discussing the extraordinary popularity of a Mexican telenovela in Russia in 1992. More generally, I would argue, serials have been regarded as some form of trash by critics and commentators virtually everywhere their popularity has prompted public comment: as waste-of-time women's trash (US daytime soaps); glitzy, tasteless trash (*Dallas* and *Dynasty*); glitzy, tasteless, American cultural–imperialist trash (*Dallas* in France); badly-produced trash (Mexican serials); adolescent trash (*Neighbours*); adolescent, colonial-revenge trash (*Neighbours* in Britain); etc., etc.

In the US the very term *soap opera* marks out the serial's ironic relationship both with high art and the dirt soap is bought to eliminate. The "soap" in soap opera alludes to the use of the serial form from its earliest days to the present as an advertising vehicle for laundry detergents and household cleaning products. The "opera" in soap opera signals a travesty: the highest of dramatic art forms is made to describe the lowest. (Similarly, western movies were called "horse operas" in the 1930s).

As a "soap opera" the serial is a drama about two kinds of dirt. In calling his study of the British serial *EastEnders*, *Public Secrets*, David Buckingham points to the tendency of serials to be "about" trash: they seem to revel in the concealment (to other characters and initially to the viewer) and revelation (to some other characters and to the viewer) of the dirty little secrets of characters' lives.[4] One of the most common ways for a serial character to demonstrate his or her villainy is to obtain and threaten to disseminate some "dirt" about another character: his mistaken parentage, her previous lover, his extramarital liaison, her child given up for adoption.

In the US and in other countries where serials function within commercial broadcasting systems to attract female viewers there is another dirty drama going on in the commercials that interrupt the narration of the serial. Characters in the soap opera commercial have, quite literally, dirty secrets: dirty laundry, dirty floors, dirty toilets, dirty bodies, dirty appliances, dirty children, dirty homes – which require the cleansing only this particular brand and type of soap can offer. Not coincidentally, it is female characters who are associated with dirt in the commercials. According to the commercials' logic, it is their inadequacy in controlling dirt that creates a problem, and it is their responsibility to eliminate the home's sources of filth.

Wherever they are shown, the act of watching serials seems to generate another kind of dirt: the dirty discourse of gossip. Perhaps more than any other form of television, serials encourage viewers to extend the pleasure of watching to the pleasures of talking about what they watch. Dorothy Hobson has documented the pleasures viewers take in gossiping about serials: what has happened, what might happen, what consequences whatever happens might have on the intricately patterned set of relationships that constitute any serial's social world.[5]

Like the trash generated by consumer capitalism, the serial has been associated with the masses and mass culture. For cultural critics such as Dwight MacDonald and Ernest van den Haag in the 1950s the spectator was being diverted from "serious" art by mass-produced, predigested works of mass culture, anonymously manufactured and distributed in bulk. The sheer quantity of mass culture was drowning real art, they argued, while its easy pleasures stupefied the spectator and rendered him or her incapable of aesthetic discrimination. MacDonald even singles out radio serials as a prime example of mass-produced mass culture that threatened to inundate authentic culture "by its sheer pervasiveness, its brutal, overwhelming *quantity*."[6] Thus, condemned for its ubiquity and written off as the unfortunate consequence of progamming for the least common denominator of audience taste, the soap opera's very popularity has served as an obstacle to its serious scrutiny. With a few notable exceptions, the television critic writing in magazines and newspapers has shown about as much interest in writing about soap operas as the restaurant critic has in writing about McDonald's – and for much the same reason: they are both regarded as "junk."

Although the mass appeal of soap operas was an obstacle to their critical analysis, it quickly prompted studies of the soap opera audience, as broadcasters and advertising agencies attempted to measure the popularity of radio serials. The first audience studies in the 1930s were called "mail hooks": during a commercial, an announcer would offer a free gift (a packet of flower seeds, for example) to anyone sending proof-of-purchase of a product advertised on the show. By extrapolating from the number of letters received and noting their addresses, broadcasters and advertisers could gain a rough idea of the size and geographic distribution of the serial's audience. In 1933 the Pilsbury Company received more than 250,000 responses to such a mail hook when it was broadcast during an NBC serial, *Today's Children*.[7] Another such offer in 1934 generated more than 1 million letters.

Initially, at least, broadcasters and advertisers had little interest in examining the soap opera audience beyond determining its size, constitution, and geographic distribution. By the early 1940s, however, soap operas and their audiences became caught up in a more general controversy surrounding the possible deleterious effects of radio listening upon particularly vulnerable segments of the audience. In March 1942 a New York psychiatrist, Louis Berg, claimed in a speech that listening to soap operas caused a variety of emotional and physical disturbances, ranging from gastrointestinal distress to nocturnal fright. He also compared soap opera listeners with "emotionally distorted" individuals who enjoyed lynchings and who "in the past had cheered on witch burnings."[8] Berg's outrageous charges were eventually revealed to have been based on nothing more than his own reactions to listening to soap operas, but not before they had received wide publicity as "scientific" findings.

Berg's jeremiad fed a widely-expressed fear that radio could be used as an effective instrument of mass persuasion and propaganda, and, particularly among more susceptible members of the audience, directly influence behavior and attitudes. Broadcasters were in no position to deny entirely the potential "effects" of radio – the sale of air time to advertisers was predicated upon the hypothesis that broadcast messages were effective in influencing beliefs and behavior, at least when it came to the purchase of commodities. However, they feared that Berg's attack on soap operas would precipitate a wider, and, perhaps, government-sponsored inquiry into radio's power to mold political opinion and provoke social action. Thus, their response to Berg was not direct refutation of his charges but reframing the issue of soap opera listening from one of (negative) effects to one of audience needs.

In a series of studies over the next severals years – some of them commissioned by broadcasters – soap opera listening was investigated in terms of the social, psychological, and emotional needs it fulfilled among its (presumed female) audience. The more generous of the studies concluded that soap operas were a source of advice regarding family and domestic problems and a temporary escape from the tedium of household responsibilities. Others cast the relationship between soap operas and their fans in less positive terms:

> Women of the daytime audiences are having physical and psychic problems that they themselves cannot understand, that they cannot solve. Being physical, they feel the thrust of these problems. Being poor, they cannot buy remedies in the form of doctors, new clothes, or deciduous coiffures; being unanalytical, they cannot figure out what is really the matter with them; and being inarticulate, they cannot explain their problem even if they know what it is. . . .[9]

In short, American audience research in the 1940s cast soap opera listeners as a distinctively different audience group with special needs and lacks, which, presumably, the (male) audiences for other types of programming did not have. The female fans of soap operas listened so loyally – so the argument went – because soap operas spoke to their particular "feminine" needs. Whether conclusions were drawn on the basis of an effects or functionalist model of media engagement, early soap opera audience research in the US constructed the "average" serial fan as a woman suffering from some deficiency – whether emotional, psychological, social, relational, or some combination of them all. This image of the soap opera viewer persisted in both "serious" and popular discourse for decades after the research that produced it was conducted, in part because of the dearth of subsequent studies in the 1950s and 1960s. Despite the form's having made a successful transition from radio to television two decades earlier, a 1972 article in *Public Opinion Quarterly* could still note that "despite the magnitude of the phenomenon, there has been no published research on television serials."[10]

Soap operas in contemporary media and cultural studies

Given the antipathy of most literary critics to mass culture in general, television more specifically (with the exception of anthology drama in the "Golden Age" of television in the early 1950s), and soap operas in particular, it is hardly surprising that it was not until the 1980s that soap operas began to be taken seriously as texts. To be sure, social scientists had subjected television soap operas to quantitative "content analysis" in order to compare the construction of some aspects of social reality in the world of the soap opera with their bases in "real life." Such studies assume that fictional texts are (and are understood by their readers to be) direct reflections of objective social reality and further assume that the features of that reality fastened upon in the study (occupational and sex roles, communication

6

patterns, causes of death and disease, etc.) function within the text in the same ways they do outside of it. In general, content analysis tells us little about the way soap operas work as texts, generate meanings, and allow pleasures for their viewers because its procedures deny the soap opera any status as a complex fictional text.

Within this historical context, then, Tania Modleski's discussion of American daytime soap operas in her dissertation and book, *Loving With a Vengeance* (1982), was important for several reasons.[11] Demonstrating the usefulness of applying the methods of post-structuralist criticism to serials, Modleski situates soap operas and their study squarely within the context of feminist theory. She argues that soap operas, along with several other forms of popular culture, position their female "readers" quite differently than more male-oriented texts and make possible quite different pleasures and meanings. This is not to say that Modleski celebrates soap operas as feminist or progressive texts; indeed, she sees their formal structure and thematic concerns meshing all too neatly with the domestic demands placed upon women within patriarchal capitalism. Denied the omnipotent reading position to be found in more closed narrative forms, soap opera viewers are asked to relate to the diegetic families of their serials as they are expected to do to their own. They must exercise patience and tolerance in the face of unending tribulation, wresting pleasure from consolation and sympathy rather than from any expectation of final resolution. The narrative structure of soap operas – cutting in the middle of conversations from one plot line to another, interrupting constantly with commercial messages – mimics the rhythms of the mother/reader's domestic life.

Although Modleski's approach is textual rather than ethnographic, it also points to the importance of understanding soap operas and other forms of popular culture within the contexts of their reception and use. That concern for the reader or viewer also underlies my own study of American daytime soap operas, which appeared a few years later (*Speaking of Soap Operas*, 1985). In it I address the paradox of the soap opera's cultural status in the US: on the one hand, the soap opera is the most successful broadcast advertising vehicle ever devised; on the other, it is among the most disdained forms of popular culture of the last half century. At the crux of this paradox, I argue, lies the "gendered" nature of the soap opera's appeals and popularity. Soaps are both highly valued (by advertisers and broadcasters) and dismissed (by critics) as a "woman's" form.

Furthermore, soap operas operate according to very different narrative and dramatic principles than more closed narrative forms: they are predicated upon the impossibility of their ever ending. Hence, the critic attempting to "read" an episode of a soap opera comes to a story already years in the telling, and one that will be unaltered by anything occurring in that episode. Put in semiotic terminology, US daytime soap operas trade an investment in syntagmatic determinacy (the eventual direction of the overall plot line) for one in paradigmatic complexity (how any particular event affects the complex network of character relationships). The long-term, loyal viewer of the soap opera is rewarded by the text in that her knowledge of the large and complex community of characters and their histories enables her to produce subtle and nuanced readings, whereas a single episode of any given soap opera, viewed out of context by a textually-naive critic, appears to be so much pointless talk among undistinguishable characters about events of maddenly indeterminable significance.

The early 1980s also saw the first important critical work on British soap operas. The BFI monograph on *Coronation Street* (1981) and Dorothy Hobson's book on *Crossroads* (1982)[12] mark the inclusion of the serial form as an object of inquiry on the agenda of the emerging field of cultural studies. As any British television viewer knows, since 1960 semi-weekly episodes of Granada Television's *Coronation Street* have chronicled the lives of the residents of its eponymous working-class neighborhood set in a fictional northern city. The working-class milieu of *Coronation Street* and, since 1985, its chief rival in the ratings, the BBC serial *EastEnders*, has made class a central issue in critical analyses of British serials and set them apart from both American daytime and prime-time serials. The nature of class, the constitution and character of the working class, and the academic study of both were foundational issues for British cultural studies, in part because they figured so prominently in the work of such key figures as Richard Hoggart, Raymond Williams, E. P. Thompson, and Stuart Hall. Because *Coronation Street* emerges from the same cultural moment as Hoggart's influential study of working-class culture, *The Uses of Literacy* (1958),[13] and in the wake of the Angry Young (Working-Class) Man movement in British literature, theater, and cinema, it is a privileged and sustained instance of popular culture's engagement with questions of class and, as such, a convenient springboard for Richard Dyer, Terry Lovell, Christine Geraghty, and the other contributors to address the more general theoretical and methodological questions it gives rise to.

Ironically – given the contemporaneous struggles in the US to admit the critical study of soap operas to the academic agenda – *Coronation Street* was of scholarly interest to Dyer and his co-contributors because it enjoyed substantial scholarly sympathy and critical acclaim, albeit in spite of its status as "soap opera." The same definitely cannot be said of the object of Dorothy Hobson's 1982 book, *Crossroads: The Drama of a Soap Opera*. If *Coronation Street* was marked in the early 1980s as a program that transcended the conventions of its genre, *Crossroads* was frequently singled out by critics and broadcast regulators as the most egregious example of soap opera – and, by extension, commercial television – at its technical and aesthetic worst. As is frequently the case when such charges are made about soap operas, the only people who disagreed (or could have cared less) were the millions of devoted viewers who watched each week: in the early 1980s, *Crossroads* was battling *Coronation Street* for supremacy in the weekly ratings.

Hobson's book contributed importantly to the early critical literature on soap operas in several ways, although its influence was felt much more and more immediately in Britain than in the US: with *Crossroads* not shown on American television, her book was not widely distributed in the US. Based on research for her dissertation at the Centre for Contemporary Cultural Studies at the University of Birmingham, Hobson's published account is organized around a pivotal moment in the diegetic, institutional, and reception history of the serial: after seventeen years as its central female character, Meg Mortimer was to be written out of the show and the contract of the actor playing her, Noele Gordon, not renewed. This decision became the subject of enormous controversy in the popular press and prompted thousands of angry letters from Meg's fans. Meg's demise provided Hobson with an opportunity to examine the meaning of *Crossroads* for the company that produced it; the writers, producers, cast, and crew that made it; the press that covered it as "news"; and the audience that watched and read about it.

Methodologically, what distinguishes Hobson's study is what might be called its ethnographic orientation. Hobson is not concerned with *Crossroads* as text but how – as production challenge, enacted script, subject of public discourse, or viewing experience – it takes on meaning for the various groups that encounter it in any of its varied manifestations. Her role, then, is not so much critic as observer and commentator on the observations of those whom she interviews about *Crossroads*.[14] Hobson's account of the audience for *Crossroads* replaces the American functionalist model of viewer/text interaction with one that foregrounds the production of meanings and pleasures. Furthermore, she argues that those meanings and pleasures cannot be "read off" the text in isolation but rather are deeply embedded in the social contexts of its viewing. Thus, they vary from viewer to viewer: *Crossroads* is a different experience for the young mother who feeds her child while she watches than for the widowed grandmother who views alone. Hobson's finding of the diversity of meanings and pleasures connected with watching *Crossroads* also suggests that they may be quite different than those assumed by its producers, writers, actors, or sponsors.

The investigation of the pleasures of soap opera viewing and their relationship to both genre conventions and the gendered nature of the serial audience also forms the focus of *Watching "Dallas": Soap Opera and the Melodramatic Imagination*, Ien Ang's study of the reception of *Dallas* in Holland. Published in Dutch the same year as Hobson's work (1982) and translated into English in 1985, *Watching "Dallas"* is the first book-length work to examine the cross-cultural reception of serials.[15] Based on forty-two letters from *Dallas* viewers solicited in a Dutch woman's magazine, *Watching "Dallas"* is not so much a study of the audience for soap operas as it is an extended essay on relationships among gender, genre, and ideology generated by a "symptomatic" reading of viewer discourse on *Dallas* at a time when the show's popularity was a controversial issue in Holland.

Like Hobson and Modleski, whose work she acknowledges, Ang is concerned with the pleasures associated with soap opera viewing, particularly the pleasures available to female viewers (all but three of her respondents were female). However, Ang also investigates the ironic pleasure some viewers seem to take in hating *Dallas* or in disliking the values they see it representing so much that they enjoy watching the show in order to condemn and ridicule it. Ang relates this pleasure in displeasure to both an implicit critique of mass culture and to concerns about the influence of American popular culture on Dutch life.

More than any work to that point, *Watching "Dallas"* foregrounds the complex and sometimes contradictory nature of the pleasures watching soap operas produces for some of its viewers. Many of the letters expressing considerable enjoyment of the act of watching *Dallas* also confess to finding some aspects of the program politically problematic, implausible, silly, insulting, or excessive. Serials, Ang suggests, engage their viewers along a number of different axes, and deriving enjoyment from the viewing experience would seem to depend upon the negotiation of multiple tensions. For example, being a regular serial viewer involves resolving or at least accommodating the tension between recognizing the soap opera world as fictional construct and accepting its "as-if-it-were-real" character – an issue Louise Spence takes up in her essay. As both Hobson and Ang demonstrate, female soap opera viewers – frequently charged in the popular press with an inability to distinguish soap opera fiction from "real life" – move easily and knowledgably in their discourse about soaps between pleasure in soaps' status as fabricated products of the show business industry and the different kinds of pleasure to be derived from involvement with soap characters as if they were (but still knowing they are not) people.

Sparked in part by these and other early critical investigations of serials, the late 1980s and early 1990s have witnessed a burgeoning of work on the form around the world among scholars operating within what might be called "media studies" or "cultural studies" academic paradigms. Charlotte Brunsdon, whose own early essay on *Crossroads* complemented Hobson's more extensive analysis, discusses in her chapter the centrality of the serial form to the emergence of feminist media criticism. Critical work on soap operas also expanded as theories of media derived from structuralism and post-structuralism supplanted or at least were allowed to coexist with more empiricist models in academic curricula. Studies of serial audiences benefited from the increased interest in ethnography among media scholars in the wake of David Morley's *Nationwide* monograph (1981) and his *Family Television* (1986), as well as John Fiske's celebration of such studies in his work. David Buckingham's *Public Secrets: EastEnders and Its Audience* (1987) certainly reflects this interest as well as a concern to link institution, text, and audience in the study of serials.[16]

The other major locus of recent critical work on serials has been Latin America, particularly Brazil. As Maria Teresa Quiroz has noted, although serials have been a part of Latin American broadcasting since the 1940s, they have attracted the serious attention of critics and scholars only recently.[17] Interest in the Latin American television serial, the telenovela, has been prompted not only by the enormous contemporary popularity of the form from Mexico to Chile, but also by the rise of Brazil, Mexico, and Venezuela as major serial exporters both within and outside of Latin America. Brazil's TV-Globo sells telenovelas to more than 100 countries around the world; serials produced by Mexico's Televisa have been number one hits in Korea and (as Kate Baldwin discusses in her chapter) Russia; and Venezuelan serials have engendered "novelamania" in Spain.

Scholars of Latin American serials, such as Ondina Leal, Tomas Lopez-Pumarejo, Michèle and Armand Mattelart, Jesús Martín-Barbero, Renato Ortiz, Nora Mazziotti, Monica Rector, and others[18] have seen telenovelas as well as imported US serials as opportunities to explore questions of national identity, cultural authenticity, the relationship between television and everyday life, and the gaps between serials' representation of social reality and that experienced by serial viewers. But more than anything else, the telenovela has been discussed in terms of its relationship to modernity: the economic, cultural, and psychic reorganization of society around the demands of consumer capitalism. Modernity has certainly been an important issue to scholars in Europe and North America, but principally as a historical phenomenon and in relation to its epochal successor, postmodernity. For scholars of Latin America, however, the project of modernity is of current not just historical interest. Television has been seen as an important instrument of modernity in Latin America – supplanting premodern modes of experience, suppressing linguistic and cultural differences, addressing the viewer as consumer, and offering a window onto a high-tech, secular, market-driven world into which the viewer is somehow expected to fit. Jesús Martín-Barbero, along with Mattelart and Mattelart, views telenovelas as a mixture of modern and more traditional modes of storytelling and reception. The attenuation of the story over a period of weeks and months evokes the slow, cyclical rhythms of the seasons and family life. But within each daily episode, the viewer encounters the frenetic pace and fragmentation both of contemporary television style and of modernity itself. As Mattelart and Mattelart put it,

> It would seem that this mix defines well that part of our symbolic needs catered to by the cultural industries. They can appear as the time of pathos, of emotions, of the family libido, in contrast to the elliptical, fragmented time that explodes in the video clip, for example, in the era

11

of postmodernity. What is characteristic of the novela is the combination of a broken narrative from the point of form with the structure of long duration. The fragmented rhythm corresponds to our visual immersion in the modern world of technology and satisfies the contemporary modalities of aesthetic perception.[19]

Soap opera scholarship: the next generation

The chapters in this volume might be said to represent the second and third waves of serial research. In many cases they build upon scholarship conducted and published a decade or more ago or, at the very least, no longer feel obliged to make the case that serials are an appropriate object of scholarly inquiry. These essays also reflect both continuities in the serial form and changes occurring since the early 1980s.

One of the most striking of those changes is the degree to which serials have become a global phenomenon. In a number of countries, serial production predates the advent of television. Many radio serials were produced in Cuba in the 1940s; there were more than 200 broadcast over that decade in Australia; and *The Archers* has been a staple of BBC radio since the early 1950s. But the global circulation of broadcast serials on a massive scale is a function of technological, institutional, and political changes occurring in the 1980s.

The development of cable and satellite technologies expanded the delivery capacity of many national television systems. At the same time and in response to some of the same forces, governments across Europe began to shift from a public-service model of broadcast policy to a "mixed" or entirely commercial model. The expansion of channel capacity and the growth of the commercial broadcasting sector combined to produce the need to build new audiences for television and to find relatively low-cost sources of entertainment programming. Importing serials from other countries became an attractive programming option for several reasons. In addition to being internally self-promoting – each episode is implicitly an advertisement for the next – serials also advertise and promote the medium through which they are delivered to consumers. As Roger Hagedorn notes in his chapter, serials encourage viewers not only to consume them, but also to consume other types of texts offered through that medium. In order to realize any pleasure from their engagement with serials, the viewer must "stay tuned." Given the number of hours of progamming they represent and the size of audience they can attract, imported serials are relatively inexpensive (US$4,000 to US$8,000 per episode in Greece or Spain, for example) – especially when compared to the cost of locally-produced dramatic programming. To the expansion and "privatization" of television services in Western Europe and other capitalist countries since 1980 must be added the establishment of commercial or quasi-commercial television services in the countries of the so-called Eastern Bloc.

As Kate Baldwin's chapter makes clear, such resource-poor enterprises find in serials that have long since traveled around the world once an affordable source of popular programming.

For decades it has been axiomatic that the international circulation of television programming occurs from north to south and from west to east: that is to say, US and, to a lesser degree, European program producers maintain their hegemony over the global television market by selling their programs at a low cost to foreign broadcasters, particularly to broadcasters in the "developing" nations of Latin America, Asia, and Africa. They can do so because their production costs have been recovered in the far larger and richer domestic market. Thus prices for foreign sales can be kept at a level low enough to discourage domestic drama production elsewhere but still high enough to be profitable to the producer.

Interestingly, however, it was not US producers who benefited most from the increased demand for serial programming in the 1980s, although a few US companies scored spectacular successes in the early part of the decade with such shows as *Dallas*, *Dynasty*, and *Falcon Crest*. Rather Latin American producers, particularly Brazil's TV-Globo and Mexico's Televisa, moved aggressively into the international arena, both benefiting from their near-monopoly domestic positions. TV-Globo, which in 1991 captured 60 percent of the Brazilian television advertising market, began exporting telenovelas to Europe in 1975. Within a decade, its annual profits on foreign telenovela sales to nearly 100 countries had risen to US$20 million. Export revenue increased more than fivefold between 1982 and 1987. In 1992 it announced plans to build a new US$45 million studio facility in Rio de Janeiro, mainly for the production of telenovelas.[20] Serials account for almost half of the output of Mexico's private communications giant Televisa, which are now being exported to fifty-nine countries around the world. They have topped the ratings in Korea, Russia, and Turkey.

Globo and Televisa have been joined by other distributors of Latin American telenovelas. Although based in the US (Miami), Coral Pictures primarily represents Latin American producers, 70 percent of its catalog being programs made by Venezuela's Radio Caracas TV. Coral exports Radio Caracas telenovelas to thirty-six countries around the world, including Thailand, Israel, and Singapore, and is credited with "opening" Spain to the Latin American serial through the success there of its *Cristal*, the last episode of which was seen in September 1990 by more than 11 million viewers.[21]

A further instance of the "flow" of television programming from south to north, periphery to center, is the export of Australian serials, particularly, as Stephen Crofts discusses in his chapter on Grundy Television's *Neighbours*. Originally produced for Australia's Seven Network in 1985, it was cancelled after seven months, then picked up by the competing Network Ten. A surprise hit on its new network, *Neighbours* was launched on commercial television in Great Britain in November 1986, becoming the first serial there to be "stripped:" shown each weekday. Its success in the UK was even more surprising than its ratings-topping popularity in Australia. It is now regularly among the ten most-viewed shows of any given week, attracting an audience of more than 24 million. Grundy Television claims that the *Neighbours* cast is the first of any television series to have traveled to Britain at the request of the royal family for a Royal Command Performance. *Neighbours* is now seen in some twenty-five countries around the world, from Bulgaria to Zambia.

Grundy's latest serial venture aimed at the European market involves co-production arrangements with Dutch and German companies for the making of a daily soap opera entitled *Good Times, Bad Times*. The show is actually a recycled version of a now defunct Australian serial called *The Restless Years*. Grundy writers in Los Angeles rewrite the script for each episode, resetting it in Holland and Germany. It is then shot by the co-production partners in the local language with local casts. So far as the audience knows and so far as local broadcasting regulators are concerned, *Good Times, Bad Times* is a domestic production. Both versions debuted in the summer of 1992 and are doing well. In Holland, it is regularly among the top ten shows of the week. Grundy executives in Sydney say they hope to enter into more co-production arrangements for this and other serials, particularly in countries where there is little indigenous tradition of serial production.[22]

Ironically, producers of US daytime serials are now in the position of taking lessons from their Latin American and antipodean competitors, as they turn to the export market to offset domestic declines in viewership and revenue. Although they continue to be profitable, the future of US daytime soap operas is perhaps more uncertain than at any time since the genre made its successful transition from radio to television in the early 1950s. Total network viewership, both prime-time and daytime, is steadily falling, as more viewers have access not to three or four channels but to thirty or forty.

For the three major commercial networks, dispersed viewership across an increasingly fragmented market means lower ratings, reduced total advertising revenue, reduced advertising rates, and, with program production or licensing costs not declining, reduced profit margins, especially for daytime. Although soap operas have gained in some audience segments over the past ten years – men and adolescents especially – these are not groups traditionally targeted by the companies whose advertising has sustained the genre for a half century. Total viewership among the most valuable segment of the soap opera audience – women between the ages of 18 and 35 – has declined since 1980 as more women have entered the paid workforce and as women at home defect to other programming alternatives.

The penetration of the VCR into the American market over the same period (currently over 75 percent of US homes have a VCR) has had a curious impact on soap opera viewership. Although soap operas are one of the genres most "time-shifted", soap opera viewing on videotape does not figure into audience ratings data, and even if it did, advertisers would discount such viewership, believing (probably accurately) that most viewers "zip" through the frequent commercial messages.

As they scramble to staunch the flow of audience to cable, satellite, and independent stations, the networks have turned to programming forms that require minimal start-up investment and carry low production budgets: game and talk shows. Both these genres represent increasingly serious competition for soap operas. Few new network soap operas have been launched in the past five years, and only two, *The Bold and the Beautiful* and *Loving*, are still on network television.

Ten years ago, as cable systems enlarged their channel capacity and new cable programming services began to target specific audience segments ("narrow casting," as opposed to the commercial networks' traditional strategy of "broadcasting"), some predicted that cable programmers would turn to the soap opera as a way of attracting and maintaining viewership. This vision of different soap operas for every audience segment has, for the most part, not come to pass, although MTV did experiment with a serial for teenagers and the Black Entertainment Network did for a while produce new episodes of *Generations*, a multi-racial soap opera initially produced for and then cancelled by NBC. Cable programmers have not commissioned new soap operas for several reasons. First, even though production costs are still far less than dramatic programming shot on film, the weekly budget for an hour-long soap opera can be US$500,000. Although soap audiences can be extraordinarily loyal, viewership and viewer loyalty can take years to build. For cable progammers attempting to program for a tiny sliver of the available audience, with advertising revenues a fraction of those for the commercial networks, and, consequently, with minuscule programming budgets, buying network series reruns from syndicators and developing new programs within cheaper genres (particularly talk shows) seems a better risk than starting new soap operas. Significantly, the cable channel competing most directly for the soap opera audience, Lifetime, has still not taken the plunge into soap operas.

After decades of largely ignoring the export potential of daytime soaps, some US producers are following Globo and Televisa into the international serial market. *The Bold and the Beautiful* has been hugely popular in Italy, Egypt, and Greece, among other countries. After being originally purchased by the Greek state-run channel ET-1, *The Bold and the Beautiful* became the object of the country's biggest television bidding war, when a private channel, Antenna, offered an unprecedented US$8,000 per episode. Now broadcast on Antenna in the early afternoon, *The Bold and the Beautiful* attracts more than a 50 percent audience share.[23] For independent producers and Procter & Gamble, the giant food and household products company that still owns six daytime serials, the prospect of significant income from foreign sales might enable them to lower or hold steady the license fee they charge US networks. Procter & Gamble is also perfectly positioned to "sell" their soap operas to foreign commercial TV services through a barter arrangement, by which the program itself is provided at little or no cost in return for commercial time during the show for the advertising of Procter & Gamble products sold in that country.

The crowning irony, of course, would be the conquest of the US market by Latin American serials. Although this has not yet occurred, Latin American serials have become staples in one segment of the US television market, and the much-hyped prospect of 500 channel delivery systems increases the likelihood of their further penetration. Telenovelas have become mainstays of Spanish-language cable, satellite, and broadcast channels, now available throughout the US. However, because they are not subtitled in English and since most Americans living north of the southern rim of the country do not speak Spanish, the impact of Latin American serials on US television is greatly circumscribed.

From its beginnings in the late 1940s, US commercial network television has been informally closed to foreign programming. With a huge domestic television production infrastructure, the world's richest consumer market to absorb high production costs, and program suppliers able to offer programming to the networks for less than their actual cost of production (because of lucrative syndication, foreign, and other ancillary rights accruing to a series with a successful network run), there was no incentive to seek alternative, offshore sources of programming. Furthermore, using wonderfully circular logic, the networks reasoned that since there was no tradition of watching programs dubbed or subtitled, or even programs with different English accents on network television, audiences would not tolerate such programs. Thus, the only national broadcasting service that has relied heavily upon imported programming has been public television, which has provided a venue for British drama, documentary, situation comedy, and, recently, with the importation of *EastEnders* from the BBC, serials.[24] But PBS is a distinctly minority service, attracting on average about 3 percent of the available prime-time viewing audience.

It is possible, however, that the continuing explosion of television viewing options in the US, the decline of power exercised by the three principal commercial networks, and the accompanying fragmentation of the viewing audience will work together to create a more favorable climate for foreign programs in general and serials in particular. Programmers may have to go further and further afield – geographically and linguistically – to secure programming to fill thousands of hours of weekly schedules on hundreds of channels. As they do so they will find a number of countries – Mexico, Brazil, Venezuela, and Australia among them – that have demonstrated their ability to produce serials that "travel" well beyond their own cultural and linguistic boundaries.

As the chapters by Daniel Miller, Marie Gillespie, Kate Baldwin, and Stephen Crofts all make clear, this circulation of serials around the world raises any number of interesting and important questions. Among them are: how does a serial made to "speak" to an audience in one culture manage to speak to other audiences in other cultures around the world? And what role does the cultural provenance of a particular serial play in its reception by "foreign" audiences?

Open and closed serials

Regardless of their circumstances of production, distribution, or reception, serials share a distinctive narrative form, one recognized by their viewers around the world. A brief discussion of that common form and some key distinctions within it might be helpful as background for reading any of the chapters that follow.

The term "serial" draws our attention to the one feature *Kewang*, *Coronation Street*, *Guiding Light*, *Dallas*, *Ramayan*, *Los Ricos Lloran Tambien*, and even the programs that make up *Masterpiece Theatre* all share – their seriality. True serialization – the organization of narrative and narration around the enforced and regular suspension of both textual display and reading activity – produces a very different mode of reader engagement and reader pleasure than we experience with non-serials. As literary theorist Wolfgang Iser has noted, the act of reading any narrative involves traversing textual terrain over time, as the reader moves from one word, sentence, paragraph, and chapter to the next. Or, in the case of cinematic or televisual narratives, from one shot, scene, sequence, or episode to the next. As readers or viewers we take up what he calls a "wandering viewpoint" within the text as we move through it, looking back upon the textual terrain already covered (what Iser calls retention) and anticipating on that basis what might lie around the next textual corner (protension). Both processes occur in the gaps between words, sentences, and chapters (or shots, scenes, and sequences) – those necessary textual silences where we as readers/viewers are called upon to connect the words, sounds and/or images of the text to form a coherent narrative world.[25]

The serial, then, is a form of narrative organized around institutionally-imposed gaps in the text. The nature and extent of those gaps are as important to the reading process as the textual "material" they interrupt. Each episode ends with some degree of narrative indeterminancy: a plot question that will not be answered until the next episode. In the US, where daytime serials are broadcast Monday through Friday, the greatest indeterminancy is left with the viewer at the end of the Friday episode, encouraging her, as the announcer's voice used to say, to "tune in again next time" on Monday. These gaps leave plenty of time for viewers to discuss with each other both the possible meanings of what has happened thus far as well as what might happen next. Thus, regardless of the cultural context of their production and reception, regardless of their plot or themes, television serials around the world seem more than any other form of programming to provoke talk about them among their viewers. Indeed in her recent book on television serials and women, Christine Geraghty sees this as their defining quality:

> Soap operas . . . can now be defined not purely by daytime scheduling or even by a clear appeal to a female audience but by the presence of stories which engage an audience in such a way that they become the subject for public interest and interrogation.[26]

Lisa Rofel analyzes the soap talk provoked by the broadcast of *Kewang*, the first domestic serial produced in China since the Cultural Revolution. For both factory workers and academics, *Kewang* opened up a non-political space for the discussion of gender, the effects of the Cultural Revolution, the role of intellectuals in Chinese society, and other contested issues.

Non-serial popular narratives tend to be organized around a single protagonist or small group of protagonists and to be teleological: there is a single moment of narrative closure (obviously involving the protagonist) toward which their plots move and in relation to which reader satisfaction is presumed to operate. The classic example of this type of narrative is the murder mystery, in which the revelation of the murderer at the end of the story absolutely determines the movement of the plot. By contrast, the serial spreads its narrative energy among a number of plots and a community of characters, and, what is even more important, sets these plots and characters in complex, dynamic, and unpredictable relationship with each other. Because serials cut between scenes enacting separate plot lines, the viewer is prompted to ask not only "Where is each of these plot lines going?," but also "What might be the relationship between different plot lines?"

It is at this point that we need to distinguish between two fundamentally different, but frequently conflated, forms of television serial: what I call "open" and "closed" serials. US daytime, British, and Australian serials are open narrative forms. That is to say they are the only forms of narrative (with the possible exception of comic strips) predicated upon the impossibility of ultimate closure. No one sits down to watch an episode of one of these programs with the expectation that this episode might be the one in which all individual and community problems will be solved and everyone will live happily ever after.

In a sense, these serials trade narrative closure for paradigmatic complexity. Just as there is no ultimate moment of resolution, there is no central, indispensable character in open serials to whose fate viewer interest is indissolubly linked. Instead, there is a changing community of characters who move in and out of viewer attention and interest. Any one of them might die, move to another city, or lapse into an irreversible coma without affecting the overall world of the serial. Indeed, I would argue that it is the very possibility of a central character's demise – something that is not a feature of episodic series television – that helps to fuel viewer interest in the serial.

US daytime soap operas are "open" in another sense as well. Events in a daytime soap are less determinant and irreversible than they are in other forms of narrative, and identity, indeed ontology itself, is more mutable. For example, generally, when a character dies in a fictional narrative (assuming we are not reading a gothic horror tale or piece of science fiction) we expect that character to stay dead. In soap operas, it is not unusual to witness the resurrection of a character assumed to be but not actually dead, even after the passage of years of intervening story. I remember one character on a now cancelled soap opera called *The Edge of Night* who was presumed drowned in a boating accident in the Caribbean literally for five years before she returned. It turned out she had been rescued by a passing French yacht and discovered to be suffering from amnesia. She was taken to Paris where she lived for five years before recovering her memory and returning to her husband and family in the States. On *The Guiding Light*, one character, Roger Thorpe, was killed off twice more than ten years ago, only to have now returned to the show, where he awaits, we presume, yet another possible reversible demise.

Another distinguishing feature of open serials, particularly US daytime serials, is their large community of interrelated characters. More than half of all US daytime serial episodes are 1 hour in length and all are broadcast five days each week. As a result, it is not uncommon for the cast of a daytime soap to include more than thirty regularly-appearing characters – not counting a dozen or more others who have moved away, lapsed into comas, been incarcerated or otherwise institutionalized, or are presumed dead. Furthermore, the audience comes to know some of these characters quite literally over the course of decades of viewing. In the nearly forty years that actress Charita Bauer played the role of Bert Bauer on *The Guiding Light*, her character evolved from young bride to great-grandmother. Viewers of *Coronation Street* have followed events in the life of character Ken Barlow since he was introduced in the show's first episode in December 1960. Thus, the community of soap opera characters shares with the loyal viewer a sense of its collective and individual history, which, in some cases, has unfolded over decades both of storytelling and viewing: the viewer who began watching *The Guiding Light* in 1951 as a young mother caring for infants might herself now watch with her grandchildren. Truth to tell, writers seldom draw upon their characters' or viewers' specific knowledge of story events from decades past, although some viewers are quick to chastise writers when they inadvertently violate that shared history.

The size of the open serial community, the complexity of its character relationships, and the fact that these characters possess both histories and memories all combine to create an almost infinite set of potential connections among characters and plots events. As Laura Stempel Mumford discusses in her chapter, the revelation of hidden parentage – a plot device common, so far as I can determine, to television serials around the world – is emblematic of this feature of serials, in which to whom someone is or might be related is frequently more important than anything that character might do.

The open serial's emphasis on relationships among characters also helps to explain a frequently commented upon feature of open serials: their redundancy within a given episode. Such a program might devote most of an episode to relating a single piece of narrative information – the revealing of parentage, let's say. One character overhears someone telling someone else, who then tells another character, who telephones yet another with the news, etc., etc. This reiteration does nothing to advance the plot, and the uninitiated viewer might well regard it as redundant. However, to the experienced viewer, who tells whom is just as important as what is being related: each retelling affects relations among the community of characters.

It is not uncommon to hear people who don't watch open serials complain that "nothing ever happens" in them. "Why bother watching every day or even every week," they puzzle, "when you can keep up with the plot by watching an episode a month." This complaint is grounded in two fundamental qualities of open serial narrative, but it also reveals an equally fundamental misunderstanding of how these narratives function and the nature of the pleasures they might generate. It is true that no story event will push the open serial narrative any closer to ultimate closure. It is also true that, compared to other types of popular narrative, the emphasis in soap operas is on talk rather than action. But, as we have seen, events in open serials take on meaning for viewers not so much in relation to their place in a syntagmatic chain but rather in terms of the changes in the paradigmatic structure of the community those events might provoke: if, after twenty years, Jason's father is revealed to be Ralph, then Jason must call off his engagement to Jennifer who is now revealed to be his half-sister, and he must come to terms with the fact that Jeremy, his nemesis, is also his half-brother! But, because he is not a regular viewer, the soap opera critic is ignorant of this complex paradigmatic structure and its history. Soap operas are to him merely so much syntagmatically inconsequential talk. To him, little changes from year to year in the soap opera community; to the competent viewer, however, each episode is loaded with important adjustments or possible alterations to that world.

The centrality of paradigmatic structure in the open serial thus helps to account for the emphasis on talk over action as well as for the typical settings in which this talk occurs, and, in the case of US daytime soaps, at least, the kinds of occupations soap opera characters are given. Open serials tend to be organized around locations where characters regularly have occasion to meet: restaurants, hospitals, nightclubs, doctors' offices, lawyers' offices, corporate headquarters, etc. And characters are given occupations that depend on "talk": doctors, nurses, lawyers, entrepreneurs, police officers, entertainers, and, recently in *The Guilding Light*, the staff of a local television station. All US daytime soap operas are middle to upper middle class in their social settings, and working-class characters seldom figure prominently in plot lines. British soaps, on the other hand, tend to represent working-class social worlds. Still, their key settings are places where characters come to talk: the most important location in both *Coronation Street* and *EastEnders* is the local pub.[27] These locations and occupations also facilitate the introduction of new characters, who enter the story as hospital patients, newly assigned doctors or nurses, bar patrons, crime victims, criminals, etc., in the case of US daytime soaps, and newly arrived residents of "the street" or Albert Square, in the case of *Coronation Street* and *EastEnders*. Conversely, US daytime and British soaps typically do not give characters occupations that are non-social, solitary, or non-verbal: farmers, factory workers, computer programmers, night-watchmen, or lighthouse keepers.

The absence of a final moment of narrative closure also indefinitely postpones any moment of final ideological or moral closure in the open serial. This probably makes the open serial a poor vehicle for the inculcation of particular values, but it does mean that open serial writers and producers can raise any number of potentially controversial and contentious social issues without having to make any ideological commitment to them. The viewer is not looking for a moral to the story in the same way he or she is in a closed narrative, even a closed serial.[28] This is not to say that open serials are not ideological constructs, but it is ultimately not in their interest (or that of their producers or sponsors) to be seen to take sides on any particularly issue or to appear to be overtly didactic. *Brookside* creator Phil Redmond has said that his serial

> remains, always has and always will remain, neutral with no particular view or axe to grind. The characters within the programme can be as extreme in their views as the story, characterization or reality demands – although the programme itself must not be seen to take any particular viewpoint.[29]

For the most part, the worlds of open serials – at least in the US, Great Britain, and Australia – do not express a particular ideological "message" (except in the broadest sense of supporting the socio-economic status quo – an orientation shared by every other commercial television program) so much as they mark out more general normative territories.

At the center of this normative space are those values, attitudes, and behaviors implicitly or explicitly believed by producers to be held by the core group of intended viewers: in the case of US daytime serials, middle-class women between the ages of 18 and 35. These norms form, for the most part, the unarticulated givens of the serial social structure. However, in their continuing efforts to keep storylines "current" and interesting to viewers, writers frequently introduce plot lines dealing with controversial social or moral issues. The narrative structure of open serials enables these plot lines and the implicit values they carry to be tried out and allows their fates to be influenced (if not determined) by viewer response. If viewers lose interest in a given plot line or find it offensive, it and the character(s) to which it is attached can be dispensed with or the character can be divested of it (drug use, prostitution, radical political views, etc.). As Joy Fuqua discusses in her chapter on the representation of homosexuality and AIDS in US daytime serials, another strategy for dealing with aberrant values is to attach them to a character on the margins of the serial's core value systems and thus keep them at the edge of the serial's normative territory.

Indeed, the open serial frequently provides a more politically acceptable venue for the airing of controversial issues than more determinant forms of television drama. The first successful television serial in the Republic of Ireland was *The Riordans*, which ran from 1965 to 1978. This story of family life in a rural community dealt with a wide range of highly charged social issues: the living conditions of farmworkers, sexuality and the use of contraceptives, alcohol and tranquilizer addiction, and the role of the church in Irish society. That it was able to do so on government-controlled television, in a society where the majority, as late as 1986, opposed divorce, and under the ever vigilant gaze of the Catholic Church, was a direct consequence of its open serial form. It could raise these issues without taking a perceptible stand or proffering solutions.

But it is important to note that the nature of the paradigmatic structures of US daytime and other examples of open serials themselves carry implicit ideological valences. For example, there are three basic types of relationships among characters in a US daytime soap. One might be related to another character through kinship (as a mother, father, brother, sister, uncle, cousin, etc.), through romance (husband, wife, lover, former lover, potential lover, secret admirer, etc.), or through social bond (employer, co-worker, friend, neighbor, enemy, etc.). White, heterosexual characters move easily among these three categories: a neighbor becomes a lover and is later revealed to be a father as well, the possibility of romance developing among colleagues is ever-present, and even criminals and their victims become romantically involved. However, Joy Fuqua's analysis shows how blacks and homosexuals are consigned to much more restricted positions in this paradigmatic matrix, more because of the underlying ideological values of that structure than any direct consequence of biology or sexual orientation. Although there have been homosexual characters in soap operas, they have in the main been treated like contentious social issues: introduced from outside the community as a part of a specific and limited story line and, after a while, disposed of without lasting impact upon the community. The presence of more than a token gay character among the paradigmatically embedded central characters of a soap opera would call into question the very structure of that community. Similarly, with interracial heterosexual romance still outside the normative bounds of the soap opera community, black characters are relegated to "second-class" citizenship on soap operas: because they are disqualified as actual or potential romantic partners for white characters and not likely to be revealed as their parents, brothers, or children, black characters are restricted to a relational ghetto, operating freely only among their own tiny subcommunities and appearing in the larger community only as co-workers, neighbors, friends or acquaintances.

Unlike the open serial, the Latin American telenovela and other forms of closed serial are designed to end and their narratives to close – although this closure might not be achieved until after several months or 200 episodes. It has been said that the narrative trajectory of the Brazilian telenovela, which usually is broadcast nightly for four to six months, can be divided into three stages. The initial episodes introduce a variety of characters and open up a number of plot lines. In the next twenty or thirty episodes two or three major themes emerge, central characters are defined in greater detail, and plot lines are further complicated. The final third of the telenovela is devoted to bringing the major plot lines to some form of resolution.

To Nico Vink, closure represents a key difference between Brazilian and North American serials. The teleological thrust of the telenovela privileges the final episodes institutionally, textually, and in terms of audience expectation and satisfaction. The ending of a telenovela is heavily promoted, and, in the case of particularly popular telenovelas, becomes the subject of anticipatory public and private discourse: "how will everything work out?" "Who will win and who will lose?" "Who will live and who will die?" Two endings were shot for *Roque Santeiro*, a telenovela broadcast in 1985. The nature of each was publicized as the serial approached its final revelatory episode and a public opinion poll taken to determine which the audience preferred. Both commentators and ordinary viewers (through letters to newspapers) attempted to see in each ending a meaning that extended well beyond the narrowly textual. One critic saw one ending as transforming the serial into an allegory for the socio-political situation in Brazil. A viewer responded by published letter that the alternative ending provided moral closure for the world of the text in compensation for the lack of it in the real world. "Everyone knows," she wrote, "that in reality the powerful never go to prison. Just for that reason at least a [tele]novela should offer this satisfaction."[30]

As the public discourse surrounding the ending of *Roque Santeiro* suggests, closed serials also offer viewers an opportunity after closure to look back upon the completed text and impose upon it some kind of moral or ideological order. In this sense, closed serials are, as Ana Lopez notes, inherently melodramatic in nature. To use Peter Brooks's phrase, melodramas are narratives of the "moral occult."[31] They offer us worlds in which the unthinking decision, the chance encounter, the accidental occurrence, the meaningless tragedy all seem connected to some deeper but obscure pattern of significance, some hidden moral order. Each twist of the plot implicitly prompts us to ask "what does this mean?" "Why is this happening?" The

23

melodrama defers providing any answers until the end, when the outline of the operative moral or ideological universe comes into view through the way in which resolution and closure are imposed upon the narrative. The attenuation of the narrative in closed serials combined with the privileging of closure – both within the text and in intertextual discourse – invites the viewer to supply or discern a moral to the story.

The open serial's lack of closure enables it to accommodate a wide range of interpretations among its viewers. Indeed, the elaborate discourse about serials – generated by viewers as they watch, among viewers on a work break or on the playground, and in the pages of magazines devoted to serials – reflects the process that occurs within each viewer as she or he comes to terms with the serial text. Because of the gaps created by its serial structure, even the closed serial, for a time at least, opens up issues, values, and meanings that the text itself cannot immediately close off. In her essay on the Chinese serial *Kewang*, Lisa Rofel attests to this phenomenon. Despite the government's attempt to impose meanings upon the text through extratextual discourse about it, the very seriality of the narrative rendered these attempts at textual and ideological closure ineffective.

The collection of essays on both open and closed serials that follows is not designed to map completely the near global terrain now covered by soap operas in one form or another. Rather, it suggests something of their range and diversity while addressing some of the important issues their production, distribution, and reception raise for scholars in media and cultural studies. Nor is this project intended as an uncritical celebration of the soap opera. For the most part, serials are created as vehicles for selling viewers to advertisers, and, as such, they first and foremost serve the interests of the institutions that produce, broadcast, and sponsor them. These interests may well be at odds with those of some of their viewers. By the same token, however, the serial form itself and its various manifestations on television systems around the world clearly engage viewers in ways and on a scale that is perhaps unprecedented in the history of storytelling. To attribute this phenomenon either to the hypnotic power of the media or the mental inadequacies of soap opera viewers (both of which have been proposed in the past) accounts neither for the meanings or the pleasures they generate. This collection represents a snapshot of the kind of serious and productive work being done on the serial form by scholars around the world. It is work that, like the form it analyzes, is necessarily "to be continued."

Notes

1 Robert C. Allen, *Speaking of Soap Operas* (Chapel Hill, NC: University of North Carolina Press, 1985), pp. 114–122.
2 See, among other testimonials to the popularity of serials, Matt Moffett, "All the World Sobs Over Mexican Soaps," *Wall Street Journal* (January 9, 1992), p. 1;

and Everett M. Rogers and Livia Antola, "Telenovelas: A Latin American Success Story," *Journal of Communication* 35 (4) (1985).

3 Allen, *Speaking of Soap Operas*, pp. 8–29.

4 David Buckingham, *Public Secrets: EastEnders and its Audience* (London: BFI, 1987).

5 Dorothy Hobson, "Soap Operas at Work," in Ellen Seiter, Hans Borchers, Gabriele Kreutzner, and Eva-Maria Warth (eds), *Remote Control: Television, Audiences, and Cultural Power* (London: Routledge, 1989), pp. 150–167.

6 Dwight MacDonald, "A Theory of Mass Culture," *Diogenes* 3 (summer 1953), pp. 10–17.

7 *Broadcasting* March 1, 1935, p. 12.

8 Max Wylie, "Dusting Off Dr. Berg," *Printer's Ink* (February 12, 1943), p. 44.

9 May Wylie, "Washboard Weepers," *Harper's* (November 1942), p. 635.

10 Natan Katzman, "Television Soap Operas: What's Been Going On Anyway?," *Public Opinion Quarterly* 36 (1972), pp. 200–212.

11 An article on soap operas taken from her dissertation was published in 1979. See "The Search for Tomorrow in Today's Soap Operas," *Film Quarterly* (fall 1979). See also her *Loving With a Vengeance* (Hamden, Conn.: Archon Books, 1982).

12 Richard Dyer, Christine Geraghty, Marion Jordan, Terry Lovell, Richard Patterson, and John Stewart, *Coronation Street* (London: BFI, 1981); Dorothy Hobson, *Crossroads: The Drama of a Soap Opera* (London: Methuen, 1982).

13 Richard Hoggart, *The Uses of Literacy* (London: Penguin, 1958).

14 Hobson's insistence on examining *Crossroads* as the result of a dynamic set of institutional practices and a different but equally complex set of reading (viewing) practices can also be seen in one of the first scholarly books on Australian serials: John Tulloch and Albert Moran's *A Country Practice: 'Quality Soap'* (Sydney: Currency Press, 1986). They speak of the meaning of the serial they investigate (*A Country Practice*) arising from its "performance," not just by actors but by all those involved in its production, distribution, and reception.

15 Ien Ang, *Watching "Dallas": Soap Opera and the Melodramatic Imagination*, trans. by Della Couling (London: Methuen, 1982).

16 See, in particular, Fiske's *Television Culture* (London: Methuen, 1987). David Morley, *The "Nationwide" Audience* (London: BFI, 1980); Buckingham, *Public Secrets*.

17 Maria Teresa Quiroz, "La Telenovela peruana: antecedentes y situacion actual," in Nora Mazziotti (ed.), *El espectaculo de las pasion: Las telenovelas latino-americanas* (Buenos Aires: Ediciones Colihue, 1992), pp. 111–132.

18 See Monica Rector, "A televisao e a telenovela," *Cultura* 5 (18), pp. 112–117; Ondina Leal, *A novela das oito* (Petropolis: Vozes, 1985); Tomas Lopez-Pumarejo, *Aproximacion a la telenovela* (Madrid: Catedra, 1987); Michèle and Armand Mattelart, *The Carnival of Images: Brazilian Television Fiction* (New York: Bergin & Garvey, 1990); Jesús Martín-Barbero, "Communicacion, pueblo y cultura en el tiempo de las transnacionales," in M. de Moragas (ed.) *Sociologia de la comunicacion de masas* (Barcelona: Gustavo Gili, 1985); Renato Ortiz, Silvia Hebera, Simões Borell, José Mário, and Ortiz Ramos, *Telenovela: historia e producao* (São Paulo: Editorio Brasiliense, 1988); Nora Mazziotti (ed.), *El espectaculo de las pasion: Las telenovelas latinoamericanas* (Buenos Aires: Ediciones Colihue, 1992).

19 Mattelart and Mattelart, *The Carnival of Images*, p. 51.

20 Mattelart and Mattelart, *The Carnival of Images*, p. 13; *Variety* (March 23, 1992), p. 82; Jose Marques de Melo, "Brazil's Role as a Television Exporter Within the Latin American Regional Market," paper presented at the International Communication Association Conference, 1992.

21 Moffett, "All the World Sobs"; *Variety* (March 23, 1992), p. 78, (September 28, 1992), p. 58.
22 Interview, Ric Burns and Don Battye, Grundy Television, Sydney, Australia (September 1992).
23 *Variety* (October 5, 1992), p. 60.
24 Of course, PBS has been a key venue for serialized British fiction for decades; the *Masterpiece Theatre* slot on Sunday evenings showcasing such "quality" multi-part dramas as *The Jewel in the Crown* and *The Forsyte Saga*. But until PBS stations were offered *EastEnders* in the late 1980s, public television viewers in the US had not seen anything British audiences would recognize as a "soap opera." *EastEnders* has not been a huge success, even by PBS's modest standards. Not all PBS affiliates choose to run it, and it has no regular prime-time slot. In my market, two episodes of *EastEnders* are shown at 11:30 p.m. on Sunday evenings, scheduling that guarantees it will have a tiny, if devoted, audience.
25 Wolfgang Iser, *The Act of Reading: A Theory of Aesthetic Response* (Baltimore, Md.: Johns Hopkins University Press, 1978).
26 Christine Geraghty, *Women and Soap Opera: A Study of Prime Time Soaps* (London: Polity, 1991), p. 4.
27 The late (and, by some, lamented) British serial *Crossroads* used a motel for the same purpose. An exception to the above – sure to be noted by British readers – is Channel Four's *Brookside*, which debuted in 1982. Creator Phil Redmond quite consciously rejected the idea of centering the serial around a pub, feeling that British social life in the 1980s no longer revolved around pubs. Instead he set *Brookside* in an eponymous suburban cul-de-sac, where, as in *Neighbours* three years later, character interaction could develop among its residents. See *Phil Redmond's Brookside: The Official Companion* (Weidenfeld & Nicolson, 1987).
28 It is interesting in this regard to note the efforts of western social agencies and Third World governments to use "soap operas" to instill "pro-social" values: progressive farming practices, family planning, AIDS prevention, etc. So far as I am aware, in every case the vehicle employed has been the closed serial. This has been for some obvious, but perhaps also some not so obvious reasons. Empiricist-oriented social scientists need to bring their experiments to closure in order to test attitudes, behaviors, ideation, "before and after" – something difficult if not impossible to do with an open serial. Also, television programming is expensive, and no government agency is likely to fund a new program indefinitely. But it is also the case that the closed serial can impose an ultimate and determinant "message" upon the text (whether or not the audience chooses to take it up in the same way the producers and writers "intend" is another matter) in a way that the open serial cannot. The latter always leaves open the possibility of reversal. See Larry Kincaid, "The Pro-Social Soap Opera in Changing Behaviors in a Variety of Third World Settings," and Joseph Potter and Emile McAnany, "Popular Culture, Public Policy and Communication Theory: Brazilian Novelas and Family Practice Change," both papers presented at the 1993 Conference of the International Communication Association, Washington, DC.
29 *Phil Redmond's Brookside*, p. 7.
30 Nico Vink, *The Telenovela and Emancipation: A Study on Television and Social Change in Brazil* (Amsterdam: Royal Tropical Institute, 1988), p. 179.
31 See Peter Brooks, *The Melodramatic Imagination: Balzac, Henry James, Melodrama, and the Mode of Excess* (New York: Columbia University Press, 1985).

1

Doubtless to be continued
A brief history of serial narrative

Roger Hagedorn

Introduction

In a section of *S/Z* entitled "contract-narratives," Roland Barthes asserts that narrative is not only production (the story as it "unfolds") but product. As such, it is "legal tender, subject to contract, economic stakes, in short, *merchandise*, barter." Narrative's material basis is an often overlooked fact. When it comes to serial narrative, however, this fact cannot be ignored because it is at the heart of what distinguishes a serial, to what purposes serials have traditionally been put, and how this narrative form developed.[1]

Contrary to popular belief, the serial is not limited to a particular medium nor genre. Consider for a moment the following example serials: *Pickwick Papers* and *Les mystères de Paris*; *The Perils of Pauline* and *The Phantom Rider*; *Amos 'n' Andy* and *Ma Perkins*; *Buck Rogers* and *Little Orphan Annie*; *NYPD Blue*, *All My Children*, and *Wild Palms*. The first thing one may notice is the variety of media represented: part-issue print publications and newspapers, film, radio, newspapers again, and television. The reader may also recognize the diversity of narrative types invoked: novels, fiction films, comic strips, long-running radio and television programs, and the television miniseries. As for the traditional narrative category of genre, one can easily identify yet another degree of difference. Among serials, one finds comedies (*Soap*), mysteries (*Twin Peaks*), westerns (*Railroad Raiders*), courtroom dramas (*L.A. Law*), adolescent adventure tales (*Jack Armstrong, the All-American Boy*), science fiction (*Flash Gordon*), political satire (*Amerika*), erotica (*The Pearl*), and domestic melodramas (*Search for Tomorrow*). All things considered, it may appear as though serials have no particular narrative specificity. Certainly this is true in so far as surface narrative content, generic affiliation, and medium are concerned.

Serials are distinguished as a narrative form by the discourse they trace between the producing industry and the readers/spectators/listeners who consume them. In other words, one must look to the mode of production, distribution, and consumption of serials; that is, how and when individual texts are materially presented to the consuming public. Serials are defined through the practice of offering a narrative text to consumers in isolated, materially independent units available at different but predictable times: in a word, in successive episodes. Episodicity is *the* crucial trait which distinguishes the serial (and the series) from the "classic" narrative text – that is, the single-unit realistic narrative, including the novel in book form, the feature film, the radio play, and so on. While a classic text can be consumed however the consumer wishes, because he or she generally has material control over the text in its entirety before beginning to consume it, serials' mode of presentation places consumers at the whim of the medium that presents them (or, more precisely, at the whim of those who command the medium that presents serial texts). Episodicity functions as a textual sign of the serial's material existence as merchandise and, therefore, of the discourse established between the producing industry and the consuming public.

Episodicity works in conjunction with reified forms of the two sequential codes Barthes elaborates in *S/Z* in such a way that serials break with the three classical unities. Multiplying the elements of time, space, and character allows for infinitely greater narrative complication. Furthermore, serials differ from classic narratives in multiplying the number of narrative enigmas as well as partial answers, snares, delays, and so on that are activated in the course of the narrative. A more striking difference is in regularly setting up delays *across the narrative breaks* which result from the serial's episodic presentation. This kind of suspension functions obviously to stimulate consumption of later episodes. Though by no means the only kind of enigmas activated by a serial, the suspension of predication across the various narrative breaks is behind the colloquial term for the serial, the "cliff-hanger." It is precisely the way in which what Barthes calls narrative's "instinct for preservation" is mobilized over textual breaks that allows us to account for the difference between the classic text and the serial.[2]

These differences between classic texts and serials are not particularly radical, which prompts the question: why do serials exist? In a word, because from their beginnings, serials have been used to accomplish three tasks. At the most basic level, an episode of any one particular serial functions to promote continued consumption of later episodes of the same serial, which is specifically why the cliff-hanger ending was developed. In addition to self-promotion, serials have traditionally functioned to promote product loyalty. For example, any Pathé film serial in effect promotes all other Pathé serials or, to offer a contemporary example, the broadcast of a television mini-series such as *Menendez: A Murder in Beverly Hills* includes heavy promotion of the network's regularly scheduled programming.

It is serials' public which has consistently provided the dependable mass of consumers essential to any "mass media." Obviously, individual serials function to increase newspaper circulation, the sale of theater tickets, or provide audiences for advertising spots. More significantly but indirectly, in attracting a large audience to a particular medium, serials also serve to promote the very medium in which they appear. This explains why serials have been introduced into every medium precisely at the point at which they are emerging as a mass medium: because they constitute a remarkably effective tool for establishing and then developing a substantial consuming public for that medium. Once attracted, that audience is then available and predisposed to consume other texts the particular medium provides. And for this same reason, serials have also been used to expand an existing audience base by targeting specific subgroups of the population, generally women or children. When a medium needs an audience, it turns to serials.

Long before the development of serial fiction, many narrative works contained elements associated with serials. For example, the *Arabian Nights* is not merely episodic but includes stories embedded in other stories and its characters appear in several levels of discourse, the effect of which is to create a diegetic world inhabited by a large cast of recurring characters, some of whom talk to or of others (much like the gossip one finds in contemporary soap operas). The visual arts too offer precursors to serial narrative. Greek and Roman reliefs, for example, present elaborate narratives in fragmented, horizontal bands which must be read sequentially, much like strip serials. Yet none of these is a serial. What is lacking is the production and distribution of fragmented narrative in a mass medium that is consumed at regular intervals. Historically, for this to occur, one needs a social context characterized by three essential elements: a market economy, a communications technology sufficiently developed to be commercially exploited, and, as Barthes suggests, the recognition of narrative as commodity.

Publishing mysteries: part-issue print, magazine, and newspaper serials

The first such technology to be exploited was the printing press. Serial publication has existed for centuries, having proved itself a viable technique for circulating voluminous episodic narratives such as *L'Astrée* and *Le Grand Cyrus*. Despite increased commercial use of movable type printing in the seventeenth and eighteenth centuries, books remained a premium item available to only a select few. So to reduce the purchase price, expand the market, and thereby increase profits, publishers produced editions of large works in fascicles available to subscribers in low-cost installments. This practice became known as part-issue or publication in numbers.[3]

The earliest instance of this practice was the publication in England of Joseph Moxon's *Mechanik Exercises; or The Doctrine of Handy-Works* in 1678. Part-issue publication initially made available histories, geographies, encyclopedias, romances, and the Bible. By the nineteenth century, however, the mainstay of part-issue publication was original fiction, beginning in 1836 with the publication of Charles Dickens's *Pickwick Papers*. Monthly periodicals quickly followed suit. Throughout the century authors, including Anthony Trollope and Thomas Hardy, offered completed works or contracted to write original fiction which was serialized in magazines like *Graphic* and *Cornhill Magazine*.[4]

The first acknowledged production of a newspaper serial also occurred in England. The Stamp Act of 1712 imposed a halfpenny tax on half-sheet newspapers and a penny tax on full-sheet newspapers, but classified all publications larger than one page but not of book-length as pamphlets subject to only a 2 shillings per page tax. Capitalizing on this legal loophole, many publishers produced one and a half page newspapers, identifying them as pamphlets. When news articles did not fill the additional space, publishers often reprinted fiction. By the time Parliament revised the Stamp Act in 1724, closing the loophole, readers had developed a taste for daily installments of fiction, so publishers continued the practice as a means of maintaining readership.[5]

The introduction of this practice in France completely revolutionized French newspapers and made newspaper serials a worldwide phenomenon. Until 1830 French newspapers were *"journaux d'opinion"* which promoted various political positions. As such, their circulation depended upon the relative influence of the position they represented and was, in the main, stable. Between 1830 and 1845, however, the French press was radically transformed by the repeal of official censorship. *Journaux d'opinion* were gradually replaced by anonymous commercial ventures whose *raison d'être* was simply the development of capital revenue through purely commercial means.[6]

This transformation came about largely due to the rivalry between two publishers: Emile de Girardin and Armand Dutacq. On July 1, 1836 Girardin launched *La presse*. On the same date Dutacq, who had collaborated with Girardin during the planning phase of his paper, turned rival and began publishing *Le siècle*. Rather than charging the going subscription rate, both papers were conceived as "2 penny papers" whose subscription rate was half that of competing papers.[7]

Girardin's strategy was to cut prices while expanding production and sales. In order to offset the fall in the profit margin per unit sold, Girardin counted on substantially increasing the number of subscriptions sold and selling advertising space. The catch was to develop a broader reading public by providing non-political, hitherto unavailable material. He chose to exploit original fiction in serial form. To ensure the success of this gambit, Girardin approached the most famous novelist of the period, and Honoré de Balzac's *La vieille fille* began its run in *La presse* on October 23, 1836. Its success was quickly imitated by other newspapers and by 1842 the serial publication of original fiction had become an integral component of every newspaper in France.[8]

The most famous French newspaper serial is Eugène Sue's *Les mystères de Paris*, which set the standard for successful serial writing. Its 147 installments, appearing in *Le journal des débats* during 1842–1843, drew literally thousands of new subscribers. A rival publisher quickly bought Sue's

Le juif errant and saw his circulation rise from 3,600 subscribers to approximately 23,000. Sue's phenomenal success was due in part to the author's sensational subject – matter, which included convicts, suicides, murders, foundling children, conspiracies, and a mysterious avenging angel; it was also due to his elaboration of the serial narrative technique.[9]

Les mystères de Paris is a multiple focus *"roman-fleuve"* that exploits an enormous cast of characters and shifts the space of action frequently, creating an effect much like cross-cutting in film. As a consequence, readers become involved with dozens of characters and the incredible amount of action they are involved with at any one time. Furthermore, Sue's narrative strategy successfully exploits the inherent formal limitation of serial publication: each installment ends at a point of unresolved narrative tension, precisely in order to leave the readers in suspense. Sue cannot take credit for having invented the cliff-hanger, but he can for being the first to exploit it so elaborately and consistently. Finally, Sue and his editors also established the pattern of writing at the same rate as the novel was published so that its course could be modified according to reader reaction.[10]

Sue's work demonstrated the importance of serials in expanding newspaper circulation in general and *daily* newspapers in particular. It also made clear serials' ability to stimulate truly mass appeal, especially among people who might not otherwise purchase a newspaper. Not only did businessmen and lawyers consume his fiction; so too did chambermaids, domestic cooks, shopkeepers, and day laborers. Although countless authors wrote successful serials, including Alexandre Dumas and Emile Zola, Sue first demonstrated the potential for mass consumption of serial narrative and the profits that could be made by publishing it. So successful were his works that when translated and published throughout Europe and South America, they incited an international vogue for serial fiction in newspapers which lasted until the First World War.[11]

Illustrating humor: the comic strip

An industry rivalry resembling that between Dutacq and Girardin was also responsible for the development of the comic strip. The invention of photoengraving in 1873 made possible inexpensive newspaper illustration and newspaper publishers including William Randolph Hearst, Joseph Pulitzer, and James Gordon Bennet, Jr quickly harnessed its potential by incorporating illustrations into their papers. Then in 1895, Hearst acquired the *New York Morning Journal*. In order to outsell his rivals, Hearst determined that the *Journal* would feature the first complete comic supplement – "eight pages of polychromatic effulgence that make the rainbow look like a lead pipe" – and he lured Richard Felton Outcault away from Pulitzer to develop a series of comic drawings featuring a bald child dressed in a nightshirt.[12]

The previous year, while a staff artist on the *New York World*, Outcault had developed a weekly, large-panel comic illustration in association with E. W. Townsend: "Hogan's Alley." When Outcault went to the *Journal*, he transformed one of its characters into the central character and the strip became known as "The Yellow Kid," considered the first American comic strip. The series was so popular that the *Morning Journal* quickly became the largest American newspaper, with a circulation of over 1.5 million in 1907.[13]

Though the first strips constituted series, it wasn't long before strip serials developed. Judith O'Sullivan asserts that Winsor McCay's "Little Nemo in Slumberland" "is the first sustained comic-strip narrative, its epic story unfolding over a five-year period (1905–1910)." Other historians point to Rudolph Dirk ("The Katzenjammer Kids") and Lyonel Feininger ("The Kinder-Kids") as artists who early on expanded serial narrative possibilities. The most obvious serial trait, the cliff-hanger, was introduced by Charles W. Kahles's "Hairbreadth Harry" in 1906 and became a featured element of Harry Hershfield's "Desperate Desmond" beginning in 1912.[14]

The heyday of strip serials, however, were the 1930s and 1940s when, in addition to humor, adventure and crime became central subjects of daily and weekly strips. A few established strips developed serial adventures in the late 1920s, including Harold Gray's "Little Orphan Annie," but it was primarily new strips like Rex Maxon and Harold Foster's "Tarzan" (1929) and Alex Raymond's "Flash Gordon" (1934) that set the trend for serialized adventure and science fiction. The sequential linking of both daily and Sunday episodes then became a standard practice of the *Chicago Tribune–New York Daily News* syndicate in strips such as Chester Gould's "Dick Tracy" (1931) and Milton Caniff's "Terry and the Pirates" (1934).

The first comic strip series were directed at the entire family, but in the 1930s and 1940s comic syndicates used strip serials to target an adolescent, primarily male, audience. The portrayal of adventure and science fiction narratives through dynamic visual design and color provided just that audience, which was also being courted by the movie and radio industries at that time. All three media had only recently discovered this hitherto untapped potential audience of potential consumers and each used serial narratives to exploit them, in direct competition with the others.

One serial strip, however, eschewed adolescent males and targeted instead a female audience: Martha Orr's "Apple Mary," begun in 1934. When its creator married, John Saunders and Dale Connor transformed its heroine into the wealthy widow Mary Worth. Initially a commentary on the Depression, "Mary Worth" developed into a sort of strip soap opera focusing on the emotional and romantic problems of women in glamorous professions – artists, advertising writers, business executives, and the like. This and similar strips, such as Harold LeDoux's "Judge Parker," continue to appear, but there has never been a vogue for them, perhaps because the main rival to this kind of strip emerged in a competing medium, the radio soap opera, which also developed in the mid-1930s.

Weekly wonders: American movie serials

Throughout the early years of film production, newspaper publishing remained, on the surface, an aloof and disinterested spectator. But the involvement of the newspaper industry in film production grew once it recognized that movies could be a significant tool for boosting newspaper circulation. Two major publishers correctly thought they could attract additional readers to their newspapers by having episodic films made to illustrate the serial fiction appearing in their newspapers.[15]

When Hearst decided to expand his publishing empire into the Chicago market, he embroiled his *Evening American* in bitter competition with Cyrus McCormick's *Chicago Tribune*. In 1912, the cover of the *Ladies World*, the *Evening American*'s women's supplement, featured an artist's rendering of the ideal American woman. The magazine's director then decided to illustrate her adventures, leading to the Edison Company's 1912 *What Happened to Mary?*, a twelve-part episodic film presented on a monthly basis coinciding with the newspaper's publication of the story. In 1913 *What Happened to Mary?* was followed by one of the earliest sequels, the six-episode *Who Will Marry Mary?* As before, its story was serialized in the *Ladies World*, thus successfully linking episodic film production to weekly newspaper publication.[16]

At this point defections and industrial espionage between Hearst and McCormick played a key role in the development of film serials. Due to a series of defections from Hearst's Chicago office, McCormick learned of the *Mary* film while it was still in production. As a result, one of the defectors developed the 1913 Selig serial, the *Adventures of Kathlyn*, for McCormick; episode summaries were published throughout the week prior to the film's release. The result generated 50,000 new readers for the *Tribune*. However, the head of Hearst's King Features Syndicate learned of McCormick's plans through Selig, and so Hearst bought the rights to a film already in production, *The Active Life of Dolly of the Dailies* (1914), and serialized its narrative in his papers. He also ordered the production of *Lucille Love, Girl of Mystery* (1914) and *The Perils of Pauline*, the first serial produced by Pathé (with whom Hearst would develop a long-standing relationship). *Pauline*'s story was also serialized in Hearst's *Chicago Evening* and became, in Anthony Slide's words, "the first of the big-money serials." McCormick responded with *The Million Dollar Mystery*. Costing US$125,000, it grossed a reported US$500,000 and "the return to the stockholders was 700 per cent."[17]

By the end of 1914 twenty film serials were in general distribution and theaters regularly carried serials developed in conjunction with newspapers. More than fifty serials were made in 1915, and the numbers continued to mount in subsequent years. Curiously, *Kathlyn* and its immediate followers were designed as support material to the print media rather than films produced on the initiative of film studios. Early serials were developed in order to increase newspaper sales, just as newspaper serials had done so successfully in the previous century. This industry link only lasted a few years, however. Almost from the start, film serials were also produced independently of the publishing industry, including many of the most successful serials, such as *Gloria's Romance* and *A Lass of the Lumberlands* (both released in 1916). By the mid-1910s, serials had proven themselves such an effective tool for establishing and then developing a substantial consuming film-going public that producers no longer needed newspaper support, nor did they wish to share the profits.[18]

Serial films had also proved themselves particularly successful in cultivating specific subgroups of the consuming public. As suggested by the majority of titles cited above, serial film producers generally targeted a female audience by intertwining romance with action. After all, 75 percent of the film-going audience in the mid-1910s consisted of adult males, so for further market expansion to take place, producers needed to cultivate female consumers. By the 1930s, however, women had become accustomed to regular movie consumption and, in the wake of the transition to sound, serial production companies turned their efforts to the exploitation of a new target audience, children, with serials like *Undersea Kingdom* (1936). As one exhibition manual pointed out, "The kids of today are the men and women of tomorrow – and you can bank their money just as easily as you can adult admission."[19]

During the 1930s and 1940s, film serial producers' fiercest competition for the adolescent consumer came not from other film producers, but from those of rival media: radio and comic serials. Often as not, their solution was to adapt material. For example, *Flash Gordon* (1936) and *Dick Tracy* (1937) were based on adventure strips, while radio provided *The Lone Ranger* (1938) and *The Green Hornet* (1940). This solution worked well enough until television came on the scene in the 1950s, at which point serial films ceased to be produced.[20]

Exploiting the air waves: radio serials

In 1926, the Radio Corporation of America founded the National Broadcasting Company, the result of years of convoluted machinations between American Telephone and Telegraph, RCA, General Electric, and Westinghouse who, only seven years earlier, when they formed an illegal trust to control the industry, had no thought of broadcasting. As William White of GE remarked: "We had everything except the idea."[21]

However, the industry moved quickly. Michele Hilmes notes that by 1927 "radio broadcasting had taken on most of the structural, economic, and regulatory features that were to characterize the radio, and later television, industry for the next fifty years," notably advertiser-based commercial broadcasting. Between NBC's founding and 1932, broadcast radio became completely dominated by advertising interests. Despite the fact that the network's stated purpose was "to provide machinery which will insure a national distribution of national programs, and a wider distribution of programs of the highest quality," programming was created with the specific idea of attracting sponsors. In fact, sponsors and/or their advertising agencies maintained direct involvement in the production and scheduling of programming until the mid-1950s.[22]

By the early 1930s radio broadcasting was a thriving entertainment industry dependent upon delivering substantial audiences on a regular basis to the programs' sponsors. Networks were thus forced to develop more attractive programming than the musical and talk shows they had depended upon in radio's first decade. One solution for attracting such an audience was suggested by vaudeville, the movies, and theater: use star-power. Hence the development of variety programs featuring established stars like Fred Allen and Will Rogers. The talk show and the quiz or audience participation show, on the other hand, used gossip and the possibility of prizes to stimulate audience interest.[23]

The tremendous success of *Amos 'n' Andy*, however, demonstrated the potential of serial programming to attract a large audience. Created by Freeman Gosden and Charles Correll in 1926 and, according to various reports, based on the comic strip "Andy Gump" or "Mutt and Jeff," *Amos 'n' Andy* relied for its appeal on audience interest in character and narrative. By the end of its first year on NBC's Blue Network in 1929, *Amos 'n' Andy* had become the most popular show on the radio, drawing some 40 million listeners weekly. The unprecedented popularity of the program demonstrated that listeners would follow serial programs and the industry took note.[24]

In the early 1930s NBC introduced other comic serials modeled on *Amos 'n' Andy*, including *The Rise of the Goldbergs, Just Plain Bill*, and *Myrt and Marge*, while CBS developed *Easy Aces*. Like their model, these programs were broadcast in the early evening. Serials came to dominate radio, however, once attention was turned to the afternoon schedule. Soap operas, domestic serials that featured prominent female protagonists coping with Depression-era dilemmas, were developed as advertising vehicles for health and beauty products; hence the term "soap opera." These products' manufacturers were attracted to the earlier time period by the reduced rates of daytime broadcasting and the time slot's accessibility to women in the home. (Women had long been recognized as the primary domestic consumers and, thus, the ideal audience for these products' advertisements.) Sponsors believed that the kind of loyalty and dedication listeners developed for serial characters might be transferred to their products.[25]

Robert C. Allen notes that in early 1930

Henry Selinger, station manager of WGN, approached the advertising firm of Lord and Thomas with the idea of developing a daytime serial

35

story that would be of special interest to women, and, hence, to manufacturers of products used in the home.

Actress–writer Irna Phillips then drafted several scripts for the project which became *Painted Dreams*, a daily 15-minute serial that went on the air as a sustaining program in October 1930. Concerning Mother Moynihan and her children, the program lasted less than a year but established the practice of linking corporate sponsorship, serial narrative, and women consumers. Within two years, daytime programming would be dominated by this practice, thanks in part to the efforts of Frank and Anne Hummert, of the Blackett–Sample–Hummert advertising agency, who developed early serials such as *The Romance of Helen Trent* and *Ma Perkins* for clients that included Colgate, Lever Brothers, and Procter & Gamble.[26]

In 1933 *Just Plain Bill* and *Easy Aces* were rescheduled for afternoon broadcast, seven new soap operas were introduced, and more were being developed. As Allen writes,

> Between 1933 and 1937 serial drama became a staple of daytime programming, and companies like Procter and Gamble, Pillsbury, American Home Products, and General Foods came to rely more and more upon the soap opera as their primary radio advertising vehicle.

In 1937 Phillips introduced *The Guiding Light* and *The Edge of Night*, while the Hummerts began *Lorenzo Jones* and *Stella Dallas*, four of the longest-running soaps. By 1940, sixty-four different soap operas were in regular broadcast, including all ten of the highest-rated daytime programs. Though their numbers declined slightly thereafter, on average some thirty-nine soap operas were broadcast throughout the 1940s.[27]

By 1941 serials represented nearly 90 percent of all advertiser-sponsored daytime programming. Not all radio serials addressed a female audience, however. Beginning in 1931 with *Little Orphan Annie*, based on the comic strip serial, many of the same agencies that developed soap operas produced programs targeted at children, including Blackett–Sample–Hummert, the advertising agency responsible for *Jack Armstrong, the All-American Boy* as well as *Little Orphan Annie*. Like soap operas, they were broadcast in 15-minute episodes Monday through Friday, but adolescent serials filled the late afternoon, when children were home from school. Their sponsors, manufacturers of foodstuffs like Ovaltine and Ralston cereal, offered premiums – flashlights, decoder rings, and the like – in exchange for box-tops, which allowed them to estimate their audience and encourage listeners to consume their products. And like soap operas, the story-lines were distinctly extended. In serials like *Bobby Benson* and *Tom Mix*, an adventure might occupy the characters for weeks or months, at which point a new mystery was immediately introduced.[28]

From the mid-1930s through the 1940s, radio's adolescent serials relied on successful strip and film serials that emphasized crime-fighting to draw listeners to the likes of *Dick Tracy* and *Terry and the Pirates*, while the 1940s added war heroes such as *Captain Midnight*. In the late 1940s adolescent serials were extended to half-hour episodes. Many of the older serials such as *Tom Mix* were replaced by newer ones like *Mark Trail* during the early 1950s. But the advent of television brought a competing medium into the picture. Television transferred very few of these serials from radio, created even fewer new ones in direct competition with radio, and, most significantly, siphoned off radio's sponsors. Only five radio serials remained in the 1952–1953 radio season, two in 1954–1955, and none by 1956.[29]

Invisible waves of gain: television serials

In the postwar era, television quickly replaced radio broadcasting as the primary entertainment medium in the United States. The development of commercial television did not follow the same path as had radio. While television's early history too involved patent battles, corporate strategies, and regulatory decisions, these had been resolved in the 1930s and 1940s, allowing the broadcast giants to maintain their control and transform a new technology into a mass medium. As NBC network executive, Sylvester Weaver, stated in 1950, "Whereas in radio we had to find our way through hit or miss methods, we now have a pattern we believe will enable us, with great economy, to do a tremendous job in television without too much experimentation."[30]

When it came to programming, television avoided experimentation by cannibalizing radio, stripping radio programming to the bone, and leaving for the most part only what radio began with: news reports, talk shows, and recorded music. As a result, Hilmes notes that "the advent of regular television broadcasting caused radio ratings to fall precipitously throughout the industry."[31]

Curiously, television only briefly offered adolescent serials. Although the DuMont network ran *Captain Video* from 1949 until the network's demise in 1955, networks generally preferred developing series programming for children and adolescents. As for comic serials, they had virtually disappeared from radio by 1935 and none was developed for television. Only the daytime soap survived the transition to television.[32]

Throughout the late 1940s radio soap operas held their own, but the transitional years of the early 1950s brought a loss of sponsorship and audiences. Radio soaps including *Just Plain Bill,.Lorenzo Jones*, and *Stella Dallas* were cancelled in 1955; 1959–1960 saw the end not only of *Mary Noble: Backstage Wife* and *Ma Perkins* but of all radio soaps. By then, however, soap operas were an established television genre.

Experimentation with televised soap operas began in the late 1940s. In 1947 DuMont broadcast *A Woman to Remember*, a short-lived program that never found a sponsor. A televised adaptation of *Ma Perkins* was Procter & Gamble's first attempt at the genre. This was also unsuccessful, possibly because its radio fans had their own conception of the serial's characters. Procter & Gamble decided instead to create made-for-TV soaps. Their initial attempt, *The First Hundred Years*, was broadcast on CBS in 1950 but lasted only two years. However, Procter & Gamble followed in 1951 with two other original serials, *Search for Tomorrow* and *Love of Life*, both of which lasted some thirty-five years. In addition, several popular radio soaps, notably *The Guiding Light* and *The Brighter Day*, were adapted for television in the early 1950s while still broadcast on radio. In the mid-1950s, Procter & Gamble also developed the first half-hour soap operas, *As the World Turns* and *The Edge of Night*. In all, thirty-five television soaps were introduced during the 1950s.[33]

In subsequent decades, soaps have undergone numerous changes and a few challenges. The 1960s brought the advent of several of the most successful soaps of all time, including *General Hospital*, *Another World*, and *Days Of Our Lives*. In the 1970s the latter two were the first to be expanded to 1-hour episodes. This development was a response to changes in audience demographics that took place in the 1960s and 1970s – notably a drop in the number of daytime viewers as more and more women sought work outside the home. Television soaps have also retained or regained a considerable audience by introducing increasingly controversial subject-matter – notably concerning sexual matters – and orienting plot lines to attract younger viewers. For the most part, these tactics have been successful. As Allen observes, since 1960 "the number of soap operas running during any given year has never dropped below ten." Only in the past few years have soap operas shown a significant decline.[34]

Following the success of British programs including *The Forsyte Saga* on the Public Broadcasting System, commercial networks began to develop what for the American audience was a new form of serial, the television miniseries, beginning in 1977 with *Roots*. Mini-series are serialized adaptations of best-selling novels whose episodes, generally four to six in all, are broadcast over successive nights. Though much more expensive than regular programming because of their high production values, location shooting, and star casting, these elements contribute to garnering a large viewing audience, as does the existence of a pre-established audience – those who read the book on which a particular mini-series is based – and these serials' often sensational subject-matter. Finally, networks use mini-series to attract viewers who would not generally watch television, including up-scale viewers sponsors are interested in reaching. Mini-series are therefore scheduled during "sweeps" periods and promoted by networks as special media events. As such, networks deliver an especially large and potentially diverse audience to their sponsors but also use this occasion for self-promotion – by advertising their regularly scheduled programs during the mini-series they hope that those audience members who enjoy a particular mini-series will be lured to the network's other offerings.[35]

Mini-series began to decline in number and success in the mid-1980s, in part because of a general glut of them, but also because what had lured their large audiences became more generally available through regularly broadcast evening serials. Beginning with *Dallas* in 1978, viewers could find the same production values, glamorous stars, and scandalous personal behavior in night-time soaps as they had found in mini-series like *Lace* or *Scruples*. *Dynasty* and the like also included the kind of big-business allure and narrative complexity that had contributed to the success of mini-series like *Rich Man, Poor Man* and *Master of the Game*. And while networks once attempted to draw viewers who would not generally watch television with mini-series such as *Holocaust* and *QBVII*, which presented more adult, sophisticated material than generally broadcast in the 1970s, much of the same material became available in other night-time serials of the 1980s, including *St. Elsewhere*, *Hill Street Blues*, and *Wise Guy*. For these reasons it would appear that, with the occasional exception such as *Wild Palms*, mini-series have largely been supplanted by regularly scheduled evening serials and made-for-television movies.[36]

By the early 1990s *Dallas*, *Dynasty*, *Knots Landing*, *Falcon Crest*, and the other evening soap successes of the 1980s had been canceled. Despite more recent offerings such as *Sisters* and *Melrose Place*, it may be that the night-time soap opera is, like the mini-series, an endangered species. However, other adult serials such as *Picket Fences*, *I'll Fly Away*, and *NYPD Blue* still flourish, in part because the content of these serials includes interpersonal turmoil as well as courtroom drama and law-enforcement action. Further-more, in addition to actual serials such as the above-mentioned programs, the historical success of televised serial drama has affected contemporary programming in a more widespread if diffuse manner: elements of serial narrative have been introduced into most series programs, resulting in various hybrid forms. In one hybrid form, each episode presents one or more problems which are then resolved at the conclusion of the episode, thereby identifying the program as a series. However, at the same time there exists at least one other problem, generally involving a developing relationship between central characters, which is left unresolved from one episode to the next. Jane Feuer aptly refers to this phenomenon as the serialization of the series and invokes *Cheers!* as an example. *Star Trek: Deep Space Nine* offers another kind of hybrid. In addition to using two-part episodes at broadcast season breaks, its writers often refer to elements of one episode in subsequent ones and, even more significantly, link eposides with characters and events from the original *Star Trek* and *Star Trek: The Next Generation* series, the effect of which is to create a sense of fictional space, history, and character development that is far more sophisticated and intricate than that of classic series programming. To a lesser extent, any significant, long-term change in the development of a series character – such as getting married (for example, *The Cosby Show*) or changing partners (*Law and Order*) – represents an instance of serialization. Sometimes these instances are developed to re-vitalize a floundering series by slightly altering the given situation (changing jobs in *Bob*). In short, serials continue to be broadcast by networks, serial–series hybrids have developed, and more traditional series now incorporate elements of serial narrative.[37]

The current situation

Today serial narratives are omnipresent. They may in fact be the dominant form of narrative presented through the mass media. Consider what is currently available in the United States. Though newspaper serials are a truly rare phenomenon, several magazines still occasionally offer serial fiction, including *Rolling Stone* (Tom Wolfe's *Bonfire of the Vanities*) and *Premiere* (John H. Richardson's *The Blue Screen*). Berke Breathed's "Outland" is one of the few remaining comic strip serials, but Tod McFarlane's *Spawn* and Dale Keown's *Pitt* demonstrate that serials have invaded the contemporary comic book market. People may no longer flock to the cinema on Saturdays to see the latest episode of their favorite serial, but the current inundation of sequels (*Rocky* I, II, III, and IV) and films such as *Back to the Future* illustrate this industry's renewed interest in profiting from successful narratives through continued elaboration. The *Star Wars* trilogy, whose films carried episode numbers, has also been broadcast over public radio as a ten-part serial, suggesting that there may still be a place for serial radio drama. (Certainly this still holds true in Great Britain.) As for television, not only does one find countless serials in the form of soap operas, night-time dramas and mini-series, but even PBS relies on serials in programs such as *Master-piece Theatre* (which offers a succession of serials) and *Mystery* (offering a combination of serials and series). In addition, in *Square One* and *Ghost Writer*, PBS has begun to exploit serials in their educational programming for children. Television commercials have also turned to serial strategies to sell products ranging from coffee (Tasters' Choice) and breakfast serials (Lucky Charms) to batteries (the most recent Eveready commercials). In short, serials continue to appear in every mass medium and dominate the television programming schedule.

By way of conclusion

Serials first came about in order to develop the commercial exploitation of the printing press. As subsequent media technology developed, serials were introduced in order to stimulate consumption of that medium's product. Thus, when advances in printing technology allowed for mass consumption of newspapers, the industry incorporated serial fiction on its front page, and when photoengraving became available to these publishers, the comic strip was developed; with the development of film as an exploitable medium, so followed the film serial; with radio broadcasting came *Amos 'n' Andy*, followed by countless soap operas and adolescent adventure narratives, and so on. In addition, when media industries decide to target a new sector of the population in order to expand their market share, they have consistently turned to serials as a solution, especially when interested in targeting women and children. Finally, while an individual serial might succeed or fail, the most significant competition any serial could face is any serial in a newly emerging mass medium. Thus film serials continued to be profitable until the success of radio serials, which in turn faded into memory as television came into being. In the so-called "information age," as technology evolves and media corporations merge, we can expect to see new developments not only in the realm of the mass media, but also in that of serial narrative. For this reason alone, this brief history of serials will undoubtedly need to be continued at a later date.

Notes

1 Roland Barthes, *S/Z*, trans. Richard Miller (New York: Hill and Wang, 1974), pp. 88–89.
2 The hermeneutic and proairetic codes that Barthes develops are particularly useful concepts for distinguishing between the classic text and serial narrative. They clarify how serials differ from classic narratives by increasing the number of enigmas, partial answers, snares, delays, and so on that are activated in the course of the narrative. In addition they elucidate the importance of creating delays across the narrative breaks between episodes. As a consequence of this concerted functioning of the two sequential codes, the serial more than the classic text appears to have what Barthes suggests as an "instinct for self-preservation" and it is precisely the way in which the "instinct for preservation" is mobilized over textual breaks that allows us to account for the difference between the classic text and the serial. See *S/Z*, pp. 18–20.
   The hermeneutic and proairetic codes Barthes identifies are also useful in distinguishing the serial from the series. Like the serial, the series is made commercially available in material units known as episodes and the series centers around a restricted set of characters – anywhere from one (extremely rare) to many, but generally centered on either some variation of the "family unit" (for example, *Father Knows Best* or *My Two Dads*) or a group of colleagues (for example, *The Adventures of Sherlock Holmes* or *Car 54, Where Are You?*). Unlike a serial, however, each episode of a series achieves closure. The hermeneutic code is engaged anew at the beginning of each episode, but the enigma or enigmas – for it often occurs that series mobilize pairs of enigmas, often tonally opposed (for example, one humorous, the other serious) in each episode – is resolved at the conclusion of that same episode, as are all actions begun during that period. This would explain why David Marc suggests that "each episode may appear to resemble a short, self-contained play." Because enigmas and proairetics are not carried over between episodes, series, unlike serials, do not establish temporal continuity between episodes. Thus, even though within each episode of a series, the narrative is subject to what Barthes refers to as the logico-temporal order, there is no corresponding relationship between its episodes. As a consequence, series

produce no notion of succession or causality from one episode to the next, nor any sense of process, development, or growth. For the series, there is at most some "basic story concept" or situation which is broad enough to allow for the creation of a large number of adventures, but these actions or situations bear no consequences for later episodes. In a sense, individual episodes of a series function like cards in a deck – they can be shuffled without distorting the deck. Episodes of a serial, however, are like interlocked links in a chain – missing even one risks the integrity of the whole. See David Marc, *Democratic Vistas: Television in American Culture* (Philadelphia, Pa.: University of Pennsylvania Press, 1984), p. 12.

3 Robert L. Patten, "*Pickwick Papers* and the Development of Serial Fiction," *Rice University Studies* 61 (1) (winter 1975), p. 52. See also Roy McKeen Wiles, *Serial Publication in England Before 1750* (New York: Cambridge University Press, 1957), pp. 1–14.

4 J. Don Vann, *Victorian Novels in Serial* (New York: MLA, 1985), pp. 1–6.

5 Ibid, pp. 1–2. See also Wiles, *Serial Publication*.

6 As Richard Terdiman notes, "once a paper's political position was established, its circulation was relatively insensitive to variations in the paper's specific daily or weekly content and depended much more upon changes in the fortunes of the party behind it." See *Discourse/Counter-Discourse* (Ithaca, NY: Cornell University Press, 1985), p. 128.

7 More detailed accounts of these developments can be found in Nora Atkinson, *Eugène Sue et le roman-feuilleton* (Paris: A. Nizan and M. Bastard, 1929), p. 6. See also Josette Pare Young, "Emile de Girardin, le 'journal à deux sous' et la littérature romanesque à l'époque romantique," *French Review* 56 (6) (May 1983), pp. 869–875.

8 Girardin remarked in the first issue of *La presse* that "the price of advertising being a function of the number of subscribers, we have to reduce the subscription fee to the bare minimum to raise the level of subscription to its maximum . . . . It is the advertising that pays for the newspaper." See John Lough, *Writer and Public in France* (Oxford: Clarendon, 1978), pp. 294–295, translation mine. The reader may note a parallel with the development of commercial radio and television in the United States and the role advertising played in developing serials in those media. It should be pointed out nonetheless that the development of serial fiction did not simply spring fully formed from the forehead of Girardin; its development was considerably more gradual. As Marguerite Iknayan demonstrates, serial publication went through a series of transitional phases. See *The Idea of the Novel in France: The Critical Reaction 1815–1848* (Paris: Librairie Minard, 1961), p. 73. See also Georges Jarbinet, "Les antécédents littéraires," *Les mystères de Paris d'Eugène Sue* (Paris: Société Française d'Editions Littéraires et Techniques, 1932), pp. 85–91. As for the serial's introduction into every French newspaper, see René Guise, "Balzac et le roman feuilleton," *L'Année balzacienne*, (1964), p. 285.

9 Anne-Marie Thiesse, *Le Roman du quotidien* (Paris: Chemin Vert, 1984), p. 84. Priscilla Clark reports an even greater increase; according to her figures *Le constitutionnel*, the paper in question, reached 40,000 subscribers after running *Le juif errant*. See Priscilla Clark, "The Beginnings of Mass Culture in France: Action and Reaction," *Social Research*, 45 (2) (summer 1978), p. 281. These events also made Sue the highest paid writer in France. During this period a day laborer averaged 2,50 francs a day; *Le siècle* guaranteed Sue 100,000 francs a year for fifteen years in return for his exclusive collaboration.

10 For an overview of the kinds of letters readers sent to Sue, see Anne Marie Thiesse,

"l'Education sociale d'un romancier – le cas d'Eugène Sue," *Actes de la recherche en sciences sociales* 32–33 (April–June 1980), pp. 51–63; and Guise, "Balzac et le roman Feuilleton," esp. pp. 283–337. It should be noted that contemporary soap opera writers also respond to viewer reactions and suggestions.

11 Although the rise of the novel as the most popular narrative form is generally linked with a female reading public, Anne-Marie Thiesse's research on serials represents the first compelling demonstration of a similar link between the success of newspaper serials and the development of a female reading public. As she states, "By virtue of the traditional opposition between a masculine (public) and a feminine (private) universe, women read newspapers less than men or, rather, they did not read the same columns as their husbands" (Anne-Marie Thiesse, *Le Roman du quotidien*, p. 19, trans. mine.) As for Sue's work inciting an international vogue for serial fiction, see Angela Bianchini, "Le roman-feuilleton en Italie" and Pina Maria Arnoldi Coco, "Le roman-feuilleton au Brésil," both in René Guise and Hans-Jörg Neuschäfer (eds), *Richesses du Roman populaire* (Nancy: Centre de Recherches sur le Roman populaire, 1983), pp. 389–397 and pp. 399–406, respectively. On a related note, during the 1932–1933 American radio season, *The Mysteries of Paris* was offered as a non-sponsored, sustaining half-hour broadcast on CBS on Monday nights at 9:30. It did not, however, attract the same attention as *Amos 'n' Andy*. See Harrison B. Summers (ed.), *A Thirty-Year History of Programs Carried on National Radio Networks in the United States: 1926–1956* (New York: Arno, 1971), p. 35.

12 Clark Kinnaird, "Cavalcade of Funnies," in D. M. White and Robert Abel (eds) *The Funnies: An American Idiom* (New York: Free Press of Glencoe, 1963), pp. 88–89.

13 See Bill Blackbeard's entry in *The World Encyclopedia of Comics* (New York: Chelsea House, 1976); as well as Blackbeard and Martin Williams's "Introduction: The Comic Treasures of the American Newspaper Page," in *The Smithsonian Collection of Newspaper Comics* (Washington, DC: Smithsonian Institution Press, 1986), pp. 11–18; and Denis Gifford, *American Comic Strip Collections, 1884–1939: the Evolutionary Era* (Boston, Mass.: G. K. Hall, 1990). Curiosity surrounding how the Kid's nightshirt became yellow involves its connection with the term "yellow journalism." On this note, Stephen Becker states that the Kid became yellow when "Charles Saalburgh, foreman of the color press room, needed an open patch of white space which the presses could print yellow. Saalburgh apparently chose the Kid's nightgown as his test area." More recently, Richard Marschall has stated that the historical explanation for how the character's shirt became yellow remains obscure. See Stephen Becker, *Comic Art in American* (New York: Simon & Schuster, 1959), pp. 2–3; and Richard Marschall, *America's Great Comic-Strip Artists* (New York: Abbeville Press, 1989), p. 22.

14 Judith O'Sullivan, *The Great American Comic Strip: One Hundred Years of Cartoon Art* (Boston, Mass.: Little, Brown & Company, 1990), p. 14. Blackbeard and Williams, "Introduction," p. 15.

15 To illustrate the inter-media hostilities, Daniel J. Czitrom reports that during the spring of 1907, "responding to pressure from the *Chicago Tribune*, the city's police department set up a 'nickel theater bureau' charged with investigating movie theaters and penny arcades." See *Media and the American Mind* (Chapel Hill, NC: University of North Carolina Press, 1982), p. 51.

16 The *Ladies World* represents a growing tendency among newspaper publishers to develop special Sunday supplements in order to interest women and children, "the new readers sought by newspapers for the rising department stores," as Alfred McClung Lee states. Lee stresses in particular the role of fashion notes, society

news, cooking recipes, ads for household products, and serial fiction in cultivating women readers. See Lee, *The Daily Newspaper in America: The Evolution of a Social Instrument* (New York: Macmillan, 1937), esp. pp. 586–588 and 595. For further information on the Hearst–McCormick circulation war, see Raymond W. Stedman, *The Serials: Suspense and Drama by Installment* (Norman, Okla.: University of Oklahoma, 1971), pp. 3–7; and Jean Mitry, *Histoire du cinéma*, vol. 2: 1915–1925 (Paris: Editions universitaires, 1969), pp. 22–24; see also Benjamin B. Hampton, *History of the American Film Industry From its Beginning to 1931* (New York: Dover, 1970), p. 103; and Jim Harmon and Donald F. Glut, *The Great Movie Serials: Their Sound and Fury* (Garden City, NY: Doubleday, 1972), pp. 1–3. There is a certain amount of confusion over the exact status of *What Happened to Mary?*. While many historians regard it as a series film, others including Raymond W. Stedman have dubbed it the first serial, arguing that it followed a continuing main character and general story-line. Actually, given the fact that this film no longer exists, it is difficult to determine if it constitutes a film series or serial. It seems very likely that *What Happened to Mary?* was yet another Edison series similar to its 1913 offerings, *The Chronicles of Cleek, Mr. Wood B. Wedd's Sentimental Experiences, The Adventures of Andy*, and *Octavius, the Amateur Detective*, and that most or all of these series were structured around some basic equilibrium which is repeatedly disrupted. In any case, its success spurred the development of serial films. For further information, see Stedman, *The Serials*, pp. 6–7; and Mitry, *Histoire du cinéma*, p. 16.

17 Anthony Slide, *Early American Cinema* (New York: A. S. Barnes, n.d.), pp. 158–159. Mitry confirms the figure, *Histoire du Cinéma*, p. 24; as does Stedman, *The Serials*, p. 9. "The first of the big-money serials" quotation is from "News of the World," *Variety* 47 (9) (July 20, 1917), p. 28. Concerning the Hearst–Pathé link, consider that Pathé became known as "The House of Serials" in large part due to its particularly close links to Hearst. As *Variety* reported in September 1917, "It is conceded in film circles that Pathé has a most comprehensive selling organization, which is further strengthened by the Hearst alliance, which enables it to secure almost invaluable publicity via the Hearst–Pathé weekly and the Hearst publications." The *Exhibitors Herald* confirms this important link, commenting about Pathé's 1919 serial *Bound and Gagged* that "in one hundred of the largest daily newspapers in the United States, paid advertising and publicity material covering all angles of exploitation will be found in prominent positions." See "Counter Amalgamations Rise Like Mushrooms Over Night," *Variety* 48 (4) (September 21, 1917), p. 30; and "Pathé Opens Advertising Drive for *Bound and Gagged* Serial," *Exhibitors Herald* (November 8, 1919), p. 72. Concerning *The Million Dollar Mystery*, see Stedman, *The Serials*, pp. 14–15; Mitry, *Histoire du cinéma*, p. 25; and *Variety* 34 (13) (May 29, 1914), p. 16. One reason for the exceptional success of *The Million Dollar Mystery* is that the producers offered a cash prize to the person who provided the most exciting conclusion to the serial. See "$10,000 for 100 Words," *Chicago Tribune* (October 4, 1914), "Color section," p. 7. The article reports that "The prize of $10,000 will be won by the man, woman, or child who writes the most acceptable solution of the mystery."

18 All information pertaining to serials published in newspapers or magazines derives from *Variety*, the *Exhibitors Herald*, and other primary sources; no secondary sources (i.e., film histories) were relied upon. An example serial film whose story was published in a popular magazine is Metro's *The Great Secret* (1917). *Beatrice Fairfax* (1916) was based on a well-known advice to the lovelorn column.

19 Information on audience composition is from Russell Merritt, "Nickelodeon Theaters 1905–1914: Building an Audience for the Movies," in Tino Balio (ed.), *The American Film Industry* (Madison, Wisc.: University of Wisconsin Press,

1976), p. 75. As for the claim that early film serials targeted a female audience, consider the predominance of female protagonists (for example, *The Hazards of Helen, Gloria's Romance*, and *Lucille Love, Girl of Mystery*) and female stars (for example, Pearl White, Ruth Roland, Helen Holmes) in these productions. Roughly one-third of serial films produced during the 1910s bear a "sign of the feminine." I should mention as well that newspaper ads for serial films typically appeared in the women's sections, generally between the society page, the household hints, and the advice for the lovelorn. Finally, various exhibition practices and promotional campaigns demonstrate the industry's attempt to target women. Perhaps the most ingenious strategy for increasing ticket sales was designed for the serial *Runaway June*. Ben Singer notes that the winner of its promotional contest "won a free trip to California on a train equipped with a special car converted into a hair and nail salon. The contest was open only to women, and was publicized only in women's magazines and sewing-pattern monthlies." See Singer, "Female Power in the Serial-Queen Melodrama: The Etiology of an Anomaly," *Camera Obscura* 22 (January 1990), pp. 91–129. The quotation on children is from Universal Pictures Corporation, *How to Make Money With Serials – A Universal Text Book for the Use of Motion Picture Exhibitors* (New York: Universal Pictures Corporation, n.d.), p. 12.

20 See Stedman, *The Serials*, pp. 97–167 for further information on source material for film serials.

21 White's statement is cited in Eric Barnouw, *A Tower in Babel* (New York: Oxford University Press, 1966), pp. 73–74.

22 Michele Hilmes, *Hollywood and Broadcasting – From Radio to Cable* (Chicago, Ill.: University of Illinois Press, 1990), p. 49; NBC's policy statement is reprinted in Barnouw, *A Tower in Babel*, p. 187 *bis*. For a discussion of radio's commercial basis, see Hilmes, *Hollywood and Broadcasting*, pp. 50–60; and Robert C. Allen, *Speaking of Soap Operas* (Chapel Hill, NC: University of North Carolina Press, 1985), pp. 101–110. For a short introduction to radio industry history, see David Cook, "The Birth of the Network: How Westinghouse, GE, AT&T and RCA Invented the Concept of Advertiser-Supported Broadcasting," *QRFS* 8 (summer 1983), pp. 3–8.

23 For a discussion of programming strategies, see Robert E. Summers and Harrison B. Summers, *Broadcasting and the Public* (Belmont, Calif.: Wadsworth Publishing, 1966) pp. 54–63; and Allen, *Speaking of Soap Operas*, pp. 103–107.

24 Discussing this program's phenomenal success, J. Fred MacDonald writes that

> by 1930, there were Amos 'n' Andy toys, candy bars, comic strips, and phonograph records. The sales of radio sets jumped from $650.5 million in 1928, to $842.5 million in 1929 (the year their WMAQ program was nationally aired by NBC). Six times a week their 15-minute serialized program engaged the national consciousness.

See McDonald, *Don't Touch That Dial! Radio Programming in American Life, 1920–1960* (Chicago, Ill.: Nelson-Hall, 1979), pp. 27–28 and 113; see also Stedman, *The Serials*, pp. 227–233; and Barnouw, *A Tower in Babel*, pp. 224–231. On the comic strip inspiration for the characters, see Barnouw, *A Tower in Babel*, p. 226; and the 25th anniversary broadcast of February 14, 1953 available on CBS records. Incidentally, the comic strip "Andy Gump" eventually inspired *The Gumps*, a daytime radio serial in 1934. See Stedman, *The Serials*, p. 278.

25 Ed Trach, Proctor & Gamble's manager of daytime programming, states the desire to link listeners' interest in serial characters with sponsored products in *Procter & Gamble: The House that IVORY Built*, n.a. (Lincolnwood, Ill.: NTC Business Books, 1989), p. 185. Procter & Gamble was the leading sponsor of soap operas,

controlling the most daytime time slots. Spending slightly over US$2 million for network radio in 1935, Procter & Gamble reports spending close to US$4.5 million in 1937 and almost US$8.8 million by 1939, when it sponsored twenty-one soap operas. By 1945, Procter & Gamble was spending US$15 million on radio, about twice as much as it did for all other media. For these reasons Alfred Lief, a Procter & Gamble executive, boasted that "P&G virtually built daytime radio for the networks." See *Procter & Gamble: The House that IVORY Built*, pp. 18–19. Procter & Gamble may take credit for developing the first serial designed to sell soap with its 1922 advertising campaign for Ivory Soap. Designed by Mark Wiseman in the form of a comic strip about the Jollyco family, it appeared in newspapers' Sunday supplements for months. See Allen, *Speaking of Soap Operas*, p. 108.

26 The quote is from Allen, *Speaking of Soap Operas*, pp. 110–111. Due to a legal dispute, Phillips left *Painted Dreams* and became an independent producer. In this capacity her first soap opera was one of the more successful ones, *Today's Children*, which garnered General Foods as its sponsor in 1932, followed by Pillsbury in 1933. As for the role of advertising agencies in programming, Michele Hilmes notes that

> Llewellyn White, reporting for the Commission for the Freedom of the Press, links the entry of advertising agencies into broadcasting with the rise of the daytime "women's" serial, the comedy series, and the adventure and mystery drama .... Stephen Fox supports this conclusion and further emphasizes the large part played by advertising agencies in creating the so-called "soap opera" form."
>
> (see Hilmes, *Hollywood and Broadcasting*, pp. 52–53)

Ralph M. Hower's remarks concerning one advertising agency illustrate the nature of sponsorship in radio (as well as early television): after 1930,

> the Ayer firm rapidly developed the view that an agency must start with the client's sales problems, determine whether radio can help, and then devise a program which will achieve specific ends in terms of sales .... The actual program in many cases is built completely by the agency, including idea, script, and production. In some cases, however, it may be built in cooperation with a "package producer" or selected from the wide variety of available shows created by package producers or networks, which are constantly under review by the agency's program division. In this way the type of show recommended to the client is evolved out of the needs of his selling problem as the agency sees it. The determining factor is not an established program which someone wants to sell, nor a famous star performer who is available for a leading role, but rather a specific job to be accomplished as part of the client's total promotional plan."
>
> (see Ralph M. Hower, *The History of an Advertising Agency: N.W. Ayer & Son at Work* (Cambridge, Mass.: Harvard University Press, 1949), pp. 153 and 286)

Finally, I should note that Frank Hummert told Stedman that his idea for soap operas was predicated on the success of serial fiction in newspapers and magazines. According to Hummert, "It occurred to me that what people were reading might appeal to them in the form of radio dramas" (quoted in Stedman, *The Serials*, p. 235). On the other hand, Robert LaGuardia claims that Hummert was inspired by comic strip serials: see his *From "Ma Perkins" to "Mary Hartman:" The Illustrated History of Soap Operas* (New York: Ballantine, 1977), p. 12.

27 Allen, *Speaking of Soap Operas*, p. 117. For statistics, see Summers and Summers,

Broadcasting and the Public, p. 57; and Stedman, *The Serials*, pp. 155–156.

28 The statistic is taken from Allen, *Speaking of Soap Operas*, p. 19. For additional information on adolescent radio serials, see Stedman, *The Serials*, pp. 168–210; and MacDonald, *Don't Touch That Dial!*, pp. 27–32.

29 Stedman, *The Serials*, p. 209.

30 Weaver is quoted in William Boddy, *Fifties Television – The Industry and Its Critics* (Chicago, Ill.: University of Illinois Press, 1993), p. 16. Boddy's discussion of early television broadcasting and its links to radio is particularly useful; see ibid., pp. 15–27.

31 Hilmes, *Hollywood and Broadcasting*, p. 66.

32 *Captain Video* was so popular that in 1951 it was made into a film serial by Columbia. As for comic serials, there are two obvious exceptions to the statement that none was developed for television. Following the phenomenal success of television soap operas, two satires on the genre were developed in the mid-1970s: *Mary Hartman, Mary Hartman* (1976) and *Soap* (1977).

33 See *Procter & Gamble: The House that IVORY Built*, pp. 185–188; Allen, *Speaking of Soap Operas*, p. 126. Allen's discussion of soaps' transition to television is particularly insightful; see ibid., pp. 122–129.

34 Since 1991 NBC canceled both *Generations* and *Santa Barbara*. It currently airs only two soaps (*Days Of Our Lives* and *Another World*) as compared with the other two commercial networks, both of which air four (ABC's *All My Children*, *General Hospital*, *Loving*, and *One Life to Live* and CBS's *As the World Turns*, *The Bold and The Beautiful*, *Guiding Light*, and *The Young and the Restless*). With both viewership and advertising revenue down, networks have developed alternative programming and allowed their affiliates to broadcast syndicated programming of a similar sort: primarily talk/interview shows, magazines, and "infotainment" programming, all of which is less expensive to produce and more successful at attracting viewership. Traditional sponsors of daytime soaps have also turned to alternative fare. P&G reports that in response to audience deterioration in the late 1970s, it began to expand into other areas of TV, sponsoring mini-series like *A.D.* and *Marco Polo*, made-for-TV movies such as *The Corn is Green*, and even cable TV series including *The Catlins* for Superstation WTBS. See *Procter & Gamble: The House that IVORY Built*, pp. 185–188. Though not written for a scholarly audience, LaGuardia, *From "Ma Perkins" to "Mary Hartman"* offers descriptions of the general plot-lines of the soaps mentioned. For an insightful discussion of soap opera's appeal to women (as well as other minorities), see Martha Nochimson's *No End to Her: Soap Opera and the Female Subject* (Berkeley, Calif.: University of California Press, 1992).

35 David Bianculli reported in 1987 that a network can count on approximately US$750,000 in foreign and domestic syndication and an additional US$75,000 in video rentals for every US$3 million in production costs. "Thus, for the approximately $6 million production of *Celebrity*, NBC will realize about $1.5 million in foreign sales and approximately $150,000 in cassette rights." See Bianculli, "The Roots of the Problem," *Channels of Communication* (January, 1987), pp. 32–33. For a discussion of the use of star-power in mini-series, see William MacDougall, "TV Miniseries Shift Focus to Big Stars," *U.S. News & World Report* (November 26, 1984), p. 71. Concerning ratings, *Roots* (still the highest rated mini-series) earned a rating of 45.0. It should be pointed out that one Nielsen ratings point equals 1 per cent of the 90 million or so homes equipped with a television. For a discussion of ratings, see Neil Hickey, "Do You Know Why Miniseries Usually Start on Sunday?," *TV Guide* (December 7, 1985), pp. 39–40. For the contention that mini-series attract non-traditional television viewers, see Bob Knight, "Skinny Minis Flourishing During Web's Hard Times,"

Variety (Wednesday, July 30, 1986), pp. 34 and 61.

36 It should perhaps be noted that *Dallas* was not the first regularly scheduled night-time serial in the United States. From 1964 to 1969, ABC offered twice-weekly episodes of *Peyton Place*, an Irna Phillips production. It was reportedly inspired by the success of Britain's *Coronation Street* and its success prompted an evening serial spin-off of the daytime soap *As the World Turns* called *Our Private World*. See Stedman, *The Serials*, p. 406–415. It should also be noted that even after *Peyton Place* was canceled, the commercial networks sporadically developed several other prime-time soap operas in the late 1960s, including *Bracken's World*, *Family*, and *The Survivors*. The first prime-time soap of the 1970s was *Beacon Hill* in 1975; a lavish adaption of *Upstairs, Downstairs*, it is most notable for its immediate failure in the ratings. Special mention should be made concerning PBS and imported serials. PBS may not live up to its mandate to provide alternatives to commercial television, but it has been a consistent conduit for high-quality British serials including *I Claudius* and *Upstairs, Downstairs*, in addition to the previously mentioned *Forsyte Saga*. Current competition with the Lifetime and Arts and Entertainment networks over many of the same British imports threatens PBS's future effectiveness, but it did set precedents for night-time serials as well as the mini-series.

37 Jane Feuer, "Genre Study and Television," in Robert C. Allen (ed.), *Channels of Discourse* (Chapel Hill, NC: University of North Carolina Press, 1987), pp. 113–133. For a brief illustration of *Star Trek: Deep Space Nine*'s intertextuality, consider that its first episode, "Emissary," picks up on events previously related in the two-part episode of *The Next Generation* entitled "The Best of Both Worlds," while "Crossover" is a continuation of "Mirror, Mirror," an episode of the original *Star Trek* series.

2

The role of soap opera in the development of feminist television scholarship

Charlotte Brunsdon

In recent years I have more than once set an examination question for third-year undergraduates along the lines of, "Why have feminist critics been so interested in soap opera?" To my recurring disappointment, no student has yet attempted this question, which I think is probably a tribute to their much underrated ability to identify their teachers' research agendas, and the way in which these tend to frame unanswerable questions. There is also a way in which the answer can seem very obvious – because soap operas are women's programs – which may make it very unattractive in the competitive context of an examination. This essay is my attempt at an answer to this question, but I should make clear that I think this bald and simple answer, in the west, in the key period of feminist interest, is fundamentally correct, and that all that I shall do is to make things a little more complicated. This I shall do in two main ways. Initially, by sketching a rather broader semi-historical context for feminist analyses of soap opera – a "when" of this interest – and then by tracing the different modalities of this interest – a "how." In this process, I hope to provide an account of the role of soap opera in feminist television scholarship. Before I start though, I want to spend a moment on establishing why I think the question is itself interesting.

First, despite what I am going to say later in the essay, I think there is still a piquancy in the juxtaposition of "feminists" and "soap opera." Each noun connotes a different engagement with femininity. The common-sense under-standing of "feminist," a much more problematic term within common sense than "soap opera," is partly constructed through the negation of more familiar modes of femininity. In the popular imaginary, feminists are still women who don't shave their legs, don't approve of page three girls, and don't like soap opera. Given the extent of feminist scholarship on soap opera in the 1980s, this residual piquancy is intriguing. What is at stake in the relationship between feminists and soap opera?

Second, the very extent of recent scholarship on soap opera, much of it within, or influenced by feminist paradigms, provokes reflection. Ann Kaplan,

49

in her 1987 review of feminist television criticism points to the centrality of feminist work on soap opera to the increased attention to the genre from the mid-1970s[1]. Robert Allen traces the contours of research on soap opera in his 1985 book, *Speaking of Soap Operas*, outlining the growth in social science research on the genre between 1972 and 1982.[2] It is toward the middle of this period that the feminist work starts being published, as I outline below. The status of soap opera, as an object of academic study, has changed radically in the last twenty years. At its simplest, this is to say that soap opera is at present studied within the academy in a wide range of disciplines – something that would have been quite inconceivable in 1970. This collection, in its very commissionability and existence, testifies to this point. Soap opera has been peculiarly significant for the development of feminist television criticism, and I think it is arguable that it is for the study of soap opera that this criticism is most visible in the wider arena.

So underlying my question about why feminists have been interested in soap opera is the paradox that, on the one hand, there is a perceived incompatibility between feminism and soap opera, but, on the other, it is arguably feminist interest that has transformed soap opera into a very fashionable field for academic inquiry.

The general context of feminist television scholarship

Many commentators have pointed out the significance of what are usually called "the media" to post-1960s feminism. Key texts of second-wave western feminism such as Betty Friedan's *The Feminine Mystique*, Germaine Greer's *The Female Eunuch*, or Sheila Rowbotham's *Woman's Consciousness, Man's World* all have central concerns with the available repertoire of images of femininity, with the way in which women are represented.[3] This feminist movement was, from its inception, a believer in the reality and importance of images. The twenty years or so since these founding texts were written have seen enormous changes in the analysis of images of women. For our purposes, perhaps the most significant is that this type of analysis has shifted from being primarily a political, extra-academic project to having a substantial academic existence. Many courses, in subjects such as English, history of art, communications and media studies, offer units on "the representation of women" or "images of women." With the percolation of feminist ideas into the academy, which has happened differentially across disciplines, there have been several key debates which have taken place in rather different forms across different disciplines. At a general level, one of the most significant of these can be seen as the debate about realist paradigms.

Early feminist approaches to the media were usually within a realist paradigm, comparing real women, or the reality of women's lives, with the available images thereof. Real women were found to be imperfectly formed, hard-working, multi-ethnic, and extremely various in contrast to the dominant ways in which they were represented.[4] This important strand of criticism, which still has relevance today, was challenged theoretically by feminists who wanted to break with the realist paradigm, and what they saw as the false distinction between "real women" and "images of women." These feminists wanted to argue that what we understand as real women, indeed, how we experience ourselves as such, is inextricably bound up with these images of femininity. That is, they argued that it is not clear what "a woman" is, except through representation.[5]

These theoretical arguments, and the related debate about "essentialism," structure feminist academic endeavor in a range of fields. Indeed, Michèle Barrett and Anne Phillips have recently argued that we can make a periodizing distinction between "modernist" 1970s feminism, with its optimism about discovering the cause of women's oppression, and postmodern 1990s feminism, with its sense of the fragmentation of the category "woman," and its stress on the significance of difference.[6] In relation to the study of the media, we can mark a move away from the study of images of women to the study of the construction of femininity, or the inscription of sexual difference. So if the general theoretical terrain involves the move from the affirmation of the presence of "woman" in the 1970s to doubt about the validity of this category in the 1980s, there are also marked changes in attitudes to conventional/traditional femininities. The recognition that women were perhaps rather more engaged with, and constituted by, available discourses of femininity than second wave-feminism had first insisted, fundamentally shifts the objects and purposes of feminist media analysis. This we can see most clearly in the changing attitudes to the mass produced genres of femininity: romance fiction, film melodrama and "weepies," women's magazines, and television soap opera. Key feminist books of the early 1980s, such as Rosalind Coward's *Female Desire* and Janice Radway's *Reading the Romance*, articulate a much more sympathetic engagement with mass media femininities, even as writers such as bell hooks challenge the racism of these femininities and feminisms.[7] It is these changes which are most relevant to the construction of soap opera as an object of study central to feminist television scholarship, and which are most interesting in the answer to my question, why were feminists so interested in soap opera? Before proceeding to this issue, it is necessary to outline some distinctions in the expanding field of feminist television research.

Feminist research on television

Feminist scholarship on television can be found in a series of academic disciplines: film studies, communication studies, mass communications, cultural studies, sociology, English, women's studies. These different disciplinary contexts govern the construction of the object of study and the methodologies employed. What researchers are interested in, and how they proceed to explore it has to be understood partly within each disciplinary context. Thus, for example, work within sociology is more likely to be concerned with the pattern of women's work within the television industries than work within English, which may be more concerned with narrative structure of particular programs. However, many of the disciplines that have proved most permeable to feminist concerns, such as cultural or media studies are themselves only semi-institutionalized – only intermittently recognized as proper subjects. This fact, in combination with the relative youth of feminist scholarship on television, and the common political origins of much of the research, means that there is also a high degree of interdisciplinarity, and a determined tendency to breach disciplinary boundaries. Widely cited work like that of Ien Ang, Ann Kaplan, Tania Modleski, or Michele Wallace which is to varying degrees directly concerned with television, cannot be contained by just one discipline.[8]

So, within a framework in which we initially understand feminist research on television to be both interdisciplinary and dispersed across academic disciplines, we can distinguish four main categories of scholarship.

The real world of women working in television

Scholarship in this area investigates patterns of employment, promotion, and power of women in television. There are two main issues here. First, the exploration and documentation of the manifest and continuing discrimination against women at nearly every level of program-making apart from secretarial work. This was a particular focus for feminist work in the 1970s, in some countries coinciding with the period before discrimination on grounds of sex became illegal.[9] Unless otherwise specified, "women" here is usually a unitary category, as is characteristic of early second-wave feminism. Margaret Gallagher has continued to produce extensive data for UNESCO, and Abrahamsson and Kleberg's "Gender and Mass Media" newsletter consistently reports on new work in the area.[10] It is, however, surprisingly difficult to obtain recent information for some professions and countries, which might be seen as symptomatic of what Margaret Gallagher identifies as an overall retreat from the public political arena in feminist media research.[11]

Second, more theoretically, there is the issue of the extent to which the gender of the producers does determine media output. The notion of the "male-dominated" media was a popular explanatory factor in the early days, but has become noticeably less prominent. There is an almost total lack of what might be termed feminist political economy, which perhaps points to the difficulties of using gender alone as an explanatory category. There has not been much theoretical discussion of this issue either, although Liesbet van Zoonen reviews what literature there is in her 1994 book, *Feminist Media Studies*.[12]

Instead, although relatively undocumented in the academic literature, there are the accounts by individual women and groups of women of their attempts to break into the industry and make programs. These accounts have many different forms and emphases, depending partly on their addressees. For example, Annette Kuhn uses a letter form in a feminist journal for her reflections on working in the Pictures of Women collective, while Karen Alexander is interviewed on her video work in the same publication.[13] Helen Baehr and Angela Spindler-Brown discuss their involvement in Broadside (a feminist company producing news/current affairs programs for early Channel 4) in an article in an academic collection, while there are now several survey articles, such as those by Marilyn Crafton Smith and Linda Steiner which include television work by women in accounts of (mainly US) women's work in a range of media.[14]

For our purposes, it should be noted that soap opera is not a positive term in work in this category. With some exceptions, like the lesbian soap, *Two in Twenty*, feminists have not been drawn to making alternative or feminist soaps, nor has it been in relation to this genre that inequality of opportunity or employment discrimination has been felt most acutely. It has been in relation to news and current affairs that the aspiration, and the exclusions, have been felt.

Content analysis of the presence of women on the screen

Although early feminist critique had generally involved some notion of counting – how many women appeared on screen to read the news? what sort of roles did women generally have? which women? – it has been mainly within the discipline of mass communications that questions about gender have been added to the array of quantifying projects. Gaye Tuchman's 1978 formulation of "the symbolic annihilation of women" provided a vivid hypothesis about the absence of women on television, as well as specifying their generic presence: "with the excepton of soap opera, where men make up a 'mere majority' of the fictional population, television has shown, and continues to show, two men for every woman."[15] There have been a series of studies which have focused on soap opera in the investigation of the type of roles available for women, and the type of women likely to fill them since Tuchman's article, and the early piece on the heroine of the daytime serial by Downing, such as Cassata and Skill's 1983 *Life on Daytime Television* or Matelski's later *Soap Opera Evolution*.[16] The extensive collecting of statistics about gender is not, of course, necessarily informed by a feminist project.

Alongside this type of analysis, which remains very much within the paradigms of mass communications, there has been a strong critical current which mobilizes feminist argument to support a methodological and sometimes epistemological attack on the practices of mass communications research. Key texts here would be Noreene Janus's 1977 attack on the assumptions of quantitative methodology, published, indicatively, in the *Insurgent Sociologist*, Lana Rakow's work, and a series of journal special issues, such as the 1986 issue of *Communication* edited by Paula Treichler and Ellen Wartella.[17] This feminist attack on dominant disciplinary paradigms has been frequently associated with a more general ferment in the field, and the increased influence of critical/cultural studies methodologies. So within this category of research, soap opera is a significant, but methodologically contested site.[18]

Textual or program studies: "heroine television"

The detailed analysis of television programs as "texts" is a relatively new practice, and has generally been conducted by scholars whose first training is in a text-based discipline such as English literature or film studies. Feminist textual analysis has in the main been directed at two types of fictional programs: those addressed *to* women and those centrally *about* women characters. It is perhaps thus not surprising that soap opera is such a presence in this category of research. The two other main genres that have attracted feminist interest are sitcoms with distinguished comediennes, such as the "Lucy" and Mary Tyler Moore shows, and, interestingly, one of the main sites for "positive images," the crime series, most significantly *Cagney and Lacey*.[19] Both these genres, given the type of feminist interest that has been manifested, could be subsumed into a larger category of "heroine television" which includes all the later fictional programs which have been attractive to feminists such as *Kate and Allie*, *The Golden Girls*, *Designing Women*, and *Murphy Brown*.[20] "Heroine television" is centrally about female characters living their lives, usually working both inside and outside the home, usually not in permanent relationships with men, sometimes with children, and trying to cope. It is the "trying to cope" which is critical. These shows are all, in some fundamental way, addressing feminism, or addressing the agenda that feminism has made public about the contradictory demands on women. Sitcoms seem to be the dominant form – the irresistible comedy of being a modern woman – but certainly in Britain there has been considerable exploration of the crime series, most notably through *Prime Suspect* and the work of Lynda La Plante.[21]

Soap opera isn't quite "heroine television," but it was mainly attractive to feminists as an object of analysis because it was perceived to be both for and about women. I discuss this at more length below, as I do the multi-referentiality of the portmanteau "soap opera." Here it is important to note that the early work on soaps tended to come out of work concerned at a more general level with media directed at female audiences. Thus Carole Lopate wrote about US daytime television in general in 1976.[22] Dorothy Hobson started off her research with an investigation of women's daytime radio listening.[23] Tania Modleski looked at soaps along with other mass-produced fiction aimed at women.[24] It is also historically significant that 1978 saw the launch and subsequent international success of *Dallas*. So the interest in television programs directed at women/housewives displayed by feminist critics coincides with popular serial melodrama as a worldwide phenomenon. Feminist work on soap opera develops alongside studies of the international reception of *Dallas*.[25]

Audience studies

As is clear from the section above, the feminist interest in television programs was from the beginning formulated through ideas about the audience. Several early analyses of soap opera make hypotheses about how women respond to soap opera, and many later studies attempt to test these ideas.[26] Thus the Tuebingen/Volkswagen study explicitly tests some of Modleski's formulations, and Andrea Press asks questions drawn from a variety of cultural studies work.[27] Ien Ang offers both an extensive reading of *Dallas*, and an audience study.[28] This work, too, needs to be seen in the broader context. Thus while feminist researchers were particularly concerned with the way in which women "read" or enjoyed television programs, there was a new attention to audience "decoding" in general, as any review account of media research in the 1980s indicates.[29]

We can quickly note two tendencies in recent studies, in both of which feminist research is prominent. First, there has been an increased emphasis on the domestic environment and familial relationships therein. Ann Gray's work about the use of the video recorder offers one example of this, while Lynn Spigel's research on "making room for the television" is another.[30] Second, there is a growing literature on audiences-as-fans and fan identity as such, which would include Constance Penley's work on Star Trek fans, and that of Lisa Lewis on music videos.[31]

As with the textual analysis of programs, I think we can observe a pattern in which feminist work is initially clustered round soap opera but then begins to move away from the mid-1980s onwards.

Within the context of this brief mapping, I can now offer a time-line of feminist work on soap. This is not meant to be exhaustive – a task which would, given the interdisciplinarity of the research indicated above, be very difficult – but it is meant to signal when key articles and books were written in relation to each other.

Feminist research on soap opera: time-line

1974

* Helen Butcher, Ros Coward, Evaristi, Garber, Harrison, and Janice Winship, "Images of Women in the Media," (Universtiy of Birmingham, CCCS Stencilled Occasional Paper no. 31).

1976

Carol Lopate, "Day-Time Television: You'll Never Want to Leave Home," *Feminist Studies* 3 (3–4) (spring–summer), pp. 69–82.

† Horace Newcomb (ed.), *Television: The Critical View*, 1st edn (Oxford: Oxford University Press). Includes: Renata Adler, "Afternoon Television: Unhappiness Enough and Time," *New Yorker*, February 12, 1972.

1977

Richard Dyer, Terry Lovell, and Jean McCrindle, "Soap Opera and Women," *Edinburgh International Television Festival Official Programme*, pp. 24–28.

1978

Lesley Stern, "Oedipal Opera: *The Restless Years*," *Australian Journal of Screen Theory* 4.

* Gaye Tuchman, Daniels, and Benét (eds), *Hearth & Home: Images of Women in the Mass Media* (New York: Oxford University Press).

1979

Tania Modleski, "The Search for Tomorrow in Today's Soap Operas," *Film Quarterly* 37 (1), pp. 12–21.

1980

Richard Dyer, Christine Geraghty, Marion Jordan, Terry Lovell, Richard Paterson, and John Stewart, *Coronation Street*, (London: BFI Television Monograph, no. 13).

1981

Ellen Seiter, "The Role of the Woman Reader: Eco's Narrative Theory and Soap Operas," *Tabloid* 6.

Charlotte Brunsdon, "*Crossroads*: Notes on Soap Opera," *Screen*, (April 22).

Michèle Mattelart, "Women and the Cultural Industries," *Media Culture and Society* 4 (4), pp. 133–151.

Gillian Swanson, "*Dallas*," *Framework* 14, pp. 32–35.

1982

Dorothy Hobson, *Crossroads: The Drama of a Soap Opera* (London: Methuen).

Ellen Seiter, "Promise and Contradiction: The Daytime Television Serials," *Film Reader* 5 (Evanston, Ill.: Northwestern University).

Ien Ang, *Het Geval Dallas* (Amsterdam: Uitgeverij SUA).

Tania Modleski, *Loving With a Vengeance* (Hamden, Conn.: Archon Books, Shoe String Press).

1983

E. Ann Kaplan (ed.), *Regarding Television* (essays by Allen, Flitterman, Modleski) (Los Angeles, Calif.: AFI).

1984

Jane Feuer, "Melodrama, Serial Form and Television Today,' *Screen* (January 25).

Annette Kuhn, "Women's Genres," in ibid. Later reprinted in Christine Gledhill (ed.), *Home Is Where the Heart Is* (London: BFI, 1987).

1985

Ien Ang, *Watching "Dallas*," trans. and rewritten (London: Methuen).

Robert C. Allen, *Speaking of Soap Operas* (Chapel Hill, NC: University of North Carolina Press).

1986

† Elihu Katz and Tamar Liebes, "Mutual Aid in the Decoding of *Dallas*," in Philip Drummond and Richard Paterson (eds), *Television in Transition* (London: BFI).

Mary Ellen Brown, "The Politics of Soaps," *Australian Journal of Cultural Studies* 42, pp. 1–25.

Jane Root, *Open the Box* (London: Comedia), chapter on soaps.

† John Tulloch and Albert Moran, *A Country Practice: Quality Soap* (Sydney: Currency).

1987

* Helen Baehr and Gillian Dyer (eds), *Boxed In: Women and Television* (London: Pandora).

† David Buckingham, *Public Secrets: EastEnders and its Audience* (London: BFI).

1988

Sandy Flitterman-Lewis "All's Well That Doesn't End," *Camera Obscura* 16, pp. 119–129.

E. Ann Kaplan, "Feminist Criticism and Television," in Robert C. Allen (ed.), *Channels of Discourse* (New York: Routledge).

1989

† Sonia Livingstone, *Making Sense of Television: The Psychology of Audience Interpretation* (Oxford: Pergamon).

Ellen Seiter, Hans Borchers, Gabriele Kreutzner, and Eva-Maria Warth (eds), *Remote Control* (London: Routledge).

1990

Mary Ellen Brown (ed.), *Television and Women's Culture* (London: Sage).

Prabha Krishnan and Anita Dighe, *Affirmation and Denial: The Construction of Femininity on Indian Television* (Delhi: Sage).

Andrea Press, *Women Watching Television* (Philadelphia, Pa.: University of Pennsylvania Press).

† Tamar Liebes and Elihu Katz, *The Export of Meaning: Dallas* (Oxford: Oxford University Press).

1991

Christine Geraghty, *Women and Soap Opera* (Cambridge: Polity Press).

* Ien Ang and Joke Hermes, "Gender and/in Media Consumption," in James Curran and Michael Gurevitch (eds), *Mass Communication and Society* (London: Edward Arnold).

* Liesbet van Zoonen, "Feminist Perspectives on the Media," in ibid.

1992

* Margaret Gallagher, "Women and Men in the Media," *Communication Research Trends* 12 (1).

Christine Geraghty, "British Soaps in the 1980s," in D. Strinati and S. Wagg (eds), *Popular Media Culture in Post-War Britain* (London: Routledge).

Christine Gledhill, "Speculations on the Relationship Between Soap Opera and Melodrama," *Quarterly Review of Film and Video* 14 (1–2) (July).

† Richard Kilborn, *Television Soaps* (London: Batsford).

* denotes that the work is important in feminist approaches to the media, but only deals tangentially with soaps.

† denotes that the work is about soaps, but is not strongly (or at all) informed by feminist approaches.

Why and how were feminists interested in soap opera?

Having established some sense of the distribution of feminist research on soap opera – that feminists have indeed been interested in the genre – and that some of the best-known feminist television criticism, such as that of Ang, Hobson, and Modleski is on this topic, I want finally to move toward an answer to my motivating question. So – why were feminists interested in soap opera?

Because soap opera is a woman's genre

From their origins in the US radio serials directly sponsored by detergent manufacturers, soap operas have been specifically aimed at female audiences. This is less true now than at any earlier point, but the connotational femininity of the genre remains overwhelming. The early research on radio soap opera conducted by Herta Herzog, Rudolf Arnheim, and Helen Kauffman, under the aegis of the Radio Research bureau only investigated female audiences.[32] Thelma McCormack has analyzed the assumptions about the female audience in other US research literature on the genre.[33] Ellen Seiter has revealed the commitment of Irna Phillips to educating women, as well as exhorting them to buy.[34] Christine Gledhill has examined the gendering of soap opera in the context of a discussion of the melodramatic mode in general.[35] In short, women have been targeted by the makers of soap opera, women have been investigated as the viewers of soap opera, and the genre is widely and popularly believed to be feminine, despite stubborn evidence that it is not only women who watch.[36]

Early feminist writing on the media, which was strongly dependent on the idea of "stereotyping," characterized the representation of women as dominated by two figures, the sex-object and the housewife. If the former was found in beauty competitions and ads for cars, the latter lived in soap operas and ads for washing-powder. So one of the early feminist responses to soap opera was simply hostile. The programs were one instance of the brainwashing project of the mass media, the project to keep women thinking that all they could do was be housewives. The women who watched soap opera, in this type of analysis, needed consciousness-raising, while the women portrayed were without interest. Feminists were interested in soap opera only to the extent that they purveyed ideologies of femininity and family against which feminism was defining itself. It was a combative interest, a commitment to knowing thine enemy.

But it was also more complicated than that.

Because "the personal is political"

"The personal is political" is the most resonant and evocative claim of 1970s western feminism. This slogan reminds us of the particular flavor of the anglophone feminist movement that emerged from the political and social upheavals of the 1960s with its fierce belief in the significance of individual experience, but its absolute determination to understand this experience socially. This slogan, while evoking a specific political movement also has a certain familiarity which is not specific, and which indicates to us something of the influence of this movement. The radical redefinition of the personal and the political associated with 1970s feminism affected a wide range of fields, among them, media research. I want to suggest here that it is partly the direct political challenge of "the personal is political" which contributes to the changing emphasis of media research in the 1970s and 1980s away from hard news/current affairs to softer programs. Further, I want to suggest that soap opera, and the feminist influenced analysis of soap opera, is pivotal to an understanding of this structural shift in the field. Thus we cannot understand the impact of a book such as John Fiske's *Television Culture*, with its radical shift away from "hard" programming, without noting the attention paid therein to a feminist agenda.[37] For it is feminist criticism which has insisted that the home and personal life are in and of themselves significant, and not some mystified "effect" of an economic determination elsewhere.

In arguing for the historical significance of the assertion that "the personal is political" for an understanding of certain patterns in media research I don't dispute the deconstruction of the personal/political opposition as specific to white middle-class women that has been offered by scholars such as Aida Hurtado.[38] Jacqueline Bobo and Ellen Seiter map out some of the implications of this argument for media research, and particularly for domestic ethnographies, in their article on *The Women of Brewster Place*.[39] The point here, though, is that it was precisely those women not subject to state surveillance and harassment in their homes and personal lives who argued not only that the personal was political, but who also turned their attention to the media representation of women's lives. It is the same moment, the same movement, which declared that the personal was political, and which saw that this might change the significance of soap opera to radical analysts of the media.

If the personal is political – if it is in the home, in relationships, in families, that women's intimate oppression – or the oppression of women as women – is most consensually secured, then the media construction and representation of personal life becomes fascinating and an urgent object of study. If the traditional leftist critique of the media, with its structuring sense of class conflict, was drawn to the reporting of the public world – to industrial disputes, to the interactions of state and broadcasting institutions, to international patterns of ownership and control – emerging feminist scholarship had quite another focus. The theoretical impulse of feminism pushed scholars not to the exceptional but to the everyday. There was, as discussed above, research into patterns of employment for women in the media, but textually the concern to look at the representation of women of necessity led away from hard news and current affairs. So the theoretical conviction that there was a politics to everyday life and that women's hidden labor in the home was essential to capitalism coincides with the actual generic distribution of (white) women on television. If the project was to analyze the representation of women on television, there was of necessity a focus on genres other than the traditional objects of critical analysis because, in the main, women neither read nor featured in hard news and current affairs.

Because "soap opera" has a metaphoric meaning

It is evident that in the late 1970s and the 1980s the term "soap opera" was used about programs that are in fact rather distinct: South American telenovelas, US daytime serials, British social realist serials, US prime-time shows. What do they have in common that attracts feminist scholars to all of them?[40] Here the answer is again the perceived femininity of the programs, but here in a rather more metaphorical sense – the feminine as contemptible, as banal, as beneath serious critical attention. Thus the unity of these different programs – the reason why, in a certain sense, it was correct to call them all "soap" in a particular period – lies in their shared place at the bottom of the aesthetic hierarchy. It was to this gendering of aesthetic judgment that feminist critics were partly addressing themselves, as we see in this comment from 1981 by Terry Lovell: "Yet *within this almost universal denigration*, soap opera does provide the pleasures of validation, and of self-assertion, which must surely go some way to accounting for its lasting popularity with women."[41]

Because they shouldn't be: feminist ambivalence

Early feminist work on soap opera is marked by a profound ambivalence. On the one hand, there is the repudiation of the genre that I have discussed. On the other, this sense that these programs are something that "other women" – non-feminists – watch, offers a political rationale for an engagement with the genre. The drive here is to make a political analysis of pleasure – pleasure that is seen to be politically regressive. However, sometimes, underneath this explicitly feminist repudiation/ re-engagement structure, there is a more elusive presence, a ghost of past femininities. For many feminists, writing about soap opera – and, I would argue, comparable genres and media such as romance fiction and women's magazines – entailed an investigation of femininities from which they felt, or were made to feel, a very contradictory distance.[42]

Ien Ang discussed this directly in her *Dallas* project where she inscribed a sense of generally condemnatory attitudes toward soap watching in her original advertisement: "I like watching the tv serial *Dallas* but I often get odd reactions to it."[43] She is, in the first instance, concerned to investigate what she names the "ideology of mass culture," but later in the book explicitly criticizes a tendency toward "the overpoliticizing of pleasure" present in much feminist work on popular fiction. Janice Winship has written about this vividly in the introduction to her book on a related genre, women's magazines, published in 1987:

> Admitting within feminist circles that I was doing research on – of all things – women's magazines used to make me feel just as comfortable as when I hastily muttered an explanation of my "study" to politely inquiring friends of my parents . . . . Whether feminist friends voiced it or not I felt they were thinking that if I really had to do research . . . I should do it on something more important politically . . .
>
> Yet I continued to believe that it was as important to understand what women's magazines were about at it was, say, to understand how sex discrimination operated in the workplace. I felt that to simply dismiss women's magazines was also to dismiss the lives of millions of women who read and enjoyed them each week. More than that, *I* still enjoyed them, found them useful and escaped with them. And I knew that I couldn't be the only feminist who was a "closet" reader.[44]

The self-conscious use of "closet" here points to the way in which the first feminists doing academic studies of these popular forms really did face opposition not from just the academy, but also from within feminism. Some parts of 1970s feminism were very keen to construct a distance between feminist identity and more conventional forms of femininity. We see this tension again when, writing five years earlier, Terry Lovell defends both the watching and the study of the British soap opera, *Coronation Street*, in these terms:

> *Coronation Street* offers its women viewers certain "structures of feeling" which are prevalent in our society, and which are only partially recognised in the normative patriarchal order. It offers women a validation and celebration of those interests and concerns which are seen as properly theirs within the social world they inhabit. Soap opera may be the opium of masses of women, but, like religion, it may also be, if not "the sign of the oppressed", yet a context in which women can ambiguously express *both* good humoured acceptance of their oppression *and* recognition of that oppression, and some equally good humoured protest against it . . . .[45]

This mild defense of soap opera comes after nine pages of closely argued theoretical writing about why the genre is worthy of notice.

It is this final reason "why" that brings me back to my starting-point, that of the perceived piquancy in the relationship between feminism and soap opera. Because of the sedimented gendering of the genre, there was no way in which a political movement which was challenging gender definition could ignore soap opera. But neither could it, finally, repudiate these pleasures and identification, nor simply celebrate them. Feminists were interested in soap operas because they were women's programs, but each of these terms proves unstable on closer inspection. What was referred to as "soap opera" often had little more than seriality and lack of prestige in common. "Women," as I have repeatedly found while tracing this history, has proved a very tricky category for feminism, both necessary and impossible, often excluding more people than it includes. And finally, feminist interest in these programs has had rather different forms and motivations at different moments. And in this intricate dance of attitudes and categories a little subfield of academic study has been created.

Conclusion

Through tracing a set of interwoven histories I have tried to suggest what was most significant about the feminist encounter with soap opera. The tense is important, for I think we can date the key period of this encounter between 1976 and 1984, and it is in these years that we see both feminism and soap opera first becoming established in their much disputed and often ridiculed academic identities. In crisis in the political arena, feminism began to establish some toe-holds in the academy, sometimes in "its own" discipline, women's studies, sometimes in the newer disciplines such as cultural or media studies, and occasionally in more established fields. The study of television, too, changed, and the interest in popular genres, perhaps partly focused by the international success of *Dallas*, was enriched and explicitly feminized through the attention to soap opera.

Second, the study of soap opera provided a particular generic site in a new medium for the investigation of the female viewer. The question of the female reader/viewer/spectator/audience has been a recurring topic to occupy feminist scholars in a range of disciplines at both a theoretical and an empirical level. Soap opera, perceived as so evidently gendered, while also very popular internationally, provided an excellent site for the analysis of this figure, whether she was theorized as a textual construct or investigated as a sociological fact.

Finally, I think we could say that feminist media scholarship explores and defines itself a little in this encounter. Taking soap opera seriously – and perhaps, most significantly, taking soap opera fans seriously – as this early feminist work began to do, also involved taking the skills, competencies, and pleasures of conventional femininities rather more seriously. Doing research with "real people" raises complex and difficult ethical issues. It has been partly through the exploration of this "woman's genre" and its audiences that some of the simplicities and blindnesses of second-wave feminism have been challenged. So if feminism has been important in producing a context in which soap opera can be taken seriously, soap opera has been significant as a site in which feminism can learn to address its others with respect.

Notes

1 E. Ann Kaplan, "Feminist Criticism and Television," in Robert C. Allen (ed.), *Channels of Discourse* (Chapel Hill, NC: University of North Carolina Press, 1987), pp. 211–253.
2 Robert C. Allen, *Speaking of Soap Operas* (Chapel Hill, NC: University of North Carolina Press, 1985).
3 Betty Friedan, *The Feminine Mystique* (New York: Dell, 1963); Germaine Greer, *The Female Eunuch* (London: Paladin, 1971); Sheila Rowbotham, *Woman's Consciousness, Man's World* (Harmondsworth: Penguin, 1973).
4 For example, Josephine King and Mary Stott (eds), *Is This Your Life? Images of Women in the Media* (London: Virago, 1977).
5 An early contribution to this argument can be found in Elizabeth Cowie, Claire Johnston, Cora Kaplan, Mary Kelly, Jacqueline Rose, and Marie Yates, "Representation vs. Communication," in Feminist Anthology Collective (ed.), *No Turning Back* (London: The Women's Press, 1981), pp. 238–245.
6 Michèle Barrett and Anne Phillips, "Introduction," in Michèle Barrett and Anne Phillips (eds), *Destabilizing Theory* (Cambridge: Polity, 1992).
7 Rosalind Coward, *Female Desire* (London: Paladin, 1984); Janice Radway, *Reading the Romance* (Chapel Hill, NC: University of North Carolina Press, 1984); bell hooks, *Ain't I a Woman?: Black Women and Feminism* (Boston, Mass.: South End Press, 1981).
8 Ien Ang, *Watching "Dallas"* (London: Methuen, 1985); E. Ann Kaplan (ed.), *Regarding Television* (Los Angeles, Calif.: American Film Institute, 1983); Tania Modleski, *Loving With a Vengeance* (Hamden, Conn.: Archon, 1982); Michèle Wallace, *Invisibility Blues* (London: Verso, 1990).
9 For example, Maurine Beasley and Sheila Silver, *Women in Media: A Documentary Sourcebook* (Washington, DC: Women's Institute for Freedom of the Press, 1977); Margaret Gallagher, *Unequal Opportunities: The Case of Women and the Media* (Paris: UNESCO, 1981).
10 Margaret Gallagher (ed.), *Women and Media Decision Making: The Invisible Barriers* (Paris: UNESCO, 1987); Ulla Abrahamsson and Madeleine Kleberg (eds), *Newsletter: Gender and Mass Media* (Stockholm: Department of Journalism, Media, and Communication, Stockholm University, and Audience and Programme Research Department, Swedish Broadcasting Corporation). Between 1981–1988 this publication was called *Newsletter: Sex-Roles and Mass Media*.
11 Margaret Gallagher, *Women and Men in the Media*, Communication Research Trends 12 (1) (1992), p. 14.
12 Liesbet von Zoonen, *Feminist Media Studies* (London: Sage, 1994).
13 Annette Kuhn, "Dear Linda" and "Karen Alexander: Video Worker," *Feminist Review* 18 (1984); pp. 112–120 and 28–34.
14 Helen Baehr and Angela Spindler-Brown, "Firing a Broadside: A Feminist Intervention in Mainstream tv," in Helen Baehr and Gillian Dyer (eds), *Boxed In: Women and Television* (London: Pandora, 1987), pp. 117–130; Marilyn Crafton Smith, "Women's Movement Media and Cultural Politics," in Barbara Creedon (ed.), *Women in Mass Communication* (Newbury Park, Calif.: Sage, 1989), pp. 278–298; Linda Steiner, "The History and Structure of Women's Alternative Media," in Lana Rakow (ed.), *Women Making Meaning* (New York: Routledge, 1992), pp. 121–143.
15 Gaye Tuchman, "The Symbolic Annihilation of Women," in Gaye Tuchman, Arlene Kaplan Daniels, and James Benét (eds), *Hearth and Home* (New York: Oxford University Press, 1978), p. 10.

16 Mildred Downing, "Heroine of the Daytime Serial," *Journal of Communication* 24 (2) (1974), pp. 130–139; Mary Cassata and Thomas Skill, *Life on Daytime Television* (Norwood, NJ: Ablex, 1983); Marilyn Matelski, *The Soap Opera Evolution* (Jefferson, NC: McFarland, 1988). As will be evident, I am not, in this chapter, trying to survey the voluminous and rapidly expanding recent mass communications literature on soap opera.

17 Noreene Janus, "Research on Sex-Roles in the Mass Media: Towards a Critical Approach," *Insurgent Sociologist* 7 (3) (1977), pp. 19–32; Lana Rakow, "Rethinking Gender Research in Communication," *Journal of Communication* 36 (4) (1986), pp. 11–26; *Communication* 9 (1) (1986); *Journal of Communication Inquiry* 11 (1) (1987).

18 Prabha Krishnan and Anita Dighe discuss the serials based on the *Ramayana* and *Mahabharata* epics in their *Affirmation and Denial: Construction of Femininity on Indian Television* (New Delhi: Sage, 1990). They use a mixture of traditional content analysis and much broader specific contextual analysis, which Gallagher argues is exceptional among current feminist analysis of television in its attention to the political (Gallagher, *Men and Women in the Media*, pp. 4–5).

19 Patricia Mellencamp, "Situation Comedy, Feminism and Freud," in Tania Modleski (ed.), *Studies in Entertainment* (Bloomington, Ind.: Indiana University Press, 1986), pp. 80–98; Serafina Bathrick, "The Mary Tyler Moore Show: Women at Home and at Work," in Jane Feuer, Paul Kerr, and Tise Vahimagi (eds), *MTM: Quality Television* (London: British Film Institute, 1984), pp. 99–131; Julie D'Acci, "The Case of *Cagney and Lacey*," in Baehr and Dyer (eds), *Boxed In*, pp. 203–225. There is an extensive feminist literature on *Cagney and Lacey* which D'Acci's book on the show references (*Defining Women: The Case of Cagney and Lacey* (Chapel Hill, NC: University of North Carolina, 1994).

20 Lauren Rabinovitz, "Sit-Coms and Single Moms: Representations of Feminism on American TV," *Cinema Journal* 29 (1) (1984), pp. 2–27; Sandy Flitterman-Lewis, "The Production of Social Reality and the Reality of Social Production: The Pre-Quayle *Murphy Brown*," paper to "Console-ing Passions" conference, Los Angeles 1993.

21 *Prime Suspect* written by Lynda La Plante and starring Helen Mirren as a senior policewoman investigating serial killing of women attracted enormous popular and critical acclaim when shown on British television in 1991. Gillian Skirrow wrote on an earlier La Plante series, *Widows* in "Women/Acting/Power," in Baehr and Dyer (eds), *Boxed In*, pp. 164–183.

22 Carole Lopate, "Daytime Television: You'll Never Want to Leave Home," *Feminist Studies*, 3 (spring–summer 1976), pp. 69–82.

23 Dorothy Hobson, "Housewives and the Mass Media," in Stuart Hall, Dorothy Hobson, Andrew Lowe, and Paul Willis (eds), *Culture, Media, Language* (London: Hutchinson, 1980), pp. 105–114.

24 Modleski, *Loving With a Vengeance.*

25 Tamar Liebes and Elihu Katz, *The Export of Meaning* (Oxford: Oxford University Press, 1990).

26 Thelma McCormack offered a feminist critique of assumptions about female audiences in mass communications research in her "Male Conceptions of Female Audiences: The Case of Soap Operas," in Ellen Wartella, D. Charles Whitney, and Sven Windahl (eds), *Mass Communication Review Yearbook* (Beverly Hills, Calif.: Sage, 1983), pp. 273–283.

26 Ellen Seiter, Hans Borchers, Gabriele Kreutzner, and Eva-Maria Warth, "Don't Treat Us Like We're So Stupid and Naive," in Ellen Seiter, Hans Borchers, Gabriele Kreutzner, and Eva-Maria Warth (eds), *Remote Control* (London:

Routledge, 1989), pp. 223–247; Andrea Press, *Women Watching Television* (Philadelphia, Pa.: University of Pennsylvania Press, 1991).

28 Ang, *Watching "Dallas"*; but see also her book on audiences as such, *Desperately Seeking the Audience* (London: Routledge, 1990).

29 For example, John Corner, "Meaning, Genre and Context," in James Curran and Michael Gurevitch (eds), *Mass Media and Society* (Sevenoaks: Edward Arnold, 1991), pp. 267–284.

30 Ann Gray, *Video Playtime: The Gendering of a Communications Technology* (London: Routledge, 1992); Lynn Spigel, *Make Room for TV* (Chicago, Ill.: University of Chicago Press, 1992).

31 Constance Penley, "Feminism, Psychoanalysis, and the Study of Popular Culture," in L. Grossberg, Cary Nelson, and Paula Treichter (eds), *Cultural Studies* (New York: Routledge, 1992), pp. 479–494; Lisa Lewis, "Consumer Girl Culture: How Music Video Appeals to Girls," in M. E. Brown (ed.), *Television and Women's Culture* (London: Sage, 1990), pp. 89–101.

32 Herta Herzog, "What Do We Really Know About Daytime Serial Listeners?," in Paul Lazarsfeld and Frank Stanton (eds), *Radio Research 1942–3* (New York: Duell Sloane and Pearce, 1944), pp. 3–33; Rudolf Arnheim, "The World of the Daytime Serial," in ibid., pp. 34–85; Helen Kaufman, "The Appeal of Specific Daytime Serials," in ibid., pp. 86–107.

33 McCormack, "Male Conceptions of Female Audiences;" Allen, *Speaking of Soap Operas*.

34 Ellen Seiter, "'To Teach and To Sell': Irna Phillips and Her Sponsors, 1930–54," *Journal of Film and Video* 40 (1), 2 (1989), pp. 223–247.

35 Christine Gledhill, "Speculations on the Relationship Between Soap Opera and Melodrama," *Quarterly Review of Film and Video* 14 (1–2) (July 1992), pp. 103–124.

36 For example, essays in Suzanne Frentz (ed.), *Staying Tuned: Contemporary Soap Opera Criticism* (Bowling Green, OH: Bowling Green State University Press, 1992) use data about male and female audiences although this is not the object of investigation in most cases.

37 John Fiske, *Television Culture* (New York: Routledge, 1987).

38 Aida Hurtado, "Relating to Privilege: Seduction and Rejection in the Subordination of White Women and Women of Color," *Signs* 14 (4) (1989), pp. 833–855.

39 Jacqueline Bobo and Ellen Seiter, "Black Feminism and Media Criticism: *The Women of Brewster Place*," *Screen* 32 (3) (1991), pp. 286–302.

40 Allen discusses the lack of precision in the use of "soap opera" from a slightly different angle in his "Bursting Bubbles: 'Soap Opera,' Audiences and the Limits of Genre," in Seiter *et al.* (eds), *Remote Control*, pp. 44–55.

41 Terry Lovell, "Ideology and *Coronation Street*," in R. Dyer, Christine Geraghty, Marion Jordan, Terry Lovell, Richard Paterson, and John Stewart, *Coronation Street* (London: British Film Institute, 1981), p. 51 (emphasis added).

42 I have argued this point more thoroughly in "Identity in Feminist Television Criticism," *Media, Culture and Society* 15 (1993), pp. 309–320.

43 Ang, *Watching "Dallas"*, p. 10.

44 Janice Winship, *Inside Women's Magazines* (London: Pandora, 1987), p. xiii.

45 Lovell, "Ideology and *Coronation Street*," p. 51.

3

Social issues and realist soaps
A study of British soaps in the 1980/1990s

Christine Geraghty

One of the characteristics of British television is the way in which the home-produced soaps have undertaken a realist function in their representation of British society. *Coronation Street* began in 1960 at a time when the British "new wave" in the theater, literature, and cinema was stressing the importance of drawing on different kinds of experience based on the lives of "ordinary" people. While soaps always have a tendency to deal with the everyday and the mundane even in their most extreme moments, in British soaps this emphasis on the quotidian inevitably intertwined with issues of class and region. The working class, as a specific group, not just as ordinary people, was represented in *Coronation Street* so that the drama of personal relationships so characteristic of a soap was placed within a homogeneous community living in the backstreets of a town in northern England. A sense of place and of class was thus written into British soaps at an early stage with the consequence that *Coronation Street*'s stories were more likely to be concerned with the tensions and pleasures of the community rather than the elaboration of dramas in the family home.

If *Coronation Street* was always concerned with the social, its story-lines tended to emphasize the drama of human relationships rather than the exemplification of social issues. While problems were placed firmly in a social context, it was the characters who drove the plots and set limits on what stories could be worked through them. Although realism was important, other factors were to contribute to the program's success – the strong female characters, the emphasis on comedy and the sense of nostalgia for a lost way of life which meant that the point of reference for contemporary *Coronation Street* always seemed to be set in the past. It was not until the 1980s when *Brookside* (1982) and *EastEnders* (1985) were both launched that British soap operas took up social issues more overtly and handled social problems in a more direct way which went beyond the plight of individual characters and dealt with the public sphere as well as the personal. In doing so, the new programs sought to engage an audience which included those not normally attracted to soaps – young people, men, those concerned about political and social issues. This essay attempts to map out some of the consequences of this change and to look at how the the new soaps handled the social issues which they claimed as their own.[1]

Brookside and *EastEnders* did not break with the *Coronation Street* model of rooting stories in a particular region and class. *Brookside*, produced independently by Phil Redmond for the commercial Channel 4, is set in a new housing development on the edges of Liverpool and the credits draw the audience into Brookside Close through a series of pictures of Liverpool's most characteristic buildings and landscapes. Similarly, *EastEnders*, made in-house for the BBC, starts with credits which feature a map of London's East End with the great curve of the River Thames marking out the boundary. This is *EastEnders*'s territory with the focus on a run-down square with its pub, street market, and multi-occupied houses. Both programs also use class as a way of developing characters and engaging the audience. The majority of the characters are working class and, while that does not make them auto-matically sympathetic or correct in their judgments, the audience is invited to understand the programmes from that class perspective. But the traditional issues of class and community were allied in the 1980s soaps to other questions of race and sexuality, and new problems like AIDS, harassment, and rape were put on the agenda.

Realism is a key concept for these new British soaps and is called on as a justification or a rationale for the world which they depict. The claim to reflect reality helped the producers to combat those who asserted that the 1980s soaps were too outspoken and brutal in what they showed. "We don't make life, we reflect it," Julia Smith, the producer of *EastEnders*, told viewers who complained about the program's direct approach.[2] But the British 1980s soaps promised more than *Coronation Street*'s original claim to reflect the mores of a working-class community. They were concerned not so much with what holds a community together but with what threatens to splinter or disrupt it. In extending their audience, they had to demonstrate that they were breaking new boundaries, moving out of what was deemed to be the cosy world of women's problems. The soaps of the 1980s claimed to appeal to a diverse audience and to deal realistically with difference and conflict; therein lay their appeal and the source of some of their problems.

It is a mark of the impact of the new soaps that it was in the 1980s that British soaps became a matter of public debate, and judgments about how they handled sensitive issues were continually being made. Comment came, as was to be expected, from those who traditionally feared the power of popular television such as Mary Whitehouse's National Viewers' and Lis-teners' Association;[3] Peter Dawson of the Professional Teachers Association described *EastEnders* as "evil" and warned that "the whole nation is drugged by *EastEnders*."[4] Other groups also intervened in a way which indicated a concern for how the 1980s programs were taking responsibility for the new issues that were on the soap agenda. On *Right to Reply*, a program for viewers' comments put out on Channel 4, gay and lesbian viewers questioned the representation of gay men and lesbians in soaps, arguing that

> Many gay people find it hard to identify with any of the three gay characters currently seen in British soaps and since there is no such thing as a typical heterosexual or homosexual person, why are the gays in these series shown as bland and two-dimensional characters?[5]

The call here is for greater plausibility and a less precious acceptance of the reality of gay and lesbian sexuality. In the specialist magazine *Nursing Times*, the "Media Watch" page featured Carmel, then the health visitor in *EastEnders*, and remarked that she "has come in for quite a bit of stick from HVA [Health Visitors Association] members who haven't felt that the character gives a good impression of their role." Disappointment was expressed that the character "has not developed in a way which promotes the role of the health visitor more positively," and Roma Iskander, who discussed the role with *EastEnders* scriptwriters on behalf of the HVA, remarked that "Carmel isn't a positive image of a black woman or a health visitor."[6] *Midweek*, a giveaway London magazine, interviewed a black London Labour local councillor, Merle Amory, about her political career; the interviewer reported that

> She is a fan of *EastEnders* . . . although she feels the rebellious side of Kelvin's character has been played down: "In politics, when black people are seen to be achieving something that's received positively then people get a little scared." She also doesn't like the way Naima's character has become "the stereotypical hardened Asian business-woman with a scheming cousin."[7]

One doesn't have to be a soap opera scriptwriter to reel a little at the range of the comment and the scope of the demands. *EastEnders* was accused of raising the suicide rate when Angie attempted to overdose, *Brookside* of increasing anxiety about AIDS when Paul Collins, speaking as an anxious father and not an expert, gave wrong information about the HIV virus. But both *EastEnders* and *Brookside* have been quite overt about their commitment to social issues, and the publicity aroused by their handling of some of these issues is presumably not unwelcome. Cynics might indeed describe the whole phenomenon of the socially realist soap as an exercise in increasing the audience and feeding the tabloids' need for scandal. But much of the tension exemplified in the quotations above arises from a conflict in the 1980s soaps between a desire to be positive about a particular issue and a commitment to credibility in terms of characters and setting. The HVA, it would appear, want Carmel to be a model health visitor, demonstrating a wide range of skills in a professional manner. But the credibility of Carmel's character in the soap depends on her being a character who is part of the life of the Square, a professional who makes mistakes and whose personal life is also a source of interest. Quite clearly, the demands for a positive image for health visitors as a profession are less pressing than the necessity for the program to be able to deploy Carmel as a soap opera character. Those making the programs are quite certain that this is the way it must be. Both programs are besieged by a plethora of groups wanting space for their particular cause, but not all can be accommodated. Julia Smith and Tony Holland are clear that "issues, like everything else in a realistic soap, must come naturally out of the characters and community,"[8] and John McCready argues that *Brookside* has to resist the "constant pressure from social and political agencies who want this or that issue to be brought into the programme. If they had their way, *Brookside* would become nothing more than a documentary with a scouse accent."[9] The emphasis in both cases is on raising the issues naturally rather than adopting a heavily didactic or documentary approach.

But the dilemma is not always resolved, as in Carmel's case, so readily in favor of British soap opera's traditional mode of working through credible and engaging characters. Both *Brookside* and *EastEnders* have a commitment to dealing seriously with social problems and indeed to appeal to viewers who watch these soaps and not *Coronation Street* or *Neighbours* precisely because they attempt to deal with social issues in a positive way. This phenomenon is recognized by the program-makers. Writing in 1987, the creator and executive producer of *Brookside*, Phil Redmond, argued that

> it must cover in a realistic and responsible way issues such as AIDS – something that was not even heard about when the programme started five years ago. The programme will have to explore these issues and reflect their development if it is to retain its reality and its relevance.[10]

Tony Pearson suggests that *Brookside* appears to have a special appeal for viewers who appreciate "a blend of serialized entertainment with the responsible handling of hard topical issues."[11] Similarly, Julia Smith, *EastEnders*'s first producer, told David Buckingham, "We decided to go for a realistic, fairly outspoken type of drama which could encompass stories about homosexuals, rape, unemployment, racial prejudice, etc, in a believable context."[12] Clearly, social issues are integral to the dramas and to the audience which is being appealed to. It is hardly surprising then given the nature of these issues and the conflicting conventions of soap opera and realism that the handling of such material can become a somewhat fraught exercise.

Before moving on to discuss how particular examples of issues of conflict and difference are dealt with in *EastEnders* and *Brookside*, it is worth noting that both soaps take the family as the basis of their structure. This may be a surprising assertion in the light of their apparent emphasis on family breakup and tensions. Family life was an important element in the network of relationships in *Coronation Street* but in the main it was the community which sustained its individual members whether they were part of a family or not and ensured no one was without support.[13] *Brookside* and *EastEnders* specifically turned their back on what were seen to be nostalgic notions of neighbors turning to each other for help. In *Brookside*, the Close was divided on class lines and it was rare for the boundaries to be breached. When Jonathan held a party for his yuppie friends, the young working-class Corkhills, far from joining in, held their mocking parody of the event in the garden next door, the garden fence marking a symbolic as well as a literal boundary. In *EastEnders*, the notion of community was certainly invoked, but it was not always seen to be effective; it belonged to the "good old days" about which the older women reminisce but whose very existence is questioned by the younger characters. The notion of the community was thus rendered problematic and a vacuum left in *Brookside* and *EastEnders* which had to be filled; somewhat ironically, it was the family which emerged as the model.

The loss of the community as a practical force and a sustaining ideal drove characters back into family relationships at key moments in the narrative. Certain ideals were set up in both *EastEnders* and *Brookside* which centered on a white, working-class family offering each other support and reassurance in the face of the harsh reality of unemployment and financial crisis. In *Brookside*, this model was initially represented by the Grant family and subsequently by the Corkhills, the Rogers, and the Dixons; in *EastEnders*, this role was undertaken by the Beale/Fowler extended family. In each case, there were clearly tensions within the family, struggles over male and female roles, arguments over the adolescents' attempts to escape the over-close family embrace, disagreements over priorities and loyalties. Despite this, in both programs, characters aspired to a notion of family unity and harmony even if it was rarely achieved, and support from members of the family was looked for although not always found. Moments of happiness or sorrow were marked by the coming together of the family, the return of those who had strayed, and the momentary suspension of rivalry and tension. Even when such moments do not actually occur they are consciously sought. Christmas in these soaps offers a good example of this. Christmas was nearly always marked in the programs by a series of disagreements over how the celebrations should be organized, who should spend time with whom, and what was appropriate behavior on the "Day." But it was always quite clear what ideal lay behind the pressures to have a proper family Christmas and the arguments tended to be about how that could be achieved rather than the desirability of · the ideal itself. The audience was thus invited to identify with these families and to see their struggles toward family unity as a realistic reflection of the difficulties which face families in the audience.

This model of an imperfect family working toward an harmonious ideal has important consequences for the way in which the social issues identified by the program-makers have been dealt with. The notion of the family at the heart of the new soaps implied the existence of deviants from that model.

These deviants divided into two groups – those who could be part of the family but have chosen not to be, and those who never can be. Into the first group fall those whose behavior has pushed them out of the family structure or who have rebelled against some of its restrictions. In *Brookside*, different members of the Grant family fought for independence and the ability to control their own lives but all turned to the mother, Sheila, for support at critical moments. On a less momentous level but no less typically, Sam Rogers's interest in green politics caused her parents concern when it took her out into the public world of demonstrations and action. In *EastEnders*, both Mark and Michelle Fowler have had to fight for their independence against their mother's demands in the same way as Arthur Fowler had to assert himself against the domination of his mother-in-law, Lou. In these cases, conflict could be expressed within the family and resolution of differences could be achieved, however tenuously, within the family model.

The other group raised problems for the programs because they were much more difficult to accommodate within the family. The white working-class family, however extended and open, does not readily or realistically (in the programs' terms) accommodate black people or lesbians and gay men, for instance, and yet their presence was essential in the 1980s to the programs' claims to deal with current social issues. These characters thus hovered on the fringes of the central families, sometimes allowed in to observe the drama, but never quite part of the action. Their treatment tended to be exemplary rather than passionate and they represented problems to the audience rather than demanding the viewers' identification. This can be seen in the handling of gay men and black characters in *EastEnders*. Colin, the main gay character in *EastEnders*, was warmly treated by the Fowler/Beale family who offered him sympathy but not a sense of belonging. Neither Colin nor his erstwhile lover Barry were seen in the context of their own families and they thus lacked a crucial dimension in the program's own terms. The treatment of black characters in *EastEnders* also proved problematic in the 1980s; none of the black families rivaled the Fowler/Beale position at the heart of the program's structure and black characters were pushed to the margins of the story-lines. Carmel and Darren clearly had an extended family along the lines of the Beale/Fowler nexus but its other members were rarely seen. Kelvin Carpenter hung around with Ian, Michelle, and Sharon but his personal life got little attention and he disappeared from the program while the other young characters have been able to grow up in it. Darren operated on the fringes of the criminal world to which Den was central, and the treatment of Naima was sketchy compared with that given to the white female characters. It seems indicative that *EastEnders*, during this period, should have got rid of certain black characters, including Naima and Tony Carpenter, by sending them "home" to Bangladesh and Trinidad, as if they had never been at home in the Square.

In *Brookside*, similar problems have been experienced in the representation of gay and black characters. Gay characters were represented

71

through Gordon Collins and his lover Chris, but the program made no attempt to place them in the context of the gay community and they moved somewhat uneasily in and out of the Collins's family home. *Brookside* did not, during this period, have a black family and its black characters appeared on the margins of the program. Thus, isolated black characters like Jonah, Kate, and Nisha had to represent the issues of race which the program aspired to accommodate.

This emphasis on the family as a supportive structure and the difference between deviant or troublesome characters within the family and those outside it helps to explain why certain issues are taken up in the way in which they are. In soaps, as we have seen, problems are attached to or worked through with particular characters and the handling of a specific issue depends very much on the way in which that character has already been established. Some social issues can be taken up through a character in one of the established families and derive much of their impact from that setting. In 1986–1987, for instance, Arthur Fowler went through a traumatic period of redundancy, unemployment, and debt which led to a mental breakdown and a prison sentence for stealing. Clearly, Arthur was being used by the program to exemplify the pressures and problems which were facing the 4 million then unemployed and to draw drama out of a national issue. One trades union newspaper commented that through Arthur's plight "*EastEnders* has brought the evils of unemployment to people's attention."[14] Sympathy was demanded for Arthur himself, particularly in the moving scenes when he could no longer cope mentally with his situation, but emphasis was also placed on the strains on his family. Arthur's character was already known to the audience before this particular series of events and the story developed gradually out of Arthur's position in the program (he was unemployed when the serial began). In other words, this was a classic example of Julia Smith and Tony Holland's dictum that issues must arise naturally from the characters and the story fitted well into the traditional soap opera ethos of the family pulling through.

Brookside, too, dealt with unemployment in the 1980s through an emphasis on its consequences for the family. In the main, unemployment was seen to be a male problem. Women like Sheila Grant, Doreen Corkhill, and Chris Rogers had part-time work outside the home but it very rarely impinged on their stories. The shattering and debilitating effects of unemployment were presented through male characters such as Damon Grant, Billy Corkhill, and Terry Sullivan. For Billy, like Arthur Fowler, unemployment threatened his standing in the home, eating away at his pride and sense of usefulness so that his energy turned into violence which was painfully and searingly redirected against his wife and children. For Damon and Terry, unemployment condemned them to be "one of the lads" with an eye out for a quick buck; it trapped them into dead-end jobs with no hope and prevented them from establishing their own families. Bobby Grant blamed unemployment for his son's death; his assessment had a symbolic aptness since it was Damon's move out of the protection of the family to look for work which led him to his death.

But other issues fitted more problematically into the structure provided by the family model. The stories about Gordon Collins in *Brookside* provided an interesting example of soaps' drive to solve problems, if at all possible, within rather than outside the family. Gordon had been in *Brookside* from the start and had, as it were, a pre-gay existence and a role in the Collins's family. His coming out as gay caused his parents and particularly his right-wing father much anguish and his lover Chris was not a popular figure within the home. Indeed, Paul Collins's intolerance provided Gordon and Chris with the opportunity to lecture him (and the audience) about their right to lead their own lives as a gay couple without interference or condemnation. The program addressed some of the difficulties faced by gay men such as "queer-bashing" and put Gordon through an HIV test. It is striking, however, not only that Gordon consistently returned home (a move demanded by the soap convention that the program is organized around the houses in the Close), but in times of crisis was able to turn to his parents and particularly his father for support. Thus, when Chris and Gordon were beaten up and arrested outside a gay club, it was Paul Collins who got up in the middle of the night to get them out. He stood by them in the subsequent feud when, significantly, the attack by the gang was made not merely on Chris and Gordon but on the family home. It was also to Paul that Gordon turned when he decided to have the HIV test; during the tense period of waiting Paul tried to reassure him about the outcome and anxiously watched over his health. There was no indication that Gordon had other gay friends to turn to for reassurance and there was little reference to more organized gay support systems in Britain such as Gay Switchboard or the Terence Higgins Trust. During this story, *Brookside* realistically represented the panicky and uncertain attitudes of many parents faced with a gay son and it could be argued that Paul Collins's defense of Gordon was a positive and exemplary approach within a family setting. But the representation was unlikely to satisfy those in its audience who were looking for a positive representation of the gay community or for a hint that gay politics could challenge the ideology of the family rather than be incorporated within it.

Given this framework, it is hardly surprising that both *EastEnders* and *Brookside* found HIV/AIDS a very difficult issue to deal with as information on the syndrome developed in the 1980s. It was of course a subject which they were expected to take on precisely because of their self-proclaimed stance of dealing with social issues. But positive images were difficult to develop given the prevailing metaphors of plague and punishment and the soaps' approach was initially a cautious one. Both *EastEnders* and *Brookside* were careful to avoid AIDS being automatically linked to gay characters. *Brookside*, for instance, had a relatively self-contained story in which Bobby Grant had to deal with a trades union member with AIDS who was being ostracized by his own workmates as well as being discriminated against by his employers. Again, the issue was directly brought into the family and was presented through the reactions of Bobby's wife Sheila who was fearful for her child's safety; the story was in fact about Sheila working through her own prejudices and coming to terms with her irrational fears. Like Paul Collins, in his dealings with Gordon, Sheila's position was offered to the audience as representative of the way in which ignorance and fear can be overcome. *EastEnders* also ran a story in which one of Den's fellow prisoners was identified as being HIV positive and had to cope not only with his own fears but those of his wife. As with the *Brookside* example, however, this was a relatively self-contained story and the prisoner was not one of the serial's long-running characters. In both cases, AIDS as an issue for heterosexuals was dealt with through characters who appeared to have been brought into the programs specifically for that purpose.

So far as the gay characters were concerned, AIDS during this period was an issue which could not be ignored but was never confronted. Colin in *EastEnders* talked of the deaths of friends but they were in the United States. Chris in *Brookside* lent his flat to a friend who was dying of an AIDS-related illness but this was something of a plot device, forcing Gordon and Chris back into the family home and the opportunity to show the experience of care and bereavement was not picked up. Instead, AIDS tended to be used as a suspense element when any one of the gay characters was ill. Thus, Barry, Colin, Chris, and Gordon were all suspected of "having" AIDS and the audience was invited to share a period of anxious waiting with them while they went through the test. During this period, the "all clear" verdicts relieved the programs of having to pick the issue up more seriously.

If it is difficult to fit gay issues into the model of the white, working-class family which underpins the soap structure, it is impossible for it to accommodate issues around race. Black characters cannot fit into the model and all too often during the 1980s their differences were presented as deviancies. One clear example of how this occurred, despite the programs' good intentions, was offered by the stories in which both *Brookside* and *EastEnders* featured the problems of Asian schoolgirls. In many ways, this was an ideal social problem for the 1980s soaps. It combined issues of race with stories about the relationships between parents and children, an element which has featured strongly in both *EastEnders* and *Brookside* with sympathetic emphasis on the adolescents' point of view. In *Brookside*, Nisha was introduced into the program through her schoolgirl friendship with Sammy, the elder daughter of the Rogers family. She and Sammy both had part-time jobs in the local supermarket and Nisha gradually let slip the difficulties she faced in dealing with her parents, the restrictions they placed on her social life, and the work they demanded of her in the family business. The pattern which emerged was a contrast between the normal, white girl getting ready to enter the world with the loving if anxious support of her parents and the deprived Asian girl whose unseen parents were behaving unreasonably and whose life deviated unsatisfactorily from the British norm. Nisha thus followed the *Brookside* tradition during the 1980s of using a single black character as a focus for a particular set of problems without making them central to the program as a whole; the black family was hardly seen and the audience was forced to conclude that it was different from and less supportive than its white counterpart.

EastEnders fell into similar difficulties in its handling of a similar story. As is usual in *EastEnders*, the narrative was much more highly compressed than in *Brookside* and the melodramatic speed with which the plot moved forced the issues into the open very quickly. The Bengali family in the Square took over the running of the corner shop but did not feature as a family in any of the stories, and so the audience had no real familiarity with their characters before the issue of the Asian daughter began to emerge. Shireen, the teenage daughter, began a relationship with a white boy, Rick, and as in *Brookside* the restrictions placed on her were emphasized, so that while the program was careful to emphasize that Shireen loved her parents and did not want to hurt them, the impression given was of an unusual and undesirable way of life. Any sympathy that might be felt for the Asian parents' view that white teenagers were too wild and free was undermined by the father's commitment to the concept of an arranged marriage and his determination to arrange one for the schoolgirl Shireen as soon as possible. An arranged marriage was thus presented in the worst possible light, as alien to the values of the white families and as a punishment for Shireen for her relationship with Rick. The representation of Mr Kamir's genuine concern for his daughter was finally destroyed for the audience by his outrageous demands that Dr Legge test his daughter to establish that she was still a virgin; the doctor's response that no doctor in the country could do such a test underlined the deviancy of the father's request. The audience was thus drawn to Shireen's distress and to her demand that she be treated as a person in her own right, not as an object to be manipulated at her father's will. As with Nisha in *Brookside*, the parents were presented as abusing their daughter by refusing to adopt an approach more in tune with British mores.

The *EastEnders* example is a particularly interesting one because of the program's genuine efforts to include a much wider range of black characters than is usual on British television. Shireen's story provides an example of how the conventions of 1980s soap opera, a particular use of social problems for realist purposes, and a demand that black characters be treated positively, can clash in a way that undermines the black family. The Kamir family were not well established in soap opera terms; unlike the Beales and Fowlers, they had not been known to viewers over a number of years and the audience was given little access to the internal discussions within the family. Mr Kamir could claim little credibility with the audience before the story started, and what he had was lost almost immediately through his extreme attitudes. The mother was seen to be subservient to her husband in a way that was in line with the program's "realistic" attempt to present traditional attitudes within the Kamir family but out of tune with the normal emphasis in soaps on a strong matriarchial presence in the family, thereby once again calling attention to the Kamir family's difference from the norm. Intellectually, the program went to considerable lengths to present positively Mr Kamir's determination to maintain his own culture. He pointed out forcibly to Dr Legge that the isolation of the immigrant community was not a matter of choice but a means of protection in the face of the hostility of the white community; even Frank Butcher, Rick's father, was given a speech in which he pointed out that arranged marriages might have a better chance of success than western marriages based on romance. Emotionally, though, the audience was asked to identify with Shireen's rejection of her father's values and her desire to be more integrated into the life of her friends. In presenting Shireen positively, the program did scant justice to the Kamir family as a whole and invited the audience to make its judgments from the point of view of a white family.

The structural deviancy of gay and black characters, illustrated by these examples, was a particular problem for 1980s soaps given their proclaimed intention of treating social issues positively. Indeed, lying behind the dilemma which gay and black characters pose for soaps is the demand that they be at the same time realistic, representative, and positive. By their very isolation, Colin and Gordon "stood for" homosexuality in Britain in a way that was never demanded of the heterosexual characters. A bad, boring, or bland gay character is dissatisfying to gays precisely because they find it difficult to identify with them, but no one is concerned if they cannot identify with unsympathetic white men like Pete Beale or Paul Collins. Heterosexual problems are presented across a whole range of characters; those of gays through only one or two per soap. Similarly, black characters run the risk of being read as representative, as standing for the black community as a whole, in a way in which white characters do not. The likelihood of this happening is increased because in the soaps "ethnic minorities" are represented by one or two characters and are presented in isolation. The representative nature of the black characters causes particular tensions when the realism on which the program-makers pride themselves clashes with notions of a positive image. Realism may demand a recognition that "bad" black characters exist, and thus black Darren was set up as a counterpoint to the white Dirty Den, but it is all too easy for a character like Darren to be read as representing all young black males as skiving, irresponsible, and up to no good. Realism may also demand that black characters are represented in recognizable and familiar situations, but such a strategy again runs the risk of reinforcing rather than challenging stereotypes. Thus, Naima and the Kamir family ran the corner shop, inviting criticism that *EastEnders* had fallen into the trap of automatically associating the Asian community with shopkeeping and acquisitiveness. David Buckingham argues that "The crucial question is not whether *EastEnders*'s black characters are 'realistic', but how the serial invites its viewers to make sense of questions of ethnicity – and in particular, how it defines ethnic difference and inequality or racism,"[15] and he is right to try and move the argument away from questions of accuracy. Nevertheless, it is important to recognize that it is precisely because of the contradictory claims of realism and representativeness that problems arose over the way in which the 1980s British soaps presented their black characters.

As we move into the 1990s, it is possible to see how the new soaps have become part of the established pattern of British television. In conclusion, therefore, this essay points to the way in which some 1980s issues have bedded down into the conventional pattern of British soaps while others have disappeared or changed. The soaps have continued to develop their concern with social issues and in some cases have been able to integrate issues and characters more strongly because they can now call on the audience's greater knowledge of and involvement with the fictional world being presented. One example of this would be the way in which the HIV/AIDs issue has moved from being addressed through peripheral characters brought in for that purpose to being a story which affects a major character. In *EastEnders*, Mark Fowler finally told his family that he was HIV positive and the issue is now being dealt with on a long-term basis. This means that at some points it is given prominence, as it was when Mark re-established his relationship with his girlfriend Gill (in a dramatic story-line she herself died of AIDS just after their wedding); at other times, it is one of a number of factors which affect Mark's responses to particular situations and for long periods it is not referred to directly. The audience knows that Mark is HIV positive and can bring that information to bear when it seems appropriate to understanding his behavior; so the issue is thus rooted in character and story. In effecting this shift, *EastEnders* has continued the practice of grounding issues in the family rather than in a wider social setting. Although Mark sometimes finds his family's response inadequate, he has little access to support outside the family and acceptance by his father in particular was understood to be crucial to his own ability to come to terms with his position.

Brookside, too, has maintained its tradition of using strong, topical issues to make stories. It has continued the convention of using soaps' traditional appeal to women viewers to base stories on contemporary women's issues; in this way it has drawn on debates outside the program about date rape, sexual harassment at work, and prostitution and used them as the basis for long-running stories. The introduction of the Jordache family was particularly significant in providing the basis for a series of stories which brought together issues of incest and violence against women. The dominating and brutal Trevor Jordache was shown to make violent attacks on his wife and it was revealed that he had sexually abused his teenage daughter and was a threat to the younger girl in the family. His eventual murder by his wife and teenage daughter provided a classic example of the way in which dramatized social issues could be welded with more traditional soap values of female solidarity to powerful effect. Significantly, the murder scene was the subject of a formal warning by the Independent Television Commission which ruled that it had breached the codes for what could be shown at the tea-time transmission time (the problem arose over the Saturday repeat which is screened between 5:00 and 6:30 p.m.). Thus soaps continue to challenge ideas of what is appropriate for family entertainment.

Along with a commitment to issues, the programs continue to struggle with the task of representing a broader group of characters than the traditional soaps. The most striking disappearance in the range of characters represented has been the departure of the gay characters. However flawed the treatment of Colin and Barry or Gordon and Chris was, the attempt to develop gay characters in the 1980s now looks like a brave one and their disappearance has meant the loss of a distinctive voice. The involvement of black characters continues in both programmes but has developed in slightly different ways. The black characters in *EastEnders* are still limited in number and seem to have been incorporated into the working-class culture of the Square rather than offering something different from it. The focus for the black characters in the early 1990s was the Afro-Caribbean Carpenter family which for a while had the mixture of generations and attitudes which characterized the Fowlers and gave them such a dominant position in the Square. Somewhat typically, however, the family broke up leaving the teenage Hattie on her own. The presentation of the most recent addition, the Asian couple Sanjay and Gita, seems to be marked by class similarities with the rest of the Square rather than racial or ethnic differences. They run a stall on the market; Sanjay shares the capacity for ducking and diving which traditionally characterizes the program's "cockney" men such as Frank and Grant, pushing Gita into the role of nagging wife. *Brookside* has extended its very limited range of black characters with the establishment of Mick as a regular. Bringing up his two small children on the Close, he has a network of relationships with the other men – Sinbad, Frank Rogers, Ron Dixon – while being involved in his own stories, focusing on his relationships initially with his wife and subsequently with his girlfriend Marianne. The black characters in *Brookside* are now involved in stories which do not specifically address black issues and their representative quality as characters whose function it is to raise black issues is therefore less marked.

The position of Mick as a single father is also significant in identifying a trend which has been prominent in *Brookside*. It is inevitable that, as the years pass, soap families break up both because actors/actresses want to leave and stories need the drama generated by failed relationships. What is striking in *Brookside*, however, is how often the breakup of the families in the Close has left the father and not the mother in place. Thus, it was Mick who was left with the children when his wife disappeared and who has to worry about schooling and paying the rent; it was Frank Rogers who stayed with the family when he and Chris split up and who had to try and cope with the difficult pregnancy of his elder daughter and the schoolgirl rebellions of the younger; as the Dixons' marriage foundered, it was D-D who left and Ron who stayed behind to face the opprobrium of his children over his affair with a much younger woman. This realignment of the family structure is in strong contrast to *Brookside*'s earlier years which featured a series of strong mothers – Sheila Grant, Doreen Corkhill, Marie Jackson, Annabelle Collins – who controlled and negotiated family life within the home. The number of male single-parent families is odd in realist terms since it does not reflect the reality of such families in Britain, but it is also an indication of the way in which *Brookside* in the 1990s seems to be troubled by how the male role in the family should be represented and, in particular, what the role of the father should be. The 1980s soaps had challenged the secure gender positions of traditional soaps by giving men a greater role and placing more emphasis on the development of complex male characters like Bobby Grant and Arthur Fowler. *Brookside* now seems to have gone further and, whether by accident or design, is challenging the mother's traditional dominance of the soap family. The program's dominant point of view now tends to be that of the father, uneasy in handling personal relationships, somewhat baffled by his children's needs, and confused about how to handle his own role as a father. The debates about power in the family which so strongly marked the relationships between Bobby and Sheila Grant and Billy and Doreen Corkhill have been replaced by the struggles of rather weak, middle-aged men to organize the lives of their motherless families. If *Brookside*'s strength continues to be its handling of social issues, its reorganization of the family around the father has pushed to the limits its challenge to the pleasures of recognition and reinforcement that women viewers are traditionally offered by soaps.

Although *EastEnders* has not gone down this particular road in the 1990s, it too has experienced problems in its handling of the family. Significantly, the Beale/Fowler axis which was at the heart of the program began to loose its hold. The death of the matriarchal Lou Beale, Kathy's divorce from Pete Beale, and the development of Michelle Fowler's life at college contributed to this process but the crucial factor has been the split between Pauline and Arthur Fowler. This shift was marked by Pauline's long break in New Zealand, Arthur's year-long affair with Christine, and finally in October 1993 by Arthur's temporary departure from the serial. While Pauline remained a significant character after this, she was no longer the mother to whom everyone could turn and became increasingly irritable and isolated. Significantly, however, a family crisis resolved the situation. Pauline and Arthur were united in thwarting the threat that the Beale market stall might be sold to someone outside the family and, with the support of their daughter Michelle and an uncharacteristically sentimental gesture from their nephew Ian Beale, they bought the stall for their son Mark. Success in re-establishing the Beale/Fowlers at the heart of the market, and hence the community, was suitably celebrated when, that evening, Pauline welcomed Arthur back to her bed again and the family unity was restored, on as permanent a basis as it ever can be in a soap . . . .

Notes

1 For influential accounts of the relationship between women viewers and soap operas see Charlotte Brunsdon, "*Crossroads*: Notes on Soap Opera," *Screen* 22 (4) (1981); and Tania Modleski, *Loving With a Vengeance* (London: Methuen, 1982). For comments on the change in the intended audience for 1980s soaps and the effects for the women viewer see my *Women and Soap Opera* (Oxford: Polity Press and Basil Blackwell, 1991).

2 Comment made on BBC Television's *Open Air* (February 19, 1987). See Geraghty, *Women and Soap Opera*, pp. 31–35, for a more extended discussion of the use of an appeal to realism in this way.

3 David Buckingham offers an interesting account of the kind of criticism made of *EastEnders*, in particular by Mary Whitehouse, in *Public Secrets* (London: BFI, 1987), pp. 146–152.

4 Reported in *Guardian* (August 2, 1989).

5 These dissatisfactions were voiced by viewer Tony Gregory on *Right to Reply*, Channel 4 (June 4, 1988). Andy Medhurst's views, also expressed on that program, prompted me to try to think through some of these issues and I acknowledge my debt to him.

6 *Nursing Times* 84 (26) (June 29, 1988), p. 25.

7 Quoted in an interview with Pete May in *Midweek* (April 23, 1987), p. 10.

8 Julia Smith and Tony Holland, *EastEnders: The Inside Story* (London: BBC Books, 1987), p. 204.

9 *Phil Redmond's Brookside: The Official Companion* (London: Weidenfeld & Nicolson, 1987), p. 11.

10 Ibid., p. 7.

11 Ibid., p. 111.

12 Buckingham, *Public Secrets*, p. 16.

13 For an analysis of *Coronation Street*'s invocation of community see the essays in Richard Dyer (ed.), *Coronation Street*, TV Monograph 13 (London: BFI, 1981).

14 Mary Maguire in an interview with the actor Bill Treacher (who plays Arthur Fowler), *Public Service* (May 1987), p. 5.

15 Buckingham, *Public Secrets*, p. 102.

This article was written before the introduction of lesbain story-lines in both *Brookside* and *EastEnders*.

4

National and cultural identity in a Welsh-language soap opera

Alison Griffiths

This chapter considers the growing interest in the popular Welsh-language soap opera, *Pobol Y Cwm* (*People of the Valley*), and the extent to which discourses of Welshness and definitions of cultural and national identity contribute to the appeal and longevity of the soap. Welsh-language broadcasting has been largely neglected in debates surrounding popular culture and pleasure in the 1970s and 1980s; little English-language research has been done in Wales, and most Welsh-language research remains unavailable in English. This marginalization is in many ways symptomatic of the larger politico-historical structure that characterizes Wales's relationship to England; Raymond Williams argues that the process of subordination imposed on the Welsh by the English, in the form of English law, administration, and the suppression of the Welsh language, led to the Anglicization of Welsh institutions. Identifying these processes as "forms of political and cultural colonization," Williams points to the movement of English capital and management into Wales that slighted the rural economy and internal needs of the small, developing country.[1]

As a consequence of these political structures and the relatively recent introduction of Welsh-language programming on S4C (*Sianel Pedwar Cymru/* Channel 4 Wales), a regional television channel introduced in 1982 after considerable Welsh political lobbying, there is a paucity of research conducted into the reception of S4C and how Welsh identity is negotiated in popular televisual forms.[2] Furthermore, critics are generally quick to deride pleasurable Welsh-language genres and draw upon conventional aspersions on the soap opera genre.[3] In order to redress this imbalance, this chapter will trace discourses within *Pobol Y Cwm* that explore definitions and redefinitions of "Welshness" and contribute to (re-)formations of cultural identity, those codified systems and ideological forms that contribute to the sense of a collective experience based on a range of shared assumptions and ideas. The main areas of investigation are structured around three key concerns: first, the role of culture in contributing to a sense of Welsh identity through an investigation of the social, cultural, and institutional forms of *Pobol Y Cwm*; second, analysis of textual ideologies in the soap with specific focus on a controversial story-line; and, third, the role of *Pobol Y Cwm* in the lives of its young viewers and their understanding of ideological concerns.

The three small nations that together with England make up the United Kingdom have been represented in multifarious forms on national television since the early 1950s. A polemic voiced by many critics is that professionals engaged in television production in Wales are encouraged to merely reproduce "dominant" UK mainstream broadcasting in the Welsh language.[4] Moreover, according to Michelle Ryan, the main concern of the "white, middle-class elite" who run the broadcasting institutions in Wales has been to preserve all that is traditional in Welsh culture, secure in the knowledge that such a policy will not compromise their allegiances within the British Establishment.[5]

The form of this relationship between London and regional centers, together with the effect this "marriage" has had on program content and dominant representations, has been discussed by Colin McArthur in relation to Scottish television. He argues that there has been pressure on Scottish television to privilege an image of Scotland that is nationally marketable. Furthermore, just as British television is increasingly dependent on dramatizations and serializations which will attract co-production finance and international sales, so Scottish television looks for financial and critical approval from London and the independent network. The result is a marketable image of Scotland that confirms rather than challenges the dominant discourses of Scottishness.[6]

One of the inadequacies of Scottish television for McArthur is the absence of any sense of its engagement with a *developed* notion of national culture or national identity which goes beyond the reflection of an always already constructed "Scottishness."[7] This criticism is also frequently leveled at *Pobol Y Cwm*; opponents attack the soap for its presumed lack of engagement with any "progressive" notion of "Welshness," arguing that *Pobol Y Cwm* is content to reproduce tried and tested forms of representations that are regressive and vacuous. Absent from these critiques, however, is any form of *real* engagement with the soap or considerations of its generic conventions and popular pleasure. Critics seldom refer directly to the text and are content to make judgments frequently based on their memory of the program's early format which was much slower paced (one of the major narrative settings during episodes from 1974 to 1988 was an old people's home) and appealed to an older audience. Such criticism also raises the vexed question of what a "progressive" Welsh cultural identity might look like.

Developing from definitions of culture which appeared in the 1950s and 1960s work of E. P. Thompson, Raymond Williams, and Richard Hoggart, theoretical accounts of Welsh national culture could locate points of identification around which individuals or groups discover or recognize their "Welshness," a Welshness held together as a unique identity in the face of pressures toward nationless and classless homogeneity.[8] In applying this model to "Scottishness," John Caughie argues that such identification exists in both regressive and progressive forms: in its regressive forms, national culture becomes the "celebration of national identity, a national identity which is always already given," while in its progressive forms, it is concerned with "positive images, with the establishment by discovery or recovery of . . . identity and traditions which can be mobilised as the basis for political action."[9]

This notion of an "already given identity" is a particularly interesting argument to apply to the paradigm of "Welshness" and the role of Welsh television in defining and contributing to a national culture. McArthur argues that discourses of Tartanry and Kailyard (defined respectively by Peter Meech and Richard Kilborn as "a nostalgic and overly sentimental parochialism," and "heavily romanticized depictions of heroic deeds of yesteryear against spectacular Highland backdrops")[10] are both frozen and regressive in that they provide a reservoir of Scottish "characters," "attitudes," and "views" which can be drawn upon to give the "'flavor of Scotland,' a petrified culture with a misty, mythic, and, above all, static past."[11] Attempts to recover a "pure" and quintessential cultural identity rooted in a mythical past are animated by contemporary ideological projects, as Paul Willeman argues:

> Cultural identity no longer precedes . . . discourse as something to be recovered; it is by trying to put an understanding of the multifarious social–historical processes at work in a given situation into discourse that the national–cultural–popular identity begins to find a voice. Tradition(s) can no longer be seen as sacred cows: some are to be criticized, others to be mobilized or inflected.[12]

The extent to which representations of Wales and "Welshness" on popular television are steeped in the frozen and petrified past of Willeman's "recovery" model could only be established through textual analysis of discourses and character types that have appeared in a range of genres. There are undoubtedly certain institutions that have become synonymous with notions of "Welshness," including rugby, beer drinking, male-voice choirs, coalmining, the Welsh *mam* (mother), and the Welsh chapel, while more mythic, "Celtic" images, particularly those associated with notions of stoicism and striving in the face of adversity, have characterized Welsh literature and other arts. Williams argues that these images of the past have been created as ways of "amending images of the present and of finding images of the future" and are a direct consequence of "enduring, understanding and then trying to find ways of resisting subordination."[13]

However, as Williams notes, discussions of Welsh cultural identity frequently neglect its complex and contradictory qualities:

> If there is one thing to insist on in analyzing Welsh culture it is the complex of forced and acquired discontinuities: a broken series of

radical shifts, within which we have to mark not only certain social and linguistic continuities but many acts of self definition by negation, by alteration and by contrast. Indeed it is this culture of Wales, profoundly and consciously problematic, which is the real as distinct from the ideological difference from a selective, dominant and hegemonic English culture.[14]

Moreover, as Marie Gillespie argues, notions of national culture with unique customs and practices understood as "pure" homogeneous nationality can be disabling, and need to be challenged; ideas and idea systems surrounding *Pobol Y Cwm* cannot in any simplistic sense be isolated or perceived as containing any "common-sense truth" about "Welshness" or what is understood by the term "Welsh identity."[15] Discussion of differentials of culture, then, unearths a number of problematics, for example, discourses of cultural nationalism, as Stuart Hood argues, tend to view nations as monolithic givens without considering the importance of subcultures, and their potential for "re-creation" within regional divisions.[16] Furthermore, David Morley and Kevin Robbins argue that debates around questions of cultural identity have existed within a largely uninterrogated model of what cultural identities actually are, and warn of the dangers of essentialist models that perceive national and cultural identities as "pre-given objects."[17] Philip Schlesinger's account of identity and difference, sensitive to the risks of such essentialism, is useful; he argues that "the critical factor for defining the ethnic group . . . becomes the social *boundary* which defines the group with respect to other groups . . . not the cultural reality within those borders."[18] For Schlesinger, therefore, constructing a binary based on inclusion and exclusion invites a more dynamic view of identity, and recognition of the discursivity of identity politics, and of its shifting boundaries and contradictory sites.

Despite periods of re-formation that fissure and destabilize essentialist notions of Welshness, as Williams points out, it is important not to neglect the areas of continuity within Welsh culture. Clearly the central shared marker of cultural identity in Wales is the Welsh language which distinguishes Wales as a country within both the United Kingdom and a broader European community. In recent years the language has enjoyed a modest yet significant revival, boosted by its status as a core national curriculum subject in Welsh-language schools and elective subject in all other schools. The language is unquestionably the foundation upon which Welsh culture and a sense of national identity resides; many characteristics and definitions of Wales have been constructed around the language, which acts as a re-affirmation of Welsh autonomy. Serving as the most important and noticeable differential, the Welsh language, as Williams argues, "is significant both as a cultural dimension of an otherwise merely geographical or administrative area and, against heavy pressures of standardization, as an unforced and steadily available community."[19]

Welsh is characterized by two distinct dialects of the language; one situated in the north, the other in the south. The growth of various media institutions in Wales, particularly the introduction of S4C, has underlined the difference in sound and expression; each form of the language has striven for national recognition as the superior paradigm in both fictional and non-fiction television programming. Just as other UK soaps are positioned in localities with distinct, though frequently contrived and romanticized, discourses and speech patterns, so *Pobol Y Cwm* is firmly situated in a region of Wales characterized by a specific linguistic mode and rural diegesis.

In this regard as in others, *Pobol Y Cwm* presents a compromise between a static and petrified national culture identified by Colin MacArthur and the more dynamic notion of national and cultural identity found in the Irish soap opera *The Riordans*. Produced autonomously in the Irish Republic, free from the restraining hand of a British- (London) based governing body, *The Riordans* made several historic inroads during the 1950s and 1960s. By disengaging the rural family from the cycle of inhibition, authority, and conservatism in which it had been traditionally enclosed, the soap played off a dominant ideology which looked to the family and the family farm as the basis of Irish society.[20] Moreover, the very seriality of *The Riordans*'s textual form opened up a space for discussion of controversial social issues which would not have been permitted in other dramatic genres such as the single play. Situated somewhere between these two paradigms of national identity, *Pobol Y Cwm* is becoming increasingly self-conscious in terms of addressing issues socially and culturally specific to Wales.

Pobol Y Cwm has undergone several changes in format and editorial style since its inception in 1974. It was first broadcast on BBC1, for 30 minutes on Sunday evenings as a trial thirteen-week series. Following favorable audience response, the series was extended for fifty-two twice-weekly episodes. In 1982, the soap moved to S4C and in September 1988 was broadcast in the new time slot of 6:40 p.m. in the form of daily 20-minute episodes with a lunchtime repeat the following day with English subtitles. *Pobol Y Cwm* has since abandoned the lunchtime repeats in favor of a 2.5 hour omnibus edition on Sunday afternoons, and evening episodes have moved to 7:00 p.m. and been extended to 30 minutes. A unique production feature of *Pobol Y Cwm* since 1988 was the decision to broadcast episodes taped earlier the same day; this facility offered *Pobol Y Cwm* an immediacy unparalleled in the UK soap market. Unlike the three other major national soaps, *Coronation Street* (ITV, Granada Television, 1960–), *Brookside* (Channel 4, Mersey Television, 1982–) , and *EastEnders* (BBC1, 1985–), which tape material for broadcast four to six weeks later, *Pobol Y Cwm* could introduce significant national and regional topical material, albeit in a sometimes glancing fashion, while recording a particular day's episode.

An example of this facility arose in a December 1988 episode transmitted on the evening after the Lockerbie airplane disaster. As the producer explained, a decision was made to include a reference to the bombing and crash as the tragedy dominated the national media's attention. At the same time, the program-makers were concerned about the form the reference should take, especially if the remainder of the evening's episode was humorous. Eventually a decision was made to shoot an opening scene with a close-up of a tabloid newspaper's front-page headline on the crash that widened to reveal the shocked and saddened face of the landlord. The scene, shot in total silence, then shifted to the planned opening with no other mention of the disaster; the producer considered the reference effective in conveying a sense of horror and loss without sensationalizing the incident in pursuit of topicality. Significantly, following a disturbing spate of national "disasters" in the 1988 to 1989 series (the Lockerbie plane crash, M1 motorway plane crash, Clapham Common rail collision, and Hillsborough football incident where scores of fans were crushed to death through overcrowding), such incidents were scrutinized by the program's producers and did not automatically receive coverage. In fact, none of the other incidents were integrated in this way, highlighting the production and ethical pressures involved in last-minute production changes possible in daily taping.

An area of interest that did receive topical treatment during the 1988–1989 season was the game of rugby. In that year Wales had fared dreadfully in all their matches and were facing the "wooden spoon" (a tournament term referring to the team who loses every game against the five competing nations of Wales, England, Scotland, Ireland, and France) unless they were victorious against England in the last match of the tournament to be played at Cardiff Arms Park. A pub scene during Friday's episode featured much speculation on the outcome of the next day's match, as Wales playing against England stirred up strong nationalist sentiments in the national media. The following Monday's episode predictably chronicled the victorious outcome of the match and the sense of relief in retaining national pride. Despite the enormous benefits of this immediacy in contributing to the sense of realism and "unrecorded existence" of *Pobol Y Cwm*, great attention is paid to maintaining a sense of balance, as there is a danger that the daily lives of the characters and aspects of their existence and identities will be marginalized if current news events are dramatized. In other words, the production team are sensitive to the "gimmick-potential" of this device, and have resisted introducing extra-diegetic references if it means altering the tone of a particular episode or jarring the way one reference or scene segues into the next. The producers wish to minimize the strain imposed on characterization when, in certain episodes, characters are required to function as news "mouthpieces"; if the reference can be predicted in the scriptwriting – a previously known event, for example – then less pressure is imposed on members of the production team.

The characters that make up the "imagined" and demographically highly-constructed community of Cwmderi, a fictitious village located in the Gwendraeth Valley in south-west Wales, speak the Welsh language in distinct regional dialects. In an attempt to bridge the gap caused by the linguistic divide between North and South Wales and to attract viewers from all regions of Wales, there are a few North Walean characters in the soap; interestingly, the most prominent of these, Meic Pierce, a local café owner, is a comic character and frequently the butt of humorous story-lines. The north/south mix is clearly an arbitrary device as small West Wales villages seldom have such a broad mixture of dialects represented in the community. Despite its lack of realism, the device does contribute to the soap's broad appeal across the Principality; differences between the North and South Walean are often framed in comic terms in popular culture, with numerous reworkings of stereotypical traits.

Humor has occupied a prominent position in the soap; the form of Welsh humor embedded in the narratives of *Pobol Y Cwm* derives both from the classic "gossipy" nature of stereotyped rural village people, and from the slightly macabre rugby club culture and macho sensibility derived from post-rugby match beer drinking sessions where bawdy songs are sung and rude jokes told. (It could be argued that the former is less a distinctive *cultural* feature and more a formulaic device and character type found in most popular UK soaps). The second form of humor is best captured in the image of the slighly morose yet stubbornly optimistic Welshman lamenting the loss of his favorite team but looking forward to another match. Most significantly then, entertainment has evolved as the medium through which issues are raised and explored in the soap. This was apparent in the introduction of what one senior script editor terms the "Invasion" story-line that examined the effect of unwelcome English immigration into the area.

Ron Unsworth, a pub landlord from Birmingham, had taken over a quiet and traditional local village pub, The Farmer's Arms, and planned to modernize it through introducing gimmicks such as a happy hour and Sunday morning striptease shows. Much of the ensuing humor resided in the clash of cultures between Ron's brash, anomic personality and the locals' bemused, tolerant response. The nub of the humor emerges in a joke two of the locals play on Ron. One of them pretends he cannot speak English as he was brought up by his "Bible-thumping grandmother on a farm in the mountains" and did not attend school. Though amazed by this story, Ron nevertheless believes it to be true. In the ensuing dialog, the two locals use many Welsh stereotypes to fuel and sustain the humor; these encompass religion, un-pronounceable Welsh names, uncivilized existence, and stupidity of the Welsh figure "Taffy" (a term which connotes both stupidity and cunning, deriving from the River Taff which flows through the capital Cardiff). The self-denigrating device is itself quintessentially Welsh and a convention in comic exchanges in the soap. Unfortunately, much of the humor is linguistically specific and therefore lost in the subtitled translation for non-Welsh speaking viewers. The scene, nevertheless, is ideologically loaded with references to perceived Welsh and English stereotypes.

While popular genres cannot adequately be conceived of as mere vehicles for the transmission of ideology, the most emotionally saturated entertainment will produce ideas certainly locatable in terms of ideology.[21] The Ron Unsworth story-line, for example, demonstrates that the characters in *Pobol Y Cwm* are continually involved in recirculating notions of Welshness which do not exist in a vacuum, but must be defined in relation to another culture.[22] According to one commentator, aspects of Welsh life which have traditionally contrasted with England (besides the language) are *Brogarwch* (love of locality), *Cyndogaeth* (good neighborliness), egalitarian social attitudes, a tradition of home-ownership, strong kinship ties, scattered and small-scale close-knit communities, a passion for education, and an historical experience of colonialism.[23] It is primarily through the characters that these aspects obtain meaning within the narrative. However, the "Welshness" of *Pobol Y Cwm* is created less via individual characters than by the community and networks of social interaction through which their lives are played out and assume meaning.[24] These social aspects of the Welsh identity can perhaps be summarized by the term *Cydymunedaeth* (literally, "co-communityism"), a contrast to the anomic, impersonal, large-scale, techno-bureaucratic society represented by Ron and his family who "invade" Cwmderi.[25] "Welshness" is consequently framed in direct opposition to English culture via a series of binary oppositions: rural/urban, personal/impersonal, caring/uncaring. Ron is thus defined as the outsider within the community and positioned in stark contrast to the locals on a number of levels.

Throughout history, the Welsh, who claim to have been the earliest inhabitants of the British Isles, have been continually subject to attacks from the Irish, Anglo-Saxons, or English; numerous historians have identified the importance of specific myths, ideas, and images in giving the Welsh self-consciousness down the centuries.[26] The presence of binary oppositions brings the soap's text into culturally mythic territory as Ron's synecdochal role embodies this fear of "otherness" and potential "invasion." Moreover, the threat of invasion by the English strikes an historically familiar chord in a nation whose very foundation stems from a self-consciousness derived from the challenges and crises from invading neighbors. The fictional content of the "Invasion" story-line is generated and sustained by culturally familiar sets of oppositions that magnify the cultural "void" between Ron and members of the community and highlight the lack of shared cultural capital.

In addition to drawing upon a reservoir of issues that have much cultural resonance for Welsh audiences, discourses circulating around regional news and other newsworthy specific socio-cultural events are regularly unpacked and explored within *Pobol Y Cwm*, as innovative story-lines transcend conventions of the genre and cut across many boundaries. This shift in style and content has been most noticeable since 1988, when *Pobol Y Cwm* producers moved to increase socio-political references in the soap. One example involves the publicly sensitive issue of the sale of Welsh property to the English. This issue has aroused much political and social controversy since a series of arson attacks on English-owned cottages in the 1970s, and the media coverage of the quasi-terrorist Welsh Nationalist group *Meibion Glyndwr* (Sons of Glyndwr) in 1988 and 1989 triggered the inclusion of a story-line exploring the political ramifications of the conflict.

The narrative centered on Gladys, an elderly woman who put her small cottage on the market following the death of her husband. Disappointed that several local potential buyers couldn't afford the asking price, she was tempted to sell to Ron Unsworth's brother, Billy, who would use the cottage as an occasional weekend retreat from Birmingham. However, she began to receive threatening phone calls from the Sons of Glyndwr, warning her about selling to English immigrants. After much trauma and deliberation, she was relieved to sell to Meic Pierce, an entrepreneurial local café owner who persuaded her to drop the price, only to resell the cottage himself to Billy Unsworth at the higher price. The ironic resolution of the story-line complicates the ideological message critical of property sales to the English, as it signifies the underlying financial imperative and represents to many viewers the most realistic outcome. Furthermore, on a subtextual level, the North Walean regional identity of the pivotal character in this story line, Meic Pierce, adds another dimension in terms of stereotyping as North Walean characters in Welsh popular fiction are commonly constructed as money-orientated.

One of the ideological strands of this story-line concerns an individual's right to enter the housing market, as buyer or seller, without harassment or threats from political pressure groups. However, the "structures of feeling" of the story-line challenge this simplistic reading. Gladys's position in the narrative exemplifies a moral dilemma experienced by Welsh home-owners who want to secure a realistic price for their property, but feel guilty about selling to non-Welsh, thus contributing to English immigration and the destruction of Welsh communities. Gladys is sympathetic to the nationalist cause and expresses *some* concern for the preservation of cultural traditions and institutions. Encouraged by her brother to attain the highest possible price, she is at the same time subject to pressures from political lobbyists not to sell to Billy Unsworth. Gender relations and the pressures on single women represent another rich ideological strand in this story-line. With little experience of dealing with financial issues, and still traumatized by the sudden death of her husband, Gladys typifies the uncompromising reality many widows are faced with when their husbands had previously managed economic decisions. Gladys is also manipulated by her brother who encourages her to sell the house and live with him and his wife (so they can share some of the proceeds) and displays very little compassion regarding the harassment and threats she receives from Welsh nationalists. Such competing pressures and subtexts indicate the ideological complexity of the soap's engagement with topical issues.

The very seriality of *Pobol Y Cwm* allows complex issues and ideas to be explored and yet remain narratively unresolved. Moreover, the diegetic memories of characters constructed by the story editors are available for resurrection at a later date in the open-ended narrative. Discourse and meaning constantly evolve as story-lines and characterizations shift ideological sites into new territories and spaces. Issues with cultural currency in Wales, such as the sale of second homes to the English, depopulation of rural areas and increasing urbanization, and unemployment, as well as problems facing the agricultural community can be explored through the familiar framework as the personal is inserted into a network of economic and communal relations.[27]

It would be misleading to assume that *Pobol Y Cwm* embodied a single, consistent ideological position in relation to notions of national and cultural Welsh identity; as a site of discursive struggle, meaning in *Pobol Y Cwm* is not transmitted in any fixed or static way; certain readings may be privileged over others, while allowing viewers to produce meaning in a number of complex and possibly contradictory ways. Responses elicited from a range of young Welsh viewers in relation to *Pobol Y Cwm* richly illustrate the extent to which the soap privileges certain ideas and values over others, and constructs a specifically Welsh discourse. I conducted research into the role of *Pobol Y Cwm* in affirming and redefining notions of nationhood and culture through a series of English-language interviews in a bilingual comprehensive school in a village in South Wales. Despite its bilingual status, the school is Welsh in ethos and is known locally as the "Welsh school." My aim was to explore the forms of identification young people have with *Pobol Y Cwm* and the extent to which they believe it constructs and contributes to a specific Welsh identity and discourse. I had identified four key areas (representation, narrative, ideology, and didactic text) and hoped to elicit responses in relation to these concerns. It was my intention not to exclude other issues, but to encourage an open agenda so that students could identify their concerns on their own terms.

The methodology employed consisted of screening the launch episode of the "Invasion" story-line to three groups of approximately eight students. The main structuring determinant was age (11 to 18), with the sample preselected by the headmaster of the school prior to my arrival. The complexity of my role as "outsider," researcher, invited guest of the headmaster, female teacher, and young adult, cannot be ignored in any analysis of my findings. Moreover, it is generally accepted that what children disclose in any situation does not necessarily correspond in any simple way to what they "think"; the existence of an "approved" and what David Buckingham has described as a "distanced or critical" discourse about television must be taken into account and measured against other readings.[28]

Added to this is a risk of unintentionally setting an agenda concerned with "serious," "teacher-like" concerns, when actual viewing and discourse around a program may be quite different, for example, singing the theme tune, mocking characters, or applying subversive readings. The unnatural, public setting for the discussion of an activity normally carried out in the private familial space must also be acknowledged, together with the privileged connotations of the selection process despite its supposed random nature. What the children said or felt able to say was, therefore, influenced by a range of factors, one of the most significant being my perceived cultural identity.

The students' expectations of the "*Pobol Y Cwm* lady" (as I was referred to by staff and students) would have been influenced by the language I spoke (and its associated cultural codes) and my perceived class position as an "English," middle-class academic. I therefore anticipated a slightly hostile response from the pupils, though in reality only sensed discomfort with the older students who were the most reticent and made remarks about the subtitled episode I screened. It did, however, emerge in each of the interviews that I could in fact understand Welsh, although the only group this had any impact on was the 16–17 year olds, who relaxed once they realized I was Welsh.

What emerged across all three groups of respondents was their strong sense of identification with the representations on offer in *Pobol Y Cwm*. However, their identification with the representations of the soap did not extend to urban representations of Wales perceived in the rival Welsh language soap *Dinas* (*City*), which, set in an urban diegesis (Cardiff), had been pejoratively labelled a Welsh version of the US soaps *Dallas* and *Dynasty*, and mocked for its "yuppie" characters and unrealistic narratives.[29] Emma, a 12-year-old student, believed *Pobol Y Cwm* was "more like our village. It's not like *Dinas* with big skyscrapers and big buildings . . . . It's more like us, so we're sort of used to it then." In fact all three groups adopted a derisive attitude towards *Dinas* and condemned it for its Anglo-American style and diegesis:

Sara (aged 14): It's just like an English soap opera, except they're trying to speak Welsh . . . *trying*!

Sarah (aged 14): Yes, trying! (Group laughter)

Andrea (aged 14): I think *Dinas* appeals to the people say who live in Cardiff or in the cities and I think that *Pobol Y Cwm* appeals more to us who live in small villages.

Einir (aged 17): It's like a Welsh *Dynasty*; *Dinas* is. I don't like it at all – it's horrible!

To some extent the distinctions made between English and US prime-time soaps are collapsed in this exchange as the students construct an opposition between the "foreign" soaps (and *Dinas*) and *Pobol Y Cwm*.

Many of the respondents applied their "expertise" and superior knowledge of social and cultural institutions when viewing *Pobol Y Cwm*, and were able to measure its "realism" against their own lived experiences and cultural competences. Owen, a 12-year-old, felt that the soap was "portraying a typical Welsh village with nothing much happening," while Rhys and Dafydd, also 12, commented on the soap's realistic style: "I think they may have based it on somebody, you know, the characters" (Rhys); and "It looks like they've just gone into somebody's house and put a camera there, hidden, and recorded what goes on" (Dafydd). The respondents' discussion of the realist modality was quite complex and sophisticated, perhaps because the representations constructed in *Pobol Y Cwm* were close to their lived experience of a small rural community. However, when asked if they felt the soap should contain less anachronistic and more "progressive" representations, they recognized the need for realism and plausibility to be balanced against a remit to entertain through the introduction of dramatic and comic story-lines. Siwan, aged 12, felt the soap was "just meant to be entertainment for the Welsh. But the thing is, if we have it like that, it's more like a documentary than about the Welsh . . . we're not thinking about these things in *Neighbours* and things like that." Interestingly, throughout the interviews, *Neighbours*, a "lightweight" non-socially realist soap from Australia with a cult teenage following, is "forgiven" for its lack of realism, low production values and unsubtle use of soap conventions such as the cliff-hanger ending. *Neighbours* was referred to with warmth as it invited a particular kind of identification and subject positioning and could therefore be made sense of within those terms. Furthermore, its scheduling in a traditional children's television slot (5:30 p.m.) contributes to young audiences claiming the soap as their own (it used to broadcast to a small daytime audience before the BBC decided to repeat lunchtime episodes before the early evening news).

All three groups of respondents firmly believed that *Pobol Y Cwm* contained positive and realistic representations of Wales and Welsh people. Adjectives such as "caring," "respected," "friendly," and "humorous" were used to describe characters. The description "natural" was frequently applied: "They lead a more *natural* life, the Welsh;" "It's all *natural*;" "It would lose its *naturalness* – there's nothing false about it." Other aspects of Welshness transmitted by the soap included the close-knit community and cultural traditions and values.

A series of oppositions becomes apparent when notions of Welshness were compared to an English existence in the student responses. Some spoke of an opposition between urban and rural: "The countryside, because in England a lot of it is buildings and cities" (Rhodri, aged 14); between the anomic and the social: "In England they don't care, you know, they just lead their own lives and just leave everyone else to get on with theirs, but they're all close community in Wales" (Nerys, aged 14); between friendliness and hostility: "And the friendliness of the Welsh people. We seem to be more adaptable, help people out, whereas the English tend to be more arrogant and do things to suit themselves" (Lisa, aged 17).

The respondents were also quick to identify the social and cultural stereotypes of Wales and the Welsh visible in other genres and discourses. Some Welsh cultural "institutions" were viewed more positively than others; examples of negative stereotyping included the label "Taffy" and representations of the Welsh as slow or "backwards" as in the naive and gauche Welsh constable who frequently forms a comic double act with his sergeant in television police series. (The television comedy series *Minder* and crime fiction series *The Bill* have made use of this negative stereotype, reminiscent of the English stereogtype of the Irish).

The main narrative discussed in each group interview was the "Invasion" story-line and the characterization of Ron Unsworth. From the outset, several of the respondents offered a particular understanding of what they perceived to be the "reasons" for the story-line and Ron Unsworth's role in the diegesis. Virtually all the respondents supported the polemical nature of the story-line, the negative effects of English families moving into the close knit community, both in their perceptions of the role of Ron Unsworth and the program-makers' intentions. The following comments are typical and reflect a consistent attitude across the age ranges:

> *Owen (aged 12)*: Ron, he's just come in from outside and he expects to be able to turn everything around his little finger and stop "Welshness."

> *Dafydd (aged 12)*: I think he's anti-Welsh. The Welsh are just nothing, it's just another accent.

> *Andrea (aged 14)*: And he thinks he can come to Wales and take over and doesn't realize that they were there before him . . . he's arrogant in his ways.

> *Elin (aged 14)*: I think he's meant to be compared to the Welsh people to try and show the two different sides; what the English think of the Welsh and what the Welsh think of the English.

What emerged was a strong sense of approval of this story-line, particularly its ability to address a controversial issue and fulfill a consciousness-raising role. Many of the respondents related anecdotes of English families moving into their villages and communities and the harmful effect on institutions such as the Welsh language and local chapels. Additionally, many respondents felt that the soap should be tackling this issue and making itself accountable to its viewers while addressing a "real" socio-political concern. Elin, aged 17, felt it was an issue that was "becoming more and more obvious in Wales . . . people should be aware of it." Older respondents were able to apply an economic analysis of the situation and could cite evidence drawn from everyday interaction with Welsh media and as part of their socialization:

Nona (aged 17): It shows what's happening in a lot of communities in Wales.

Wyn (aged 17): English people coming down, buying houses really cheap, selling their houses up there for fortunes and coming down here.

Nona: Thinking they can take over the communities as well.

Coupled with this economic analysis was an anti-imperialist discourse which in some instances was incisive and indicated an historical awareness:

> It's the same with the Scots. They've lost their language, the Gaelic language and the same with the Irish, Northern Ireland. That's why there's so much fighting going on in Ireland; it's because they want their territory back, because it was theirs in the first place.
>
> (Dafydd, aged 12)

Two respondents did resist this consensus reading, particularly of Ron Unsworth's characterization, which they felt did not present a fair or accurate portrayal of English people. Andrea, aged 14, voiced the following viewpoint: "Some stories, like they've introduced Ron Unsworth, well, I've got to admit that not *all* English people are like that. Some people do make the effort to learn the Welsh language, so I wouldn't portray the character like that personally." The fact that Ron functions as an ideological type, a caricature of a "Brummie" (a native of Birmingham), rarely entered the respondents' agenda on regionalism and identity. As far as the majority of respondents were concerned, Ron was not atypical and therefore not anomalous to their lived experience. This would suggest that their undiscerning impression and overall view of English people derives from the fact that they had little or no direct experience of many of the representations and situations presented on television. As an ideological structure, the approved reading of the effect of Ron's entry into the community was inextricably linked to their world-view of English social and cultural traditions. The following analyses were not untypical:

> *Betsan (aged 14)*: People *are* like that; some English people are really ignorant and make fun of the Welsh accent, not understanding that Welsh is one of the oldest Celtic languages.

> *Katrin (aged 17)*: His attitude was very characteristic of some English people.

The respondents also felt able to identify what they understood to be a characteristically "English" view of Wales: Nerys (aged 14): "Yeah, because the English people, from England, they think that the Welsh are only coal tips and choirs, but it's not, it's more interesting." Their understanding and interpretations of "Welshness" were frequently defined in terms of what they considered were "un-Welsh" and typically English traits. Discussing

Ron Unsworth, they felt he was "always making a big fuss when everyone else is basically quiet and just wants to be left alone" (Owen, aged 12), and "the people from Cwmderi [Wales], they're sociable, but he's just loud" (Rhys, aged 12).

The consensus expressed by the group was that the particular English representation apparent in *Pobol Y Cwm* served the purpose of embarrassing English people in Wales. Sara, aged 17, felt that it was "an insult to the English, showing how loud and ignorant they [were] and unsophisticated too." This position was also imputed to the producers of the soap: "I think they brought him [Ron] in deliberately, because they're embarrassing the English." There was little ambiguity in the respondents' reading of the role of the "Invasion" story-line and its invited ideological argument. In defining an albeit stereotypical English identity, they felt that the representation was a fairly accurate portrayal of the English presence in Wales. Another possible reading of Ron's character not voiced by the respondents relates to the somewhat hyperbolic qualities of his characterization; it could be argued that in making Ron such an uniquely obnoxious person, the writers are deflecting the story away from an indictment of the English *per se* – Ron is Ron irrespective of his English identity.

An underlying anti-imperialist reading of Wales's historical and cultural past was repeatedly suggested by the students; the prominence of nationalist discourses was surprising, associated with the "perceived" threat of Ron Unsworth's characterization:

He's just come in from England so he thinks that the English are better than the Welsh. He just thinks he can rule our country. . . . Really the English are being very selfish and cheeky coming into Wales because they're coming into Wales to try and turn it into England. The Irish don't do it, the Scots don't do it and the Spanish don't do it – why the English?

(Emma, aged 12)

A salient point is the extent to which their education and acculturation had framed the views of the respondents and perhaps reinforced Welsh nationalist positions. The respondents' negotiation of *Pobol Y Cwm*'s political themes was clearly framed against what they believed were the producer's intentions. When invited to comment on the perceived "motivation" of the story-line, the students' response was direct and unswerving: "To get us thinking it's a bad thing and we've got to stop it" (Owen, aged 12). Moreover, oppositional readings were virtually non-existent: Dafydd, aged 12, who had previously compared Wales's colonialist experience with that of Scotland and Ireland, was now seen to shift position: "I don't think they should go too fanatical over Welsh, not go too much over the top." His compromised view was quickly challenged by his peers who forced him to modify his position and agree with the consensus, a fact that illustrates the crucial role of group dynamics and peer pressure on ethnographic research findings. Moreover, the negotiation of subject positions within the group structure underscores the complex and contingent nature of the research data and the danger of overly determinist readings of their themes and concerns. While the students' pleasure and enthusiasm for *Pobol Y Cwm* suggest a unified position in relation to its realist story-lines and high production values, more nuanced readings may have been obtained in different research contexts.

Conclusion

An attempt has been made in this chapter to highlight the way concepts of culture and nationhood are deployed in a popular generic form, and how this might be used to delineate wider discourses associated with media representation of small nations and distinct ethnicities. Clearly, there is considerable scope for detailed and extensive ethnographic research to be carried out in this area: *Pobol Y Cwm* represents *one* paradigm of popular Welsh-language broadcasting. Research into Welsh sitcoms, drama series, youth programs like *Video 9,* and regional news output would broaden the investigation and provide a more rigorous analysis of how "Welshness" is negotiated and made sense of in both indigenous and non-Welsh broadcasting.

Notes

1 Raymond Williams, "Wales and England," in John Osmond (ed.), *The National Question Again: Welsh Political Identity in the 1980's* (Llandysul: Gomer Press, 1985), p. 26.

2 The Welsh-language channel, S4C, has broadcast programs scheduled alongside network Channel 4 output since its inception in 1982. The effect this "marriage" has had on channel identity has been criticized by both Welsh and non-Welsh-speaking viewers who argue that Channel 4's experimental productions produce a "jarring" effect sitting alongside mainstream Welsh-language soaps and chat shows. As S4C's remit does not require innovation or alternative programming, it has catered for the needs of its minority audience by commissioning, producing, and broadcasting what many consider to be "safe," bland programming that reflects a popular, "balanced" television schedule. Critics have argued that Welsh speakers are, therefore, addressed as an homogeneous group with experimentation absent from the current output. Moreover, now that S4C carries all Welsh-language broadcasting and is seen to be conveniently serving the needs of Welsh language speakers, organizations whose remits also include programming for Wales (BBC2, BBC2 Wales, and HTV Wales) have been condemned for their complacency and Anglocentricism. Consequently, so the argument goes, non-Welsh-speaking Welsh viewers have become invisible and are assimilated into the broader UK audience. The problem is likely to be exacerbated following deregulation and market penetration of cable and satellite systems. For a discussion of this argument see *The Media Show* (editor Jane Root, Channel 4, transmitted on January 28, 1990); and Michelle Ryan, "Blocking the Channels: TV and Film in Wales," in Tony Curtis (ed.), *Wales: The Imagined Nation. Essays in Cultural and National Identity* (Bridgend: Poetry Wales Press, 1986), pp. 181–196. For an account of the introduction of S4C see Angharad Tomos,

"Realising a Dream," and Jonathan Coe, "Sianel Pedwar Cymru: Fighting for a Future," both in Simon Blanchard and David Morley (eds), *What's this Channel Four?* (London: Comedia Publishing Group, 1982), pp. 35–61. For an overview of the political ramifications and background to introduction of S4C see John Osmond, "The Dynamics of Institutions," in Osmond (ed.), *The National Question Again*, pp. 225–256.

3 See, for example, Wynne Lloyd, "Soap 'Sianel' Boasting a Trio of Home-Grown Productions," *Western Mail*, October 22, 1988, n.p.

4 Ryan, "Blocking the Channels," p. 87.

5 Ibid.

6 John Caughie, "Scottish Television: What Would it Look Like?," in Colin McArthur (ed.), *Scotch Reels: Scotland in Film and Television* (London: British Film Institute, 1982), p. 114.

7 Ibid., p. 115.

8 Ibid., p. 116.

9 Ibid.

10 Peter Meech and Richard Kilborn, "Media and Identity in a Stateless Nation: The Case of Scotland," *Media, Culture and Society* 14 (2) (April 1992), p. 254.

11 Caughie, "Scottish Television," p. 116.

12 Paul Willeman, "The Third Cinema Question: Notes and Reflections," in Jim Pines and Paul Willeman (eds), *Questions of Third Cinema* (London: British Film Institute, 1989), p. 20.

13 Williams, "Wales and England," p. 25.

14 Ibid., p. 23.

15 Marie Gillespie, "Technology and Tradition: Audio-Visual Culture Among South Asian Families in West London," *Cultural Studies* 3 (2) (May 1989), p. 238.

16 Stuart Hood, "The Couthy Feeling," *New Statesman and Society* (August 12, 1988), pp. 30–31, cited in David Morley and Kevin Robbins, "Spaces of Identity," *Screen* 30 (4) (1989), p. 16.

17 Philip Schlesinger, "On National Identity: Some Conceptions and Misconceptions," *Social Science Information* 26 (2) (1987), p. 234, cited in "Spaces of Identity," p. 14.

18 Ibid., p. 235.

19 Williams, "Wales and England," p. 22.

20 Martin McLoone and John McMahon (eds), *Television and Irish Society: Twenty One Years of Irish Television* (Dublin: RTE/IFI, 1984), p. 43.

21 Terry Lovell, *Pictures of Reality: Aesthetics, Politics and Pleasure* (London: British Film Institute, 1983), p. 51.

22 Roger Tanner, "National Identity and the One-Wales Model," *Planet* (April–May 1973), p. 32.

23 Ibid.

24 Ien Ang, *Watching "Dallas:" Soap Opera and the Melodramatic Imagination* (London: Methuen, 1985), p. 29.

25 Tanner, "National Identity," p. 59.

26 Ibid.

27 McLoone and MacMahon (eds), *Television and Irish Society*, p. 37.

28 David Buckingham, "Seeing Through TV: Children Talking About Television," in Janet Willis and Tana Wollen (eds), *The Neglected Audience* (London: British Film Institute, 1990), p. 89.

29 *Dinas* received mixed reviews from critics and audiences and was taken off the air in July 1991.

5

Global *Neighbours*?

Stephen Crofts

An irresistible epigraph, from Jerry Hall, when she was the taller half of Mick Jagger, speaking on the *Clive James Show* in the United Kingdom on New Year's Eve, December 31, 1989: "Before I saw *Neighbours*, I didn't know there *was* an Australia."

This chapter contrasts the receptions accorded to the Australian soap opera, *Neighbours*, in Britain, the USA and France. Produced by the Grundy Organisation in Melbourne and written by Reg Watson, it first screened in Australia on March 18, 1985, and has, for much of the time since, been Australia's most popular soap. It has been exported to some twenty-five countries.

I would like to advance a key concept for the analysis of the success or otherwise of cultural exports. It pivots around the question: how assimilable are the cross-cultural differences involved? National cultural differences, say, will present consumers with no reading problems provided these differences are culturally assimilable by the importing country. Similarly between different cultural populations within a given nation state. In television, the acceptability of cultural variation is likely to increase as the size of targeted audience decreases: the range, say, from the highly standardized, culturally restricted material of US network television to the culturally varied material of Channel 4 in the UK and SBS in Australia. Yet, this presupposes that the texts have received adequate exposure in the importing country for a judgment to be made. This is acutely the case for soaps, whose dispersed narrative structure and incremental characterization make of them an acquired taste. Institutional and cultural factors, in other words, can be the preconditions for an imported text being given a market chance.

Britain: *Neighbours* as post-colonial success story

This section traces the reasons for *Neighbours*'s phenomenal success across the UK. Between 1988 and 1992, when research for this chapter was completed, it regularly tussled with the UK's home-grown soap, *EastEnders*,

98

for top spot in the British ratings.[1] It has proved to be sufficiently compulsive viewing to be one of only two scheduled TV programmes to survive the carpet bombing of Gulf War coverage on UK television on the war's first day, January 18, 1991 (the other survivor on that day was another Australian soap, *Home and Away*).

Before treating the institutonal and textual factors which contributed to *Neighbours*'s success in the UK specifically, I propose ten textual reasons for its success in a range of territories. Several of these factors are noted in British press commentary, which accounted retrospectively for the massive success of *Neighbours*. *Neighbours* persisted in its success, similarly to *Crocodile Dundee* in 1986 in the USA, where it obliged two major film critics, Vincent Canby and Andrew Sarris, to reconsider it after they had farmed out reviews to second stringers on the film's first appearance (Crofts 1992: 223).

1 *The everyday* The programme urges identification with profoundly every-day experiences: personal problems, desires, worries, fears, minor mis-understandings, romance, low-key domestic arguments. In negative accounts, the "everyday" becomes "trivial" and "banal" "dog-attacks-cat" stories, or, in the words of one French journal, "these clumsily intrusive neighbours whose greatest existential anguish consists in having to choose between two colours of wallpaper" (Brugière 1989: 51). *Neighbours*'s ordinariness and predictability largely shun the melo-dramatic, the concatenation of incidents, the excessive. In the words of producer, Mark Callan:

> We try to keep everything as simple as possible and direct it at the ordinary things that occur in every household and within every neighbourhood. We are often tempted to use a sensational story, but we pull back and say: "That's not likely to happen." We do best when we portray the mundane in an entertaining way.
>
> (quoted by Galvin 1988)

Testimony to the success of this strategy is found in the observations of Lucy Janes, a 15-year-old Scot whose age is typical of the program's principal demographic target. She talks about

> the plot – predictable, filled with clichés and relatively simple (particularly compared to *Dynasty* and *Dallas* where each character has been married to each of the others at least twice). You can play an amusing little game because of the predictability. Try to guess what he/she is going to say next. It's easier than you think and gives the viewer a feeling of participation and achievement.
>
> (Janes 1988)

Identification is encouraged by the everyday tempo and rhythm, the invariable use of eye-level camera and a thoroughly utilitarian visual style which draws no attention to itself (even *Home and Away* appears a little mannered in comparison). (As at July 1992, when research for this section of the chapter was completed, there were signs of *Neighbours*'s adopting a flashier and more sexually explicit style.)

2 *The domestic, the suburban* Ian Craven has noted *Neighbours*'s "populist segregation of the worlds of work and leisure" (Craven 1989: 15).[2] The private sphere is elevated over the public sphere, leisure over work, family and suburban manners over social and political issues. Such a focus is *ideally* suited to the domestic address of daytime soap operas. The representation of the outside world, especially the bush, as threatening, disorienting, abnormal is entirely consonant with such domestic address. Witness *Neighbours* as transmitted in Australia on April 15, 1992: Doug and Jim's canoeing trip involves their being kept awake by feral animals outside their tent, being drugged by wild mushrooms, and then losing their canoe. Crime, violence, and murder – the staples of many soaps – emphatically do not occur in this program's almost exclusively domestic realm, though the program still adopts the soap opera's narrative logic of intensifying and concentrating everyday life.

3 *Women as doers* as well as carers are common, and thus mesh with the employment aspirations/practice of the predominantly female audience for daytime soaps. The most famous example is the girl mechanic Charlene, played by Kylie Minogue. The elevation of the private over the public sphere, however, does not generate a surplus of female characters: alongside some women with jobs outside the home, most Ramsay Street households have a man who works from home or one who seems not to need to go to work. A numerical gender balance is accompanied by a conventional gender politics modified in a progressive direction only, one suspects, in so far as audience demographics are perceived to require.

4 *Teen sex appeal* Young stars such as Minogue, Peter O'Brien, Craig McLachlan, and Jason Donovan have exercised often huge appeal over the teen audience which comprises the bulk of *Neighbours*'s viewers. Embodiments of youth, vitality, and health, they appeal to older viewers too.

5 *Unrebellious youth* These young characters, however, overwhelmingly uphold sensible adult values. Contributing to a fundamental domestic harmony, they are, like Brandon in *Beverley Hills 90210*, often 15 going on 40. Sex is rare, loving, and discreet. Parents could breathe a sigh of relief to see girl-next-door Kylie displace Madonna as their teenage children's pop idol.

6 *"Feelgood" characters* Walt Disney-like, these characters are predominantly nice, ordinary people, with a few devious or egocentric exceptions such as Mrs Mangel, Paul Robinson, and Fay Hudson. Sympathetic elders complement decent youth.

7 *Wholesome neighborliness* Good neighborliness and wholesome, traditional, suburban values eliminate behavioral extremes and set up the
moral certainties of hard work, decency, compassion. *Neighbours* resembles the down-home, wholesome populism of a Frank Capra comedy
except that its suburban protagonists are saved the trouble of traveling to
and from a big city to discover their true values.

8 *Differences are resolved, dissolved, or repressed* The characters are
"almost compulsively articulate about problems and feelings" (Tyrer
1987). Crises are solved quickly, usually amicably. Conflict is thus
managed almost psychotherapeutically by and within the inner circle of
family, and the outer circle of Ramsay Street. Witness the episode
broadcast on April 23, 1992 in Australia: after fire destroys much of
Gaby's clothes boutique, three female neighbors remake the lost stock,
while three male neighbors clear up the debris from the shop. As the theme
song has it: "Neighbours should be there for one another." Incursions of
conflict from the social world beyond these charmed circles are treated
tokenistically or spirited away. The program blurs or represses differences
of gender politics, sexual preference, age, and ethnicity. Domestic
violence and homosexuality, male or female, are unknown. Age differences are subsumed within family love and tolerance. Aboriginal
characters manage a two-episode plot line at most (Craven 1989: 18), and
Greeks, despite the real Melbourne being the third largest Greek city in
the world, figure rarely. *Neighbours*-watchers could likewise be forgiven
for not knowing that Melbourne has the largest Jewish community in
Australia. The program elides questions of disability, alcoholism, or
religious difference. It displaces drug addiction on to a friend outside
immediate family circles (Cousin 1992). Unemployment as a social issue
is subordinated to the humanist characterization of Brad, for instance, as
dopey, happy-go-lucky surfie. *Neighbours* counterposes suburban escapism to the high-gloss escapism of *Santa Barbara*.

9 *Depoliticized middle-class citizenship* These "cosy parish pump narratives," as Ian Craven calls them, depoliticize the everyday (Craven 1989:
21). Such good middle-class suburban citizenship is roundly condemned
by no less than Germaine Greer:

> The world of *Neighbours* is the world of the detergent commercial;
> everything from the kitchen worktops to the S-bend is squeaky
> clean. Everyone's hair and underwear is freshly laundered. No one
> is shabby or eccentric; no one is poor or any colour but white.
> *Neighbours* is the Australian version of the American dream, owner-
> occupied, White-Anglo-Saxon-Protestant paradise.
>
> (Greer 1989)

In this blithely comfortable middle-class ethos, the characters seem never to have problems with mortgage repayments. Commenting on the opening episodes of *Neighbours*, a British critic underlines its property-owning values:

> Max Ramsay is the cardboard cutout Ozzie clod who warns his son, Shane, against dating Daphne because she works as a stag-night stripper. His main fear seems to be the effect the newly arrived Daphne might have on the price of his property.
>
> (Smurthwaite 1986)

As Grahame Griffin notes, "the closing credit sequence . . . is a series of static shots of suburban houses singled out for display in a manner reminiscent of real estate advertisements" (Griffin 1991: 175). Small business abounds in *Neighbours*: a bar, a boutique, an engineering company, with no corporate sector and no public servants or bureaucrats apart from a headmistress.

10 *Writing skills* must be acknowledged. It is very hard to make the mundane interesting, and indeed to score multiple *short* plot lines across a *small* number of characters (twelve to fifteen), as is appropriate to representing the local, the everyday, the suburban. As Moira Petty remarks, *Neighbours* is successful because "it's very simple. The characters are two dimensional and the plots come thick and fast. The storylines don't last long, so if you don't like one, another will come along in a few days" (quoted by Harris 1988).

These ten textual reasons doubtless contribute, differentially across different export markets, to *Neighbours*'s success in many countries of the world. Its wholesome neighborliness, its cosy everyday ethos would appear to be eminently exportable. However, lest it be imagined that *Neighbours* has *universal* popularity or even comprehensibility, there remain some 150 countries to which it has not been exported, and many in which its notions of kinship systems, gender relations, and cultural spaces would appear most odd. The non-universality of western kinship relations, for example, is clearly evidenced in Elihu Katz and Tamar Liebes's comparison of Israeli and Arab readings of *Dallas* (Katz and Leibes 1986). And, indeed, there are two familiar territories to be considered later – the USA and France – in which it has been screened and failed. Significantly, the countries screening *Neighbours* are mostly anglophone and well familiar with British, if not also with Australian soaps.

But why does *Neighbours* appeal *so* forcibly in the UK? In the UK market, I suggest, five institutional and cultural preconditions enabled *Neighbours*'s phenomenal success. Some of these considerations are, of course, the *sine qua non* of *Neighbours* even being *seen* on UK television.

The first precondition was its price, reportedly A$54,000 per show for two screenings; with *EastEnders* costing A$80,000 per episode, *Neighbours* was well worth a gamble (Kingsley 1989: 241).

Scheduling, too, was vital to *Neighbours*'s success. This has two dimensions. *Neighbours* was the first program on UK television ever to be stripped over five weekdays (Patterson 1992). BBC Daytime Television, taking off under Roger Loughton in 1986, while Michael Grade was Programme Controller, was so bold in this as to incur the chagrin of commercial television, constrained at the time from such a move by Independent Broadcasting Association regulations (Willock 1992). *Coronation Street* and *Crossroads* had been stripped across three evenings, and *EastEnders* across two. Stripping across five days/nights had long been common in Australian television. This was first done for *Number 96* (1972–1977) by Ian Holmes, later the Grundy Organisation's president. So successful was the stripping of *Neighbours* across five days that the same principle has since been adopted in the UK for *Home and Away*. David Liddiment, Head of Entertainment at Granada, which produces *Coronation Street* and *Families*, both *Neighbours* competitors, went so far as to say: "In future, no-one will contemplate running a daytime serial in the UK except as a strip. It's inevitable that you build success more quickly when you strip a soap" (Liddiment 1989: 20).

Second, on scheduling, Loughton made the schedules more cost-effective by repeating each edition daily (Patterson 1992). "The time-slots chosen by the BBC were 1.30 pm, with a repeat the following morning at 9.05. It attracted a typical audience of housewives, shift workers, the unemployed, people home sick" (Oram 1988: 48). After the unexpected success of *Neighbours*' first year, it was decided to reschedule the next morning repeat for the same evening, at 5:35 p.m. This was to cater for working mothers, but most of all for schoolchildren who had previously played truant to watch the series. The most famous story attributes the schedule change to the representations made to no less than Michael Grade himself by his daughter. Rescheduled in January 1988, *Neighbours* nearly doubled its audience to 16.25 million within six weeks. By Christmas 1988, audiences topped 20 million. Five-day stripping and repeat screenings, then, offered a regularity and familiarity significant in capturing such huge audiences, representing one-third of the UK population.

The third precondition was the UK "mediascape." This included a very broad familiarity with Australian soaps. When *Neighbours* was launched on October 27, 1986, *The Sullivans*, *A Country Practice*, *Young Doctors*, *Flying Doctors*, *Richmond Hills*, *Prisoner: Cell Block H*, and others had broadened the paths already beaten by many Australian films released in the UK. Michael Collins, executive in charge of production at JNP, producers of *A Country Practice*, maintains that the serial, screened in the UK since 1983, "was a forerunner in getting audiences used to Australian drama" (Collins 1991). And one factor contributing to *Neighbours*'s topping the ratings late in 1988 would have been the demise of *Crossroads*, the British soap created by Reg Watson, in spring 1988 after a twenty-four-year run.

Fourth, tabloids, television, and un(der)employment. Under Thatcher and Murdoch, the tabloid press in Britain expanded in the mid-1980s, producing what one television executive described, albeit parodically, as "one page of news, one page of sex, and twenty-two pages of television and sport" (Patterson 1992). So when *Neighbours* was stripped over five days, "the papers really noticed it" (Willock 1992). Together with *Woman*, *Woman's Day*, *Jackie*, *Scoop*, and other teen magazines, the tabloids ran myriad stories on Kylie, Jason, Peter O'Brien, and so on, as is indicated by the three sample headlines from three successive days:

> Floored by Kylie Haymaker: She Wallops like a Kangaroo – How Tiny Kylie Thumped Hunky Jason.
>
> *(People*, August 21, 1988)

> Heartless Neighbours Jibe That Made Kylie Cry.
>
> *(Sun*, August 22, 1988)

> Why Kylie's Driving Me [Jason] Crazy.
>
> *(Sun*, August 23, 1988)

Also significant is the contemporaneous Thatcherite swelling of the ranks of the unemployed and underemployed. Writing in the *Guardian*, Hugh Hebert noted of the "new daytime audience" that

> there is a huge pool of unemployed and under-employed people and the daytime phenomenon is tapping into that market. *Neighbours* has been lucky enough to take off as that audience has grown. But it has a lighter touch than *EastEnders* or *Coronation Street* – it doesn't have such deep social problems.
>
> (quoted by Harris 1988)

Finally, media publicity has continually stoked the boilers of *Neighbours*'s success in the media in the last four years. Kylie and Jason launched their singing careers, threatening no less than Cliff Richard at the top of the charts in Christmas 1988. As well as the Royal Family, the Archbishop of Canterbury also let it be known that he, too, watched *Neighbours*. Since 1989, cast members have been invited to Royal Command Performances and to participate in Christmas pantomimes. *Neighbours* became a political football in 1991, with Michael Fallon, a junior education spokesperson, denouncing it for "making teachers' jobs even harder" (*Independent*, May 19, 1991), and Jack Straw, his Labour counterpart, joining the fray in similar terms. It has also spawned a British version, *Families*, first screened on April 23, 1990. This revolves around two families, one British and one Australian, and the British father's visiting Australia to find his lover of twenty years ago. In 1992 *Neighbours* appears to have incited its first murder, or at least manslaughter:

LONDON: A man who killed his neighbour over a blaring television says he was driven mad – by the theme tune of *Neighbours*. Eric Seall, who walked free after being convicted of manslaughter, said: "It was that *Neighbours* tune that finally did it. That stupid song made my life hell." A court was told that Seall, 32, came to blows with John Roach, 37, who fell downstairs at their flats in Hampshire and fractured his skull.

(*West Australian*, June 27, 1992)

Supported as they are by these five institutional and cultural factors, the ten general textual factors set out above would seem to encounter no import restrictions to the UK. But there remain four other factors. These constitute apparent points of difference between Australia as represented in *Neighbours*, and Britain, the importing market. The four features of significant climatic, cultural, and linguistic differences between the two countries put to the test the questions raised earlier: how assimilable are the cross-cultural differences involved? Under what circumstances can such differences be assimilated?

First, weather. In the words of Barry Brown, Head of Purchased Pro-grammes at the BBC, "The weather [in Australia] is always hot and the characters are casually dressed. [This] gives the series a freedom and freshness which is new to us" (quoted by Tyrer 1987). Ruth Brown observed that "the cast complain of having to perform in unseasonably thin clothing because the Poms like to think it's always hot in Oz" (Brown 1989). The production company, Grundy, denies anything of the sort: "We don't make the show for world consumption, international consumption . . . . What we get back from overseas wouldn't pay for it" (Fowler 1991). Warm weather can be associated with a casual lifestyle and the singlets and shorts sartorially prominent in *Neighbours*. Such weather and lifestyle, then, can represent idealized projections for Britons seeking sunny holidays away from grim, grey skies and drear British drabness.

The second difference takes off from two aspects of Australian suburbia: higher rates of home-ownership and much lower rates of population density than obtain in the UK. As represented in *Neighbours*, readily accessible home-ownership can exercise an evident appeal for Britons, especially during the late 1980s property boom, when rapidly rising prices excluded yet more from joining the propertied classes. Moreover, the spacious homes and gardens of Erinsborough are a function of a low population density which enables British viewers to imagine in the Melbourne suburb a comfortable self-distancing from the violent evidence of class and ethnic differences so widespread in a Conservative Britain. Allied to this is the relative affluence enjoyed by the neighbors. A quotation from the 15-year-old Scot, Lucy Janes, brings together differences of weather and suburbia in a comparison of *Neighbours* with the socially conscious *EastEnders*:

If you turn on a British soap such as *EastEnders*, you see a pub, dirty houses, dirty streets and the British weather. *Neighbours*, on the other

105

hand, is set in a clean, bright little street with swimming pools in every garden and SUN. To us *Neighbours* offers the taste of a world beyond the wet and fog-ridden British Isles.

(Janes 1988)

A bathetic referential parenthesis: the much-vaunted quarter-acre plot of Australian suburban real estate discourse has in actuality more than its share of loneliness, domestic violence, lack of nearby educational facilities, commercial and social services, and so on. An Australian television pro- gramme, *Lost in Space* (Channel 2), screened on September 2, 1992, cites a British emigrant relocated, and unemployed, in an outer Brisbane suburb, blaming *Neighbours* for having misled him to Australia.

The third difference pits Australian egalitarianism against British class hierarchies. The myth of Australia as egalitarian circulates widely in the UK as well as in Australia. It readily enables an elision of any working-class or unemployed populations. That elision was literally as well as metaphorically bought by Barry Brown, BBC Head of Purchased Programmes: "There isn't a class system in Australia – or, if you like, everyone in Australia is middle class" (quoted by Tyrer 1987). In this way, *Neighbours* can focus British viewers' notions that there is a safe, middle-class/classless suburban heaven down under. Wholesome neighborliness is highly pertinent here. Peter Pinne, executive producer of *Neighbours*, is quoted as ascribing its success to the fact that "it provides a vision of something that is lacking in the personal lives of many people in Britain today, particularly a sense of personal commitment and caring in the community" (Solomon 1989).

The fourth difference concerns Australian accent and idiom, and their differences from British English. Acceptability of these differences has been facilitated not only by the steady succession of Australian television and film product screened in the UK since the early 1970s, but also within UK television production by the growing recognition of regional and ethnic accents since the early 1960s first moves away from plummy upper-class enunciation. Thus when "bludger" is noted in a *Daily Telegraph* (February 2, 1988) review as not being understood, it is *not* a matter of criticism or condescension, as in some reviews of *Crocodile Dundee* (see Crofts 1992: 210–220). The opening of the review indicates a ready acceptance of difference: "'I was just goin' to put the nosebag on. Fancy a bit of tucker yourself?' This is the essential tone of *Neighbours*, BBC-1's usually [sic] successful bought-in Australia soap. It is just quaintly foreign enough to please without confusing" (Marrin 1988).

Of these four differences, then, between Australia and Britain, three (concerning the weather, suburbia, and egalitarianism) are virtually dissolved in that they enable the projection of British fantasies on to *Neighbours*. The last difference functions as a marker of cultural difference so familiar as to present no problems of assimilation.

In sum, *Neighbours*'s huge success in the UK can therefore be traced in the three general categories of explanation set out above. Its ratings suggest beyond doubt that all of the general textual "success factors" of *Neighbours* apply in the UK; indeed, almost all have been commented on by British reviewers anxious to make sense of the *"Neighbours* phenomenon."

It is worth noting, second, that the institutional and cultural facilitators of *Neighbours*'s UK success are both very powerful, and also often historically fortuitous. Recall the opening up of daytime television on BBC1 and the expansion of tabloid coverage of television in 1986. Factors such as these are likely to escape the most assiduous attentions of program producers and buyers, as well as of governmental cultural and trade agencies concerned with promoting media products overseas.

Third, the dissolution of apparent differences achieved in *Neighbours*'s UK success is likewise partly dependent upon conjunctural coincidences of the 1980s, as well as on cross-cultural familiarities bred of histories linked by colonization. Not only can it be claimed that "every next person in Britain has a relative in Australia" (Fowler 1991). It is also arguable that *Neighbours*'s UK popularity arises because it can reduce almost all cultural specificities to projections of relief from a grey, cramped, class-divided, Thatcherized society (one might remember here that such cultural specificities as *Neighbours* might have had are already severely etiolated by the program's anodyne, easily generalizable, and depoliticized ethos). Indeed, there is a remarkable congruence between *Neighbours*'s introverted, mutually supportive community and Thatcherite anti-welfare doctrines of self-help. *Neighbours*'s Australia represents a distant home, I suggest, for residents of the "scepter'd isle" long since bereft of Empire apart from Hong Kong and the Falkland Islands, and simultaneously having acute difficulties connecting with Europe. Ruth Brown notes in British responses to *Neighbours* a twilight gasp of colonial condescension toward a remnant of Commonwealth: *"Neighbours* seeks to persuade us that middle-class neighbourliness is alive and well and living in Australia, Britannia's infant arising . . . to glad her parent's heart by displaying her glories shining more brightly in another sphere" (Brown 1989).

Given Britain's uncertain self-image in the world it once bestrode, an "invasion" of cultural products from a former convict colony can bring out a certain snobbery. In the case of Nancy Banks-Smith's remarks on *Home and Away*, cultural snobbery perhaps overlays class snobbery: "One is aware of *Home and Away* as one is aware of chewing-gum on the sole of one's shoe" (Banks-Smith 1990). Such views recall the comment of the Australian poet, Les Murray: "Much of the hostility to Australia, and it amounts to that, shown by English people above a certain class line can be traced to the fact that we are, to a large extent, the poor who got away" (Murray 1978: 69).

That both major British political parties could take up *Neighbours* as political football testifies not just to the category of youth as ongoing focus

STEPHEN CROFTS

of moral panics in a country deeply prone to such motions, but also to the continuing ubiquity of *Neighbours*. If *Crocodile Dundee* supplied Australian tourists with cab-driver conversation around much of the world for at least a year, *Neighbours* has sustained its impact much longer in Britain. Acknowledged by government, royal family, and Church of England, it has achieved journalistic benchmark status for things Australian.

USA: lost in *Dallasty*

Neighbours is probably the most successful international soap opera that's ever been.

(Cristal 1992)

The Americans are probably the most parochial people on earth.

(Fowler 1991)

Needless to say, they didn't like it over there [in the USA].

(Harvey 1991)

Thus Grundy's account of the failure in the US of its most successful soap, as voiced respectively by the company's Senior vice-president of marketing in Los Angeles, its senior vice president of business affairs in Sydney, and its Sydney publicity manager. This tale of failure contrasts starkly with that of *Neighbours*'s British success. Grundy's tried out the US market by syndicating the program in a thirteen-week batch, episodes one to sixty-five, to two independent stations, KCOP/13 in Los Angeles and WWOR/9 in New York. In Los Angeles it screened Monday–Friday at 5:30 p.m. from June 3–28, 1991 before being rescheduled at 9:30 a.m. Monday–Friday from July 1–August 30, 1991. In its first and third weeks *Neighbours* rated 4 per cent of TV sets in the Los Angeles area, which has forty-one channels; in its fifth week, the first at 9:30 a.m. the figure dropped to 1 per cent, and thereafter it never picked up (Inouye 1992). The program was also stripped by WWOR in New York. There it ran at 5: p.m. from June 17 to September 17, 1991, with its audience averaging 228,000 – a poor figure – in its best month, July (Stefko 1992). Plans to extend its screenings to Chicago, Philadelphia, Washington, Atlanta, and Phoenix appear to have foundered.

Unlike the British case, explanations of *Neighbours*'s failure in the US market are drawn more from its seller, Grundy, and its buyers, KCOP and WWOR, than from the press, which in Britain sought to account for the program's colossal success. Press coverage heralded the opening of *Neighbours* in the US, and subsequently ignored it (the commentaries come from seven dailies and weeklies and *Variety* in Alexander 1991; Goodspeed 1991; "Gray." 1991; Kelleher 1991; Kitman 1991; Mann 1991; Rabinowitz 1991; Roush 1991). Belonging mostly to the journalistic genre of announcing a likely new popular cultural success arriving with a remarkable foreign track-

108

record, these commentaries were closer to advertorial than to the customarily more "objective" genre of film reviewing. But since they were not advertisements as such, they did give indicative prognostications of the acceptability of a program such as *Neighbours* in the US market.

The commentaries' treatment of the ten textual factors contributing to *Neighbours*'s global successes yield important insights. The last eight categories gave these commentators no pause: women as doers, teen sex appeal, unrebellious youth, wholesome neighborliness, "feelgood" characters, resolution of differences, depoliticized middle-class citizenship, and writing skills. Indeed, all eight are clearly instanced in the highly successful *Beverley Hills 90210* with the marginal modifications that their neighborliness is more school- than home-based, "middle class" is defined upwards from petit bourgeois, and writing skills are devoted to less prosaic representations. That five of the commentaries are positive in their evaluation of *Neighbours*, two neutral, and only one negative suggests the broad potential acceptability of the program to the US market (only one publication, the *Wall Street Journal*, has the kind of highbrow readership which might encourage its television critics to sneer at popular material such as soaps).

The two textual features of *Neighbours* which do draw comment – the everyday, and the domestic and suburban – point to a crucial first feature of the US "mediascape," in particular its "soapscape," namely the preference for the exceptional, the non-domestic, the non-suburban. In US soaps, it is well known, the pole of melodrama exercises greater attraction than the pole of realism (cf. Geraghty 1991: 25–38) – in contrast to Australian and British soaps. These two textual aspects of *Neighbours* are a central theme of the US commentaries, combining under the rubric of the non-exceptional, the "realistic."

All the commentaries bar the sole negative one (Kitman 1991: 23) refer positively to *Neighbours'* "realism," often in contradistinction to the perceived artificiality of US soaps. Peter Pinne, the program's executive producer, is twice quoted to just this effect (Goodspeed 1991: 22; Mann 1991: 28), while *USA Today* (Roush 1991: 15) applauds "how close the residents of Ramsey Street seem to our own suburban counterparts," and notes that "its casual gossip and unexceptional lifestyle [are] closer to the early days of *Knots Landing* than to any current soap." The redoubtable *Wall Street Journal* does not sneer, but praises

a television version of middle- and lower-class life that is at ease with itself and singularly lacking in ... the self-consciousness and discomfort that attends American television's efforts to portray uneducated white working-class types .... [Its] characters ... ought to be more recognisable to Americans than the peculiar beings that inhabit the worlds of our home-grown TV dramas .... [They] actually converse with one another in the way that people do – without declaiming or the rat-a-tat of one-liners, or recitals of a position on the latest hot social theme. If the beat of their daily lives is unhysterical – quiet, in fact – it is also eventful.

(Rabinowitz 1991: 17)

The *Wall Street Journal* takes a refreshing distance from the infamous "Greed is good" dictum voiced in Oliver Stone's film, *Wall Street*! Given *Neighbours*'s atypicality in the realm of US soaps, its American reference points are either *Knots Landing* – which one British journalist described as "the nearest the Americans can bear to get to a soap about ordinary people" (Kingsley 1989: 226) – or US sitcoms (Kelleher 1991: 36; Rabinowitz 1991: 17).

Buyer and seller agreed that its non-exceptional "realism" was one reason for *Neighbours*'s failure in the US "soapscape." KCOP described it as "less raunchy than US soap operas, too wholesome" (Moran 1992). Its seller, Bob Cristal, added that

Neighbours, as Reg Watson said, was the softest concept he had ever come up with, and he thinks the success of the show worldwide is the softness; whereas in this country when you're dealing with a foreign accent in a soft premise, you have a tougher row to hoe.

(Cristal 1992)

Here, Cristal touches on the second, and major, incompatibility between *Neighbours* and the US mediascape: its foreignness. He elaborates:

The real problem . . . is that the American marketplace – and I don't agree with it, but so be it – is, has been anti-foreign material for as long as I can remember . . . . The one show that broke through – and it was on a network – was *Prisoner* with Patrick McGoohan.

(Cristal 1991)

Variety, more hard-nosed in its trade prognostications than the more "newsy," advertorially-oriented commentaries cited above, frankly notes that "it's questionable whether [*Neighbours*] will achieve the level of runaway success it's found elsewhere . . . . International pop–cultural exchange seems to be one-sided for the US, which is generally xenophobic about embracing fare from other nations" ("Gray." 1991: 72; this rare acknowledgement of American media ethnocentrism does not, of course, undercut *Variety*'s servicing role in relation to the US media's domestic and overseas markets). The Americanization of non-American film and television is big business. Hollywood versions of foreign film successes as varied as *The Vanishing* and *La Cage aux Folles* represent a significant proportion of Hollywood production. One sizable company, Don Tafler International, specializes in Americanizing foreign television programs. *Till Death Do Us Part* is a major example of a foreign program which "had to be remade . . . because the original was not acceptable in this country . . . and yet *Archie Bunker, All In The Family* . . . which was a direct lift from that show ... became a classic in our country" (Cristal 1992). Grundy's themselves supported the sequelling and Americanization of *Prisoner: Cell Block H* with *Dangerous Women*, an American production with Peter Pinne as its executive producer. If the Patrick McGoohan *Prisoner* was exceptional in its status of being foreign material which gained entrance to the fiercely ethnocentric US television networks, few more successes have been registered with independent stations. The bulk of such material – and overall there is precious little of it – finds its way into the US market by way of the more upmarket route of public service television, most of whose imports are British, largely genteel and respectable, though extending to include *East-Enders*. With this point in mind, Cristal remarked: "I would think that *Neighbours*, in retrospect, might have been more appropriate to a public broadcaster" (Cristal 1992). In the year of *Neighbours*'s attempt on the US market, public service television screened *The Shiralee* and *Dolphin Cove*, and *Bangkok Hilton* was shown on cable. This is a far, far cry from the broad swathe beaten to the British market by soaps ranging from *The Sullivans* to *Flying Doctors* and from *Prisoner: Cell Block H* to *Country Practice* which preceded the *Neighbours* phenomenon there.

"The accents" were constantly cited as a crucial point of resistance. KCOP: "People couldn't understand the Australian accent" (Inouye 1992). WWOR: "We received some complaints about accents, but maybe that's not the real issue" (Darby 1992). KCOP: "The actors are unknown, and it takes place in a country that few people know about" (Inouye 1992). WWOR: "One problem with anything from out of this country is making the transition from one country to the next. We're all chauvinists, I guess. We want to see American actors in American stuff" (Leibert 1992). The tenor of these reflections in fact gainsays the *New York Daily News*'s own report five days prior to *Neighbours*'s first New York transmission:

> The program was test-marketed in both cities, and viewers were asked whether they prefer [*sic*] the original Australian version or the same plots with American actors. "All of them chose the Australian program over the US version," Pinne said. It won't hurt, he added, that a program from Australia will be perceived as "a little bit of exotica" without subtitles.
>
> (Alexander 1991: 23)

The station's verdict within three months was clearly less sanguine. Australian material did not stay the course, even as exotica.

Two additional factors militated against *Neighbours*'s US success: scheduling, and the length of run required to build up a soap audience. Scheduling was a key factor of the US "mediascape" which contributed to the foundering of *Neighbours*. Schedule competition tends to squeeze the untried and unknown into the 9–5 time slots. Whatever its British track-record, the Australian soap had no chance of a network sale in the face of the American soaps already locked in mortal combat over the ratings. The best time for *Neighbours* on US television, between 6:00 p.m. and 7:00 p.m., could be met no better by the independent stations. For the 6:00–8:00 p.m. period, when the networks run news, are the independents' most competitive time slots, representing their best opportunity to attract viewers away from the networks – principally by rerunning network sitcoms such as *The Cosby Show* and *Cheers*. An untried foreign show, *Neighbours* simply would not, in executives' views, have pleased advertisers enough; it was too great a risk. Even the 5:00–6:00 p.m. hour, which well suited *Neighbours*'s youth audience, was denied it in Los Angeles after its first month, with its ratings dropping from 4 per cent to 1 per cent as a consequence.

Cristal lamented most the fourth factor contributing to *Neighbours*'s demise: the stations' lack of perseverance with it, giving it only three-month runs either side of the States. This is the crucial respect in which public service broadcasting might have benefited it, by probably giving it a longer run. Until the late 1980s, when networks put on a daytime soap, they would normally trial it for two years, both for it to catch on with its audience and, if applicable, to amortize establishment production costs. Shows as famous and successful as *Cheers* and *Cagney and Lacey* suffered poor ratings in their first two years, but were persevered with. Recent years of recession and cable's effect of fragmenting the market have generated what Cristal calls the networks' "ultra-conservatism." The expansion of cable meant that by 1991 Los Angeles residents might choose from some forty-one channels, while the figure elsewhere in the country tops sixty. This enables advertisers to diversify their expenditure, spending, for instance, US$30,000 on ten different ads, rather than risk US$300,000 per minute on *The Cosby Show*, or somewhat less on a *Neighbours*. Such a situation encourages deep caution among television station executives once ratings fail to measure up.

A final factor was mentioned by none of the reviews or interviewees. It is, though, reasonable to speculate that the age of the show – episode one dates from March 1985, pre-Kylie – may have combined with its lack of crisis-a-minute plot lines and strange accents to discourage viewers. For the fashion, interior decor, and casual deportment of *Neighbours* 1985-model would in 1991 in the US have seemed light years beyond those of daytime soaps such as *General Hospital*, not to mention those of *Dallasty*. The sitcom appearance would not have yielded enough jokes to compare with a *Roseanne*, while its plot lines would have appeared to belong on another planet from those of *Days of Our Lives* – certainly outside the orbit of the American soapscape.

Neighbours's failure in the US market, then, can be seen to proceed from its non-exceptional realism, its foreignness, the gridlock of US television scheduling for such a soap, the brevity of its run, and, probably, the quaintness of its six-year-old material. The preceding material authorizes some further conclusions, about American acceptance of other countries' media product.

In so far as the Australianness/non-Americanness of *Neighbours* was the sticking-point for US television executives, there are two significant indices of the degrees of acceptability of Australian/non-American material for American network television. The first is the unashamed (though not broad) Australian accent of Tristan Rogers, who plays leading man and long-time heartthrob, variously police commissioner and secret agent, Robert Scorpio, on the "goliath of daytime soaps" (Twan 1984: 13), the ABC network's *General Hospital*. On his 1981 debut on the show, he expressed pride in being "the first leading man who's been allowed to retain his Australian accent on American television [Rod Taylor had not], and I'm very pleased it's proving successful" (quoted by Church 1981: 24). In subsequent publicity and advertorial, Rogers's Australian origin has taken a key position in a discursive set of permutable qualifiers such as "suave," "handsome," "charming," and 'heartthrob." Its function as a distinguishing marketing tag is evident from such descriptions as "Robert Scorpio (Tristan Rogers) whose Australian accent and smouldering good look" (Tormey 1982: 119); "Tristan . . . introduced the suave Aussie, Robert Scorpio, to *General Hospital*'s large audience" (Goldstein 1983: 26); and "Here was an Australian with a wry sense of humor and gruff charm [this was post-*Crocodile Dundee*], equally alluring to men and women" (Brown 1987: 33). In other words, Robert Scorpio is conveniently – if not tokenistically – played by an Australian. The limits of tolerance of the non-American for the world of network soap are instanced in *General Hospital*'s casting criteria for an (American) actor to play Robert Scorpio's long-lost brother, Malcolm. The actor, John J. York, is quoted in the ABC house journal, *Episodes*, saying: "They didn't want a strong dialect [*sic*] . . . . They didn't want a Paul Hogan type, because that accent is too strong. They were saying 'just a hint'" (Kump 1991: 29). The Australian is more "exotic" than Peter Pinne may have wished: *too* exotic. Just the accent, though, if muted, can have an appealing otherness.

The second index of the acceptability of the non-American, again Australian, has yet to be tested on the American market place. Called *Paradise Beach*, it is not a ready-made Australian soap seeking overseas sales, but a co-production between the Australian-based Village Roadshow, Australia's Channel 9, and the American New World Entertainment, which has secured pre-sales to the CBS network at 7:30 p.m. week-nights (beginning June 14, 1993) and Britain's Sky Channel as well as in nine other territories worldwide (Gill 1993; Chester 1993; Shohet 1993). As an Australian-based soap directed primarily at a teen audience, it recalls *Neighbours* and *Home and Away*. As a youth drama serial set in a beach tourism center, it recalls *Baywatch* and summer holiday editions of *Beverly Hills 90210*. And like *Melrose Place* and the Australian *E Street*, each episode includes what one report breathily calls "an MTV moment . . . a two-minute montage of sleek shots of beautiful bodies and plenty of sun, surf and sand set to the latest pop music hit" (Shohet

1993: 5). Set in and around Surfers Paradise on Queensland's Gold Coast, it recalls, for Australian viewers, the 1983 film, *Coolangatta Gold*, which celebrates Australian beach culture (see Crofts 1990). It is noteworthy indeed that most of the performers are recuited from a model agency, not an actor's agency. An American actor, Matt Lattanzi, plays an American photographer, and Australian actor, Tiffany Lamb, sports an American accent. There is a concern, understandable in a program sold overseas, to make Australian colloquialisms comprehensible (Gill 1993: 2). In terms of physical geography, the locations are Australian; in terms of cultural geography, Queensland's Gold Coast is substantially indistinguishable from much of Florida and parts of California and Hawaii. The era of the co-production re-poses the question of the degree of acceptability of non-American material in the American market-place by begging the question of the distinguishability of the two. But given the unequal cultural exchange long obtaining between Australia and the US, with shows like *Mission: Impossible* being filmed in Australia to take advantage of cheap labor; given the tight money of *Paradise Beach*'s shooting schedule of 2.5 hours of soap per week; and given New World's Head's, James McNamara, ignorance of Australian soaps ("*Paradise Beach* is the first soap to be skewed at a teen audience" (quoted by Gill 1993: 2)), one might wonder which party is defining the elimination of cultural difference. McNamara assured an Australian journalist: "The show is Australian through and through" (quoted by Gill 1993: 2). At the time of writing, neither American nor Australian responses are known. However, the summer release in the US – like that of *Neighbours* – is significant. This is the holiday season, the season when stations introduce material in which they place less market faith.

Neighbours's failure in the American market begs questions about the differential circulation there of Australian televisual and filmic texts. Jon Stratton and Ien Ang have argued the centrality of television to

> the modern nation-state's basic reliance on . . . the nuclear family as the basis for social order, as the site of morality and for the organization of desire . . . . Through (modern) television, the nation could be forged into an encompassing imagined community in a way which was both more extensive and intimate than the newspaper – Benedict Anderson's exemplary medium endowed with this role – was able to achieve.
>
> (Stratton and Ang 1994)

Television's homogenizing rhetorical space appears to be particularly resistant in the American case to incursions from outside its boundaries. Film differs somewhat. While both film and television production in the US are safely dominant in their local market, film eludes the familiar and familial domestic space of television. *Crocodile Dundee* succeeded strikingly in lowering the threshold of recognition of Australian media product in America. Yet, despite the film's massive success in Australian terms

(US$174 million US gross box-office, far above *Crocodile Dundee 2*, second at US $109 million, and *Mad Max Beyond Thunderdome*, third at US$36 million), it has made less great waves in *US* market terms. Among *Variety's* "All-Time Champs of the 1980s," it ranked only twenty-third, sandwiched between *Honey, I Shrunk the Kids* and *Fatal Attraction*, and earned only 31 percent of the takings of the top film, *E.T. (Variety* 1993: 10). *Neighbours's* failure in the US television market should be measured not only in terms of the fact that US television is more strenuously resistant to foreign imports than is US film distribution–exhibition, but also in terms of the relative lack of success, by American standards, of even Australia's greatest film export success.

France: "Viewers have been bluffed by vandals"

Neighbours play a particular role in Australia. In that country of infinite spaces, the sparse population must practise solidarity and good neighbourliness to survive. In an urban environment, however [*sic*], caring quickly descends to malevolent snooping. Faced with this soap, it is difficult to observe the evangelical precept of loving one's neighbours as one loves oneself.

(A.W. 1989: 7)

In France, *Neighbours*, dubbed as *Les voisins*, was launched by Antenne 2 in August 1989. Screened twice daily at 11:30 and 5:45, it secured ratings of 24 per cent of the market, in fact Antenne 2's average for that year. However, for reasons which Antenne 2 is unwilling to disclose, the evening screening was shifted after only ten editions to 6:30. This put it up against stronger competition from others of the then five channels, and its rating dropped to just below 16 percent of market share. A further scheduling change briefly preceded its demise after a total of only seven months' screening. The 185 episodes purchased only just included the debut of Kylie Minogue at episode 169.

According to its French agent, Rolande Cousin, Antenne 2 bought *Neighbours* exclusively on the basis of its colossal British success (Cousin 1992), a phenomenon mentioned by all six articles heralding *Neighbours's* arrival on French screens; its Australian success was referred to by four articles (Baron 1989; Brugière 1989; Lepetit 1989; Pélégrin 1989; Thomann 1989; and A.W. 1989). The Minogue factor also appears significant. Her singing career peaked in 1988–1989, and among the six articles she rated one cover story (*Télé 7 jours*), an exclusive interview and a cover story with Jason Donovan (in *Télé poche*), and two other references (Brugière 1989; and Thomann 1989). Cousin identifies five other potential appeals in the program for French viewers: its sun, its "acceptable exoticism," its lack of blacks (a sensitive topic in France, as witness the racist political career of Jean-Marie

115

Le Pen), its lack of other disturbing social material, and its everyday issues (Cousin 1992). For all this potential appeal, Antenne 2 still delayed transmitting by three months, pushing its opening into August, when most of France goes on holiday, and opted instead for the American *Top Models* (Baron 1989: 25). This lack of confidence in its purchase instances what Cousin called a "Pavlovian reflex" against non-US serial fiction (Cousin 1992), and points to broader issues than the fame of two of the program's principals.

The French commentaries differ noticeably from the American in their assessment of the ten textual features of *Neighbours* singled out above. One feature – women as doers – is not mentioned at all. All other features are mentioned at least once. The two most often referred to are the everyday, and the domestic and suburban. But *Neighbours*'s non-exceptionality, its everyday realism, had a different status for French than for American reviewers. For most of the latter it offered a desirable antidote to the spectacular confections of home-grown soaps. For French reviewers it was treated in one of two ways. While some derogated the program's perceived banality (Brugière 1989; Pélégrin 1989), others, whether high(er) brow or plugging the Minogue factor, remained curiously non-committal about its everyday realism. There was a similarly curious abstention from either positive or negative evaluation of the program. Commentators' apparent unease with this centrally distinguishing feature of *Neighbours*, its everyday realism, suggests that it represented something of a conundrum in the mediascape, in particular the field of television serial fiction screened in France, and may well echo the unease evidently felt by its buyer. The reasons require some clarification.

Within this field of serial fiction, American product leads, French ranks second, and British third. This triangular force field explains *Neighbours*'s anomalous position in the French market. American serial fiction is, in the form of *Dallas* especially, very well known in France. Such American imports are treated with a culturally characteristic ambivalence: admiration for the narrative drive and polish of American product counterposed by distaste for its spectacularization and superficiality. As seen with reference to the American market, a serial fiction market dominated by *Dallas* and *Santa Barbara* offers a less than congenial soil for a *Neighbours* to take root.

French serial fiction production offers few more televisual referents to make *Neighbours* accessible/familiar/popular on French screens. Crucial here is a long history of French distaste for *continuous* television serial fiction: "you might say that French serial fiction quickly runs out of steam" (Bianchi 1990: 92). One French forte in this field is the series, the sequence of narratively discrete stories engaging the same characters (more or less) across (usually) weekly transmissions for some months. The best known examples are *Les cinq dernières minutes*, dating from 1958, *Commissaire Moulin*, and *Maigret*. Besides the series, the other forte of French television serial production is the mini-series. And the reasons underpinning the dominance of these two modes, especially the mini-series, will explain both the limited field of the French soapscape and the difficulties for a *Neighbours*. First, a cultural snobbery attaches to the mini-series, indicated by one critic's sneering at the genre as representing "a serial of interminable insipidity, the television equivalent of the photo-novel or romance, destined above all to housewives [*sic*]" (Oppenheim 1990: 43; the sexism of this account may further point to certain assumptions about soaps among French television executives). High(er) cultural literature, in other words, commonly supplies the mini-series' source material and cultural cachet. Second, then, French television scriptwriters have long traditions of the skills of literary compression and visualization of the psychological, skills which would be seen as wasted on scripting soaps. A further occupational/industrial factor working against the imminent success of soaps focuses on the reluctance of directors of mini-series and longer series to cede the dominant creative role to scriptwriters, the major creative force in continuous serials. And finally, actors in a country with vibrant film and theater industries are loath to commit themselves to the lengths of term required by soaps (Bianchi 1990: 96). These factors militate against the continuous fictional serial which involves a large number of characters engaged by multiple, interweaving plot strands of indeterminate duration and with limited resolution at the end of any given episode (usually 30 minutes long, and often stripped across three–five days weekly). Thus there were, at the time of *Neighbours*'s launch on French television, only four home-grown French soaps, of which the longest-running, *Voisin, voisine*, launched by La Cinq in September 1988, ran to only 360 episodes; contrast the British *Coronation Street* which started in 1960 and is still going! French soaps, then, "were far from proven successes" (A.W. 1989: 7). "The French have been uneasy about soaps" (Pélégrin 1989: 37). Indeed, rumour had it that one of them, *En cas de bonheur*, was nicknamed *En cas de déprogrammation* (*In Case of Happiness/In Case of Cutting from the Schedules*) (Pélégrin 1989: 37).

The third and least powerful element in this force field is the British contribution to French TV serial fiction. As the French preference for the high(er) cultural mini-series might lead one to expect, British production is represented by BBC-style middle-brow costume dramas such as *The Forsyte Saga*, rather than by such soaps as *Coronation Street* or *EastEnders*, neither of which had been screened in France when *Neighbours* opened.

This triangular force field of high-gloss prime-time American soaps and high(er) cultural French and British costume and psychological dramas afforded no familiar televisual footholds for a *Neighbours*. It landed in a limbo, possibly ahead of its time, but certainly lost in 1989. Whereas its register of the everyday proved readily assimilable to the British aesthetic discourse of social realism exemplified by such community-based soaps as *Brookside*, *EastEnders*, and even *Coronation Street*, such a discourse is in France found less in soaps than in quite another genre, the *policier*. Simultaneously, *Neighbours* fails to measure up to two key expectations of

French television serial fiction: its psychological characterization with psychologically oriented *mise-en-scène*, and its polished, articulate dialog involving word-games and verbal topping (Bianchi 1990: 100–101).

The second and third factors working against *Neighbours*'s French success are linguistic and to do with television imports. Both the unfamiliarities of the English language and of other Australian televisual product doubtless played their part in *Neighbours*'s failure in France. Linguistically, France is more chauvinist than such European countries as Holland, Belgium, and Germany, where Australian and British soap operas and mini-series are much more widely screened. And apart from short runs of *Young Doctors*, *A Country Practice*, and a few oddball exports, Australian televisual material is known best through the mini-series *All the Rivers Run*, *The Thornbirds*, and *Return to Eden* (which was successful enough on TF1 in 1989 for La Cinq to rescreen it in 1991). This is a far cry from the legion Australian soaps which paved the way for *Neighbours* in Britain.

All in all, the prospects for *Neighbours* in France were not promising. In the event, as in the USA, it secured no opportunity to build up its audience. Antenne 2 declined to discuss the brevity of its run or its (too) frequent rescheduling. Catherine Humblot, *Le Monde*'s television commentator, sees a "French mania for change in television scheduling" as a widespread phenomenon: "if a programme has no immediate success, then they move it" (Humblot 1992). Rolande Cousin, the passionate advocate of *Neighbours* who had previously sold *Santa Barbara* and *Dallas* in France, adds that Antenne 2's lack of confidence in the Australian soap may have been exacerbated by its employment policy of the time of offering golden handshakes to its experienced management and installing young blood. This would have arisen from Antenne 2's difficulties finding adequate advertising revenue to support its operations following the 1986 deregulation of the French television market. Since the buyers declined to comment, it might be fair to let the selling agent have the last word: "Viewers have been bluffed by vandals . . . . They were not passionate enough" (Cousin 1992).

> It's inescapable. Every channel needs to create a regular and loyal audience without spending too much on doing so. There aren't a thousand different solutions. I'll bet you that in ten years every channel will run one or two soaps. The question is: will they be French or bought in from other countries?
>
> (Cousin, quoted by Pélégrin 1989: 37)

Conclusions

The major conclusion will already be clear, namely that importing countries' cultural and televisual norms, especially the contours of their "soapscapes," constitute the crucial determinant of the success or otherwise of an imported soap. Massive success is predicated, as for *Neighbours* in Britain, upon the recognizability/acceptability of the textual features described above; upon such favorable – and sometimes fortuitous – cultural and institutional features as Kylie Minogue's singing career and the expansion of British tabloids; and upon the acceptability of difference across such axes as weather, accent, and home-ownership. Culturally and televisually, Britain is far closer to Australia than are the other two territories. In the USA and France, given the time taken to build a soap audience, *Neighbours* barely achieved the threshold of visibility which would have enabled its potentially attractive textual features to come into play with viewers. In both countries, executive decisions to cut the program arose from the challenging, deregulationary ethos of the late 1980s.

A second conclusion concerns the conceptualization of audiences. In writing of audiences as defined by various nation states I have, of necessity, homogenized hugely diverse audience responses. As I have argued elsewhere, to hypostatize the national is to deny both the subnational and the supranational (Crofts 1993). What is entailed in this essay, on this topic, is the necessity to work at a certain level of abstraction. There is no contradiction between such work and that of Marie Gillespie in this collection (Chapter 18). Methodologically, journalistic commentary and interviews with buyers and sellers are as appropriate to the former as are surveys of, participant and non-participant observation of, and interviews with viewers to Gillespie's ethnographic research into the social use-value of *Neighbours* for Punjabi youth in the outer London suburb of Southall. Macro- and micro-levels of research are both valuable and complementary.

Notes

1 According to the BARB ratings, which may disadvantage a show with no weekly omnibus edition.
2 This essay is indebted to Craven's attentive analysis of the stylistic specificities of *Neighbours*, although I disagree with some of his case for a "melodramatic" input into the program's visual style.

Acknowledgment

I would like to thank Kate Bowles for her comments on the first part of this chapter.

Bibliography

Alexander, Paul (1991) "Is Aussie Soaper our Dish?," *New York Daily News*, June 12.
A.W. (1989) "Les aimer comme soi-même?," *Le monde*, Supplément Radio-Télévision, August 20–21.
Banks-Smith, Nancy (1990) *Guardian*, September 13.
Baron, Claude (1989) "Kylie Minogue: le feuilleton mystère," *Télé 7 jours*, June 24–30.

Bianchi, Jean (1990) "Français, nous avons le souffle court. . . . La fiction de série à la française," in Réné Gardies (ed.), *Les feuilletons télévisés européens*, Paris: Cinémaction.

Brown, Meredith (1987) "Tristan Rogers Has the Last Word," *Soap Opera Digest*, December 15.

Brown, Ruth (1989) "Caring What the Neighbours Say," *Guardian*, February 18.

Brugière, Anne-Juliette (1989) "Les gens d'en face," *Télé K7*, August 14.

Chester, Rodney (1993) "Surf, Sex – and Sales," *Courier-Mail* (Brisbane), 29 May.

Church, David (1981) "Tristan Rogers: The Man From Down Under Goes Straight to the Top," *Soap Opera Digest*, July 2.

Collins, Michael (1991) Interview, Sydney, October 2.

Cousin, Rolande (1992) Interview, Paris, January 20 and 21.

Craven, Ian (1989) "Distant Neighbours: Notes on Some Australian Soap Operas," *Australian Studies*, 3.

Cristal, Bob (1992) Interview, Los Angeles, February 12.

Crofts, Stephen (1990) "*Coolangatta Gold*: Men and Boys on the Gold Coast," in Jonathan Dawson and Bruce Molloy (eds), *Queensland Images*, Brisbane: University of Queensland Press.

—— (1992) "Cross-Cultural Reception Studies: The Case of *Crocodile Dundee*," *Continuum*, 6 (1).

—— (1993) "Reconceptualising National Cinema/s," *Quarterly Review of Film and Video* 14 (3).

Darby, Ross (1992) Interview, New York, February 7.

Fowler, John (1991) Interview, Sydney, October 1.

Galvin, Cathy (1988) "The Neighbours," *Daily Express*, October 17.

Geraghty, Christine (1991) *Women and Soap Opera: A Study of Prime Time Soaps*, Cambridge: Polity Press.

Gill, Roy (1993) "Exporting *Paradise*," *Age Green Guide* (Melbourne), 27 May.

Goldstein, Toby (1983) "Tristan Rogers, the Not-So-Secret Agent Man," *Soap Opera Digest*, July 5.

Goodspeed, David (1991) "Have You Met the *Neighbours*?," *Total*, August 4–10.

"Gray." (1991) "*Neighbours*," *Variety*, June 17.

Greer, Germaine (1989) "Dinkum? No, Bunkum!," *Radio Times*, March 11–17.

Griffin, Grahame (1991) "Landscape and Representation of Space in Australian Popular Culture: A Study in Cultural Geography," in Deborah Chambers and Hart Cohen (eds), *Australian Cultural Studies Conference 1990 Proceedings*, Sydney: University of Western Sydney.

Harris, Margaret (1988) "Why the British Love *Neighbours*," *Sun Herald* (Sydney), January 31.

Harvey, Liz (1991) Interview, Sydney, October 2.

Humblot, Catherine (1992) Interview, Paris, January 21.

Inouye, Joyce (1992) Interview, Los Angeles, February 12.

Janes, Lucy (1988) "Coming Clean on Soap Addiction," *Scotsman*, August 18.

Katz, Elihu and Leibes, Tamar (1986) "Mutual Aid in the Decoding of *Dallas*: Preliminary Notes from a Cross-Cultural Study," in Phillip Drummond and Richard Paterson (eds), *Television in Transition*, London: British Film Institute.

Kelleher, Terry (1991) "There's a New Soapie in Town," *New York Newsday*, June 22.

Kingsley, Hilary (1989) *Soap Box: The Australian Guide to Television Soap Operas*, Sydney: Sun Macmillan.

Kitman, Marvin (1991) 'Super Suds It Isn't," *New York Newsday*, June 16.

Kump, Theresa (1991) "Oh, Brother!," *Episodes*, November–December.

Leibert, Phyllis (1992) Interview, New York, February 7.

Lepetit, Mirella (1989) "Kylie Minogue raconte le feuilleton de tous les records," *Télé poche*, August 26–September 1.

Liddiment, David (1989), Interview, quoted in *"Street's* Boss Predicts Demise of Twice Weekly Soap Opera," *Broadcast*, December 22.

Mann, Virginia (1991) "Globally Warming to a Show," *Record*, June 17.

Marrin, Minette (1988) "Good Neighbours Preach Their Sermons in Soaps," *Daily Telegraph*, February 2.

Moran, Elizabeth (1992) Interview, Los Angeles, February 7.

Murray, Les (1978) "Bread and Dripping," in *The Peasant Mandarin*, Brisbane: University of Queensland Press.

Oppenheim, Jacques (1990) "A la recherche de solutions originales: La fiction télévisée à Canal Plus," in Gardies (ed.) *Les feuilletons télévisées européens.*

Oram, James (1988) *Neighbours: Behind the Scenes*, Sydney, Auckland, and London: Angus & Robertson.

Patterson, Mark (1992) Interview, London, January 9.

Pélégrin, Dominique-Louise (1989) "La soupe populaire," *Télérama*, 2006, August 16.

Rabinowitz, Dorothy (1991) "Real Life from Down Under," *Wall Street Journal*, July 1.

Roush, Matt (1991) "Pleasant Newcomers," *USA Today*, June 17.

Shohet, Rachel (1993) "Life's a Beach in Paradise," *Sunday Mail Magazine* (Brisbane), May 16.

Smurthwaite, Nick (1986) *"Neighbours,"* *TV Today*, November 20.

Solomon, Les (1989) "The Oz Invasion," *Age* (Melbourne), March 23.

Stefko, Stephanie (1992) Interview, New York, February 7.

Stratton, Jon and Ang, Ien (1994) *"Sylvania Waters* and the Spectacular Exploding Family," *Screen*, 35 (1), pp. 1–21.

Thomann, Serge (1989) "'Les voisins' arrivent mais sans Kylie Minogue," *Télé 7 jours*, August 19–25.

Tormey, Carol (1982) "The Crush Is On! Tristan Rogers and Jackie Zemen Come to Brooklyn," *Soap Opera Digest*, February 2.

Twan, Kenneth (1984) "Do I Take the Money and Bury My Ego?," *TV Guide*, September 22.

Tyrer, Nicola (1987) "A Street That's in a Class of Its Own," *Daily Telegraph*, May 27.

Variety (1993) "All-Time Film Rental Champs, By Decade," *Variety*, February 22.

Willock, Simon (1992) Interview, London, January 30.

6

The end of civilization as we knew it
*Chances** and the postrealist soap opera

Ien Ang and Jon Stratton

Bill Anderson is watching television in a bar. The news reports that an unknown longhaired man wearing only a lap-lap has got into the zoo and castrated one of the animals. Bill reports this to Sharon, who is working behind the bar:

- some pathetic sleazoid walks into the zoo and cuts the knackers off a Zambucan warthog.
- Why for God's sake?
- Because the thin tissue of civilization is coming crashing down around our ears, mate. Because society is going straight to hell on a greased pig. . . . I mean whatever happened to family values and a bit of common bloody decency?
- Well, what did happen to them?
- Gone to the shit house.

Bill Anderson is one of the original characters of the Australian soap opera *Chances*. He was a neighbor and best mate of Dan, head of the Taylor family. They were in Vietnam together, where Bill heroically saved Dan's life. But in the postrealist world of *Chances* all this doesn't matter: Bill is just a bloke trying to live his life and make the best sense he can of things. Not that there is a lot to make sense of – now that family values and common decency have "gone to the shit house." A Tarzan look-alike castrating an animal in the zoo: well, it just happens in *Chances*, hitting the news today and forgotten tomorrow, and life goes on anyway. In *Chances*, the moral order based on family values and common decency, which guarantees the thin tissue of civilization, is no more. In this respect, *Chances* signals a qualitative departure from the familiar world of soap opera, a genre that has been traditionally founded precisely on the naturalization of a repertoire of moral values which is claimed to underpin social order, modern "civilization."

One of the enduring formative features of soap opera, as well as a major source of its pleasures, has been its reliance on the creation and slow consolidation of a unified, fictional community, a community whose rules and logic form an ordered normative system to which all characters – despite their differences and antagonisms – are ultimately subjected. In this sense, the traditional soap community can be seen as a metaphor for (the ideal of) modern society. What we will argue in this essay is that the Australian serial *Chances* articulates the breakdown of that ideal. *Chances* problematizes the traditional soap's stress on the moral consensus of community by privileging *radical excess*: that which is excessive to, and therefore is generally excluded from, the prevailing moral order of soap opera. This shift forms the basis of what we will call soap opera *postrealism*.

This transformation in the soap genre can be connected with the much debated more general social and cultural transition from modernity to post-modernity which western societies are undergoing at present. Abercrombie, Lash, and Longhurst have recently written that realism – and as we will argue, the soap opera is essentially a realist genre – is "a socially and historically delimited cultural paradigm"[1] which has dominated popular cultural pro-duction in the last 200 years, but that by the end of the twentieth century – or, to put it somewhat apocalyptically, the end of modernity – postmodernist cultural forms are proliferating. In contrast with realism, these forms articulate non-order and contingency rather than order and rationality. This is one way of approaching the shift we are exmaining here.

However, we think it would be too easy to see a soap such as *Chances* – another example would be *Twin Peaks*[2] – as a straightforward reflection of the "postmodern condition." After all, the relationship between text and historical context is a problematic one, a circumstance we want to emphasize by designating this soap text as "postrealist." Postrealism, we suggest, is an ambiguous and ambivalent realism: on the one hand, it no longer depends on the claim of the representation of a naturalized social and moral order, as was the case with classical realism. But on the other hand, it remains formally linked to the project of realism in that it is still concerned, formally speaking, with representing "the real world," although it is no longer sure how that world should be represented. That is to say, postrealist soaps are marked by the recognition that there is no longer a privileged point of view from which "the real world" can be determined. What *is* civilization as we know it? That's the question, and the question is no longer answerable.

The brief history of *Chances*, one of the most controversial recent Australian soaps, began in January 1991, when it was first broadcast on Channel Nine at 8:30 on Tuesday and Thursday evenings. Each episode lasted an hour. The network cancelled the serial in December 1992. In total, 127 episodes went to air. Toward the end it only ran for one hour a week in the later time slot of 11:00 p.m., a marginalization which is in itself suggestive of, and probably further reinforced, the program's failure to attract a loyal audience on a continuous basis. The radical changes in the format of the serial in the short period of its existence is another indication and cause of this (relative) failure. The show went through three phases. When it started

Chances was constructed as an adult soap. It then became a soft-core pornographic soap. In the third and last phase it can be described as a postrealist soap.

As indicated above, it is in this last, postrealist phase of *Chances* that we are particularly interested here. However, in order to appreciate fully the import of *Chances*'s postrealist turn in effecting a transformation in the conventional assumptions related to the soap opera genre, a brief consideration of the two preceding phases is useful. One of Australia's first soap operas, the tremendously popular *Number 96*, was an adult soap. Adult soaps include themes usually excluded in the traditional soap operas. Shown between 1972 and 1977, *Number 96* included homosexuality, terrorism, and, just like *Chances*, female nudity. When *Chances* was launched, it was repeatedly compared with *Number 96*, but it soon became a soft-core pornographic soap. The porno-soap might best be described as a particular inflection of the adult soap, in which the serial becomes pornotopic. According to Steven Marcus, pornographic fantasies have a particularly utopian quality – they seem to take place outside space and time.[3] Elaborating Marcus, we can define a pornotopia as a fictional world in which sexual activity – and in the case of visual media we could add associated nudity – is the determining reason for all narrative action. Pornotopias are usually constituted for the male gaze, and privilege the female body over the male body. However, the pornotopic soap requires a privileged male actor to anchor the sequential flow of naked women in the narrative. In *Chances* this took the form of an increasing focus on one particular male character whose serial sexual relations with a potentially infinite number of women paralleled the potentially infinite seriality of the soap. The plots were downgraded in importance and became more excuses for the introduction of new female characters into Alex's bed than narrative moments in their own right. However, this does not mean that the narrative was non-existent and, in a formal sense, *Chances*' soft-core phase marked an important transitional moment in the move from soap opera realism to postrealism.

The soft-core phase required an interrogation of the necessity of many of the features usually associated with the generic conventions of the soap opera. The construction of the adult soap, and more obviously that of the porno-soap, denies the conventional linkage between soap opera and a female audience. In textual terms, the inclusion of action-based themes and of female nudity tends to be associated with an attempt to capture a male as well as female audience, a tendency shared by American prime time soaps such as *Dallas* and *Dynasty*. More importantly (and more radically), however, the soft-core phase of *Chances* transgressed the naturalized repertoire of moral values – the claimed moral order which holds the soap community together – upon which the conventional soap opera, including the American prime-time soaps, have always been premised. In this phase of *Chances* the sexual activity depicted never occurred between a married couple and rarely between people with an established relationship. It sometimes took the form of extramarital affairs but always emphasized sexual relations as a totally pragmatic function of sexual desire. In this way *Chances* uncoupled sexual behavior, in an entirely non-moralized way, from the overdetermining moral order. In the postrealist phase, we will argue, this non-moralizing uncoupling has been generalized, resulting in a soap which marks the end of civilization as we knew it.

Later in this chapter we will examine the postrealist phase of *Chances* more closely. We will do this by contrasting it with *Neighbours* and, briefly, *A Country Practice*, two very popular soaps commonly heralded as quint-essentially Australian. We will argue that what makes *Chances* different is that it opens itself up to what in the fictional worlds of *Neighbours* and *A Country Practice* is constructed as radically excessive, and therefore either excluded or contained. Perhaps this is the reason why *Chances* was not very popular. But first we need to make a number of general theoretical observations about soap opera realism and its relation to excess.

Realism, melodrama, and radical excess

The realist base of soap opera can be usefully understood in the context of the general dominance of realism as a cultural form in modern western capitalism. As Raymond Williams has put it, "The historical signficance of realism was to make social and physical reality (in a general materialist sense) the basis of literature, art and thought."[4] But since realism, as Ian Watt has argued,[5] originated in the concerns and aspirations of the emerging European bourgeoisie, the "reality" represented and naturalized in realist texts is not just any reality: it is the world as experienced and preferred in bourgeois ideology; the lived reality, if you like, of capitalist modernity.

The rise of the bourgeoisie and the concomitant secularization of belief led to the ongoing attempt to give absolute status to a new moral repertoire which articulates bourgeois ideology. In this hegemonic project, what Habermas would call the incomplete project of modernity, realism has played an important role by naturalizing bourgeois values, turning them into the universal moral "truths" on which the modern social order, western capital-ist modernity, is based. It is familiarity with and acceptance of this particular construction of the world which the reality effect of realism both depends upon and reinforces.

The site credited with being the cornerstone of this modern order is the nuclear family, in which the wife/mother occupies a central role as guardian and reproducer of the moral repertoire. The importance of the family enables us to understand the cultural significance of soap opera, a genre which draws, as several authors have remarked, on the nineteenth-century genre of do-mestic fiction.[6] It is generally through the domestic context of the family – or more precisely, the fleshing out of familial relations in the home – that the soap community establishes itself. It is for this reason that soap opera realism has such an ordinary, everyday feel to it. Our argument is that one of the distinctive features of the postrealist soap is the disappearance of the family as the foundation of community, and the subsequent disappearance of community itself.

It is important to stress the significance of soap opera as a site for the naturalization of what functionalist sociology – the core discipline of capitalist modernity – calls the central value system. In his book on American daytime soaps, Robert Allen describes how this naturalization is achieved:

> At times, the underlying normative perspective of the soap opera is exposed: family is to be valued over career; "feminine" fullfillment ultimately involves marriage and parenting; the social system is shown to be ultimately fair and just; virtue is ultimately rewarded and evil punished; and so forth. For the most part, though, the world of the soap opera does not express an ideological "message" . . . so much as it marks out a more general normative "territory." At the center of this normative space are those values, attitudes, and behaviors believed . . . to be most dearly held by the "average" viewer. These norms form, for the most part, the unarticulated "givens" of the soap opera social structure.[7]

It is precisely this unstated naturalization of the moral order which forms the basis for soap opera realism. The realism is a normative one, what Watt called a "realism of assessment:"[8] soap operas are commonly held to be about how the world works, about what is good and bad, about the ultimate legitimacy and authority of the prevailing moral order. Thus Hilary Kingston, in a popular soap opera handbook, has this to say about soap operas:

> My own view on the importance of soap is simple. I think it binds us together as a society . . . . To watch soap is affirmation of social piety, a declaration that we share the beliefs, hopes, fears and prejudices of the rest of Western mankind [sic].[9]

It is this cultural positioning of soap operas as modern morality plays which underlies the often heard call that soap operas should be "socially responsible," which is held to involve giving a "realistic" view of the world. At the same time it is also precisely because of this cultural positioning that soap operas trigger criticism whenever they are considered "unrealistic."[10]

The "unrealistic" is a discursive category designating that which is excessive to what is considered "real." In soap opera narratives, the excessive pertains to that which disturbs or disrupts the naturalized moral order on which the genre's realist claims are based. Important for our argument here is not just a consideration of what, from the perspective of soap opera realism, is defined as excessive, i.e., beyond the bounds of its rendition of the "real," but also how excess is *structurally* related to the realism of the soap world. In this respect, we want to distinguish between two kinds of excess: melodramatic excess and radical excess.

126

If soap operas, particularly American ones, are often disparaged for their melodramatic quality, the implication is generally made that this is what makes soaps lacking in realism. In such a view, melodramatic narratives, which often include "improbable" events, are seen to violate – to be excessive to – a realist representation of life. However, this is to mis-comprehend melodrama's structural relation to realism – a relationship which has to be defined, as Jon Stratton has argued in an earlier article, in terms of ultimate complicity rather than antagonism.[11] What needs to be specified, then, is the narrative function of melodramatic excess *vis-à-vis* the world constructed in the text.

In *The Melodramatic Imagination*, Peter Brooks describes melodramatic excess in terms of "the effort to make the 'real' and the 'ordinary' interesting through heightened dramatic utterance and gesture that lays bare the true stakes."[12] We would add here that by making the "real" and the "ordinary" interesting in this way, the normalization of what is constructed as "real" and "ordinary" is reinforced: they are "the true stakes." As Stratton has put it, "[melodrama's] strategy of excess operates to assert – and naturalize – certain values by placing them under threat."[13] In other words, while realism works to naturalize the moral repertoire of the social order, melodramatic excess works in relation to this order by disrupting it: excess is constituted "in a narrative project which generates plot as 'extraordinary' to the 'ordinary' life out of which the plot develops."[14] It is precisely because the "extraordinary" is founded on the "ordinary" that the disruption caused by melodramatic excess will ultimately confirm the "normality" of a pre-established order naturalized by realism. As Brooks put it, "melodrama [is] the principle mode for uncovering, demonstrating, and making operative the essential moral universe in a post-sacred era."[15]

In the open-ended narrative format of soap opera, the continuous inter-change of melodrama and realism results in a simultaneous, and permanently extended, problematization and affirmation of the stability of the soap community. According to Stratton,

> in the melodramatic serial where the acceptance of ongoing narrative development is coupled with a lack of final closure, the image of a static moral universe of "ordinary" life is much less clearly defined and the threat to it more amorphous, because it is precisely the permanent characters who constitute the basis of the serial who also appear to present a threat to the world of the serial.[16]

However, Stratton continues, it is precisely because of this constant imminent threat that the viewer is required to bring to bear a greater implicit knowledge of, and complicity with, the prevailing moral universe of the serial in order to be drawn into it. That is to say, s/he must know the constant succession of crises experienced by the individual characters – the site of the melodramatic – ultimately takes place in the context of a "fundamental continuity of characters and of moral premises"[17] – the site of the everyday, the ordinary, the normal. This ties in with Allen's observation that "the soap opera community is a self-perpetuating, self-preserving system little affected by the turbulence experienced by its individual members or the fate of any one character."[18]

To take this point further, one of the appeals of soap opera may be located precisely in the ultimate reassurance provided by a long-term investment in watching a soap: the certainty that despite all the difficulties and problems, the order of the community will survive. This is the ideological context for what Ien Ang called the "emotional realism" of the soap experience: despite the empirical "improbability" of soap events, viewers can experience the emotional ups and downs in soap as "just like real life" because of their tacit attachment to the prevailing moral order.[19]

Melodramatic excess, then, unsettles realist closure only to reaffirm it. By contrast, radical excess fundamentally unsettles the premises of realism itself. This kind of excess does not reaffirm the naturalized moral order of "real life" as constructed by realism, but rather threatens its very foundations. While melodramatic excess is structurally defined in a binary relation to the "normality" of the everyday as represented in realism, radical excess is that which cannot be incorporated into the unitary moral order which traditionally undergirds the soap community. It exists outside, and exposes the limits of, that order.

Radical excess can be defined as that which makes realist closure impossible. In narrative terms, the disruption caused by radically excessive events and story-lines would not just be temporary (as in the case with melodramatic excess), but would lead to a fundamental disintegration of the soap's creation of everyday "normality." Therefore, the radically excessive cannot be allowed to go unchecked. If the private sphere of the family is the key site of melodramatic excess (although melodramatic excess can also be constructed in the public domain), radical excess generally exists in the public domain and is held in check – kept at bay – by the moralizing power of the family and, by extension, the community based on the family. As we will see, in realist soap operas radical excess is either excluded (*Neighbours*) or contained (*A Country Practice*). *Chances*, on the other hand, operates with a narrative structure in which radical excess is rampant. As a result, the normal and the excessive, the ordinary and the extraordinary become indistinguishable; the fundamental opposition between order and disorder which underlies the interchange of realism and melodrama has been erased. Instead, *Chances* constructs a world no longer held together by a central moral order, where there is no ultimate reassurance of a "normal" everyday life in a binding, family-based community, where there is non-order.

Christine Gledhill has observed that "The degree of melodramatization . . . varies according to the particular soap opera in question and the national cultural characteristics it draws on."[20] For reasons we cannot go into here, most Australian soaps are not very melodramatic, which is highlighted in their relatively secure, unproblematic invocation of family and community. Against this background, *Chances*, which in equally unproblematic (i.e., non-melodramatic) fashion does away with family and community, is an interesting departure.

A particular national context can, of course, give rise to a diversity of soaps, while at the same time setting limits to and giving direction to the kinds of "real world" represented and naturalized in these texts. Thus, "Australian reality" is complexly articulated in *Chances* in very different ways from soaps such as *Neighbours* and *A Country Practice*. Before we go into *Chances*, we will look at these two more traditional Australian soaps in order to clarify how *Chances* pronounces a crisis in the representation of "Australian reality," without offering any clear alternatives.

Neighbours: a world without excess

At the heart of *Neighbours*'s construction of Australian reality is its insistence on the ordinary, the everyday. As Stephen Crofts puts it (Chapter 5), "*Neighbours* urges identification with profoundly everyday experiences: personal problems, desires, worries, fears, minor misunderstandings, romance, low-key domestic arguments." This sense of everydayness is constructed in *Neighbours* in and through the absolute normality of Ramsey Street. Ramsey Street is a street dominated by nuclear families with teenage children. The nuclear family is normative here by virtue of its taken-for-granted normality. This echoes what Marion Jordan has observed about *Coronation Street*. Although there are virtually no nuclear families in the British soap,

> one is never conscious of this when watching the programme, because it insists (impudently) that it is about the family, and the word itself, and the kitchen table which repeatedly symbolises it, have such powerful connotations that we are left, as viewers, unable to question it.[21]

What is most characteristic about how the inhabitants of Ramsey Street interact is what Crofts calls their "wholesome neighborliness:" "Good neighborliness and wholesome, traditional, suburban values eliminate behavioral extremes and set up the moral certainties of hard work, decency, compassion" (p. 101). It is through this emphasis that the *Neighbours* community is constructed as almost totally harmonious. This is further reinforced by plot structures in which problems and crises are quickly and amicably resolved. In other words, even the melodramatic excess is toned down – it should not disrupt the everyday too much – with the effect that the moral values which bind the soap community never have to be clearly articulated.

One of the distinctive features of *Neighbours* then, as Ian Craven puts it, is the reduction of "the moral and emotional range, leaving it almost unnecessary to make explicit the 'norms' against which relative character-positions are assigned."[22] What results is a plenitude of community, a world of utter, unproblematic ordinariness. The general impression, as Craven explains, is that "*Neighbours'* characters live in the world of an over-whelming 'averageness' that's just attainable but lying for the moment somewhere beyond the lived experience of the mere 'majority.'"[23] The very idea of "average" reflects the program's success in generalizing a particular reality as natural and self-evident. It is the fictional reality of the Great Australian Dream. From this point of view the utopian dream of being average is actually the internalization of moral values and the desire for a concomitant lifestyle which underpin the Great Australian Dream.

Such a dreamworld is an ideological construct which can only be attained by the exclusion of what is considered beyond its bounds. Even the program's producers concur on this. Reg Watson, head of drama at the Grundy Organisation, is quoted as saying: "There is a point beyond which you don't go and that is where you get into the sensational aspects that don't really apply to the majority of people. So you pull it back and keep it real and entertaining."[24] But what is considered "real" for the "majority" is an imagined fantasy, from which anything will be excluded which will highlight or threaten – and in the context of the "ordinary" and the "average" highlighting is itself threatening – the naturalization of that fantasy.

Thus, the community of Ramsey Street is, to all intents and purposes, racially and culturally homogeneous. It is Anglo-Celtic Australian. Craven quotes Germaine Greer's criticism of this aspect of *Neighbours*. Greer notes that Australia has never had such a homogeneous population. She argues that the "neighbourly exemplum [of *Neighbours*] is based on frighteningly illiberal presuppositions."[25] That is, all non-Anglo-Celtic racial and cultural groups are excluded in order to achieve the apparent liberal harmony of the soap. The basis of this liberal utopia is an underlying homogeneity of interest, a shared value system. The politics of modernity has always been a politics of exclusion and toleration. Who was to be excluded and who tolerated was decided in relation to the given repertoire of norms and values conceptualized as the moral basis of social order.

Above all, *Neighbours* naturalizes middle-class values and assumptions. The setting is suburban and, as Craven comments, "Ramsey Street's resid-ents seem able to afford their mortgages on substantial detached properties on relatively modest incomes, whilst the serial pays endless lip-service to the problems of income-generation."[26] Crofts (Chapter 5. p. 102) notes that, "small business abounds in *Neighbours*: a bar, a boutique, an engineering company, with no corporate sector and no public servants or bureaucrats apart from a headmistress." Crofts describes these people as middle-class, and certainly that is the program's *mise-en-scène* and ambience but, in technical

Marxian terms, they are petit bourgeois, self-employed people running small firms, often in the service sector. Nevertheless, *Neighbours* has a classless quality to it, an effect of the lack of any clear enunciation of the class basis of the Ramsey Street community.

In *Neighbours*, then, everything that, from the point of view of the utopia of Anglo-Celtic Australian, middle-class normality, is constructed as excessive, is excluded. Even the youth is, as Crofts observes, sensibly unrebellious. Here realist closure is virtually absolute: the world of *Neighbours* is a world without melodramatic excess, let alone radical excess.

But what *Neighbours* constructs as excessive (and therefore excludes) may not be seen that way once one leaves its claustrophobic normative system. What is at stake here is the very definition of what constitutes "Australian reality." In a discussion on Australian soaps, talk show host, Peter Couchman, made the following point in relation to another Australian soap, *E Street*:

> The interesting thing is . . . [that] *E Street* has been experimenting with realism and in a sense getting into strife with the network with it because *E Street* introduced a serial killer and the network felt people didn't like it. But serial killers exist in real life. You never see them in a soapie. *E Street* had a go at it. I read that *E Street* is in strife again over the sort of violence that they're portraying.[27]

Couchman's point is revealing. What status do serial killing and other violence have? For Couchman they seem not to be a part of the excessive but an integral part of contemporary "real life." However, how can they be integrated to the world of soap opera without destroying the realist construction of community which keeps a soap going? In its "experimenting with realism," *E Street* developed a story-line in which a serial killer was an ordinary member of the E Street community. It is precisly this positioning of what, from the perspective of the prevailing morality, is unremittingly evil *within* the community which apparently proved too uncomfortable, too radically excessive. *E Street* did not succeed in containing the threat posed by the serial killer character to the integrity of the community; its narrative structure could not melodramatize and, therefore, finally neutralize that threat. In the end, the character had to be killed off in order to remove the radical excess from the show.[28] This is one example of how present-day "real world" occurrences such as serial killing and other violence expose the limits of what soap opera realism can handle.

Chances, for reasons we shall explain, would have no qualms about including serial killers in its diegetic world. However, a serial killer in Ramsey Street is utterly inconceivable. So inconceivable in fact that, commenting on Couchman's point, Barbara Angell, script editor for *Neighbours*, joked "We've been planning the Ramsey Street massacre for years but nobody will let us do it."[29] Such a scenario would be so radically excessive that it could not possible be countenanced, let alone included in the program.

If serial killers are now accepted as a part of daily life, as are non-nuclear families, then we must ask how the ideological claim that *Neighbours* represents "real life" is legitimated. The answer is that *Neighbours* is not set in the present. As a utopian fantasy it is set back in a timeless past. Barbara Angell put this very clearly on Couchman's program:

> Apart from being totally realistic and very confronting *Neighbours* also tries to fantasize, if you like. We deliberately set *Neighbours* some- where back in the past. We're not trying to be of today .... We deliberately try to entertain people by taking them out of everyday life, out of today and perhaps putting them into a period when things were softer, maybe nicer. Maybe that time never existed, I don't know. But that is certainly what we try to do.[30]

It is interesting to note Angell's conflation of "everyday life" with "today," a time when the "average," the ordinary in the sense that we have been using the term, not only no longer exists (if it ever did), but when its ideological claim to represent a generalized acceptance of a unitary and harmonious moral and social order can no longer be made in Australia. Nuclear families are no longer the dominant family form; anybody might be a serial killer; violence – in particular domestic violence – is endemic throughout society; massacres can happen anywhere.

The popularity of *Neighbours*, then, is fundamentally nostalgic. It articu- lates the desire for a world which no longer exists. If such a world ever existed, it did so sometime in the post-Second World War period. This was the time of the postwar economic boom, of middle-class affluence, and working-class upward social mobility. It was also the time of nuclear families and large-scale suburban growth, as well as the White Australia Policy.[31] It was the time of the welfare state, the managed economy, and low to negligible unemployment. It was the time of the novelty of the new consumer goods, from fridges to cars to vinyl records. All these things, and the system of morality which sustained the lifestyle, the everyday life, have been put in question or swept away.

If *Neighbours* disarticulates itself almost completely from this contempor- ary Australian reality, a soap such as *A Country Practice* attempts to take account of it through its issue-based approach. *A Country Practice* is set in a small bush town, Wandin Valley, which provides the site of integration and inclusion not only of families but also of individuals bonded into a com- munity of shared and often unstated moral values. Shirley, the childless wife of Frank the community's policeman, operates as the benign matriarch outlined by Christine Geraghty as so typical of the families in British soaps.[32] The villain within the community was Councillor Muldoon, a local business- man with an eye for making money. He used his position as a councillor as a way to further his own business dealings without any regard for its effects on the community of Wandin Valley and its infrastructure. Where Shirley, the woman, was the Valley's benign matriarch overseeing its private sphere, Muldoon was the metonym of the evil, male public sphere, the business and bureaucratic world which threatened the integrity of the community.[33]

In the issue-based story-lines, a new social concern is raised in *A Country Practice*'s two 1-hour episodes each week. The community deals with and resolves the problem. The narrative offers instruction as to the "appropriate" (i.e., morally acceptable in liberal pluralist terms) way of dealing with the problem, marking the explicitly pedagogic intention of A *Country Practice*. The concerns have ranged from alcoholism, unemployment, white-Aboriginal relationships, teenage abortion through to a wide range of illnesses. However, as these themes are included in the program as "issues," they are never a fundamental threat to the stability of the community; they do not form an ongoing, integral part of Wandin Valley's everyday life. The issues somehow appear in the community, usually brought from outside. After the resolution of the issue the "outsiders" who brought them in, the "guest appearances" who do not belong to the community, disappear again, off-stage, into the world beyond Wandin Valley. The narrative always explains how the threats posed by the "issues" can be dealt with, preserving Wandin Valley's charmed existence as a part of the past – rural white Australia – still present today. As *A Country Practice* scriptwriter, David Allen, says: "The solutions are often easy because this is popular television and you have to pull the story together, but the problem has at least been stated, which I think is extremely commendable."[34] The "solutions" of *A Country Practice* always amount to a restoration of realist closure: by putting the "issues" *outside* of the community, they are constructed as radically excessive to everyday life in Wandin Valley. Once again, radical excess is excluded from the realist experience, in favor of the representation of an unmarred social and moral order. In other words, while *A Country Practice*, contrary to *Neighbours*, alleges not to shy away from the complexities of the present "real world" (which is why David Allen finds the program "commendable"), its pedagogic message is ultimately conservative: as long as we all keep to family values and common decency, the world will always return to "normal." What would happen if radical excess were allowed to take over is exemplified in the following response from a 15-year-old schoolboy to the question, "if you could write *A Country Practice* for the next few weeks, what would you make happen?:"

> A mad trucky comes through the town and Franky tries to stop him but gets killed so then they call in Mad Max to help get rid of the trucky. As he chases him the truckdriver drops a bomb and blows the town sky high. But Vicki and Simon escape and go to another valley and get down to repopulating the country and then they call it Bowen Valley.[35]

It is interesting to note that this boy's fantasy remains caught by the conservative realist pull of community harmony. He reinstates community after having invented a radically excessive destruction of it. Compare the boy's recognition of how radical excess is excluded from *A Country Practice* with what one viewer wrote to Channel Nine about why she thinks *Chances* is "a good show:"

> It deals with the issues of today, divorce, incest, schoolgirl drug adventures, murder, etc. I think it's really important to have issues like that on TV, because a lot of things are happening in this world that people don't take notice of.

For this viewer the inclusion of radical excess is what makes *Chances* realistic and "good."

Chances and the normalization of excess

When *Chances* began, it was presented by the Nine Network as "the story of the dramatic and irreversible changes that occur in the lives of an ordinary Australian family after discovering they have won $3 million in a lottery." In one sense, then, the serial began like a traditional soap. It was based on one particular family, nuclear but with the usual extensions, and followed their changing relationships with each other and with friends and associates. The Taylors lived in the same suburbia in which the families of Ramsey Street live. Dan Taylor, the father, worked as a drainage and landscaping contractor. He was as petit bourgeois as any of Ramsey Street's self-employed. His wife, Barbara, looked after the house and the family. Dan and Barbara had two daughters and a son. One early story concerned the eldest daughter's marriage.

So the Taylors were constructed as the ordinary, everyday family of Anglo-Celtic Australian soap opera. However, unlike those families, something fundamentally not everyday happened to them. This "average" family won what, in the context of the ideological fantasy of the average, is an impossibly huge amount of money. Now, the Ewings of *Dallas* and the Carringtons of *Dynasty* were also extremely wealthy. However, in both these soaps the Ewings and Carringtons were always already rich. Being wealthy was normal in these shows. Their lives were remote and yet, because their world was ruled by the same moral order as "ours," they were also in a sense neighbors. In *Dallas* and *Dynasty* the rich and famous, despite the magnifying glass of melodramatic excess, essentially live ordinary, everyday lives.

In contrast, the effect of the Taylors' *gaining* wealth was to cause a rift in the experience of the everyday. They could neither be the "ordinary" fantasy family of bourgeois ideology, the family we could all desire to be, nor could they be the "ideal" family of bourgeois ideology, the family we could never be but love to observe. From the outset, then, *Chances* placed the traditional family in a crisis of the everyday. By the time the serial entered its pornotopic stage, the whole idea of the family as moral center became irrelevant. As one commentator put it, *Chances* "started with an interesting premise – how an extended family would cope with a big lottery win – [but] quickly slipped into becoming an excuse to explore every licit and illicit brand of coupling."[36] Had *Chances* been a realist soap, then it would have focused precisely on how the family would cope, that is, how it would attempt to maintain its own moral integrity as a family. Instead, the Taylor family began to disintegrate. The daughters were written out, many neighbors and family friends began to disappear, and, finally, Dan and Barbara Taylor separated.

Pornotopias have no ideological space for the nuclear family. The soap family, the ideological site of the production and reproduction of the bourgeois moral order, is inimical to the pornotopic view of the world. In these circumstances the dismantling of the Taylor family was a necessary prologue to the construction of a pornotopic world. More importantly, this dismantling also provided the basis for the move into postrealism. In its postrealist stage, *Chances* articulates a world without a center, a world where the moral values constituted as a system and reproduced through the family no longer prevail. It is the loss of the centrality of this moral system which marks the shift from the realism of *Neighbours* to the postrealism of *Chances*. In order to explain how this can be and what its effects are, we now want to look at how the serial has been reconfigured in its postrealist stage.

Bill's comments quoted at the beginning of this essay – that family values and common decency have gone to the shit house – make the narrative drive of *Chances* very explicit. The postrealist world of *Chances* is one of permanent non-order: it is a never ending succession of random and idiosyncratic events. In the good old days the show's stories were set around marriages and affairs, the human dramas of everyday life – and of soap opera realism. In the postrealist stage, however, *Chances* is no longer bound by the constraints of that realism. It is set in a fictional present, with story-lines in which contemporary "real world" references are mixed with mythic elements, such as the buying of nuclear weapons from "Boris" (Yeltsin), decadent Nazi cabals, tribes of women on remote Pacific peninsulas who use cordless phones, DNA transfer, televized sex instruction, large-scale drug trafficking, subliminal conditioning, trade in human organs, necrophilia, and so on. Now, from a realist point of view such events are beyond the bounds of everyday life, and can only be marked as excessive. In *Chances*, however, where there is no normality of everyday life against which the excessive can be defined, such "extraordinary" events become not only the order of the day, but ordinary. This lack of a "normal" situation providing the background for non-normal things to happen is reflected in the very title of the show. While both "neighbours" and "a country practice" connote stability and security, "chances" suggests flux and uncertainty, accident and contingency. What happens in *Chances*, then, is the normalization of radical excess.

135

Chances does not incorporate the excessive by melodramatizing it, nor does it contain it by relegating it to a space external to the soap community's social and moral order, as happens in *A Country Practice*. Instead, a world is created in which the radical excessive has become structural, and therefore, in the context of that world, ceases to be excessive.

With the dismantling of the Taylor family there is, as we have already noted, no longer a familial organization upholding the world of *Chances* as a community. The characters behave as isolated individuals connected mainly through their work and their sexual desire. Residues of nuclear families still exist. Alex's parents are still around although they are separated and Alex, in common with all the characters, lives on his own. Further, two father/daughter pairs play an important role in the serial: Crowley Lander, the extraordinarily rich manipulative villain, and his daughter Imogen, and Bogart Lo, the rich Chinese–Australian villain, and his daughter Lily. Both father/daughter pairs have evil intentions towards the rest of the characters, and on each other. Any hint of a mother figure is glaringly absent. With the exception of Barbara Taylor there are no mothers in the soap, and no matriarchal figures. Significantly, Barbara Taylor's presence progressively declined during the pornotopic and postrealist stages. The only other character who turned out to be a mother is Bambi, a former porn queen and prostitute with a Ph.D. in psychology turned sex therapist, whose daughter, herself a single mother, turns up out of the blue and berates Bambi for being a bad mother.[37] The effect is to get Bambi to give up her career in order to look after the granddaughter she did not know she had. The fact that this narrative line was used to write Bambi out of the show, illustrates that there is no place for mothers in the world of *Chances*. The absence of the mother from the villainous part-families and the lack of any general matriarchal figure (as is common in traditional soaps) helps to reinforce the decentering of a unitary repertoire of moral values.

With the disappearance of the family as the privileged site of the moral order, the foundation for community ceases to exist. As we have seen, both Ramsey Street and Wandin Valley are the sites of secure, enclosed communities which can be thought of as extensive private spheres, sustained by a hegemony of family values and common decency. In *Neighbours* this hegemony is simply claimed through the complete absence of any larger public sphere; in *A Country Practice* it is explicitly displayed by asserting the "normality" of the community to ward off radically excessive elements intruding from the greater world beyond.

In *Chances*, with no families, the distinction between the private and the public spheres has been erased. It is instructive here to recall Charlotte Brunsdon's observation that "the action of soap-opera is not restricted to familial or quasi-familial institutions but, as it were, *colonises* the public masculine sphere, representing it from the point of view of the personal."[38] But this does not apply to *Chances*. Here the opposite takes place: there is no longer a separate private sphere. The public sphere, associated in soap opera realism with the site of radical excess, is all-pervasive. There is no place of recourse, no ideal world where family values and common decency will always triumph, a world held together by a shared moral order.

There is, for example, no distinction between the domestic and the workplace in *Chances*. All the characters, female as well as male, work, and domestic tasks can as much take place in the work situation as work can take place in the flats where the characters live. The advertising agency has become an important focal site of action in the serial. However, it does not serve as a family metaphor like the motel in the British soap *Crossroads*. The agency is important only as a site where the isolated individuals are accidentally brought together. Their social and sexual relations are negotiated through the workplace; they often occur as a result of work contacts.

In both *Neighbours* and *A Country Practice* work for the main characters is limited to respectable petit-bourgeois activities, jobs which help build the community or keep it functioning smoothly. These jobs include Dan Taylor's original work and span those of shopkeeper, local builder, teacher, police-person, doctor, vet, and so on. Since winning the lottery, however, Dan runs a boat-yard, providing moorings and hiring out boats. This is a different kind of work. It is non-productive and, therefore, in the realist terms of the traditional soap, not worthy. Alex now runs the advertising agency, together with his colleague Angela. Again, this implies non-productive work in traditional terms. It is work which depends on the creation of images and illusions. In short, work in *Chances* is related to the construction of a society of leisure and spectacle, characteristics of the postmodern emphasis on consumption and information.

Money is increasingly dislocated from the productive labor of industrial capitalism. Crowley Lander seems to make most of his money in currency transactions, bonds, and shares. Thus, he makes money through speculation, not through honest hard work. Without the traditional value system in place labor is not only no longer the main site of the production of wealth, it also holds no moral worth of its own. Bogart Lo's most successful enterprises are a casino and a brothel, both of which operate illegally in relation to Australia's gambling and prostitution laws. The state, however, is absent in *Chances*. In *A Country Practice*, and also in *E Street*, the local police are an integral part of the community and act as the benevolent patriarchal enforcers of the law which articulates the moral order on which the community is founded. In *Chances* the police make only brief and in-effective appearances, usually in relation to routine crimes like break-and-enters and burglary. The viewer has no way of judging the legality or illegality of Bogart Lo's enterprises and, therefore, has no guide as to the moral status of this line of work.

The appearance as regular characters of the racially Chinese actors playing Bogart and Lily Lo suggests a clear shift away from the homogeneity of the mythic communities of Ramsey Street and Wandin Valley.[39] When non-Anglos do appear in Australian soaps it is usually in the context of moral statements about racism. For example, in Couchman's discussion program, Greg Stevens, the story editor for *Home and Away*, told how the show had been approached by the Human Rights Commission as part of their Different Colours One People program to tackle the issue of racism. The producers agreed but did not want to be overtly moralistic about racism. The solution was to introduce an Asian girl for eight weeks and to make her just like the Anglo-Australians:

> The only time there is any reference to her Asian background at all is in the one week racism story within the overall eight week story. And that is the best way to treat it otherwise it becomes the worst kind of tokenism you can imagine.[40]

Ironically, Stevens's attempt to combat racism remains firmly within the ideological preoccupation with community and homogeneity which characterizes the traditional soaps, and with Australia's assimilation policy of the post-Second World War period which was the complement of the White Australia Policy referred to earlier. If difference describes the radical excess excluded by homogeneity then here we have another example, albeit couched in liberal pluralist terms. There is in Stevens's discussion of the problem not even a hint of a multicultural recognition of the coexistence of different cultural identities in the same space of the community. Of course, given the exclusivism dominating the traditional Australian soap, recognition of multi-culturalism would surely begin to dismantle the closed unity of the soap community, and therefore the basis of soap opera realism itself.

With no community, *Chances* is a soap driven by what Derrida has termed *différance* – radicalized difference, or, very briefly, difference that cannot be contained by any unifying system. Commenting on Stevens's concerns, *Chances* producer Gwenda Marsh had this to say about Bogart and Lily Lo, the two Chinese–Australian characters:

> We have two Asian characters at the moment. They are both Chinese and they are both bad. We don't really have to be nice about racism and the actors who are playing these roles – both Chinese – absolutely love it because they can play baddies. They've said to me, "Everyone is always so gentle, walking around someone of a different ethnic persuasion because you're not all game enough to say that we can be bad." So both ours are bad, really bad, killers, murderers.[41]

In *Chances*, Bogart and Lily Lo are baddies (Bogart used to be a triad killer in Hong Kong), but they are as much part of the network of practical and sexual relations that make up the world of the serial as the other characters.

The position of the villain deserves to be looked at more closely here as it effectively illuminates *Chances'* postrealism. In the traditional soap the villain is the bearer of melodramatic excess. The villain is constructed as villainous precisely because she or he transgresses the moral values natural-ized in soap opera realism. The function of the villain, due to melodrama's ideological complicity with realism, is to place the community (or parts of it) under threat in order to enable the reassertion of the moral order. In a discussion of the villain in soap opera in her analysis of J. R. Ewing in *Dallas*, Ang argues that J. R. "constantly ignores the laws and rules of society and bends developments to his own will."[42] The important point about this positioning of the villain is that s/he is always a member of the community s/he threatens. As Ang writes, referring to J. R. Ewing in *Dallas*:

> Not only is [the villain] not an outsider, set apart from an other-wise harmonious community, but he also belongs to the community. Moreover, he is the one who brings the community to life and sees to it that things happen. The evil is therefore woven into the community itself, so that the community is by definition conflictual because it bears the core of the conflict within itself: harmony only exists as unattainable Utopia.[43]

However, *Dallas* is an American soap, where, as Christine Geraghty has noted,[44] relations between family and community, or "self" and "society," have always been presented as much more fraught – in fact, it is this problematic tension that often forms the ideological basis for the melo-dramatic in American soap operas. In contrast, Australian soaps are much less melodramatized. This is articulated, as we have shown, in a much less problematic and rather more positive, mutually reinforcing relationship between family and larger community. In *Neighbours* and in *A Country Practice*, where the internal threat from the bad Councillor Muldoon is always quite muted, especially when compared with the constant threats from outside the community, the communities do have a utopian quality of harmony. The very idea of utopia as harmony is an inflection of modernity's image of social order, in which villains are either quite harmless or excluded and defeated. Were the villain ever to win in any final fashion, the community would cease to exist and the whole "real world" of soap would crumble. As we have suggested, this is what made the introduction of a serial killer in *E Street* beyond the pale.

The fact of the matter is that the villain's evil is only evil when set in the context of the naturalized order. In the postrealist context of *Chances* where there is no community and no ruling moral order, in this world where radical excess is the experience of daily life, there can be no villains in the traditional sense. This does not mean that people do not struggle for power. They do, and the power they achieve can be defined in terms of control and manip-ulation. These people cannot, however, be described as evil in the same way as J. R. in *Dallas*. In relation to Bogart and Lily Lo, this is another way of saying that they can be bad and Chinese because they cannot represent, stereotypically, the excluded radical excessive threat to the community – the white middle-class community to which they could have been constructed as a threat does not exist in *Chances*. In a sense, this is a radicalization of the tenets of multiculturalism which none of the traditional soaps has been able to deal with. What is disturbing, however, is that this articulation of *différance* can only be done in a postrealist context. The implication of this is that "multicultural Australia" can only be imagined as a reality without identity, without guiding meanings and values. What *Chances* exemplifies, then, is a crisis in how to represent contemporary Australian reality.

In the absence of a principle of moral ordering which regulates the private life of a community, the interactions between the individuals in *Chances* are governed almost completely by the public sphere concerns of sex, power, and money. Lily Lo craves power separate to her father's power. Indeed, the struggle between the two has a distinctly Oedipal quality. Bogart Lo wants to be more powerful than Crowley Lander. Quite why these people want to be so powerful is unclear, but it is interesting that both Lander and Bogart Lo are men. The one time Lily Lo achieved a certain amount of power, it was quickly destroyed by her father. She later marries Lander (but never has sex with him) in order to gain access to power. As a result, Bogart no longer wants to antagonize Lander because the latter is now Bogart's son-in-law. That both Lander and Lo are fathers suggests an assertion of patriarchal values. Alex, too, seems to want power. He kidnaps Lander's daughter, marries her, and has a son to ensure that he will inherit Lander's fortune. Power is articulated with wealth. The more wealthy a person is, the more powerful he is.

The preoccupation with power, sex, and money is utterly alien to the traditional Australian soap which is centered on "family values and a bit of common bloody decency," that is on the private sphere, but it is of course well represented in the American prime-time soaps where these "male" concerns of the public sphere often overlay the concerns of the private sphere. The Ewings, for example, were a family company as well as a family. What is peculiar about *Chances*, however, is the absence of any balancing, redemptive force provided by the security of the private sphere.

A case in point is the character of Crowley Lander. He is immensely wealthy but he is also condemned to physical immobility. Like Howard Hughes, Lander controls his empire remotely. He seems to have cameras everywhere, and in a literalization of Foucault's theorization of the panopticon Lander watches everything on a bank of television screens from his bed in his completely white room. Lander's preoccupation is with reproducing himself. He tries to do this by DNA transfer technology which would transform Alex into Lander. From one point of view, then, Lander seems to want to cheat death. Certainly, given Lander's removal from the world and the overwhelming use of white around him the connotations of a secular divinity are present. The paradox here makes quite explicit the problem of the villain discussed above. From another point of view, which is complementary, Lander is acting out the modern male fantasy of finally appropriating the female power of reproduction.

For men the wealth/power structure seems to have an inverse relation to sexual activity. Neither Crowley Lander nor Bogart Lo engage in any sexual activity whatsoever. It is as if the more patriarchal the position occupied by a male, the more the women to whom he relates get positioned as daughters. This makes him less able to indulge his sexual desires. The Law of the Father pervades and organizes the structure of *Chances*. In contrast to the men, however, on the evidence of Lily Lo, for women wealth relates to an increasingly active sexual desire. This signals both a position as an assertive female and a construction of this on male terms. Angela, as a powerful woman in the advertising agency, also has a degree of active sexual desire. She reminds us of the stereotypical post-feminist career woman: successful in work, but craving love and romance. However, her romantic cravings – a residue of old, realist concerns – are themselves represented as excessive: she falls not only for the Tarzan look-alike, but also for Dr Caldura, the vampire/organ bank surgeon.

This – necessarily very brief – analysis suggests that the absence of a moral order does not mean that there are no ideological assumptions in *Chances*. Clearly there are. However, these assumptions tend to be those of an unshackled, "male" public sphere, a world represented as fundamentally devoid of stable and shared meanings, where people make sense of things as they go along. In the world of the realist soap meaning is shared; it is a world based on communication. This is why there is so much emphasis on dialog in soap operas; as Gledhill has noted, "talk in soap opera *is* action."[45] The utopia of perfect communication is the effect of a belief that meaningful human interaction will sustain, and will be sustained by, an all-embracing, fundamental commonality of meanings and values. *Chances*, by contrast, is a world of arbitrary, personal semiotics rather than a society based on communication. It is a perfect illustration of Baudrillard's assertion that:

> meaning ... is only an ambiguous and inconsequential accident, an effect due to the ideal convergence of a perspective space at any given moment (History, Power, etc.) and which, moreover, has only ever really concerned a tiny fraction and superficial layer of our 'societies'.[46]

That superficial layer of "society," of course, is the thin tissue of civilization, which has been effectively removed in *Chances*. What remains is the non-order of flux and uncertainty which is the contemporary world of postmodern capitalism.[47]

The end of civilization as we knew it?

As we have said in the introduction, we do not want to suggest a direct, reflectionist connection between the emergence of the postrealist soap and the postmodern condition. Rather, *Chances*, in the Australian context, might be read as a discursive articulation of the impossibility of representing a plausible world, because what is plausible – the stability of the "real" – is no longer certain. Up till now, realist soaps have thrived on the assumption that everyday life in Australia is knowable – and therefore representable in a "realistic" fashion: its familiarity and predictability, resulting from the hegemony of a unitary social and moral order, was utterly dependable. *Chances* breaks away from this construction. When producer Gwenda Marsh exclaims, "we don't even attempt to do realism in any form,"[48] she is not only commenting on the limit(ation)s of the realist soaps, but also on the inability of soap opera realism as such to include difference and diversity in its construction of the "ordinary." Consequently, *Chances* could only capitalize on *différance*, on what from a realist point of view would be "extraordinary" and therefore excessive, by moving toward postrealism, no longer claiming to be a faithful representation of the "real world" at all.[49] Only under such a condition could *Chances* represent radical excess as normal, as the stuff that daily life is made of.

But in the end, this might all have been too close for comfort. If the popularity of soap operas has depended on their success in naturalizing the prevailing moral order, a soap opera which does not establish a sense of order – of "normality," the everydayness of modernity – at all can only be disturbing, offering no reassurance. This might help explain the fact that *Chances* eventually failed as a soap opera (as did *Twin Peaks*) in spite of achieving a small but committed following. Given this context, it is suggestive that the last few episodes were increasingly centered on the threat of the imposition of an order of some kind – a terrifying New World Order dominated by a rejuvenated Crowley Lander, now showing Hitlerian despotic qualities and known as the Leader. So in the end Lander did become constructed as the ultimate modern Evil. But Alex manages to kill him and, despite Lily's attempt to forge the will, inherits Lander's power and money. Nevertheless, he immediately wants to get back to work at the advertising agency. In the very last shot we see him throwing a bundle of lottery tickets in the air: life in the postmodern world is a matter of chance – as the title song says, "some win, some lose."

Notes

* *Chances* was a production of the Beyond International Group for the Australian Nine Network. We would like to thank especially Steve Amezdroz, one of the program's executive producers, and his personal assistant Annie Parsons for their help in supplying material relevant to this project.

1 Nicholas Abercrombie, Scott Lash, and Brian Longhurst, "Popular representation: Recasting Realism," in Scott Lash and Jonathan Friedman (eds), *Modernity and Identity* (Oxford: Blackwell, 1992), p. 116.

2 We do not have the space here to examine the particular ways in which *Twin Peaks*

can be considered a postrealist soap. Suffice it to say that this American cult soap announces the end of civilization as we knew it by constructing the "normal" (American suburbia) as structurally excessive. This is in contrast to *Chances*, which, as we discuss in this chapter, presents the excessive as normal, or more precisely, presents the normalization of excess itself.

3 Steven Marcus, *The Other Victorians*, 3rd edn, (New York: Norton, 1985), p. 268.

4 Raymond Williams, *Keywords* (Glasgow: Fontana 1976), p. 220.

5 Ian Watt, *The Birth of the Novel* (Harmondsworth: Penguin 1963).

6 See, for example, Robert C. Allen, *Speaking of Soap Operas* (Chapel Hill, NC; University of North Carolina Press, 1984), pp. 140–1; Christine Gledhill, "Speculations on the Relationship between Soap Opera and Melodrama," in *Quarterly Review of Film and Video* 14 (1–2) (1992), pp. 103–124.

7 Allen, *Speaking of Soap Operas*, p. 173.

8 Watt, *The Birth of the Novel*, pp. 327–329.

9 Hilary Kingston, *Soap Box. The Australian Guide to Television Soap Operas* (Melbourne: Sun Books 1989), p. 11.

10 See, for example, Ien Ang, *Watching "Dallas"* (London: Methuen, 1985); also Pertti Alasuutari, "'I'm Ashamed to Admit it but I Have Watched *Dallas*:' The Moral Hierarchy of Television Programmes," *Media, Culture and Society* 14 (4), 1992, pp. 561–582.

11 Jon Stratton, "Watching the Detectives: Television Melodrama and Its Genres," *Australasian Drama Studies* (April 1987), pp. 49–66.

12 Peter Brooks, *The Melodramatic Imagination* (New York: Columbia University Press, 1985), p. 15.

13 Stratton, "Watching the Detectives," p. 64.

14 Ibid., p. 61.

15 Brooks, *The Melodramatic Imagination*, p. 15.

16 Stratton, "Watching the Detectives," p. 61.

17 Ibid., p. 59.

18 Allen, *Speaking of Soap Operas*, p. 70.

19 Ang, *Watching "Dallas"*, pp. 41–46.

20 Gledhill, "Speculations," p. 104.

21 Marion Jordan, "Realism and Convention," Richard Dyer, Christine Geraghty, Marion Jordan, Terry Lovell, Richard Paterson, and John Stewart, *Coronation Street* (London: BFI, 1981), p. 32–33.

22 Ian Craven, "Distant Neighbours: Notes on Some Australian Soap Operas," *Australian Studies* 3 (December 1989), p. 17.

23 Ibid., p. 17.

24 Watson quoted in Jim Oram, *Neighbours: Behind the Scenes* (London: Angus & Robertson, 1988), p. 158. Quoted here from Craven, "Distant Neighbours," p. 17.

25 Germaine Greer, "Dinkum, No, Bunkum!," *Radio Times* 260 (3405) March 11–17 1989), quoted in Craven "Distant Neighbours," p. 18.

26 Craven, "Distant Neighbours," p. 17.

27 *Couchman on Soaps*, Australian Broadcasting Corporation (September 1992).

28 This is also why Brett Easton Ellis's novel *American Psycho*, and the film *Henry: Portrait of a Serial Killer*, where the serial killers were represented as "normal," met with so much controversy. On the problems posed by the normalization of serial killing see Jon Stratton, "(S)talking in the City: Serial Killing and Modern Life," *Southern Review* 27 (1) (1994),

29 *Couchman on Soaps*.

30 Ibid.

31 The White Australia Policy refers to a set of immigration regulations which

resulted in a hierarchy of desirable potential immigrants according to "race." In practice, the policy led to the virtual exclusion of non-Europeans. This policy was officially abandoned in the early 1970s.

32 Christine Geraghty, *Women and Soap Opera* (Cambridge: Polity Press, 1991).

33 A useful account of the production, textual concerns, and reception of *A Country Practice* can be found in John Tulloch and Albert Moran, *A Country Practice: Quality Soap* (Sydney: Currency Press, 1986).

34 Ibid., p. 39.

35 Ibid., p. 257.

36 Bob Millington, "MP Chances His Arm on Nudity," *Age* (May 28, 1992).

37 As if to highlight the anomaly of Bambi's motherhood, the character is played by the actress Abigail, who became famous as the most audacious bare-it-all character in *Number 96*.

38 Charlotte Brunsdon, "*Crossroads*: Notes on Soap Opera," *Screen* 22 (4) (1981), p. 34 (emphasis in original).

39 When *A Country Practice* started, Wandin Valley had one non-Anglo resident. She was matron of the Wandin Valley hospital. However, even this threat to the Anglo-Australian racial and cultural homogeneity was mitigated by an Anglo-Australian actress, Helen Scott, playing the part. When Helen Scott/Marta Kurtesz left the serial Wandin Valley became as completely Anglo-Australian as Ramsey Street.

40 *Couchman on Soaps*.

41 Ibid.

42 Ang, *Watching "Dallas,"* p. 77.

43 Ibid.

44 Geraghty, *Women and Soap Opera*, p. 84.

45 Gledhill, "Speculations," p. 115.

46 Jean Baudrillard, *In the Shadow of the Silent Majorities* (New York: Semiotext(e), 1983), p. 11.

47 See also Ien Ang, "In the Realm of Uncertainty: The Global Village in the Age of Capitalist Postmodernity," in David Crowley and David Mitchell (eds), *Communication Theory Today* (Oxford: Polity Press, 1994), pp. 193–213.

48 *Couchman on Soaps*.

49 In this respect, Marsh described the soap as "adult fantasy," although this label does not take account of the formal realism that the soap opera format as such entails.

7

"I'm not a doctor, but I play one on TV"

Characters, actors and acting in television soap opera

Jeremy G. Butler

Upon the death of soap opera actor Don MacLaughlin, who played Chris Hughes on *As the World Turns* for some thirty years, the program's producers elected to have his character die also. Consequently, an episode was presented in which the news of the character's death was announced. At the conclusion of this episode, a framed photograph of him, placed on the Hughes family's piano, dissolved into a montage of shots from previous episodes – some of which were black and white kinescopes dating from the days when the program was broadcast live. A memorial was chromakeyed over the shot of the framed photograph: "Don MacLaughlin, 1906–1986." In so doing, the death of MacLaughlin was elided with the death of the character, Chris Hughes. The photograph – set within a diegetic "frame," literally and figuratively – served to signify two complementary, almost contradictory, signifieds: the actor and the character. Was the photograph wholly within the fiction (Chris Hughes) or was it a signifier of "reality" (Don MacLaughlin)? Was it within the diegetic world or without, or could it have been somewhere in between, drawing on both reality and fiction?

To date, academic interest in the soap opera has generated narrative/ thematic studies (in the work of critical theorists), audience demographic and content analyses (in social science-based research), and ethnographic considerations of fan culture (drawing upon cultural studies).[1] This work, I would argue, is significant but incomplete. In order to understand soap opera one must confront the ambiguities of the actor–character relationship and precipitate out the position of the performer and the significance of his/her work, performing. For it is actors who incarnate the characters in soap opera narrative structures, providing character types for content analyses; and it is actors' bodies and gestures – as much as the dialog scripted for them or the actions plotted for them – in which viewers invest deep-seated emotions and long-standing empathies.

145

Several factors, both practical and theoretical, militate against the comprehension of the significance and signifying functions of the soap opera actor. First, the genre's low status in the acting hierarchy has encouraged neglect of or disdain for the work of soap opera performers. Moreover, the genre itself has long operated to efface the presence of the performer; individual actors are practically treated as ciphers by the soap opera's stylistic, spectatorial, and economic structures – the genre's *apparatus*. On a more global level, the meanings of actors' images and the discourse(s) of their performances are awash in the flow of contradictory meanings, the polysemy, that defines contemporary US television (see Raymond Williams).[2] And finally, the semiotics of performance, as it has developed in the antecedent performance media of theater and film, is still in a rather primitive state; there is no established set of analytical tools that one may merely borrow and apply unmodified to television studies.[3]

The following thoughts on soap opera characters, actors, and acting do not pretend to resolve each of these difficulties, but they do aspire to a clearer understanding of the parameters of the issues involved, as well as to a suggestive mapping of heretofore uncharted semiotic territory relating to performance and soap opera. Further, this essay begins the work of contextualizing the soap opera actor within more general notions of performers and performance in related genres and media – such as the prime-time series and the cinema.

The prison-house of narrative[4]

Soap opera actors currently find themselves in a position that strongly resembles that of film actors before the institution of the "star system."[5] At that time, film producers promoted a film's story rather than its actors, many of whom were themselves embarrassed to be performing "pantomime" in silent "photoplays." It was not until just before the First World War that producers began to actively cultivate – and exploit – acting "personalities."[6] Contemporary trade and popular publications began carrying advertisements for favored performers and the actors' names were finally given credit on the screen. "Fan" magazines developed concurrently. Initially they began as summaries of plots rather than features on the performers – as is suggested by the titles *Motion Picture Story Magazine* and *Photoplay*.[7] Soon, however, fan magazines turned their attention from narrative and began providing a discourse about the stars' publicly available personal lives. The intertwining aesthetic, ideological, and economic systems of film exhibition/production and the print media thus evolved into the system of cinematic star construction.

In comparison to this cinematic model, the daytime soap opera has no true "star system." Networks and sponsors such as Procter & Gamble seldom if ever promote specific actors, preferring instead to advertise certain storylines. Even learning the name of the actor who plays a character can be difficult for the viewer, because cast lists are run just once a week and very quickly; and casts are not provided in *TV Guide* or similar program-listing services. Although there are, naturally, actors who are better known or receive more money than others, none function economically the way stars do in the cinema, where they form the economic substratum of the industry. Most major films today are based on a "package" involving at least one star to guarantee the return on the bank's investment. Stars' "bankability" has become one of the few semi-certainties of Hollywood finance.[8] This bankability stems from the cinema's reliance upon what John Ellis calls a "narrative image."[9] A variety of media texts – promotion, publicity, previous films, and reviews of the films – construct a narrative image of the star,[10] but that image is incomplete without the film itself. Thus, argues Ellis, media texts invite the viewer to the theater to complete/cohere the star's narrative image. Soap opera actors as *stars*, by contrast, have only a feeble support system of media texts, a circumscribed intertextuality.[11] The soap opera viewer has comparatively little contact with actor promotion/publicity.[12] He/she has usually not seen an actor in a role other than the present one; and even if the actor has transferred from another soap opera, the producers do little in advertising or in the story-line to exploit the actor's previous role/image. So, the idea of a "star vehicle" holds no currency in soap opera. All actors in a soap opera's ensemble cast are more or less equally prominent/obscure in the multitudinous narrative lines. Further, there are no reviews of soap opera narrative lines, individual episodes, or performances *per se*, though some soap opera magazines do critique the programs in general terms, with reference to characters' activities rather than actors' performances.

In short, the soap opera viewer is not drawn to a day's episode to complete the media text-produced, extra-diegetic, *narrative image* of star actors performing certain roles. Rather, the soap opera uses other diegesis-based mechanisms to maintain viewer interest: primarily, the never-fully-resolved narrative enigmas themselves. Typical print advertisements and broadcast promotional announcements use only the characters' names and pitch the programs in terms of narrative questions: "Will Holly discover that her daughter, Blake, has been having an affair with her (Holly's) ex-husband, Ross?" (*Days Of Our Lives*). Thus, while the cinema sells narrative images of stars, the soap opera sells solely the characters and/as the narrative, thus de-emphasizing the importance of actors as performers or "stars."

This de-emphasis is reflected in the contracts under which soap opera actors work. Most soap opera performers, for example, sign a relatively stable, three-year contract, but the producers have the option to cancel that contract every thirteen weeks (more established players are allowed twenty-six weeks). No actor is indispensable to a soap opera. Programs have lost or fired significant "stars" without appreciable effect on their narratives or their rating share. Anthony Geary and Genie Francis (Luke and Laura, *General*

Hospital) may well have been the most widely publicized actors in the history of television soap opera. The fact that *Days Of Our Lives* promoted Francis, as *actor* not character, when she shifted to that program, testifies to the exceptionally high level of her visibility as an individual actor.[13] Yet her and Geary's departure from *General Hospital* did no irreparable harm to its popularity – just as Geary's return to the program *as a different character* in the 1990s did not catapult it to the top of the ratings. Clearly any specific "star" is a rather disposable element of soap opera.

This disposability is further exemplified in the soap opera press. The elements of soap opera that it chooses to stress are emblematic of the actor's position in the genre. Similar to the early movie magazines, major soap opera publications such as *Soap Opera Digest* still devote as much space to plot summaries as to actors' "personal" lives. Further, every cover photo of *Soap Opera Digest* identifies *both* the actor and the character he/she plays. Apparently, its editors assume no soap opera "star" is significant enough to be recognized wholly outside of the context of his/her character. In so doing, they publicize the *character* as much as the actor.

Even the profiles of actors' personal lives stress their relationship with their characters. Characteristically, one *Soap Opera Digest* piece poses this question: "Where Does *The Young and the Restless*'s Jill Abbott (The Character) End and Brenda Dickson (The Actress) Begin? Sometimes, It's Hard to Tell."[14] Without fail, every interviewer asks the actor how he/she compares with his/her character. Of course, this tack is frequently taken in interviews with cinema actors also, but, I would argue, the soap opera actor differs because he/she has little or no star image outside of the character he/she plays. The intertextuality of the film star – his/her appearance in promotion, publicity, previous films, previous interviews/reviews – cannot be presumed for the soap opera actor. Each magazine article must first *create* a soap actor's star image – his/her image outside of the context of the character he/she plays – and, having first separated image and character, must then compare/contrast that star image with that character. Thus, one may still see soap opera magazines attempting the same comparisons between actor and character that are performed between star image and specific roles in the cinema, but without being able to rely upon the context of a star's intertextuality.

In film studies, this star–character relationship has been summarized by Richard Dyer in terms of the ways in which the star image is used to construct characters. He believes it falls into three categories: the "perfect fit," the "problematic fit," and the "selective use" of the star image.[15] A star's image may fit a role precisely, or it may work against type, or the role may depend on select elements of his/her star image. Even though the soap opera fan magazine cannot rely on a previously constructed star image as the cinema does, one can still find parallel examples of Dyer's star–character categories in *Soap Opera Digest*. For example, to suggest that one cannot distinguish actor Brenda Dickson from character Jill Abbott is to posit a "perfect fit" between the two. The soap opera has been known to capitalize diegetically upon "perfect fits" between real and diegetic life: for example, when actor Jeanne Cooper had cosmetic surgery it was worked into her character's storyline on *The Young and the Restless*; the operation itself was videotaped and used in the program. Similarly, representing Don MacLaughlin's death as the death of *As the World Turns*'s Chris Hughes also presumes a morbid "perfect fit" between the actor and the character.[16]

But despite these dramatic anecdotes in which an actor is confused with his/her character, the "perfect fit" is not the most common way soap opera actors are represented in fan magazines and the occasional piece in *TV Guide* and other more general interest publications. Quite the contrary, the print media usually represent the soap opera actor as making selective use of his/her "real life" personality or even performing in a role that is diametrically opposed to his/her offscreen image (in other words, Dyer's "problematic fit"). Meredith Brown, writing in *Soap Opera Digest*, describes Frank Runyeon, at the time an actor in *As the World Turns*:

> In person he is different. Frank is taller, lankier, tan and dark and sensual with those puppy brown eyes and full lips. But unlike [his character] Steve, who acts before he thinks, Frank Runyeon stores, processes and dissects information. Then he makes a decision . . . .
> When first found, Frank has just come out of rehearsing a scene where Steve has been shot. He literally limps down the stairs, forgetting that he isn't acting anymore. Hours later he does the same thing and a production assistant has to remind him that it's just make-believe. "Well, I have to stay in character," Frank complains with a shy grin, only half-kidding.[17]

This article constructs Runyeon as *both* Steve and not-Steve, or, perhaps, Steve as both Runyeon and not-Runyeon. Offscreen, the actor looks different from his onscreen role, Brown suggests, and behaves unlike his character, but, still, he is so fully immersed in the role that he has difficulty emerging from it. That an actor would be thus consumed with living a role plays into the discourse of the dominant (and, for the general public in western culture, the only) system of performance, the Method. When Brown writes of Runyeon in these terms she uses the assumptions of the Method discourse to conflate character and actor – that is, that good acting = the use of selective emotional memory in order to live the part. Ambivalences arise, however, as she struggles in the same essay to distinguish Runyeon from his character.

The article constructs an image of Runyeon as a conservative, born-again Christian who has some indiscretions in his past.[18] The character, Steve, uses some aspects of this image, but blocks others. Steve is a relatively positive character, with strong, ethnic ("Greek") values, but not without moral faults. "Steve" selects the strong, moral qualities of "Runyeon," but ignores the specific aspects of born-again Christianity. If Runyeon were a film star, his star image would be constructed across several texts, but, in soap opera "stardom," this activity must be compressed into just a few paragraphs of a single article.

Instances in which the soap opera press reports that an actor's "life," his/her public image, departs completely from that of the character are less common, but they do occur. Most often one reads about this sort of image/character split when actors are playing villains and do not wish to be associated with their characters' actions. Susan Lucci, for example, who plays the role of Erica on *All My Children*, was represented in the press during the 1970s as a homebody who cherished her husband and children above all. Her character at the same time, however, was a mischievous troublemaker who secretly took birth control pills to avoid conception.

For film actors, the relationship or "fit" of actor to character is only one means by which they are constructed as culturally meaningful, but for television soap opera performers it takes on predominant importance. The cinema star's intertextuality (his/her visibility in various media texts in addition to a particular role in a particular narrative) undergirds a broader cultural significance, but the vast majority of soap opera actors rarely establish a public image apart from their characters. All but a few are sequestered within the prison-house of narrative, their cultural prominence heavily dependent upon the uncertain tenure of a specific character. When a soap opera actor is furloughed to another genre or medium, he/she is significant, is visible, only in terms of his/her relationship to his/her character. Hence, commercials, when done by soap opera actors, rely upon their *character* images, not their star images. And those character images are manipulated in complex, sometimes odd, fashion. A shaving cream commercial featuring Laurence Lau and Kim Delaney – then performing on *All My Children* as young, mostly chaste sweethearts (Greg and Jenny) – presents the two of them as an unmarried couple bantering with one another the morning after having slept together. This commercial selectively uses elements of the soap characters' narrative meanings (here, the characters' unconsummated romance), ignoring any potential meanings associated with the actors themselves. The star images of Lau and Delaney have become wholly subsumed by the character images of Greg and Jenny.

Even more striking in its use of soap actors for their characters' narrative signification was a late 1980s advertising campaign run by Vicks cough medicine.[19] The potency of various soap opera actors (all men) declaring, "I'm not a doctor, but I play one on TV," lies in the overweening emphasis on character in soap opera. Even though the actors manifestly deny any medical training or expertise, the viewer is clearly meant to impute such knowledge to the authoritative voices addressing him/her. Why else should he/she trust these actors' opinions on medicine? The ideal viewer of this commercial – someone familiar with soap opera doctors – is conditioned to view the actor through the filter of the character, having little or no other context in which to place him. Still, the actor declares the "reality" of his existence as a human being who may perform in several roles. Mimi White paraphrases the commercial's message: "I'm not really a doctor, but I really am an actor; and as an actor in another television text, I really play a doctor."[20] But this affirmation of the reality of an actor's performance submerges within the hyperreality of television texts' competing meanings: the commercial text says he is not a doctor; the soap opera text says he is. Moreover, if he did not carry the semiotic residue of his role as a doctor then he would have no significance in the context of medicinal advertising.

Because soap opera actors are so dependent upon their characters' "lives," a few comments on the precariousness of those characters' existences will further illustrate the tenuous situation of actors in soap opera, as well as suggest further problematic areas for those attempting to analyze the contribution of actors' images and performances to readings of these programs. This precariousness of soap characters is the result of the genre's unique narrative structure. Soap operas are not limited to one or two protagonists. Their casts are much larger than those of any other TV program; thus, individual characters have less specific impact on the overall design of the narrative. No one character's contribution is critical to the functioning of the soap opera apparatus. As Robert C. Allen has noted, "the soap opera remains a textual system dependent upon not individual characters but an entire community of characters for its aesthetic effect and popular appeal."[21] Second, the soap opera narrative is not structured around one core dilemma, but an overlapping chain of *successive* dilemmas and enigmas. If one dilemma – for example, the paternity of a child – is enervated by the departure of a character, then the soap opera merely moves on to another. As Charles Derry comments,

> Conflicts may develop quickly, and then suddenly be suspended (in soap opera parlance, being "put on the back burner"), characters' problems may be solved haphazardly without a climax; a character may dominate the narrative and then suddenly become irrelevant . . . . Other times, a main character suddenly dies and the narrative simply and cruelly continues . . . *things just keep happening* . . . .[22]

The imperative of maintaining a number of simultaneous narrative enigmas steamrollers any concern for story details. Characters come and go quickly, without regard for the conventional narrative logic one might expect in a classical film.

It is evident, then, that the soap opera actor's presence is largely "invisible," repressed by a variety of ideological, economic, and aesthetic factors. On the relatively rare occasions when he/she does become "visible" outside of the context of his/her program – in, say, a *Soap Opera Digest* profile – then he/she is slotted into "star" patterns inherited from the cinema

(Dyer's "fits" of star to character). The repression of the actor's presence within a program is never complete, however. In certain circumstances a soap opera program cannot help but foreground the actor's presence *as actor*.[23] This is particularly evident in the phenomenon of recasting, which within the context of film and television is virtually unique to the daytime soap opera. Suddenly, and usually without warning for most viewers, a new face speaks the dialog of a familiar character, a new set of performance signs supplants the old one. By examining these performance signs in the flux of recasting we may best understand their significance to the soap opera text.

Soap opera recasting: "a body too much"?

While commenting on Pierre Renoir's performance as Louis XVI in *La Marseillaise*, Jean-Louis Comolli observes:

> If the imaginary person [i.e., a character], even in a historical fiction, has no other body than that of the actor playing him, the historical character, filmed, has at least two bodies, that of the imagery [constructed in previous films and paintings] and that of the actor who represents him for us. There are at least two bodies in competition, one body too much.[24]

Most films, Comolli contends, attribute imaginary characters to actors' real bodies: *one* character to *one* body, with the extremely rare exception of a film such as Luis Buñuel's *That Obscure Object of Desire* (1977). Historical fiction, however, finds two or more bodies (the actor and the historical figure) competing, as it were, for one character: a body too much.

Soap opera, also, occasionally has a body too much. In the recasting process an actor may be hired to play a character who possesses a personal history and has already been associated with a previous actor/"body," much as in the historical film. Characters in historical fiction, according to Comolli, "presuppose a referential model": "These characters have a past, they have a history before the film began and without needing it: other scriptwriters, the historians, have dealt with them."[25] Parallels with soap opera may be drawn: first, in soap opera recastings there is a "referential model" – the previous actor who em*bodied* the character – to whom the new actor is inevitably compared; second, the character has a clearly defined past; and third, other scriptwriters (quite literally) have dealt with the character. Comolli argues that this excess of bodies generates significant, but ambiguous pleasure in *La Marseillaise*:

> The more he [Pierre Renoir] is him [Louis XVI], the more difficult it is to believe it: the more we believe in it, the more we know all the same that he is not him, and the more we believe in it all the same. The pleasure here is not without its unease, it derives from the unease that reignites it.[26]

Thus, the "role" of Louis XVI was "recast" in just the same fashion as the role of, say, Bo (*Days Of Our Lives*) was recast in the 1990s. The recasting of Pierre Renoir as Louis XVI activates the distinctions between his (Renoir's) image and performance, and the real Louis XVI's historical image and his "performance" within the narrative that constitutes historical textuality. These distinctions may provoke a certain semiotic distress, according to Comolli, but yet they still "ignite" narrative pleasure. Could soap opera recasting also be a source of spectator pleasure, of *jouissance* based on the foregrounding of actors *performing* characters? Let us examine the issue in a specific instance of recasting.

In 1984 Meg Ryan elected to leave the role of Betsy Stewart Andropolous on *As the World Turns*. Ryan had not originated the role and, indeed, had played it for just two years, but had quickly become a popular, central character.[27] As always in the case of a departing integral actor, the producers and writers were left with two options: recast the role, or discontinue the role through either the character's death or his/her departure. According to *As the World Turns* producer, Michael Laibson, the decision was made to recast the role, because the producers and writers felt it would annoy the audience to have Betsy discontinued so soon after her *long*-delayed marriage to Steve.[28] One might also surmise that the recasting was done to keep the still popular character/actor of her husband on the narrative "front burner." To eliminate Betsy would have necessitated diminishing the role of her husband as well.

In soap opera, once the decision to recast has been made, the producers and writers may elect either to provide a diegetic motivation for the change in appearance and voice, or, more commonly, they may simply insert the new body into the old role. In Betsy's case, the change in appearance was diegetically motivated: she was in a car accident and had plastic surgery. Ryan performed as Betsy in the car wreck, but when Betsy reappeared, her face covered in bandages, she was being played by a new actor. Indeed, as Laibson explained, because they were having trouble recasting Betsy, two women – whose faces were never seen under the bandages – played the role before the permanent replacement, Lindsay Frost, was located.[29]

Recasting illustrates the overwhelming pulsion of the soap opera narrative. Meg Ryan may leave, but Betsy's story continues. Her disappearance causes little more than a ripple on the surface of the text because another body may fill her same function within the network of familial and romantic relationships. As Allen emphasizes, soap opera viewing pleasure stems more from the *relationships* among the characters than it does from the characters individually.[30] Recasting allows those relationships to be continued with little alteration, while the force of powerful, long-established narrative enigmas works to submerge (new) actors and their performance styles once again. After the accident, the amnesiac Betsy/*Frost* was separated from Steve – mistakenly transported to a hospital in Vermont. Before the accident, Betsy/*Ryan* was also separated from Steve, due to a variety of misunderstandings.

Regardless of the actor, the character functioned similarly in the narrative pattern – still another link in the hermeneutic chain based on the enigma: will Betsy reunite with Steve?

Does this mean, however, that recasting generates *no* change in the soap opera text's production of meaning? Is a soap opera recasting the equivalent of soap opera's seamless use of a double in a twins story or the cinema's use of a stunt performer or a nude scene stand-in? In those instances, as John O. Thompson notes, the doubles

> supply presences to the screen which have to seem indistinguishable from those of the actor or actress who is being stood in for: here much trouble is taken to ensure that the actual substitution of one body for another makes no difference to the text.[31]

Does the soap opera substitute, or *commute*, one body for another with no appreciable difference to the text? The answers may reside in the semiotician's "commutation test" as applied to the case of soap opera recasting.

Soap opera performance and the commutation test

In 1978 Thompson suggested that the commutation test might well be imported from the writings of Roland Barthes to a discourse on film performance.[32] The basic principle of the commutation test, in this instance, is that one could hypothetically substitute one actor for another, contrast the performance text of each, and precipitate the semiotics of performance in the differences between the two. In sum, the "meaning" of each performance could be articulated in terms of their differences – much as structural linguists do with meaning production in language. It could, in theory, be a more rigorous version of the parlor game film critics sometimes play in which they imagine the results of different casting decisions:

> Suppose Cary Grant had been the detective [in *Vertigo*], then vertigo would become an annoying weakness "I should *really* get over" and not the abyss at James Stewart's feet. Grant is too secure to be quite the victim made of Stewart. But play Grant as the photographer in *Rear Window*, and the nocturnal spying becomes more cold-blooded, more the sport of curiosity cut off from compassion.[33]

David Thomson here playfully exemplifies the premise of the commutation test, but John O. Thompson had hoped to extend it into a full theory of screen acting.

Seven years later, Thompson dismissed the commutation test as "unworkable-with" in an article titled, "Beyond Commutation" (1985).[34] This piece criticizes his early approach as sterile and unable to cope with several analytical problems. First, the paradigmatic substitution of alternative actors is infinitely open-ended. One may hypothetically exchange thousands upon thousands of actors in one specific role. The task could be endless. Second, the meaning generated by the difference of performance must be *intuited* by the critic. Individual intuitions may vary considerably. Clearly this is no "science" of meaning-production, as linguistics is. Third, the later Thompson objects to the commutation test's reliance on difference to generate meaning. He maintains in the 1985 piece that a theory of performance must account for the "positivities" of each character – that is, "that which is what it is independently of the network of difference, of any relation to what-is-not."[35]

The interpretation of acting may well always be retarded by the intuitive nature of the interpretive act and the reliance upon difference can limit analysis, but I feel Thompson was premature in rejecting the commutation test entirely. For the soap opera commonly provides an instance in which the substitution of alternative actors is finite and quite tangible. Indeed, in the remarkably commonplace phenomenon of recastings, it provides specific examples of two actors playing the same role. Because recastings are so rare in night-time television series and the cinema, it would be misleading to develop a global theory of the significance of the actor, of his/her position in cultural and ideological production, from the daytime soap opera, but recastings do facilitate examination of one element of all actors' work – the semiotics of performance – in the comparison and contrast of two actors performing the same role. Moreover, the commutation test also defines the limits of the soap opera actor's significance, suggesting how his/her work as a performer may occasionally, rarely, become evident and perhaps annoying or distressing to the viewer.

To begin our commutation of performance we must first specify the signs of performance – those elements which comprise the performance text. In soap opera, as in the cinema, these signs may be grouped in four categories, as have been outlined by both Dyer and Barry King (the exact terms are King's):

the facial
the gestural
the corporeal (or postural) and
the vocal.[36]

A performance text is constructed out of this material. Certain elements, or "features" (Thompson),[37] of a performance will construct meaning when contrasted with similar, but different, features in a second performance. These features, Thompson argues in his 1978 piece, are "thematized"; they create meaning through difference. Other, "unthematized" features lack this ability: "Unthematized features could be altered or redistributed without any change in the meaning of the film resulting."[38] A commutation of soap opera performance may best be understood by returning again to a specific example: Betsy in *As the World Turns*. To test this procedure I have analyzed two scenes chosen largely at random: in one, Meg Ryan performs as Betsy and

in the other, Lindsay Frost fills the role.[39] In the former, newly-wed Betsy/
Ryan and her husband Steve/Frank Runyeon discuss the mystery of Steve's
paternity and then engage in some casual romantic horseplay. In the latter,
Betsy/Frost and Steve/Runyeon prepare for his departure to Greece. It should
be noted at the outset that this is no true commutation test, because Ryan and
Frost do not perform precisely the same scene. In a recasting situation an
actor rarely speaks exactly the same lines that another actor has already
spoken. The story must move forward even if there is a large quotient of
conventional narrative redundancy. Still, two distinctly different performances in a role that the *As the World Turns* text labels "Betsy" can illuminate
the significance of performance in soap opera.

Vocal performance in soap opera is at once the most significant and the
most difficult performance sign to interpret without falling to the microscopic
level of phonetic analysis. This arena of signification dominates soap opera
because of television's reliance on sound and the genre's heavy emphasis on
dialog.[40] In recasting, the scriptwriters attempt to minimize the signifying
difference in the written dialog in order best to smooth over the transition.
The dialog style remains constant because the script is still being created by
the same writers who, especially at the beginning, cannot design dialog
unique to the new actor. His/her acting strengths and viewer appeal are at
first mostly unknown quantities. Still, although the scripted dialog style
remains the same, the performance style shifts and thematized features may
be affected. Frost's voice is deeper than Ryan's, for example. The deepening
of Betsy's voice may be interpreted as signifying more sophisticated, less
childlike speech – if we presume a culturally coded semiotics of vocal
expression that puts Marlene Dietrich at one end of the scale and Shirley
Temple at the other. This signified – "more sophisticated" – is not as
strongly connected with its signifier – deeper pitch – as one would prefer for
the clarity of interpretation. Additional signifieds crowd in around the
signifier of deeper pitch: masculinity, a persistent cold, a tough sexiness. All
are equally valid; the commutation test provides no way to curtail the range
of interpretation. Here we may see the limitations of the commutation test:
its reliance upon critical intuition to determine cultural meaning(s), and its
inability to specify how performance signs will be read by individual viewers.

If soap opera sound is structured around dialog, the image is predicated
upon the importance of the close-up, arrayed in conventional shot–reverse
shot patterns. Obviously, the preponderance of close-ups privileges facial
signs of performance. However, the semiotics of film and television is still
lacking a mechanism for "reading" the minutiae of facial expression –
though viewers comprehend easily a certain range of meaning in the smallest
facial movements. Still, a few comments may be made. As is common in soap
opera recasting, Frost was chosen largely for her facial resemblance to the
departing Ryan. Reportedly, this resemblance was commented on even before
Frost auditioned for the role.[41] One can easily observe innate similarities in

the two actors' facial structure, eye color, and hair color which would approach zero difference and thus zero meaning. These similarities were heightened through hairstyling; Frost's hair was cut to resemble Ryan's coiffure.[42] Hairstyle, especially for women, can be a major source of signification within our culture. Coiffure can signify a person's politics, musical preference, sexual orientation, moral perspective, and so on. Ryan's hairstyle was moderately short and tousled. Indeed, it was so casually styled that occasional letters to *Soap Opera Digest*'s "Sounding Board" complained about it. Why couldn't a woman like Betsy – the daughter of a wealthy family – get her hair "properly" styled? they queried. Ryan's hairstyle thus signified a carefree, maybe even impudent, attitude toward social convention for many viewers. For them the *difference* between Ryan and soap opera's more elaborately coiffured women generated meaning. The early similarity of Frost's and Ryan's hairstyle created inappreciable difference/meaning when Frost first assumed the role. Since that time, Frost's hair has been allowed to grow out. Comparing Frost in 1986 with Ryan in 1984, I would suggest that Frost's hair has become increasingly conventional – increasingly similar to the "average" soap opera hairstyle and increasingly dissimilar to that of Ryan (with whom she is no longer compared by the press).

In corporeal terms the major difference between the two women is that Frost is 2 or 3 inches taller than Ryan. This would tend to give her a more imposing presence in a scene. It is offset, however, by Frost's gestural style. In comparison to Ryan, Frost gestures less actively and mostly *in response* to other actors' movements. She seldom makes initiating gestures. Ryan, in contrast, gesticulates in a sometimes unexpected fashion. Her quirkiness is confirmed in publicly available comments about her behavior. In one interview, Runyeon comments: "She doesn't always play a scene the way I think she's going to, which can be difficult . . . . She has a unique personality. But it would be wrong for me to say that whenever we work together it's just wonderful."[43] As well as a certain eccentricity, her performance contains an "excessiveness" of gestures. In the scene used for the present study, she *over*extends her arms when initiating an embrace with Steve and waving goodbye to a departing friend (a gesture so broad that it violates the edges of the frame); she also frequently pats Steve's back without narrative motivation. This sort of movement draws the viewer's attention and creates a stronger visual presence – suggesting, perhaps, strength or significance of character. Further, the "quirkiness" of Ryan's movements – for example, kissing her upside down husband – serves to confirm the sprite-like "unconventionality" of her character. Consequently, though Frost is the taller woman, I would suggest that her presence is not as strong as Ryan's.

Whether it is Ryan or Frost playing Betsy Andropolous, the overall significance of her performance is largely determined by her relationship with Runyeon (Steve Andropolous). The constancy of the actor playing Steve provides a benchmark to which Ryan and Frost may be compared. As has been noted above, most of Betsy's significance in the overall narrative system of *As the World Turns* is in relationship to Steve. Potentially, the change in Betsys could modify her relationship with Steve and thus threaten her position in that system. Runyeon himself has commented on the impact of performance on character in the context of Steve and Betsy's relationship:

> I always thought of Meg as a fragile bird. She has the beautiful blue eyes and the sweet, perky blonde hair. And Lindsay I always think of more as a lioness. And it's like two lions and just a completely different story as a result. A good story, but the contrast between Lindsay and myself is not nearly as dramatic. We were partners. Where I was this black leopard, if you will, and she was the lioness.[44]

As Runyeon suggests, narrative is affected by contrasting performances. Or, in other terms, *thematized differences* between Frost and Ryan become particularly evident when we contrast the Runyeon/Frost performance with the Runyeon/Ryan performance. Here Frost's additional height and deeper voice become significant, lending the character a certain strength and sophistication. Frost's gestures, however, either mirror or are sympathetic to Runyeon's, unlike Ryan's which tend to contrast with his movements. Frost's less active gestural performance, in conjunction with elements such as her more conventional hairstyle (in 1986) make her a less distinctive, less eccentric figure – one who more closely resembles the codified norm of gesture and hairstyle of Runyeon and the other actors on *As the World Turns*. In sum, Betsy/Frost's relationship with Steve has been, as Runyeon suggests, less contrasting than Betsy/Ryan's was.

The atypicality of Meg Ryan

Ryan's career since *As the World Turns* has been quite atypical, when compared to most soap opera alumni. A quick overview of it brings the position of the soap opera actor and the significance of soap opera performance into sharp relief. In 1982 when the unknown actor Ryan assumed the role of Betsy from Lisa Denton, she was initially defined in terms of her difference from Denton and the other actors who played the role. During the course of her time on *As the World Turns* she was defined in terms of her difference from the actors she played opposite (especially Runyeon) and the characters to which Betsy was counterposed (especially her husband, Steve). When Frost became Betsy in spring 1984, the *image* of Ryan was retroactively defined in terms of her difference to Frost. This could have marked the final significance of Ryan to the media textuality – as it has many actors who have left soap opera, seeking more prestigious work, only to disappear from television and film entirely. However, Ryan's departure from soap opera turned out to be the beginning of her construction of a true, though still nascent, star image. As a soap opera actor, she was defined solely in terms of the character and she had little intertextual significance. But since leaving soap opera, she has begun to construct an *intertextual* identity by entering new media arenas: theatrical films (notably, *When Harry Met Sally . . .* (1989)), magazines aside from the soap opera press, television talk shows (promoting her films), MTV (a non-singing, guest appearance), and so on. Her individual roles are now defined in terms of her star image and her other media appearances, in addition to the juxtaposition with other actors in a specific film or TV program. Upon her newfound intertextuality will be constructed a star image.

Because they have virtually no intertextual potential, most soap opera actors do not ever attain the traditional star status toward which Ryan is moving. Their actor images remain imprisoned within their narrative personae, unable to be exploited in other media or to establish images independent of their roles. This does not mean, however, that the soap opera press does not treat these actors like "stars," but only as "stars" in relation to a specific character role. Indeed, as I have argued, articles on soap opera actors have inherited the cinema's assumptions of the actor–character relationship (Dyer's "fit" of star to character). These articles, most of which appear in the media ghetto of the soap opera press, are generally the sole source of soap opera "star/image making," in contrast to film actors and other celebrities who become constructed as stars intertextually in several media through many different means. Film star and soap opera actor are united, just the same, in the construction of a performance text through the signs of the human body/voice and its movement/speech. The commutation test, when applied to soap opera recasting, illustrates how difference of performance style generates meaning that contravenes the "invisibility" of the soap opera actor, marking his/her work as (briefly) noticeable and semiotically significant.

Through a close reading of performance texts such as the work of Ryan, Frost, and Runyeon in *As the World Turns*, one can perceive a faint, indistinct imprint of the functioning of performance signs, of the semiotics of acting. But at this stage in the analysis of film/TV performance, our understanding of the significance and signifying function of soap opera actors continues to be obscured by several factors:

1 *Aesthetic*. The soap opera actor's low standing in a hierarchy of "good," acceptable acting styles diverts attention from analysis of *how* performance constructs meaning. The discourse of acting aesthetics would itself be worthy of semiotic analysis, particularly in terms of its rather obvious interface with twentieth-century intellectual currents (for example, how does the Method depend upon Freud?).
2 *Ideological*. The hierarchy of acting styles resonates with class prejudice, where the taste in acting of the working class and women working within

the home (the audience of soap opera) is subordinated to that of the bourgeois theatergoer or viewer of, for example, Meryl Streep films. To better illuminate this connection of taste and class, Pierre Bourdieu's "social critique of the judgment of taste" might well be applied to the evaluation of acting.[45]

3 *Semiotic*. By applying the commutation test to television recasting we can identify the raw material of signification in TV acting (the signs of performance) and we can observe how paradigmatic differences pattern these signs into meanings that go beyond the motivations of the character. But the ideologically determined codes structuring those meanings are so amorphous that the range of paradigmatic associations is difficult to limit. Meaning remains allusive and intuitive, even for the scholarly analyst.

4 *Spectatorial*. By stressing textual analysis, this essay has relied on a rather unreconstructed model of the television subject/viewer. Further work needs to be done on the relationship between TV actor/character and viewer, addressing the psycho-social dynamics of that interaction and the connection between the discourse of the performance and the discourses of the viewers.[46]

The significance of the actor within film studies was neutralized decades ago with Kuleshov's often-cited (and never seen) experiment: a seemingly expressionless actor does "nothing" while meaning is created for him by the intercutting of various semiotically potent images. But, as I have argued and as seems quite obvious, actors do embody meaning within our culture and performance does generate meaning within a narrative text such as a television program. The emergent field of television criticism needs, therefore, to grapple with performance semiotics in order to come to a more global understanding of the televisual text.

Notes

1 Tania Modleski inaugurated the current critical interest in soap opera. See Tania Modleski, *Loving With a Vengeance: Mass-Produced Fantasies for Women* (New York: Methuen 1982), pp. 85–109. The chapter on soap opera enlarges an article originally published in 1979. Social science-based research on soap opera is illustrated by Mary Cassata and Thomas Skill (eds), *Life on Daytime Television: Tuning-in American Serial Drama* (Norwood, NJ: Ablex, 1983), which includes an annotated bibliography. The ethnographic approach is illustrated by the chapters on soap opera in Ellen Seiter, Hans Borchers, Gabriele Kreutzner, and Eva-Maria Warth (eds), *Remote Control: Television, Audiences, and Cultural Power* (New York: Routledge, 1989).

2 Raymond Williams, *Television: Technology and Cultural Form* (New York: Schocken, 1974).

3 See, for example, Keir Elam, *The Semiotics of Theatre and Drama* (London and New York: Methuen, 1980). Two anthologies bring together what work there is on film performance and stardom: Jeremy G. Butler (ed.), *Star Texts: Image and Performance in Film and Television* (Detroit, Mich.: Wayne State University

Press, 1991); Christine Gledhill (ed.), *Stardom: Industry of Desire* (New York: Routledge, 1991).

4 With apologies to Fredric Jameson.

5 See Richard DeCordova, "The Emergence of the Star System in America," *Wide Angle* 6 (4) (1985), pp. 4–13; Janet Staiger, "Seeing Stars," *The Velvet Light Trap* 20 (summer 1983), pp. 10–14.

6 Staiger, "Seeing Stars," p. 14.

7 Noted by Janet Staiger; see ibid., p. 13.

8 Other financial semi-certainties include the sequel and the remake. Note: *Friday the Thirteenth, ad infinitum*; and *D.O.A.* (1949), remade as *Color Me Dead* (1969) and *D.O.A.* (1988).

9 John Ellis, *Visible Fictions: Cinema:Television:Video* (London and Boston, Mass.: Routledge & Kegan Paul, 1982), p. 126.

10 These terms come from Richard Dyer. According to his sense of them, "promotion" refers to studio–agent–distributor–exhibitor produced publicity. "Publicity" proper refers to news about the stars *presumably* not under their control. See Richard Dyer, *Stars* (London: BFI, 1979), p. 60.

11 For substantive considerations of the importance of intertextuality to TV's flow of heterogeneous texts, see Mimi White, "Crossing Wavelengths: The Diegetic and Referential Imaginary of American Commercial Television," *Cinema Journal* 25 (2) (winter 1986), pp. 51–64; and John Fiske, "Intertextuality," in his *Television Culture* (New York: Methuen, 1987), pp. 108–127.

12 During the 1980s, soap actors became slightly more visible in the general print media, as the recently begun "Soaps" section of *TV Guide*'s "Insider" feature illustrates. Still, in this and other instances, soap actors news is segregated from the news about "normal" TV actors, functionally "ghettoizing" the soap opera performer and limiting his/her intertextuality.

13 See the advertisement in *TV Guide* (May 3, 1987), A–99 (Northern Alabama edition).

14 Michael Logan, "Where Does *The Young and the Restless*'s Jill Abbott (The Character) End and Brenda Dickson (The Actress) Begin? Sometimes, It's Hard to Tell," *Soap Opera Digest* (May 5, 1987), pp. 124–128.

15 Dyer, *Stars*, pp. 142–149. Ellis pursues a similar concept, *Visible Fictions*, pp. 102–104.

16 This somewhat macabre congruence of real and diegetic death is seldom equalled in the cinema – occurring only in rare instances such as John Wayne, himself infected with cancer, playing a character dying from the disease in *The Shootist*. Cf. James Naremore's discussion of the ailing Nicholas Ray's performance in Wim Wenders's *Lightning Over Water*: James Naremore, *Acting in the Cinema* (Berkeley, Calif.: University of California Press, 1988), pp. 19–21.

17 Meredith Brown, "Frank Runyeon: Beyond the Heat," *Soap Opera Digest* (September 13, 1983), p. 9.

18 Runyeon has also lectured publicly on behalf of his faith.

19 Soap opera actor Peter Bergman (who played Dr Cliff Warner in *All My Children*) and others were used.

20 Mimi White, "Ideological Analysis and Television," in Robert C. Allen (ed.), *Channels of Discourse, Reassembled* (Chapel Hill, NC: University of North Carolina Press, 1992), p. 162. White's argument pursues a different tack to the present one, using this advertising catchphrase "to initiate a consideration of the ideological functioning of television" (p. 163).

21 Robert C. Allen, *Speaking of Soap Operas* (Chapel Hill, NC: University of North Carolina Press, 1985), p. 57.

22 Charles Derry, "Television Soap Opera: 'Incest, Bigamy, and Fatal Disease,'" *Journal of the University Film and Video Association* 35 (1) (winter 1983), pp. 5–6.

23 Cf. the foregrounding of the celebrity as celebrity when well-known, intertextual figures make guest appearances on soap operas: Whitney Houston on *As the World Turns*, Elizabeth Taylor on *General Hospital*, Carol Burnett on *All My Children*, and so on.

24 Jean-Louis Comolli, "Historical Fiction – A Body Too Much," *Screen* 19 (2) (summer 1978), p. 44.

25 Ibid., p. 43.

26 Ibid., p. 48.

27 Patricia McGuiness (1971), Suzanne Davidson (1972–1980), and Lisa Denton (1981–1982) had previously played the part. Source: Christopher Schemering, *The Soap Opera Encyclopedia* (New York: Ballantine Books, 1985), p. 34.

28 Author's interview with producer Michael Laibson.

29 Frost began the role in the episode broadcast July 24, 1984.

30 See Allen, *Speaking of Soap Operas*, pp. 61–95.

31 John O. Thompson, "Screen Acting and the Commutation Test," *Screen* 19 (2) (summer 1978), p. 58. Reprinted in Gledhill (ed.), *Stardom*, pp. 183–197.

32 Thompson, "Screen Acting,", pp. 55–69.

33 David Thomson, "The Look on an Actor's Face," *Sight and Sound* (autumn 1977), p. 244.

34 John O. Thompson, "Beyond Commutation," *Screen* 26 (5) (September–October 1985), p. 64.

35 Ibid., pp. 64–65.

36 Barry King, quoted in Andrew Higson, "Film Acting and Independent Cinema," *Screen* 27 (3–4) (May–August 1986), p. 112; see also Dyer, *Stars*, p. 151.

37 Thompson, "Screen Acting," p. 59.

38 Ibid., p. 60.

39 Ryan's scene was broadcast June 6, 1984, Frost's December 18, 1986.

40 Regarding sound in soap opera, see Jeremy G. Butler, "Notes on the Soap Opera Apparatus: Televisual Style and 'As the World Turns,'" *Cinema Journal* 25 (3) (spring 1986), pp. 64–66; and on television in general, see Stephen Heath and Gillian Skirrow, "Television: A World in Action," *Screen* 18 (2) (summer 1977), pp. 7–59.

41 Marianne Goldstein interviewed Frost for *Soap Opera Digest*:

> Lindsay remembered a friend of hers once mentioned that "I looked something like this woman on this soap. I watched the show once last winter, and I didn't think we looked so much alike. But that's all I've been hearing for a while."
> (Marianne Goldstein, "Meet the Brand New Nina, Betsy and Blaine," *Soap Opera Digest* (December 18, 1984), p. 131)

42 Laibson reported that Frost's hair was cut just before Betsy's head-covering bandages were removed. The cast and crew, he said, were startled by her resemblance to Ryan.

43 Brown, "Frank Runyeon," p. 15.

44 Robert Rorke, "Frank Runyeon: A Fond Farewell," *Soap Opera Digest* (December 16, 1986), p. 93.

45 Pierre Bourdieu, *Distinction: A Social Critique of the Judgement of Taste*, trans. Richard Nice (London: Routledge & Kegan Paul, 1984).

46 The analysis of viewer positioning before the television actor/character has already begun. See Sandy Flitterman, "Thighs and Whiskers: The Fascination of

Magnum, P.I.," *Screen* 26 (2) (March–April 1985), pp. 42–58. For discourse analysis, see the work of Stuart Hall and others of the University of Birmingham Centre for Contemporary Cultural Studies, summarized in John Fiske, "British Cultural Studies and Television," in Allen (ed.), *Channels of Discourse, Reassembled*, pp. 284–326.

8

Plotting paternity
Looking for dad on the daytime soaps[1]

Laura Stempel Mumford

The attribution of paternity is something of an obsession on daytime soap operas. Critics and viewers familiar with the form remark on the frequency of unplanned pregnancies (often from a single sexual encounter), the prominence of story-lines involving secrets or mistakes over paternity, and the importance characters attach to discovering who has fathered a particular child. In fact, the preoccupation with questions and mysteries about paternity is almost a defining characteristic of the genre. Every single daytime soap opera – as well as each prime-time serial – deals with the issue of paternity on a regular basis, and the most heavily freighted single piece of information on any given show is commonly the knowledge of paternity. From a feminist perspective, the issue seems almost overdetermined – so much so that, if it is possible to describe soap operas as being "about" any one thing, they are about paternity.

The predominance of this subject, which is presented through what I will call the *paternity plot*, raises a number of questions about how and why women viewers enjoy soap operas, and about the genre's political and ideological role. In particular, it is a paradigmatic example of the methods by which soap operas provide competent viewers with an opportunity for pleasurable anticipation and utopian, woman-centered fantasy, while ultimately containing and managing the disruptive aspects of that fantasy through the inevitable re-establishment of patriarchal order.

Although I make reference in this paper to other serial forms, my focus throughout is on American daytime serials. It may be possible to extend many of my points to other genres – especially, as I indicate below, so-called "prime-time soaps" such as *Dallas* and *Dynasty*. However, because the basic narrative structures and the contexts of production and reception differ considerably from genre to genre and from country to country, I am reluctant to make any specific claims for my argument's application even to British serials like *Coronation Street*, much less to Spanish-language telenovelas.

Before considering the paternity plot's role, let me briefly sketch the way paternal identity itself functions in feminist theory. This is in no way a thorough examination of feminist interpretations of paternity, but, rather, an outline of the ideas that some feminist theorists have expressed about the meanings of fatherhood. Such analyses of the historical, social, and psychological significance of paternity can provide a useful ground against which to read the soap opera paternity plot. In addition, although I would not want to argue that all soap opera viewers are always thinking consciously about the cultural meanings of paternity while they watch the programs, those meanings do circulate through both discourse and social practice. Whether or not they bring them directly to bear on the shows they consume, culturally competent viewers understand paternity's social significance, and that understanding provides one of the lenses through which they interpret soap opera narratives.[2]

For many feminist theorists concerned with the origins of women's oppression, the prehistoric discovery by men of their role in reproduction is a key moment.[3] Before the recognition of paternity, by some accounts, women were assumed to reproduce on their own or in concert with deities or nature, and were consequently viewed with awe. The power to create life seemed to put women on a par with other aspects of the natural world, and to position them above men, who appeared to be the only ones unable to exercise this creativity. Once men's role was discovered, however, this interpretation of women's reproductive capacity dissolved, and new rituals evolved that emphasized men's importance, including the development of elaborate kinship networks that depended on exogamy.[4] Efforts to prove that men were the "true" – that is, the culturally significant – parents extended to biological explanations of reproduction, and attempts persisted well into the scientific age to demonstrate that women were merely vessels for *men's* magical ability to create life.[5]

This view of women's symbolic fall from reproductive power does not fully explain the oppression of women, but there is no doubt about men's anxiety over the question of paternity. As many feminist theorists have pointed out, this anxiety springs from the fact that no man can ever be as certain of his children's identity as is the woman who bears them: only mothers know beyond any doubt that their children are their own. (It is important to note that changes in reproductive technology could ultimately place women in the same position as men in this regard. Even as social relationships like surrogacy increasingly complicate the legal definition of motherhood, embryo transplants and other techniques are likely to complicate the biological meanings of parenthood for both sexes.) Fatherhood is, in this sense, a myth, an ultimately unprovable claim that we agree to accept as fact.[6] Elaborate legal, social, and religious barriers have been raised in an attempt to ensure the "fact" of paternity, but the very existence of these regulations only serves to underline the profound anxiety that surrounds the issue. In the words of Mary Ann Doane,

> Paternity and its interrogation . . . are articulated within the context of
> . . . *social* legitimacy. To generate questions about the existence of
> one's father is, therefore, to produce an insult of the highest order . . . .
> Knowledge of maternity is constituted in terms of immediacy . . . .
> Knowledge of paternity, on the other hand, is mediated – it allows of
> gaps and invisibilities, of doubts in short. It therefore demands external
> regulation in the form of governing social relations . . . .[7]

Soap operas speak directly to the anxiety that demands such regulation, demonstrating the uncertainty of paternity in endlessly repeated story-lines. But these stories do not just stir up anxiety. They inevitably resolve it by re-enacting the discovery that men – specific men – are fathers. Soaps thus perform what Thomas Elsaesser and others have called a "myth-making" function,[8] and although there is rarely any such guarantee in real life, the question of fatherhood is always given a definite answer.

Before I begin, let me offer one caveat. While I will make references in the following discussion to the differences (and occasional similarities) between "real life" and the fictional world of soap operas, I do not intend any rigid opposition. Nor do I mean to read any television program as an unmediated mirror-image of some objective "reality." The ways in which television imitates and/or recuperates viewers' conceptions of reality are extremely complex, but I assume that soap operas and other apparently "realistic" programs present a version of life that viewers can recognize as in some ways coherent with their own experience. Soap operas are thus distinct from fantasy and science fiction programs, although some soaps, such as ABC's *General Hospital*, have incorporated elaborate fantasy plots that try viewers' efforts to believe in the shows' realism.

Definitive resolution is one of the paradigmatic characteristics of what I have defined as the paternity plot. The plot itself begins at or just before conception and rests on a simple premise: a woman character becomes pregnant but does not know or will not reveal the father's identity. Other characters – usually including but never limited to the men who might have fathered her child – become involved in the pregnancy or with the child, depending on the stage at which the mystery becomes known. According to their relationships to the woman and in keeping with their functions as "good" or "evil" figures, these characters attempt to discover, repress, or reveal the pregnancy's origin. Predictable soap opera complications ensue and varying lengths of time may pass between conception and revelation, but the identity of the true father eventually becomes public knowledge. There are numerous variations on this basic plot, the most common of which revolve around the woman's engagement or marriage to a man other than the lover responsible for her pregnancy or that lover's marriage or engagement to another woman. Various characters' lies or misapprehensions about paternal identity are also often central.

166

The paternity plot is so pervasive that examples can be chosen almost at random, but one should be enough to suggest the mechanisms by which it is typically worked out. In the summer of 1986, ABC's *One Life to Live* unfolded a story-line about young lovers forcibly separated and meeting again some twenty years later, and this particular embodiment exhibits many of the paternity plot's standard features. Clint Buchanan had been unaware that he had a grown son, Cord, by his former lover Maria, because his own wealthy and powerful father had bribed the young woman's mother to keep it a secret. Although knowledgable viewers could guess that it would only be a matter of time before the secret became known to everyone, elaborate steps were taken to conceal it. Typically, one of the prime manipulators in this story-line was the unacknowledged son's new wife, Tina, herself the illegitimate daughter of another wealthy man; and Clint himself has a brother whose questionable paternity took months to resolve, and who was involved in a paternity mystery concerning his cousin's putative child. In fact, each of these characters was at one time the focus of a story-line whose essential elements made it almost indistinguishable from the one in which Clint was unwittingly entangled.

Such complex family trees and the tension and suspense that surround them are relatively rare in real life, but the ubiquitousness of the paternity plot makes them typical of kinship relations on soap operas. It is common to find soap opera families in which a majority of members have been involved in some kind of paternity mystery. (Since the *One Life to Live* example outlined above, for instance, Cord, Tina, Clint's wife, Viki, and his father, Asa, have all been embroiled in new story-lines about mysterious parentage. Some, like Cord and Tina, have even been involved in more than one such plot.) Ironically, however, while the immediate effects of such mysteries are profound, it is also rare for such a dispute to resonate very far beyond the revelation of the true father. Although post-revelation resentment occasionally lasts a few weeks (or a few months on prime-time shows), it is a rare soap opera character who continues to harbor negative feelings beyond the moment of confrontation and acknowledgment. (When such resentment does last longer, it tends to be a function of the resentful character's already well-established "evil," selfish, or spiteful nature.) Despite the fact that it initially threatens to destroy the family structure, then, the paternity mystery is in fact only a temporary disruption of family life, one whose long-term effects consist almost entirely of the realignment of specific family ties, rather than the undermining of essential family or community frameworks.

Although it is easiest to focus on fairly recent examples, I want to note at the outset that the paternity plot has been a fixture in soap operas at least since their earliest days on television. Less than six months after *The Guiding Light* became the first radio soap to move to television, for instance, writer Irna Phillips was planning a story-line in which Kathy Lang Grant, pregnant by her dead first husband, tried to attribute the baby to her second husband.[9]

Regular soap opera viewers will be able to come up with many other examples of paternity mysteries on long-running serials like *General Hospital* and *Another World*. Programs that have been on the air long enough to allow multiple generations to be born and grow up inevitably contain adult characters whose mysterious paternity provided plot interest in the 1950s, 1960s, and 1970s. (For instance, the Tara–Chuck–Phil love triangle which reigned when *All My Children* began in 1970 as a soap featuring adolescents led eventually to an elaborate paternity plot, and although the mystery was settled years ago, the child in question, Charlie Brent, is now a recurring adult character.)

The repeated eruption of story-lines that center on questionable paternity is striking on statistical grounds alone, but an even more telling aspect of this chain of secrecy and revelation is the fact that paternity can always be proven absolutely. Although it may seem to the casual viewer that the women characters are so promiscuous that they cannot be sure who has fathered their children, it almost always turns out that any given woman knows the truth. She has lied about having an affair, was actually pregnant earlier or later than other characters realized, or for some other reason can demonstrate that there is no real question. If all else fails, blood tests are infallible – assuming that no one bribes the lab technicians or tampers with the computer records. Although in real life such tests have until recently only been able to prove who is *not* the father, on soap operas they have long proven paternity beyond dispute, even when the choice has been between close relatives. The recent incorporation of new technologies like DNA testing (used in February 1992, for instance, to prove Sean Donely's relationship to son Conner on *General Hospital*) thus merely provide up-to-date scientific support for well-established soap opera fact.

On the surface, such story-lines seem to fit easily into the daytime soaps' fixation on their characters' private lives. As Tania Modleski has pointed out, soap operas' preoccupation with private questions – family, love, sex, loyalty, jealousy – reassures the traditional daytime audience of home-centered women that their focus on the private world is not merely legitimate, but fascinating.[10] By presenting not only women, but men who are as bound up with private concerns as the most stereotypical housewife, these programs glamorize those interests and reassure viewers that such men do – or could – exist. (Janice Radway makes an analogous point about the male heroes of romance novels, who can be seen at their first appearance to express a "feminine" sensitivity that she suggests contrasts with the men in romance readers' daily lives.)[11] This characterization of the shows' bias toward the private explains their almost exclusive focus on the family, but we might expect that, for home-centered women viewers, issues of *maternity* would be far more compelling than issues of paternity. And indeed, there are cases in which maternity is in question – usually involving babies switched at birth[12] – although it is not a common plot device. The very rarity of this plot twist, however, highlights the extent to which *male* uncertainties and anxieties are manipulated and reversed in soap operas.

Why, however, does paternity figure so prominently in a genre directed primarily at women? A simple but inadequate explanation, of course, is that mainstream, mass media-generated popular culture reflects the ideology of the dominant culture, in this case patriarchal interests which privilege the father's role and identity over the mother's. But a consideration of the differences between soap opera presentations of uncertain maternity and paternity may help to illuminate the choice to emphasize the latter.

First of all, the paternity plot is narratively both far simpler and far richer in potential complications than one centered on mistaken or unknown maternity. For a child's father to be unknown, no intentional act of deception is needed. It is only necessary for a woman character to have had or appeared to have had sex with more than one man around the time of conception. Although the woman herself may be actively plotting to conceal the information, or to pin the pregnancy on an "innocent" man, there are many other possible explanations, including an unreported rape, a secret love affair, or that time-honored soap staple, the sudden return of a long-lost husband or lover. This is largely a narrative consideration, but it helps to explain why such a theme would prove popular among soap opera writers. While simplicity of premise is not necessarily the overriding concern, extremely complicated plots do not often become staples. Since a daily serial quickly exhausts new plots, this wide range of possible explanations and the suspense inherent in them makes paternity an excellent subject for a continuing serial in which new story-lines must constantly be introduced. Questions about a character's paternity can be introduced at any time, even "retrofitted" years later.

In contrast, the physical facts of reproduction make maternity a relatively less abundant source of either suspense or mystery. For a child's *mother* to be unknown, someone must act – and act after its birth – to confuse things. Although it is possible for the error to be innocent – not part of a plot to confound identity or custody – it cannot be truly inadvertent. And because maternal identity itself cannot usually be as mysterious as paternity, it is far more difficult to introduce the idea of questionable maternity after the fact, and there are probably fewer potential permutations to a maternity-centered plot. While such secrets are not unheard of, it is far more difficult for a woman to hide a pregnancy than for a man to conceal a sexual liaison, and it is far easier to prove, whether through eyewitness testimony or medical examination, that a woman has given birth than that a man has fathered a child.

Once again, this is likely to change as reproductive technologies such as embryo transplants and *in vitro* fertilization find a permanent place in soap opera plots. Although adoption and adultery have been the soaps' traditional solutions to characters' fertility problems, changes in the social and techno-logical relations of reproduction will no doubt mean changes in fictional "solutions" as well. (Both *All My Children* and *General Hospital* have already made brief use of surrogacy plots; *One Life to Live* has already employed an embryo transplant, and *General Hospital* introduced one in the spring of 1993.) It is easy to imagine a future maternity plot whose central mystery is whether a pregnancy was the result of an embryo transplant or "normal" conception.

But the difference between unknown mothers and fathers goes far beyond the writers' need to come up with potentially intriguing story-lines. After all, this particular story-line takes place in a fictional context which consistently presents pregnancy and maternity as passive conditions. One of the most obvious tactics for establishing this passivity is rhetorical. Women characters almost always describe themselves (and are described by others) as "carrying" their lovers' children. This description seems most prominent when a woman is pregnant by a man who is for some reason unavailable to her (usually because he is married to someone else), so that it may express the woman's willingness to settle for the small part of him she possesses through his child. But even more important, it implies that the woman sees herself as a passive receptacle for the more active male progenitor.

The rhetoric of soap operas also has women "giving" children to men, a dramatic verbal admission of who controls the family. Although this may suggest a certain degree of activity (versus merely "carrying" a child), it is activity in the service of passivity, so to speak, rather than real active agency. By positioning a woman in the role of recipient, an August 1989 episode of ABC's *General Hospital* incidentally highlighted the rhetoric by which a woman "carries" a child for another parent. When Bobbie Spencer Meyer accidentally discovered the identity of the woman whose baby she was waiting to adopt, her conversation with the adoption agency representative included a question about when she had discovered that this woman was carrying "her" (i.e., Bobbie's) child.

Added to this rhetorical characterization of pregnancy as a passive activity is the remarkable fact that few soap opera women seem able to recognize the symptoms of pregnancy on their own, but must be diagnosed by a (usually male) doctor. They frequently go to the doctor because of vague or mysterious symptoms – faintness, nausea, fatigue – but almost never does a woman note a missed period and deduce her own condition. (This is, of course, perfectly in keeping with soap opera women's striking ignorance of their own reproductive systems, including their apparent lack of information about or access to contraception and their constant surprise at unplanned pregnancies.) Thus, despite other instances of active agency, the presentation of pregnancy on the soaps highlights women's passivity. In fact, activity and awareness of pregnancy are often associated with villainy; "evil" women characters frequently plot to become pregnant in order to exert control over a man, and often claim to know they are pregnant immediately.

The soaps' treatment of abortion and miscarriage is also relevant here.

Miscarriage is unrealistically frequent on soap operas, and often occurs under truly ridiculous circumstances (as on *General Hospital* several years ago, when a character was pregnant for fourteen months and finally miscarried in a fall down the stairs). Abortion is virtually always wrong, even in cases of rape, and this judgment frequently turns openly on the inappropriateness of a woman's autonomous decision to abort. Other characters – including men not directly involved in the pregnancy – may interfere by telling the would-be father, who attempts to prevent the abortion, or the woman may be struck with sudden feelings of guilt as she is about to undergo the procedure. If the abortion takes place, the woman is almost always assailed by regret afterwards, often accompanied by the imagined crying of babies, and, inevitably, the would-be father sees the abortion as a betrayal of his rights to the child.

The "immorality" of abortion provides a logical counterpoint to the prominence of plots about women unable to become pregnant or carry a child to term. But beyond this, both the highly charged negative portrayal of abortion and the alarming frequency of miscarriages support the soaps' insistence on pregnancy as something that *happens to* women, and whose end is beyond their control. This aspect of women's passivity is emphasized by the fact that the decision over abortion is frequently rendered moot when a woman considering the procedure conveniently experiences a miscarriage. It is also likely, however, that extratextual considerations are at work here: namely writers' and producers' unwillingness to present abortion as a positive choice in the context of an intense social debate over women's reproductive rights. Convenient miscarriage permits them to entertain the possibility of abortion without actually having to approve or reject it.

It is easy to see why voluntary abortion should be so threatening in a fictional world in which men have invested great significance in family life, for a woman who willingly terminates a pregnancy also terminates a tie with the would-be father, and cuts off his power to control the situation, the woman, and the child to come. The fact that, through abortion, a woman can intervene to permanently forestall a man's future ability to exert control makes abortion an exercise of real power (as it may sometimes be in real life), and thereby gives significance to the nearly uniform soap opera rejection of this choice as a moral one. Thus it is consistent that there are only two "appropriate" conclusions to a soap opera pregnancy: carrying a baby to term or inadvertently miscarrying. The other obvious choice, a voluntary abortion, represents an active exertion of control by the pregnant woman that violates her identification as passive.

This is underlined by the fact that "evil" women characters who want to trap a man into marriage, or at least the acknowledgment of paternity, often play on this fact by threatening abortion. This is just one instance in which villainesses demonstrate their understanding of the soap opera "rules." Women viewers may, of course, read quite different lessons in the continuing struggle between good and evil, and may identify in some way with the manipulative villainesses.[13] I would argue, however, that the very fact that such women are identified as villainesses highlights the soaps' equation of "proper" femininity and passivity, at least within the framework set up by the narratives themselves.

The question then becomes why control in this particular area is so important. We might begin to answer this question by recognizing that on the soaps, as in real life, paternity is more than a biological fact. It means inheritance of name and property, defines kinship patterns, and seems to carry the weight of loyalty, family traits, and even day-to-day behavior. On soap operas, the assimilation of all family members into the family of the father is so complete that, for example, a woman who marries into a family often takes on whatever traits are typical of the new family.

The fact that inheritance of wealth and property is so frequently the key to attributions and misattributions of paternity suggests that for many soap opera women, the power to name the father represents a concrete form of economic power. Although the attribution of paternity is often presented in terms of love, it is also often a question of money: if he thinks (or knows) this child is his, he'll have to marry me and give my child his name, money, and position. Or, from the child's point of view, the concealment of my father's identity has denied me access to money and power that are mine by right.

But the correct assignment of name and kinship position appears to be even more important, for questionable or misattributed paternity occurs even among soap opera characters of relatively modest means. When we remember soap operas' focus on private life, however, the reason for this becomes clear: if the family is the most important structure in the world of the soaps, a character's relationship to a particular family is a central pole of his or her identity. Despite the use of workplace settings and the relatively recent introduction of exotic mystery and suspense plots, romantic and family relationships and conflicts remain the story-line staples, and such conflicts make the exact definition of a character's position in the family crucial. Just how important it is for soap opera characters to know their exact kinship positions is underlined by the occasional threat of brother–sister incest posed by unknown or misattributed paternity – as occurred, for instance, in 1989 between Cricket Blair and her half-brother Scott Grainger on CBS's *The Young and the Restless*, and, several years earlier, on *All My Children*, between Erica Kane and her half-brother Mark Dalton.

In the soap opera world, the power to define another person's family position is often the only power women are permitted to exercise with impunity, and the only exertion of power that generates even short-term satisfaction. Although women characters wield other forms of power – through money, ownership of property or businesses, political influence, and so on – these women are usually villainesses, and they have often acquired financial or political power through marriage, divorce, or, more commonly, widowhood. "Good" women, even those who are wealthy and/or fully

172

employed outside the home, exert power indirectly, primarily through family ties and most often by their private influence on other family members. This makes the ability to name, and thereby control, the father and define the family a crucial route to autonomy, however limited and temporary it may be.

The same larger context that identifies women's reproductive role as passive also defines soap opera women as dependent creatures. Women characters almost never achieve money, success, or political power through their own exertions, and if they do, it becomes insignificant in contrast to their unhappy personal lives. (*All My Children*'s Erica Kane is an archetypal example of this.) With few exceptions, women who would in the real world be seen as highly successful (such as prominent doctors and lawyers) expend all of their emotional energy sorting out their marriages, and seem to get little satisfaction and almost no public acclaim for their hard-won careers. In contrast, the men who seem so caught up in personal concerns continue at the same time to advance in their careers and to receive recognition and rewards for their performance in the public sphere.

The equation of paternity with inheritance and name is particularly noticeable on night-time serials, largely because programs like *Dallas* tend to emphasize money and power over the daytime soaps' focus on love and family. While Elsaesser's suggestion that melodrama is particularly adept at reproducing "the patterns of domination and exploitation in a given society, especially the relation between psychology, morality and class-consciousness," is an apt description of the power differentials implicit in daytime soap operas' gender relations, it is almost transparently appropriate to the prime-time serials' obsession with financial power.[14] On *Dallas*, for example, family feelings – loyalty, say, as exemplified in the Barnes–Ewing feud – are couched almost entirely in terms of money and power, although lip-service is paid to the importance of romantic love, respect for ties of blood, traditional values. Because the show actually revolves around the central "character" of Ewing Oil, other bonds tend to be subordinated to the maintenance of the oil company. The families – both the Barneses and the Ewings – *are* their financial interests, and in this context, naming the father (as in the questionable paternity of John Ross Ewing and Pamela Barnes, among others) resonates with particular strength.

But the attribution of paternity is not only a function of power and money, for fatherhood is more than a social or economic role. Daytime soaps also posit an almost mystical bond between biological parents, and most notably, between father and child. Western culture tends to promote the idea that *mothers* and children experience such a bond, and recent feminist theory has paid particular attention to the mother–child relationship.[15] But the focus of the soap opera paternity plot is instead the profound feelings that *fathers* experience. A man's discovery that he has fathered a child arouses powerful feelings of love and attachment, frequently drawing him to the child's mother

– often regardless of his previous feelings for her or his attachment to any other woman – and almost always drawing him to the newly recognized child. The soap opera assertion of the power exerted by all family ties is evident here, but, equally importantly, such a plot invests paternal feelings with a special kind of significance and weight. For instance, the child may be presented as forcing a couple to admit their love for one another, but such "love" is frequently indistinguishable from lack of interest or even dislike before the pregnancy. Shared parenthood is sometimes even capable of overcoming all other considerations, including infidelity or other betrayals, and couples not only get married and stay together because of a child, they often stay *happily* married – or as happily married as the exigencies of the soaps permit.

The positing of this special bond between fathers and their children may be an important source of pleasurable fantasy for women viewers all too aware that, if the statistics on child-support payments are any indication, men in the "real" world do not universally feel such attachment. Thus, it is possible to see the soap opera version of fatherhood as a particularly "feminized" one. Needless to say, however, the depth of fathers' feelings toward their children is never the route to a feminist transformation of the soap opera family into one characterized by equal parenting or a sharing of domestic responsibilities. Although soap opera men are obsessed with private concerns, this obsession never extends to an interest in the maintenance work that family life requires. Of course, few soap opera women not clearly marked as "working class" actually perform this work either, and such domestic labor as is performed onscreen is usually done by housekeepers or other domestic helpers. Nevertheless, soap opera women are presented as bearing primary responsibility for the domestic routine through their planning of parties, dinners, and holiday gatherings, and their direct supervision of household staff.

Soap operas always feature elaborate family crises that threaten to embroil all members, but the supposed bond between father and child makes the revelation of paternity perhaps the most extreme case. The impact of paternity extends beyond the lives of the would-be parents and their relatives. Weddings are cancelled and relationships ended because of it. "How can I marry you when another woman is carrying your child!" exclaims the soap opera bride-to-be (usually on her wedding day, since suspense demands that this information be revealed at the last possible moment). Regardless of the circumstances surrounding conception, the discovery of a pregnancy almost always interrupts ongoing relationships because the creation of a child equals the creation of a bond between parents. Significantly, even when the father or father-to-be claims to feel nothing for the woman he has impregnated, his would-be wife often *insists* on the primacy of the biological father–mother–child triad. This is especially true if the wife or fiancée is herself unable to bear children, and indicates the success with which "good" soap opera women have absorbed the prevailing wisdom.

The mystique of the father–child bond is also demonstrated when a woman lies about a pregnancy or about her child's paternity in an attempt to force a man to marry her. Such situations usually rest on the woman's desire to make a man fall in love with her (although sometimes marriage alone is the goal), and her conviction that this will happen is one of the most stubborn feelings on the soaps. On *All My Children*, for instance, Natalie Hunter, pregnant by her recently deceased husband, claimed that her stepson and former lover Jeremy was actually the father, and insisted beyond all reason that his feelings for the child would lead inevitably to love for her. As always, a blood test resolved everything, but until that moment, no other arguments could persuade her that her belief was groundless – including Jeremy's obvious hatred of her, his commitment to another woman, and his suspicion (correct, as the audience knew) that he and Natalie had not actually had sex. Such insistence obviously draws on the folk convention that intense hatred is actually a cover for love. The fact that this sometimes turns out to be true for soap opera characters makes it even more significant that "true love" never follows from a woman's lies about pregnancy or paternity.

These twists will all be familiar to any regular soap opera viewer. But the fact that, year after year, soap opera women intentionally misattribute paternity brings us back to the question of why a television genre directed primarily at women should emphasize fatherhood rather than motherhood. One plausible explanation is that these plots offer viewers an opportunity for the vicarious experience of power, permitting women simultaneously to acknowledge and to manage feelings of powerlessness and emotional deprivation, a function Janice Radway suggests is performed by romance novels.[16] In contrast to the traditional male-dominated family of real life, where power resides in the husband/father, the soap opera family confers very real power on women: the power to name, or to mis-name, the father. As I have already suggested, while they are unable to act directly concerning their pregnancies, soap opera women hold the key to family relations and are therefore in a position, however briefly, to define the most important structure on these shows. Although their control over this structure may be temporary, and is always resolved by incontrovertible biological fact, these women exert a form of power denied to their male counterparts and thus offer the traditional soap opera viewer an opportunity to imagine a world in which women like themselves (i.e., centered on the family) are in control of the central fact of family life.

But this focus on paternity also provides evidence that, however much they may appear to be shaped by women's interests, soap operas are no more radical or woman-centered than any other form of mass media commercial entertainment. While the open-ended serial format breaks the traditional narrative structure and therefore brings soaps somewhat closer to "real life," individual story-lines do have a certain degree of closure (although it may take years to achieve it), and their resolutions inevitably signal acceptance of the values of the dominant culture. Nowhere is this closure so evident as in the resolution of the paternity plot. Regardless of the degree of immediate disruption it may cause, such a plot always ends with the restoration of family order.[17]

In fact, that very restoration demonstrates the strength of the traditional family, presented in soap operas as a structure able to withstand all assaults and to triumph in the face of the greatest threats. Thus, despite the suggestions of critics like Modleski that the active villainesses of soap operas represent a significant departure from traditional portrayals of female passivity, the constant eruption of the paternity theme and the meaning and prominence given to the inevitable identification of the father continually undermine whatever progressive or woman-centred message we might see in "evil" women shaping the circumstances of their lives.

A detailed discussion of the ways in which a popular culture form like the soap opera may or may not work to reinforce the dominant ideology as a whole is too complex to attempt here. Even setting aside questions about what exactly constitutes "the" dominant ideology, the general methods of its enforcement, and the extent to which resistance is possible, there are still major unanswered questions about precisely what television's role could be. In particular, the exact mechanisms by which a television serial aimed at women might participate in regulating ideology have yet to be delineated to anyone's satisfaction. This is hardly surprising, since arguments persist about such basic issues as how women viewers consume and/or resist television, and whether film – and, if only by implication, television – even constructs any possible viewing position for women.

However, as the recent fascination among feminist critics with "women's" texts such as soap operas, film melodramas, and romance novels testifies, we can move closer to an understanding of those issues by exploring specific aspects of popular texts and by considering what contributions they may make to progressive or regressive social messages. It should be apparent by now that I understand the conventional daytime soap opera as having an implicit political agenda. I would argue that it cooperates in the "teaching" of patriarchy – at the very least, by persuasively restating male dominance and the related oppressions of racism, classism, and heterosexism in such a way as to make them seem inevitable, if not necessarily "natural." Because of its reiteration of the power of the father, the paternity plot plays a particularly important role in this restatement.

But that role entails more than the simple repetition of the principle of male dominance. In order to appreciate fully the intricacies of soap opera plots, viewers must have developed competence in understanding and predicting events on the programs. In fact, it seems likely that a good deal of viewers' pleasure arises from the recognition that they are superior in knowledge to the shows' characters, a superiority that is especially evident in the presentation of the paternity plot, where regular viewers usually know the father's identity long before the father himself. This advantageous position is usually crucial to such a plot's suspense, but at the same time, the very familiarity that aids in building suspense includes a knowledge of how paternity plots are conventionally resolved. For experienced viewers, then, the pleasure of watching the mystery unfold must inevitably exist in tension with the realization that it will not remain a mystery for long. And most important for my reading of the paternity plot, that familiarity includes the recognition that whatever family-shaping power the woman has exerted will end when some particular man is finally identified as her baby's father.

It is, of course, profoundly ironic that women viewers should enjoy watching programs that recapitulate what some feminist theorists see as the first stage in women's oppression. As Hilary Radner points out, however, "to say that something is pleasurable for women does not ultimately justify this practice as feminist."[18] The fact that soap operas re-enact as fact what in real life could until recently never be more than myth – the absolute identity of the father – makes them a particularly striking example of the way in which popular cultural forms restate and thereby indirectly reinforce the dominant ideology. (The inevitable reiteration of the father's identity and power may also help to explain the popularity soaps have attained among male viewers.)

But I do not want to suggest that viewing soap operas is simply an exercise in masochism, for there is an important utopian aspect to the repeated reworkings of the paternity plot. I use "utopian" here in the same sense as Janice Radway (who has in turn adopted it from Fredric Jameson), to refer to an "oppositional moment" that permits readers – or in this case, viewers – to participate in a brief fantasy about a more satisfying world.[19] Although many other parts of the viewing experience undoubtedly contribute to women's pleasure in the soaps, I think that the paternity plot itself – or at least that part of it that precedes the final and absolute establishment of paternal identity – constitutes a significant aspect of the enjoyment. The pleasure it produces resides partly in the hope such a plot holds out that women *can* define the family structure, *can* attribute paternity with impunity, *can* name the father according to their own desires and without reference to blood tests. The centrality of the paternity plot also means that, even as the identity of one father is established, viewers can look forward to the eruption of another paternity mystery down the road – another opportunity, however short-lived, for utopian pleasure. If this is so, then the fantasies viewers spin about the shows they watch may be the most radical aspect of them.

However, as Radway repeatedly cautions, while its enjoyment depends on the (often unconscious) recognition of a basic dissatisfaction with things as they are, such a moment of opposition may in fact stand in the way of garnering support for a movement for social change, since it provides a temporary fulfillment of desires unmet in daily life. But the paternity plot's implication in this process goes far beyond its power to distract women from their complaints by offering a fictional substitute for social action. In my view

177

it is in fact one of the chief methods through which soap operas repress the very resistance women enjoy – not only by incorporating what might be a feminist or proto-feminist utopian fantasy into an essentially conservative narrative, but by defusing and ultimately cancelling out that fantasy through its inevitable resolution in favor of the father-centered family.

In what has been in part an effort to claim the soap opera as a genre worth taking seriously, feminist critics have tended to argue that its narrative or formal disruptions are sites at which the "feminine" successfully undermines the dominant, or to insist that the serial form and its attention to women's private concerns are themselves inherently progressive. Instead, I would argue that the genre of the soap opera is able simultaneously to vent and to contain those concerns. Laura Mulvey has questioned the common assumption that contradiction automatically undermines ideology, pointing out that "no ideology can even pretend to totality: it must provide an outlet for its own inconsistencies."[20] Her identification of 1950s melodramas as a "safety valve" for the contradictions inherent in the dominant ideology suggests a way of talking about television soap operas.

Mulvey's claim that "ideological contradiction is the overt mainspring and specific content of melodrama"[21] can, I think, be adapted to soap operas – with an important qualification. In soap operas, contradiction and disruption are raised as content but are then repeatedly smoothed over, resulting in a narrative that maintains rather than undermines the dominant ideology. While these shows allow for the play of women's fantasies – particularly through the workings of the paternity plot – and may therefore provide a pleasurable utopian dream-space, that space is finally both carefully managed and ultimately closed off by the reassertion of the conservative, male-centered ideology the genre promotes.

My reading of the paternity plot suggests several directions for future work on soap operas. For example, although I have argued that this plot is now the driving force of daytime soap opera narrative, it is not clear when it assumed this dominance, and I am reluctant at the moment to speculate very far about whether its current primacy is the result of a unique historical moment or is instead a long-standing central feature of the genre. It is, I think, safe to say that the paternity plot – like many other aspects of the soaps and like television in general – has come over the last forty years to involve many more open expressions of sexuality, and this has no doubt multiplied the plotting possibilities. In other words, opportunities for more overt television representations and discussions of sexual behavior have probably expanded soap opera writers' repertoire of paternity plots – permitting them, for instance, to include more plots involving non-marital relationships, rather than relying (as in the early days of *The Guiding Light*) on husbands who conveniently die shortly after conception. Whether there are, however, *more* paternity plots now than there were in the 1950s or 1960s still has to be established.

The importance of this issue becomes apparent when we try to think about whether and how soap operas respond to specific changes in the culture at large. For example, it may be that current versions of the paternity plot owe their parameters, even their origins, to feminist and other challenges to paternal authority. It is tempting to see certain aspects of the paradigm – the intense father–child bond, the reiteration of paternity as the cornerstone of family identity – as responses to specific changes in the family, such as the increasing numbers of female-headed households. On the other hand, what seems like a reaction may simply be a change in the details writers use to work out a theme that actually remains consistent over time. In considering the ideological role of television soap operas, we need to examine not only how they work today, but how they have evolved across the last forty years.

There are also many questions still to be asked about the structure of soap operas, and once again I see the paternity plot as exemplary. Critics have focused on the constant interruptions and deferred endings that characterize soap opera narrative, but far less attention has been paid either to the ways in which closure is achieved or to the satisfactions that may be provided *between* moments of interruption. If we are to understand the popularity of soap operas – what it is that tempts women to keep watching for years, even for decades – we need to give more thought to the temporary pleasures afforded by plots like those organized around paternity mysteries.

There are potentially profound implications here for the study, not simply of soap operas, but of popular culture in general. We still have much to learn about how and why the members of non-dominant groups take up commercial cultural artifacts, and especially about what enjoyment they find in fictions that seem to assist in perpetuating their secondary status. As an example of both a "women's" genre and a highly successful mass-produced popular cultural form, soap operas have a special role to play in this inquiry. They can be an important focus for theorizing and in the end, they may even provide the key to understanding the political meaning and ideological function of popular culture itself.

Notes

1 A slightly different version of this essay appeared in *Genders* 12 (winter 1991), pp. 45–61. Thanks to JoAnne Castagna, Lynn Spigel, Barb Klinger, and Ellen Berry for their help.
2 I want to acknowledge here television viewers' work as collaborators in the construction of the soap opera text. Nevertheless, the following argument emphasizes their role as recipients of a text produced elsewhere (by writers, producers, and actors, as well as commercial television networks), a text that in some sense pre-exists their consumption of it. For some idea of the complexities of negotiating between a text-centered criticism of soap operas and an audience-centered ethnography, see Charlotte Brunsdon, "Text and Audience," in Ellen Seiter, Hans Borchers, Gabriele Kreutzner, and Eva-Maria Warth (eds), *Remote Control: Television, Audiences and Cultural Power* (London: Routledge, 1989),

pp. 116–129. Especially important for me is Brunsdon's insistence that, "difficult as it may be, we have to retain a notion of the television text" (p. 125). See also her "Television: Aesthetics and Audiences," in Patricia Mellencamp (ed.), *Logics of Television: Essays in Cultural Criticism* (Bloomington, Ind.: Indiana University Press, 1990), pp. 59–72.

3 The most famous exposition of the role of paternity in women's oppression is of course Engels's in *The Origin of the Family, Private Property, and the State* (1884; reprinted New York: Pathfinder Press, 1972). Among feminist theorists, see, for example, Simone de Beauvoir, *The Second Sex*, trans. H. M. Parshley (New York: Bantam Books, 1961), pp. 61–73; Gerda Lerner, *The Creation of Patriarchy* (Oxford: Oxford University Press, 1986), pp. 149, 185–186; and Peggy Reeves Sanday, *Female Power and Male Dominance: On the Origins of Sexual Inequality* (Cambridge: Cambridge University Press, 1981), esp. ch. 3.

4 Two basic feminist analyses of the meaning of the exchange of women, both of which address its significance as an enforcer of paternal identity, are Gayle Rubin, "The Traffic in Women: Notes on the 'Political Economy' of Sex," in Rayna R. Reiter (ed.), *Toward an Anthropology of Women* (New York: Monthly Review Press, 1975), pp. 157–210; and Juliet Mitchell, *Psychoanalysis and Feminism: Freud, Reich, Laing and Women* (New York: Vintage Books, 1975), pp. 370–381.

5 For example, the homuncule theory claimed that sperm contained complete beings that were simply implanted in women. For some of the implications of the association between women and nature, see Sherry Ortner, "Is Female to Male as Nature Is to Culture?," in Michelle Z. Rosaldo and Louise Lamphere (eds), *Women, Culture and Society* (Stanford, Calif.: Stanford University Press, 1974), pp. 67–88.

6 Two very different feminist approaches to the mythic quality of male uncertainty over paternity are Jane Gallop, *The Daughter's Seduction: Feminism and Psychoanalysis* (Ithaca, NY: Cornell University Press, 1982), pp. 39, 47; and Mary O'Brien, *The Politics of Reproduction* (Boston, Mass.: Routledge & Kegan Paul, 1981), pp. 30, 48–49 and *passim*.

7 Mary Ann Doane, *The Desire to Desire: The Woman's Film of the 1940s* (Bloomington, Ind.: Indiana University Press, 1987), pp. 70–71.

8 Thomas Elsaesser, "Tales of Sound and Fury: Observations on the Family Melodrama," in Christine Gledhill (ed.), *Home Is Where the Heart Is: Studies in Melodrama and the Woman's Film* (London: British Film Institute, 1987), p. 44. Cf. Ien Ang's application of this insight to soap operas, in *Watching "Dallas": Soap Opera and the Melodramatic Imagination*, trans. Delia Couling (London: Methuen, 1985), p. 64.

9 "Projected Storyline for The Guiding Light" (November 24, 1952, July 31 and October 15, 1953), Irna Phillips Papers, Film and Manuscript Archive, State Historical Society of Wisconsin. Phillips's correspondence with the advertising agency controlling the program also provides evidence that patrilineage was an important source of identity even in these early days. A story about Paul Fletcher, whose parents were unmarried and whose father is unknown, focuses on Paul's conviction that he is no one – because he has no father. At one point, Phillips even draws an explicit parallel between this plot and the Kathy Lang Grant paternity plot: see "Projected Storyline for The Guiding Light" (April 27, 1957), pp. 10–14.

10 Tania Modleski, *Loving With a Vengeance: Mass-Produced Fantasies for Women* (New York: Methuen, 1982), pp. 88, 108.

11 Janice Radway, *Reading the Romance: Women, Patriarchy, and Popular Literature* (Chapel Hill, NC: University of North Carolina Press, 1984), p. 148.

12 For example, several years ago on *One Life to Live*, well-meaning friends told a former prostitute that her baby had died and gave the child to a former nun, who did not know that her baby *had* died. Although paternity plots figure prominently on this show, the writers of *One Life to Live* also seem to be unusually interested in cases of mistaken or unknown maternity. Two separate maternity mysteries were featured during 1989 alone, one a particularly complicated story-line involving the recovery by Viki Lord Buchanan of a daughter born to her twenty-five years earlier, the other a version of the standard baby-switching plot. Like paternity mysteries, maternity mysteries are always resolved through the absolute identification of the mother and/or child.

13 See Modleski, *Loving With a Vengeance*, p. 95.

14 Elsaesser, "Tales of Sound and Fury," p. 64.

15 See, for example, Nancy Chodorow, *The Reproduction of Mothering: Psychoanalysis and the Sociology of Gender* (Berkeley, Calif.: University of California Press, 1978); and the writings of Adrienne Rich and Sarah Ruddick, among others.

16 See, for example, Radway, *Reading the Romance*, p. 141.

17 For a range of approaches to this question, see for example Robert C. Allen, "On Reading Soaps: A Semiotic Primer," in E. Ann Kaplan (ed.), *Regarding Television: Critical Approaches – An Anthology* (Los Angeles, Calif.: University Publications of America, 1983), pp. 97–108; Sandy Flitterman-Lewis, "All's Well That Doesn't End – Soap Operas and the Marriage Motif," *Camera Obscura* 16 (1988), pp. 119–127, who argues that what would mark closure in other genres is, in soap operas, only the beginning. Among many other iterations of soap operas' apparent lack of closure, see also John Fiske, *Television Culture* (London: Methuen, 1987), p. 181. I obviously disagree with this assessment, and believe instead that soap opera plots do close, although they may reopen at a later date. In fact, I would argue that certain kinds of plots – including those involving crimes and those centred specifically on questions of family identity – actually exhibit the full closure associated with classical narrative. The details of this argument are beyond the scope of this essay, but I attempt to address the issue in "How Things End: The Problem of Closure in Daytime Soap Operas," *Quarterly Review of Film and Video* 15 (2) (1993), pp. 57–74.

18 Hilary Radner, "Quality Television and Feminine Narcissism: The Shrew and the Covergirl," *Genders* 8 (summer 1990), p. 123.

19 Radway, *Reading the Romance*, pp. 214–215.

20 Laura Mulvey, "Notes on Sirk and Melodrama," in her *Visual and Other Pleasures* (Bloomington, Ind.: Indiana University Press, 1989), p. 39.

21 Ibid.

9

"They killed off Marlena, but she's on another show now"

Fantasy, reality, and pleasure in watching daytime soap operas

Louise Spence

The title of this essay comes from a conversation between two daytime soap opera viewers, my mother and grandmother. Both watched NBC's *Days Of Our Lives*. My grandmother hadn't seen the show in some time:

> My mother informed her: "They killed off Marlena, but she is on another show now."
> My grandmother asked: "Who did it?"
> My mother answered: "The same guy who's been trying to for a while."

What interested me about the conversation was that, without effort or confusion, they were switching from the narrative world of the characters and the plot to extra-narrative information about the performer:

> "They [the writers/producers] killed off Marlena [a character on *Days Of Our Lives*], but she [the actress, Deidre Hall] is on another show now [the prime-time series *Our House*]."
> My grandmother's "Who did it?" refers to which character on *Days Of Our Lives* killed Marlena.
> And my mother's "The same guy who's been trying it for a while," refers again to the character.

One of the most popular images of a daytime soap opera viewer is someone who can't tell the difference between reality and fiction – women attacking the performer who plays a villain on the street or sending wedding presents to characters who marry on the show. And one of the more passionate complaints of non-viewers is that soaps lack credibility – they lack plausibility. Soaps are unfaithful to someone's idea of reality. The extravagance, the unlikeliness, the hyperbole, departs from the limits of common sense.

My experience talking to women who watch daytime soap operas suggests that viewers always bring some idea of "reality" into the viewing process, testing the fiction for "plausibility" according to the worlds they know (both fictional and real) and adding their private associations to the specific sounds and images broadcast.[1] This added information quietly transforms what they see and hear into their interpretations, so that some textual idea of fact and some textual idea of fiction are always acting at the same time. Soap operas' extravagant feelings, extravagant behavior, and extravagant circumstances may strain credibility, but they are also an important source of energy and excitement. Viewers often refer to instances of excess and folly as "great." This essay will attempt to call into question the validity of the terms "fantasy" and "reality," and, perhaps even more importantly, problematize the idea of fiction and fact, fantasy and reality *as dualities* – as separate and opposed entities.

But first, let's look at the ideas of "unlikeliness" and "credibility" to see how they might relate. Nancy K. Miller, in a fine essay on plots and plausibility in women's fiction, quotes Bussy-Rabutin's critique of *La Princesse de Clèves* where he complained that Mme de Clèves's confession "is extravagant, and can only happen in a true story;" he goes on to say that "when one is inventing a story for its own sake it is ridiculous to ascribe such extraordinary feelings to one's heroine."[2] The reasoning is that in life anything can happen, so we really can't complain of unlikeliness. In fiction, however, we should be more responsible and not violate the readers' expectations. Could this be related to the early English novelists' ritualistic denial of authorship by claiming to be simply recording or editing someone else's true story (i.e., the facts)?[3] It is possible that the "veracity" of the story left them more leeway for extravagance and exaggeration. That is, the disavowal may have had the double benefit of making the story seem more acceptable to readers and giving the authors a certain amount of rhetorical freedom.

At the turn of the twentieth century, Dorothy Richardson's American autobiography discussed the reading habits of her fellow workers in a box factory, women who "will not read stories laid in the past, however full of excitement they may be [and who] like romance of the present day, stories which have to do with scenes and circumstances not too far removed from the real and the actual." But Richardson also tells us about describing the plot of Louisa May Alcott's *Little Women* to her co-workers and the reaction of one who complained "that's no story at all – that's just everyday happenings. I don't see what's the use putting things like that in books . . . They sound just like real, live people."[4]

This tension between the ordinary and the out-of-the-ordinary seems to operate today on daytime soap operas. Soaps are populated with "real" people in a knowable landscape, people and places we are familiar with. Familiar in the sense that we have seen them on soap operas before and familiar in that they have aspects that are not too dissimilar to people and places we know or know about from real-life texts, such as news stories or a friend's account (or community gossip). Of course, many of these texts are fashioned after soap opera conventions, sometimes even in installments, and often only loosely based on reality. However, since they seem so familiar, they seem almost accessible. Soaps have few superheroes (equipped with powers superior to or unimaginable in common folks), few fairies or sorceresses, or truly repugnant freaks. Yet these people are not *just* like we might be, they are exceptional. They are exceptional because they are on display (via *mise-en-scène*), and also because they have only significant qualities and significant circumstances. Their lives are very concentrated, so they can be, simultaneously, ordinary and outrageous.

As one soap opera story is intertwined with another, so are our other stories and the days' chores and dreams. We can never see a structured whole from our interminable moment in the middle. Peter Brooks, writing about nineteenth-century serialized novels, suggests that time in the representing was felt to be a necessary analogue of the time represented.[5] Soap opera viewers also speak about the sense of "real time," the life-likeness of the slow pace. Although they often joke about "children who grow up in a hurry" (reaching sexual maturity quickly) or days that take weeks to happen, despite obvious discrepancies in representation time and represented time, they also find comfort in characters who pass time as they do and while they do.

The time of the story is both analogous to and separate from the time of the storytelling.[6] Unlike novels, whose verb forms temporally situate us *in relation* to the tale, soap operas by their very present nature (a story forged before our eyes) situate us *with* them; we are in the same time. We seem to experience a reality that coincides temporarily with our own reality. The past tense is generally treated as a mental state, remembering. It is signaled by optical devices and audio effects similar to those used for dreams and other interior fantasies. The iterative is seldom used; soaps are the here and now. They conform to real-life seasons and holidays and often refer to contemporary social issues like AIDS, sexual harassment, and homelessness. They will sometimes adapt recent news stories: in 1985, for example, *All My Children* had a story remarkably like New York City's Mayflower Madame, even playing with Sydney Barrows's name for their character, Mickey Barlowe. *Capitol* had a story in March 1987 about a doctor who was accused of an unauthorized implant of a mechanical heart, soon after a Texas case was in the newspapers. A couple of months later *The Young and the Restless* had a highly moralistic summer story involving a teenage pregnancy.[7] That same summer, *The Young and the Restless*, *Guiding Light*, and *Loving* all had story-lines that acknowledged adult illiteracy. Several soaps have had stories situated in homeless shelters.[8]

These references to current affairs, even while they suggest a certain insecurity about the categories of fact and fiction, serve to fix and displace a fundamental defense of the truth of their stories, permitting soap operas a margin for excess. That is, the "veracity" of these stories may leave them more leeway for extravagance and exaggeration.

Soap opera publicity and promotion also encourage a conflation of the fictional and the real. Some make associations between the daily life of the performer and the life of the fictional character. The October 18, 1988 issue of *Soap Opera Digest*, for example, had a cover story about the "Real-Life Triumphs over Drugs and Alcohol" of Jeanne Cooper and Jess Walton. The article was about the substance abuse of the performer who plays *The Young and the Restless*'s alcoholic Katherine Chancellor and of the performer who had played a drug addict on *Capitol*, extending their personal experiences to their acted roles.

A few years earlier, Jeanne Cooper's face-lift became a story line as her character Kay Chancellor underwent the same procedure on the soap opera. There was a strange collapse of the actual and the acted as the character Kay, explaining her reasons for the face-lift to another character, demonstrated the tricks of the television trade and revealed on camera the off-camera make-up secrets that had made her look younger. Then, with suitable publicity, Cooper's operation was taped and shown as Kay's on the show.[9] *TV Guide* awarded "cheers" to *Days Of Our Lives* for writing the actress Suzanne Rogers's neuromuscular disorder into her story-line so that she can cope with it on air.[10] When the wife of Doug Davidson (who plays Paul Williams on *The Young and the Restless*) played opposite him in a temporary role as his girlfriend, fan magazines forecasted hot love scenes.[11] The off-screen romance of Margaret Reed and Michael Swan, who were playing the spatting lovers Shannon and Duncan on *As the World Turns*, was highlighted with their appearance on CBS's *Morning Program*.[12]

Much publicity functions to stimulate the illusion that the fictional places (for example, Genoa City, Pine Valley, Springfield) and the characters coexist with us or that there is a homology between their daily lives and ours. For example, in the November 15, 1988 issue of *Soap Opera Digest*, the news section by Seli Groves asked readers if they had ever been helped by a soap plot in their own life and requested that readers send in their experiences.[13] A month earlier, the magazine published results of a romance survey. Readers had been asked to respond to eight questions. Six of the eight questions related the reader's own romances to those represented in soap operas. One asked readers about some of the values they felt were important in "real-life" romances. Only one question referred solely to the representation of romance on screen. With this emphasis on the factual worthiness of the fictions, it is not surprising that the magazine found

An overwhelming majority of our readers admitted that they did get ideas about how to conduct their personal romances from watching the soaps, and that they had, at some point in their lives, dealt with the same kind of problems soap characters have had to deal with.[14]

The following issue ran a feature entitled "How to Dress Like A Soap Bride," which included instructive "do's and don'ts" from costume designers.[15] In February 1986, *Search For Tomorrow* mailed a special edition of the soap's *Henderson Herald* to subscribers of *Soap Opera Digest* reporting on Henderson's flood situation. *Another World* placed a two-page advertisement in the October 4, 1986 *TV Guide* inviting viewers to audition to be members of a jury (as extras) for an on-screen murder trial and to actually participate in the decision on the guilt or innocence of the defendant. More recently, the show asked fans to telephone a 900 (pay per minute) number and participate in a survey to decide which of the five back-up bands they were featuring on the program should be selected for (the character) Dean Frame's new music video.[16]

Soap opera publicity often indulges in public anecdotes about performers, casting, and backstage antics. Many of the articles, photographs, and recipes in *Soap Opera Digest* educate us on how to look like, eat like, or furnish your home like a soap opera performer – a person who may have more visibility and a higher income than we have, but does not seem to have richer tastes. These "celebrities" are seldom pictured in more than fantasizable middle-class luxury. The performers in the photo sessions, and, perhaps even more importantly, the characters on the screen, wear ready-made clothing, purchased off-the-rack and generally available to the viewer as well. *Soap Opera Digest*'s "How to Dress Like A Soap Bride" feature included the name of a store in Brooklyn where many of the television bridal gowns are selected and the added assurance that the actresses sometimes return to the store to purchase gowns for their own weddings.[17] Such comments, the personality profiles, and the backstage stories in the magazine's "news" columns remind us that these people (even more than the characters) are people like us, or people we know, not only subject to wages, contracts, negotiations, and competition in the workplace, but to the vicissitudes of home life as well. In a January 1983 interview, Marc Liu, who was at the time the new president and publisher of *Soap Opera Digest*, explained that the magazine's "entire treatment of the soap opera field treats people as people . . . We don't treat the characters and actors as *stars*."[18] The scenic designer of *All My Children* told me that the show often gets letters from people inquiring where a particular lamp or piece of furniture might be purchased.[19] How we respond to a show certainly must depend on how it connects to not only our dreams and dissatisfactions but to what's available.

Fan magazines not only relate the viewer's daily life to that of soap opera characters and performers, they also promote the importance of decoration, personality, and individual behavior (that which is changeable, moldable, extrinsic). This is in tune with commercials on the soaps for the sweepstakes, press-on nails, diet pills, and the cures for sinus headaches, greasy stains, boring dinners, and bad breath: all atomized solutions. It's also compatible with the many advertisements in soap opera fan magazines for self-improvement products which promise you "stronger, thicker hair," "a golden tan overnight," "the perfect bottom," a "round sexy bosom," or "surgery free facelifting." Or the numerous weight loss plans and training offers (such as computer-based paralegal training or home art instruction); or Dale Bronner's videotape "How to Find and Keep a Husband in one year or less. Guaranteed!!!;" or money-making schemes involving home work or door-to-door marketing ("Get a LOT of Spare Cash for a LITTLE Spare Time" and "How to start your own big profit home import business").[20] Our lives, too, are always at the intersection of uncompleted stories.

An ad in the magazine, *Daytime TV*, offered "THE ULTIMATE FANTASY TRIP – BE A SOAP STAR" (a networking enterprise where a participant is able to "design [his or her] own character and determine what he or she does," interacting by mail with other participants for an ongoing narrative).[21] Sigmund Freud, in a somewhat ominous tone, wrote of our "unfulfilled but possible futures to which we still cling in phantasy, all those strivings of the ego which adverse external circumstances have crushed, and all our suppressed acts of volition which nourish us in the illusion of Free Will."[22] He reminded us that our fantasies are a reality of sorts, a psychic reality, clearly not the same as material reality, but none the less worthy of investigation.[23] Fantasy and reality are not opposed dualities, but coexist in a dialectic, as differentiations. In trying to come to terms with our lives we are always trying out new possibilities. If new information makes any of our beliefs problematic, the displaced beliefs do not cease to exist; they continue as mutual complements of the new. Difference, as Trinh T. Minh-ha points out, is an ongoing process.[24] New positions, new "authenticities," need displaced ones as oppositions which give meaning. Perhaps, then, the notions of fiction and truth, fantasy and reality, are more useful when they are viewed, "not in terms of dualities or conflicts but in terms of degrees and movements within the same concept," always interrelating.[25]

Soaps are fictional and yet are about the world. We gently imagine, are immersed, but never completely leave familiar ground. Or as Wolfgang Iser says of works of fiction, they are not about contingent reality, but about "models or concepts of reality."[26] Soap operas might be seen as both representing and interfering with (or challenging) our formulations of the world. As well as being the product of everyday thoughts, they are, for many, a departure from the limitations of those thoughts. In fact, these plays of fantasy may come to signfiy a critical arena of reality. As Robert Musil observed in his novel, *The Man Without Qualities*, "If there is such a thing as a sense of reality, there must also be a sense of possibility."[27] Our real is seldom very static.

Hanni Lederer, one of the soap opera viewers whom I have been speaking to, told me about her displeasure with what she called the "unnaturalness" of *As the World Turns*, especially its convoluted families.[28] "Nobody lives with their parents; everybody has been married to somebody else. I don't think that real life is as mixed-up as this show is." That is, she wants (or expects) the show, or the writers, to know something of life. Yet she considers herself an experienced woman and doesn't easily cede authority if her beliefs don't coincide with those in the show. The idea that a coherent and rationalizing authority creates an orderly world is not a given; it is negotiated. What is real is not universally acknowledged but is problematically at stake with each viewing and each viewer. As Mieke Bal has noted, each interpretation is a proposal, a well-founded proposal which must make logical connections if it is to be accepted.[29] We speculate, form propositions, formulate views of our worlds. This is a way of historicizing the fictions, of naming and transforming them, making them our own.[30]

Watching soaps is experiencing a fantasy which we believe to be true enough to warrant drawing moral conclusions, forming opinions, and comparing to what we know from the real world. The more detailed our experience is with the subject or similar subjects, the more likely that pieces of it will infiltrate the screen. Hanni reflected on the situation of some of the characters on *The Young and the Restless* and said,

> I was thinking today what if [Brad] would have told Tracy when Lisa first came into the picture, "I have been married before." You see, I'm a very honest person. He could spare Tracy and himself all this grief now if he would come out and explain it to her . . . . I would have told it, and there wouldn't be a threat, but then there wouldn't be a story . . . .

One reason soaps are so compelling is that they make us believe that we are actually getting to know about people and life. However, at the same time they are clearly constructs. We know that it's not the same as our lived experience and the characters are not real people.

If the line between image and reality, the real and the acted, is constantly being challenged, is the line erased when guests (such as Hulk Hogan, Ron Darling, or Stevie Wonder) appear as themselves? Is it also erased when well-known film and television stars such as Liz Taylor, Carol Burnett, or Sammy Davis Jr appear in temporary roles as "characters?" What happens when performers change soaps, or when characters are played by a new or substitute performer? Or when a performer appears on commercials "in character?"[31] Were we thrown into a tailspin when Daniel Pilon appeared as both Max Dubujak (on *Ryan's Hope*) and as Alan Spalding (on *Guiding Light*) simultaneously (November 1988)? Or at the end of a week of auditioning back-up bands, Dean Frame and his manager, Matt, in costume, make-up and on the set, look directly at the camera to say, "Now you watch, watch next Friday, watch *Another World* to see if your choice is the winning band." Is there a blurring of distinctions between illusion and reality, sign and referent – rendering *both* artificial, as Baudrillard might say? Is it, as Lawrence Grossberg claims, that television's indifference to this line has changed its effectivity? That the distinction collapses and becomes ir-relevant?[32]

It seems to me that it is not a matter of failing to distinguish between fact and fantasy or a narrowing of the distance between reality and fiction; they coexist. I remember an involuntary shudder that once came over me when an actor who was playing a rapist came in to check the call-board as I was interviewing one of the crew members in the lunch room of *All My Children*. Representations may come to vie with our lived experiences as we attempt to structure meaning. If there *is* a blurring of distinctions, it is because neither fact nor interpretation can be taken as given.

How we relate to the soaps and their publicity and promotion is complex; soaps articulate subject-positions that are often multiple and contradictory and our identification operates in relation to difference and dreams as well as to resemblance. It is not simply that we "are" or "want to be," or that we can put ourselves in the place of or occupy the perceptual space of a particular character. Our feelings for a character are certainly other than simply feeling at one with that character; they involve both psychological processes and critical ones. Hanni spoke to me several times about how she felt characters *ought* to behave (if they had the same scruples that she has). However, in the next sentence she would often remark on the story-line and the acting. For instance, commenting on Carline Forrester on *The Bold and the Beautiful*, she said, "I don't know how I would feel if I were marrying the guy, but I think that I would say that he had a last fling. Why cancel the wedding?," and a moment later, "Wait 'til she finds out . . . what a sleaze her father is!" When I asked her, "Do you think she will?," she replied, "Of course why would he be like that if she [weren't going to find out]?" Soon after, she said, "You knew that Ridge wouldn't die because then he would be out of the picture, right? Then there would only be half the story."

Our feelings for a character or a situation surely also have some elements of desire. Part of the process of watching soap operas is making friends with characters. In fact, we may feel that we know a character in a soap opera better than we know some of our own friends or colleagues. One women I spoke to told me that she felt that she knew some characters on the show that she had been watching for eighteen years better than she knew herself. Or we may feel we know characters that we might not be friends with in the course of our daily activities.[33] As such, our connections are multifocal and promiscuous (even the particularity of gender may be ignored), and they can be the result of highly ambivalent feelings. One viewer discussed Jack Abbott on *The Young and the Restless* and said, "I like him as entertainment. I wouldn't want to meet him, I mean I wouldn't want to get involved with him. I probably *would* like to meet him because he's sharp and sarcastic and . . . I can be like that!"[34]

I would argue against the idea that we locate ourselves *in* characters, or merge with characters – or that the strong bonds between viewer and

189

characters replace or overcome the weak bonds of family and friends. Many theorists account for the pleasures of soap opera viewing as surrogate companionship substituting for face-to-face interaction.[35] This doesn't account for our critical capacities, the thinking and imagining that is certainly a part of the viewing experience. Even emoting can be reflexive. For example, although we often weep at a particular feeling of sadness (generally connected with a situation or an event), there is also another type of tears, tears that are admittedly self-conscious and enjoyed, where pleasurable feelings are sought for their own sake (a sensuous delight in weeping).[36] Although tears of sensibility seem "justified" by a moving work, tears of sentimentality are thought by many to be an artificial and gratuitous indulgence.[37] None the less, many of the women I spoke to mentioned "the pleasure of a good cry," and, though not everyone admits to weeping, those that do feel that is a significant part of the experience. One woman told me, "You know, I really *live* [soaps]," and with a change of tone which seemed to indicate some embarrassment, she explained, "I cry."

Marilyn Morales, herself a mother, told me that she cried when one of the characters on *All My Children* was sobbing over the fate of her kidnapped child. "Don't you cry when Dixie's thinking about the baby and crying . . . that's emotional, right?" And later when we were talking about the child's father, Adam Chandler, an evil character, "He's terrible, but you imagine if it happened to you, how would you feel? I cried then."

Lee Metz, who also watches *All My Children*, said that she cried for days when Jenny died. Later, when I asked how she felt about the prospect of us watching the show together, she admitted a bit of anxiety, "I *react*, you know. Like, 'Oh my god, what happened? Why did this happen?'" Awilda Valles bragged that she was crying so much when Jenny died, even after the broadcast was over, that her grandmother came to find out what was the matter. But she also wrote to the production company to tell them off for killing her. Peggy Orr admitted crying when Jenny died, but then went on to justify her reaction by telling me what a "good" character Jenny was: good because she was such a nice person *and* because she was central in the narratives, affecting the lives of many other characters.

What we think of as a knowing suspension of our disbelief, or our simultaneous interest in characters as people or story as event and characters or story as fictional devices, or our appreciation of the suspense of a tale whose ending we already know – all this involves a certain disjunction in our viewing experience, but one that is seldom disconcerting. Candy Lampropoulos, for example, was telling me how much she cried when the young daughter of Brooke Chandler and Tom Cudahy died: "I was very upset." She then laughed and said, "I was really upset because for years a creepy kid played her but then when they got a cute kid they killed her." When I asked another woman if there were some characters she liked better than others, she paused, referred to Jack Abbott, smiled and said: "He's a bastard. But then you give him credit for good acting, so you don't really dislike him!"

The anonymous letters to the editor of *Soap Opera Digest* regularly comment on writing, performance, and other aspects of craft. Couldn't these be the same people who give advice to characters or send wedding presents? Are different viewing attitudes indicative of different viewers, or different postures, or the complexity of the viewing relationship?

One issue of *Soap Opera Digest* printed two letters to the editors commenting on the realism of the recent death of the character Jesse Hubbard on *All My Children*. Each letter both acknowledged the story as a construct performed, and discussed the truth in the performance. The letter from P. B. in Washington, DC, began,

> As a faithful viewer of *All My Children*, I was very sad to see Darnell Williams leave his role of Jesse Hubbard. I never cried so much for an actor on a soap opera. Every time I saw Angie [the character, his wife] after his death, I would cry. It all felt so real.

The writer goes on to wish Williams luck in the world and thanks the writers for Angie's and Jesse's story-lines. K. H. in Detroit wrote that

> Debbi Morgan [who plays Angie] deserves an Emmy. She is an excellent actress who constantly performs with such strong emotion and sensitivity that she can't help but touch everyone's heart. Her portrayal of grief at Jesse's death was so moving that I felt as though a member of my immediate family had taken the deadly bullet. I was able to feel deeply the hurt, pain and agony that she portrayed at that particular time. I cried when she cried, and I cried when she tried to be so strong. So, Debbi, I hope you get the prize you so richly deserve.[38]

The performance is true because it has a special relation to our feelings and our fantasies. It is familiar, and as its familiarity adds to its plausibility, it becomes true.

There has been much recent scholarly concern for how popular culture shapes the way we perceive reality; less has been written about how our perceptions of reality shape how we view our fictions. Our opinions and convictions may be partially formed by the fictions we imagine; however, our fictions are also infused by our opinions and convictions. New understanding exists within and because of our previous knowledge and experience (even if it opposes them). We know our fictions through our histories, so most of the time there is a truth in every fiction. Truth and fiction can only be analyzed as a network of reciprocating processes. Fantasy and daily life are not opposed dualities, but coexist in a dialect, as differentiations that inform each other.

Any narrative is a social transaction, "a medium of exchange," writes Roland Barthes.[39] More than structures, they are acts. If we admit that an act of viewing is also an act of interpretation, we must also admit that our insights and perception are produced, in part, from other textual experiences, from a sensitivity to the subtleties of our own life, and from the worlds we observe and dream about. If, as Freud claimed, unsatisfied wishes are the driving power behind fantasies, if every separate fantasy contains the fulfillment of a wish and improves upon satisfactory reality,[40] then perhaps soap operas take up and improve on dissatisfaction: wishes rooted in fundamental desires, fears, anxieties, and needs. Fantasy, if seen as a process, rather than a particular scenario, is part of what constitutes us as human subjects.[41]

Many of the women that I spoke to seem to take a critical stance and test the stories against their experiences and those of others. But this does not seem to prevent the viewer from becoming involved in the fictions. Awilda Valles, for example, talking about the birth of Adam Chandler's son (*All My Children*, summer 1989), said: "That part was phoney – he wanted a boy and he got a boy. Get out of here . . ." But she also told me that she cried a day after the birth when the infant's life seemed to be in danger. And Marilyn Morales commented on the "realism" of some exorbitant occurrence and tried to justify the relevance: "It *does* happen but it doesn't happen in – in every day form of life, you know. It happens to someone else, not to me." (As does, I might add, most of what we read about in the newspapers.)

Marilyn spoke about the easygoing nature of Melanie on *All My Children* as "dull" and "not too realistic:" "Why's she acting like that? People in 1989 do not act like that!" Later, she and Awilda agreed that they didn't like Erica Kane as much since she had had her baby because she is now "more steady, more realistic," and they remembered with relish one of her more grandiose stunts: "Right, oh, that part was good!" Describing an ingenious incident on another show, Marilyn said, "I liked that part! Like, that's interesting. I said, let me see this. What *is* this? I can't believe that this is going on!" On soap operas, it sometimes seems that the commonplace, the down-to-earth, is most radically unthinkable.

The outlandishness of soap operas' excesses (antithetically) reinforces the status of the domestic. In order for the middle-class family to construct itself – however unsuccessfully – as the site of respectability and emotional security, it must construct danger, excitement, and thrill as degraded otherness. It may be that this act of exclusion encourages us to produce an "other domestic" out of the outrageousness of soap operas, an identity-in-difference that is nothing other than a negative symbiosis with that which we "reject" in our social practices and yearnings. The limits we feel are necessary to the social formation may be simultaneously, at the level of our imagination, an impetus to fantasy. Do we use soaps as our own Petit Guignol, the very attributes and actions that horrify us become exotic costumes we can try on in order to play out the disorders of our own situation.[42] The blandness that makes a soap opera character appear "unrealistic" is in fact nothing other than the critical negation of the "outrageousness," the "colorfulness," and the "madness" upon which the legitimacy of domestic life is partially dependent, the structural inversion of our ordinary daily experience.

Peter Brooks writes that nineteenth-century theatrical melodrama constantly reached toward a sublimity of expression, maintaining a state of exaltation, where hyperbole became the "natural" form of expression because anything less would convey only the apparent, banal drama, not the "true" moral drama.[43] Perhaps the excesses of the daily soap opera broadcast might also be seen as a form of emphasis, markings of intensity, italicized versions of the real. New soaps, or an unfamiliar soap opera, at first seem almost tongue-in-cheek, so excessive that they might be a parody.[44] However, generally once we become involved with the stories and the characters, the excess is no longer so laughable.[45] Daytime soap operas are so conventionalized that viewers know what to expect when they tune in. We are not so much spectators awaiting a *coup de théâtre*, as we are watching to see the familiar happen. And we have a good idea what will happen. The conventions of soap opera storytelling are so strong that we can hardly say that we are watching to see *what* will happen. Rather, we watch anticipating what we know will happen once again and to see *how* it will happen this time, a bundling together of memories and expectation. Like little Alice's White Queen, we remember best the things that happened the week after next.[46]

Between the time we realize what story this is (and thus what will happen) and the time it does happen, a lively anticipation imbues the happenings. All that happens, happens as though conventional happenings were certainly following. Though things to come are not yet, we still have an expectation of them in our mind, an expectation that acts as a structuring presence. Perhaps much of the satisfaction comes from the excitement produced by waiting? That is, the pleasure is not in knowing, but in the process of knowing, in experiencing the new telling of what is recognized as the same old story. There is a to and fro between an excess – which catches the imagination and almost seems to wink at the viewer – and the knowledge that it will, eventually, settle down to a more ordinary and predictable probability. One pulls against and expands the limits of the other.

If, as Audre Lorde put it, "we have been raised to fear the *yes* within ourselves,"[47] if desire pulls us toward self-denial, then perhaps watching soap operas offers us the possibility to explore the tensions between our own finiteness and our longing to push our limits. Perhaps soap operas' constant state of exaltation exhorts the world to live up to our impassioned expectations of it. We are able to provide ourselves with our own space, an elsewhere of our own pleasure and will. Rather than denying values and feelings, watching soaps is the act which carries them to their limits, where the "yes" inside us reverberates, implicating and questioning everything, in a scintillating world, a world without shadow and twilight, a world where the divine functions.

LOUISE SPENCE

Notes

1 This essay is part of a larger work, a much broader study of watching US daytime soap operas. In it, I use ethnographic methods to investigate the pleasures and displeasures of watching and talking about soaps. I would like to express my appreciation to the viewers who have given me so much of their time and their feelings. When it comes to acknowledging my debts, I am moved by how much this seems to be a collective inquiry. Parts of this essay were presented at the Columbia Seminar on Cinema and Interdisciplinary Interpretation, in NYC, in 1992; and sections were presented at "Consol(e)ing Passions: Television, Video and Feminism," at the University of Iowa in 1992. In 1989, earlier versions of the research were presented at the Florida State University's Fourteenth Annual Conference on Literature and Film and the Speech Communication Association's Doctoral Honors Seminar at the University of Georgia.

2 "Emphasis Added: Plots and Plausibility in Women's Fiction," in Elaine Showalter (ed.), *The New Feminist Criticism: Essays on Women, Literature and Theory* (New York: Pantheon, 1985), p. 339.

3 As in, for example, Samuel Richardson's original preface to *Pamela*. On the phenomenon in seventeenth- and early eighteenth-century novels, see Lennard J. Davis's "A Social History of Fact and Fiction: Authorial Disavowal in the Early English Novel," in Edward W. Said (ed.), *Literature and Society* (Baltimore, Md.: Johns Hopkins University Press, 1980).

4 As quoted in Michael Denning's *Mechanic Accents: Dime Novels and Working Class Culture in America* (London: Verso, 1987), p. 200. Denning notes that, although little is known of Richardson, it seems that she was of a middle-class background and didn't share the culture of the other workers (ibid., p. 197). Originally written in 1905, Richardson's *The Long Day: The Story of a New York Working Girl* is reprinted in William O'Neill (ed.), *Women at Work* (New York: Times Books, 1972).

5 *The Melodramatic Imagination: Balzac, Henry James, Melodrama and the Mode of Excess* (New Haven, Conn.: Yale University Press, 1976), p. 21.

6 See Christian Metz's *Film Language: A Semiotics of the Cinema* (New York: Oxford University Press, 1974), p. 18, on the "doubly temporal sequence" of narrative which "invents one time scheme in terms of another;" and Gérard Genette's *Narrative Discourse: An Essay in Method* (Ithaca, NY: Cornell University Press, 1980), p. 34, on the "pseudo-time" of the text, which metonymically borrows "with a combination of reservation and acquiescence" from the reading time.

7 School-age children are more likely to be watching in the summer months.

8 These stories, no matter how sympathetic to the life of homeless people, however, did not investigate or expose the social roots of the problem. They used the problem as a setting for more conventional plots. For example, the homeless woman Brooke befriended (as a journalist writing about the shelter) turned out to be her long-lost mother, and Jack Abbott, sentenced to work time in a shelter, fell in love with the shelter's director (*All My Children*, spring 1986, and *The Young and the Restless*, fall 1986, respectively). The *Capitol* story about the unauthorized implant explored the doctor's personal motivation and the personal repercussions, not medical regulation or institutional policy.

9 Jeremy G. Butler discusses the "ambiguities" of the character/performer relationship in chapter 7 of this collection.

10 August 22, 1987, Rogers plays Maggie Horton. Publicity sometimes assures viewers that performers do not have some of the less than admirable traits that

194

their characters exhibit. The December 26, 1987 *TV Guide*, for example, wrote that Ilene Kristen who played the flighty, childish, manipulative, outrageous Delia on *Ryan's Hope* was more caring off-camera and spent three days a week visiting children in welfare hotels.

11 See, for instance *TV Guide*'s August 29, 1987 issue, which announced that the two were married and suggested, "Maybe that's why their love scenes seem so convincing" (p. 28).

12 July 2, 1987.

13 *Soap Opera Digest*, November 15, 1988, p. 70. *Soap Opera Digest* is published biweekly and is sold by subscription, in supermarket checkout racks, and at newsstands. With a circulation of almost 1.5 million (estimated by the Audit Bureau of Circulation, December 1989), it was, at the time of this research, the most widely read of the US soap opera fan magazines.

14 *Soap Opera Digest*, (October 4, 1988), p. 96. The questions included:

> Do you ever get ideas about how to conduct your own personal romances from watching the ones on soaps? Have you ever dealt with a problem that a soap couple had to deal with and dealt with it the same way? Do you think you handle your own romantic problems and challenges better than most soap characters? Do you get ideas for romantic settings, clothing, presents, dinners or surprises from watching soaps?

As an indication of the pervasiveness of this discourse, see Herta Herzog's 1944 essay, "What Do We Really Know about Daytime Serial Listeners?" in Paul Lazarsfeld and Frank Stanton (eds), *Radio Research, 1942–1943* (reprinted, New York: Arno Press, 1979, p. 25, where she claimed that the listeners in her study looked to radio soap operas as an important source of advice.

15 *Soap Opera Digest* (December 13, 1988), pp. 20–24.

16 August 5–9, 1991. I am grateful to Krin Gabbard for drawing my attention to these episodes. In the New York City area, the spot was included among ads inviting viewers to dial free 800 numbers to join Jenny Craig's "Introductory Weight Loss Program" or to become a Sprint Priority Customer, and such other 900 enterprises as your personal daily horoscope.

17 *Soap Opera Digest* (December 13, 1988), p. 22. Of course, this ellision of fiction and reality is not unique to soap operas or soap opera viewers. The day that I was writing this part, I turned the radio on to get the weather forecast and tuned in to Jeffrey Lyons's review of a Canadian animated film, *The Man Who Planted Trees*. Lyons opened by saying that the film "tells the story, which I hope is true, of a man who . . ." The next piece was an ad for a Channel 2 news special report on Soviet spying which began, "You've seen it in James Bond movies, you've read about it in spy novels, tonight you'll see the real thing, startling undercover footage of a Soviet agent spying in your own back yard . . ." Later, investigative reporter Jack Anderson's novel, *Control*, "a story written from tomorrow's headlines," was advertised with the tag line "based on a truth so frightening it had to be fictionalized to tell it" (CBS Radio, November 2, 1988). The implication in all of these examples is that knowledge of life is to be learned from fiction, and that our knowledge of real life contributes to our understanding of fiction. In some cases, the fictions may even throw the very definition of reality into question.

18 *Magazine & Bookseller* (January 1983), p. 16, emphasis in original.

19 Interview, January 16, 1986.

20 All quotes are from the February 1989 issue of *Daytime TV*. Spelling, punctuation, and capitalization thus in original.

21 Ibid., p. 45. Correspondence with the company indicated that there was not much interest in the venture at that time. Recent work by Henry Jenkins and Constance Penley on fan writing of *Star Trek* stories raises some interesting questions on what sorts of narratives and modes of spectatorship seem more open to this type of input. See, for example Jenkins's "Star Trek Rerun, Reread, and Rewritten: Fan Writing as Textual Poaching," *Critical Studies in Mass Communications* 5 (2) (1988); and Penley's presentation of research to the Columbia Seminar on Cinema and Interdisciplinary Interpretation, Museum of Modern Art, New York City (February 1990).

22 "The Uncanny" (1919), *Studies in Parapsychology* (New York: Collier, 1971), p. 41.

12 "The Paths to the Formation of Symptoms" (1917), in *Introductory Lectures on Psychoanalysis* (New York: W. W. Norton, 1977), p. 368.

24 "Of Other Peoples: Beyond the 'Salvage Paradigm,'" transcription of a discussion in the Dia Art Foundation's *Discussions of Contemporary Culture*, edited by Hal Foster (Seattle, Wash.: Bay Press, 1987), p. 140. Trinh is speaking specifically about the production of differences between the "First World" and "Third World."

25 As Trinh suggests about "sameness" and "otherness," ibid.

26 *The Act of Reading* (Baltimore, Md.: Johns Hopkins University Press, 1978), p. 70.

27 Robert Musil, *The Man Without Qualities* (New York: Capricorn Books, 1965), p. 11. He goes on to elaborate,

> A possible experience or a possible truth does not equate to real experience or a real truth minus the value 'real'; but, at least in the opinion of its devotees, it has in it something out-and-out divine, a fiery, soaring quality, a constructive will, a conscious utopianism that does not shrink from reality but treats it, on the contrary, as a mission and an invention."
>
> (p. 12)

28 Different disciplines have different views on naming informants. Issues of privacy, confidentiality, and rapport are involved along with the political aspects of identity. Although many of the ideas and feelings that were expressed by the women I interviewed are shared by others, I have not assumed that they wished them openly conveyed. In formal interviews, I asked the interviewee whether, if I happened to refer to her or quote her in my writing, she would like me to use her name or not. Many later read a draft of my work and I reconfirmed permission to use comments. I have conformed to their wishes and used names where they requested and left out names where they preferred.

29 *Narratology: Introduction to the Theory of Narrative* (Toronto: University of Toronto Press, 1985), p. 10.

30 Of course, the rebelliousness of viewers must not appear too evident in the halls of the networks. Ironically, although the mass-market nature of soap operas makes viewer involvement a necessity, an ideal of passivity and conformity, and the comfortable myth that the viewer is under the thumb of the sponsor is the major operating restraint ("the reality") of the institution.

31 As, for example, when *One Life to Live*'s Erika Slezak, or her character, the sweet family-oriented Viki Buchanan, advertises prunes. Or when the actor who plays Benny Sago on *All My Children* appears in a pizza commercial, still in his vaguely ethnic, working-class guise. Colleen Casey, while playing the whole-

some Faren (on *The Young and the Restless*), starred in a cream of wheat commercial, portraying the woman in the commercial in such a corresponding way that it almost seemed like Faren was endorsing the product. The performer's fictive persona and the strong performer/character association has been used to advantage in a series of commercials where a soap opera actor (Peter Bergman of *All My Children*, for example), in his white jacket costume as one of the serial's doctors, recommends the use of Vick's® cough syrup by confessing, "I'm not really a doctor, but I play one on TV. And when you have a cold at home, you often play doctor, too." This advertising campaign has been discussed by both Jeremy Butler (op. cit.); and Mimi White in "Ideological Analysis and Television," in Robert C. Allen (ed.), *Channels of Discourse: Television and Contemporary Criticism* (Chapel Hill, NC: University of North Carolina Press, 1987).

32 "The In-Difference of Television," *Screen 28* (2) (spring 1987), p. 42.

33 In an interview quoted in the *Village Voice* (October 11, 1988), *As the World Turns*'s head writer, Doug Marland, tallking about a new gay character on the show, said, "For a lot of people in the audience, Hank may be the first gay person they'll come to know."

34 There are not only differences between viewers and between interpretations, but also sometimes within viewers.

35 As do, for example, Robert Cathcart, "Our Soap Opera Friends," in Gary Gumpert and Robert Cathcart (eds), *Intermedia: Interpersonal Communication in a Media World* (New York: Oxford University Press, 1986), p. 217; and Ruth Rosen, "Soap Operas: Search for Yesterday," in Todd Gitlin (ed.), *Watching Television* (New York: Pantheon, 1986), p. 45.

36 What the French call a *volupté des larmes*.

37 See Sheila Page Bayne's *Tears and Weeping: An Aspect of Emotional Climate Reflected in Seventeenth-Century French Literature* (Tübingen: Gunter Narr Verlag, 1981), pp. 55–56.

38 *Soap Opera Digest* (October 18, 1988); the passages quoted are on pages 13 and 14, respectively. These letters may have been edited "for style and brevity," as the magazine maintains is their right. I quote them not as pure testimony, but as part of the discourse surrounding soap opera viewing which fan magazines help to create as well as perpetuate.

39 *S/Z* (New York, Hill and Wang, 1974), p. 90.

40 Sigmund Freud, "The Relation of the Poet to Day-Dreaming" (1908), *On Creativity and the Unconscious* (New York: Harper & Row, 1958), p. 47.

41 Cora Kaplan notes that romantic and sexual fantasies shouldn't be seen simply as the mark of our subordination, because they are always simultaneously the mark of our humanity: "*The Thorn Birds*: fiction, fantasy, femininity," in Victor Burgin, James Donald, and Cora Kaplan (eds), *Formations of Fantasy* (London: Methuen, 1986), pp. 149–150.

42 See Peter Stallybrass and Allon White's *The Politics and Poetics of Transgression* (Ithaca, NY: Cornell University Press, 1986), p. 200.

43 *The Melodramatic Imagination*, p. 40.

44 Over the years there have been many actual parodies of soap operas such as the television serials *Soap* and *Mary Hartman, Mary Hartman*, Carol Burnett's sketch "As the Stomach Turns," and skits on Nickelodeon and *SCTV*.

45 Although it is possible that even after becoming involved in the stories, there will be some moments that, for some viewers at least, still provoke irony and distance.

46 "'What sort of things do *you* remember best?' Alice ventured to ask. 'O, things that happened the week after next,'" Lewis Caroll, *Through the Looking*

Glass, in Martin Gardner's *The Annotated Alice* (New York: Bramhall House, 1960) p. 248.

47 Audre Lorde, *Sister Outsider* (Trumansburg, NY: The Crossing Press, 1984), p. 57.

10

"There's a queer in my soap!"
The homophobia/AIDS story-line of
One Life to Live

Joy V. Fuqua

Soap Opera Digest lists ten things that you will never see on a daytime soap opera:

1 Nudity
2 Homosexual Kissing
3 Cruelty to Animals
4 Abortion Without Disaster
5 A Dentist
6 Women With Runs in Their Stockings
7 Characters with "Personal Problems" [such as jock itch]
8 Old People in Nursing Homes
9 The Weekend
10 Heroines Who Smoke[1]

What is interesting about the list, besides the fact that viewers will never have the opportunity to see Erica Kane floss her teeth as she whips a French poodle, is the positioning of homosexuality or its synedoche, "homosexual kissing." The placement of "homosexual kissing" between "nudity" and "cruelty to animals" suggests that "cruelty to animals" is more acceptable an image than the dread representation of "clothed" same sex desire, and that the latter is somehow safer than full-scale "heterosexual" nudity. The reluctance to represent homosexuality and homosexual desire needs to be examined in relation to conventional soap opera narrative structure, institutional pressures, and the various contexts of reception.

In "Out of the Mainstream: Sexual Minorities and the Mass Media," Larry Gross argues that the appearance of gay men and lesbians is "inherently problematic and controversial for the mass media" and that when gay or lesbian characters *do* appear in mainstream media, the focus is consistently "on the heterosexual characters and their reactions" (Gross 1991: 130). Further, Gross suggests that when gay or lesbian characters *are* represented by mainstream media, they are always "defined by their 'problem.'" In other

199

words, the "social issue" which is addressed by the particular televisual text is precisely their identity as gay male or lesbian characters. As a result, the representation of the social issue of homosexuality is dependent upon the ways in which the character "embodies" his or her sexual identity.

When Gross argues for a critique of mainstream media in relation to the representation of gay men and lesbians, his article is indebted to the debate over positive v. negative imagery or the role of the "stereotype."[2] In fact, much of the theoretical work which has addressed the question of gay/lesbian representation in and by specifically mainstream media has been framed by a discussion of positive/negative imagery and the either liberatory or damning effects of figures such as the "flexible" C. J. Lamb (*L.A. Law*) or campy Dwayne and Antoine (*In Living Color*'s "Men on Film"). Frequently, the discourse of positive imagery leaves little room for contradiction, for negotiation, or for an analysis of the complex ways in which these popular images circulate and are received by viewers. This, of course, is not to say that the critique of positive/negative imagery should be abandoned and replaced with another evaluative model. Rather, it is a question of recognizing how the discourse of positive imagery contributes to the production of common-sense readings of gays and lesbians in popular media.

When considering the specificity of daytime television soap opera and its structural and institutional imperative to maintain legitimacy by presenting timely narratives through the (now conventional) social issue story-line, one must account for the ways the particular "problem" of homosexuality is then embodied as a social issue. That is, the television soap opera form, generically speaking, has long accommodated specific social issues such as incest, alcoholism, abortion, rape, homosexuality, and, most recently, AIDS. Conventionally, the *issue du jour* is introduced to the soap opera community (Pine Valley, Llanview, Oakdale, etc.) through the arrival of a new and oftentimes marginal or peripheral character. Soap operas deploy tentative story-lines through the introduction of these marginal characters so that if the narratives prove too problematic, the new character(s) can be written off or redirected. By tying problematic social issues to marginal characters, soaps, in comparison to other television narratives, are able to "openly" embrace daring issues. As Robert C. Allen states:

> It is precisely this openness that has enabled the soap opera to give the appearance of normative daring without embracing anything other than normative values. A soap opera might deal with interracial marriage, abortion, incest, homosexuality, child abuse, or some other controversial issue, but any threatening values connected with those issues are attached to particular characters, who can be disposed of or attitudinally "defused."

(1985: 171)

However, a character's marginality should be understood as more than just a narrative symptom; marginal positionality may be representative of structural and institutional concerns for positive audience response. Hence, although the social issue story-lines of soap operas have historically spoken from a didactic and oftentimes classically liberal humanist position, the teaching of "tolerance" of race, class, and recently sexuality, has always been tempered by the constant, material necessity to sell advertisers' products to the target audience of 7 million women 18–49 years of age.[3]

Although conventional soap opera narrative codes generally use marginal characters to introduce taboo social issues, these characters are occasionally made a permanent part of the soap opera community if the problematic issue can be "disembodied" or, rather, "detached," from the character. For instance, the social issue of the "wanton woman" remains a favorite narrative device and adequately illustrates the ability of problematic issues to be detached from characters.

Of the many available examples on every soap, let's take the characters of Donna Tyler and, more recently, nurse Gloria Marsh from ABC's *All My Children*. Both characters were "redeemed" through disembodiment; that is, Donna's life of prostitution ended with her marriage to one of the prominent, wealthy male characters (Dr Chuck Tyler), and nurse Gloria Marsh was "redeemed" from her partnership with con man Craig Lawson by a romance with Stuart Chandler and subsequent marriage to Adam Chandler. Thus, heterosexual marriage and class mobility provided the means by which "social issues" (such as prostitution represented by Donna and her former pimp Billy Clyde Tuggle) can be dissociated from characters. And, even though both Donna and Gloria were introduced as marginal characters, through the negation of controversial social issues, they attained core character status.

In contrast, homosexuality as a social issue is so uniquely tied to the marginal character (and in fact constitutes the identity of that character) such that the problem of "gay sexuality" can never be disembodied from that same marginal character. Tania Modleski indicates that there are only certain social issues which can be represented on daytime soap operas:

> As a rule, only those issues which can be tolerated and ultimately pardoned are introduced on soap operas. The list includes careers for women, abortions, premarital and extramarital sex, alcoholism, divorce, mental and even physical cruelty. An issue like homosexuality, which could explode the family structure rather than temporarily disrupt it, is simply ignored.
>
> (1990: 93)

While it may be compelling to argue for the potentially disruptive power of homosexual characters in relation to conventional soap opera narrative structure (which is dependent upon the assumed and taken-for-granted heterosexuality of the particular community), it would be shortsighted to say that the mere representation of homosexual characters and of homosexuality is adequate to threaten narrative structure. I would add this qualification to Modleski's argument: it is not the case that homosexuality is not represented, nor is it even a matter of the prohibition of a "homosexual kiss." On the contrary, the "homosexual kiss" and homosexuality more generally have been and are represented, but only after they have been sanitized, so to speak, for the viewer's protection.[4] As Mandy Merck says with regard to the narrativization of homosexuality and AIDS in relation to popular fiction, it is not necessarily the case that homosexuality consistently threatens narrative or heterosexual "familial" conventions: "I write 'can' threaten . . . in uneasy recognition of recent attempts by post-AIDS authors like David Leavitt to *suburbanize* the gay novel, maintaining its object choice while domesticating its stories and settings" (1993: 45).[5] This is to say that the representation of homosexuality, and I would argue of AIDS, on daytime soap opera is a conditional and qualified one. What needs to be accounted for are the conditions which delimit and proscribe the circulation of particular representations of homosexuality and AIDS and the ways in which these images are received.

It is important to note that while AIDS has wrongly been situated in the public imaginary as virtually synonymous with male homosexuality, these two social problems have historically received quite different treatment on daytime soap operas. As far as the history of the ways in which soap opera has addressed HIV/AIDS, the "face of AIDS" has been dominated by the image of the heterosexual, white, middle- to upper-class female who happens to contract HIV from former intravenous drug-using husbands, embodied through the character of Cindy from *All My Children*.[6] To date, there has been practically no attempt to address homosexuality in relation to AIDS on a soap opera.[7]

The dissociation of homosexuality from AIDS emphasizes the ways in which AIDS both is and is not a "gay disease." However, I do not believe that through this gesture of dissociation of homosexuality from AIDS, soap operas are somehow being "progressive" (that is, preventing the all too often synonymous linkage of AIDS and gay men) or more "accurate" according to epidemiological statistics. Rather, soap operas have gone out of their way to avoid and/or disembody gay men with AIDS while consistently deploying the convention of the "innocent victim." While I certainly acknowledge the problematics of maintaining the linkage between gay men and AIDS, it is likewise as important and necessary to not deny or erase the history of this pandemic, nor the continued loss of both gay and straight lives. The consistent absence of gay HIV positive characters on soap operas has resulted in the conventional and sanitized way in which AIDS is and can be represented on daytime television. Interestingly enough, the reverse is the case in relation to the HIV serostatus of soap opera *actors*: *As the World Turns* actor Joe Breen (Scott) was "outed" as HIV positive by the *National*

Enquirer, but has apparently received support from the soap opera as well as from fans.

The complex and oftentimes convoluted ways in which AIDS is and is not associated with gay men on daytime television can be seen by turning to the Margo rape story-line on *As the World Turns*. This 1992 award-winning story-line focuses on the central character of Margo, a white, heterosexual police detective who is raped by a man who is HIV positive.[8] The story-line sets a six-month time period within which Margo faces the results of the HIV antibody test. Given Margo's positioning within a heterosexual, assumed monogamous relationship, the HIV testing procedure is terminated after one or two negative results. However, during this testing period (drawn out as is conventional with soap opera time), Margo attends weekly group counseling meetings for people who are HIV positive. At a counseling session, Margo befriends an HIV positive man and accompanies him to a hospital room as he visits his gay lover who has an undisclosed AIDS-related illness. As Margo's new friend approaches his lover's bedside, he leans over and kisses him on the forehead. So, one might then ask: when is a kiss considered to be "homosexual?" Can this gesture not be read and recognized as a "homo-sexual kiss?" When and under what circumstances is AIDS represented through homosexual characters?

I would argue that the representation of the "homosexual kiss," in the above instance, is only rendered visible under certain conditions which call for it to be situated within the context of HIV disease and the potential gesture of compassion as it is offered through the *mise-en-scène* of the hospital AIDS care unit. The representation of homosexual kisses on both daytime and prime-time soaps is either sanitized through *mise-en-scène* (the sterile context of the hospital) or suspended via strategic cut-aways.[9] Thus, in the following pages, I will raise questions about the "risk" of representing gay male sexuality and its "corollary," AIDS, as exemplified by yet another soap opera: ABC's *One Life to Live* and the 1992 homophobia/AIDS story-line.

During the summer of the Democratic and Republican National Conven-tions, *One Life to Live* represented the issues of AIDS, gay sexuality, and homophobia. This story-line was named in different ways depending upon the particular production or reception contexts. That is, the writers of *One Life to Live* named the story "The Accusation," while fans called it "The Billy Douglas Story" or the "Virginia Douglas Story," and the Soap Opera Digest Award Show, which nominated it for the 1992 Best Social Issue Story-line called it "Homophobia in Llanview."[10]

The story-line centers around two characters and the struggles within their particular families: Rev. Andrew Carpenter and the gay teenager Billy Douglas. The AIDS portion of the story-line deals with Rev. Carpenter and his efforts to force his homophobic father, retired General Sloan Carpenter, to come to terms with and accept the AIDS-related death of the Reverend's gay brother, William. General Carpenter remains steadfast in his rejection of

William's gayness and death until Rev. Carpenter brings the NAMES Project AIDS Memorial Quilt to Llanview. At the display of the quilt, Rev. Carpenter and his brother's surviving lover present a dedicatory panel. General Carpenter watches as his son places the panel in the larger structure of the quilt and, in a moment of cathartic grief, allows himself to feel the loss of his dead, gay son. Thus, through the affective power of the quilt, the father is redeemed and reunited with both sons.

The homophobia half of the story-line focuses on Billy Douglas, a non-sexually active gay teenager, and his relationship with his family and with Rev. Carpenter. The town "wanton woman," Marty Saybrooke (who happens to be in love with the Reverend), overhears Billy tell Rev. Carpenter that he is gay. Marty then deceives Billy's parents and tells them that Rev. Carpenter seduced their son. Upholding the principle of privacy, Rev. Carpenter refuses to clear his name of the accusation of his alleged "homosexuality," while Billy publicly declares his gayness and defends Rev. Carpenter from false charges. Mr Douglas refuses to believe that Billy is gay and finally "disowns" him. Billy subsequently moves into the home of his best friend, Joey Buchanan, thus coming as close as he possibly can to "core character" status by literally inhabiting the domestic space of the core family of the soap opera.

At the center of the narrative, then, are two sets of relationships between sons and fathers: Rev. Carpenter and General Carpenter are reunited through the quilt and the shared remembrance of William, while Billy Douglas and his father are separated due to intransigent homophobia. However, while the Rev. Carpenter, father/son drama achieved a mini-closure through resolution at the NAMES Project AIDS Memorial Quilt, the relationship between Billy and his father continued to deteriorate and eventually was allowed to fade from view. That is, the homophobia story-line, at least in terms of Billy, was not resolved or closed but rather, it was abandoned. Presumably, the Douglases still exist as part of the community of Llanview, albeit as completely peripheral and tangential characters.

However, I argue that the sheer presence of a gay character, in this instance Billy Douglas, is enough to cause a type of generic pressure upon the most elemental of the soap opera codes. In particular, the peripheral positioning of Billy as a character specifically developed for this story-line emphasizes the limitations and constraints upon the representability of gayness in relation to the basic generic conventions of soap opera. That is, most often in soap opera the action of the narrative has to involve main, core characters. The implications of representing gay male sexuality and homophobia through the device of a peripheral gay character suggest that these issues are not a continuing part of the narrative of the soap opera. That is, once Billy Douglas is gone, there is no more gay male sexuality nor is there any more homophobia.

But, another struggle which occurs at the *generic* or aesthetic level points to the representational necessity of the peripheral positioning of the gay male character. In terms of the larger narrative structure of the soap opera, Billy's non-core position is one of the factors which enables gay sexuality to be represented at all. However, due to the fact that Billy Douglas was not a core character and that the homophobia story-line was then not a core story-line, the issue of homophobia could not be incorporated permanently into the existing narratives of the soap opera. And, Billy as a peripheral character was lost, for all intents and purposes, after the summer's story-line ceased.

The risk of representing gay male sexuality in terms of the story-line of *One Life to Live*, then, raises contradictions not only on a generic level. The perceived risk of gay male sexuality also affects the institutional or network levels of production. On the institutional level, there was an apparent structural antagonism between the interests of the network and the strategies of the producers and writers. This structural antagonism can be understood as an institutional struggle over the setting of the terms through which gay male sexuality could be represented. The network ensured that the representation of a peripheral gay character would not be read as offensive and thus cause loss of audience and advertising revenues. In defiance of network sensitivity about the representation of homosexuality, the producers and writing staff had originally storyboarded a core character as gay.

During an interview at ABC studios, New York City, the institutional struggle was described in these terms: "The idea for the homophobia storyline came from headwriter Michael Malone who wanted to produce a gay character. His first idea was to make Joey Buchanan gay. But the network didn't think that was a great idea."[11] Presumably, the network was hesitant about having Joey Buchanan as the gay character because the Buchanans are the core, main family of *One Life to Live*. The representation of gay sexuality would have been automatically moved from the narrative's periphery to the very center of the soap opera. The network was then faced with the possibility of having to deal in a more substantial and, more importantly, *sustained* manner with the issue of gay male sexuality and potential "homosexual kisses." Joey Buchanan's gayness could not be easily written off or placed on hold in the same way as a non-core or peripheral character most certainly could be abandoned or terminated at the end of a story-line. And, it must be remembered that what is also at stake, as far as the network is concerned, is advertising revenue or economics. That is, one cannot simply argue that it was a completely ideological decision on the part of the network not to produce a core gay character.[12] The network had a particular idea of the audience in mind when they vetoed the production of the core gay character story-line. And, in this case, the network's concept of the taste of the viewers was radically different from the ways in which *One Life to Live*'s producers and writers had imagined it. However, even if the writers and producers lost on their idea for the core gay character, at the very least they placed Billy

205

Douglas as close as possible to the core family by making Billy the best friend of Joey Buchanan.

Embedded within the institutional struggle over the representability of the figure of the gay male is an implicit conception of viewership, of reception, from the perspective of both the network and the producers/writers of *One Life to Live*. From the producer's point of view, as exemplified by program executive Robyn Goodman, it is necessary to first account for the intertextual context within which the story-line was produced and received. That is, in order to problematize the context of reception of the summer 1992 story-line which explicitly addressed homophobia, it is productive to situate the soap opera in relation to the televisual event of unbridled hatred and homophobia which was represented by the Republican National Convention. Goodman and executive producer of *One Life to Live*, Linda Gottlieb, understand their production of the AIDS/homophobia story-line very much in *activist* terms; that is, when Goodman describes the work of the story-line, she situates the production in relation to the spectacle of Republican homophobia and the potential critique of homophobia provided by *One Life to Live*.[13] Goodman describes the intertextual relation between the story-line and the Republican convention in these terms:

> I was very proud of the storyline when I saw that convention. It was one of the most horrific things that I have ever seen in this country . . . . People make fun of daytime but that was a very courageous story and an important story . . . . On the whole in this country there is so much hate-mongering going on and fear and homophobia. Linda Gottlieb said she wanted to speak out early on and say "this will not do" . . . I wish Gottlieb could do the same story again on prime time. I think it's incredibly important and I don't think that television is addressing homophobia at all.[14]

Goodman, then, places the story-line and the work of *One Life to Live* within specific relation to the homophobic spectacle of the Republican convention and understands her work in terms of a specific and timely intervention. She critiques the notion that daytime television is somehow less than prime time with a reading of the potential affective power of daytime to intervene – at the level of production and reception – in the perpetuation and circulation of homophobia. It is important to understand that Goodman, Linda Gottlieb as executive producer, and head writer Michael Malone, all consider themselves to be informed by a political position which is committed, in whatever way this is possible, to a critique of homophobia from *within* the institution of television. As ABC Daytime president, Mary Alice Dwyer-Dobbin, said with regard to the ironic simultaneity of the broadcast of Pat Buchanan's address to the Republican National Convention and the screening of the AIDS/homophobia story-line by network executives, "I would like Pat Buchanan to see the shows."[15]

The reception of *One Life to Live*'s story-line was "overwhelmingly positive," according to head writer Michael Malone, and he describes the power of fans to, in fact, rewrite the story-line to fit their particular readings:

> Though we had originally considered [Rev. Carpenter] to be at the center of the storyline, we were amazed to find that it was not considered to be "the accusation" story but, rather that it was becoming "The Billy Douglas Story" and the "Virginia Douglas Story" [Billy's mother]. Characters that were to us originally simply catalysts took on something more – through the power of Billy Douglas's predicament, his courage was so strong that it moved to the center of story.[16]

Interviewed in *Soap Opera NOW!*, actor Wortham Krimmer (Rev. Andrew Carpenter) offered these comments on his role as well as fan response:

> That storyline was like a gift. There was an amazing audience response. I'm still sifting through letters and so many of the letters just demanded handwritten responses. I feel like the ordinary man who was put into extraordinary circumstances . . . . My role was small but it really felt good to play a role, no matter how small in something that was obviously very relevant in having a major impact on the audience.[17]

The gay press also covered the story-line and one magazine, New York City's now defunct *QW*, even included a weekly update on young Billy's trials and tribulations: "Recognizing that some members of the gay community may work for a living and have been missing the remarkable storyline on *One Life to Live*, 'Q-in' [the column] will provide weekly peeks at what's been percolating on the ABC daytime soap."[18] The praise from gay and lesbian organizations appears to have been supportive and even revelatory. In fact, the Gay and Lesbian Alliance Against Defamation recognized Ryan Phillipe, the actor who played Billy Douglas, for his efforts.

As evidenced by this letter to *Soap Opera Digest*, the fans wanted the storyline to continue:

> After presenting a well-researched, well-written and timely storyline on homophobia, *One Life to Live* has apparently deserted the character of Billy Douglas. Head writer Michael Malone probably crafted the finest work since joining the program when he addressed gay prejudice. *One Life to Live* has yet to be as enthralling as it was during the summer of 1992. Certainly Billy's life did not end once the AIDS quilt was packed up and shipped away. Malone is doing viewers a great disservice by not opening the next chapter in this character's life.[19]

The fans, particularly as represented by the text of *Soap Opera Digest*, were disappointed that this AIDS/homophobia story-line did not continue. In fact, *Soap Opera Digest* noted Billy's absence by saying that several of the topics which are "out" (so to speak) on daytime soap operas include the representation of gay characters:

It was good while it lasted: Putting the spotlight on *OLTL*'s gay teenager Billy Douglas (Ryan Phillippe) did wonders for *OLTL*'s image and AIDS awareness, but now that the tale's been told, where is Billy? Even Joey (Christopher McKenna) rarely talks about his friend.[20]

Interestingly enough, the trendy "in" social issue for soaps includes AIDS awareness – but specifically through *heterosexual* characters:

Soaps do their part to raise AIDS awareness, and *As the World Turns* is at the forefront. Memorial Hospital established an AIDS unit (funded by annual AIDS balls), and the soap is telling the story of Dawn Wheeler (Lisa Emery), an HIV-positive single mom who can't get health insurance and is struggling to raise her son, Jerry (Sam Rovin). *One Life to Live* rolled out the AIDS quilt to dramatize the epidemic's impact, and *All My Children*'s Stuart wears a red ribbon to honor his wife, Cindy, who died of AIDS.[21]

In fact, it seems that one of the most acceptable ways in which AIDS is signified on soap opera is through the wearing of the red ribbon as a signifier of compassion and of absence or loss.

Billy Douglas as a gay character has, for the most part, disappeared from *One Life to Live*, but he was brought back to the show for an interesting conjunctural moment: the "AIDS Awareness" day observed by all of the network soap operas. On this day, June 21, 1993, the ABC, CBS, and NBC soap operas were asked to address the social issue of AIDS in some way – most of the address took the form of the red ribbon pinned to the lapel of actors such as Scott and Dr Bob Hughes from *As the World Turns*.[22] However, with the exception of this brief reappearance, Billy Douglas will, in all likelihood, not be making any more encore appearances – at least he will not be played by the same actor, Ryan Phillipe. Evidently, the gay teen/ homophobia story-line was causing some difficulty for Phillipe:

Although viewers saw them [Billy and his boyfriend, Rick] do little more than dine out, *OLTL* had planned to push the envelope further by sending the duo on a double date with straight teen Joey Buchanan (Chris McKenna) and a girl. These (and future) plans were dashed when Phillipe – who, according to sources on the set, was extremely un-comfortable with the gay theme – took a role on NBC's prime-time soap miniseries *The Secrets of Lake Success*.[23]

And according to *One Life to Live* head writer, Michael Malone, the potential risk of continuing the Billy Douglas portion of the story-line was simply too much for the conventions of daytime television to handle: "It's one thing to explore homophobia. It's quite another to explore the life of a gay couple – a life that includes sex and such problems as whether or not to adopt children. I doubt that day will come."[24] Therefore, it is the representation of the "everyday" in relation to gay characters which causes the difficulty for soap opera. Gay characters can certainly be represented, but only in terms of the sexuality-as-a-problem paradigm. So, Billy Douglas made his final curtain call (at least as played by Ryan Phillipe) while Llanview turned its social conscience to other pressing issues such as rape as represented by the Marty Saybrooke/Kappa Alpha Delta fraternity story-line of summer 1993.

Notes

1 Robert Rorke, "Ten Things You'll Never See On a Soap," *Soap Opera Digest* (December 8, 1992), pp. 74–78.
2 In relation to the representations of gay men and lesbians by the popular media, one of the most persistent forms of critique of these images has concentrated on alleged oppositions between "positive" or "negative" versions of homosexuality or of the non-representative and even damaging aspects of the "stereotype." This "images of" analysis, however, falls short at a crucial point, according to Richard Dyer:

> Much image analysis seems only to demonstrate that everything is the same and it's awful. There is something deadly about such reductive work: it tells one little and thus does rather little politically. It is important not to lose the fire of "images of" work but it needs to be tempered by considerations that get more nearly at the complexity and elusiveness, the real political difficulty, of representations.
>
> (1993: 1–2)

As Dyer has also noted, it is not the representation of "positive" or "negative" or "stereotypical" images of gay men and lesbians which *in itself* constitutes a problem. It is, rather, an issue of "who controls and defines them [the images], what interests they serve" (ibid., p. 12).
3 This didactic impulse of television soap opera was emphasized by a group of panelists during a seminar held on July 8, 1993 at the Museum of Television and Radio, New York City, in honor of *One Life to Live*'s twenty-fifth anniversary. The panel consisted of creative personnel including Agnes Nixon, Mary Alice Dwyer-Dobbin, Sr VP, daytime programming, ABC; Linda Gottlieb, executive producer, *OLTL* and Michael Malone, head writer, *OLTL*. Agnes Nixon, the creator of *One Life to Live*, *Loving*, and *All My Children*, emphasized the ways the production staff believe *OLTL* was conceptually different from the other soap operas in the representation of social issues. She said it had been her "desire to take soap opera narrative out of 'WASP Valley' because it was pretty sanitized and white bread."
4 Notwithstanding the fact that during spring/summer 1993, images of lesbian "chicness" appeared on magazine covers at an overwhelming rate (*New York*, *Newsweek*, *Vanity Fair*), the begged question is not whether homosexuality *can* be represented but in what ways is lesbian or gay male sexuality represented through popular media and what knowledges are made available through these "social issues." As a critique of "lesbian chic," see Alexis Jetter, "Goodbye to the Last Taboo," *Vogue* (July 1993). In this article, Jetter questions whether "lesbian chic reflect[s] a New Visibility of the Old Voyeurism" (ibid., p. 86).
5 See Mandy Merck, "A Case of AIDS," in Mandy Merck, *Perversions: Deviant Readings* (London: Virago Press, 1993), pp. 45–61; and Judith Williamson,

"Every Virus Tells A Story," in Erica Carter and Simon Watney (eds), *Taking Liberties: AIDS and Cultural Politics* (London: Serpent's Tail, 1989), pp. 69–81.

6 For an indispensable text addressing the specificity of women and HIV see Cynthia Chris and Monica Pearl (eds), *Women, AIDS, and Activism* (Boston, Mass.: South End Press, 1990).

7 However, AIDS has provided the means by which to remove a character from a soap opera, for example, with the character of Hank in CBS's *As the World Turns*. In a gesture of verisimilitude, Hank was called away from Oakdale so that he might take care of his ill lover who lived in another city.

8 *As the World Turns* won 1992 Best Story-line from the 1992 Soap Opera Awards conducted by *Soap Opera Digest*. It is worth noting that the award was accepted by head writer Douglas Marland just weeks before his death.

9 Homosexual kisses provided moments of narrative disruption during the spring of 1994 with outbursts on *Roseanne* as well as the FOX's Network prime-time soap opera *Melrose Place*. The season finale of *Melrose Place* caused major controversies in relation to the depiction of a gay kiss involving the show's resident gay boy, Matt, and Billy's "best man" Rob. The camera tracked in for an emphatic yet teasing slow-motion close-up of Matt and Rob as their lips almost touched and then quickly cut away to a reaction shot of Billy gazing – appropriately – from between the mini-blinds of his distant window. In this case, the homosexual kiss is framed through the gaze of the heterosexual spectator, Billy, and is represented as *his* crisis of knowledge. As Doug Savant (Matt) says in an interview from the savvy gossip text, *Entertainment Weekly*: "I don't understand the controversy. [The kiss] is very tame. It's more about Billy's reaction to finding out that his best man is gay and he didn't know" (see Alan Carter, "The Hard-Bodied Men of 'Melrose Place' Ponder Life Playing Soft-headed Himbos," *Entertainment Weekly* 223 (May 20, 1994), pp. 12–22).

10 During the 1992 *Soap Opera Digest* awards, two of the nominations for Best Storyline addressed AIDS – *As the World Turns* and *One Life to Live*. Interestingly, though, *OLTL* was not nominated for "Outstanding Drama Series Writing Team," "Outstanding Drama Series," nor for "Outstanding Young Actor" at the 1993 Daytime Emmy Awards. *Soap Opera NOW!* express their dismay at the neglect of *OLTL* with comments such as:

The homophobia storyline was groundbreaking and the AIDS quilt shows were exceptional . . . . what happened to *OLTL*? Surely, Linda Gottlieb did every-thing she could to attract attention, aided by the ABC publicity machine. And it had the shows to back up the hype! Still, no nom . . . *OLTL*'s Ryan Phillippe (Billy) had the storyline with the most visibility and he did an excellent job as a teenager coming to terms with his homosexuality.

(Soap Opera Now! 11 (14) (April 15, 1993) p.2)

11 The source for this statement must remain unnamed due to network sensitivity regarding the representability of gay male sexuality. This information, therefore, cannot be verified. However, the inability to provide accreditation allows the remark to circulate as "rumor" or "gossip" – one of the narrative conventions most closely associated with soap opera.

12 Although it may be the case that the network and program executives may share views concerning the representability of homosexuality and AIDS, the institu-tional positioning of the network executives may very well conflict with their "personal" views.

13 Many of the soap opera publications such as *Soap Opera Digest* and *Soap Opera NOW!* have noted the "theatrical" and often "filmic" style of *OLTL*. And, as a

way of complicating the distinctions between film and television, it is important to note that several of the producers of the soap opera have vast amounts of film and theater experience, including executive producer Linda Gottlieb, who has also been the executive producer of such films as *Dirty Dancing* and Home Box Office's *Citizen Cohn* about the late Roy Cohn (one of the characters featured in Tony Kushner's award-winning *Angels In America*). Also, program executive Robyn Goodman brings many years of avant-garde theater experience to *OLTL*.

14 Robyn Goodman, personal interview, ABC/Capital Cities, New York (October 1992).
15 Dwyer-Dobbin's remarks were made in the context of the ABC network executives' screening of *OLTL*. She was quoted in the August 31, 1992 issue of *Soap Opera NOW!*.
16 Michael Malone, telephone interview, New York/Capital Cities (March 1993).
17 Joanna Coons, "*OLTL*'s Wortham Krimmer Is Just a Country Gent At Heart," *Soap Opera NOW!* (December 21, 1992), pp. 4–5.
18 Andrew Jacobs, "Can't Live Without *One Life*!," *QW* 39 (August 2, 1992), p. 7.
19 Letter, from H. H., Fredericksburg, Virginia, *Soap Opera Digest* (March 3, 1993), p. 191.
20 *Soap Opera Digest* (July 6, 1993), p. 109.
21 Ibid., p. 108.
22 "The Ribbon Project," started in 1991 by the Artist's Caucus of Visual AIDS and now joined by Broadway Cares/Equity Fights AIDS, has achieved fame as a signifier (albeit a controversial one) primarily through televised award shows such as the Academy Awards. And while most soap opera stars are willing to wear a red ribbon and some are especially vocal as well as active in their own participation in the fight against AIDS, *Days Of Our Lives* star Deidre Hall (Marlena) has loudly protested the campaigns of "extremist activists who resort to harassment to compel actors and actresses to wear these ribbons" and concludes that these "militants" are "practicing a '90s brand of McCarthyism – and their behavior is deplorable." (From Deidre Hall, "Why I Won't Wear a Red Ribbon," *Soap Opera Digest* (June 8, 1993), p. 77. Ms Hall's diatribe is preceded by a brief article "Seeing Red: Is the AIDS Ribbon Project Creating More Controversy Than Concern?" (pp. 74–75).)
23 Michael Logan, "Daytime Taboos – Any Left?," *TV Guide* (September 25, 1993), p. 37.
24 Ibid.

References

Allen, Robert C. (1985) *Speaking of Soap Operas*, Chapel Hill, NC: University of North Carolina Press, p. 171.
Coons, Joanna (1992) "*OLTL*'s Wortham Krimmer Is Just a Country Gent At Heart," *Soap Opera NOW!*, December 21, pp. 4–5.
Dyer, Richard (1993) *The Matter of Images: Essays on Representations*, London: Routledge, pp. 1–2.
Gross, Larry (1991) "Out of the Mainstream: Sexual Minorities and the Mass Media," in Ellen Seiter, Hans Barchers, Gabriele Kreutzner, and Eva-Maria Warth (eds), *Remote Control: Television, Audiences, and Cultural Power*, London and New York: Routledge, pp. 130–149.
Hall, Deidre (1993) "Why I Won't Wear a Red Ribbon," *Soap Opera Digest*, June 8, p. 77.

Jacobs, Andrew (1992) "Can't Live Without *One Life!*," *QW*, 39, August 2, p. 7.

Jetter, Alexis (1993) "Goodbye to the Last Taboo," *Vogue*, July, p. 86.

Logan, Michael (1993) "Daytime Taboos – Any Left?," *TV Guide* September 25, p. 37.

Merck, Mandy (1993) "A Case Of AIDS," in Mandy Merck, *Perversions: Deviant Readings*, London: Virago, pp. 45–61.

Modleski, Tania (1990) "The Search For Tomorrow in Today's Soap Operas," in *Loving with a Vengeance: Mass-Produced Fantasies For Women*, London and New York: Routledge, pp. 85–110.

Rorke, Robert (1992) "Ten Things You'll Never See On a Soap," *Soap Opera Digest*, December 8, pp. 74–78.

Williamson, Judith (1989) "Every Virus Tells A Story," in Erica Carter and Simon Watney (eds), *Taking Liberties: AIDS and Cultural Politics*, London: Serpent's Tail, pp. 69–81.

11

The consumption of soap opera

The Young and the Restless and mass consumption in Trinidad

Daniel Miller

It is hardly surprising that the spread of soap opera is closely linked for most people with the rise of mass consumption. There is a specific version of this linkage which unites the two in terms of the global reach of American soap operas such as *Dallas* and *Dynasty*. The argument is often that these and their "clones" focus on an affluent scion within American society and thereby appear as a showcase for American goods and more generically the American wealth that is juxtaposed with the American "way." This is seen as part propaganda and part a symbolic token of a process termed "Americaniz- ation" in which soap opera seems to form a triumvirate with Coca-Cola and McDonalds as the key symbols of the global expansion of American culture.

The less specific version of this linkage is based on the wide reach of soap operas as a media form linked with the general spread of mass consumption. There is the obvious link between the increasing availability of television and the subsequent association between soap opera and advertising. There may be more structured links as in the selling of goods through the commercial sponsorship and patronage which, for example, may require certain branded goods to be visible in sponsored Brazilian telenovelas. Overall we have a colloquial discourse in which the images of these two phenomena are closely linked.

The juxtaposition of these images is almost always used as the basis of a condemnation of their effects in colloquial discussion. There are three main elements to this critique which single out these effects as, first, homogen- ization, second, a new superficiality/vulgarity, and, third, commodification. In brief the argument is, first, that both the lifestyle and the goods which are associated with soap opera emerge from a core culture often seen as synonymous with Americanization, which results in the destruction of all local and diverse traditions through their replacement by the emulation of a single model of modern affluent life. Second, it is argued that soap opera and its associated consumer goods tend to favor a transient fashion-based and superficial attachment to people and things and lead to a subsequent lack of

213

depth. This point has been the particular focus of the now voluminous literature on postmodernism. Third, it is argued that this same lifestyle favors the commoditization of what previously had been affective and personal relations, and forms part of the general tendency which Marx proposed between the rise of capitalism and an inexorable tendency to commoditize.

In this essay I wish to subject this critique to an ethnographic case-study of the actual consumption of an American soap opera in Trinidad. Each of these three assumptions will be shown to be problematic. I will argue that there is indeed a relationship between the soap opera and commodification but the reasons behind this linkage and the effects may not be those that are commonly supposed, but lie rather in the manner by which soap opera transforms the nature of gossip, applying ideas on modernity which were formulated by Simmel rather than Marx.

The Young and the Restless

The Young and the Restless may be introduced through a particularly Trinidadian perspective. Below is an edited transcript of one of the two calypsos launched in 1988 called *The Young and the Restless*. This one was rapturously received by audiences from the moment it starts with a copy of the soap's theme tune, and the laughter, provoked by what is largely a summary of plot, usually continued to the end.

The Young and the Restless by calypsonian *"The Contender"*

> Hear how it go,
> Philip and Cricket did love bad.
> For some reason Jack Abbott dohn like Brad.
> Nina, the old lady dohn like she,
> Nina stick Philip with a baby.
> Jack Abbott, he went crazy
> over Cricket' mummy,
> so though the woman got Aids
> he still went and marry she.
>
> You talk of commess
> check the young and restless,
> commess at its best
> check the young and restless.
>
> Everyday at noon precisely
> old and young in front their tv.
> Well believe me this ain no joke
> some people carry tv to work,
> to watch the bacchanal
> to watch the confusion,

I tell you the picture
is a sensation.

It was Dallas and Dynasty
that had tv fans going crazy,
then came Falcon Crest
but they can't touch Young and Restless,
when it comes to bacchanal
when it comes to confusion.

The Young and the Restless fits the narrow category of true soap opera, as given by Cantor and Pingree (1983), of afternoon serials as opposed to the prime-time series such as *Dallas*. It has been produced since 1973, though by Columbia Pictures for CBS rather than the original "soap" group produced by Procter & Gamble. The targeted audience is the housewife, reflected in the emphasis on dialog rather than visual content, because this is compatible with domestic work. According to these same authors, *The Young and the Restless* is one of a group which tends to a greater orientation toward sex and social breakdown than the prime-time series and within the field of soap opera, *The Young and the Restless* is situated in the "liberal" group which is particularly so inclined (ibid.: 94).

The Young and the Restless was introduced to Trinidad following other lunch-hour soaps and was not therefore expected to have the same weight as serials such as *Dynasty* and *Dallas*. Advertising space was consequently cheaper at that period which is seen as the housewives' slot, although by the end of fieldwork (1989) retailers were insisting that the producers target this time slot. Evidence that the effect of this soap opera emanates from the salience of its content and is not merely the product of well targeted television comes from the manner by which it has completely overthrown the power of the prime-time slot, and that Trinidadians have refused the logistical constraints and insisted on watching the series even when conditions should have constrained them. The case reveals something of the flexible potential of television as technology. Many of the favorite stories surrounding the aura of *The Young and the Restless* are about the extremes people go to in order to see what is generally termed the "show" on a daily basis, although it is repeated in full at weekends. Particularly important are battery operated miniature televisions, which are vital for those wishing to see the show at work. These are particularly conspicuous in retailing, where shop assistants have one eye to the screen, even as they serve, but many also find their way into office lunching areas. The disruptive impact of the show on work was heightened by the desire of those without access to a television to use the subsequent hour topick up the details they had missed.

Much less common was the use of videos to reschedule watching to a more convenient time, owing to their relative scarcity. Those with low incomes, for example, a large squatting community among whom I worked, were among the most resourceful in gaining access. The bulk of these homes have neither water nor electricity, but given the imperative to watch the "show" many homes have televisions connected to car batteries which are recharged at a small fee every week by those with electricity supplies.

A local marketing survey carried out early in 1988, before I suspect *The Young and the Restless* had peaked, suggested 70 percent of those with TV watched the show regularly, slightly more than the news; both of these being well ahead of the third highest rating which was less than 30 percent. In my own survey of 160 households, out of the 146 who had access to a television all but twenty watched *The Young and the Restless* regularly. There was no evident association with ethnicity, but only five out of seventy-one in the lower income bracket did not watch this show, while fifteen out of seventy-five in the higher income bracket did not watch. In a separate question where forty-four households mentioned their favorite programs, thirty-seven gave *The Young and the Restless* as one of these.

The viewing of the soap opera is often both a social and a participatory affair. Few televisions fail to attract a neighbor or two on a regular basis. Individuals may shout derogatory comments or advice to the characters during the course of the program. Afterwards there is often collective commentary and discussion. There is a considerable concern to spread news of important events quickly. I was slightly "shocked" in my sense of vicarious propriety, when an important Muslim festival I was viewing was interrupted by three ladies who collectively announced to the assembled group some new development which we had missed by taking part in the ceremony. Typically people telephone each other to confirm that they knew all along that some event was going to occur.

I had no intention when embarking upon my fieldwork of studying a soap opera. My primary concern was with mass consumption and subsequently with more general issues concerning the nature of modernity (Miller 1994a). The study took place in four communities: a middle-class suburb, a government housing estate, an area of squatters, and a village which had been incorporated into a town, all in the vicinity of the town of Chaguanas. The problem with this project was that for an hour a day, fieldwork proved impossible as no one would speak with me, and I was reduced to watching people watching a soap opera. It seems likely that this anecdote could be cloned by many other contemporary anthropologists from India to Brazil. Most of my evidence comes from the manner in which the program was referred to in conversations about other topics rather than in direct response to questions asked about the watching of the soap opera, and it is therefore mainly concerned with the manner by which the influence of the program manifests itself in the daily lives of the communities studied.

For most of this century, and particularly since the stationing of American troops there during the Second World War, Trinidad has been the recipient of sustained influences from the United States, reinforced by the number of

216

families with relatives who have emigrated to North America, by macro-economic pressures, and by the American dominance of the media. The nature of American society and the implications of its current influence upon Trinidad is certainly a contentious issue, and one might have expected that this would be a major issue in the reception of the soap opera by viewers. However, a review of the conversations in which the soap opera is discussed or used for illustrative purposes shows that this is not the case. Indeed, one of the most common comments about the show was its relevance to contemporary conditions in Trinidad. Typical would be:

> "the same thing you see on the show will happen here, you see the wife blackmailing the husband or the other way around, I was telling my sister-in-law, Lianna in the picture, just like some bacchanal woman."
> "It really happening this flirtatious attitude, this one they living together that partner working this partner, and have a date with the next one or in bed with another."
> "People look at it because it is everyday experience for some people. I think they pattern their lives on it."

From this sense of relevance comes also the ideas that there are direct lessons to be learnt from the narrative content for moral issues in Trinidad, for example,

> "it teach you how husbands could lie and cheat and how a wife could expect certain things and never get it, the women always get the short end of the stick."

> "I believe marriage should be 50–50 not 30–70 the woman have to be strong she have to believe in her vows no matter what . . . that make me remember *The Young and the Restless*, Nicky want her marriage to work but Victor is in love with somebody else, but she still holding on."

Or (as in a current story):

> "You always go back to the first person you loved, in my own family my elder sister went with a Moslem boy, and so was married off by parents to a Hindu man, but she left her husband, gone back to the first man and had a child by him."

As shown by the study of *Dallas* in Israel (Katz and Liebes 1986), this moral use of the show will depend upon the perspective it is being viewed from. The Trinidad evidence supports Buckingham in arguing that the audience feels quite able to retain both a sense of critical distance which breaks the frame of realism and yet have an intense involvement in the "as if scenario" which results (Buckingham 1988: 200; see also Vink 1988: 232–240). This may emerge in the desire to intervene in or comment upon the manner by which the producers have decided to construct the story, as in the following two comments on AIDS:

"we find that Jessica so nice they shouldn't have given her AIDS they should have given Jill, somebody nice shouldn't have been given Aids."

"I like the idea of AIDS, since there was an episode which explain to Cricket how you get it, that you can't get it through swimming pools, so I find that was good, it's educational especially to housewives."

There can also be criticism of over-identification as in: "with my mother in the USA she so involved you would actually think it is some of she children she is talking about."

Bacchanal and localization

From both the chorus of the calypso and the above quotations it is clear that many Trinidadians have developed their own set of ideas which account for the attraction and success of this particular soap opera. This is encapsulated in the phrase "they like the bacchanal." Outside of Trinidad, this term would connote some kind of orgiastic or frenzied celebration, and so it is not surprising that the term is also frequently applied to the annual carnival. But within Trinidad, bacchanal has far more complex connotations. If one looks at the use of the term in calypso, the first synonym is clearly "scandal." In 1988 David Rudder sang "Bacchanal Women, sweet scandal where she walks," while Carl and Carol Jacob sang, "We people like scandal. We people like bacchanal." In the 1988 carnival queen competition, there was an entry with the title of Bacchanal Woman; the costume consisted of a voluminous pink/scarlet dress with exaggerated breast and buttocks, but above this was a spreading fan of layers like a peacock's tail emblazoned with a series of open eyes.

The second clear connotation of the term bacchanal is confusion or disorder. The two major connotations are linked by the other unfamiliar term in the calypso that is "commess." In dictionaries commess is translated as extreme confusion, but it will normally carry the connotation of confusion which results from scandal or idle chatter. Indeed, it seems that Trinidadian language has retained a set of terms from earlier French patois for constructing a network of concepts which are not well covered by English. My work as anthropologist in uncovering or listening in to gossip rendered me a Maco, or Macotious, potentially instrumental in spreading news, or Movay-Lang (*mauvaise-langue*) which again leads to commess and to bacchanal.

A final semantic linkage is the connotation of the term bacchanal as truth, as in the notion of bringing to light. It is not just that scandal reveals the hidden, but for many Trinidadians there is a moral value in this exposure. Scandal and confusion have highly ambiguous moral overtones, at once undermining patiently constructed systems of order and stability but also bringing us closer to the true nature of social being. The benign element of bacchanal is most evident in the affection for carnival which is the moment of the year given to the exploration of bacchanal as an ideal. Indeed the central motif for many in carnival is the ritual of Jouvert, where groups dressed in mud and ashes organized into bands such as "Barbarians" or "Kids in Hell," full of ironic commentary parodying topical items such as advertisements, TV evangelists, or *The Young and the Restless*, throng the streets before dawn. The event is dominated by dawn itself, the bringing into light of that which is normally hidden.

The context for interpreting this semantic network may be derived from one of the most influential anthropological accounts of Caribbean society. Wilson (1973), generalizing out from his particular case-study, divides Caribbean societies into two opposing cultural projects, which he terms respectability and reputation. Respectability is seen as the abiding influence of colonial pressures towards the kind of domesticity which is enshrined by the colonial female. This includes the drive to social stratification, religiosity, familial forms sanctioned by the church, and its major enshrinement is through women's involvement in the construction of a domestic domain. This becomes, however, in the Caribbean context an even more gendered distinction since most men are entirely uninvolved in this arena. Rather they embody an oppositional tendency termed reputation in which they are mainly engaged in male-only activities with transient peer rivalry but longer-term egalitarian pressures, involving drinking, gambling, and, above all, verbal play, resistant to the hierarchizing and constraining pressures of the domestic. Working from the perspective of Trinidad, I would wish to modify elements of Wilson's portrayal of the origins and implications of these projects, and a dualism he associates most closely with gender, I see as being projected equally on to ethnicity in Trinidad and class in Jamaica. I use the terms "transcendence" and "transience" in preference to the terms "respectability" and "reputation" in order to lay greater stress on the differences in temporal orientation and the relationship of interior and exterior.

The relationship between transcendence which finds its apotheosis in the cult of domesticity and with the event and style-based exteriorizing project of transience is not merely one of a simple symbolic opposition. Some people manage to live almost entirely within one or the other; a greater number have elements of both but lean to the transcendent at Christmas and embrace the transient at carnival. Also common is to spend one's youth in transience and move rather suddenly into religion, a home, and marriage, reversing one's previous values. This structural opposition manifesting the intrinsic contradiction of modernity as expressed through Trinidadian culture is the point of departure for the formation of the concept of bacchanal, which may be a key concept in relating the two modes to each other.

As in other accounts of soap opera it is clear that the "realism" with which it is identified has little to do with the environmental context of domestic presentation; the scenes cannot look like Trinidad. Realism rather is based on the truth of the serial in relation to key structural problematics of Trinidadian culture. It is the realism of myth. The soap opera is a meta-commentary on the nature of truth itself. It explores through its stories the processes by which natural forces such as lust and gossip break open the global discourse of the domestic into the confusion and disorder of true life.

A major preoccupation in the soap opera is the manner by which individuals are, as it were, thrown off course or driven to extreme actions by sexual desire. So a person writing a critical biography, almost against her will, starts an affair with the object of her work. A female working hard to integrate within the respectable family of her child's father is seduced from these efforts by a good-looking male recruited for the purpose. Here as in the Trinidadian ideology of the domestic, it is often the females who assert one morality but find themselves inexorably drawn through sexual attraction into overturning these same principles. The viewer notes "look how she is a commess maker, just so some women come to some people house and do the same thing." For some of the squatters there is not enough bacchanal:

> "people in *The Young and the Restless* can't have fun like people in Trinidad, their sort of fun is boring. There's more bacchanal here than in *The Young and the Restless*, in each soap you can tell what's going to happen but around here you can't tell."

Clearly this concept of bacchanal arises from the very specific contradictions that are experienced within Trinidadian social life. Indeed, when Trinidadians were asked to describe their country in one word, by far the most common response was the term "bacchanal," said with a smile which seemed to indicate affectionate pride triumphing over potential shame. It seems quite common in media research, for example, Marchand's (1985) study of American advertising, to argue that a genre represents collusion between media creators and consumers to construct a set of images which comment on and possibly help resolve contradictions in contemporary culture. Marchand suggests advertising related to the contradictions between aspirations of modernity and nostalgia for tradition. In Trinidad, a small country quite self-conscious about the degree of wealth, education, and sophistication enhanced by the experience of the oil boom, there is considerable participation in debates over the proper nature of Trinidadian television, and, as noted by Wilk for Belize (1990), the implications of such images for cultural development. The audience may well attempt some intervention in program scheduling of imports, as in the "protest" calypso by David Rudder, the chorus goes "dey take Kojak off de TV, but what about *Dallas* and *Dynasty*." More commonly, however, the core concern is with television programs which are made within Trinidad.

In general, political and official culture is associated with respectability and transcendence; politics should be a "serious" (in the sense used by Abrahams 1983) matter. The flagship of local television is the news, which may be complemented by an hour of extremely dull discussion of, for example, problems involved in ministerial planning. There is considerable concern with the degree of quality and significance of locally-made television, and a ready tendency to contrast it unfavorably with imports. There have been several locally-made drama serials. The series current at the time of my research (called *No Boundaries*), which had the open-ended structure of a soap opera, focused on ethnic distinctions, which are recognized as the "proper" problematics of Trinidadian society with a considerable political impact. The stereotypes were exaggerated, with the East Indian Trinidadian involved in an arranged marriage, something virtually extinct in contemporary Trinidad.

In the world of bacchanal, however, ethnicity is dissolving, as all ethnic groups are represented on both sides of its boundaries. It is, however, hard for local television to construct images this close to the ground (unlike the newspapers for which see below). One large female comedian does succeed in portraying a fairly anarchic sense of bacchanal in advertisements and on her own program, with few pretensions to quality props or realism, and based on local dialect humor, but this is exceptional.

In contrast to Wilson (1973), I do not want to suggest that transience is authentic to the historical experience of the peoples of the Caribbean while transcendence is derived from colonial culture. The seriousness of the transcendent has arisen at the same time in the same structural tension, and both are the products of a continual dialog with global discourses. The point here is a slightly narrower one: that there are strong constraints upon an institution as serious as Trinidadian television in producing clear expressions of bacchanal. There is a sense, then, in which the imported program has the potential to articulate that aspect of the "local" which the locally-produced cannot incorporate given its continuous eye on the external judgmental gaze. A point of particular concern to anthropology is that it is *The Young and the Restless* (more than, for example, Shango religion) which in daily conversation is associated with the wise adages and saws of folk knowledge. When dealing with a key dilemma of moral life it is the soap opera which is referred to for analogy. The two most popular television programs are those devoted to the two kinds of truth: *Panorama*, the news program, which reveals the serious truth, and *The Young and the Restless*, which reveals the truth of bacchanal.

This clearly is not a case of simple global homogenization or Americanization. Within Trinidad itself there is a powerful discourse which argues that given the forces of cultural imperialism, the airbases stationed there during the last war, and similar factors, the country has been the passive victim of Americanization, a theme picked up by the Trinidadian novelist V. S. Naipaul in his book *The Mimic Men* (1967). There are many reasons why Trinidadians might want to comment upon the nature of American culture and use the soap opera to do this, but the evidence from conversations in which the program is mentioned shows that this is not in fact the way *The Young and the Restless* is employed.

Instead, the program is directed against one of the most specific elements of Trinidadian culture. What is significant is that, on the one hand, bacchanal is the term many people gave as their one-word description of the essential character of Trinidadian society, and at the same time the principal form used to exemplify bacchanal in 1988 was not an indigenous production but an imported American soap opera. The mistake made by some studies is to assume that we are dealing with an "American" product which others may not have the cultural knowledge to "properly" interpret, or that it simply slips into some local context (for example, Schroder 1988; Katz and Liebes 1986). Although in terms of production, we are dealing with what might be called the unintended consequence of international media marketing for profit, at the level of consumption we can observe both the re-creation of the soap opera as Trinidadian and also its role in the refinement of the concept of Trinidad as the culture of bacchanal.

It is not hard to account for the particular significance of *The Young and the Restless* at the time of this study. Trinidad is an extraordinarily dynamic society. With the oil boom post-1973 it was catapulted into the world of mass consumption, but with the decline of the oil price, especially in 1986, it has suffered an almost equally precipitous recession. I would argue that bacchanal is more important than wealth *per se* in determining the local equivalent of class. The disdain felt by the suburban community for the squatters is based on the uncontrolled commess of the latter. Wealth, however, is of considerable importance in allowing groups to struggle toward the respectability of transcendence and its instruments of interiorization and enclosure.

The oil boom gave a tremendous impetus to the growth of the middle class to the extent that they emerged at its peak as dominant both numerically and culturally. With the recession, however, many of the more fragile pretensions of the *nouveau* element within this class were exposed. There is a continual discourse about the financial plight that exists behind the closed doors of the domestic household, which is only brought to light by events such as cutting off the phone through unpaid bills. Even in the suburbs there were frequent rumors about how many properties were back in the hands of the banks or deserted by migrants to Canada. Therefore, this unprecedented orientation toward an imported soap opera may well have its roots in the near exquisite tension that had built up between transcendence and transience and which was highlighted by the focus upon bacchanal.

Many of the writings on soap opera and serials tend to assume that these lend some reassurance, stability, and so forth as part of their power. Much of this may stem from the legacy of the mass culture critique which treated soap operas as a kind of visual valium that stupefied its audience in the interests of some dominant will. In certain cases this may well be the impact, but not in Trinidad. Here, so far from patching up a wound, or "functioning" in the interests of social cohesion, the attraction of the program is that it forces its point into the key fissure which manifests the basic contradiction of Trinidadian culture, at a time when this is especially sensitive. This is precisely why Trinidadian television cannot produce a program of this kind. *The Young and the Restless* reinforces bacchanal as the lesson of recession which insists that the domestic and the façade of stability is a flimsy construction which will be blown over in the first storm created by true nature. It thereby colludes with the local sense of truth as exposure and scandal. The soap opera in its consumption is therefore not just Trinidadian, but as in a popular local expression "True True Trini." This suggests that while producing one's own culture as indigenously created forms may provide for easier cultural appropriation, nevertheless imported forms may also have transformative potential as vehicles for objectification (in the sense used in Miller 1987). To achieve a balance a case-study such as this one needs to be seen in conjunction with the findings of Mattelart (1983) on the deleterious effects of international media imperialism.

Style and the superficial

Almost all the literature on soap opera emphasizes the forms of identification between the audience and the characters portrayed as central to the attraction of the genre. When reviewing the occasions upon which informants noted personal identifications, it became evident that these almost always take a particular form that I had not encountered in the comparative literature (though see Vink 1988: 227–228, 236, on the work of Milanesi). It is rarely the character or personality of the individual which is seen as the point of identification. In the first instance it is almost always the clothing which mediates the act of identification as in the following quotes:

> "I love Lauren, how she dresses and I identify with her."
> "I like Nicky the way she dresses, my name is Nicky too, she is a loving person."
> "I look mainly at Dynasty I like the way Alexis dresses, she is so sophisticated and I like the way Kristle dresses."
> "I like Nicky's and Lianna's dress I always look at Nicky's hair, her braids and bows and stuff, Mrs Chancellor does dress nice."
> "even if you don't like what is happening you could admire their earrings or their pearl necklaces . . . I would copy Brad's wife though I wouldn't like a husband like Brad."

This identification may often translate into direct copying of clothes, so that seamstresses may conceive of watching the soap operas as part of their job. Although it was a different program being described this quote illustrates the point:

"Nah when you see that show is about to start, the phone does ring. Gloria yuh watching it . . . like every dress she see she say "Oh God I want one like that," and how many yards to buy and I think she was writing on the other end."

Another seamstress waits for someone to request a copy from *The Young and the Restless* and then watches the repeat at the weekend in order to note the style, in this case, a low cut across with a frill and mini worn by Ashly, but the colors dictated by the fact that they were watching on a black and white TV.

At another level it is fashion which dictates the identification with the particular show as opposed to the particular individual:

"It is so modernized with AIDS, up-to-date music wise, clothes wise, when you look at the shoes you say this is nice this is really up to date, it's modern it's now, that why you appreciate it more, I admire the earrings, necklaces."

"the first thing I like about *The Young and the Restless* is the way they dress, I find it look right up-to-date fashion, all the women are so beautiful."

"I like the way they do their make up, the Australian soap operas seem very dull make up, but this one outstanding shades of lipstick, eye-makeup, earring and kinds of jewelry, the way they dress and everything goes with everything else."

A retailer of jewelry noted the importance of the program for his trade:

For *Young and Restless* – big rhinestone, anything big and shiny, big rings from Mrs Chancellor [a character within this soap]. That is the biggest influence right now, so I take an interest. There is a lot of parties and weddings in that show. Even the buyers have to keep up with *Young and the Restless*. I watch it and have to keep up, because when a woman say I want something like came on *Young and Restless*.

The point was summarized in another retailer's laconic comment: "What is fashion in Trinidad today – *The Young and the Restless* is fashion in Trinidad today."

Clearly this demonstrates that the link often supposed between the popularity of soap opera and the desire for certain commodities certainly operates in Trinidad. Indeed, in this case it actually mediates in one of the key relationships which all studies of soap opera stress: that is the identification with the main characters. There is a close association between the desire to look like one of the people portrayed and the degree of empathy with them as fictive individuals.

At first glance this seems to provide clear evidence in favor of one of the

224

main critiques made of soap opera: the superficial level at which identification is made, and by implication the effect of the soap opera in creating a shallowness to social relations and identifications. The problem, however, is that this critique assumes that the general ontology of "depth" and "appearance" which is presupposed by the use of the term "superficial" and is found equally in western philosophy and western colloquial discourse, would also operate in Trinidad.

What the larger ethnographic study reveals, however, is that, contrary to this assumption, the use of clothing demonstrates not the superficial level at which the program is absorbed, but quite the opposite. Clothing and style have for a long period had a much more significant position in many Trinidadians' conception of themselves and their identities than may be the case in other regions. This may be directly linked to the dualism of transcendence devoted to the domestic regime, the interiorization of values, and the cultivation of "roots" or religiosity, as against the transience associated with individualism, the outside or exterior, and a refusal of institutionalization. From the latter perspective the proper cultivation of the self is through style; it is the surface which is "true" to the person, and allows them to express their genuinely transient nature. The opposition is to any form of interiorization in which people hide their true selves by pretensions to a deep unchanging nature.

In European philosophical traditions a kind of "depth" ontology is prevalent where "being" is associated with inwardness but also with realness, firmness, solidity, something deep down that changes slowly if at all. Façade is by definition on the outside facing outwards, and always implies superficiality. For the transient the aesthetic of being works in a very different manner. Interiorization is more like hoarding, trying to keep private, keep away from proper public scrutiny in whose gaze being is constantly reconstituted. From this perspective there should be no interior space. Rather to know who one is depends upon the public response to a constructed exterior, locally to one's sense of "style." For these Trinidadians bacchanal is largely benign; it may lead to confusion fighting, etc., but still it is a welcome return to a kind of natural state. Friendship in bacchanal is spontaneous, relationships are dyadic and transient without the constraints on freedom imposed by social convention and structure.

The cultivation of style is indeed a major element in Trinidadian culture, but this is not because of the arrival of soap operas or even increased commoditization, since it may be traced historically to before these events, although it clearly has been subject to increased commoditization in recent times. Some (for example, Gates 1988) would link this concern with the surface which in relation to verbal style he terms Signifyin(g) to a particular West African tradition. Others have concentrated more on the effects of slavery. In Trinidad it pertains to more than one ethnic community and any precise linkage with an historical source is difficult. It can, however, be argued more generally that it expresses a wider concern to avoid being institutionalized by hierarchical and oppressive forces and to retain the freedom of an identity based on transience and the surface.

Within this exteriorizing, centrifugal aesthetic, the use of clothing as the media of identification demonstrates the centrality of the program to that aspect of Trinidadian culture. In this approach to ontology it is precisely in the response to stylistic display that one finds out who one really is. This being is based on the event and is not accretative or institutionalized in social structures, but reconstructed with each performance which ideally requires a new set of clothing. During the oil boom, when families who had been brought up in poverty obtained wealth, they outdid the hegemonic classes in the transience of their fashions, not out of some "crass" materialism, but rather as an appropriation of goods which opposed their incorporation into longer-standing accretative structures. The identification through fashion is therefore evidence for the profundity of the experience of this program rather than its inverse, and quite accounts for the degree to which viewers appraise the program in large measure in terms of the appearance of the characters (for more details of this critique of the application of the concept of superficiality see Miller 1994b).

Gossip, narrative and commoditization

If the localization of *The Young and the Restless* via the concept of bacchanal demonstrates the importance of gossip, and the identification with characters via jewelry and clothing demonstrates the impact on commoditization, then what remains is to demonstrate the nature of the link between gossip and commoditization. This will be attempted through a closer examination of the relationship between gossip, narrative, and the event, through which it can be seen how the soap opera illustrates some general philosophical statements about the growing importance of the relationship between these elements in the modern world.

There is considerable evidence for the centrality of gossip to social relations and the control of access to potentially revelatory information in Trinidad. For the village context, a Ph.D. thesis by Harrison (1975) constructs an ethnography of a village in 1971–1972 with particular emphasis on the place of gossip. He notes the concern over how information about a household is obtained, even the conveyance of innocuous information may be condemned as "carrying news." He also documents the particular channels by which information about third parties is transmitted, usually with disclaimers about the truth of the rumors such as "I hear that, . . . I ent know if it's true nah." Gossip then is both highly stylized and frequently leads to confusion.

For the transient of the squatting community there may be a positive identification with this culture of gossip, as they see themselves as the true objectification of bacchanal. This was the area where you would hear the most elaborate cussing out, where gossip flowed free and far, where the walls of houses built from the boxes in which car parts are imported could scarcely hope to conceal the activities of the domestic arena. From their perspective it is the connotations of truth and nature which are particularly important. It is they who can condemn as façade the "social" (meaning anti-social) ways of the suburbs, and who insist that eventually all such attempts to respectability will fail, as all will succumb to the natural drives which lead them into scandalous situations. One of the strongest instruments of bacchanal is clearly the sexual imperative, and the term nature is as equally connotative of sex itself as it is of the male's world in nature outside of the domestic.

The impact of soap operas such as *The Young and the Restless* is to enter into this world of gossip, but as a clearly displaced version. It is almost a metaphor for an "event" focused perception of the world, a narrative which is, then, also a challenge to narrative itself as an ordering mechanism in the world. Not that displacement is itself entirely new. Bacchanal is generally associated with innuendo and is not entirely provenanced. "Town talk" as it used to operate was also often based on the circulation of generalized genre suspicions before they could be pinned onto any particular person or place. Nevertheless, *The Young and the Restless* is still more displaced which means that a considerable amount of gossip can take place in which people's actual interests are not involved:

> "I prefer that, you see it is safer to talk about the celebrities' business than to talk about people's business. You won't get into trouble, nobody will cuss you if you say Chancellor was with this one husband . . . but it is just bacchanal . . . all them soaps is bacchanal."

Trinidad provides clear evidence for the commoditization of this form of gossip as applied to soap opera through reference to the articulation between the soap opera and another key media: weekly newspapers. For a considerable period the print media was similar to television in that it was a largely "serious" form represented by the daily press of the *Guardian* and the *Express*, but the 1970s and 1980s saw the appearance of a new genre of bacchanal weekly newspapers such as the *Bomb*, the *Punch*, the *Blast*, and the *Heat*. Such newspapers include a fair number of "girlie" shots usually in swimsuits with suitable titles such as "Chick in Heat," but also a new genre of reportage which includes local cultural materials, but which are dominated by the exposé story. The *Punch*, which is the most risqué and was also, according to marketing research, the most widely read newspaper in the country, is seen as equally well informed on matters of style from clothing to music as on matters of gossip.

Stories may focus on prominent individuals and their supposed misdeeds, or recent crimes, especially of passion, but also include a fair amount of fairly general and unsubstantiated gossip intended to promote bacchanal. A person (unnamed) from a particular area (named), who drives a particular (though

227

common) brand of car of a given color is scandalizing the neighborhood with his/her overt homosexual relationship/use of obeah (magic), etc. One of the most discussed examples of weekly gossip during fieldwork was the following: "Police have been unable to confirm that a man known to have AIDS was seen walking into a well-known fast-food restaurant in Chaguanas and squeezing blood from a cut into a bottle of tomato ketchup." Such articles certainly work as media interventions into typical "town talk." Everybody "knew" which particular fast-food outlet was implicated, indeed the rumor may well have predated the article.

These weekly newspapers clearly represent a successful bid to commoditize gossip. They also represent a kind of homogenization through technology by which gossip, instead of being reliant on local observation about, for example, whose car was seen parked all night in front of whose house, becomes instead a nationwide form such that a politician or media personality can be discussed by all. This clearly has affinities with the impact of television soap opera which also unites the entire country in terms of the common knowledge of the current behavior of key characters. The two forms came together when an enterprising weekly newspaper (*Blast*) took advantage of the fact that several soaps are shown in the United States prior to their arrival in Trinidad, and printed the stories in advance. As a result marketing surveys showed this weekly newspaper leap-frogging *Punch* and all other newspapers to become the best-read newspaper in the country. Since then the coverage has become more sophisticated as the original reporting of the week ahead has been joined by a summary of the previous week and snippets of information about the actors and actresses taking part. For example, the *Blast* of December 11, 1992 tells, first, how "Jeanne Cooper was given a big welcome back when she returned to the show after a bout of pneumonia," second, how the actress who plays Ashley also sings in a nightclub, and, third, how other actresses noted the numbers of men who admitted watching when they attended a charity-raising function. In addition, predictions are made or "scoops" given of future events and comments are made by participants about the reception of the show: for example, the *Blast*, January 8, 1993 reported: "'I imagine there are some segments of the audience still distrustful of Ryan – even though he's done a lot of things to redeem himself' comments Bill Bell . . . 'I was always surprised that the audience reacted so strongly.'"

In addition, the advertising agencies have become involved with adverts that pastiche the show or with competitions based around the show. In July 1989 a company was running an advert in the *Guardian* which "invites you to enter the *Young and the Restless* competition; new grand winner will take off to meet the stars in person at a filming of The Young and The Restless." This meant a trip to California plus spending money. Those entering had to give evidence of purchase of this company's products, and in addition answer five questions such as "in what month and year was little Phillip Chancellor IV born" or "who was in the car accident with Nina on the way to her wedding." The *Blast* was one of the sponsors of a concert in Trinidad on July 21, 1990 by members of the cast flown over for the occasion and accompanied by local calypso singers. The newspapers therefore increasingly combine with television to build up the sense of anticipation and revelation constituted by "events" while at the same time increasingly rendering these as fictive industrial forms which are available for commoditization.

Even more than in newspaper coverage, it is the soap opera itself which creates a narrative structure within which this style of "event" based gossip can be elaborated both as soap opera text and in its consumption through gossip about the fictive characters by real Trinidadians. To consider the implications of this, we must see the narrative function of soap opera as much more than merely a resonance with everyday life. As evident in the use of the terms transience and transcendence, it is the consciousness of temporality which seems to be the key to the Trinidadian response to the contradictions of modernity (Miller 1994a). The philosopher Ricoeur provides a substantial argument for the centrality of narrative to modernity; indeed he takes narrative as perhaps the key component of philosophical understanding. For Ricoeur (1984–1988), narrative is often that by which ordinary humanity as well as abstract philosophy brings forth meaning. There is a proper imperative to narrative – to tell the stories of humanity and its suffering – but one which potentially leads in many directions. Like other modern philosophers, Ricoeur rejects the pretensions of metanarrative associated with the Hegelian tradition and looks also to dilute some of the more pretentious forms of historiography by relating them to the more creative multiple senses of narrative embodied in fiction. Ricoeur seizes on narrative as a key moment in relating morality, temporal consciousness, and the sense of cause and goal. It is narrative which makes metaphor intelligible. The purpose of "narrativity is to mark, organize and clarify temporal experience" (1983: 177). Narrative is thereby credited with tremendous significance in helping us make sense of experience. Of course, as a philosophical work, Ricoeur's study is largely based in "high" rather than popular traditions; the conflict over the place of narrative is first posed as a conflict between St Augustine and Aristotle. The sense of the event and recapitulation are evoked with Proust not soap opera. In many ways this is a pity. It is precisely in the semi-industrialized massive production field of soap opera (for example, see Allen 1985: 45–60) and its multiple readings that perhaps a better sense of the actual place of narrative in human relations could be revealed (Abu-Lughod forthcoming; Das forthcoming). Can, for example, the antipathy to ending as closure given in philosophical consideration of narrative be related directly to the open-ended structure of soap opera? Certainly the sheer scale of soap opera provides persuasive evidence in support of Ricoeur's focus upon narrative. It is soap opera which above all today gives that sense of a morally infused and communally shared fictive past without the dangers of a more parochial nationalistic sense of history. Indeed, it might be argued that Trinidadians have been carrying out in practice some of what Ricoeur attempts through philosophy, that is the reconciliation of the sense of "event" with the sense of narrative. In both cases there seems to be an appeal to narrative as an instrument which provides order and moral understanding of ordinary life, but equally a reliance on the event as that which disrupts the pretensions of narrative and brings the story back in articulation with ordinary people's experience of time as action.

The advantage of such ethnographic material is in preventing easy generalizations which tend to arise from the narrowness of many academic traditions. For example, Giddens (1991: 70–108) has recently provided a much simpler interpretation of narrative in relation to the repair of autobiographies that seems much too parochially Anglo-American in its assumptions about the way modernity may operate. For many Trinidadians there is much less concern with narrative as a kind of accretative process than is assumed by philosophers and sociologists who have concentrated on European models. Gossip is clearly a form of narrative which highlights the "event," the immediacy, and present context of action at the expense of the longer term. The favorite event as subject of gossip is one that undermines the gradual accumulation of reputation and is irresponsible with regard to longer-term consequences.

The problem is that the European tradition tends to emphasize the place of narrative as ordering, often providing simple unilineal sequences that evoke a sense of causation combined with the moral implications of our *déjà vu* sense of responsibility for what led up to an event. This certainly occurs in the reading of *The Young and the Restless*, but there is a deeper more subversive temporal consciousness at work which celebrates bacchanal, that is the disordering outcome of events which disrupt attempts by narrative to impose order. What is interesting is the degree to which the soap opera's narrative form is subjected to a kind of radical presentness, a highlighting of the exhilaration of the event. As such the Trinidadian consumption of soap opera, when mediated through their concept of bacchanal, can help illustrate a key tension discerned by Ricoeur as a philosopher between "narrative" and "event" based time.

The Young and the Restless needs to be understood as among a series of objectifications of bacchanal available to contemporary Trinidadians. Indeed, one of Trinidad's best-known cultural events, the carnival, may also be viewed as a symbolic/displaced objectification of bacchanal, but it is a seasonal, in a sense, more formal expression of transcendence breaking down into transience and revelation as bringing into light. The soap opera, by comparison, is closer to the everyday activities of those for whom bacchanal is a more constant experience. It may thereby comment more directly on the current dynamics of the domestic, while carnival reflects more on a slower moving structural dualism within which the domestic is implicated. This is the sense in which Trinidadians echo the more academic commentary on soap opera as a new realism, aware of the linkage to social life as itself an open-ended tension between narrative continuity and the event.

Both in its own terms and in combination with the weeklies, the soap opera represents an abstraction of one of the most important forms of social communication: gossip. It is this rather than the use of such programs in influencing people to buy goods that is perhaps the more important link to commoditization *per se*. As Simmel (1978) argued, one result of the spread of money and the intervention of monetary transactions into everyday life is the ability of money to exchange as abstract equivalence what otherwise were seen as qualitatively incommensurable spheres of exchange. It is part of that general process of increasing abstraction which we usually term "modernity" and is thereby fundamental to the rise of both the modern sense of alienation and that of freedom.

Soap opera may be understood as analogous with money in so far as it also takes a key media of exchange, in this case gossip, as a form of communication and again renders it more abstract and interchangeable than the highly localized and relatively personally provenanced earlier forms of gossip. Although the structure of soap opera gossip mimics non-televised forms as based around key characters and their social interactions, the fictive nature of these figures and the homogenization of the knowledge of all observers as television viewers transforms the consequence. It is this which enables soap opera, perhaps more than traditional gossip, to be an instrument for commenting on key contradictions which pertain more generally to modern Trinidadian life, notwithstanding its American origins. As with money itself, it may have the contradictory effects which Simmel analyzed of both enhancing freedom and internal mobility, while at the same time creating a sense of generalized knowledge which is cosmopolitan but potentially also uncommitted and blasé. I do not think that the soap opera as gossip replaces more localized equivalents which seem to continue to flourish; perhaps as with the weeklies it is more a response to the other new technologies which result in more frequent social interactions between peoples from diverse backgrounds and parts of Trinidad and which therefore require a kind of meta-gossip which derives from the creation of this global but also specific locality.

Conclusion

There is, indeed, an important link between the spread of soap opera and the spread of commoditization, but this link may be quite different from the simple assertion that one is merely the instrument for promoting the other, which would then fail to account for the many varieties of soap opera (for example, in Britain) where the setting is generally one of relative poverty. Instead by focusing upon what remains perhaps the best theoretical account of the social consequences of commoditization, Simmel's *The Philosophy of*

Money (1978), we can trace through important analogies with one of the most commonly observed cross-cultural effects of soap opera. This is the manner by which its foundation in a form of "real-time" narrative structure makes it far more amenable to consumption through means of displaced gossip than other television genres. In combination with Ricoeur's observations in *Time and Narrative* (1984–1988) on the centrality of narrative itself to our temporal consciousness, we can, perhaps, appreciate why soap opera has the extraordinary appeal that is evident cross-culturally while still being able to discern the very particular imperatives that determine its consumption in specific communities.

Acknowledgments

This chapter is a revised version of Miller 1992. Thanks are due to many friends and helpers in Trinidad who provided assistance during fieldwork and particularly my research assistant Shanaz Mohammad. Financial assistance toward various aspects of this project has been given by the British Academy, the Nuffield Foundation, the University of London Central Research Fund, and the Wenner-gren Foundation for Anthropological Research. Thanks also to Rickie Burman, Mike Rowlands, Roger Silverstone, and Eric Hirsch who commented upon a draft of this chapter.

Note

Much of the substantive material overlaps, though in the earlier version it was used to explore a rather different theoretical problematic concerned with the terms local and global and the domestic.

References

Abrahams, R. (1983) *The Man of Words in the West Indies: Performance and the Emergence of Creole Culture*, Baltimore, Md.: Johns Hopkins University Press.

Abu-Lughod, L. (forthcoming) "The Objects of Soap Opera: Egyptian Television and the Cultural Politics of Modernity," in D. Miller (ed.), *Worlds Apart. Modernity Through the Prism of the Local*, London: Routledge.

Allen, R. (1985) *Speaking of Soap Operas*, Chapel Hill, NC: University of North Carolina Press.

Buckingham, D. (1988) *Public Secrets: EastEnders and its Audience*, London: British Film Institute.

Cantor, M. and Pingree, S. (1983) *The Soap Opera*, Beverly Hills, Calif.: Sage.

Das, V. (forthcoming) "On Soap Opera: What Kind of Anthropological Object Is It?," in D. Miller (ed.) *Worlds Apart. Modernity Through the Prism of the Local*, London: Routledge.

Gates, H. L. (1988) *The Signifying Monkey*, Oxford: Oxford University Press.

Giddens, A. (1991) *Modernity and Self-Identity*, Oxford: Polity Press.

Harrison, D. (1975) "Social Relations in a Trinidadian Village," unpublished Ph.D. thesis, University of London.

Katz, E. and Liebes, T. (1986) "Mutual Aid in the Decoding of Dallas: Preliminary Notes from a Cross-Cultural Study," in P. Drummond, and R. Patterson (eds), *Television in Transition*, London: British Film Institute.

Marchand, R. (1985) *Advertising the American Dream*, Berkeley, Calif.: University of California Press.

Mattelart, A. (1983) *Transnationals and the Third World*, London, Mass.: Bergin & Garvey.

Miller, D. (1987) *Material Culture and Mass Consumption*, Oxford: Basil Blackwell.

—— (1992) "*The Young and the Restless* in Trinidad: A Case of the Local and the Global in Mass Consumption," in R. Silverstone and E Hirsch (eds), *Consuming Technologies*, London: Routledge, pp. 163–182.

—— (1994a) *Modernity – An Ethnographic Approach*, London: Berg.

—— (1994b) "Style and Ontology." in J. Friedman (ed.), *Consumption and Cultural Strategies*, London: Harwood.

Naipaul, V. S. (1967) *The Mimic Men*, Harmondsworth: Penguin.

Ricoeur, P. (1983) "On Interpretation," in A. Montefiore (ed.), *Philosophy in France Today*, Cambridge: Cambridge University Press.

—— (1984–1988) *Time and Narrative*, 3 vols, Chicago, Ill.: University of Chicago Press.

Schroder, K. (1988) "The Pleasure of *Dynasty*: The Weekly Reconstruction of Self-Confidence," in P. Drummond and R. Paterson (eds), *Television and its Audience*, London: British Film Institute.

Simmel, G. (1978) *The Philosophy of Money*, London: Routledge.

Vink, N. (1988) *The Telenovela and Emancipation*, Amsterdam: Royal Tropical Institute.

Wilk, R. (1990) "Consumer Goods as Dialogue About Development," *Culture and History* 7, pp. 79–100.

Wilson, P. (1973) *Crab Antics*, New Haven, Conn.: Yale University Press.

12

Not all "soaps" are created equal

Toward a cross-cultural criticism of television serials

Gabriele Kreutzner and Ellen Seiter

In a period marked by rapid political developments, the advent of the single European market, and the call for the establishment of a "common house of Europe" (Mikhail Gorbachev), questions of cultural identity have taken on an ever-more pressing significance. While media and communication processes are undoubtedly of major significance in the formation of such identities, David Morley and Kevin Robins have pointed out that deterministic models of communication are quite inadequate to explain how such identities are constructed and maintained or changed.[1] In this chapter, we address the question of how particular forms of entertainment popular in the 1980s preconstituted cultural identities for their audiences. For the purposes of our micro-study, we will look at prime-time television serials deriving from two differing national and socio-cultural contexts. We will investigate a television serial which has been extremely popular with its national audience, namely *Die Schwarzwaldklinik* (1985–1990) of the public service German network ZDF.[2] In comparison, we will discuss *Dallas* (CBS/Lorimar, 1978–1991) and *Dynasty* (ABC/Aaron Spelling/Fox-Cat, 1981–1990) as examples of nationally and internationally successful US television serials of the 1980s. Our decision to compare prime-time serials across cultures is motivated by their intimate relationship to melodrama as a popular tradition appealing particularly to female audiences, and to critical discussions about the television serial's semantic and ideological openness. Our analysis is also motivated by the troubling observation that the question of gender has yet again been repressed in recent discussions of national identities and television's role in their construction.[3]

We wish to situate our work within the context of feminist studies of the daytime soap opera and to extend its perspective to popular forms of melodramatic prime-time entertainment. Critics such as Tania Modleski, Charlotte Brunsdon, and Carol Lopate were interested in the possibility that soap operas offered women an entertainment vehicle which was inextricably bound up in the problems in their lives caused by the split between public and private cultures, and the burden placed on women for the psychological nurturance of the family.[4] Initially, the main focus was on the representation of gender and women's oppression as portrayed in these programs and as a motivating interest on the part of the viewers in the story-lines. Throughout their history US daytime soaps have emphasized women's relationships with one another to a much greater extent than other kinds of programming. Irna Phillips, one of the originators of the genre, devised all of her early programs with a matriarchal figure and a series of daughters or daughter figures.[5] More recently, work on the prime-time serials and on the internationalization of family melodrama has been less concerned with these issues. For example, a discussion of *Die Schwarzwaldklinik* in *East of Dallas* fails to problematize gender dynamics in the drama.[6] It is our intention to apply feminist concerns to serial forms that can be subsumed only problematically under the generic signifier of "soap opera" as a form of popular entertainment targeted at an audience constructed in exclusively female terms.[7] More specifically, we shall look at how gender relations are constructed in prime-time serial drama in the context of US network and German public service television.

In what follows, we approach our examples in two stages: we situate each form in the respective context of a particular cultural technology and a specific media institution; that is, US network television as a commercial medium, and German public service television. Then, we describe the popular traditions enshrined in specific forms of melodramatic prime-time entertainment in the 1980s. These traditions account for considerable differences which are of major importance for the readings that can be produced from these texts.

Prime-time serials on US network television in the 1980s

As a commerical medium, US network television is primarily interested in the production of profit by selling the largest possible audience to advertisers. In order to materialize this goal, the medium developed three main strategies for addressing the audience, each of which depended on placing given shows within the network schedule. The first of these strategies addresses the television audience as female. This strategy clearly dominates network televison's daytime production and determines the characteristics of daytime texts. Although daytime shows (such as soap operas) are actually watched by women and men, interviews with network researchers and production personnel of daytime soap operas in 1987 showed that producers and network executives (still) consider the male audience during daytime as negligible.[8] The second strategy addresses the television audience as a familial one. This mode of address dominates the early evening hours. Evidence for this strategy is provided by recalling the debate about the so-called family hour in the 1970s or by looking at the situation comedy as the genre which dominates this time slot.[9] The hours after 10:00 p.m. are determined by a third strategy which constructs the audience as "adult." Generally speaking, texts within that time slot used to follow what one might call the "sex and crime" formula. Up to the second half of the 1970s, this slot was dominated by the crime, detective, and lawyer genres, that is by generic texts culturally coded as "male." In terms of the narrative form preferred within these time slots, the television serial – with its characteristic resistance to closure and its multiple plot structure – was and is the dominant fictional narrative on daytime television. Until the second half of the 1970s, prime-time slots used to be the exclusive domain of the episodic series.

The combination of narrative form and strategic mode of address leads to two well-known interrelationships: the first between the open serial narrative and an address to an audience constructed as female; and the second between the narratively self-contained episodic series and an audience constructed in familial or adult, that is in male terms. This well-established nexus began to be untied in exactly that time slot designed to reach an "adult" audience in the 1980s.[10] The success of the prime-time serial *Dallas* caused the production of a whole wave of *Dallas* "successors," all of which combined serial form and a synthesis of the figures of the extended family and the corporation as narrative subject. Instead of regarding these serials as a modification of the US daytime soap opera, we suggest that it is more productive to consider them as an expression of significant changes within the category of texts geared toward an adult audience. In this context, it should be noted that the similarities between prime-time serials and other shows for "adult audiences" are not restricted to their position in the television schedule. Rather, we are confronted with a category of texts determined by a common mode of production (on 35 mm film) and by a considerable number of shared visual characteristics and generic conventions.[11] Moreover, prime-time television's appropriation of the serial narrative was not limited to texts in a melodramatic vein such as *Dallas* or *Dynasty*, but spread out to shows like *Hill Street Blues* (NBC/MTM, 1981–1987), *St. Elsewhere* (NBC/MTM, 1982–1988), *L.A. Law* (NBC, 1986–), and, more recently, to the latest fad on US network television, *Twin Peaks* (NBC, 1990–1991), initially directed by David Lynch, *Northern Exposure* or *Love and War*.

Serials produced by public service television: the case of *Die Schwarzwaldklinik*

Die Schwarzwaldklinik was conceived and produced at a time when the public networks, ARD and ZDF, were becoming increasingly concerned about their future. At that point, commercial channels outside West Germany, such as RTL in Luxembourg, could be received in a limited number of areas in (West) Germany. The response to these commercial channels by (regional) audiences was watched and anxiously researched by the public networks.

Soon, studies revealed that viewers who could receive the new channels were rapidly changing their attitude toward commercial television. Having initially complained about the frequent advertising breaks, they soon expressed their acceptance of the commercial channels, mainly because they provided them with a wider variety of choice among (US) theatrical films and television series.

In their study of differing national television productions in Europe, Alessandro Silj concludes that the influence of audience ratings on "the decisions taken by those responsible for programming is a relatively recent phenomenon."[12] However, a consideration of the context in which the conception and production of *Die Schwarzwaldklinik* took place suggests a rather different perspective. While audience ratings have always played a role in the decisions taken by (public) network executives, the advent of commercial channels changed the very conditions of competition in (West) Germany. Because of "the need to minimise costs and as a result of the initial[ly] very low coverage in the 'cable ghetto,'" the new commercial channels offered a television schedule which predominantly consisted of (US) theatrical films and television series.[13] In contrast to the commercial channels' policies, the public networks (financed by obligatory license fees and only partially through advertising) operate under the legal obligation to provide not only "entertainment," but also educational, political, and other material "in the public interest." However, in contrast to their commercial competitors who started out with small audiences and limited budgets, the public networks' well-established position enables them to rely on a broad national audience and a much larger budget. Unlike the commericial channels, they can afford to offer fictional entertainment made in Germany (which is much more expensive than purchasing and dubbing US television shows). Thus, *Die Schwarzwaldklinik* was made with the expectation that such a "homegrown" series would not only attract a large national audience, but would also give ZDF the edge over commercial channels. In short, *Die Schwarzwaldklinik* was conceived not only as a "homegrown" competitor to US prime-time serials like *Dallas* and *Dynasty*, but also as public television's answer to the much bemoaned "Americanization" of the German media.

Die Schwarzwaldklinik was at once very popular and very expensive. Scheduled on Saturday nights at 7:30 p.m., it was designed as a "family show" aimed at attracting the broadest possible audience. Like the US prime-time serials of the 1980s, *Die Schwarzwaldklinik* was not targeted at women, as daytime soap operas are in the US, where women between the ages of 18 and 49 are singled out as the "purchasing agents" for the household.

For those readers not familiar with German public television, it is important to describe the type of schedule in which *Die Schwarzwaldklinik* made its appearance. The serial was scheduled as one of the prime-time programs which included theatrical films (mainly US and German from the 1930s onwards), weekly *Krimis* (crime series), studio variety shows, game shows, political and cultural "magazines," and productions such as *Aktenzeichen XY Ungelöst* (ZDF), the prototype for recent US shows such as *America's Most Wanted* (NBC/Fox, 1988–) and *Unsolved Mysteries* (NBC, 1988–). At that time, only one other serial, *Die Lindenstraße* (ARD, 1985–), also followed a serialized melodrama format, but this show was heavily steeped in domestic realist traditions (as well as following the model provided by British soap operas) and was not broadcast during prime-time. Family melodrama tends to figure primarily as background story in popular German and European crime series (such as *Tatort* (ZDF, 1971–) or *Eurocops* (ZDF, 1988–)) where it explains a crime's motivation but remains peripheral to its investigation. It is significant that (public) programming produced in Germany, with its emphasis on "something for everyone," provides something less for women. It was only through the rise of the commercial channels that daytime soap operas (from the US as well as from South America) have been imported and now form a part of the daytime television schedule. With regard to the overall programming, there is a decidedly male orientation to all except for a portion of the American imports.

For ZDF, as a public broadcasting institution, *Die Schwarzwaldklinik* provided a means of securing large audiences by a domestic production. The high ratings of US series are often publicly bemoaned and overestimated: as Silj has shown,[14] domestic programs always beat American ones when available, and one audience study discovered that German viewers found *Die Schwarzwaldklinik* more pleasurable than *Dallas* or *Denver-Clan* (the dubbed German version of *Dynasty*) even though they might watch all three. In a sense, the success of the American imports provoked the producers of *Die Schwarzwaldklinik* to produce a certain version of and a certain overemphasis on "Germanness."

Schwarzwaldklinik and the traditions of the *Heimat-* and *Ärztefilm*

Die Schwarzwaldklinik was a "homegrown" television product in that it combined elements of popular national genres and traditions with conventions of US prime-time serials. Indeed, the resemblances to the latter are in some ways superficial. For example, the title sequence mimicked *Dallas* with its jaunty theme music, its use of split-screen landscape shots, and of aerial photography of the stories' buildings and locations, and there was a heavy reliance on local color. The title shots already suggest that this is an insular, geographically remote world, confined to the clinic building and the homestead of Professor Brinkmann, the new director of the clinic, and his family. Through the program's several seasons and renewals, individual scenes became shorter in length. In looking at the first year's episodes, however, the scene length and especially the absence of "mini-climaxes" which precede the commercials and are so much at the heart of the US daytime soap opera

238

tradition (taken up by the prime-time serials), are striking – particularly for an American viewer. In many ways, *Die Schwarzwaldklinik* was more in tune with the conventions of German television productions, with their emphasis on sequence shots preserving the integrity of the actor's performance, and a slow build up through dialog than with US serials such as *Dallas* and *Dynasty*.

Die Schwarzwaldklinik was also less serialized than its US counterparts. In an astute analysis of the program's first season, Rotraut Hoeppel[15] demonstrates the gradually increasing reliance on serialized narratives and the decreasing number of discrete "guest star" appearances. Guest stars (prominent German actors) frequently appeared in single episodes which typically included three plot lines (roughly a tragedy, a melodrama, and a comedy) involving patients whose stories would be completed during the episode. The cast of characters also owed much to the functional format of the episodic series set in an institutional environment (a clinic, a hotel, etc.): chief doctor (Professor Brinkmann), young doctor (son Udo), nurse/love interest (Christa), elderly woman housekeeper to the Brinkmann family (Katie), irksome administrator, stiff head nurse, handsome lovable conscientious objector (Mischa). As the producer, Rademann, explained, the clinic was the focus of the series,

> not only a first-rate transfer point for fate, but also a collection spot for the different characters. Every viewer can find something amusing in every episode: older women like Katie, young girls like Mischa, young intellectuals identify with Udo and his struggles with women's liberation.[16]

In this respect, the show bears a strong resemblance to certain Aaron Spelling productions of the 1970s and 1980s which were shown on ZDF: *Hotel*, *Love Boat* and *Fantasy Island*. We will return to the specific configuration of the family melodrama, which involves a striking Oedipal conflict between Udo and Professor Brinkmann, and to the position of women in the narrative, after considering the popular traditions that *Die Schwarzwaldklinik* drew upon.

Heimatfilm refers to a German genre particularly popular during the Third Reich and again in the 1950s, and recently reworked in many different forms (including the mini-series *Heimat*) in German film and television. Typical themes of the *Heimatfilm* are agrarianism, the importance of a spiritual tie to the German land, and the decadence of the urban and the intellectual. In *Prodigal Son* (*Der Verlorene Sohn*, 1934), a prototype for the genre, Luis Trenker plays the prodigal son, Toni, who leaves his home in the Bavarian mountains with an American femme fatale, Lillian, who has asked him to take her on a dangerous mountain tour. When a friend who has come along on the tour dies, he refuses to return home and leaves for New York. In Manhattan, Toni faces unemployment, eviction and destitution. When he re-encounters Lillian, she claims she still loves him but cannot live in Europe. Toni decides to return home. He arrives during a winter solstice celebration, and, since everyone is wearing folk masks (strong National Socialist connotations here), he disguises himself. Despite the disguises, he and his hometown sweetheart recognize one another and are reunited. The film very explicitly codes the city, the United States, and corruption as female; the mountains, Germany, and folk values as male. This structure is mapped out on a male *Bildungsroman* (filled with phallic symbolism – from the tree trunks of the forest to the skyscrapers of Manhattan): as the local teacher says: "you have to leave in order to come home." Thus, the hero is reintegrated into the homogeneous community of the mountains, reunited with the land, with his paternal inheritance, and with the native girl who will bear him children.

In the pilot episode of *Die Schwarzwaldklinik*, "Die Heimkehr" (the home-coming), *Heimat* conventions were very apparent. In the opening scene, Professor D. Klaus Brinkmann and his housekeeper, Katie, drive along the steep, winding roads of the Black Forest before pulling over to look at the view. Brinkmann remarks that he has not been back since his father's funeral. Gazing down at the clinic below, he says philosophically: "birth and death, luck and bad luck, pain and joy: all the things that make up our lives." Thus begins a reattachment of Professor Brinkmann to the nuclear family and to his *Heimat*. While his words convey the traditional terrain of the melodrama – fate and emotion within the family – they also convey his privileged mastery over them. Later in the pilot episode, we learn that Professor Brinkmann's wife (Udo's mother) is dead, that he has traveled throughout Europe, practicing in Paris, Zürich, and Karlsruhe, and that he has recently ended a relationship with his anesthetist girlfriend. After scratching his finger on a rusty nail, he enters the hospital for the first time in "disguise" (as a patient), observing his new employees incognito. The return under an assumed identity, the connection between land and his paternal inheritance are, therefore, quite explicit. Although later episodes are unable to repeat this premise precisely, the themes of *Heimat* remain, and Professor Brinkmann is often placed in a situation where he passes as a local, while keeping his distinguished identity a secret. It was important that the pilot episode made these familiar generic patterns so explicit. In later episodes, like a good son of the *Heimat* films, when troubled or out of sorts, Professor Brinkmann takes a hike on the hills.

In one episode, he meets an elderly man (a *Landstreicher* (hobo)) using his cabin, but Professor Brinkmann pretends he too is living off the land and humbly takes lessons about gardening and cooking soup. Over and over again, Professor Brinkmann enjoys a special closeness with "peasant" figures: elderly men with thick Swabian accents, farmers, hobos. There is only one ethnicity in this fictional Black Forest: that of true Germanness, of traditional life. "Guestworkers," immigrants, and radicals (anyone who might challenge the authority of the good doctor) have no place in this world. Thus, local color (of the guidebook kind) emphasizes the pre-industrial agrarian nature of the Black Forest and forms the background of many episodes. Fishing, swimming, and hiking, depicted in scenes which produce precisely the visual conventions of the travel brochure, are the rewards that await the hard-working doctors during their leisure time. Emotional states are projected onto the landscape, with pathetic fallacy commonly used (storms reflect the characters' agitation; sunshine mirrors their happiness). After Udo was rehabilitated as a character, in part due to his discovery of true love with a simple, earthy, uneducated, and uncomplicated woman (nanny to his infant half-brother), the couple regularly commune with nature and their sexual relationship is approvingly associated with the outdoors. Indeed, the association with nature helps to naturalize the astonishing blatancy of the incestuous themes within the Brinkmann family.

A 1988 episode makes the *Heimat* themes explicit. Brinkmann has had a minor heart attack and is housebound while Christa (who has attended medical school, become a doctor at the hospital, married him and given birth to their son) is out working. The first part of the episode focuses on his predicament at home, with nothing but time on his hands. His professional competence at the clinic is in complete contrast to his incompetence in the home: he changes diapers awkwardly, plays the piano badly, begins talking too much at meals, irritating everyone else in the family with his complaining and restlessness. Finally, he leaves for the United States to see a specialist, hoping he can return to work. Disappointed by his wife's lack of attentiveness, he meets an attractive woman on the plane, who turns out to be a local Black Forest girl, a "farmer." In San Francisco, he discovers the modern city and technological nightmare: airports, skyscrapers, and the hospital (the doctor Brinkmann visits has his office in a skyscraper). It is an entirely impersonal world and he is very anxious to leave, a situation which again strongly echoes the wanderings of the hero in *Der Verlorene Sohn*. The woman he meets on the plane invites him to a barbecue on an enormous ranch complete with country-and-western singers. German viewers know this United States, for it is "Southfork." Brinkmann and his new flame hire a mobile home and set out for the Grand Canyon. America is represented in the landscape symbolism by a valley – the inverse, mirror image of the German mountains that are his home. But there is a great economy here in this symbolism (United States, valley, feminine – Germany, mountains, masculine), representing the US as the opposite of German culture and values, and doing so by geographic symbolism (another hallmark of German film). In a shot reminiscent of his arrival in the Black Forest during the pilot episode, Professor Brinkmann stands at the precipice, above the valley, gazing below, and floats a paper airplane down into the canyon before heading back home.

As in the *Heimatfilme* of the 1950s, these elements are conservative through and through. The Black Forest is here an idyllic world where, not coincidentally, everyone knows his place, and is satisfied with it. The people honor traditions and celebrate their very own Professor Brinkmann, who holds the center of this order of things.[17]

Some of the classic themes of the medical story (as in the German *Ärztefilme*) are interwoven with the conventions of the *Heimatfilm*. Professor Brinkmann replaces the now outdated figure of the aristocrat, whose place he still occupies structurally within the narrative and who proves both his wisdom and the justification of his exalted position by showing he is still in touch with the common folk and the land. Medical stories about the impact of modern life, or modern technology on individuals are always set against this background. Patients routinely arrive at the clinic as a result of hair-raising car accidents at high speeds along the curvy mountain roads of the Black Forest. But these are often played off against another story, about elderly natives who are also guests of the hospital, who cling to the old ways, and have arrived on foot or by bicycle.

In an episode entitled "Sterbehilfe" (mercy killing), Professor Brinkmann is called to testify at a hearing involving an old childhood friend accused of mercy killing. His friend is a "country doctor" who still delivers cows as well as babies, and objects to the use of "unnatural" technological means of prolonging life. Professor Brinkmann is able to prove that he still understands life – that he is not a mere slave to the advanced technology we so often see at the hospital, and his testimony essentially absolves his friend. Professor Brinkmann is equally committed to protecting the old ways and helping to translate and explain the need for the new to his worried, frightened patients. Professor Brinkmann can also be tough when he has to: he angrily reprimands his son Udo for his personal and professional behavior. While father and son regularly display a murderous rage in their interactions, the problem eventually turns out to be reconcilable. Udo eventually sees that his womanizing interferes with his practice of medicine. Initially portrayed as intensely resentful of his father at work (as he describes his father to another intern: "He knows everything. He makes you feel like nothing"), Udo's admiration for his father's skill and wisdom (granting him the status of a "natural" authority) ultimately wins out, and he too grants Professor Brinkmann the status of natural authority.

Popular traditions, narrative form, and popularity

Like the German serial, the US prime-time serials of the 1980s also relied on popular traditions, in this case ones pre-existing in US media culture. It was the Hollywood family melodrama of the 1950s which served as the model for successful serials of the 1980s such as *Dallas* and *Dynasty*.[18] Thus, in an era determined by the political shift toward conservatism, both media systems revitalized traditions which had been successful during the restoration phase of the 1950s. In both countries, the war period arguably meant a "disturbance" of the patriarchal order in so far as women were called upon to hold social positions and responsibilities usually reserved for men. Following this period of considerably altered social positions for women, the patriarchal order had to be firmly restored in the 1950s. In that process, popular entertainment undoubtedly was of major importance. But if the German *Heimat-* and *Ärztefilm* unequivocally confined women to their "natural" place as (house)wives and mothers, and if both German genres reinstalled the "good" patriarchs and male authority figures, the Hollywood family melodrama arguably suggested much more ambivalent lessons about patriarchy and the family to its female audience.

Die Schwarzwaldklinik asked viewers to admire Professor Klaus Brinkmann as the lovable incarnation of the patriarchal order. Plots and stories around his son Udo or guest stars featuring as Professor Brinkmann's old school buddies practice what Roland Barthes called inoculation: "One immunizes the contents of the collective imagination by means of a small innoculation [*sic*] of acknowledged evil; one thus protects it against the risk of a generalized subversion."[19] Within the framework of sanctified patriarchy, a small dose of sexism is introduced, the better to convey the sense that the system still really works, as represented by the ideal man, Professor Brinkmann. It is hardly surprising that female characters who do not fulfill the norm of an unthreatening and acceptable femininity are negatively evaluated. One of Udo's fiancées, a dedicated doctor, was repeatedly denounced as a women's libber; the clinic's head nurse was cast as the stereotypical old termagant sticking her nose into everybody else's business. Even Professor Brinkmann's love interest and later wife Christa (Gaby Dohm), virtuous in her uncomplicated femininity, was narratively abused in order to heighten the patriarch's glory. By the serial's third season, Christa, a former nurse who has, meanwhile, become a doctor herself, is practicing medicine full time. In scene after scene, we are made to feel the wrongness of her placing her professional commitments first. Eventually, her son develops a psychosomatic illness and she cuts back to half time. But Christa's sufferings – and they are many – form only a kind of feminine dystopia to the background of Professor Brinkmann's control of the family and the world. In one episode, Christa must face a suicidal woman patient who, after picking up her beloved father from a long stay at the clinic, and convincing him that she could drive despite her inexperience, is involved in a car accident which fatally injures him moments after leaving the clinic. Christa tells the woman that her father was dying of cancer anyway, and the patient is cured. But her husband Professor Brinkmann harshly rebukes Christa for "playing God" – a role that he himself has assumed so gracefully throughout the series.

Die Schwarzwaldklinik presented an archaic, idealized rural microcosm in which harmony and order signified the familial status quo. While that harmony was threatened by events and happenings within the plot structure, the narrative (within the single episode and beyond) ultimately worked toward the reconciliation of contradictions and conflicts within the hospital community and the Brinkmann family. Compared to such a politics of representation, US prime-time serials such as *Dallas* and *Dynasty* confronted viewers with chaos and conflict as the usual state of things, both within the public (in this case, the corporate) and the familial sphere. Here, contradictions and conflicts were not resolved by containing them within the family, since "the family is the very site of economic struggle and moral corruption."[20] Jane Feuer's analysis of strategic differences in dealing with the family between the episodic series format (exemplified, in her analysis, by the US situation comedies of the 1970s) and the melodramatic prime-time serials is useful in illuminating the differences between German television and its US counterparts. If both the German and the American form are constituted by television's "economically derived need for perpetual self-reduplication," *Die Schwarzwaldklinik* is much more closely related to the episodic format of the US sitcom in that both forms depend upon the continual reintegration of the family. In contrast to this, self-replication in the US prime-time serials "depends upon the continual disintegration of the family."[21] And whereas the US family sitcom of the 1970s tried to convey its "liberal" messages within the narrative framework of the episodic series, *Die Schwarzwaldklinik* combined that (narratively) conservative form with a revitalization of extremely problematic traditions.

Critical work on US prime-time serials points to a close interrelationship between the paradigmatic change toward the serial form on US network television and a tendency within serial texts to be open to multiple readings.[22] In the case of the melodramatic US prime-time serial, it can be argued that its narrative openness is inextricably related to a greater openness in terms of gender relations and to its allowance of and fascination with female transgressions. In our view, these characteristics account for much of its popularity, especially with its female audiences. However, one should not conceive of such textual characteristics of these serials as a cause for critical praise of their "democratic" qualities. A better way of understanding such textual traits is to consider a serial like *Dynasty* as a new kind of *bricolage*, i.e., as an assemblage of bits and pieces of various forms into a new textual structure, designed to meet specific economic and cultural requirements.

But what are these requirements and how do they manifest themselves in a given prime-time serial made in the US? A general answer is provided by considering the commercial character of US network television and the specific socio-cultural context in which it must operate today. In this respect, we have to bear in mind that US prime-time television searches for the largest possible audience in a society and culture marked by a particularly high degree of heterogeneity, if not fragmentation. Consequently, the goal of selling the largest possible number of viewers to advertisers ultimately requires some kind of acknowledgment of the audience's socio-cultural diversity. This does not mean, however, that US television producers and network executives consider all audiences equally desirable. Desirability is measured in terms of the viewer's capacity for consumer spending. Thus, economically affluent sub-audiences (among them women holding high positions in the workforce) whose cultural identity is not identical with that constructed by the traditional television text (which is that of a white, male heterosexual) have increasingly gained significance for advertisers and, consequently, for the networks. The introduction (and success) of the prime-time serial in the 1980s arguably suggests that the narratively self-contained episodic series geared toward an audience constructed in male, white, and heterosexual terms had become inadequate for meanings and pleasures produced by viewers.

The historical and cultural specificity of the situation which facilitated the US prime-time serial's rise to popularity becomes evident by a comparison with the situation established by the tradition of German public programming. The number one "homemade" popular form which occasionally even wins the praise of television critics is that of the crime series. Until recently, programs made for women simply did not exist on German television, with the rare exception of an occasional fashion show broadcast on a Saturday afternoon. Apart from US and South American soap operas which have been introduced only recently under pressure from commercial channels, there is presently only one show broadcast by public television which explicitly addresses women (while stressing that men are not excluded from the show): *Mona Lisa* (ZDF, 1988–), a magazine show scheduled for early Sunday night – 6:10 p.m. It is ironic that the German public television system, with its explicit obligation to do justice to the variety of "socially and politically relevant" groups and perspectives, could simply neglect the cultural interests and preferences of (more than) half of the German population for more than thirty years.

It is this context which may help to explain why *Die Schwarzwaldklinik* gained such popularity, particularly with a female audience. It may also be that the choice of an upper middle-class family invited more identification on the viewer's part than the outrageously conspicious consumerism which characterized the fictional US family clans. But if US prime-time serials such as *Dallas* and *Dynasty* – and, to an even greater extent, a serial such as *Knots Landing* – were marked by concessions to a female audience in that to various degrees they have taken on board the daytime soap opera's traditional emphasis on female friendships and solidarity, no such love and friendship were on offer in *Die Schwarzwaldklinik*. The show was based on Professor Brinkmann's relations with his hospital staff and domestic staff, son Udo and wife Christa. At the outset Christa had been dating Udo and discovered that he was unfaithful. By the Christmas break, Christa and Professor Brinkmann were married, and Udo was engaged to another doctor at the hospital. Christa is competent, scrupulous, and most important of all, equally committed to emotional caretaking as to medicine. This emotional sensitivity was particularly worked out on her female patients, who are often suicidal or deeply disturbed. Christa is a model of uncomplicated femininity – unlike Udo's fiancée, who is shown to be overly career-oriented and self-centered: the "women's libber." This basic structure of *Die Schwarzwaldklinik* allowed Christa no relations with equals: for the other nurses, she is the boss's wife; at home, she is the housekeeper's "boss," always retaining a respectful distance from the family servant, and she had no relatives of her own. Christa was allowed no lateral relationships, no friendships with other women, no time "off the job." She goes from her husband and stepson/ex-lover at the hospital to handling them at home.

This is especially striking in contrast to the celebration of Professor Brinkmann's male bonding with staff and guest stars on the show: he hits it off right away with men of all classes and ages, and enjoys many tender moments basking in their praise. Christa has no women to confide in. Some episodes underline the hostility or abuse Christa must take at work – much of it "sexual harassment," but there is difficulty in dramatizing this point because she is so isolated as a character. Christa must endure such hardships as Udo setting her up as having administered the wrong medication just so she will continue to date him, and the clinic's head (filling in for Professor Brinkmann on sick leave) harshly challenging her and her husband's diagnosis with patients. Christa seems tense, extremely controlled, rigidly conservative and rule-abiding, anxious (and who wouldn't be under such circumstances?). Any form of feminine solidarity is a structural impossibility in Christa's world. Later on, Udo occasionally notices her troubles and intervenes on her behalf with his father. But again, we have her dramatic conflicts overlaid on to that of the father–son story: Christa and her problems function primarily in the narrative as grist for the Oedipal mill. There are some parallels between Christa and Krystle Carrington of *Dynasty*: both women exemplify one form of what Julia Lesage has called the "hegemonic female fantasy," in this case marrying the boss.[23] It is an extremely conservative fantasy, but made much more so by the firm and unchallenged position of Professor Brinkmann. As we shall see below, Krystle's husband, Blake Carrington, suffers far more outrageous upheavals, more formidable female opponents, and more open challenges to his authority.

Female transgression in US prime-time melodrama: the case of *Dynasty*

We move on to a comparative look at the 1980s ultimate female opponent to patriarchal figures and the female transgressor *par excellence* on US prime-time television: *Dynasty*'s Alexis Carrington-Colby. It is interesting to note that her character was not part of the show's original conception. Few critics and viewers may remember that *Dynasty* started out as a *Dallas* clone, distinguished from its model by the creator–producers' explicit attempt to make the Ewings look rather pedestrian and petit bourgeois. What characterized both serials as a new type of melodrama on US prime-time television was their representation of corporate capitalism as outrageously immoral, and patriarchy as excessively monstrous. *Dynasty*'s first season not only confronted us with numerous business manipulations executed by Blake Carrington, but also revealed that he hired a bunch of mobsters to beat up one of his daughter's sexual playmates, raped his loving wife, and killed his son's ex-lover. However, John Forsythe's performance as the monstrous capitalist patriarch must have been judged as either too unconvincing or too boring to stick to the initial idea of presenting Blake Carrington as a challenge to J. R. Ewing. Therefore, the Blake character was slowly turned around to eventually become a "good" patriarch and an honest businessman. However, this change did not improve the representation of the Carrington clan as a highly problematic family. This problem-ridden, if not dystopian familial figure characterizes all US prime-time melodramas in the generic vein of *Dallas*.

Since John Forsythe, alias Blake Carrington, proved himself a rather unpromising alternative to his popular *Dallas* competitor, the show's creators introduced his ex-wife into the first episode of *Dynasty*'s second season. The Alexis character linked *Dynasty* to a particular line of Hollywood melodrama, namely to those films in which a female character is granted narrative functions usually reserved for a male protagonist.[24] As feminist critics have pointed out, the presence of a female character in the function of narrative subject – rather than that of narrative object – tends to cause a considerable amount of ambiguity and contradiction within a popular text. Even though Alexis's overall significance is by no means identical with that of a protagonist in a narratively self-contained text, her function resembles that of a male protagonist in that she can be seen as the ultimate driving force behind the narrative. From her first appearance, Alexis constantly disrupts the kind of corporate patriarchy represented by Blake Carrington. Her combined private and public "war" against the familial patriarch constitutes the serial's main source of conflict and provides a structural framework into which all other conflicts are inscribed.

With regard to the meanings of the Alexis character that can be produced from a female (textual) position, two coexisting patterns emerge from the text. The first one follows the model provided by Tania Modleski's analysis of the daytime soap opera villainess.[25] According to such a reading, Alexis is a safety valve, providing an outlet for repressed female anger and frustration, while simultaneously confirming the cultural construction of female identity as egoless, passive, and powerless. As we have argued elsewhere,[26] the textual position from which such a reading of the villainess is produced implies a distinct social position, namely that of a white middle-class housewife.

The second pattern of reading Alexis turns her into a kind of (villainous) heroine; into a female character posing a constant threat to the patriarchal order upheld by Blake Carrington.[27] This pattern can be demonstrated by looking at a major narrative conflict in *Dynasty*, namely that between Alexis and Krystle Carrington, Blake's second wife. The signification of this conflict takes up the conventional opposition between a melodramatic heroine and her adversary, the villainess or vamp. What the Alexis–Krystle dichotomy signifies is a conflict between a socially accepted femininity and its transgression. Characteristic to *Dynasty*'s representation of such a conflict is its inscription by a sequence of extremely conventional contrastive traits:

Krystle	*Alexis*
good	bad
American	European
middle-class	aristocrat
blonde	dark-haired
non-smoker	smoker
altruistic	egoistic
dependent	autonomous
wife	businesswoman
unthreatening, maternal sexuality	threatening sexuality, cut off from reproductive functions
monogamous	serial monogamy, with leanings toward polygamy
passive	active, vigorous, aggressive
suffering	enjoying
rejects power	indulges in execution of power
democratic	authoritarian
material possessions submitted to ideals and values	indulges in material possessions and wealth
idealist	hedonist

As Umberto Eco once noted, a single cliché may represent an annoyance, but 100 clichés make for a true feast. With the Alexis character, *Dynasty* does not celebrate a respectable party, but indulges in an excessive orgy.

What particularly marks Alexis as a transgressor of accepted femininity is that she is represented as having appropriated traits that are conventionally coded as "male," for example, as being active, autonomous, and powerful. Thus, her character provides a female fantasy which turns the current state of gender relations upside down. Read accordingly, Alexis would also function as a kind of safety valve for female anger and frustration. However, by reading Alexis as a kind of heroine, female anger is not directed at a female character, but at the patriarchal context of the fictional world of Denver. Thus, this pattern represents a much more explicit aesthetic acknowledgment of real conflicts and desires experienced by women under patriarchy than that of Alexis as villainess.

Let us point to some textual evidence for this pattern by looking at the character in relation to the issue of power. In the fictional world of *Dynasty*, we watch Alexis's unscrupulous attempts to successfully appropriate and exercise power in both the public and the private sphere. Since the concept of power is so inextricably interwoven into the "male" cultural sphere, the synthesis between a female character and the blatant execution of power is bound to be particularly effective. What even reinforces this highly ambivalent synthesis between a female character and the execution of power still further is that Alexis is endowed with the traits of physical attractiveness. Like the melodramatic vamp, she is represented as a sexual threat to her male environment. Not only does she threaten Blake's marriage to Krystle, but his encounter with her sexuality ultimately cost the Cecil Colby character his life, and her young lover and later husband, Dex Dexter, is submitted to considerable sufferings because of his sexual addiction to her. As a woman beyond the magical age of 40, Alexis chooses and gets the men she desires. Thus, her character combines a variety of traits by which male culture has marked women as "other." She is presented as the male fantasy of woman coming true in the fictional world of *Dynasty* and saying, "Here is your worst nightmare."

The representation of Alexis by piling up melodramatic conventions layer by layer produces a televised version of the textual excess that critics have found in Hollywood film melodrama. The excessive use of melodramatic conventions to characterize Alexis turns the viewer's attention to the representation's very fictionality and, thus, enables her to read the character – with tongue in cheek – as a (not so serious) threat to patriarchy.

It should be noted, however, that this representation is not without its problems. We are not given a challenge to the conventional construction of woman as "other," but a reinforcement. Alexis by no means represents a grown-up, autonomous, and socially responsible woman; rather, a narcissistic personality, out for pleasure and power just to confirm her own grandiosity. What *Dynasty* presents to us is a distorted image of an active, autonomous, and powerful female character, yet one excessively marked as a fictitious narcissist. Since the Alexis character so vehemently rejects the traditional construction of femininity as egoless, passive, and powerless, her character allows for more pleasures than critics so far were ready to realize.

Conclusion

Die Schwarzwaldklinik maintains a much more masculinist and authoritarian ethos than serials such as *Dynasty*. Professor Brinkmann follows the tradition of the German doctor films of the 1950s with a few nuances, as Hoeppel has carefully explained:

Professor Brinkmann is a "heroic-fighting leader," not a strict patri-archal Godfather and not a christlike magical healer. He embodies the more gentle, all-forgiving god, who works in the background and only appears when it is absolutely necessary, because the little ones need help.[28]

Hoeppel has noted the long-lived popularity of the doctor in film and television shows in Germany. It might be argued that all of this is inherent in the medical series form. It is, in this context, interesting to note that medical shows in the US such as *Dr Kildare* (NBC/MGM/Arena, 1961–1966), *Ben Casey* (ABC/Bing Crosby Productions, 1960–1965), and *Marcus Welby, M.D.* (ABC/Universal, 1968–1977), so popular in the 1950s and 1960s, were also based on charismatic, authoritarian figures like Professor Brinkmann. Recent attempts to resurrect the medical series have failed: Richard Chamberlain was brought back in *Island Son* (NBC/Lorimar, 1989–1990),as a sexier, more tropical doctor, a blend of Shogun and Dr Kildare, but the show was cancelled after one season. *Heartbeat* (ABC/Spelling, 1988), about a team of women doctors, was a similar failure. The only successes have been *Northern Exposure* (Brand, Falsey/Universal, 1991–) and *Doogie Howser, M.D.* (Boccho Productions/Twentieth Century Fox, 1989–), a Stephen Boccho creation in which the good doctor is a 13-year-old boy genius. Thus, the patriarchal overtones are masked by the hero's youth, although Doogie shares the unfailing wisdom of his pre-decessors.[29] *Northern Exposure* recasts the medical series conventions by making the young, Jewish doctor from New York the frequent butt of the eccentric local whites and inuits in the small Alaskan town where he practices to work off his medical debts. The series relies on relatively few medical dramas, focusing instead on the personal lives and colorful en-tanglements of the locals. The doctor represents the voice of authority continually questioned and even ridiculed by his recalcitrant patients – a situation made possible, in part, by his ethnicity and relative youth. Still, he is subjected to kinds of humiliation unimaginable on a German medical series.

Professor Brinkmann's intense popularity with German fans speaks of the appeal, the desire for such an authority figure. Herta Herzog[30] has noted that Germans regularly seem to be in love with such authoritarian heroes. It is important that this is recognized not as an innate personality trait of Germans, but as a "structure of feeling" continually reproduced in popular culture. For a serial character, however, this brings about a very different ethos to the show, and one that is hardly open to the kinds of feminist readings against the grain, chaos, and disruption that have been found in so many US serials – be it daytime or night-time.

What we find in *Die Schwarzwaldklinik* as a hybridization of popular German genres, the *Heimat*- and the *Ärztefilm*, are many distinctly German features, and they are troubling features: the love of invincible authority, the isolation of women, the old kinds of nationalism tied to class and gender hierarchies, and historically to fascism. The narrative structure has extensively borrowed from US prime-time serials, but declined the outrageous reversals of fortune and plot which so marked *Dallas* and *Dynasty* as trash. Uniquely, *Die Schwarzwaldklinik* gives us the conservatism of *Heimat* in the form of a reductive version of the world found in tourist promotions. At the core, what has remained are the very patriarchal elements that characterize most German mass media, and a very different deal for women on the screen and in the audience. All melodramatic television serials are not created equal, and it is the historical evolutions of combinations of genre forms which provide a basis for making cross-cultural comparisons and for understanding the rigidity of popular traditions. While Hollywood is greedily eyeing the European Community as a market for its television programming and advertising – and this certainly must be a major concern to television scholars – it is worth saying that all "homegrown" television is not equally desirable, at least not from the point of view of women.

One of the pitfalls of cross-cultural television criticism may be that the text seems more singular in its meaning, and the critic is less familiar with the variety of actual readings that are produced by real audiences. Experiences and discussions about *Die Schwarzwaldklinik* with German female friends suggest that women may produce "fragmented readings" or consider the show as purely kitsch in a way that resembles the camp readings of *Dynasty* discussed by Jane Feuer.[31] One of the main factors of producing a kitsch reading – especially for younger, university educated audiences – may be the show's ultra-Germanness, its reduction of culture to a series of tourist vignettes. However, our critical analysis as well as our experiences convince us that there are rigid limits to the variety of readings *Die Schwarzwaldklinik* can produce. Unlike *Dallas* and *Dynasty*, where Blake Carrington and J. R. Ewing were deeply and regularly shaken up, their worlds turned upside down, by forces (often women) quite outside their control, *Die Schwarzwaldklinik* offers a world intact. The Father still reigns here, relatively unchallenged. Professor Klaus Brinkmann is on top, king of his mountain. *Die Schwarzwaldklinik* seems to suggest that even when German public television sets out to be popular, to make serial melodrama, it cannot or will not produce a text as open to feminist readings as commercial US television targeted at women consumers. Thus, the politics of international television criticism for feminists is bound to be endlessly contradictory and ambiguous.[32]

Postscript

Professor Brinkmann was followed by many other benevolent patriarchs on ZDF programs. Typically these shows developed a continuing plot line around the dominant character, combined with subplots involving guest stars that came to a close within one episode. The main characters are middle-aged fathers – widowed or divorced – and story-lines focus on their personal as well as professional lives. In *Forsthaus Falkenau*, set in Bavaria, a widowed ranger with three children worked his way through a series of female acquaintances before finding the right woman. *Der Landarzt*, set in Schleswig-Holstein, offered a doctor who was younger and more liberal than Professor Brinkmann, but enjoyed the same unerring judgment and authority. Both of these series, which have finished their initial runs, had strong elements of "local color" and *Heimatfilm* motifs. *Der Landarzt* was recently reintroduced, the main characters being a new doctor moving to the area and the original doctor's widow.

It is interesting that these German series have taken on the narrative emphasis on "serial monogamy" common to US soaps, yet restricted this to the male protagonist. This typical narrative pattern has, in German series, been fitted to the measure of male fantasy. Everywhere the hero goes, women wait for his attention, and as soon as one woman has decided to leave, a new one knocks at his door. In three current programs, *Vater Braucht Eine Frau* (*Father Needs a Wife*), *Unser Lehrer, Doktor Specht* (*Our Teacher, Dr Specht*), and *Sicher ist Sicher* (*Secure is Secure*), the heroes are two teachers and an insurance executive, respectively. While male professional triumphs are at the center, women come and go from the hero's life – and are often judged harshly for their unsuitability as partners.

German television continues to rely heavily on international productions that can be purchased cheaply. The growth of commercial channels – and the expanding clock of the television schedule – have increased the number and frequency of US programs on German channels. As of February 1993, commercial channels captured about 50 percent of the audience in Germany, with ARD and ZDF getting about 22.7 percent each, local public stations about 7.9 percent, and the remainder shared by RTL (with the highest rating at 16.6 percent), SAT1, Pro7, Tele5, and others.[33] For all channels, most of the programs produced in Germany tend to be the inexpensive *Volksmusik* programs, reality television and game shows. *Krimis*, or detective dramas, make up a large percentage of the more expensively produced programs.

Currently, only one commercial channel has ventured into the production of a television serial: *Gute Zeiten, Schlechte Zeiten* (*Good Times, Bad Times*), a half-hour program broadcast daily at 7:45 p.m. on RTL. The closest parallel to *Die Schwarzwaldklinik* is a twice-weekly series broadcast on ARD, entitled *Marienhof*. Centering on a family gardening business, it remains to be seen whether it will be successful. There is only one domestic German series that features a strong female character in the leading role: *Vera Wesskamp*, a program in the vein of British rather than American soaps. Vera is a widow in her 40s who owns a shipping company. She endures the same kinds of suffering visited on professional women in *Die Schwarzwaldklinik*: her younger lover leaves her because she's too busy and doesn't put his needs first, her Sirkian children constantly nag that she neglects them.

German viewers can still look to US soaps to find female characters in more plentiful supply. While US prime-time soaps have vanished from the prime-time offerings of German television, *Dallas* can be seen weekdays at 9:00 a.m. on the combined morning program produced by ARD and ZDF, while *Knot's Landing* is shown on a commercial channel at 12:30 p.m. In addition, three daytime soaps are aired on commercial programs: *The Guiding Light* (retitled *Die Springfield Story*) at 12:30 p.m. and *Santa Barbara* (*California Clan*) at 1:20 p.m. on RTL, and *General Hospital* at 6:45 p.m. (competing with *The Cosby Show* broadcast daily by Pro7) and 10:20 p.m. on Kabelkanal. In addition the telenovela *Sinha Moca* is broadcast on EINS PLUS, a spin-off of ARD. Many US series are now available on a daily basis on German television.

The supply of US prime-time serials to television markets such as Germany's, however, will soon dry up. Two events of February 1993 symbolize important changes in US television since the 1980s: *Knot's Landing* was cancelled after fourteen years on the air, and Joan Collins appeared as a guest star on the situation comedy *Roseanne*. By the end of *Knot's Landing*, three women had displaced the show's patriarch as chief executives of the major corporation and female characters outnumbered the males by about three to one (the producers desperately imported a couple of old boyfriends just to wrap up the plot). The lack of male characters had created a situation where the five most important women on the show were all connected to the show's villain: as sister, niece, mother who adopted his child, lover, and wife.

The manic energy of the prime-time villainesses as well as the treatment of marriage, motherhood, and female friendship has migrated from soap opera to situation comedies such as *Roseanne*, *Murphy Brown*, and *Designing Women*. Often blurring the lines between melodrama and comedy, these shows are at times more explicitly feminist than the prime-time soaps could be. When Joan Collins guest-starred as a long-lost cousin of Roseanne's, she acknowledged the passing of the guard by finishing an argument between the two women with the line, "I bow to the queen of all bitches." As the credits rolled Collins and Roseanne, walking off the set, lampooned their image as bitches in the tabloid press. (Indeed, Roseanne's publicity mirrors that of Collins in the heyday of *Dynasty*: both women have been constructed as controversial, ambivalent figures to hate and love.) In the spoof, Roseanne and Collins couldn't be nicer or more charitable: Roseanne bends down to hold the dustpan while a crew member sweeps up and Joan makes coffee for the crew. Discussing the business details of Collins's appearance, Roseanne offers to put Collins's name above her own in the credits, to which Collins replies that Roseanne needn't credit her or even pay her, for that matter.

Situation comedies have an uneven track record on German television, in part because of the problem of dubbing and the fact that cultural references in comedy are at times incomprehensible to German audiences. Primary among those cultural references would be the bawdy, aggressive, "in your face" comedy of Roseanne.[34] *Roseanne* has gained a spot on Kabelkanal, and already has a sort of cult following; *Murphy Brown* is currently shown at 2:00 a.m.; *Golden Girls* has proven very successful with some younger, late night audiences. While these shows have a cult following, it remains to be seen whether they could work their way into the prime-time schedules, and gain the kind of following *Schwarzwaldklinik* or *Dynasty* enjoyed. To begin to picture the difficulties, just imagine Roseanne as Professor Brinkmann's or Dr Specht's next date.

Notes

1 David Morley and Kevin Robins, "Spaces of Identity: Communication Technologies and the Reconfiguration of Europe," *Screen* 30 (4) (1989), pp. 10–34.
2 *Die Schwarzwaldklinik* was also shown on Channel 4 in the UK, 1988–1990.
3 There are many excellent precedents for a consideration of the intersections of German nationalism and gender ideologies published in *New German Critique*, for example, Miriam Hansen's "Dossier on Heimat" 36–7 (1985); and in works such as Klaus Theweleit, *Male Fantasies* 2 vols (Minneapolis, Minn.: University of Minnesota Press, 1987), vol. 1.
4 Tania Modleski, "The Search for Tomorrow in Today's Soap Opera," in her *Loving With a Vengeance* (Hamden, Conn. Archon Books, 1982), pp. 94–98. Charlotte Brunsdon, "Crossroads: Notes on Soap Opera," *Screen* 22 (4) (1981), pp. 32–37; Carol Lopate, "Daytime Television: You'll Never Want to Leave Home," *Radical America* 11 (January–February 1977), pp. 33–51; Ellen Seiter, "Eco's TV Guide – The Soaps," *Tabloid* 5 (winter 1982), pp. 35–43.
5 Ellen Seiter, "To Teach and To Sell: Irna Phillips and Her Sponsors, 1930–1954," *Journal of Film and Video* 41 (1) (1989), pp. 21–35.
6 See Michael Hofmann's analysis of *Die Schwarzwaldklinik* in Alessandro Silj, *East of Dallas: The European Challenge to American Television* (London: BFI, 1988), pp. 142–148.
7 The argument for a careful distinction of differing forms of television serial drama has been made by Robert C. Allen, "Bursting Bubbles: 'Soap Opera', Audiences, and the Limits of Genre," in Ellen Seiter, Hans Borchers, Gabriel Kreutzner, and Eva-Maria Warth (eds), *Remote Control: Audiences, Television, and Cultural Power* (London and New York: Routledge, 1989), pp. 44–55.
8 The interviews were conducted in the context of the research project "Soap Operas on American Television," based at the Department of American Studies, University of Tübingen, and funded by the Volkswagen foundation.
9 The sitcom's preference for an address to a familial audience is discussed by Jane Feuer, "Narrative Form in American Network Television," in Colin MacCabe (ed.), *High Theory/Low Culture. Analysing Popular Television and Film* (Manchester: Manchester University Press, 1986), pp. 101–114.
10 It must be noted, however, that these modifications with regard to narrative formats were not restricted to the time slot after 10:00 p.m. Jane Feuer has analyzed the historical changes within the genre of the situation comedy. See Feuer, "Narrative Form in American Network Television."
11 Details are given in Ellen Seiter, "Von der Niedertracht der Hausfrau und der Größe der Schurkin," *Frauen und Film* 42 (August 1987), pp. 35–59; and Gabriele

Kreutzner, *Die Fernsehserie Dynasty: Untersuchungen zu einem populären Text im amerikanischen Fernsehen der achtziger Jahre* (Trier: WVT, 1991).

12 Silj, *East of Dallas*, p. 202.

13 Udo Michael Krüger, "US Productions on West German Commercial Television," in Christian Thomsen (ed.) *Cultural Transfer or Electronic Imperialism? The Impact of American Television Programs on European Television*, (Heidelberg: Carl Winter Universitätsverlag, 1989), p. 78.

14 Silj, *East of Dallas*, p. 202.

15 Rotraud Hoeppel, "Halbgötter in Weiß – Zur Faszination des Arztes in Film und Fernsehen," in AV Medienpädogogik 615, Protokolle 1986. Bundesarbeitsgemeinschaft für Jugendfilmarbeit und Medienerziehung e.V., 1986, pp. 17–69.

16 Ibid., pp. 49–50.

17 Ibid., p. 52 (our translation).

18 See Jane Feuer, "Melodrama, Serial Form and Television Today," *Screen* 25 (1) (1984), pp. 4–16; and Kreutzner, *Die Fernsehserie Dynasty*.

19 Roland Barthes, "Myth Today," in Susan Sontag, (ed.), *A Barthes Reader* (New York: Hill & Wang), 1983), p. 140.

20 Feuer, "Melodrama, Serial Form and Television Today," p. 16.

21 Feuer, "Narrative Form in American Network Television," p. 105.

22 See, for example, Feuer, "Narrative Form in American Network Television," and "Melodrama, Serial Form and Television Today," pp. 4–16.

23 Julia Lesage, "The Hegemonic Female Fantasy in 'An Unmarried Woman' and 'Craig's Wife'," *Film Reader* 5 (1982), pp. 83–84.

24 Here, we are referring to those films that Laura Mulvey has called "female melodrama": "Notes on Sirk and Melodrama," *Movie* 25 (1977–1978).

25 Alexis is also characterized by a number of differences from the daytime soap opera villainess, but they do not affect the applicability of the Modleski model (see Tania Modleski, "The Search for Tomorrow in Today's Soap," pp. 94–98).

26 See our section, "Resisting the Place of 'Ideal Mother,'" in our article with Eva-Maria Warth and Hans Borchers, "'Don't Treat Us Like We're so Stupid and Naive:' Towards an Ethnography of Soap Opera Viewers," in Seiter *et al.* (eds), *Remote Control*.

27 Kreutzner, *Die Fernsehserie Dynasty*.

28 Hoeppel, "Halbgötter in Weiss," p. 58.

29 Joseph Turow, *Playing Doctor: Television, Storytelling, and Medical Power* (New York: Oxford University Press, 1989).

30 Herta Herzog, "*Dallas* and the German Viewer: A Comparison with *Denver Clan*," unpublished manuscript (1984).

31 Jane Feuer, "Reading Dynasty: Television and Reception Theory," in Jane Gaines (ed.), *Classical Hollywood Narrative: the Paradigm Wars* (Durham, NC: Duke University Press, 1989), pp. 275–293.

32 We would like to thank Susanne Böhmer for her support in viewing the *Schwarzwaldklinik* episodes and Eva-Maria Warth for her valuable criticism of our discussion of *Prodigal Son*.

33 "Schaubild des Tages," *Die Welt* 8 (February 8, 1993), p. 1.

34 For a discussion of Roseanne see Kathleen Rowe, *The Unruly Woman: Gender and the Genres of Laughter* (Austin, Tex.: University of Texas Press, 1994); also "Roseanne: Unruly Woman as Domestic Goddess," *Screen* 31 (4) (1990), pp. 408–419.

13

Our welcomed guests
Telenovelas in Latin America

Ana M. Lopez

An article in *Variety* describing the growth of the Venezuelan TV network Radio Caracas was boldly titled "A Novel Rise to the Top;" the "novel" referring not to the novelty of the event, but to the fact that Radio Caracas is a network built, literally, by its successful telenovelas (among others, the wildly popular and much exported *Topacio* and *Cristal*).[1] Radio Caracas is hardly an isolated example. Throughout the continent, networks and TV-based conglomerates have been consolidated upon the popularity of tele-novelas and continue to depend upon their commercial potential. In fact, the persistence and frequency of the telenovela genre is the most marked characteristic of Latin American and Spanish-language television as a whole. Whether nationally produced or imported from other Latin American coun-tries, telenovelas are the basic staple of all Latin American TV programming (day- and prime-time), of Spanish-language programming in the US, and, to a lesser degree, of TV programming in Spain.

However, early studies of telenovelas in the 1970s, under the influence of the then dominant theories of cultural dependence and media imperialism, focused almost exclusively upon telenovela's presumed alienation effect. The "alienating guest" of a study by Venezuelan scholars,[2] telenovelas were posited as a harmful influence upon popular culture and consciousness and as agents for the creation of a capitalist and consumerist international global village engineered by the US and US-allied interests. In these studies, telenovelas were simply another example of the mind-numbing program-ming of the mass media as a whole. In fact, most of the myriad empirical studies and debates of the 1960s and 1970s over north–south flows of information and the deleterious presence of imported programming – albeit their political significance – failed to notice the sleeping, slumbering giants of telenovelas and the antidote they offered to the pessimism of media–imperialism studies.[3]

Nevertheless, a "corrective" trend in 1980s research perhaps went too far in the opposite direction. Claiming a "reverse media imperialism" based on the extensive telenovela export activities of TV-Globo (Brazil) and Televisa

(Mexico), scholars like Rogers, Schement, and others argued that the success of the telenovela allowed TV-Globo and Televisa to refute the "American hegemony paradigm" by substituting imported for domestic programming and by opening up international export markets.[4] The "alienating guest" was suddenly transformed into *O Salvador da Patria* (the savior of the nation, also the title of a popular 1989 TV-Globo telenovela), and the success of the telenovela equated with development, modernization, and the growing national/international clout of Latin American TV networks. As John Sinclair has argued, this second wave of research assumed that TV was "imposed upon helpless ... nations as the ideological instrument of omnipotent international forces" without taking into consideration the active efforts of the national ruling classes to forge advantageous international connections. Furthermore, this research did not recognize

> that the most consequential factor in the establishment of television in ... Latin America was not reliance on foreign programs but the institutionalization of the commercial model of [a] broadcasting structure which geared this medium ... into the more fundamental process of the transnationalization of their economies as a whole.[5]

To Sinclair's critique, still couched within the economistic terms of the media imperialism/cultural dependency debates, telenovela scholars in Latin America and elsewhere (for example, Jesús Martín-Barbero and Armand and Michèle Mattelart[6]) have begun to add a different set of theoretical questions that address the insertion of telenovelas into daily life, the function of the telenovela *vis à vis* the "modernization" of Latin American societies, and the complicated relationship between production (and economic issues) and reception. Thus Jesús Martín-Barbero has argued that the telenovela is a site of "mediations," a place where the interaction between the forces of production and reception are crystallized. That is to say, the telenovela bears the marks of TV's commercial imperatives and responds to the demands of cultural habits and specific ways of seeing which are also in a constant state of transformation and adaptation. As Martín-Barbero, among others, has said, television only works in so far as it assumes – and therefore legitimizes – the demands and needs of spectators; but it does not legitimate these demands without redefining them according to what is acceptable within socially hegemonic discourses.

Thus refigured as a "welcomed guest" rather than an alienating poacher or national savior, the telenovela can be understood as an agent for and participant in the complex processes of Latin American modernization, nation-building, and increasing transnationalization. Although the magnitude of the telenovela phenomenon makes a synthetic analysis almost impossible,[7] I shall attempt to briefly outline the principal characteristics of the genre in order to trace some of the complex economic and cultural matrices within which it functions in Latin America and in the Hispanic US, particularly in so far as it orchestrates complex mediations among the national, the pan-national, and the melodramatic.

What is a telenovela?

As a type of televisual serial narrative, the Latin American telenovela participates in the shared history that gave rise to other serial narrative models such as the US soap opera. It is an essentially melodramatic narrative mode, with roots that can be traced back to prior (Latin American and international) melodramatic forms (in the theater, serial literature, etc.) and their re-inscription and recirculation by the mass media in the cinema and radio. But even *Variety* has recognized the specificity of the genre: "The telenovela is a Latin American popular art form as distinctive and as filled with conventions as the norteamericanos' Western .... The telenovela is not a soap opera, although clearly the genres are close blood relations."[8]

Certainly, the origins of the telenovela parallel those of the US soap: in the 1950s, soap companies (like Colgate and Lever Brothers) which had already sponsored radionovelas expanded into the new medium by sponsoring similar TV serials in a number of Latin American countries (Cuba, Venezuela, Mexico, Brazil).[9] However, from the start, the Latin American telenovelas were imagined differently from the US soaps.[10] Most significantly, telenovelas have always had clear-cut stories with definite endings that permit narrative closure. The historical development of the form and its singular place in Latin American television have also resulted in other important differences. Many US soaps continue to be sponsored by soap companies, are generally produced as daytime entertainment aimed at a female audience, are primarily destined for the national market, and are still considered a form of "slumming" by its workers (work on a soap being second best to film or theatrical work). On the other hand, telenovelas are prime-time entertainment for all audiences, financed directly by TV networks (or, most recently, by independent producers who subsequently sell advertising slots), widely exported, and definitive of the Latin American star system. Unlike the case in the US, where "stardom" – either of actors or writers and directors – is still defined by Hollywood, to work in a telenovela today is often to have reached the apex of one's professional career. In nations that are continuously struggling to sustain cinematic production (and often fail to do so), telenovelas produce indigenous star systems of great cultural (and economic) significance, for the great mass media icons are not movie stars but telenovela stars.[11] Furthermore, the star system reflects back upon the specificity of the telenovela format itself: the need to establish closure often means that the community of the text is narratively subordinate to a stellar couple with whom the audience is clearly meant to identify. Whereas the US soap's lack of closure implies a spectator that is knowledgable of the history of the fictional community, the telenovela spectator recognizes actors and stars and awaits their appearance and fictional reincarnation in each new telenovela.[12]

That telenovelas have had great economic impact hardly needs to be restated. As has been well-chronicled in studies of the development of powerful TV-based conglomerates in Mexico and Brazil, for example, the popularity of telenovelas played a crucial role in their history and continue to be central to their revenues and power.[13] At least since the 1970s, the telenovela ceased to be cheaply-produced filler material for daytime programming with content directly determined by advertisers and sponsors and began to successfully compete against the great US serials (like *Dallas*) for prime-time audiences. The telenovela (alongside the *show de auditorium*[14]) proved that national productions were attractive to audiences and could replace prime-time canned US programs. At least since the 1980s, both Globo and Televisa have imported only a small percentage of their programming from the US (in both cases, primarily feature-length films).

Furthermore, in the late 1970s–1980s, the telenovela also became prime export material. Within Latin America, the trade in telenovelas has been controlled by Mexican, Argentine, and Venezuelan producers: the airwaves of every Latin American nation have featured telenovelas from these countries in the last decade, even (as in Brazil) when airing dubbed versions. The norm for most Latin American television stations since the 1980s has been to program a steady stream of national and imported telenovelas, as many as six or seven in a programming day. In Lima in 1986, for example, an average of seven telenovelas were broadcast at one time, of which only two were nationally produced.[15] In Brazil, where TV-Globo airs only its own telenovelas – since 1987, three first-run and one rerun daily – a rival network, SBT, began to successfully import Mexican productions in the early 1980s.[16] Although historically it has been less visible in Latin America than Telemundo or Venevisión, TV-Globo was the first to establish an expansive international distribution network.[17] In the 1990s, however, Telemundo, Venevisión, and other Latin American producers have begun to catch up. Thus, in the 1990s, it is not unusual to find Latin American telenovelas from nations (and television systems) as disparate as Brazil and Venezuela in the US (on the Spanish-language networks Univisión and Telemundo), Europe (especially in Spain, but also in Italy, France, Great Britain, and eastern European countries), Asia (including China), and Africa.

Because the costs of telenovela production are usually recouped with domestic advertising revenues, export revenues are extraordinarily attractive and valuable to producers.[18] Thus competition for the export market has generated a marked increase in average production costs. Whereas in 1985, the average cost of an hour-long Globo telenovela episode was US$20,000 to $30,000, in 1992, Globo executives declared that an "ambitious" novela could cost as much as US$120,000 per episode.[19] Even less well-heeled producers, like Venezuela's Radio Caracas, are currently budgeting for increasingly more expensive productions, ranging between US$50,000 and $80,000 per segment.[20] With revenues as high as US$15,000–$25,000 per episode for each foreign sale in a pool of more than thirty potential markets, however, the additional investments seem well worth the risk.

This constant production and the increasing sophistication of telenovelas have generated a solid capital base as well as a sophisticated professional and technical television infrastructure in the larger nations. Thus, primarily based upon the success of the telenovela, national networks and producers have been able to expand prodigiously in spite of their proximity to the US programming giant and without direct state intervention.[21] Whereas film production in Latin America has rarely been able to sustain itself industrially because of the competition from Hollywood and generally requires direct state investment and protection, television has gone through a markedly different development since the telenovela secured the national market and made exports possible. It is, therefore, perhaps not coincidental that the most commercially successful Latin American film-making efforts (in Mexico and Argentina in the 1930s, 1940s, and 1950s) were premised, like the telenovela, upon a melodramatic mode of expression.

Telenovelas and melodrama

Beyond its sheer economic value, then, the telenovela's popularity and huge audiences also imply that each day a greater number of people throughout the Spanish-speaking world live with and recognize themselves in the world through telenovela melodramas. Although the melodramatic has always been central to the constitution of mass popular audiences in Latin America (in reverse historical order, through film, radio, serial literature, and popular entertainment/shows), its impact has never been as great or as focused as with the telenovela.

The trajectory of melodrama in Latin American culture differs from the European and US experiences. In the latter, as Christine Gledhill has recently argued, the melodramatic was devalued in favor of realism in the twentieth century through a gendering process: its emotionality and the centrality of socially mandated female concerns made it appealing to women and, thus, feminized, the genre became a "women's" form.[22] In Latin America, however, the devaluation of melodrama is explicitly class-based rather than primarily gendered.[23] The telenovela's melodramatic antecedents were all, in their time, scorned by intellectuals and élites as *popular* forms, as entertainment with no cultural or redeeming value for the increasingly visible, primarily urban, masses.[24] Thus the telenovela is not associated explicitly with female consumption – as are "soap" operas – and its very name actively seeks prestige by citing an élite genre – novela – and a new technological medium associated with a much desired modernization.[25] Furthermore, throughout Latin America, telenovela writers, not directors, are as respected, well-known, and well-paid as telenovela stars and often better known than their literary counterparts. Undoubtedly, the telenovela has also left its mark in Latin American literary production. Even Gabriel García Márquez argued in a recent TV interview that "the telenovela was a magnetic pole from which he could not escape."

In general, the telenovela melodrama is a specific appropriation of what Gledhill, following Peter Brooks, calls the "melodramatic project": the organizing mode of a world conceived of "on the principle of terminal conflict between polarized moral forces that run through the social fabric and are expressed in personal and familial terms extending beyond the biological family into all areas of social life."[26] Like the US soap opera, the telenovela often displaces the flamboyant use of *mise-en-scène* typical of theatrical melodrama with an emphasis on dialog and talk (because of its popular, oral tradition legacy, not because of an affiliation with women's fiction), but its narrative closure and extraordinarily persistent use of standard melodramatic devices (returns from the past, reversals of fortune, painful confrontations, etc.) square it firmly within a rather "purer" melodramatic tradition.

The telenovela exploits personalization – the individualization of the social world – as an epistemology. It ceaselessly offers its audience dramas of recognition and re-cognition by locating social and political issues in personal and familial terms and thus making sense of an increasingly complex world.[27] Thus it should not be surprising that the genre changes form historically and in different national contexts. If, in general, today's telenovelas often bear little resemblance to the products of the early 1970s, it is because within the melodramatic paradigm, national characteristics have been accentuated even while international distribution and exposure have contributed to a complex web of pan-Latin American influences. What is most intriguing about the telenovela genre today is precisely how the melodramatic works with, on the one hand, the nation and its cultural characteristics, and, on the other, a self-consciousness about other markets and other Latin American cultures.

Telenovelas and the national

The differences are so marked that almost anyone familiar with telenovelas can provide a general ahistorical sketch of the characteristics of the various national manifestations of the genre. Mexican telenovelas are notorious for their weepiness, extraordinarily Manichean vision of the world, and lack of specific historical referents. At the opposite end of the spectrum, the Brazilian telenovelas are luxurious, exploit cinematic production values, and are considered more "realistic" for their depiction of ambiguous and divided characters in contemporary (or specific historical) Brazilian contexts. The Venezuelan and Colombian telenovelas lie between these two extremes, assuming certain characteristics and establishing their own differences. The

261

Venezuelan telenovelas are like the Mexican in so far as they tend to privilege primal emotions over socio-historical context, but they substitute dialog and utterly spartan sets for the signifying baroqueness of the Mexicans' *mise-en-scène*. The Colombians, on the other hand, have followed the Brazilian model, making specific and pointed reference to the history and culture of the nation, although not by recourse to "realism," but through the use of an ironic/parodic mode that combines the melodramatic with comedy.

Despite their visibility (and potential market-value), these national characteristics – deeply ingrained in the specific history of each nation's appropriation of the genre – have begun to blur in the late 1980s and 1990s. The trajectory of the telenovela genre in most nations seems to have followed a not necessarily chronological pattern that oscillates between national, pan-continental, and international concerns.

Making nation

First, and most obviously, the telenovela has served to create a televisual "national" in which the imagined community[28] rallies around specific images of itself. Following in the footsteps of radio and cinema, television increasingly makes "living" the nation a tangible and daily possibility. In other words, the otherwise invisible unity of the (political) idea of the nation becomes a part of everyday daily life. In this mode, the telenovela has become a privileged site for the translation of cultural, geographical, economic, and even political differences into the discourse of nationness.

For example, the Brazilian telenovela began to acquire its present format and popularity in 1969, when TV-Tupi (a now defunct network that was, at the time, TV-Globo's principal competitor) challenged the Globo-style of telenovelas (usually historical, set in exotic locales, and resolutely non-Brazilian) with the wildly successful *Beto Rockefeller*, a novela that took place entirely in Brazil, was peopled with easily identifiable non-Manichean national characters like the *carioca malandro* (Rio de Janeiro scoundrel) protagonist Beto and representatives of other social classes, featured colloquial Portuguese and healthy doses of humor, and accompanied daily life by incorporating holidays into the narrative itself. As the first novela to use videotape, *Beto* was also more agile and relaxed, exploited different framing strategies, and featured some outdoor locations. Globo responded rapidly to this challenge by firing most of its novela personnel, building a new team of writers (many drawn from the theater), and developing its videotape technology and the skills of its personnel. From then on, the Globo novelas (and its competitors') have been based upon specifically-Brazilian themes, characters, and landscapes, and have featured the topography, culture, and characters of the entire nation. Once featured on TV-Globo, all differences can be subsumed under the great banner of the nation. That this process took place at a time when Brazil was governed by a strict military regime whose need to rally a "new" nation coincided with Globo's desire to interpellate the nation through the airwaves of its network (and as potential consumers) is, obviously, not coincidental.

A similar process occurred in Colombia, as Martín-Barbero recounts, when the "traditional" model was transformed in the 1980s with telenovelas that brought in *costumbrismo*, a general parodic spirit (already evident in Colombian literature, which also often provides the source material) that undermines the typical melodramatic Manicheism with humor, with explicit attention to the details of Colombian social life, and even with touches of magical realism.[29] Circulating a wide spectrum of regional differences and styles and often using national "literature" as the context for the creation of new mass media narratives, the 1980s telenovela has provided the beleaguered nation with a self-image that differs markedly from the violent narco-trafficking for which it is known throughout the rest of the world.

An even more visible example of fashioning *and* interpellating the nation through the telenovela took place in Chile in the late 1980s, when Channel 13 – the Catholic Church owned and operated national television station – "adapted" the script of the rather racy Brazilian novela *Angel Malo* (*Bad Angel*) to suit not only the specificity of the Chilean "national characters," but the station's commitment to the Catholic Church's values and standards of decency. As Gertrude Yaeger argues in her study of the adaptation process, *Angel Malo*'s success "rested on its examination of the Chilean class system and the tensions or conflict between good and evil within every individual."[30] The Chilean version diminished the social and economic distance between rich and poor families represented in the Brazilian novela, eliminated racial elements in the plot, and highlighted Chilean views about sex and the family (for example, once pregnant, the protagonist never considers an abortion). Inspired by traditional Chilean literature – of the foundational kind[31] – the telenovela depicted a simple world populated by a rich and powerful aristocracy and poor, but ambitious, lower classes. The two classes come into contact only through domestic service and (often illicit) sex because in this universe, social mobility occurs not through hard work and effort, but through marriage.

Angel Malo's "Chileanization" stratagem was successful: the telenovela averaged over a 60 percent share of the national audience and some episodes earned nearly a 90 percent share. In a country where most popular culture is imported from the US or Argentina, *Angel Malo* offered a clearly "national" alternative at a time when, nearing the end of a decade-long military dictatorship, the nation desperately needed to redefine itself and to seek solace and inspiration in its traditional foundational myths.

However, adaptation is not always necessary. As the case of Cuba demonstrates, imported telenovelas can also be used for nation-building projects. Throughout the 1960s and 1970s, Cuban television was a national laughing-stock for, to the same degree that the Cuban cinema developed prodigiously since the 1959 revolution, Cuban television had regressed from its pre-revolutionary glory. Cuban television had been one of the principal legacies of US capitalism: in 1954, only four years after the medium's official introduction in Latin America, Cuba was the fourth TV nation in the world as well as an active exporter and programming innovator.[32] But the elimination of all commercial broadcasting, the centralization and bureaucratization of production and transmission, equipment and financing difficulties, and the highly political and didactic imperatives forced upon the medium, transformed Cuban TV into a national liability. Cubans watched TV because it was there, but without loyalty and with vociferous critiques. Telenovelas, once a national staple, had almost disappeared and national serial narratives had lost their popular appeal. Shot under extreme duress – with each 30-minute show shot in one day to be broadcast a month later – serials had a rough, improvisational quality that demanded a very active audience and precluded easy identification. Furthermore, the official critique of melodrama – which equated the emotional excesses of the genre with capitalist consumerist alienation – required the development of other narrative strategies which proved anathema to the genre (or, at least, to audience desires).[33]

However, in the 1980s, when faced with the threat of Radio (and TV) Marti, the Instituto Cubano de Radio y Televisión (ICRT) reconsidered its programming practices and, in addition to livening up its own productions,[34] began to import telenovelas from other Latin American nations. The first highly popular import was TV-Globo's *La Escrava Isaura*. For the first time in decades, the nation rallied through fictional serial television: the country literally stood still during each evening's broadcast of the popular Brazilian novela and the ICRT had to arrange a morning re-broadcast to accommodate the demands of night-shift workers. Easily identifying with the historical theme of the novela (the story of Isaura, a slave who can pass for white and suffers prodigiously), the Cuban audience rediscovered the pleasures of melodramatic identification and easily worked through the "foreignness" of the text – awkwardly dubbed to Spanish and filled with Brazilianisms – and the different narrative conventions of commercial Brazilian TV.

But the popularity of *Isaura* and the many other Brazilian telenovelas that have since aired in Cuba is not an index of nostalgia or of the longevity of pre-socialist ways of being. Through the Brazilian telenovela, Cuban audiences have worked through some of the anxieties of the country's isolation, reaffirming the national in a much-desired popular encounter with cultural differences. In fact, for close to a decade, the Brazilian telenovela has functioned as a funky Caribbean glasnost; as a symbolic (and practical)[35] "opening up" of the nation toward the popular mass culture of the Latin American continent. Even under the difficult conditions imposed by the current "special period" of crisis in Cuba, Brazilian novelas are still successfully aired and continue to contribute to "national" life. Thus, for example, *Vale Tudo* (*Anything Goes*), aired in 1993, recently provided the slang name *paladares* (the tasties) for the domestic dollar-only speakeasy-like restaurants mushrooming throughout Havana in the wake of the legalization of the dollar within the Cuban economy.

Selling nation

Almost to the same degree that the telenovela has been activated in the service of nation-building projects, it has also been used to sell "nation" and specific images of the nation to others. But exporting the nation is a complicated enterprise: what is popular and/or welcomed within the nation is not always what will be understood or appreciated outside of it. For example, historical novelas, always programmed by Globo in the least popular 6:00 p.m. time slot, have proven to be its most successful exports, perhaps because, like *La Escrava Isaura*, they focus upon historical processes common to or recognizable by many nations. Its domestically successful contemporary novelas have proven to be too "Brazilian" or too insular for most other markets.

Once export potential is taken into consideration when making production decisions, telenovelas can no longer address the nation too specifically and cannot afford to be insular, but they must still retain some national specificity in order to attract audiences. One solution, exploited by TV-Globo, has been to transform internationally-known national novels – like the works of Jorge Amado – into telenovelas. Another solution, favored by Televisa in telenovelas like *Topacio* and *Simplemente María*, for example, has been to create non-nation-specific locales that exploit the urban/rural differences common to the continent as a whole. Yet another solution presented in the late 1980s was the development of telenovela stories set in multinational contexts and featuring, most often, Miami resort sites, and the experiences of world-travelers whose home base is always the national capital. Exploiting the increasing international mobility afforded to the middle and upper classes by accessible air travel (it is often less expensive to fly to Miami than to fly to the interior or to go to another Latin American country), *Amándote*, an Argentine telenovela of the mid-1980s, featured a protagonist who was a pilot on the Miami–Buenos Aires route and who oscillated between the love of a young Venezuelan girl he seduced during a Miami layover and his aristocratic fiancée back in Buenos Aires.

Mediating nation

Thus the contemporary national spectrum of telenovela production is complicated by the contradictory pull of the desire for national identification/representation/mediation and exporting (marketing) strategies which demand at the very least a more pan-Latin American focus/acceptability. This is not to say that national imperatives have disappeared. In fact, in the early 1990s, the interplay of nation with telenovela melodrama resonates more strongly than ever.

In Venezuela, for example, the story of Radio Caracas's nationally very popular 1993 novela, *Por estas calles* (*In These Streets*), was directly inspired by the antics of national politicians gearing up for the presidential election (in December 1993) and so "realistic" that episodes were often re-edited only hours before airing time so as to coincide more directly with each day's political developments.[36]

Brazil recently offered an even more extreme example of the complicated relationships among national politics, national life, and telenovela melodrama. At the same time as President Fernando Collor was being impeached by Congress for corruption, Daniela Perez, an actress of the novela, *De Corpo e Alma* (*Body and Soul*), was found brutally murdered and Guilherme de Pádua, the actor who played her abusive boyfriend in the novela, confessed to her murder. Shortly thereafter, de Pádua's real-life pregnant wife was also charged with murder and arrested. The "real" melodrama of the telenovela characters took over the national imagination and easily eclipsed the "other" drama taking place in the public sphere: the front page of the daily newspaper *O journal do Brasil* on December 30, 1992 featured headlines announcing the Senate's vote impeaching Collor, but the picture of the murdered actress and the news of de Pádua's confession were far more prominent and of greater fascination. Although the presidential saga had also acquired its own tele-novelistic characteristics, it was easily eclipsed by the real melodrama of the telenovela actors who were still appearing daily on the TV drama written by Gloria Perez, the murdered actress's own mother (*De Corpo e Alma* ran for another two months after Daniella's murder and once all the scenes she had taped had been used up, the producers and the author continued to present her in flashbacks).[37]

Inventing "nation"

An even more hybrid scenario of nation, melodrama, and the telenovela is being produced by the characteristics of the US Spanish-speaking market and its specific demands. Here the telenovela is making "nation" where there is no coincidence between nation and state.

The US Hispanic market, like the Hispanic vote, was for long considered yet another "sleeping giant," a dream of great things to come maybe in the year 2000. Yet in the last decade or so, Spanish-language television and its telenovelas have undergone radical changes that are a direct reflection of the increasing visibility and importance of a market which is no longer perceived as either transitional or ephemeral. With purchasing power of over US$205 billion in 1992 and statistics demonstrating that 65 percent of the Hispanic population prefers to or can only speak Spanish, Spanish-language television has recognized its unique and powerful position within the US: its audience pool is not only the *recién llegados* who still don't speak English, but also potentially the large group of "born-again Hispanics" who were born in the US but retain Spanish and a Hispanic or Latino cultural identity.

The two principal Spanish-language networks, Univisión and Telemundo, have been competing intensely not only for a bigger share of this market, but also to increase and improve the quality of the market itself. As *Variety* summarized it in a recent headline, "Want a Bigger Slice? You Bake a Bigger Pie."[38]

Univisión has a longer history and has historically dominated the market. Founded in 1961 by Emilio Azcárraga Vidaurreta (the Mexican media magnate, owner of Televisa until his death in 1972), his son Emilio Azcárraga Milmo (current owner of Televisa), and financier René Anselmo, Univisión was designed to function as a conduit for Mexican programming. Except for innovative news and current event programs and some variety shows in the 1970s and 1880s, Protele, Televisa's export subsidiary, provided the bulk of all programs, including its telenovelas. Hispanics in New York, Florida, California, and the south-west watched *Simplemente María* together with Mexico City. When Hallmark Inc. and First Capital bought Univisión (then called SIN or Spanish International Network) in 1988 as a result of an FCC (Federal Communication Commission) decision against the network's foreign owners, the umbilical cord to Televisa, if not severed, was fractured. Argentine and Venezuelan telenovelas were programmed more frequently, surprising viewers with their marked regional characteristics and often more sophisticated narrative styles. In this context, telenovelas like the multinational *Amándote* and its world-traveling characters and constantly shifting locales began the process of winning over new generations of viewers.

But in the background of Univisión's changes, Telemundo had also begun to assiduously court that "born-again" viewer. In development since 1985, the Telemundo network was formed in 1987, and by 1988 covered 61.3 percent of the US's Hispanic households. Its calling card was, from the beginning, a focus on domestic production.[39] In 1988 Telemundo produced *Angélica, mi vida* (*Angelica, My Love*), the first telenovela produced in the US, which featured Puerto Rican, Mexican, and Cuban immigrants as central characters. Subsequently, *El Magnate* (1991) and *MaríElena* (1992) were also produced in the US; both telenovelas were set in Latino communities and featured, as principal characters, a hodgepodge of exiles and immigrants in various stages of assimilation. Written by Delia Fiallo, a veteran Cuban writer with a long career in Venezuela, *MaríElena* was especially successful because its protagonist, the Mexican actress Lucia Méndez, had long been a favorite of Televisa's novelas and, like Fiallo, was now Miami-based (part of the community) and working for Telemundo. The impact of these telenovelas on the viewing public was remarkable: with fairly high production values, US Latinos recognized themselves through television melodrama and cherished their own, crossover, star system.

267

When Emilio Azcárraga Milmo reacquired Univisión in 1992 (in partnership with US businessman Jerrold Perenchio and the Venezuelan media magnates Gustavo and Ricardo Cisneros, owners of Venevisión),[40] Telemundo's successful telenovela programming strategies did not go unnoticed.[41] Although Univisión had increased its overall domestic production since 1988 (from 7 percent to 44 percent in 1992), it was essentially limited to news, talk shows, comedic programs, and *shows de auditorium* produced in its new extensive Miami facility. Meanwhile, Televisa's new competitor within the Mexican market, Tele Azteca Channel 13, began to import Telemundo telenovelas: *MaríElena* was the runaway success of Mexican television in 1993, beating all Televisa programming and even forcing the network to reschedule its popular news show *24 Horas* to avoid competing directly with the serial. In mid-1993, the fact that change was taking place not only at Univisión, but within Televisa itself became clearly visible with the airing of two telenovelas – *Valentina* and *Dos mujeres, un camino (Two Women, A Road)* – that represent and implicitly address and attempt to appeal to the US Latino community.[42]

Dos mujeres, un camino is the most obvious of the two. Erik Estrada, a New York-born actor of Puerto Rican descent who played Poncharelo in the US TV series *Chips*, plays Johnny, an LA-based truck driver on a route that regularly takes him across the border. He is married to Ana María (veteran actress Laura León), but while on the road, meets and falls in love with the young aspiring singer Tania (singing starlet Bibi Gaytán). The complications that ensue are not particularly surprising, but Televisa's conscious effort to enlarge the fictional space of telenovela melodrama is. The explicit representation of the border crossing scenario and the eventual blurring and disappearance of the border itself within the melodramatic work of the serial transforms it into another "lived" space consequent to those north and south of the border that unmasks the limits of official geography. That Erik Estrada – who claims to have done a Berlitz crash course in Spanish before accepting the role – speaks awkwardly and with a marked accent only adds to the serial's attractive gritty-realistic ambience produced by its frequent location shots throughout border states/cities and the Tex-Mex music of "Grupo Bronco" (in their first telenovela appearance).

Valentina is a more complicated example. Designed as a telenovela comeback vehicle (and first telenovela production effort) for Televisa veteran actress, singer, and, most recently, successful talk show hostess Verónica Castro, it was originally premised upon a complex international exchange meant to climax in the imaginary resort of Isla Escondida. The first two dozen episodes or so were visually spectacular, with complex narration, rapid editing, and much location shooting. The plot was less thrilling: his wife's botched attempt to murder him while on a cruise renders Fernando Alcántara (Juan Ferrera) amnesiac. He washes up at the resort, where he meets and falls in love with Valentina (Verónica Castro), the daughter of a once wealthy man who owned the resort, but where he is also seduced and confused by the evil Deborah Andrade (Blanca Guerra) who is the resort's present owner.

This typical melodramatic plot takes place on an island that, although ostensibly in Mexico (location shooting was done in Quintana Roo), is figured more as a mythical Caribbean locale. First of all, the island is linked more directly to Miami than to Mexico City: Fernando washes up there while on a cruise ship departing from Miami, it takes months for detectives from Mexico City to find him there. Second, it is a universe curiously bereft of marked class differences. Some characters are richer than others, there are employers, servants, employees, and even a homeless orphan boy whom Fernando befriends and unofficially adopts, but these differences are subsumed by the leveling isolation of the resort and the island itself. Owners and workers interact indiscriminately, even incestuously, and all ultimately end up on the beach. Most importantly, the central "native" character is "la negra Lucumé," an old *santera* played by the well-known Cuban salsa singer, Celia Cruz (whose only other big or small screen appearance was in the film *Mambo Kings*). Cruz's character, "imported" from the Caribbean and dropped into an inappropriate Mexican context, was obviously meant to be the serial's trump card for the US Hispanic market. Cruz's popularity and the audience's curiosity to see her acting rather than singing were activated before the telenovela's premiere and during its first few weeks on the air. Univisión featured Cruz in its talk shows, devoted a special 1-hour homage to her "Cubanness" hosted by the also Cuban-born Cristina Saralegui and featured her almost as much as Verónica Castro in commercials and in the telenovela's pre-credit sequence.

Unfortunately, *Valentina*'s emphasis on place rather than characters did not sit well with audiences. Its ratings were so poor (in Mexico and in the US) that after two months it underwent a radical transformation (engineered by a new team of writers): after disclosing that Valentina's twin sister (also called Valentina and played by Castro) had been kidnapped at birth, the two central characters were promptly killed (as they stepped out of the church after their wedding), and the action relocated to the more familiar ambience of the poor and rich neighborhoods of Mexico City, and focused upon the "other" Valentina, a typical lower class girl with an atypical profession (she drives a taxi) who is deceived and abandoned by a man she thinks she loves, but finds "true" love – and happiness, money, and her real father – across class differences.

Conclusion

Perhaps *Valentina* didn't work for audiences precisely because, in de Certeau's sense, its place was not a space.[43] The imaginary stability and located-ness of Isla Escondida was not actualized or practiced: it was too fictionally arid, too composite, its hybridity too out of context. Unlike *Dos*

Caminos, where a vibrant fictional space is created through the actions of characters that traverse through it, *Valentina*'s "place" figured primarily as backdrop (and an excuse for breathtaking long shots of the landscape) and not as a practiced signifying context. Its willful abstraction and heterogeneity denied the spectator the possibility of identifying with a cultural territory that does not coincide with administrative and political demarcations.

Valentina's failure and *Dos Caminos*'s success clearly indicate that an awareness of the larger Spanish-speaking market has generated a different mediation between the national, the pan-national, and the melodramatic. It is not simply that there is now a telenovela subgenre that addresses a multi-national audience, but that the telenovela genre itself (especially in Mexico and in the US) is undergoing a transformation where the national is melodramatically articulated in relationship to other, differentially constituted, imagined communities of viewers.

Acknowledgment

Research for this essay was funded, in part, by travel/research grants from the Mellon Foundation and the Royer Thayer Stone Center for Latin American Studies at Tulane University. My thanks to Leyda for her careful clippings and to Mami, whose faithful taping of telenovelas helped make the research possible.

Notes

1 Peter Besas, "A Novel Rise to the Top," *Variety* (October 11, 1993), p. 181.

2 Marta Colomina de Rivera (ed.), *El huesped alienanate: un estudio sobre audiencia y efecto de las radio-telenovelas en Venezuela* (Maracaibo, Venezuela: Universidad del Zulia, 1968).

3 For example, Kaarle Nordenstreng and Tapio Varis, *Television Traffic: A One-Way Street?* (Paris: UNESCO, 1974).

4 Jorge Reina Schement and Everett M. Rogers, "Media Flows in Latin America," *Communication Research* 11 (2) (1984), pp. 305–320. Also in this same issue of *Communication Research*, Livia Antola and Everett M. Rogers, "Television Flows in Latin America," pp. 185–203, and Joseph D. Straubhaar, "Brazilian Television: The Decline of American Influence," pp. 221–240. See also Everett Rogers and Livia Antola, "*Telenovelas*: A Latin American Success Story," *Journal of Communication* 35 (1985), pp. 24–35.

5 John Sinclair, "Spanish Language Television in the United States: Televisa Surrenders its Domain," *Studies in Latin American Popular Culture* 9 (1990), pp. 40–41.

6 Jesús Martín-Barbero, *De los medios a las mediaciones* (Barcelona: Ediciones Gili, 1987); and Martín-Barbero and Sonia Muñoz (eds), *Televisión y melodrama* (Bogota: Tercer Mundo Editores, 1992); Michèle and Armand Mattelart, *Le carnaval des images* (Paris: La Documentation Française, 1987), trans. by David Buxton as *The Carnival of Images* (New York: Bergin & Garvey, 1990). See also, Federico Medina Cano and Marta Ines Montoya Ferrer, *Telenovela: el milagro del amor* (Medellín, Colombia: Universidad Pontífica Bolivariana, 1989); Rosa María Alfaro Moreno, "Usos sociales populares de la telenovela en el mundo urbano," mimeo, n.d.; Teresa Quiroz Velasco, "La telenovela en el Peru," *Dia-*

logos 18 (1987), pp. 74–84; Nico Vink, *The Telenovela and Emancipation: A Study on TV and Social Change in Brazil* (Amsterdam: Royal Tropical Institute, 1988).

7 The problems facing the telenovela researcher are enormous. First of all, the "texts" in question are simply immense and the proliferation of production throughout the continent in the last decade has only aggravated the problem: by now, almost every Latin American nation has produced at least one or two telenovelas and the major producers hundreds. To add insult to injury, few of these "texts," particularly in the smaller nations, have been preserved or are available for research. With the exception of Ismael Fernandes, *Memória da telenovela brasileira* (São Paulo: Brasiliense, 1987), which identifies all the telenovelas and mini-series produced and aired in Brazil until 1986, there have been no systematic records of national production or historical assessments of the history of the genre. Thus, for practical reasons, the tendency in telenovela work has been either to focus on the output of one nation or, more specifically, on the analysis of one (or part of one) telenovela. These same practical problems have, obviously, shaped the present essay as well.

8 "Telenovela is Something Else," *Variety*, March 12, 1986, p. 142.

9 From all accounts, it seems that the Latin American radionovela and its successor, the telenovela, were first introduced and successfully marketed in Cuba. Inspired by the success of novela pioneer Felix B. Caignet (whose radionovela *El derecho de nacer (The Right to be Born*, 1948) was heard all over the continent and was subsequently remade in film, telenovela, comic book, and even book form), tycoon Goar Mestre built a Cuban media empire as powerful in its day as Brazil's TV-Globo is today. Early Cuban telenovelas were not that widely exported, but many individuals with expertise in this field, especially writers, went into exile after the 1959 revolution and subsequently played important roles in the development of the telenovela format in other countries. Thus the Cuban writer Delia Fiallo has authored a large number of successful Venezuelan *culebrones* (big snakes, the popular Venezuelan term for long serial narratives, whether on radio or TV) and Gloria Magadán (who was hired by Colgate in the US and loaned out to its Brazilian subsidiary) was essential to the development of the telenovela in Brazil in the 1960s.

10 In 1950, *Time* magazine, describing the success of Cuban radionovelas like Caignet's *El derecho de nacer* throughout Latin America (and even within the Spanish-speaking US), articulated the difference between the Caignet-style and US soaps:

> Caignet knew how to give a new twist to the radio soap opera to please Latin tastes and achieved unprecedented success. He knew how to reproduce the daily climaxes, the racking sobs, the lack of subtlety, and the sonorous disquieting narrator. But he also moved the action from the soap opera's kitchens and living rooms to places as exotic as the coffee fields of Palma Soriano. And while the North American serials tended to steer clear of sexual problems, Caignet threw himself fully into the furies of passion, abortion and illegitimacy.
>
> (cited by Reynaldo González, *Llorar es un placer* (Havana: Editorial Letras Cubanas, 1988), pp. 47–48)

11 The telenovela star system has produced fascinating ancillary markets. Besides stimulating the appearance of famous singers as characters (for example, Nydia Caro, José Luis Rodríguez, Lizette, Iris Chacón, and, most recently, Celia Cruz), telenovela actors (for example, Lucia Méndez and Verónica Castro) have also become singers and entertainers and have spilled out on to other programs and

media. Furthermore, telenovelas have generated a large-scale pan-Latin American fan and information industry, with countless magazines (for example, *Telerevista*, *TV y novelas*, *Show*, and, in Brazil, *Amiga*) and TV and radio shows devoted to disseminating information about stars, focusing on their fictional characters as well as their personal lives.

12 Tomás López Pumarejo makes a similar point in his *Aproximación a la telenovela* (Madrid: Ediciones Cátedra, 1987), p. 119.

13 See, for example, Renato Ortiz, Silvia Helena Simoes, and José Mario Ortiz Ramos, *Telenovela: historia e produção* (São Paulo: Brasiliense, 1989); Sergio Caparelli, *Televisão e capitalismo no Brazil* (Porto Alegre: L and PM Editores, 1982); Richard Paterson (ed.), *Brazilian Television In Context* (London: BFI, 1982), Raúl Trejo Delarbre (ed.), *Televisa, el quinto poder* (Mexico City: Editorial Claves Latinoamericanas, 1985); Miguel Besañez, *La lucha por la hegemonía en México* (Mexico City: Siglo XXI, 1981).

14 The *show de auditorium* or variety program is another unique Latin American TV genre that evolved through the adaptation of US programming. Like the telenovela, the *show de auditorium* originated on radio as an adaptation of the US variety show format and, after undergoing local transformations, was transferred to TV. Generally aired at weekends (when there are no telenovelas), the *shows* are extraordinarily popular. Televisa's *Siempre en Domingo* (*Always on Sundays*), for example, is beamed live to over a dozen nations and has the world's largest audience for a regularly scheduled program. (See Mark Holston, "Tuning in to Televisa," *Américas* (March–April 1986), pp. 24–29.) TV-Globo's *Fantastico*, another Sunday program, has been on the air since the early 1970s and has an audience share of close to 90 percent (based on the nationally-produced IBOPE ratings). Currently, US-based Univisión is producing perhaps the most popular of all *shows de auditorium*, *Sábado Gigante* (*Giant Saturday*). Hosted by Don Francisco, a Chilean national of German descent (real name, Mario Kreutzberger), *Sábado* is a descendent of a Chilean *show* that has aired regularly for more than thirty years and is cited in the *Guiness Book of Records* as "the world's longest running TV show with a single host without ever showing a repeat." The 3.5 hour show (a combination of game shows, documentaries, audience-participation skits, travelogues, talk shows, and beauty contests) is produced in Miami and exported to eighteen countries. It has made Don Francisco one of the most popular characters of Spanish-language television and a recognizable figure throughout the continent. Everyone loves Don Francisco. See "Univisión's Don Rules Saturday," *Variety* (March 23, 1992), pp. 74, 96; and Daisann McLane, "Couch Batata," *Village Voice* (April 26, 1988), p. 49.

15 Max. R. Tello, "Carmín: Juventud Divino Tesoro," in Ivano Cipriani (ed.), *Libro Bianco: America Latina*, mimeo (Turin: Teleconfronto, 1986), pp. 141–142.

16 To pre-empt rival networks from challenging its supremacy by airing imported telenovelas, Globo has even resorted to buying, but never programming, the most popular products. This was the case, for example, with Televisa's extraordinarily popular *Simplemente María* (a 500-episode telenovela that surpassed all sales records in the 1970s (over US$20 million) and even engendered a 1980s remake) which was purchased by Globo but never aired.

17 TV-Globo broke into the international market in the early 1980s with the success of *A Escrava Isaura* (1981), an historical telenovela set in the colonial period with a vaguely abolitionist theme. *Isaura* was sold widely throughout Latin America (its Spanish-dubbed version even aired on Univisión in the US), Europe, and Asia. It was named the best television program of the decade in Poland, caused Cuban officials to reschedule meetings to avoid competing with it, and resulted in a triumphant world tour for Lucelia Santos (the lead actress) who was féted like royalty even in China.

18 Following the pattern exploited by Hollywood interests for international trade, telenovela producers sell their product at differential rates, according to the characteristics of the market. Most often, the determining factor is the number of TV sets in the market in question, but other considerations may be taken into account as well. Thus, for example, when TV-Globo sells its telenovelas to Cuban television, it charges an average of US$250 per episode rather than its usual US$5,000–15,000 for "older" products. Furthermore, to facilitate sales to foreign debt-ridden nations, the larger producers have set up a barter system whereby programs are exchanged for advertising time. Since 1985, Televisa has demanded 4 minutes for each program hour sold to US-based multinationals. Similarly, when TV-Globo sold *A Escrava Isaura* and *Dancin' Days* to China, it accepted advertising time instead of currency. See, Mattelart and Mattelart, *Carnival of Images*, p. 12.

19 Peter Besas, "Globo Grabs the TV Jackpot in Brazil," *Variety* (March 23, 1992), p. 82.

20 Besas, "A Novel Rise to the Top," pp. 181–182.

21 The exception is Colombia, where the Colombian Radio and Television Institute (Inravisión) legislated that, as of July 1, 1987, prime-time telenovelas had to be domestically produced. However, this measure was intended to protect national producers from the popularity of Mexican and Brazilian telenovelas, and not from US serials. See Mattelart and Mattelart, *Carnival of Images*, p. 11.

22 Christine Gledhill, "Speculations on the Relationship Between Soap Opera and Melodrama," *Quarterly Review of Film and Video* 14, (1–2) (1992), pp. 103–124.

23 Nevertheless, as Robert Allen suggests in his analysis of the term soap opera in the US (*Speaking of Soap Operas* (Chapel Hill, NC: University of North Carolina Press, 1985), pp. 8–9), class denigration usually also lies behind devaluation by gender.

24 In Martín-Barbero and Muñoz (eds), *Televisión y melodrama*, pp. 39–60, Martín-Barbero sketches an interesting history of Latin American melodramas that highlights, for example, the relationship between popular serial literature and oral storytelling traditions (such as the reader in Cuban tobacco factories) and the roots of Argentine *radioteatro* (rather than radionovela) in traveling circus spectacles and their "theatrical" troupes. For an analysis of the relationship between intellectual élites and radio see Ana Maria Fadul, "Literatura, radio e sociedade," *Literatura en tempo de cultura de massa* (São Paulo: Nobel, 1984).

25 Even regional variants sustain this principle. In Brazil telenovelas are simply called novelas (but in Portuguese, the novel is more generally called a *romance*). In Venezuela, the term *culebrones* (big snakes) is often used derogatively, but its gender connotation would obviously be male rather than female.

26 Gledhill, "Speculations," p. 107.

27 Martín-Barbero and Muñoz, *Televisión y melodrama*, pp. 26–28.

28 As defined by Benedict Anderson in *Imagined Communities*, 2nd edn (London: Verso, 1991).

29 For a detailed analysis, see Martín-Barbero, "Transformaciones del género: de la telenovela en Colombia a la telenovela colombiana," in Martín-Barbero and Muñoz, *Television y melodrama*, pp. 61–106.

30 Gertrude Yaeger, "*Angel Malo* [Bad Angel], A Chilean Telenovela," *Studies in Latin American Popular Culture* 9 (1990), p. 250.

31 Doris Sommer uses the term "foundational fiction" to refer to the relationship between popular nineteenth-century romance novels and nation-building in Latin America. See her *Foundational Fictions: The National Romances of Latin America* (Berkeley, Calif.: University of California Press, 1991).

32 Jeremy Turnstall, *The Media are American* (New York: Columbia University Press, 1977), p. 293.

33 One of the earliest Cuban critiques of melodrama (cinematic, radial, and televisual) was produced by critics/film-makers Enrique Colina and Daniel Díaz Torres in "La ideología del melodrama en el viejo cine latinoamericano," *Cine Cubano* 73–74–75 (1972), pp. 14–26. Reynaldo González's study of radio serial narratives, *Llorar es un placer* (Havana: Editorial Letras Cubanas, 1988), continues in this tradition. A more subtle analysis of the place and pleasure of melodrama in television serial narratives is found in Julio García Espinosa, "La *telenovela*, ou le 'ragot' élevé à la catégorie de l'art dramatique," *Cinémas d'Amérique Latine* 1 (1993), pp. 52–55.

34 The work undertaken to improve serial narrative production has been extensive. A large number of training and informational seminars have been held for production personnel under the auspices of the ICRT. Furthermore, in the context of the 1989 Havana film festival, the ICRT organized an important seminar on the telenovela with presentations and debates among researchers and producers from various Latin American countries. The Centro de Investigaciones Sociales of the ICRT has also focused much attention on the telenovela: they have researchers dedicated almost exclusively to serial narrative, have developed an extensive dossier on telenovela research throughout the world, and have undertaken various studies of the peculiarities of the Cuban audience/context. Most recently, in an innovative experiment in conjunction with the Facultad de Cine, Radio y Televisión of the Instituto Superior de Arte, two students produced a thesis which included not only an historical study of the Cuban telenovela, but also the production *and* analysis of perhaps the first contemporary Cuban telenovela to have been a popular success: *Pasión y prejuicio* (*Passion and Prejudice*) aired in 1993. The students, Anabel Leal and Reinaldo Cruz, were simultaneously actors, assistant directors, and analysts/chroniclers of the production and reception process. They attribute the success of the telenovela not only to its story and protagonists, but also to its production strategy. For the first time in the history of the ICRT, a production was organized on a semi-industrial model: the director and producer were given free rein to hire personnel and to make budgetary decisions. Furthermore, the production team was given a financial incentive (considerable salary bonuses) to complete the project on time and under budget. See, Marilyn Bobes, "La increíble y un poco triste historia de la telenovela cubana," *Revolución y cultura* 3 (May–June 1993), pp. 4–9.

35 In a country that for decades refused to grant "star" status to domestic film/TV actors and actresses, the attention-loving and quite sophisticated personnel of the Brazilian telenovelas became instant national symbols. When visiting Cuba, even second and third-echelon actors and actresses are treated like national treasures. They are officially welcomed like diplomatic dignitaries (and regularly meet with Fidel Castro and high party officials), but they are also popularly received with an adulation that knows almost no bounds. Accompanying a Globo actor in Havana, for example, is a gruesome ordeal: chambermaids won't leave their room, every cook, *sous-chef*, and dishwasher in every restaurant must make their acquaintance, telephone operators will stay on the line during their calls, they are unable to make public appearances without causing a mob scene. Thus, even years after the airing of *A Escrava Isaura*, Lucelia Santos is still a national heroine and Maine Proença – the star of the second most-watched Brazilian import, *Dona Beija* – is still considered a national sex symbol and, despite her Germanic blonde and blue-eyed physique, a paradigmatic Brazilian beauty. More perversely, Rubens de Falco (the actor who played the villain in *Isaura*) has essentially disappeared from the Brazilian television scene, but in Cuba is still fêted and treated as a *gran galán*. It is not surprising, then, that like de Falco, many ex-Globo actors and actresses return periodically to Cuba to recharge their faltering star egos.

36 Besas, "A Novel Rise to the Top," p. 181.
37 For an interesting in-depth analysis of this period, see Alma Guillermoprieto, "Obsessed in Rio," *The New Yorker* (August 16, 1993), pp. 44–55.
38 Larry Levental, "Want a Bigger Slice? You Bake a Bigger Pie," *Variety* (January 18, 1993), p. 62.
39 Most of its non-telenovela programming – news, variety shows, music specials, talk shows, and sitcoms – is produced in the US, in Telemundo's studios in Hialeah, Florida.
40 The deal was quite advantageous: Azcárraga had sold Univisión to Hallmark for US$600 million and the new partnership reacquired it for US$550 million.
41 As this chapter was being prepared, Telemundo was unable to refinance its US$300 million outstanding debts and went into bankruptcy proceedings in August 1993. Its programming has changed little since then, but it is expected that it will have to curtail some of its more expansive production plans. See, "Telemundo Turns to Chapter 11," *Variety* (August 9, 1993), p. 43.
42 The entire menu of first-run telenovelas available on Univisión in late 1993 evidences a heightened consciousness of a larger "Hispanic" world at Televisa. In addition to *Valentina* and *Dos mujeres, un camino*, the 8:00 p.m. slot is occupied by *Corazón salvaje*, a remake of a classic historical telenovela written in the 1940s by Caridad Bravo Adams, a veteran who learned the craft writing serials for pre-revolutionary Cuban radio and TV. The stellar cast includes many well-known figures as well as César Evora, a Cuban actor who has not made a break with Cuba (and who also starred in Cuba's first successful telenovela in 1993). Replacing *Valentina* in the 7:00 p.m. slot and already airing in half-hour episodes at 7:30 since December 1993 is *Más allá del puente*, a continuation of one of Televisa's most successful serials, *De Frente al Sol*. Written by the Cuban actor/writer René Muñóz, with extensive location shooting throughout Mexico and the Caribbean, it features an expansive cast, including the special appearance of the veteran Mexican/US actress Katy Jurado (best known in the US for her role as Chihuahua in *High Noon*).
43 Michel de Certeau, *The Practice of Everyday Life* (Berkeley, Calif.: University of California Press, 1984), p. 117.

14

Memory and form in the Latin American soap opera*

Jesús Martín-Barbero

Both in and outside of Latin America, the soap opera has met with enormous success among television viewers. It is a genre which has catalyzed the development of the Latin American television industry, and, at the same time "cross-bred" new audiovisual technologies with the narrative anachronisms that form an integral part of the cultural life of the peoples of that continent.

The soap opera is first of all an industrial event. One example is *Roque Santeiro*, a soap opera whose production mobilized 800 people. Its script occupied two playwrights, a scriptwriter, and a researcher, and an average of 10 hours of editing work and was required per 50-minute episode (Marquez de Melo 1989). TV-Globo, the Brazilian network which produced it, has set up the "Casa de Creación Janette Clair," which is at once a dramaturgical laboratory, a center for audience research, and a training school for script-writers. With a total production of 100 episodes and an average of 300 minutes of fiction per week – the equivalent of more than two full-length feature films – the total cost of a soap opera is between US$1–1.5 million. This places the approximate cost per episode at US$10,000–15,000. In 1985, TV-Globo invested US$500 million, made a profit of around US$120 million, and exported soap operas to 130 countries. That same year, Mexico's Televisa made a profit of around US$150 million.

However, industrial development, the pillar of the business, cannot alone account for the soap opera's drawing power. In order to better understand this phenomenon, it is necessary to locate the soap opera within the field of transformations which make it possible for the urban masses to appropriate modernity without abandoning their oral culture. The soap opera thus proves to be the expression of a "secondary orality" (W. Ong) in which the long length of primitive stories is blended with the fragmentation of images propounded by film, advertising, and television. The connection of the soap opera to oral culture allows it to "exploit" the universe of legends, scary stories, and tales of mystery, which have traveled from the countryside to the cities (cities which have become ruralized at the same time as these nations have become urbanized) in the form of Brazilian *cordel* literature, Mexican *corridos*, or Colombian *vallenatos*.[1]

276

Within these genres, melodrama is at work. Melodrama is the reason that the moving force behind the plot is always the ignorance of an identity, be it the child's ignorance of his parent's identity, one sibling of another's, or a mother of her child's. It is present in the struggle against evil spells and outward appearances, against that which hides and disguises, a struggle *to be recognized by others*. Might this not be the secret connection between melodrama and the cultural history of the Latin American "sub"–continent? Could this not be the reason that among all popular genres, no other – neither adventure stories nor even comedies – has been able to attain a development comparable in reach and intensity to that of the melodrama? In Latin America, whether it be the form of *tango* or *bolero*,[2] Mexican cinema, or soap opera, the melodrama speaks of a *primordial sociality*, whose metaphor continues to be the thick, censored plot of the tightly woven fabric of family relationships. In spite of its devaluation by the economy and politics, this sociality lives on culturally, and from its locus, the people, by "melodramatizing" everything, take their own form of revenge on the abstraction imposed by cultural dispossession and the commercialization of life.

Melodrama and newspaper serials in the radio and cinema

Originating in the middle of the nineteenth century, the newspaper serial brought the melodrama from the theater to the press. Thus, it expanded the reading public and inaugurated a new relationship between popular readers and writing: that established by a story written in episodes and series. The "open structure" of a tale written day-by-day, carried out according to a plan, but open to the influence of its readers' reactions, propitiated the (con)fusion of fiction and life. It endowed the newspaper serial with a permeability to contemporary life that continues to constitute one of the key elements in today's soap opera, both in its configuration as a genre and in its widespread success.

In Latin America, the newspaper serial was the place where the osmosis between urban writing and oral stories took place. Beginning in 1870, Eduardo Gutiérrez published *Juan Moreira* and *Hormiga negra (Black Ant)* in installments in the newspaper *La patria argentina*. These serialized gaucho-novels, which fused the rural and the urban, constituted keys to the national imaginary. Their characters were taken not only from the verses of the *payadores* (traveling minstrels), which circulated in loose-leaf pamphlets and gazettes but also from judicial archives. The result was the configuration of a new dramatic universe, of a "frontier world" in which the changes introduced by modernization in turn of the century Latin America were expressed (Rivera 1982: 9).

But even more than in the press, the real development of the serial in Latin America took place in radio. Regarded almost with disdain by leading figures of literate culture, from its beginnings radio incorporated the oral world of songs and legends.

Melodrama came to the radio through two intermediaries: the circus in Argentina and reading aloud to groups in tobacco factories in Cuba. The *criollo* circus was the result of bringing together circus ring and theatrical stage, acrobatics and dramatic representation under the same tent. It was here that the tradition of the newspaper serials based on gaucho myths and the comic stage of traveling comedians merged. This comic stage is where the origin of the radio soap is to be found. In Argentina, companies of radio actors toured the provinces presenting the same dramas they had performed on the radio so that people could "see what they listened to!" It was for precisely this reason that radio soaps were called "radio theater" in that country. From the end of the nineteenth century on, tobacco factories in Cuba provided the setting for the reading out loud of books on politics and of serialized stories, genres which contributed themes and forms to the serialized radio play.

Fernando Ortiz (1973) has outlined key features of this practice which, originating in convents and European prisons, was introduced in the work-shops of El Arsenal in Havana where the prisoners worked rolling cigars and cigarettes. From the jails, it spread to the tobacco factories of Azcárate and Partágas. Beginning in 1936, the reader and the radio existed side by side in the tobacco factories until the radio finally took the place of readings. This radio incorporated popular forms of listening into sound expressivity and added a corporal dimension to the narration of the radio soaps. In addition, it introduced the exploration of the stories' sensory effects – tones and rhythms – which incorporated popular ways of listening to stories into the language of the radio. The genre of the radio soap opera inaugurated by *El derecho de nacer* (*The right to be born*) would be the great intermediary step between the substratum of the European serialized novel and the soap opera. This latter genre incorporates, in addition, the Latin American tradition of scary stories and songs with the world of the advice column.

The cinema also inherited the melodrama which, in its Hollywood version, worked out the visual grammar the television soap opera was to draw on. Whether it was in order to adopt it or to combat it – from Griffith to King Vidor, Douglas Sirk, or Elia Kazan – the cinema reinvented the melodrama, once again transforming it into a popular show which mobilized the great masses.

> When the spectator cheered or booed, it was not to express his judgment of the quality of the performance, but rather to demonstrate his identification with the fate of the heroes he saw on the screen. Without judging them, he made his own the adventures of characters endowed with a kind of reality which transcended the idea of performance.
>
> (García Riera 1974: 16)

This is the same kind of identification which now underlies the passion inspired by the soap opera.

For the Latin American public did not perceive the cinema as a specifically artistic or cultural phenomenon. The real reason for its success was its relation to life. This public saw the cinema as an opportunity to experiment: to adopt new habits and to see cultural codes reiterated (and dramatized with the voices that they would have liked to have and to hear). They did not go to the movies to dream; they went to learn.

(Monsivais 1980: 16)

Cinema which was largely melodramatic, like that of Mexico, played a vital role in the formation of popular urban experience and culture. According to Carlos Monsivais, this took place through three devices which shape the structure of the television melodrama. One is *theatricalization*, that is, the staging and legitimization of gestures, peculiarities of speech, and sentimental paradigms. Another is *degradation*, which identifies the popular as "lower class," characterizing it as "filial love, laziness, sentimentality, the programmed humiliation of women, religious fanaticism and a fetishist respect for private property" (Monsivais 1976: 86). The last is *modernization*: myths are brought up to date, and access is given to new ways of speaking. The soap opera learned from the movies to use the melodrama to articulate any subject, no matter what it was: the connection of the national epic with private dramas, the displaying of eroticism under the pretext of condemning incest, the tearful dilution of tragic impulses, and the depoliticization of the contradictions of daily life.

The genre and its forms in television

The site of osmosis between memory and form, the soap opera bears witness to the long experience of the market in converting the business of culture into a negotiation between the logic of the system of production – standardization and profitability – and the dynamics of cultural heterogeneity. To understand the soap opera, it is necessary to take its plural identity into account. This plurality must be understood not only in terms of the difference introduced by the diversity of the conditions of production in different countries,[3] but also in terms of the variations of the genre itself. There are two extremely different and widely recognized "variations" as well as different versions of these two "models."

The first model, based on the Cuban radio soap (Bermúdez 1979), has given form to a *serious* genre, in which heart-rending, tragic suffering predominates. This format depicts exclusively primordial feelings and passions, excluding all ambiguity or complexity from the dramatic space. That is to say, references to places and times are blurred or neutralized. In 1968, the Brazilian soap opera *Beto Rockefeller* initiated the construction of another model. This model, without completely breaking with the melodramatic one, incorporates a realism which permits the "situating of the narrative in

279

everyday life" (Pignatari 1984: 60), as well as within a specifically national reality. The first model constitutes the secret of the success of the Mexican soap opera from *Los ricos también lloran* (*The Rich Also Weep*) to *Cuna de lobos* (*Cradle of Wolves*) as well as of the Venezuelan soap opera from *Lucecita* to *Cristal*. The second model has earned recognition for the Brazilian soap opera, from *La Esclava Isaura* (*Isaura, the Slave*) to *Roque Santeiro*, and for the Colombian, from *Pero sigo siendo el Rey* (*But I am Still King*) to *Caballo Viejo* (*Old Horse*).

In the first model, the central conflicts have to do with kinship. The structure of social roles is crudely Manichean and the characters are purely signs. But in the Mexican soap opera, this simplicity of characterization is adorned with a baroque density of *mise-en-scène*, and a sophistication of wardrobe and make-up. In recent years, the modernization of the staging and the quickening of the visual rhythm have been added to the above elements. The Venezuelan soap opera, on the other hand, translates its schematicism into scenographic and visual austerity, carrying primary orality to an extreme. We find out what is happening in the story not because of what the characters do, but rather because of what they say and tell each other. This dramatic elementality and narrative austerity, expertly wielded, have met with enormous success and commanded great loyalty from viewers.

In the second model, the rigidity of models and ritualizations is perforated by imaginaries of class and territory, of sex and age. At the same time, the expressive possibilities opened up by film, advertising, and videos are explored. The characters are liberated from the weight of destiny. No longer solely great symbols, they come closer to the routines of everyday life and the ambiguities of history, to the speech patterns and customs of different regions. In the Brazilian soap opera, the reference to different areas of the country, to moments in its history and industrial transformation is depicted through a story which utilizes two different concepts of time. The sweeping time frame of the newspaper serial – in which the history of various generations unfolds – is connected with the fragmented visual discourse of advertising (Mattelart and Mattelart 1987). In the Colombian soap opera, the references to the nation are shot through with an ironic vein which incorporates a national tradition of the satiric literature of manners. In this way, it becomes possible to make fun of melodrama and to revisit the regions of the country as a recognizable and shared dimension of national plurality.

The Latin American soap opera is varied in its narrative methods, dramatic material, and visual scripts. Nevertheless, it owes a great part of its success – at least in terms of the Latin American public – to its capacity to make an archaic narrative the repository for propositions to modernize some dimensions of life. The evolution and diversification of the genre has gradually introduced new themes and perspectives. It is true that the limits of the universe represented in the soap opera are strongly defined by the absence of social conflicts whose appearance would threaten the dramatic schema. Still, despite this, the public's complicity with the genre is in part due to the soap opera's permeability to the transformations of modern life. Of course, the modernization of customs is disguised by perennial values and strait-jacketed by multiple rituals. Changes make their appearance sheltered ideologically by their links to the myth of progress and development. However, what is important is that a certain kind of soap opera has made room for itself: a soap opera in which social hierarchies lose their rigidity and in which the social fabric of loyalties and submissions is more complex. The distances between the poor and the rich, men and women, adults and young people are both exposed and turned topsy-turvy by the introduction of mediations and movements which show the other side of the tangled web of humiliations and revenges. Even in the "lowest" social sectors, the struggle for survival is shown to be also a struggle to be someone, for neither dignity nor opportunism are found on only one side.

New social actors and professions have been appearing, widening the horizons of the "soap opera-izable." They are new in so far as they are seen as life-worlds that are present in the story not to serve a function in the inevitable unfolding of the plot, but as figures which unveil new forms of social relations, of cultural breaches, and moral conflicts. Finally, these indicators of modernity, which in many cases form part of the mechanisms of construction of the credibility of a story – and of the renovation required by the business – tell us something else. They indicate how it is that the identities present in the soap opera are not purely a deceptive nostalgia but rather a dimension of living and dreaming with which Latin Americans construct their present.

Laden with heavy narrative schemas and complicitous, deceptive ideological inertia, soap operas form part of the recreational devices of the Latin American imaginary. The formation of this imaginary points to the strategic place the image-producing industries occupy today in the construction of identity. It indicates as well the marketplace's long experience in condensing knowledge that both shapes human aspirations and social demands and makes them motives of profit. This experience permits the cultural industry to use the repetitive structure of the serial to capture the ritualized dimensions of everyday life.

The soap opera in the national and transnational audiovisual space

What has made soap operas into a strategic enclave for the Latin American audiovisual production is their weight in the television market as well as the role that they play in the production and reproduction of the images Latin American peoples make of themselves, and by which others recognize them. This fact makes it indispensable to analyze the different meanings of the soap opera on the national, regional, and transnational plane, as well as its importance within these planes.

Not only in Brazil, Mexico, and Venezuela – the principal exporting countries – but also in Argentina, Colombia, Chile, and Peru, the soap opera is a determining factor in the "national capacity for television" (Portales 1987:8). It influences the extension and consolidation of television production, the industrialization of its processes, the modernization of its infrastructure – technical and financial – and the specialization of its resources: scriptwriters, directors, cameramen, sound engineers, lighting technicians, designers, and editors. Soap opera production has meant, in turn, a certain appropriation of the genre by each country, that is, its *nationalization*. On the one hand, it is true that the soap opera implies rigid stereotypes in its dramatic outline and strong conditioning elements in its visual grammar, as required and reinforced by the logic of a market with increasingly transnational tendencies. It is also true, however, that each individual country has made the soap opera into a special place for the cross-breeding between television and other cultural fields: theater, cinema, and literature. In many countries, production began by importing scripts, in the same way that scripts for radio soaps used to be imported from Cuba or Argentina. In the beginning, the dependence on the radio format was strong, especially because of the transfer of radio script-writers to television and because of the conception of the image as the mere illustration of a "spoken drama." However, this dependence was gradually broken in the process of the industrialization of television and of the production teams' "conquest" of the medium, that is, their appropriation of its expressive qualities. It was then that the soap opera became a conflictive terrain of cultural redefinition. In countries like Brazil, highly esteemed theatrical actors, film directors, and prestigious left-wing writers were incorporated into the production of soap operas. However, in other countries, television in general and the soap opera in particular were rejected by managers and workers in legitimate culture as the most dangerous of traps and the most degrading of professional fields. In all Latin American countries, however, the crisis in cinema and politics has driven many artists, writers, and actors into television and the soap opera. In spite of the commercial controls on the genre, these artists are introducing themes and styles into the soap opera which deal with dimensions of national life and culture.

The development of the soap opera and its role in the development of television in an appreciable number of Latin American countries is tied to its capacity to displace North American television series from prime-time spaces, a phenomenon that is linked to cultural and commercial reasons. The fact that the soap operas moved from the "housewives" time slot, in the middle of the day, to prime-time family hours, was because television viewers discovered something in the soap operas which North American serials, despite their visual attractiveness and narrative skill, did not offer: a complicity with certain markers of cultural identity like those pointed out previously. However, in the Latin American television industry, the soap opera's legitimization by its occupation of the "noblest" time slots in daily programming also meant taking the step to audience management (Mattelart 1989: 77ff.); that is to say, not only in terms of its quantitative measurement, but also in terms of sounding its demands and changing tastes.

These processes imply transformations which go beyond and remodel the soap opera's nation-specific dimension. Two different but intimately connected dynamics are involved: one which pushes for Latin American integration, and another which mobilizes the world market. Within the Latin American space, the soap opera uses to its advantage the long process of massive, popular identification that was put into motion in the 1940s and 1950s by the Mexican and Argentinean cinema, and by the *tango*, the *ranchera*, and the *bolero*. It is a process of sentimental integration of the different Latin American countries – a standardization of ways of feeling and expressing, of gestures and sounds, dance rhythms, and narrative cadences – made possible by the cultural industries of radio and cinema. The soap opera and the logic of its production and consumption are a landmark in the development of this dynamic of integration. That is to say, they are the place where the references and motives of Latin American integration – the countries in their national plurality and cultural diversity – are influenced by the dynamic of transnational globalization of the world market. The internationalization of the soap opera thus responds to the movement of activation and recognition of that which is specifically Latin American in a television genre which began by exporting national hits. Contradictorily, this internationalization also responds to the movement of progressive neutralization of the characteristics of Latin American-ness in a genre which the logic of the world market must convert into transnational from the time of its production.

Brazil was the pioneer. TV-Globo internationalized the soap opera by exporting its hits to Portugal beginning in 1975, and swept away geographical and political borders when it introduced its soap operas in Spain, Denmark, England, and Japan. *La Esclava Isaura (Isaura the Slave)* was declared the best television program of the last ten years in Poland and was seen by 450 million television viewers in the People's Republic of China. Meanwhile, Televisa de México concentrated first on Latin American and Hispanic audiences in the United States. Beginning in the middle of the 1980s, it restructured its international commercialization strategy, making its presence felt in Europe and North Africa with such enormous hits as *Los ricos también lloran (The Rich Also Weep)* which are broadcast from Italy to present-day Russia.

In recent years, the reordering of European national television systems, the privatization and expansion of channels, and the introduction of cable and satellite dishes have increased programming hours, opening the market to the internationalization of Venezuelan, Argentinian, Colombian, and Peruvian soap operas. However, production for a global market implies the generalization of narrative models and the thinning out of cultural characteristics. Certainly, Televisa and TV-Globo's entrance into the world audiovisual

283

market shows the level of development that has been attained by Latin American television businesses. It also signifies, in some measure, the opening of cracks in the hegemony of the United States and in the division between North and South America, that is, between countries considered to be producers and those considered to be exclusively consumers. It signifies as well, however, the tendency for Latin American audiovisual businesses to mold the image of their people in terms of audiences which are more and more undifferentiated, the tendency to dissolve cultural difference into cheap and profitable exoticism.

Notes

* Translated by Marina Elias.
1 These are forms of folk-song which recount a story and previously served the function of communicating information about events. In addition to being sung or recited, the *cordel* literature and the *corrido* were also sold in public places in pamphlet form (thus, the name of the Brazilian form, for the pamphlets were strung from a *cordel*, or cord). The *vallenato*, in addition to being a recital of events, is dance music (translator's note).
2 A *bolero* is a slow, romantic ballad (translator's note).
3 Concerning this point see the following: R. Ortiz, S. H. Borelli, and J. Ortiz Ramos, *Telenovela: história e produçao* (São Paulo: Brasiliense, 1989); M. Coccato, "Apuntes para una historia de la telenovela venezolana," *Videoforum* (1–3) (Caracas, 1979); J. González, *Las vetas del encanto: por los veneros de la producción mexicana de telenovelas*, mimeograph (Colima, Mexico, 1990).

References

Bermúdez, M. (1979) "La radionovela: una semiosis entre el pecado y la redención," *Videoforum* 2.
García Riera, E. (1974) *El cine y su público*, Mexico: FCE.
Marquez de Melo, J. (1989) *Produção e exportaçã da ficção brasileira: caso da TV Globo*, São Paulo: UNESCO.
Mattelart, M. (1989) *L'internationale publicitaire*, Paris: La decouverte.
Mattelart, M. and Mattelart, A. (1987) *Le carnaval des images: la fiction bresilienne*, Paris: La Documentation Française.
Monsivais, C. (1976) "Notas sobre la cultura mexicana en el siglo XX," in *Historia general de México*, 4 vols (Mexico), vol. 4.
—— (1980) "Cultura urbana y creación cultural," *Casa de las Américas* 116 (86).
Ong, W. J. (1987) *Oralidad y escritura*, México: F.C.E.
Ortiz, F. (1973) *Contrapunteo cubano del tabaco y del azucar*, Barcelona: Ariel.
Pignatari, D. (1984) *Signagen da televisão*, São Paulo: Brasiliense.
Portales, D. (1987) *La dificultad de inovar: Un estudio sobre las empresas de televisión en América Latina*, Santiago: Ilet.
Rivera, J. B. (1982) *El folletín*, Buenos Aires: CEDAL.

15

Montezuma's revenge

Reading *Los Ricos También Lloran* in Russia

Kate Baldwin

The reruns

It could be said that Russia's obsession with "the soap" began backwards. I say backwards, because I mean quite literally that Russia's induction into the world of television as we know it is proceeding by way of the reruns. In order to support this claim, I am going to discuss the ways in which the Mexican soap opera *Los Ricos También Lloran*, translated into Russian as *Bogaty Tozhe Plachut (The Rich Also Cry)*,[1] has made an indispensable incursion into Russian strategies of waste management: that is, the ways in which "television training" in Russia can be read as a kind of toilet training. As Penelope Leach in her book, *Your Growing Child*, advises,

> These days, most parents are able to look at toilet training as a matter of helping a child to take charge of her own excretion and waste disposal. The secret is to avoid any implication that she must. Until she makes the vital connection between the feeling and the product, your child will resent spending more than a few seconds on the box.[2]

This essay could be seen as an attempt to make that link between the feeling and the product. As you now know, the secret to making that vital connection is, of course, to avoid any implication that you must.

Russian television (which meant the two official, government-run channels) began broadcasting soap operas in order to fill the vacuum between sessions of the Congresses of People's Deputies. Up to this time, the congresses, held twice a year, consistently topped the Russian TV hit parades, which is to say that, in Russia, until 1992 there was never anything to watch on TV. At the end of the summer of 1992 Commonwealth Channel Ostankino One began to broadcast the 249-part 1970s Mexican hit series, *The Rich Also Cry*. In the fall of 1992 the show could be seen three times a week, twice a day – the evening show repeated the following morning, with a few slip-ups when a day's morning and evening programs were identical. Each episode was presented in the form of two segments of 20 minutes each, broken by a 5-minute commercial break. The opening 10 minutes of every episode replayed the prior day's closing 10 minutes, so that if you had missed the mounting tension of the last show's closing cuts, you would not be left behind; likewise, if you had been a faithful viewer, as most were, you could relive that accumulative frisson, an experience that made one all the more eager to relieve it.

Rich People continued through the end of November 1992, when the final Thursday night episode met with national grief. The following day in Moscow headlines ran "Heart be Still: 'The Rich' are Gone," and "Russia Wept Thursday." During its tenure as Russia's official soap, *Rich People* enjoyed the highest ratings of any TV show ever. It is estimated that 70 percent of the population, or 200 million viewers, tuned in regularly.[3] Such popularity was unheralded: for instance, in the summer of 1992 *Dynasty* had its try with the Russian public, as did *Dallas*. Neither show ever got off the ground. People said the plots were too difficult to follow, that there were too many characters and that things moved too quickly. The American soap opera *Santa Barbara* ran concurrently with *Rich People*, but its following never approached that of the Mexican-produced soap. Following the broadcast of the final episode, a headline in the *Moscow Tribune*[4] queried "Will *The Rich Also Cry* Beat the Congress?," and went on to assert that "of all the schmaltzy soaps currently presented by Russian television, this one has been a *ne plus ultra* hit." Similarly, the *Moscow Times* contended that "when the film started, streets became desolate, crowds gathered in stores selling TV sets, tractors stopped in the fields and guns fell silent on the Azerbaijani–Armenian front."[5] In an article published by *Moskovsky Komsomoletz*,[6] a hypothesis was voiced that the series had been more effective in increasing life expectancy in Russia than any health-promoting program, because old people couldn't bear to die before they knew how the series ended. The same newspaper reported that a publisher of collections of anecdotes had raised as many as 2,000 anecdotes about the film's characters, and that due to numerous viewers' requests, Ostankino promised to rebroadcast the serial in its entirety beginning in December 1992.

According to the press, as these clips demonstrate, viewership cut across usual lines of social stratification. *Rich People*, like its popularity, could be viewed across the expanse of Russia's eleven time zones. However, it is worth noting that when something is deemed popular in Russia by the press, there is often a conflation between Russia proper and the territories of the former Soviet Union. There is no existing data on *Rich People*'s popularity outside Russia, that is, outside Russia's main metropoles. Just as there is no definite way of accounting for the show's popularity, there is no definite way of knowing if, indeed, the show was quite so popular on, say, the Azerbaijani front as it was supposed to be. For these reasons, my argument works within a frame of Russia "proper." My argument concerns itself primarily with areas in which *Rich People* was determinedly popular – cities ethnically diverse but primarily inhabited by Russians, that is, white Russians. Of course, I am not saying that my argument need necessarily be limited to Russia. Indeed I would be quite happy if it could be extended to include all eleven time zones, but that, I fear, is the work of another station.

To return to the reports: they emphasize the specificity of the show's appeal to the people – whether on the streets, in the fields, or on the front – and it is an idea of the Russian people that reads in contradistinction to an idea of the Russian intellectual. Indeed, the show merited only disdain in academic circles. According to an article in *Literaturnaia Gazetta*,[7] the soap performed a kind of mass "psychotherapy" that replaced "real stress with artificial stress." Such emphasis on artificiality caused scholars I spoke with to deem *Rich People* not "authentic" Russian culture, and certainly not the kind of material that I, as a visiting academic, should investigate as in any way representative of or even linked to nexuses between present-day culture and politics in Russia. None the less, I will argue that *Rich People* does have quite a lot to say about such interstices. In representing a division, however banal, between the people and the intellectual, the show's popularity also has something to say about gender. Not surprisingly, *Rich People*'s viewership was made up primarily of women. And it is this intersection of the people, on the one hand, and women's place, on the other, as both outside and/or marginal to that of the intellectual (who should know better), that leads me to the site of domestic trash.

In examining the phenomenal female-biased popularity of *Rich People* in Russia, this essay will examine the implications and ramifications of *Rich People* as "recycled culture," that is, as so-called "American culture" filtered through the lens of western-style Mexican social groups, in present-day Russia. In so doing, this essay will connect a specific time/space situatedness to particular codifications of the "subject" in present-day Russia. What the show's popularity can tell us about Russian culture in and on the post-communist stage is that the switch of a good/evil paradigm from that of communist/capitalist to capitalist/communist marks a radical change in the way knowledge about gender in contemporary Russia is socially constructed. Much has been made of connections between what can loosely be termed melodrama and the feminine. Several books have been dedicated to the articulation of various links between melodrama and the female consumer.[8] Each of these investigations have in common an examination of the framework demanded by melodrama and the ways in which gender impacts upon such frames. However, as the critic Christine Gledhill has noted, melodrama and so-called "women's culture" have an uneasy relationship at best. The very

term "women's culture" requires caution. Clearly it cannot be used to suggest some pure female space where women speak freely to each other outside patriarchal constraints in that melodrama uses the female figure as a central symbol for its world as maternal icon or sexual

287

predator women's culture has been formed in an overdetermined relationship to it.[9]

In an effort to avoid the pitfall of assuming *Rich People*'s use of melodramatic plot work as necessarily indicative of an inherent girliness, and vice versa – that its very girliness constitutes its melodrama – I want to emphasize that my reading of *Rich People* presupposes that this particular serial comes to us as a fragment of such overdetermination: while *Rich People* does not tell us that its use of melodrama poses as a "feminine" genre it also does not not tell us this. Rather, in appealing to both men and women, *Rich People* affords the viewer a chance to observe the paradox of hungry eyes consuming the drama of the wealthy across a variegated tableau of genders, classes, ethnicities and sexualities. What the Russian viewer then does with, or how she forms cathexes with these various tutelary concepts reveals both modes of construction imposed from the outside as well as the contribution of fantasy and pleasure in the articulation of desires which result from a collision of Cold War ideologies. A connection between the place of the "feminine" and the place of trash as denigrated cultural spaces will become more clear as we proceed to link the eighteen-year-old soap with the gossip that circulated about its outcome and the pleasures Russian viewers found in speculating about the outcome of the Mexican family's secrets.

In addressing the desire of a Russian audience to consume foreign goods, we must keep in mind that the Russian paradigm of popular media consumption, what I am calling "television training," differs greatly from that found in western Europe. Whereas the western European television viewers find themselves within a media-saturated, fax machine gorged viewer–audience situatedness, or a realm of the "videological," the western soap opera in Russia meets a culture largely invested in written texts, the realm of the ideological. In introducing such a division between what I am calling the videological and the ideological, I mean to say that in Russian society as a whole books and not television have been the mainstay of fantasy and escapism. Until very recently, books have been extremely hard to come by, and their scarcity has made them all the more desirable, while at the same time their presence in all its paucity has provided a vital source of imaginary playgrounds: until the summer of 1991, one did not come home and flip on the TV to escape the day's hardships – one read the borrowed copy of a newly translated Philip Dick or J. R. R. Tolkien. In fact, when the failed putsch of August 1991 was broadcast, Russians were stunned, not only by the reality of a government in dramatic transition, but by the fact that they were watching it, and not reading about it. Such interfacing laid the groundwork for an entirely new relationship to the television screen; in fact, no comparison better illustrates a cross between realism and melodrama in television homes of the early 1990s: in stark contrast to vivid depictions of a crumbling government, *Rich People* offered solace to the weary eye for whom visions of marital infidelities and hints of incest demonstrated a space where

> melodrama is driven to break with the limits of representation: not to
> renew verisimilitude but rather to deal with the real as it touches psychic
> nerves or activates the moral imagination. Hence melodrama functions
> both referentially and metaphorically, bearing witness to the underlying
> desires and impulses which fuel social process. In this respect melo-
> drama feeds off the ideological conflicts that accompany social change.
> . . . Melodrama's capacity to cut short the logical processes of realism
> to arrive at overdetermined confrontations can make covertly available
> as melodrama what realism avoids or represses as too threatening.[10]

While it could be argued that the explicit televisuals of 1991 may have been
at least as melodramatic as they were "realistic," one thing is certain: they
set the scene for what was to follow, namely the privatization of at least one
channel – Ostankino – and hence the availability of a completely new set of
programmings and viewer choices. Likewise, if it can be argued that the lack
of a western-type media saturation supported *Rich People*'s popularity, then
it follows that it is such underpinnings in connection with the show's
projection of itself as marginal (that is, as not, like *Dynasty* or *Dallas*,
centrally located in the realm of the videological) that helped provide for *Rich
People*'s attraction to Russians, particularly Russian women.

Before I proceed to flesh out this argument, I'd like to give a brief plot
synopsis, for I think we find identification with the marginalized mobilized
on several levels, both for the viewer in relation to the plot diachronically,
and for the viewer as a participant synchronically, in the cultural phenomenon
of the show.

The plot of *Rich People* can be summed up rather briefly. First there is the
rich but unhappy (hence the title) Salvatierro family with a single son, Luis
Alberto, and a beautiful, poor, nubile young maid called Marianna. After
much trial and tribulation, Marianna and Luis Alberto get married and live
in marital bliss, until Marianna in an unexplained and temporary fit of
madness (you know how those young, nubile types can be) gives away her
first son to an old woman on the street.

The next eighteen years are subsequently devoted to a hopeless search for
the lost baby. Marianna finds the baby, now an eighteen-year-old *Teen Beat*
type, thanks to her daughter, Marisabel, who, incidentally, just happens to be
dating him, Beto, the long-lost son. Marianna begins to lavish all her time
and attention on her newly recovered, beloved son. Fearing anger and blame,
Marianna doesn't tell Luis Alberto about her discovery, so Luis Alberto
begins to grow jealous and suspect that Marianna is having a love affair with
Beto. Meanwhile, Marianna has confided in Marisabel that Beto is her son,
and, because Marianna declines to mention that Marisabel is herself adopted,
the daughter is immediately sent into hysterical overdrive, fearing incest

with, gasp, her own brother. The much hallowed final episode resolves itself in a showdown in which the macho Luis Alberto confronts son and wife with a handgun. As the credits roll, the father's finger is already pulling the trigger. Within 30 seconds all is righted: Marianna screams, "SON!" Luis Alberto screams, "Saint!" Beto screams, "Father!" As Beto reiterates, "Father, let me embrace you!," the family is reunited.

As you can gather, the plot turns on the question of blood relations. Once the child is returned to his blood kin, everything is straightened out. But what is the danger presented by a mixture of so to speak "bad blood," and why does it need straightening? In order to address these questions it may be useful to turn to the work of Michel Foucault to examine ways in which *Rich People* instances a coincidence of what Foucault has called "a symbolics of blood" and "an analytics of sexuality," two distinct regimes of power that "did not come about without overlappings, interactions, and echoes." Foucault writes:

> In different ways, the preoccupation with blood and the law has for nearly two centuries haunted the administration of sexuality. Two of these interferences are noteworthy, the one for its historical importance, the other for the problems it poses. Beginning in the second half of the nineteenth century, the thematics of blood was sometimes called on to lend its entire historical weight toward revitalizing the type of political power that was exercised through the devices of sexuality. Racism took shape at this point: it was then that a whole politics of settlement (*peuplement*), family, marriage, education, social hierarchization, and property, accompanied by a long series of permanent interventions at the level of the body, conduct, health, and everyday life, received their color and their justification from the mythical concern with protecting the purity of the blood and ensuring the triumph of the race. Nazism was doubtless the most cunning and the most naive (and the former because of the latter) combination of the fantasies of blood and the paroxysms of a disciplinary power. A eugenic ordering of society, with all that implied in the way of extension and intensification of micro-powers, in the guise of an unrestricted state control (*étatisation*), was accompanied by the oneiric exaltation of a superior blood; the latter implied both the systematic genocide of others and the risk of exposing oneself to a total sacrifice.[11]

I quote Foucault at length in order to emphasize the correlations between a power dynamic that Foucault locates in the late nineteenth century and the present crisis surrounding ethnicity and rising tides of nationalisms, along with long-standing and accepted racism, in Russia today. Eastern European societies are still greatly invested in the law of blood, lineages which carry the currency of sovereignty and power: the most blatant instancing can be found in the atrocities occurring in the former Soviet-bloc territories of Bosnia-Herzogovinia.

Foucault credits psychoanalysis for its interrogation of the extension of the law into the manipulation and control of the power relations aimed at administering sexuality:

> Whence the Freudian endeavor (out of reaction no doubt to the great surge of racism that was contemporary with it) to ground sexuality in the law – the law of alliance, tabooed consanguinity, and with the Sovereign-Father, in short, to surround desire with all the trappings of the old order of power. It was owing to this that psychoanalysis was – in the main, with a few exceptions – in theoretical and practical opposition to fascism. And yet, to conceive the category of the sexual in terms of the law, death, blood, and sovereignty is in the last analysis a historical "retro-version."[12]

In looking at the impact of *Rich People* in Russia, a kind of repositioning must be enacted, so that such "retro-version" suddenly seems "retro" in the sense of "backwards" and even "dated," but none the less tellingly contemporaneous. Consider the words of Anatoly Sobchak, the mayor of St Petersburg:

> In the Soviet Union, an empire of Holocaust survivors and the children of survivors, this gnawing uncertainty was the usual condition of life .... The survivor can usually imagine ... death in a generic way – the executioner's rubber apron, the ditch dug in frozen mud. But the suffering continues because there is no closure. It's as if the regime were guilty of two crimes on a massive scale: murder and the unending assault against memory. In making a secret of history, the Kremlin made its subjects just a little more insane, a little more desperate.[13]

As Sobchak makes eerily obvious, the former Soviet Union's power as a totalitarian regime demands, at the very least, reckoning. In order to reckon with it, I would argue for a provisional usefulness of psychoanalysis to investigate mechanisms at work in the residual effects of prioritizing blood and race as read in and against something so seemingly superficial, so seemingly trivial, as a soap. The problems produced by a suppressed collective memory in the face of genocide at its most "cunning and naive," and the simultaneous instancing of "generic" death, result, finally, in the desperation for superficially demarcated lines of good and evil as serialized in the Salvatierro melodrama which promises closure and likewise an "end" to suffering. But what can the family plot of *Rich People* reveal about the viewers who are so eager to witness a kind of public re-enactment of less superficial, indeed, less visible lines of racism within a framework of closure?

As the narrative reveals, on a very basic level *Rich People* can be categorized into familiar Freudian terms, namely fear of incest. However, as we recall, in *Totem and Taboo*, when Freud announced his two seminal culture-forming taboos of parricide and incest, it was parricide that got the attention.[14] This is precisely where the critic Julia Kristeva intervenes. In her book, *Powers of Horror*, she picks up the theme of incest and turns it to the abject.

The abject signifies a liminal status, it demarcates a positionality which cannot be ascribed as either inside or out. Kristeva uses the trope of "liminality" to focus upon bodily margins as demarcators of the potentially abject. Because the child issues forth from the body of the woman, the boundary between mother and child is constructed as a taboo one. The task of cultural ritual is then to ward off the danger of transgression of such liminalities. Kristeva argues,

> this is precisely where we encounter rituals of defilement and their derivatives, which, based on the feeling of abjection and all converging on the maternal, attempt to symbolize the other threat to the subject, that of being swamped by the dual relationship, the subject's fear of his very own identity sinking irretrievably into the mother.[15]

The abject is that which is cast aside, and, for our purpose, *Rich People* can be read as a kind of abjected cultural artifact, for the show is precisely a piece of Mexican pop-culture which has been discarded by Mexico only to be swept up by Russia. In recognizing *Rich People* as cultural debris, we notice that the soap has lost some of its more salient cleansing qualities; it has become its alter ego; it has become, ironically, dirt. It's no small irony that dirt only really becomes dirty when at home, or in the domestic space of the feminine. Indeed, the abject fits well into the realm of erotics so commonly associated with the soap opera as a genre, for it is precisely the erotics here, as they circulate around the figure of the mother, that can be interpreted as representative of an economy of waste. The symbiotic relationship between melodrama and soap evidences itself in such trash: melodrama's capacity to break taboos affords the soap access to socially proscribed areas, and likewise the soap resorts to melodramatic formulations when the almost unconceivable is proffered as a plot complication. Both find relief in fantasies which can be worked over and resolved when the serial is over, the viewer satisfied, the solution "realized."

Girltalk

There is much to be made of the trash status of soaps and their connection as such to the feminine. As Robert Allen has pointed out in his book, *Speaking of Soap Operas*,[16] in 1940 the *Saturday Review* called soaps "serialized drool," and soaps have historically been located within their own cultures as trash TV. Just as soap is known to produce all kinds of immaterial fluff including suds, froth, lather, and tears, its very term of self-inflicted slipperiness is emphasized through a juxtaposition to "opera." Allen points out that the terminology, bringing together "soap" and "opera," veils thinly a kind of class denigration behind that of gender. What makes *Rich People* remarkable, then, is not only the fact that the soap fluidly becomes defiled and defiling, but that this dirt is even trashier, that is, it comes cheap. One reason that *Rich People* appeared on Russian television screens is that, as an eighteen-year-old program, it simply cost less than more recent programming. As a successor to Soviet television, Ostankino needed first to build its audience by broadcasting different programs than were available before. Because of a necessarily limited budget, instead of delving into its own potentially costly productions, Ostankino chose to buy foreign programming, to find the cheapest sources of entertainment that could none the less hold the attention of a Russian viewership. Hence, *Rich People* presents itself not only as a cultural discard, as abject, but as doubly so: cheap and trashy, yes, but also dated, old trash, not new.

Once the connection between the soap and dirt has been established, and this is not difficult to maintain, given that since their inception soaps have always been called as such with no small sense of irony and derisiveness, it is worth noting that soaps were conceived of in the 1930s as a way of reaching a heretofore untapped resource of the homemaker viewership. The woman at home was the target of the serial as well as the commercials that supported them, which is to say that soaps came about as ploy to sell, among other things, cleansers and cleaning products. As Robert Allen has argued,[17] within the story-line of the soap, dirt gets positioned as a problem, a problem which takes the shape of unruly children, unfaithful spouses, and illness. The viewer is made aware of these problems as secrets, that is, the "dirty little secrets" which give the viewer a vantage point of knowledge to which all the characters are not privy. I will further address the disparities between the kinds of "knowing" that proceed and maintain the swaying power of the soap, but at this point it may be helpful to point out the connection between such "dirty little secrets" that are better off kept hidden, and the propensity of serials to provoke another kind of dirty or abjected talk among their female viewers: girl-talk, otherwise known as *gossip*. It's no secret that soap opera's mainstay of communication is conversation, and as Jon Stratton suggests, talk in soap opera is *action*.[18]

In linking the soap to the abject, we return to the mother, for in recollecting the imagined space of the pre-Oedipal, abjection works across the plane of the mother's face. And this is where we meet the *Rich People*. For what is the plot of the show if not one coded by the maternal? The story is, after all, the story of Marianna, and, as the final episode reminds us, she was not just any mother, but a sainted one. As if to emphasize this connection, the TV on which I viewed the show wore a lace curtain upon which a clay figurine of Mary was perched. Not an unlikely coupling in current Russia – the television not only as reflective box, but as mini-shrine. Indeed, throughout the series, the camera focuses on Marianna's face, using the close-up to linger lovingly over the mother's grief. Moreover, the cult of Marianna (which not surprisingly has outlived the life of the soap) depends upon the blow-up, the deified image of Mary-anna's face on everything from calendars to poster boards to teacups.

As Diana Fuss has argued, such concentration on the dis-membered image of the mother encourages a loss of reference for the viewer, a loss triggered by a face-to-face encounter with what can be termed primary narcissism – the possibility of both plenitude and loss reflected in and by the mother's, Marianna's, magnified, beautified face.[19] Moreover, as Steve Neale has argued, the powerlessness the viewer feels to change the course of the narrative and instate coincidence – the lack of which provides the continual delay, backing-up, and non-resolution of the serial – can be interpreted as not only the result of a gap between the "rightness" of a union and its delay, but as instances at which "the deep rooted fantasies of fusion, of a perfect coincidence of both communication and desire – yearnings related to the nostalgic fantasy of union with the mother, the wish for maternal plenitude."[20] Such involvement which engages the plane of the mother enables the serial to move the spectator, literally, to manipulate her emotions to a degree "beyond justification," hence the terms "weepies," or "tear-jerkers."

To clarify, I am arguing that the general appeal of the show resides in the process of identification it provides for the Russian viewer through a process of marginalization, a process which posits the Russian viewer as a decentered viewer at the same time that it provides for the repression of this recognition of the self as marginal. And this appeal becomes gender-specific when we look at the specific mechanisms through which processes of identification are deployed.

In flaunting the possibility of incest – both by presenting Beto as the mistaken lover of Marianna, and by reinforcing this idea through the love connection between Beto and Marianna's daughter – the plot strives to contain the danger of the abject, of an illegal alliance between sister and brother, a younger version of the primal taboo of mother coupled with son. Yet the very appeal of the show depends upon the calling forth of this danger, and its more specific appeal to the female Russian viewer, I would argue also depends upon the calling forth and suppression of the possibility of an illegal alliance with Marianna.

Marianna comes to the Russian viewer as a face of all that Russia promises to be: wealthy, beautiful, and perhaps even blessed. The desire to be Marianna becomes foregrounded so as to preclude a simultaneous desire to have her. I would argue that given the ways in which gender is constructed in Russia, it makes sense that women more often than men, occupy the material position of viewer. For it is the specter of the female, more specifically of the mother, that haunts the show. While I'm not saying that men don't have access to this position, I am saying that it is simply more unlikely. Suffice it to say that the position of the constructed viewer is feminized, so that gender-specificity is not necessarily identity-politics oriented: everyone, no matter what their sex, becomes a little Marianna when they view the show. Like the absenting of recognition of oneself as marginal, the specter of the mother renews itself by continually invoking its own death in much the same way as Judith Butler has argued that heterosexuality secures its identity by disavowing and calling attention to its abject, interiorized other – homosexuality.[21]

Just as the mother becomes a site of plenitude and loss, she is also a site of pleasure and excess. The desire to be Marianna is also a desire to revel in her excess, to linger in her shit. Kristeva notes such a connection between the homosexual maternal matrix and waste, writing,

> contrary to what enters the mouth and nourishes, what goes out of the body points to the infinitude of the body proper. Fecal matter signifies, as it were, what never ceases to separate from a body in a state of permanent loss in order to become autonomous, distinct from the mixtures, alterations, and decay that run through it. Psychoanalysis has indeed seen that anal dejection constitutes the first material separation that is controllable by the human being.[22]

The gesture to establish the self as separate from the mother is also a gesture which calls attention to the child's desire to be like the mother – to take pleasure in the product of her own child or little shit. Yet the reason that such conflation between one issue and the other causes such a commotion is because shitting isn't procreative. None the less, after the narrative build-up, the release of which comes in an explosive closing scene, a sense of relief manifests itself in the form of an ejaculatory pleasure most commonly associated with tears. But if we turn again to Neale we find the question, "why the pleasure in tears?" If we insert/think "tears" *pace* "shit" in the following passage, the potency of *Rich People* as a closed serial concerned with an attenuated pleasure, that is, one which builds on its own retentiveness, becomes more pointed:

> Tears in childhood arise as a consequence of loss, the loss particularly of a sense of union with the mother. However, crying isn't simply an articulation of this loss, it is also a demand for its reparation – a demand addressed most commonly to the mother who is thus situated in fantasy as a figure capable of fulfilling that demand. Crying, therefore, is not just an expression of pain or displeasure or non-satisfaction. As a demand for satisfaction, it is the vehicle of a wish – a fantasy – that satisfaction is possible, that the object can be restored, the loss eradicated.[23]

The longer such a union is put off, the more likely the faithful viewer, the one who has "held it in" all these months, is to "jerk-off," that is to "cry" at the end of the serial when the various blockages and barriers to the vicissitudes of desire that produce the narrative are allayed.

Moving from Freud's suggestion that an infant's holding back of fecal masses was a form of masturbation, taking pleasure in one's own shit has become linked to excessive forms of sexuality, or those that are supposedly going nowhere fast. Gradually the notion filtered out to the public with the outrageous subtext that one could make a child "anal" – that is, homosexual – by doing something wrong – that is, allowing the child to grow accustomed to the pleasurable experience of anal retention – in toilet training.[24] One can only wonder why it was anal retention and not anal ejaculation that was deemed masturbatory. If holding on to one's shit created such a stink, we can only imagine what tossing it out into the world might do. In either case, it is precisely such so-called wrongdoing that I commend as most definitely excess-indulgent, for it allows us to explore ejaculatory pleasure as nothing more and nothing less than the wonderful world of waste that it is. For such fantasy to be real, the richness of the seriality of this soap – its plot as goal-oriented, episodic, habit forming, and, finally, conclusively explosive – can be mined, but not undermined.

The repressive moment in *Rich People* which stifles an ejaculatory drive occurs through two simultaneous mechanisms: first, the fantasy of the rich reaches home through the thought, "I like her and I am like her. I, too, can be wealthy because I cry too." Crying and shitting become partners in an ejection which provides a kind of cleansing solace, and it is a concern with cleaning that leads to the second mechanism: it is an assumed racial superiority on the part of the Russian viewer which converges with and subsequently stonewalls the homoerotic plane of desire found in identification – "no more am I so like her, nor do I like her so much." In sum, the self-satisfied viewer leaves the set morally reaffirmed, and, finally, after the closing sequence, relieved.

It is worth noting that the racial does the work of the sexual here. In other words, the implicitly sexual level of reference between the viewer and Marianna becomes coded in terms of the racial, for it is on the level of the racial that Marianna appeals to the female Russian viewer as both beautiful and inferior. The racial aspects of Marianna are somehow more palatable, as it were, than the sexual. Part of Marianna's saliency as a cult figure can be found in her stereotypically visually marked "ethnicity:" a dark-haired, dark-eyed, tawny-skinned Mexican beauty. It is due to a foregrounding of such racial qualities that the viewer can wash her hands of a Marianna found to be "not worthy," i.e., "not wealthy," "not white" enough. Such an erasure assures the return not only to racial superiority but simultaneously to sexual superiority. To repeat, the sexual is closeted behind terms of raciality so that, in effect, we have a vivid performance of a kind of *closure* that has particular resonance in eastern Europe, that is, ethnic cleansing.

In calling up the realm of the abject, then, the show also swallows this summons, so that the popularity of *Rich People* becomes simply a phenomenon and not in any way phenomenological. The show can stand in as representative of a kind of waste-management – for the mechanisms with which it works point ultimately to a strategy of containment, both of the impact of Mexican cultural refuse on Russian society, and the desires of the not so rich Russians to be healthy, wealthy, and, dare I say it, anal erotic. In other words, aspiring to be "rich also," means eating shit, not one's own, but that of the Mexican/other. Unwittingly the Russian audience leaves the television drying its eyes and smacking its lips.

Backing the USSR

While nothing like pop-culture and/or queer – or as some might say mere rubbish – studies exist in Russia, there is none the less a great deal of critical investigation into fields of higher aesthetic appeal, namely the "arts." For our purposes, this field of legitimated study is of utmost importance, for its current stance and interests unknowingly reinforce my argument for *Rich People*. The current post-communist phase of intellectual activism has chosen for itself the title "rearguard." Just how you define "rearguard" depends on who's wearing the pants (or who's pulling them down) – artists and writers producing cultural artifacts or those who contribute to their production by consuming them. The Russian literary critic Mikhail Epstein explains "rearguard" as follows:

> What is it that constitutes the rear guard as a kind of final outlook? Contemporary aesthetics is equally weary of both a realism that corresponds to reality and an avant-garde that anticipates it. Reality turns out to be somewhere ahead, rapidly changing according to its own historical laws, *while art brings up the rear, noting and sweeping up everything along the way – though already as historical rubbish*, as the disintegrating layers of reality.[25]

Like contemporary Russian art, then, "television training" in Russia proceeds by way of the reruns. It seems that Russia has a lot of catching up to do, because they cannot even get fresh trash, but must rummage through dated and deteriorating refuse. As in the case of *Rich People*, this can be seen in the soaking up of the remnants of culture – whether it be their own or someone else's – and reingesting it as their own. If indeed the place of the end works as the place of production, then it makes sense that Russian culture would be concerned with guarding that end, along with what comes out and what goes in. Such ingestion connects again to the superstar status in which Veronica Castro, Marianna, found herself when she visited Moscow in early September 1992. Greeted by teeming crowds of adoring fans, Castro was personally greeted by Boris Yeltsin at the Kremlin. She was then carted away in his black Mercedes to lunch with parliamentary leaders, and take in *Swan Lake* at the Bolshoi Theater where, seated in the czar's box, she was ogled by frenzied fans. As Andrew Kopkind notes, [the fans] did not notice, or perhaps were too loyal to remark, that the actress had weathered considerably in the decade and a half since the series was made, and that the luscious Marianna was somewhat more ... grandmotherly than she appeared on TV.[26]

Maybe the fans did notice, but didn't care, for not looking too closely is another way to maintain the fantasy that everyone's shit looks the same, that is, of convincing themselves, in their eagerness to "talk dirty" and exchange plot forecasts, that in spite of other contradictions in their ideological make up, the "real" world occupies a space between psychic and social fantasy where ageism is not a factor.

To be sure, garbage and excrement are the overarching metaphors in contemporary Russian/Soviet art. In 1989 the well-known short-story writer Viktor Erofeev wrotes, "But is this really life? This isn't life, it's fecal waters, a whirlpool of slops, a collapse of the heart."[27] It comes as no surprise, then, that the moment of *Rich People*'s intense and overwhelming popularity is also the moment in which contemporary Russian art finds itself wallowing in a metaphysics of refuse and rubbish.

In identifying with and, perhaps, even momentarily occupying a fantasized position of the Mexican rich, contemporary Russians are simultaneously taking up the position of the southerner – a position, once recognized, whose fate follows the history of Russia's orientalizing appropriation of her own southern colonies. What Russian, indeed, what American, will not tell you about their traveling southern exposure to Montezuma's revenge? It is here that Castro's weathered looks speak for themselves; they provide a wrinkle in such dirt/logic. For perhaps even refuse in this context contains a cultural specificity that defies that old maxim "everyone's shit looks the same." Maybe Mexico's shit does look different, at least in the eyes of a Russian "rearguard" who uses the soap as a cleansing mechanism, and calls it trash so that not only will his skin seem clearer, but his shit will look better in comparison. Ironically, the intellectual's concern with maintaining a position of "rearguard" bespeaks a desire to be the housekeeper, the one with the hand on the broom, "bringing up the rear and sweeping up everything along the way." Even the intellectual wants to be a housewife, blanching age spots, ironing out those nasty wrinkles. Everyone wants to get inside where the dirt is and talk about it. Everyone can be caught taking a backwards glance at the soap.

This brings us to the bathroom. As I have suggested, *Rich People* became popular in the domestic space coded "feminine" in contradistinction to that of the intellectual or masculine coded sphere of commerce. We have seen how the intellectual calls it crap. We have seen how the housewife eats it up. And we have seen how everyone wants to wear the apron – dish it out or clean it. Despite the fact that every modern Russian flat has separate rooms for the bath and for the bow(e)l, it is precisely the conflation of these spaces

– the washroom and the toilet – that allows the soap to get down and get dirty. The cultural anxiety that accompanies the soap is not only about a containment of the feminine, "domestic trash," but also about a much more muddied area between, or what happens when your trash gets mixed up with that of your (wealthier) neighbor and everyone wants to do the sorting. Because everyone has an ass, the soap space would seem to be less about gender than about the anus. However, given a boost from Marianna, it seems that we have begun to localize a horror of the power of a potentially gender-specific eroticized end in production. It may in fact be that the move from gender to the anus in some way produces what we come to know as the "feminine." Such a displacement can only be read backwards. Focusing upon the shittyness of shit provides a decoy for talking about what is perceived but unspeakable about the "feminine," or a gender-specific end to reproduction, an inarticulation of which keeps the feminine both self-defiling and defiled.

Like other colonialisms, Russian colonialism concerned itself with the work of containment – conquering new territories and subsequently keeping a firm hand on them. The fear of internal uprisings became displaced on to the body of the colonized. Because there is no discourse of a female anal eroticism,[28] it has no specificity, and remains somewhat unspeakable, always displaced on to the body of the male. None the less, I would argue that rolling in the ruins of a "once-great" empire which never once was so great as imagined, the *Rich People* viewer is encouraged to see the specter of such an insurgence return in a Mexican mother, who, unwittingly redresses intersections between culture and imperialism, and finds them loaded with equally potent shit.

Notes

1 For the sake of clarity, excepting cases where the full title is being quoted or referenced, *The Rich Also Cry* will hereafter appear as *Rich People* in the main text.

2 Penelope Leach, *Your Growing Child* (New York: Knopf, 1990), p. 649.

3 Andrew Kopkin, "From Russia With Love and Squalor," *Nation* (January 18, 1992), p. 4.

4 *Moscow Tribune* (November 27, 1992).

5 Anya Vakhrusheva and Carey Scott, "Heart Be Still: 'Rich Also' Gone," *Moscow Times* (November 27, 1992), p. 2. See also, Adam Dawtrey and Michael Williams, "Russos Favor U.S. Fare, Ratings Report Reveals," *Variety Europe* (August 17, 1992), pp. 31–32.

6 *Moskovsky Komsomoletz* (November 28, 1992).

7 *Literaturnaia Gazetta* (December 9, 1992), p. 8. See also *Literaturnaia Gazetta* (August 5, 1992), p. 8; Michael Dobb, "Moscow Turns to Mexican Soap Opera," *Washington Post* (September 11, 1992); and Fen Montainge, "Former Soviet Union Thrilled to See that 'Rich Also Weep,'" *News and Observer* (Raleigh, NC) (July 17, 1992).

8 See, for example, Christine Gledhill (ed.), *Home is Where the Heart Is* (London: British Film Institute, 1987); Lynn Spigel and Denise Mann (eds), *Private*

Screenings: Television and the Female Consumer; Janice Radway, *Reading the Romance: Women, Patriarchy and Popular Literature* (Chapel Hill, NC: University of North Carolina Press, 1984); Mary Ann Doane, *The Desire to Desire: The Woman's Film of the 1940's*; Tania Modleski, *Loving With a Vengeance: Mass Produced Fantasies for Women* (New York: Methuen, 1982).

9 Christine Gledhill, "Speculations on the Relationship between Soap Opera and Melodrama," *Quarterly Review of Film & Video* 14 (1–2) (1992), p. 110.

10 Ibid., p. 118.

11 Michel Foucault, *The History of Sexuality: Volume 1* (New York: Random House, 1978), p. 150.

12 Ibid.

13 David Remnick, *Lenin's Tomb: The Last Days of the Soviet Empire* (New York: Random House, 1993).

14 See Freud, *Totem and Taboo* (1913), *The Complete Psychological Works of Sigmund Freud* (London: Hogarth Press, 1953–1974), vol. 13.

15 Julia Kristeva, *Powers of Horror: An Essay on Abjection*, trans. Leon S. Roudiez (New York: Columbia University Press, 1982), p. 64.

16 Robert Allen, *Speaking of Soap Operas* (Chapel Hill, NC: University of North Carolina Press, 1985).

17 Ibid.

18 Jon Stratton, "Watching the Detectives: Television Melodrama and its Genres," *Australasian Drama Studies* 10 (1987).

19 Diana Fuss, "Fashion and the Homospectatorial Look," *Critical Inquiry* 18 (4) (1992).

20 Steve Neale, "Melodrama and Tears," *Screen* 27 (6) (1986) p. 12.

21 Judith Butler, "Imitation and Gender Insubordination," in Diana Fuss (ed.), *Inside/Out: Lesbian Theories, Gay Theories* (New York: Routledge, 1991), pp. 13–31.

22 Kristeva, *Powers of Horror*, p. 108.

23 Neale, "Melodrama and Tears," p. 22.

24 See Alison Mack, *Toilet Learning: The Picture Book Technique for Children and Parents* (Boston, Mass.: Little Brown, 1978).

25 Mikhail Epstein, "After the Future: On the New Consciousness in Literature," trans. Gene Kuperman, *South Atlantic Quarterly* 90 (2) (1991) p. 433 (emphasis added).

26 Kopkind, "From Russia With Love and Squalor," p. 44.

27 Cited in Epstein, "After the Future," p. 434.

28 With the exception, of course, of the bountiful essay by Eve Kosofsky Sedgwick, "A Poem is Being Written," *Representations* 17 (winter 1987) pp. 110–143.

16

The melodrama of national identity in post-Tiananmen China

Lisa Rofel

Yearnings is a heart-wrenching Chinese television drama about the inter-twined lives, loves, and tragedies of two ordinary families, the intellectual Wangs and the worker Lius, as the vicissitudes of their joys and sorrows unfold over the two decades from the Cultural Revolution (1966–1976) through the late 1980s. A melodramatic tale of romantic loves found and lost, of a baby abandoned and raised with no one (except viewers) knowing her "true" identity, of families rent apart and tenuously held together – it is a tale that those who engage with popular culture might find moving, though other, unsympathetic critics might find sentimental.

But *Yearnings* quickly gripped vast audiences when it was aired in China in January 1991, just eighteen months after the Tiananmen demonstrations. As it experienced an explosion of popularity, it eclipsed other television programs. It moved from airing three times a week to airing every night for 3 hours, playing itself out in its entirety (fifty episodes) in one month. After dinner at a university faculty member's home, I would invariably join them in watching the show. During the day, while engaged in research in the silk factory in Hangzhou where I had previously worked in the mid-1980s, I listened as workers caught one another up on episodes they had missed because of their revolving shift system.[1] By the time I left China at the end of the month, most people I knew were heatedly debating the qualities of the heroes and villains, as they simultaneously enjoyed and critically analyzed the implications of plot and character.

How is it that a story of thwarted desires and tragic sacrifices as told through the "personal" dilemmas of family relations could stir such engaged responses in China? *Yearnings*' use of highly conventional techniques of televisual melodrama and the love content could allow one to argue that it is one of the first popular programs devoid of political content in China (especially for those who do not address the politics of gender). The *New York Times*, for example, heralded *Yearnings* as the dawn of the soap opera epoch in China (WuDunn 1991). The article congratulates China for offering, at last, real entertainment to people that enables them to escape the dreariness of socialist politics.[2]

Clearly, *Yearnings* carries many of the formal signs of what Peter Brooks (1985) has called the "melodramatic imagination," especially those to which we are so attuned in "the west." For *Yearnings* is a grandiose ethical superdrama constantly tensed to momentous turns of events that will reveal the essential Manichean conflicts of good and evil (Gledhill 1987: 20ff.). It is filled with the conventional melodramatic repertoire, including coincidences of fate, hyperbolic figures, mysterious parentage, romance, and tragedy, and the quintessential location in domestic space. It has the genre character of episodic serials (Allen 1985; Ang 1985) and, finally, it addresses the symbolic construction of woman, the maternal and the feminine, through stories of desire, personal relations, and daily family life.

These formal aesthetic features certainly account, in part, for viewers' continuous involvement in the drama. *Yearnings* created an active spectatorship through the simultaneous creation of hope for the fulfillment of desire along with forebodings of impending tragedy. Moreover, *Yearnings* was written with the explicit intention of adapting the form of melodramas that had been previously imported, with much success, from Taiwan, Japan, and Latin America. The collective group of five scriptwriters under the aegis of the state-run Beijing Television Art Center (some of whom were not regular employees of the Center but well-known popular novelists whose works have been held in disapproval by senior party leaders) adapted imported melodramas' focus on the difficulties of family unity to mainland social life by focusing upon the development of archetypal characters: the virtuous, filial woman who would appeal to Chinese men, the effeminate intellectual, the female shrew, etc.

Yet this melodrama, as with all melodramas, has its specific cultural and historical location. *Yearnings* speaks not just to other dramas of women in the home. To announce that it spells the arrival of melodrama to China is to indulge in narcissistic and orientalist cultural hegemony in defining the genre. For soap opera and melodrama have proved vital forms of socialist aesthetic production at least since the 1949 revolution. However, they have revolved around heightened dramas of landlord exploitation – whether the young woman who suffers at the hands of her landlord and flees to the mountains will be rescued in time by the Red Army (*White-Haired Girl*) – dramas of economic development – whether the forward-looking young man just returned from the city will be able to fight the lethargy and corruption of his elder cadres in the village to institute much needed modern reforms (*New Star*) – and dramas of imperialism – whether the dashing leader of a 1930s Shanghai gang will manage to live through his corrupt times (*The Shanghai Bund*).[3] The question, then, becomes not simply the current emergence of melodrama in China, but how it moved into the space of the home. How have these aesthetic productions turned away from stories about workers *qua* workers and into stories about domestic life and personal fates?

Indeed, the unexpected storm of controversy that accompanied *Yearnings'* popularity should lead us to take its politics seriously. We must ask why television viewers became so seduced by this particular narrative. How was this narrative desire constituted? In China, where official methods of ideological dissemination such as political study sessions and "thought work" lie bankrupt, consumption of television and other forms of popular culture has increasingly become the process through which people are interpellated as subjects of the nation.

In what follows, I argue that the key to understanding *Yearnings'* reception lies in the suffusion of this melodrama with re-imagined possibilities of national identity, or what Benedict Anderson has called "nation-ness" (1983: 13). Moreover, its historically specific use of the melodramatic form bound that sense of nation-ness to differential gender and class positionings of the characters but also of the viewers, thus linking it to larger debates in China about which categories of persons might stand as heroes of the nation. The identity of the nation, and which subjects speak for the nation, became acute dilemmas at a moment when China faced perhaps its greatest political and moral crisis since the socialist revolution of 1949. Further, this melodrama of national and cultural identity occurred within the contradictions created by the state's efforts to combine socialism with a free-market economy. *Yearnings* embodied the desires set loose by those transformations, as well as the resulting cultural dilemmas about what should now count as "moral." The shock of state violence at Tiananmen only heightened this sense of political and social soul-searching.[4]

Intellectuals (re)speak their bitterness

Yearnings begins in 1969, at the height of Cultural Revolutionary fervor. The Wangs, an élite intellectual family, are under attack for being the "stinking ninth category" (i.e., intellectuals) of class enemies. The family crumbles, as the father is sent to the countryside to learn manual labor from the peasants; the mother, frail with heart trouble due to the attacks upon her household, slowly sinks to her death; the daughter, Yaru, a doctor, loses her fiancé to a Red Guard labor camp after she has become pregnant by him in defiance of the state's refusal to allow such a class enemy to marry; and the son, Husheng, is sent to work in a local factory, bringing his college education to an abrupt end. Yaru, with all else lost, longs only to have her baby. She gives birth to a baby girl. But she loses her baby shortly thereafter, when her fiancé furtively returns for a brief visit, is pursued by the Red Guards while she is out, and flees with the baby, only to be forced to abandon her to an unknown woman at the bus station.

These opening episodes of *Yearnings* create a space for intellectuals, reinvigorating their memories, reminding them of old traumas, pulling them into implicit support for the current regime by replaying images of those bad old days – worse, it is implied, than these post-Tiananmen times. The *mise-en-scène* intimates that the drama will follow the conventional tale of intellectuals' senseless sufferings during the Cultural Revolution. We see the Wang family precariously living in their two-story, Beijing home, the opulence of which visually informs us that they are highly placed élites with a family genealogy of intellectuals undoubtedly going back to before the socialist revolution. But their home is an architectural palimpsest, its surface layered over with Cultural Revolution graffiti denouncing the Wangs as class enemies. The camera's sweep over the careless destruction of the family library operates to draw upon the viewers' sympathies, because, through post-Maoist eyes, this constitutes an ignorant attack against knowledge that could build China's wealth and power. The appearance of the Wangs – the youthful innocence of the children and the frailty of the mother – along with the quotidian quality of their activities – shopping, working in the hospital, working in the factory – further serve to establish the Wang family as undeserved victims who happen to be intellectuals but who otherwise share in the same desires for love, personal fulfillment, family, and career as do other human beings. Finally, the back and forth cuts that provide a sharp contrast with the worker Liu family, whose lives are initially portrayed as untouched by the political storm, intensify the Wangs' tragedies.

That these episodes, and the entire melodrama, are trafficking in icons of national identity is demonstrated through the imperceptible, taken-for-granted use of a narrative form known as "speaking bitterness." In the secondary anglophone literature on China, "speaking bitterness" is usually approached as a purely political and social tool applied in the early 1950s land reform campaigns. During that time, party cadres encouraged poor peasants to "speak pains to recall pains" (Hinton 1966: 157) in the form of public accusations against the gentry landlords. These life stories of suffering were then used to move others to adopt a class analysis and to participate actively in rebuilding the nation along Maoist lines through the redistribution of land (Belden 1949; Chen 1980; Hinton 1966).

Speaking bitterness, however, is not just a political tool, but a narrative form. If one approaches it as such, one can discern this signifying form in what others have assumed are disparate styles of political struggle. The Cultural Revolution "struggle sessions," for example, witnessed violent factions of workers and students screaming their bitter accusations against teachers, writers, former capitalists, and managers (Luo 1990; Liang and Shapiro 1983; Rofel 1991). In the first years after the Cultural Revolution, intellectuals poured out their bitterness about the sufferings they had endured as they reconstructed themselves as victims of what, in its post-Mao guise, had officially been labeled "the ten years of chaos." They wrote what came to be known as literature of the wounded, or "scar literature" (see Barme and Lee 1979; Siu and Stern 1983). In more recent years, workers have used an informal mode of speaking bitterness to contest economic reform pressures to be "productive" (Rofel forthcoming).

The importance of speaking bitterness in relation to the controversy over *Yearnings* is that the conception and construction of China as a "modern" socialist nation occurs through this politico-aesthetic practice.[5] For, if nations are imagined political communities, then we must distinguish them by the style in which they are imagined. Thus, speaking bitterness has developed into a process of political *resolution* in which subjects are called upon to articulate their oppression in order to embrace new subjectivities and claim heroic stature in the eyes of the nation. It acts as a genre that allows one to identify which social group stands as the national heroes of a particular political moment. For the greater part of the 1980s, the voices of intellectuals predominated as they claimed to speak for the nation as a result of their bitter lives in the previous era. Some did so in an attempt to wrest the nation away from socialism. But the state generally provided the ideological space for those voices as it recuperated them into projects of economic reform. At least until Tiananmen.

Yearnings, in its initial episodes, puts the intellectuals' written version of speaking bitterness into visual form. In the same way that the speaking bitterness stories have always done, those in *Yearnings* interpellated intellectuals into once again constructing their lives in this genre – to claim themselves as victims of history and therefore rightful heirs to the national mantle. One night, I watched several episodes of *Yearnings* at the home of Lao Du, an older "backbone" party cadre associated with the local university. As she and her daughter's fiancé walked me to the bus stop after the program, they began, in a tone of bittersweet irony, to tell me the story of the fiancé's family troubles during the Cultural Revolution – how his father was denounced, his schooling interrupted, and his home destroyed. His own story, he insisted, was exactly like that of the Wangs in *Yearnings*. This narrative desire engendered by the drama to speak the national tragedy from the subject position of intellectuals in turn fed back on their expectations of *Yearnings*, creating in them, as it were, a "yearning" for more of the melodrama through which they could construct meaning out of their current, post-Tiananmen lives.[6]

Yet, as *Yearnings* further unfolded its tale, an unexpected and ambiguous twist occurred. If the story had faithfully recapitulated a speaking bitterness tale of intellectuals, then the Wang family would be the only victims-*cum*-heroes. Their characters would remain sympathetic, their motives avenged, the tragedy all theirs. As the episodes progress, however, the drama jars, brushing against the grain of this expectation. Yaru, the daughter, and Husheng, the son, appear to become increasingly selfish, self-absorbed, arrogant, temperamental, sharp-tongued, and petty. They appear to be changing into the villains, as they emerge in juxtaposition to the selfless, if crude, characters of the "simple town folk."[7]

This ambiguous transformation revolves around the character of Liu

Huifang, of a humble worker background, and her selfless devotion to a baby of unknown origins. Huifang is a co-worker of Husheng in the factory, where he exists as a class pariah. Huifang feels a great deal of empathy for Husheng, though he is supposed to be a class enemy, and takes him under her wing. Huifang is engaged to an older co-worker, Song Dacheng, who longs for nothing more than to be with Huifang. But Huifang is alienated by Dacheng's use of a traditional matchmaker. Aware of her younger brother's desire for Huifang, Yaru manipulates Dacheng into thinking that Huifang is really in love with Husheng. Dacheng smashes the marriage furniture he had so happily built; Huifang then marries Husheng, as much out of his yearnings for emotional sustenance as her search for genuine love. Yaru leaves Beijing in search of the baby.

Shortly before the marriage, Huifang's younger sister returns home with an abandoned baby. Huifang begins to nurture this unknown baby, though she lives in straitened circumstances and though her husband refuses to acknowledge the baby. Yaru, when she meets the adopted child, Little Fang, several years later, has a certain feeling in her heart for her. But the child rejects her, sensing the condescension Yaru has for her mother.

After the Cultural Revolution, Yaru and Husheng have their father and their house restored to them. Husheng would like to move his family, which by now includes a son, into the spacious home, but Yaru adamantly refuses to allow him to bring in the child of unknown origins, insisting she is not of the Wang family blood. Huifang, true to her nurturing character, refuses to abandon the child, upon whom all of her desire has become concentrated. She returns to her mother's cramped home with Little Fang, while her husband lives in his home with the son.

Yearnings, then, begins with the sufferings of intellectuals but moves beyond this version of history. Or perhaps it would be more accurate to argue that *Yearnings* turns away, at least in part, from the post-Cultural Revolution project of constituting intellectuals as icons of the nation. That was a socialist realist project of pre-Tiananmen days. Instead of larger-than-life heroes, a narrative ambivalence builds at this point, between the sufferings the Wang family endures and their selfish and arrogant behavior. This is an unacceptable paradox for socialist realist stories, and one that must burst out of that form.

This ambivalence was created in part through the seriality of the melodrama. The narrative attenuation entailed in *Yearnings'* serialization created "gaps" in the text that provoked an extended process of textual reception, negotiation, and reworking carried out through the media, at work, and in informal social arenas. As Robert Allen (1985) has argued, soaps "work" because their seriality opens up spaces of ideological indeterminacy that encourage the production of a range of decodings by viewers.

The seriality of *Yearnings* certainly contributed to the sense of ambiguity about its ideological message. But the seriality of *Yearnings* encouraged controversial readings because it was multiple-layered with a "humanist" discourse that collides with and overpowers the conventional story-line of class victimization. The foreground of the melodrama becomes occupied by the painful "personal" dilemmas resulting (presumably) from that history – or do they? The "personal" in *Yearnings*, however, is not that of the bounded, unified subject of "western" humanism (Foucault 1978). The "personal" is signaled rather by the shifting meanings of family relations: highlighting the importance of spousal relations over the residual hegemony of filial obligation to parents; romantic love over the ideology of marriage as a means to reproduce family status.[8]

With such humanist representations brought to the fore as the melodrama proceeded, viewers experienced the first unexpected turn of narrative tension. Intertwined with icons of nation-ness and class, these humanist tropes created an ambivalence about whether the Wang family dilemmas were personal or historical. Were Husheng and Yaru, as they developed into self-serving, nasty people, the bitter harvest of the Cultural Revolution generation, with whom we should empathize, or were they the bearers of bad human natures? Were intellectuals prone to these types of selves or was Yaru's exaggerated mean-spiritedness – some viewers became convinced she was a case of mental illness – the natural emotions of a mother's inconsolable grief?

Kobena Mercer (1991) has argued in reference to another form of ambivalent aesthetic pleasure – Robert Mapplethorpe's photographs – that ambivalence occurs across the relations of authors, texts, and readers, because "reading" cultural meanings depends upon the historical contingency of context.[9] Thus, the phenomenon of *Yearnings* was created in and through the ways specifically situated viewers took up and interpreted its story.[10] As the intellectual protagonists did not represent the conventional socialist realist genre types, some of the people I knew became committed to the idea that the show was about fate. Yu Shifu, a retired silk factory worker and long committed party member, insisted, somewhat self-consciously, that the drama had little to do with class. Filling me in on episodes she had watched before I did, she suggested that Yaru was to be pitied her poor fate. Self-deprecating laughter followed this comment, for we had just left a Buddhist temple where she had explained to me that praying for one's fate was the stuff of superstition.

But others had a different critique. One evening, I had dinner with a group of professors from the local university. Not too far into dinner, the conversation, as it often seemed to do at that time, turned to *Yearnings*. One of the young men exploded. He declared emphatically that he was no longer going to watch the program. "This," he exclaimed, "is a show about how intellectuals have pretty words on the outside but bad hearts on the inside and how workers might have coarse words on the outside but good hearts on the inside." This program, he continued, was seriously detrimental to intellectuals. In post-Tiananmen China, the stakes for the icons of national heroism remain high, in part because they translate into systems of privilege levered in important ways by the state.

The domestication of the nation

Yearnings' middle episodes witness the emergence of the heroine, Huifang. Fragile in build – a post-Mao visual sign of female heroine material – Huifang is a paragon of good conscience (*liangxin*) and the quintessence of self-sacrifice. She sacrifices her future for her family when she enters the factory after her father's death, courageously ignores the danger to her reputation because she cares for Husheng while engaged to another, leaves behind the comfortable life she would have had married to a man of her own working-class background,[11] and gives up her son (it is never construed as abandon) when her sister-in-law and nemesis Yaru insists upon raising him in what she considers the proper milieu of the Wang home. But she sacrifices most of all for the daughter she has not even born of her own body. A serious accident leaves Little Fang without the use of her legs and, at the tender age of 7, she becomes a disabled child. Huifang then sacrifices her secure job at the factory to attend to her. She eventually decides to divorce Husheng because of their irreconcilable differences about Little Fang, but also because of the return of Husheng's old college girlfriend, with whom he renews a passionate friendship.

Huifang's ultimate sacrifices for her daughter are exquisitely captured in the crowning episode of this middle portion of the melodrama. Huifang is pregnant. She is faced with a dilemma: should she have an abortion so that she can continue her intensive studies for the college entrance examination or should she give birth and abandon her dream of becoming an intellectual? This will be her only opportunity. The state has restored the national examination system, but is giving this Cultural Revolution generation only one last opportunity to pass it before barring them as being too old for college. Undecided after a visit to the doctor, Huifang returns home to study. But she finds Little Fang slumped over the table with a high fever. We then witness a premonition of the impending tragedy when Huifang holds her stomach in pain, breathing jaggedly, as she offers medicine to her daughter. Her daughter moans with discomfort; the music swells, heightening the anxiety. With no transportation available Huifang carries her daughter on her back to the hospital. Huifang manages to get to the hospital, only to sink to the ground in pain with an oncoming miscarriage that will cause her to lose both the baby and her last opportunity to enter college.

We can begin to appreciate the storm of controversy that surrounded Huifang's character by examining how this domesticated woman became the grounds upon which nation-ness was re-articulated. Speaking bitterness narratives are less relevant here than the iconization of a model socialist citizen named Lei Feng. In the 1980s, Lei Feng coexisted with intellectuals' scar literature and vied with that genre for the sign of the nation. Lei Feng was purportedly a young worker–soldier in the People's Liberation Army who, in the early 1960s, gave his life for his country. He died when a truck backed over him as he was helping a comrade in trouble. Officially required study material during the Cultural Revolution, the figure of Lei Feng has been dusted off by the party in the post-Mao period as a belated counter to their own promotion of desire for material gain and also to dampen the "counter-revolutionary" fires of democracy threatening the very foundations of the state. In the 1990s, however, Lei Feng has been transformed into a satirical figure in the eyes of most citizens. The invocation of his name at one point in the melodrama flirts provocatively with this border between parody and seriousness. Huifang's factory girlfriend teases Huifang's soon-to-be fiancé Dacheng about his services to the Liu family by calling him Lei Feng – not for his devotion to the state, but in his search for love.

If Lei Feng has become the butt of much ironic reconfiguring, self-sacrifice has remained as an important sign of the Chinese nation. In this respect, Huifang embodies the quintessence of Chinese nation-ness. Elizabeth Cowie (1979), along with other feminist theorists of film, has argued that film, as a system of visual representations, constructs Woman as a sign whose signified incorporates more than the concept of woman. In extrapolating such a framework to *Yearnings*, I want to suggest that Huifang as a woman, or rather as Woman, represents the Chinese nation while rending that identity apart from socialist politics.[12] She is Lei Feng come home. For the domestic sphere represents that space in China in which people believe they can remove themselves from the "reach of the state" (Shue 1988). The national subject can thus maintain her integrity both within the country and in relation to other countries, unsullied by the historical degradation of state socialism. Moreover, this domesticated subject focuses attention on keeping the domestic in order at a moment when the world outside of China, especially international communism, has collapsed around it.[13] In this sense, *Yearnings* is above all a form of political allegory. It recalls Walter Benjamin's (1977) definition of allegory as composed of a history that is a landscape of ruins. The story of Huifang's destiny is an allegory of China's embattled sense of itself as a nation, of what it stands for, and whom it stands with.[14]

Perhaps the most vociferous debates about *Yearnings* revolved around the figure of Huifang. Ending the analysis with Huifang as sign of the nation would leave us still perplexed as to why this was so. To answer that question, we must examine how configurations of feminine self-sacrifice as nation-ness intersected with the constitution of Huifang as a gendered object of diverse gazes. Here we might follow de Lauretis's (1984) emphasis on female spectatorship as a site of productive relations, which supplements an understanding of woman as visual object.[15] If Huifang represents the nation, her character and that of her "other," Yaru, presented powerful female subject-positions to actual women who followed the melodrama, compelling a controversial sense-making of the inchoate experiences of womanhood during the previous decade of post-Mao economic reform. For if Huifang is a Lei Feng look-alike, she is also a character who reverberates with post-Mao reinscriptions of Confucian categories. She embodies the "virtuous wives, good mothers" homilies that have been so worked over in the 1980s (cf. Honig and Hershatter 1988). Thus, a particular gendered form of self-sacrifice is here linked to nation-ness, one that has a powerful political resonance of its own. Huifang embodies the ideal womanhood of Chinese masculine fantasies.[16]

The fierce criticisms of Huifang were, in part, directed against this fantasy. Huang Xiaolan, a woman chemist who visited with me occasionally, succinctly summarized this view when we sat down to watch the show: Huifang was insipid, uninteresting, someone without any cultural refinements. Not a model to be followed. Not, she implied, the kind of woman a man should desire.

The post-Mao social landscape has anchored this vision in a naturalized topography. The economic reform state's most pressing calls to legitimate its specific imaginary of the modern body politic have revolved around the natures of women. For it is upon this terrain that the state can so convincingly claim that Maoist politics, especially the Cultural Revolution, overturned the "natural" order of things and that state cadres now in power are simply turning the world rightside up.

This provided the social context in which *Yearnings* was aired. Women's intense engagement with the melodrama stemmed from the ways in which the naturalization of womanhood imbricated in post-Mao politics has meant that women in China lead an uneasy and provisional existence as subjects of the nation. Their debates, in effect, raised questions about the basis upon which women can claim themselves to be members of a national community whose image of itself as a community is so configured around *socially* engendered self-sacrifice. Mere personal self-sacrifice, for which essentialized, redesigned Confucian female models hold the championship, do not suffice. It may be viewed as a contribution to the nation, but not as the ground for playing its hero. Moreover, one of the implications of the narrative for female spectators is that if women don the mantle of national heroism, self-sacrifice when conjoined with gender leads to a literal crippling of one's self.

What *Yearnings* captured were the divergent stories women tell to insist upon the worthiness of their self-sacrifices. The narrative tensions and ambivalence *Yearnings* created through the intersections of gender, nation-ness, and class produced this explosion of invested arguments. The fiercest criticisms of Huifang came from those who have positioned themselves through the speaking bitterness stories of intellectuals; women who have narratively fashioned themselves as ungendered (i.e., male) intellectuals sacrificing for China's modernity through their labor. Like Huang Xiaolan,

the chemist, they angrily disparaged Huifang as a model of feudal womanhood that was old-fashioned and should be left behind. One female journalist
indignantly asked in her column how one was supposed to distinguish in
Yearnings between feudal values of "virtuous wives and good mothers"
and the communist spirit of service government cadres seemed to find in
the program (Ren 1991). By invoking "feudalism" – a historical trope
resonant with notions of "backwardness" in socialist historiography – they
implied both that the kind of woman Huifang represented was not natural,
but a culturally constructed one and that she did not fit in a "modern"
socialist state.

But other women I knew felt differently. Tang Shan, a Cultural Revolution
generation former prep worker, had risen to become the party Youth League
Secretary at one of the local silk-weaving factories. Despite our political
differences – Tang Shan was an earnest believer in the party – and somewhat
to my surprise, we had become friends. After watching the episode portraying
Huifang's miscarriage, Tang Shan confided that she had been moved to tears.
For she, too, had remained stuck in the factory because she failed the college
exam in the same year Huifang had planned to take it, when the rush of
Cultural Revolution youth stiffened the competition.

Other women, mainly factory workers or factory cadres who could but
tenuously claim to be intellectuals, also felt empathy for and defended
Huifang. Like Tang Shan, they interpreted her sacrifices as socially engendered and worthy of representing national heroism. For some, like Mo
Ying, a silk prep worker who came of age at the end of the Cultural
Revolution, the Lei Feng trope resonated most strongly. She explicitly
applauded the return of workers as heroes. Others insisted on the strength of
character in Huifang. If one could make the case that Huifang *chose* to
sacrifice rather than embodied a feminine lack of will, that she was a product
of social circumstance, then one could potentially argue that her tragedies
were the result of historically-rooted oppressions rather than the natural
outcome of femininity. In this vein, it was pointed out to me more than once
that Huifang stood up to her mother's old-fashioned attempts to arrange a
marriage for her, insisting upon a marriage built on mutual choice and love.
And again, Huifang's initiation of a divorce from Husheng was an act of
bravery in a social context in which divorced women are socially censured.

Those who disliked Huifang criticized those who defended her for advoc-
ating a return to feudal notions of womanhood. But those who took Huifang's
side were not upholding her as a model of appropriate womanhood. Tania
Modleski (1982) has persuasively argued that women in the US enjoy soap
operas and romantic novels because they provide a subversive critique of the
burdens of domesticity. This certainly appears to be a factor among those
who placed themselves in the position of Huifang. But more than this, they
were attempting to establish the grounds upon which she – and therefore they
– could claim the worthiness of her/their sacrifices and therefore the inclusion

of women's activities as contributions to the construction of the nation. They took pleasure in the character of Huifang because, through her, they were not merely an audience, but were addressed as "significant political beings" (Bobo 1988).[17]

The hero saves the nation

As an icon of the nation, Huifang is problematic in the end, for too much sacrifice on the part of China in the world of nations will lead to the kinds of crippling that Huifang finally experiences. For this reason, China/Huifang must be rescued by the intellectual hero, Luo Gang, the old boyfriend of her nemesis, Yaru. He embodies the hope that China will move forward out of suffering and will strive to succeed. The third and final section of episodes presents this one last twist. Luo Gang, restored to his position as assistant professor of literature, longs to renew his relationship with Yaru, but Yaru's fury at his losing her baby knows no bounds. His pleas of forgiveness are to no avail. In his pain and loneliness, Luo Gang writes the story of his bitter experiences in the Cultural Revolution. His book becomes a best-seller, and his students are full of adulation. One of his students is Huifang's sister. She unburdens her heartache about her older sister's troubles to her professor. The story of the adopted child peaks his interest. Luo Gang befriends the family, becoming a devoted uncle to the daughter, Little Fang. Disillusioned with Yaru's hardened ways, he takes an interest in the fragile Huifang.

Luo Gang and Huifang together eventually discover the child is the baby he lost. Huifang insists he take the child and form a family with Yaru, refusing Luo Gang's expressions of attachment. Yaru, not yet knowing the child is hers, has a change of heart after the child's accident and travels to America to learn the latest surgical procedures that will restore to Little Fang the use of her legs. Little Fang recovers, only to have Huifang fall victim to a car accident and become permanently disabled. Little Fang learns of her "true" parents, and declares that she will be their filial daughter, but only after she cares for her adopted mother, Huifang, for a time.

China needs its intellectuals in the end. But Luo Gang has the "right" kind of intellectual qualities: his willingness to place himself at the service of China/Huifang, his empathy, and his conventional use of speaking bitterness that leads to his acceptance of the political resolution of his reinstatement as a professor and, by extension, life under economic reform. Thus, his repeated assertions to Yaru that they should forget past wrongs implies not only those between one another, but those of the socialist state.

Luo Gang is recognizable as heroic material not only by his intellectual qualities, but also through the particular signs of masculinity he embodies. The mid-1980s in China witnessed an explosive search among male writers and film-makers for something they discovered they had lost or, some feared, perhaps never had: masculinity (see Louie 1991; Wang 1989).[18] They attributed their newly found castration to the state.[19] Indeed, their desire for a hyper-masculinity of forthright sexual feelings and a tough, indomitable spirit proved fertile ground upon which to mount a devastating critique of the state.[20] The politics of this masculinity, however, has played itself out over the bodies of women (Chow 1991b; Zhong 1994). In the popular novel, *Half of Man is Woman* (1986), for example, Zhang Xianliang equates male suffering with the inability to possess a woman and therefore the inability to possess the body politic. Women's agency is completely erased.

Similarly, in *Yearnings*, Luo Gang "takes over" the elements of selfless-ness and reticence from Huifang – the torch of nationhood is passed on, as it were. Modleski (1982) has maintained that in American soap operas and romance novels, the narrative progression is one of the feminization of the hero, signified by his increasing appreciation of domesticity. But Luo Gang is not the effeminate intellectual. Effeminate men, embodying the cultural qualities previously admired in intellectuals – aesthetic refinement and emotional delicacy – have been reconfigured as ineffectual political subjects. Moreover, the popularity of the hyper-masculine films and novels that have shaped cultural reading practices in China over recent years have ensured that such a figure would not capture women's admiration. Husheng plays Luo Gang's foil on that end of the gender spectrum. He is a helpless dandy, who breaks his ankle climbing a ladder to fix Huifang's roof, confirming the need for someone to "mother" him, whether it be Huifang, his sister Yaru, or his old college girlfriend.

If Luo Gang embodies the newfound masculinity of the 1980s, his character maintains a distance from the "roughest" versions of this type which belong, in most of its representations, to the working class. Song Dacheng plays this version of manhood – the broad shouldered, well-muscled, physically adept man who cannot express his feelings though they evidently tear him up inside.[21] Luo Gang represents a softer echo of this masculinity that none the less shows us that it is in intellectual male subjectivity that the Chinese nation will find its future.

The inconclusive conclusion

Yearnings ends with no one having realized their desires, everyone having experienced tragedy. The ambiguity of the entire serial is never resolved, leaving viewers with a lack of definitive narrative and ideological closure. Rather than dissatisfaction with this lack of resolution, however, most of those I knew felt that it was a fitting end in that the ambiguity reflected a corresponding ambivalence pervasive in China. That is, the conclusion, in its inconclusiveness, continued the political allegorization of nation-ness.

The fact that viewers "read" *Yearnings* as political allegory should make us wary of dismissing this program as so much apolitical fodder to distract the populace after Tiananmen. Certainly, television functions as an apparatus

for objectifying "state desires." Both the institutionalization and the ideological contours of state power in China are implicated in the decision-
making process of what will be aired on television and how a television series
such as *Yearnings* is constituted as "popular." Yet, it is crucial to acknowledge that the "Chinese state" is not a coherent entity. Thus, central
government leaders rather belatedly seized upon *Yearnings*' success to
proclaim that the program fostered socialist morality. This effort to frame
the meaning of the melodrama was only successful to the extent that women
who were critical of the heroine could use it to castigate the program's
sexual politics.

Moreover, the activity of television consumption signifies for many in
China a critically important space away from the state and socialist politics.
Television on a large scale is new to China since 1978, in terms of both the
number of households with television sets and the number of television
stations. For most, the television is experienced as at least the partial
withdrawal of the state from the realm of domestic life, which had reverber-
ated with political struggles during the Cultural Revolution.

Yet this is a complicated relationship, for the state is involved not simply
in approving programs, but more essentially in creating representations that
find their way into programs. The representation of domestic space itself is
no exception. The enclosure of *Yearnings* in a wholly domestic arena was
much remarked upon, and, indeed, the notion of the "domestic drama" gave
its name to a new genre of television programming in China. Ironically, then,
even as people experience home viewing as a haven from the heartless
socialist/market world, the "domestic space," in being brought into representation, is also opened to the gaze of the state, made subject to discourse,
and thus opened to the reach of power to colonize there. Thus *Yearnings* also
offered the potential for the extension into the domestic space of the claims
of the party to define moral character and what counts as a contribution to
the nation.

Though viewers in China experienced *Yearnings* as a realm separate from
those themes most facilely associated with the state, meanings that have
circulated through post-Mao official discourses were laced throughout the
narrative. The deep ambivalence about intellectuals, the use of gender in the
creation of that which is called "personal life," and the assertion of a
personal sphere that is felt to exist apart from the state have all been state
projects. For one of the major visions of the state about itself since the
Cultural Revolution is its claim to non-interference in that space that has
come into existence as "the personal."

If people in China, then, did not recline in a realm outside the state as they
viewed *Yearnings*, they none the less seized upon the ambivalences within
the story to read across the cultural economy of state power. The controversy
over *Yearnings* alerts us to the fact that nations are continuously reimagined
and contested through the creation of interpretive communities who have

complex stakes in specific narratives of nation-ness. The radical ruptures in who counts as a national hero and what narrative form represents these figures open up the possibility of reading these texts as not only contextualized and reflective of a national space but constitutive of that entity called China. *Yearnings* produced a powerfully seductive knowledge of viewers' lives that led them, in part, to view themselves as the program portrayed them. Thus, in making cultural sense of this television text, viewers in China were also making sense of themselves. As with other forms of discourse, it would be impossible to distinguish the way they spoke about the program from the way the program "spoke" through them, i.e., constructed their social identity.[22]

The social phenomenon of *Yearnings*, then, did not operate between two established poles of meaning and power – domination versus opposition. Accounting for the interpretative agency of people with conflicting views requires moving beyond a celebration of spectators' autonomy or resistance that relies on positivist assumptions about "choosing" meanings. But it also requires going beyond purely textual approaches with their assumptions of closed cultural worlds. The popularity – as well as the controversy – of *Yearnings* signals an emergent process, a contested moment in the making of Chinese national political culture. It reflects a similarly contested historical moment regarding how the future for the citizens of the Chinese nation state is to be fantasized.

Acknowledgments

Funding for this research in China was provided by an MIT Provost Award. Previous versions of this essay were presented at the Fairbank Center for East Asian Studies, Harvard University, the MIT Cultural Studies conference on "Melodrama," the Department of Anthropology, Stanford University, the Center for Chinese Studies, University of California, Berkeley, and the First International Women's Studies Conference in Beijing. Special thanks to Kathleen Biddick, Gail Hershatter, Sandra Joshel, and Anna Tsing for engaging with such enthusiasm and offering so many creative comments. I would also like to thank Ann Anagnost, Margaret Decker, Faye Ginsburg, Henry Jenkins, Lydia Liu, Purnima Mankekar, Renato Rosaldo, Reid Smith, Kerry Walk, Marilyn Young, and Zhang Xiulan.

Notes

1 My dissertation research, conducted from 1984 to 1986, focused on the effects of the imaginary of political economic reform in China on the creation of modernist subjectivities.

2 How one approaches this melodrama can be encapsulated in one's translation of the title. Thus, the *New York Times* talked about the success of *Aspirations*, implying that soap opera was a sign of aspiring hopes to inculcate more of "western" culture; while one of the Chinese state's magazines for foreign consumption *Women of China* (Bian 1991) praised *Expectation* for its realist portrayal of everyday life and, by implication, the expectations for a better life under the current socialist state. I have chosen to translate the title as *Yearnings*

to highlight the ambiguities in what is yearned for and to capture the blend of humanist and socialist (as they are defined in opposition to one another in China) narrative tropes in the melodrama.

3 I do not mean to imply that the melodramatic sensibility in China developed wholly out of socialist realism. Certainly the earlier part of the twentieth century and before witnessed melodramatic fiction about morality and love (Chow 1991a). Nor do I mean to conflate all socialist realism in China with melodrama. A socialist realist drama becomes melodramatic in China when the drama plays off of the realism through a heightening or exaggeration of the emotions, an emphasis upon the metaphysical dimension of moral conflict, an assertion of how things ought to be rather than merely how things are, and, finally, a melding of these elements into spectacle. The few examples I have chosen reflect these qualities. These sensibilities in literature, drama, and film produced after the 1949 socialist revolution are obviously a syncretism of Soviet realism and earlier Chinese morality tales.

4 This essay has been inspired by, and joins, recent anthropological recon-ceptualizations of cultural production in an increasingly deterritorialized world saturated by mass media. Arjun Appadurai (1991), through his concept of "global ethnoscapes," has urged anthropology to turn its attention to the intimacy of local/glocal interactions in the formation of cultural imaginations. Purnima Mankekar (1993) has written an incisive ethnographic analysis of the intersections of gender and nation in Indian television. I owe her much of my initial inspiration. Mankekar has further emphasized the importance of the ethnographic context of viewing. Faye Ginsburg (1991) has reminded us that indigenous people, in this case those who live in Australia, are not always the object of the media gaze but can also take up the tools of media for their own cultural productions. The Chinese soap opera I analyze is in dialog with these pathbreaking works, as it brings together global consumption of media with particular national and local dilemmas.

5 Rey Chow (1991a) has traced a related aesthetic formation of national culture in the literature of the 1920s and 1930s, prior to the Communist Revolution. There, the conception of national culture took the form of a literary preoccupation with various figures that connoted powerlessness.

6 It goes without saying that intellectuals were not the only audience for this first part of the melodrama. More broadly, it reconfirmed an official history of the Cultural Revolution as senseless chaos that ruined the country and delayed its economic development.

7 It is critical to the ambivalence that follows that those we might label "working class" are never referred to as such, though they carry all the tell-tale signs: working in a factory, cramped homes, etc. The melodrama assiduously avoids this label, as class labels reminiscent of Maoist politics were officially erased in 1978, when intellectuals were declared part of the working class. The ambivalence I describe below depends upon this obfuscation.

8 For more detailed discussions of marriage and family relations in socialist China, see Honig and Hershatter (1988); Johnson (1983); Wolf (1985).

9 The fact that there was no singular, fixed meaning to the text does not imply that the ambivalence was something that occurred only "inside" the text. In contrast to the claims of certain forms of academic deconstruction, the indeterminacy of *Yearnings* was not a purely linguistic event. It was a point of fierce contestation of power. Volosinov's (1973) discussion of the relationship between politics and the multivocality of linguistic signs makes this point.

10 It seems more than likely that the ambivalence also involves a very subtle parody on the part of the main authors, Li Xiaoming, Wang Shuo, and Zheng Wanlong. Wang Shuo especially is well known for subtly satirical novels that appear

innocently apolitical on the surface and therefore have eluded official criticism. One must wonder, for example, about the timing of this type of melodrama, produced when all other films and television programs were paeans to the lives of Mao Zedong and Deng Xiaoping. Cf. Zha Jianying's delineation of the making of *Yearnings* (1992).

11 This message is complicated, however; for viewers, situated in the post-Mao era, marrying an intellectual is seen as marrying up.

12 One could argue that self-sacrifice is the ground upon which the party continues to construct the domain of good citizenship. In this sense, Huifang could be seen as fostering a socialist sense of social responsibility that transcends one's own kin and family. Granting that the striking lack of blood tie with her daughter provides one means through which Huifang can be considered self-sacrificing, I would still argue that the incorporation of this daughter into kinship relations and the unfolding of the drama completely within that realm calls into question any direct homology with socialist politics.

13 Thanks to Gail Kligman for pointing this out to me.

14 I concur wholeheartedly with Ahmad's (1987) critique of Jameson's insistence that all Third World literature operates as national allegory. Jameson's essentializing, orientalist assumptions unfortunately mar some otherwise interesting insights into specific Chinese literary texts. Though I believe that in China the sense of national identity is in crisis, I do not think this necessarily informs all contemporary cultural productions.

15 Space limitations forbid an elaboration of the feminist film theorists who have influenced this essay. They have clarified dynamics of visual objectification by examining how the technical apparatus of cinema and television structures gendered relations of viewing that frame the position of women as objects of the masculine gaze (cf. de Lauretis 1984; Doane *et al.* 1984; Kaplan 1987; and the pathbreaking article by Mulvey 1975). More recently, discussion of female spectatorship and reception has begun to appear, though I still find much of it narrowly focused upon the single text of the film or television program (cf. Pribram 1988; Rabinowitz 1990). For an excellent exception that addresses gender and race, see Bobo (1988). Chris Berry (1991) offers a suggestive alternative reading of these conventions in Chinese cinema.

16 The collective group of (male) scriptwriters clarify any doubts on this score, for midway through *Yearnings'* denouement, they declared in the media that their purpose was to create a female heroine whom male viewers would find appealing (*Hangzhou Radio and Television Weekly* 1991). It should also be noted that these masculine fantasies are constructed as oppositional practices to state power (cf. Zhong 1994).

17 Bobo eloquently makes this point in reference to African American women who enjoyed *The Color Purple* despite criticisms of Spielberg's directorial editing on the one hand, and criticisms of the story by certain African American male critics, on the other.

18 For examples of this kind of literature, see Zhang Xianliang (1986); Zhang Chengzhi (1990); and Zhu Hong (1988).

19 Hong Kong writer Sun Longji, in his popular and widely read study entitled *The Deep Structure of Chinese Culture* (1983) borrows from Lévi-Strauss to attribute this problem of what he labels the "eunuchization" of Chinese men to Chinese culture *tout court.*

20 Though not explicitly theorized in either sympathetic or critical analyses of these works, the masculinity being created is imagined in the context of a global cultural economy in which China, and Chinese men, have been feminized in relation to

the masculine west. Cf. Chow (1991a) for a more general theorization of this issue.

21 Kam Louie has argued that

> Although those in the ruling classes can legitimate their political positions on any point across the masculine–feminine axis, those from the lower classes can only move in the "masculine" direction of the gender axis for a sense of achieving power.
>
> (1991: 165)

22 Teresa de Lauretis describes this process as one in which a person "perceives and comprehends as subjective (referring to, even originating in, oneself) those relations – material, economic, and interpersonal – which are in fact social and, in a larger perspective, historical" (1984: 159). See also Joan W. Scott's critique of assumptions about unmediated "experience" (1992: 22–40).

References

Ahmad, Aijaz (1987) "Jameson's Rhetoric of Otherness and the 'National Allegory,'" *Social Text* 17, pp. 3–25.

Allen, Robert (1985) *Speaking of Soap Operas*, Chapel Hill, NC: University of North Carolina Press.

Anderson, Benedict (1983) *Imagined Communities: Reflections on the Origin and Spread of Nationalism*, New York: Verso.

Ang, Ien (1985) *Watching "Dallas:" Soap Opera and the Melodramatic Imagination*, New York: Routledge.

Appadurai, Arjun (1991) "Global Ethnoscapes: Notes and Queries for a Transnational Anthropology," in Richard G. Fox (ed.), *Recapturing Anthropology: Working in the Present*, Santa Fe: School of American Research, pp. 191–210.

Barme, Geremie and Lee, Bennett (eds) (1979) *The Wounded: New Stories of the Cultural Revolution 77–78*, Hong Kong: Joint Publishing Co.

Belden, Jack (1949) *China Shakes the World*, New York: Monthly Review.

Benjamin, Walter (1977) *The Origin of German Tragic Drama*, New York: Verso (originally published 1963).

Berry, Chris (1991) "Sexual Difference and the Viewing Subject in *Li Shuangshuang* and *The In-Laws*," in Chris Berry (ed.), *Perspectives on Chinese Cinema*, London: British Film Institute, pp. 30–39.

Bobo, Jacqueline (1988) "'The Color Purple': Black Women as Cultural Readers," in E. Deirdre Pribram (ed.), *Female Spectators: Looking at Film and Television*, London: Verso.

Bian, Wen (1991) "'Expectation,' A TV Series in 50 Episodes," *Women of China*, May, pp. 14–17.

Brooks, Peter (1985) *The Melodramatic Imagination: Balzac, Henry James, Melodrama and the Mode of Excess*, New York: Columbia University Press.

Chen, Yuan-tsung (1980) *The Dragon's Village: An Autobiographical Novel of Revolutionary China*, New York: Penguin.

Chow, Rey (1991a) *Woman and Chinese Modernity: The Politics of Reading Between East and West*, Minneapolis, Minn.: University of Minnesota Press.

—— (1991b) "Male Narcissism and National Culture: Subjectivity in Chen Kaige's King of the Children," *Camera Obscura* pp. 25–26, pp. 9–39.

Cowie, Elizabeth (1979) "Woman as Sign," *m/f* 1, pp. 49–63.

de Lauretis, Teresa (1984) *Alice Doesn't: Feminism, Semiotics, Cinema*, Bloomington, Ind.: Indiana University Press.

Doane, Mary Ann, Mellencamp, Patricia and Williams, Linda (eds) (1984) *Re-vision: Essays in Feminist Film Criticism*, Frederick, Md.: University Publications of America.

Foucault, Michel (1978) *The History of Sexuality, Volume 1*. New York: Random House (first published 1976).

Ginsburg, Faye (1991) "Indigenous Media: Faustian Contract or Global Village," *Cultural Anthropology* 6 (1), pp. 92–112.

Gledhill, Christine (ed.) (1987) *Home Is Where the Heart Is: Studies in Melodrama and the Woman's Film*, London: British Film Institute.

Hangzhou Radio and Television Weekly (Hangzhou Guangbo Yingshi) (1991) "A Record of *Yearnings'* Birth" ("'Kewang' Dansheng Ji"), January 4, p. 4.

Hinton, William (1966) *Fanshen: A Documentary of Revolution in a Chinese Village*, New York: Vintage.

Honig, Emily and Hershatter, Gail (1988) *Personal Voices: Chinese Women in the 1980's*, Stanford, Calif.: Stanford University Press.

Johnson, Kay Ann (1983) *Women, the Family and Peasant Revolution in China*, Chicago, Ill.: University of Chicago Press.

Kaplan, E. Ann (1987) "Feminist Criticism and Television," in Robert C. Allen (ed.), *Channels of Discourse: Television and Contemporary Criticism*. Chapel Hill, NC: North Carolina Press, pp. 211–253.

Liang, Heng and Shapiro, Judith (1983) *Son of the Revolution*, New York: Random House.

Louie, Kam (1991) "The Macho Eunuch: The Politics of Masculinity in Jia Pingwa's 'Human Extremities,'" *Modern China* 17 (2), pp. 163–187.

Luo, Ziping (1990) *A Generation Lost: China Under the Cultural Revolution*, New York: Avon Books.

Mankekar, Purnima (1993) "National Texts and Gendered Lives: An Ethnography of Television Viewers in India," *American Ethnologist* 20: 543–563.

Mercer, Kobena (1991) "Skin Head Sex Thing: Racial Difference and the Homoerotic Imaginary," in Bad Object-Choices (ed.), *How Do I Look: Queer Film and Video*, Seattle, Wash.: Bay Press, pp. 169–210.

Modleski, Tania (1982) *Loving With a Vengeance: Mass-Produced Fantasies for Women*, Hamden, Conn.: Shoe String Press.

Mulvey, Laura (1975) "Visual Pleasure and Narrative Cinema," *Screen* 16 (July–August), pp. 6–18.

Pribram, E. Deirdre (ed.) (1988) *Female Spectators: Looking at Film and Television*. London: Verso.

Rabinowitz, Paula (1990) "Seeing through the Gendered I: Feminist Film Theory," *Feminist Studies* 16 (1), pp. 151–169.

Ren, Yin (1991) "A 'Resolute Woman' with a Morality of Self-Perfection" ("Yige Daode Ziwo Wanshande 'Jiannü,'"), *Popular Film (Dazhong Dianying)* 2, pp. 2–3.

Rofel, Lisa (1991) "Violence in the Quotidian: Fragments of a Cultural Revolution Memory," paper presented at the 90th Annual Meeting of the American Anthropological Association.

—— (forthcoming) *Imagined Modernities: Gender, Power and the State in Post-Mao China*, Berkeley, Calif.: University of California Press.

Scott, Joan (1992) "Experience," in Judith Butler and Joan W. Scott (eds), *Feminists Theorize the Political*, New York: Routledge, Chapman and Hall, pp. 22–40.

Shue, Vivienne (1988) *The Reach of the State: Sketches of the Chinese Body Politic*. Stanford, Calif.: Stanford University Press.

Siu, Helen F. and Stern, Zelda (1983) *Mao's Harvest: Voices from China's New Generation*, Oxford: Oxford University Press.

Sun, Longji (1983) *The Deep Structure of Chinese Culture (Zhongguo Wenhuade Shengceng Jiegou)*, Hong Kong: Jixianshe.

Volosinov, V. N. (1973) *Marxism and the Philosophy of Language*, trans. by Ladislav Matejka and I. R. Titunik, Cambridge, Mass.: Harvard University Press (first published 1929).

Wang, Yuejin (1989) "Mixing Memory and Desire: Red Sorghum. A Chinese Version of Masculinity and Femininity," *Public Culture* 2 (1), pp. 31–53.

Wolf, Margery (1985) *Revolution Postponed: Women in Contemporary China*, Stanford, Calif.: Stanford University Press.

WuDunn, Sheryl (1991) "Why So Many Chinese Are Teary: The Soap Opera Epoch Has Dawned," *New York Times*, February 1, p. A4.

Zha, Jianying (1992) "*Yearnings*: Public Culture in a post-Tiananmen Era," *Transition* 57 (September).

Zhang, Chengzhi (1990) *The Black Steed*, trans. by Stephen Fleming, Beijing: Chinese Literature Press.

Zhang, Xianliang (1986) *Half of Man is Woman*, trans. Martha Avery, New York: W. W. Norton & Company.

Zhong, Xueping (1994) "Male Suffering and Male Desire: Politics of Reading *Half of Man is Woman* by Zhang Xianliang," in Christina Gilmartin, Gail Hershatter, Lisa Rofel, and Tyrene White (eds), *Engendering China: Women, Culture and the State*, Cambridge, Mass.: Harvard University Press.

Zhu, Hong (ed.) (1988) *The Chinese Western*, New York: Ballantine Books.

17

All in the (Raghu) family

A video epic in cultural context*

Philip Lutgendorf

Ram incarnates in countless ways
and there are tens of millions of Ramayans.
(Tulsidas)[1]

Introduction

On January 25, 1987, a new program premiered on India's government-run
television network, Doordarshan. Broadcast on Sunday mornings at 9:30
a.m., it represented an experiment for the national network, for it was the first
time that the medium of television was to be used to present a serialized
adaptation of one of the great cultural and religious epics of India. The chosen
work was the Ramayan – the story first narrated in Sanskrit some two
millennia ago by the poet Valmiki, and retold numerous times in succeeding
centuries by poets in every major regional language, most notably, for north
India and for Hindi, in the sixteenth-century epic *Rāmcarimānas* of Tulsidas
("The Holy Lake of Ram's Acts"). The television adaptation, produced and
directed by Bombay film-maker Ramanand Sagar, was itself an epic undertaking: featuring some 300 actors, it was originally slated to run for fifty-two
episodes of 45 minutes each, but had to be extended three times due to popular
demand, and eventually grew into a main story in seventy-eight episodes,
followed after an interval of several months by a sequel incorporating the
events detailed in the seventh book (the *Uttarakāṇḍa* or epilogue) of the
Sanskrit epic. Long before the airing of the main story concluded on July 31,
1988, Sagar's *Ramayan* had become the most popular program ever shown
on Indian television, and something more: a phenomenon of such proportions
that intellectuals and policy-makers struggled to come to terms with its
significance. Why and how, observers wondered, had this serial – almost
universally dismissed by critics as a technically flawed melodrama – elicited
such a staggering response? Did its success point once again to the enduring
power of sacred narrative to galvanize the masses, or was it rather a cue to
the advent of a new force in Indian culture: the mesmerizing power of the
television screen? Inevitably, the airing of the serial provoked lively debate

over such topics as the relationship of folk and élite traditions, the marketing of religion and art, the politics of communalism and of government-controlled mass media, and indeed over the message of the Ramayan story itself.

In seeking to make a modest contribution to this debate, I will first present a brief account of the making and airing of the serial and of its public reception, and then consider its relationship to the *Mānas* epic (its principal literary source) and to older and ongoing traditions of performance. The concluding section of the essay will examine some critical responses to the serial and the debate it engendered over the impact of television on Indian culture.[2]

Sunday mornings with Ram

To suggest that the making of a TV serial began several millennia ago may appear to risk mimicking studio promotional hype, yet it must be observed that the success of India's most popular serial derives in large measure from the enduring appeal of the narrative tradition on which it draws. While the textual and historical problems associated with Valmiki's Sanskrit rendering of the Ram story have fascinated generations of scholars, only in the past decade has significant research focused on the developments that, from the eleventh century onward, contributed to the proliferation of the devotional cult of Ram in northern India, and created a religious climate in which its ultimate vernacular vehicle – the epic *Rāmcaritmānas* – could acquire throughout much of the region the status of pre-eminent text for religious performance (Whaling 1980; Bakker 1986; van der Veer 1988). Elsewhere I have traced some of the factors which contributed to the adoption of this text by ever wider audiences for both ritual and entertainment purposes; factors which included the patronage of rajas and zamindars in the post-Mughal period and of urban mercantile groups during the latter half of the nineteenth century, as well as the advent of print technology, the rise of literacy among the middle classes, and the ongoing effort to define an orthodox Hindu identity (Lutgendorf 1989, 1991b). One result of these trends was the proliferation of increasingly-standardized genres of *Mānas* performance: ritualized recitation (*pāṭh*), oral exposition (*kathā*), and dramatic enactment (*Rāmlīlā*). All three involve sustained, episodic recitation of the text and use it as a foundation for creative elaboration. As will be shown, the conventions and interpretive strategies of these still-popular genres are reflected in the screenplay of the television serial.

Another background against which the success of the serial must be viewed is the history of motion pictures in India, particularly the film genre of "mythologicals." Drawing on the story traditions of the epics and puranas and imbued with the emotional piety of regional devotional traditions, mythological films have been part of Indian cinema since the beginning. The pioneer of the Bombay cinema, the Maharashtrian Brahman Dadasaheb

Phalke, was inspired by a film on the life of Jesus to create a series of mythologicals beginning with *Rajah Harishchandra* (1912) – the first feature-length film made in India – and including *Lanka Dahan* (*The Burning of Lanka*, based on an episode from the Ramayan, 1917) and *Krishna Janma* (*The Birth of Krishna*, 1919). Although film had been on the Indian scene since 1896 (when the Lumière Brothers' *cinématographe* was unveiled at Watson's Hotel in Bombay), the actors and themes of early foreign-made films failed to engage the deepest sympathies of the Indian audience. In Phalke's films, however,

> the figures of long-told stories took flesh and blood. The impact was overwhelming. When Rama appeared on the screen in *Lanka Dahan*, and when in *Krishna Janma* Lord Krishna himself at last appeared, men and women in the audience prostrated themselves before the screen.
>
> (Barnouw and Krishnaswamy 1980: 15)

The devotional behavior of the audience – so striking to a foreign observer – would remain a common response to the screening of religious films and, as we shall see, to the TV *Ramayan*. Yet the worship of the "flesh and blood" (or celluloid or video) image, far from being a consequence of the "revolutionary" impact of film, was a response with a long indigenous pedigree, rooted in the ritualized but complete identification of actor with deity that is central to Hindu folk performance.

Over the years, a modest number of mythologicals scored as major hits with nationwide audiences – two of the most notable were versions of the Ramayana: Vijay Bhatt's *Ram Rajya* (1943; the only film, it is said, which Mahatma Gandhi would consent to see) and Homi Wadia's *Sampoorna Ramayana* (1961) – but the stronghold of such pictures has not been the Hindi film capital of Bombay, but regional production centers which cater to less urbanized audiences.[3] As was the case in the American film industry, where the 1950s and 1960s saw a flurry of epic religious films, mythologicals have tended to come in clusters, as one successful film generated a series of spin-offs. But while the occasional low-budget effort has produced an unexpected windfall – the best example is *Jai Santoshi Maa* (1975), which, through presenting a new goddess whose time had clearly come, became a runaway hit with women and one of the highest-grossing films of all time – the genre as a whole has seemed riskier than most formulas. While it was clear that an audience for such films existed, it was also evident that it was not the regular film-going crowd of young urban males at whom the majority of releases were targeted.

The advent of television did not initially create conditions favorable to the screening of religious narrative. During the 1960s and early 1970s, television sets in India served principally as technological novelties to adorn upper-class sitting rooms, where they provided, for a few hazy hours each night, a droning rendition of the day's news (read in Sanskritized Hindi by a newscaster who always looked directly into the camera – a sort of All India Radio with a face) and drably edifying cultural programming. The 1970s saw a steady increase in the number of sets and transmission centers, and the advent of color programming, yet the standard audience complaint about Doordarshan remained that it was overwhelmingly dull. The addition of a weekly program of song and dance clips from hit movies (*Chitrahaar*, which immediately became the most popular thing on television) and of a Sunday afternoon feature film sparked viewer interest, but also confirmed that the appeal of television was largely as an adjunct to the existing film industry, and that the distinctive potential of the small screen had yet to be realized.

In the early 1980s, two related developments transformed Doordarshan: the advent of commercials, and the commissioning of serialized dramas from independent studios. Maintaining the national network as a non-commercial preserve had proven a costly proposition, and powerful private-sector inter- ests were eager to pay to reach consumers over the airwaves. The decision to accept commercials in turn forced the network to provide more varied and entertaining fare, since sponsors required assurance that audiences would indeed be watching. The new commercials themselves were highly enter- taining: financed with high budgets and conceived by advertising directors who kept up with the latest American trends, they burst on the screen in 15- minute blocks, sparkling with humor, catchy music, and dazzling special effects, but their glossy look only made the regular programming appear more tired in comparison.

At the same time, Doordarshan began to face competition from video cassette recorders and a burgeoning market in rental movies, which gave viewers the option of switching off the state-controlled channel in favor of taped programs of their choice. The impact of the VCR on Indian culture during the past decade warrants closer examination – it has, for one thing, given Bombay films the truly mass exposure they never enjoyed when confined to cinema halls – but at least one effect of the machines was to jolt the officials in Mandi House (Doordarshan's New Delhi headquarters) into the realization that they were in danger of losing their audience, and, with it, revenues from private sponsorship, unless they were prepared to offer programs that could more successfully compete with the fantasies of the cinema.

The first such effort was Kumar Vasudev's *Ham log* (*Us*), a soap opera about a group of families in a middle-class neighborhood. In place of the larger-than-life heroes of the cinema, it introduced a set of believable characters with whom viewers were invited to identify. The runaway success of this fledgling effort prompted the network to commission a whole crop of serials and mini-series, of which the most popular were *Buniyaad* (*Foun- dation*, a melodramatic family saga directed by Ramesh Sippy) and *Nukkad* (*Streetcorner*). Though official parlance blessed such efforts with the newly- coined Sanskritic genre-name *dhārāvāhik* ("serialization"), the Hinglish word *sīriyal* effortlessly entered popular speech. By any name, serials had come to stay, and during the mid-1980s more than a dozen were airing during any given week. The relative popularity of each was reflected in viewer polls, advertising rates, and the eagerness with which sponsors sought 10-second slots in the blocks of commercials preceding each episode. A new industry was created, employing directors and technicians as well as many stage and cinema actors.

With the rapid proliferation of serials and the liberalization of bureaucratic policies on programming, the subject-matter of shows began to display more imagination and diversity. During 1986 two mini-series aired which drew on folklore and mythology: *Vikram aur vetal* (*King Vikram and the Vampire* – based on the folktales preserved in the Sanskrit *Kathāsaritasāgara* and in Hindi–Urdu *kissā* texts) and *Krishna avatar* (Lord Krishna, loosely based on the *Bhāgavata purāṇa*). Although both were well received by viewers, neither enjoyed enough success to eclipse the popularity of established serials like *Buniyaad*, nor did the religious content of the Krishna series provoke much controversy.

The creator of *Vikram aur vetal* was Ramanand Sagar (born Ramchand Chopra), a veteran producer/director who, together with his five sons, ran a production company responsible for several hit films, including the high-grossing musical *Arzoo* (*Desire*) and the espionage thriller *Aankhen* (*Eyes*) – but never, incidentally, for a mythological. Sagar's Natraj Studios fell on lean times in the late 1970s after a string of failures, prompting the director to turn his attention to television. While producing a second mini-series entitled *Dada-didi ki kahaniyan* (*Grandpa and Grandma's Stories*), Sagar approached Doordarshan officials with a proposal for an extended serialization of the Ramayan. By his own account a lifelong devotee of the Tulsi *Mānas*, Sagar claims to have been involved for some twenty-five years in a group that met regularly to recite and discuss the Hindi epic. His proposal was for a detailed treatment in fifty-two episodes, to be based primarily on the Tulsidas version but also drawing on the Sanskrit *Rāmāyaṇa*, the Tamil and Bengali versions of Kamban and Krittibas, and other regional retellings. Initially vetoed by Mandi House, the proposal was revised and resubmitted, but its approval was apparently delayed by concern that the airing of such a serial would arouse communal sentiments (Mazumdar 1988: 2). Even when the project was finally given the go-ahead in 1986, it is certain that neither the bureaucrats nor Sagar himself had an inkling of the response it would generate. Significantly, it was assigned a languid time slot at the start of the weekly holiday, when prior network experience indicated that few viewers would be watching.

Sagar assembled a cast that combined relatively unknown principals (such as Arun Govil as Ram, Sunil Lahri as Lakshman, and the 20-year-old Dipika Chikhlia as Sita) with veteran character actors (former wrestler Dara Singh – the serial's monkey-hero Hanuman – had appeared in some 200 action-adventures). At the secluded hamlet of Umbergaon, on the Gujarat coast some

3 hours north of Bombay, Sagar laid out "Vrindavan Studios," where the entire crew lived for two weeks each month for the duration of the project.

The serial premiered with a framing narration that situated it in the long tradition of Ramayan stories in various languages and thus introduced the theme (to be reiterated many times) of the Ramayan as a symbol of national unity and integration. The story itself opened with a parliament of frightened gods petitioning Vishnu, recumbent on his serpent-couch on the Milky Ocean, to take human form and put a stop to Ravan's depredations; this in turn led to scenes of King Dashrath's fire sacrifice and the birth of Ram and his brothers. Early episodes, while not exactly hurried, moved at a moderate pace through the first of the epic's seven books, showing scenes of Ram and his brothers' childhoods, some highly original interpretations of their education in a spartan ashram, and the familiar story of Ram and Lakshman's adventures with the sage Vishvamitra, culminating in the young hero's winning of Sita as his bride.

The rest, as they say, is history. Despite mostly acerbic reviews in the English-language media, condemning the serial as a crude commercialization and decrying its production values and sluggish pace,[4] and a few equally harsh critiques in the Hindi press,[5] the popularity of the serial rose steadily throughout its first six months on the air. In the absence of anything like Nielsen ratings for India, the most telling statistics come from advertising revenues. During its first month, *Ramayan* lagged behind the serials *Buniyaad* and *Khoj*, the weekly Hindi film, and the film-clip revue *Chitrahaar* in the number of advertising spots sold. But it caught up quickly, and the average of fifteen commercials per episode during February jumped to thirty-two by April. In June, *Ramayan* was earning more revenue than any program except *Chitrahaar*, and it passed this competitor the following month. By August, Sagar's program was generating an eighth of the total income of national television. Doordarshan was flooded with requests from some 135 advertisers anxious to pay Rs 40,000 per 10-second slot to have their products plugged at *Ramayan* screening time, and in September the number of commercials was increased to forty. From that point on, *Ramayan* consistently outgrossed every other program, generating an estimated weekly income of Rs 28 to 30 lakhs (one lakh = Rs 100,000) for the network (*Illustrated Weekly of India* 1987: 17).

What all this translates into in audience numbers is harder to say with accuracy. Conservative estimates of Doordarshan's daily viewership during the period range from 40 to 60 million, but the response to the *Ramayan* serial was unique. Many sets were mounted in public locations and drew in large numbers of people not normally exposed to TV; hence the most popular episodes may have been seen by 80 to 100 million people – roughly one-eighth of India's population. This figure may seem modest by western standards (the Superbowl reportedly engages the attention of 40 percent of Americans, while the Academy Awards telecast draws an international audience of some 300 million (Read 1985: 153, 163)), but it must be appreciated in terms of the limited number and distribution of television sets in India and the restricted availability of electricity. In fact, it represents an unprecedented regional response to a communicated message.

This response had tangible effects which were repeatedly noted in the press. The spread of "Ramayan Fever" (as *India Today* termed it) generated a flood of newspaper and magazine articles ranging from critical analyses of the serial's content to sensational accounts of its fans' behavior. Throughout most of the serial's run, *Ramayan*-related news appeared with almost daily regularity in local papers. Many reports described the avidity with which successive episodes were awaited and viewed, emphasizing that, for millions of Indians, nothing was allowed to interfere with *Ramayan*-watching. Visible manifestations of the serial's popularity included the cancellation of Sunday morning cinema shows for lack of audiences, the delaying of weddings and funerals to allow participants to view the series, and the eerily quiet look of many cities and towns during screenings – a reporter in Mirzapur observed, "Bazaars, streets, and wholesale markets become so deserted they appear to be under curfew" (*Dainik jāgaran* 1988a: 7). Other articles reported the decline of traffic on national highways during broadcasts, as truck and bus drivers steered their vehicles to teashops equipped with TV sets, where driver and passengers piled out to watch the episode. On occasion, trains were delayed when passengers refused to leave platform sets until a broadcast was over.[6]

Many articles described the devotional activities that developed around the weekly "auspicious sight" (*darśan*) of epic characters:

> in many homes the watching of *Ramayan* has become a religious ritual, and the television set . . . is garlanded, decorated with sandalwood paste and vermillion, and conch shells are blown. Grandparents admonish youngsters to bathe before the show and housewives put off serving meals so that the family is purified and fasting before *Ramayan*.
>
> (*India Worldwide* 1 1988: 56)

Local press reports detailed instances of mass devotion: a Banaras newspaper reported on a sweetshop where a borrowed television was set up each week on a makeshift altar sanctified with cow-dung and Ganges water, worshipped with flowers and incense, and watched by a crowd of several hundred neighborhood residents, who then shared in the distribution of 125 kilos of sanctified sweets (*prasād*), which had been placed before the screen during the broadcast (*Dainik jāgaran* 1988c: 3). Such ritualized public viewings were not uncommon: throughout the country, crowds gathered in front of video shops to watch display sets, and some community groups undertook to place sets in public areas. During the final months of the serial, electronics shops reported a dramatic surge in television sales and all available rental sets were engaged for the crucial Sunday morning slot – sometimes by whole villages who pooled their resources to allow residents to see *Ramayan*.

327

Sporadic incidents of violent protest resulted from power failures during the weekly screening, as when an angry mob in the Banaras suburb of Ramnagar (home of north India's most acclaimed *Rāmlīlā* pageant) stormed and set fire to an electrical substation (*Dainik jāgaraṇ* March 21, 1988d: 3).

The duration of the serial itself became a *cause célèbre*. Doordarshan initially contracted for fifty-two episodes, but as the story unfolded it became clear both that the audience did not want it to end on schedule, and that the pace of the narrative would not allow it to; indeed, by late summer of 1987 it appeared that a termination the following January would leave viewers stranded somewhere in the fifth of the epic's seven books. The slow pace consistently annoyed critics, who complained that Sagar was deliberately drawing out the story to increase his profits, but a public outcry coupled with the financial windfall from advertisers prompted Mandi House to grant two extensions of thirteen episodes each. But as the battle for Lanka raged during June and early July 1988, concerns were again voiced as to whether the series could end on schedule. At the request of Doordarshan officials, Sagar promised in writing that he would conclude with a special 1-hour telecast on July 31.[7]

The airing of the final installment was marked by festivities in many parts of the country. Sunday newspapers carried full-page articles on the serial, featuring photos of its stars and headlines like "Farewell to Ramayan" (*Āj*, July 31, 1988). In Banaras, many neighborhoods were decorated with saffron-colored pennants and festive illuminations, while residents celebrated Ram's enthronement by distributing sweets, sounding bells and conches, and setting off fireworks (*Dainik jāgaraṇ*, August 1, 1988e: 3). In the Maharashtrian city of Nagpur, canopies were erected at principal intersections and color sets installed to allow those without TVs to witness the spectacle (*Indian Express*, August 2, 1988: 5). Other municipalities reported homes decorated with earthen oil lamps to welcome Ram's return, prompting one reporter to call it an "early Divali" (similarly, the slaying of Ravan several weeks before had been observed in some areas as an out-of-season Dashahra festival (*Times of India*, August 9, 1988: 3)).

Yet amid the descriptions of rejoicing, there were intimations of grief and loss as viewers anticipated the first of many Sundays without Ram and Sita. These sentiments found expression in the press a week later, with details of the stages of what one columnist called "the national withdrawal symptom." The front-page headline of *Jansattā* on August 9 announced, "Without *Ramayan* Sunday Mornings Seem Empty." Noting that people throughout the country passed their first *Ramayan*-less Sunday "with difficulty," the article reported responses to the show's absence by people in various neighborhoods of the nation's capital. These ranged from a betel-seller in Shakarpur who observed, "After so many months, I'm finally getting some business on Sunday morning!," to a cloth-seller in Karolbagh who explained why he had sent his in-shop TV set back home by asking, "Why watch

328

television now that *Ramayan* is over?" Anticipating a promised sequel, a woman shopping on Chandni Chowk no doubt summed up the feelings of many devoted viewers: "At least we only have to wait two months. Then Ram will return! Mother Kausalya waited fourteen years for Ram to come back, but I don't know if we can manage for even two months" (*Jansattā*, August 9, 1988: 1).

The *kathā* and the camera

Clearly, viewer perceptions of the pace and duration of the Sagar *Ramayan* varied greatly. While reviewers in the English-language press complained about the agonizingly slow advance of the narrative – "what with taking practically five episodes to kill Bali and another five to behead Kumbhakarna" (Mazumdar 1988: 2) – such criticism was less common in Hindi publications, and many viewers protested that the epic was ending too quickly. When asked by *India Today* why he could not have fitted the events of Valmiki's final book into the original sequence, Sagar himself ingenuously replied, "I had no time. I was given only seventy-eight episodes, fifty-two to begin with . . . . So much had to be omitted" (Jain 1988: 81).

Perceptible beneath the various responses were varying conceptions of the Ramayan itself. The English-language critics repeatedly referred to it as a "literary treasure" which Sagar was butchering by dragging it out to enhance his own and the network's profits. Such critics, who often made reference to C. Rajagopalachari's 300-page retelling, or R. K. Narayan's even shorter synopsis, could note that films like *Sampoorn Ramayan* had reduced the whole story to 3 hours, and that the modern ballet "Ramlila," presented in Delhi each autumn, offered the epic to urbanites and foreign tourists as a 4-hour spectacle. For audiences accustomed to such handy condensations, the pace of the serial was irksome indeed.

Yet there exist other performance genres in which revered scriptures like the *Mānas* are treated less as bounded texts than as outlines for imaginative elaboration, and if a storyteller's patrons and audience are willing (as Sagar's were), such performances can be extended almost indefinitely. Indeed, the TV version's rambling main narrative, weighing in at just under 60 hours, is far from being the longest popular serialization. The *Rāmlīlā* of Ramnagar, which tells roughly the same story, averages 3 hours per night for thirty-one nights, and has been playing to enraptured audiences for a century and a half. And an oral expounder like Ramnarayan Shukla, who proceeds through the epic in daily installments at the Sankat Mochan temple in Banaras, may take more than 700 hours (i.e., two years or more) to complete a single "telling" – a feat that makes Sagar's effort seem like a condensation. Since, as I will argue, the *Rāmlīlā* and *kathā* traditions have greatly influenced the style and content of the television adaptation, it will be well to briefly summarize some of their conventions.

In Vaishnava *kathā* (narration or storytelling), a performer, usually called a *kathāvācak* or *vyās*, is invited by an individual patron or community to retell or discourse on a sacred story; a performer who specializes in the Tulsi *Mānas* (the most popular text for *kathā* in north India today) is sometimes called a *Rāmāyanī*. Until recently, such storytellers were often hired on a long-term basis to narrate the entire epic in daily installments, usually in the late afternoon when the day's work was done. However, most patrons now favor shorter programs of fixed duration (such as nine, fifteen, or twenty-one days), in which an expounder discourses on only a small section of the text. In both styles of *kathā*, the source text serves merely as the anchor for an improvised verbal meditation that may include almost endless digressions and elaborations, interspersed with relevant quotations from any part of the epic as well as from other revered texts. *Tour de force* performances in which a single line is expounded for days on end are not uncommon and are often cited by devotees as evidence of the talent of a favorite expounder.[8] Another characteristic of such narration is its tendency to "domesticize" epic characters through the retelling of incidents in a highly colloquial style and with details absent from the source text. In addition, events in the story often serve as springboards for homely excursus on matters mystical, philosophical, and even political. Though little studied by academic scholars, the *kathā* performance remains a principal form of both religious instruction and popular entertainment in many parts of India.

Rāmlīlā – which occurs mainly at the time of the annual Dashahra festival – is similarly extended and episodic, but here the emphasis shifts from hearing to seeing as oral exegesis is replaced by visual and iconographic realization of the narrative. The famous Ramnagar production (see Schechner and Hess 1977) is often termed a "visible commentary" by its aficionados, who emphasize the opportunity it affords for the experience of divine *darśan*. *Rāmlīlā* is closely related to another Vaishnava performance genre: *jhāṅkī* ("glimpse" or "tableau"), in which consecrated persons or images (usually boys, but sometimes figures of painted clay) are dressed and made up as divine characters and placed in settings intended to evoke mythic scenes. These tableaux are presented for contemplation by audiences, often to the accompaniment of devotional singing (Hein 1972: 17–30).

In the more elaborate *Rāmlīlā* cycles, as in other Indian performance genres, great importance is given to facial expression and gesture. Actors are chosen for their physical appearance and trained in all aspects of delivery. The boys in Ramnagar undergo a two-month apprenticeship during which they are taught to identify completely with their epic roles. Such training is thought to facilitate the process whereby the divinity manifests in the body of the actor – an essential element in the theology of Vaishnava performance. And although most *Rāmlīlā* plays, like *kathā* performances, are based on the *Mānas*, they too may include episodes not found in the text as well as creative

330

interpretations of its verses. Such elaborations often result in scenes and dialogs much enjoyed by the audience.

Whatever else he may be – movie moghul and shrewd businessman – Ramanand Sagar appears to have a genuine enthusiasm for the *Mānas* and a taste for *kathā*. His reported participation in an ongoing study group must have exposed him to many interpretations of the text, and his interest in the popular expounder Morari Bapu is reflected in his use of excerpts from the latter's performances to introduce several of his marketed cassettes. As the serial unfolded and as he prepared a permanent edition for international release, Sagar became increasingly concerned with his own role as storyteller, frequently appearing in the introductory or concluding portions of each cassette to comment (in typically rambling *kathāvācak* style) on the events being presented.[9] Like Tulsidas, he sought to place himself in a long tradition of Ramayan narrators, claiming little originality for his screenplay (the credits for each episode cite ten Ramayans in various languages). Yet Sagar also realized that he was creating a powerful, independent retelling – he remarked to one reporter that "Video is like writing Ramayan with a camera" (Melwani 1988: 56), and in the final, extravagant episode of July 31, he took the ultimate step of placing himself in the narrative, hovering cross-legged on a lotus in the sky above Ayodhya to join assembled deities in singing the praises of the newly-crowned Ram. Critics dismissed this as tasteless self-aggrandisement, but viewers apparently took it in their stride; wasn't he everywhere being hailed as the "Tulsidas of the video age?"

In both *kathā* and *Rāmlīlā*, performers enter a consecrated condition. The oral commentator, no less than the young Brahman actor, purifies himself through dietary and devotional practices and performs rituals before ascending the expounder's dais, where he is garlanded and worshipped as a temporary incarnation of Veda Vyas, the archetypal orator of sacred lore. Sagar was mindful of such conventions, and his widely publicized changes in lifestyle – renouncing alcohol and tobacco, and instituting a vegetarian regimen for the film crew – though mocked as hypocritical posing by critics, revealed his concern to accede to his audience's standards for epic performers.

The iconography of the serial combined *Rāmlīlā* conventions with the visual vocabulary firmly established through a century of mass-produced religious art. For the consecrated boys of *Rāmlīlā*, Sagar substituted adult actors and actresses carefully chosen to reinforce popular conceptions of each character's appearance. In casting his principals, the producer aimed for "exactly that Ram, that Sita, which is in the hearts and minds and perhaps in the souls of millions of people" (Melwani 1988: 57) – and, one might add, on the walls of teashops and the pages of comic books. That he was extraordinarily successful is attested to by numerous posters and calendars featuring garishly-colored stills from the serial, or costumed close-ups of Arun Govil with his now-famous enigmatic smile.

The "humanizing" influence of television's close focus imposed its own restrictions on iconography, and certain stock conventions were dispensed with – thus Ram and Bharat did not appear with blue complexions (though Vishnu did in his brief appearances). Yet the depiction was hardly "realistic" in other respects. The costumes and wigs of Ram and Lakshman during their long forest exile, for example, remained immaculate and perfectly arranged (down to a dandified curl at each temple) and their faces clean-shaven, a stylization that irked critics reared on more naturalistic theater (R. K. Narayan quipped that the brothers "look like Wiltech [razorblade] ads" (De 1988: 5). Hanuman and his legions were depicted according to a long-established convention, with muscular but hairless human bodies, and only long, padded tails and stylized masking about the mouth and nose to suggest a simian status; their wives were shown as fully human women.[10] Sets and costumes adhered to the garish standard of film mythologicals, which itself reflects poster art and the conventions of the *Nautaṅkī* tradition and of nineteenth-century Parsi theater. This too provoked criticism – *India Today* quipped that "Raja Janak's palace looks like it's been painted with cheap lurex paint and the clothes look like they've been dug out of some musty trunk in Chandni Chowk's costume rental shops" (Bhargava 1987: 70) – yet Sagar made considerable use of outdoor footage, including many impressive sequences of Ram's wanderings through the countryside.

The poor quality of special effects was another hobby-horse of critics, and those accustomed (as some urban Indians now are) to the standards of post-Steven Spielberg Hollywood would indeed find only laughable the pulsating, garishly-tinted "divine weapons" and the hovering demons of the TV serial, which adhered to a technical standard closer to that of *Star Trek* or *Dr. Who*. Cost-cutting was undoubtedly a factor (though some scenes – such as the burning of Lanka – were admirably executed), and Sagar may have shrewdly perceived that the bulk of his audience, accustomed to the modest stagecraft of *Nautaṅkī* and *Rāmlīlā*, would be sufficiently dazzled by cheaper effects. He must also have realized that special effects, *per se*, were not crucial to maintaining viewers' interest in the saga, and this leads me to an observation concerning the overall focus of the production. The emphasis in Ramayan was squarely on "seeing" its characters. Not "seeing" in the quick-cut, distracted fashion in which modern western audiences take in their heroes and heroines, but drinking in and entering into visual communion with epic characters.[11]

To most viewers, *Ramayan* was a feast of *darśan*, and its visual aesthetic clearly derived from an indigenous standard. Scenes and dialogs were long (interminable, critics said) and aimed at a definitive portrayal of the emotional state of each character. This was conveyed especially through close-ups (and in moments of intense emotion, repeated zoom shots – a convention favored in Hindi films), so that much of the time the screen was dominated by large heads, either verbalizing or silently miming their responses to events. Every nuance of emotion of every character – each *bhāv* of classical aesthetic theory

– was sought to be conveyed visually, and in scenes involving many characters (such as the assembly in Chitrakut, when Bharat begs Ram to return to Ayodhya), the camera focused in turn on the face of each principal to record his or her response – grief, surprise, anger, calm – to each new development. Though apallingly overstated by contemporary western standards, this technique is consonant with the mime or *abhinay* of indigenous genres like Kathakali and Bharat Natyam, in which the audience is expected to focus intently on the performer's facial expressions and gestures. The television screen is particularly suited to this kind of close-up mime, and Sagar exploited its potential to allow his viewers an experience of intense communion with epic characters.

Notable, too, was the production's tendency to periodically halt the flow of its narrative to focus on stylized, poster-like tableaux, accompanied by devotional singing. This convention has a long history, and both Ramayan texts and *Rāmlīlā* plays are usually divided into sequences of episodes, each of which is associated with a striking visual image, often presented in popular art as a visual distillation for the contemplation of devotees. In the *Rāmlīlā*, such moments as Sita's placing the marriage garland around Ram's neck, Hanuman's carrying the two brothers on his shoulders, and Ram's worshipping a Shiva *liṅga* prior to crossing the sea, all necessitate halting the action of the play. Magnesium flares are ignited to guarantee distant viewers a glimpse of the auspicious tableau, and the crowd responds with devotional chanting and cries of "*Rājā Rāmcandra kī jay!*" ("Victory to King Ramchandra!"). This custom is in turn a visual translation of Tulsi's practice of halting the narrative at such intense moments, by abandoning the storytelling meters of *caupāī/dohā* in favor of the more musical *chand*, which lovingly elaborates on the auspicious tableau set up in the preceding stanza.

These conventions are straightforwardly adapted in the television version, and every one of the scenes noted above occasions a halt in the prose dialogue, as verses are sung and the camera frames a leisurely tableau of the auspicious scene. If the technique allowed Sagar to slow down the pace, it also reflected his understanding of audience expectations. In contrast, the impatient responses of critics (such as Mimi Vaid-Fera's exasperated query, concerning the scene of Hanuman's transporting Ram and Lakshman, "Does one really have to watch Hanuman's enlarged frame against a changing backdrop for the next few minutes, in order to appreciate his strength?" (Vaid-Fera 1987: 16)) suggest ignorance of the Ramayan performance tradition. To the modern critic, apparently, all scenes are created equal – a view that accords well with the secular notion of time as a succession of discrete and equal moments. In the perception of *Ramayan*'s devoted audience, however, some scenes and characters have more intrinsic potency than others and so must be held up to view longer.

As an original retelling of the Ramayan, Sagar's screenplay presents both continuities with past versions and original elaborations of the kind common to *kathā* and *Rāmlīlā* performances. For the most part, the narrative follows the Tulsi *Mānas*, though it occasionally favors an interpretation of Valmiki or Kamban. Yet, as *Rāmlīlā* producers know, there is a vast difference between a poetic narrative and a performance script, and hundreds of interpretive decisions must be made in the representation of each scene. Such decisions are not made arbitrarily, but are guided by the thrust of traditional exegesis. Similarly, the conventions of *kathā* allow an expounder freedom to improvise on the text, yet this interpretive freedom is not unlimited, but is constrained by his training and by the audience's expectations and knowledge of the story. Certain characters and incidents have always received special attention, often because they have raised moral issues or aroused "doubts" (*śaṅkāeṃ*) which each reteller must address. The extended run of the serial gave Sagar license to explore many episodes in the kind of depth in which they are treated by traditional commentators, and to pose original "solutions" to problems that have troubled audiences for centuries. I will examine one such character, the portrayal of whom reflects both tradition and innovation and also suggests the impact of the television medium on the telling of the story.

Kaikeyi redeemed

The motives of Queen Kaikeyi – Dashrath's tempestuous junior wife and Prince Bharat's mother, whose early love for Ram is poisoned by jealousy of her co-wives and who becomes implacably bent on his ruin – have always been problematic for the Ramayan tradition, since they suggest a darker side to the epic's rosy picture of the royal family – Valmiki's treatment still hints at deception on the king's part, or worse still, rivalry among the brothers. The requirements of the narrative raise uncomfortable questions that have vexed storytellers and audiences for centuries: if Ram is so good and Kaikeyi loves him so dearly, how can she suddenly turn against him and betray him? And how is the story subsequently to deal with this maternal traitor in its midst?

Broadly speaking, we detect in many retellings a concern both to exonerate Kaikeyi from responsibility for the demands and to depict her as subsequently repentant, if not fully redeemed – a concern made all the more compelling by the greater theological weight given to the story and its characters in most vernacular versions. Tulsidas first resorts to *deus ex machina* and has the gods, anxious to get on with the business of slaying Ravan, derange the mind of Kaikeyi's hunchbacked maidservant (2.12). Later, he remarks several times on Kaikeyi's contrition (for example, 2.252.5–6, 7.6a,b), and has Ram take pains to show her special respect (for example, by saluting her first, when greeting the three mothers in the forest: 2.244.7–8). For the most part, however, he simply ignores her, merging her into a composite portrait of "all the queens." This approach is carried out visually in the Ramnagar *Rāmlīlā*, in which, following Dashrath's funeral, the three queens appear together like a spectral chorus, clad in white and veiled; their individual personalities are not further developed and Kaikeyi's emotional state is left to the audience's imagination.

Popular lore has been kinder to Kaikeyi, however. A story which I have several times heard in *kathā* programs has Ram, when granted a boon following his victory over Ravan, tearfully request that Bharat withdraw his disavowal of his mother. And in 1983 I was told a "wonderful, secret story" by a Banaras bank clerk in which it was revealed that the young Ram, in his desire to fulfill his mission on earth, himself compelled her to request the boons, since he knew that she alone in the palace loved him enough to obey even his most painful order. Concluded the amateur expounder, "Yes, and you know, it's in the Ramayan! . . . well, in *some* Ramayan."

"Television's strongest point," Neil Postman has remarked, "is that it brings personalities into our hearts, not abstractions into our heads" (Postman 1985: 123). And if, as this critic complains, the nature of the medium tends to "personalize" every kind of program, from news documentary to religious sermon, how much more powerful is its influence on the serialized narrative or soap opera, in which the acts and feelings of a limited cast of characters are explored at close range through repeated installments. Unlike the *Rāmlīlā*, television can leave little to the imagination; if principal characters are to be shown on the screen they will be shown close-up, and their emotional responses cannot be avoided. Consequently, the depiction of Kaikeyi presented Sagar with a challenge: to make believable her transformation from loving mother to cruel enemy, and then to successfully reintegrate her into the family (and into the hearts of viewers) – in short, to redeem her.

Kaikeyi's portrayal by Padma Khanna exemplifies the serial's overall excellent casting and fine (if not always subtle) acting. Manthara is played by Lalita Pawar, a veteran character actress known for her portrayal of villainous women. Although in most written versions of the story Kaikeyi's maid is unheard of until early in Book Two, when she appears on the palace balcony to fume over the preparations for Ram's consecration, Sagar inserts her into the palace milieu right from episode one, when she hobbles ecstatically into Dashrath's chamber to announce Prince Bharat's birth. The audience feels a thrill of anticipation – here is the woman who is destined to destroy the king – yet the effect is also to humanize Manthara and to underscore her powerful loyalty to Kaikeyi and her clan. This theme is further developed during several scenes that depict the women's response to the news of the princes' impending marriages. While the queens rejoice together for all their sons, Manthara can chortle only over "My Bharat! My Bharat's wedding!" In a telling and (to my knowledge) entirely original scene, she orders lamps lit in private celebration of Bharat's good fortune, and when Kaikeyi protests that "Didi" ("Elder Sister" – an affectionate reference to Kausalya) is seeing to all the festive arrangements, the hunchback replies

335

scornfully, "'Didi, Didi' – you always talk about Didi! What she does, she does only for her Ram. You have to look out for your own son" (episode 10). At this point, Kaikeyi dismisses this sour remark with obvious impatience, yet the audience perceives that the seed of dissidence and jealousy is already being sown.

For the most part, the powerful confrontations that follow as the events of Book Two begin in episode 12 – between Manthara and Kaikeyi, between the latter and the king, and so on – closely follow Tulsidas (who in turn follows Valmiki here), and it is only after the princes and Sita have departed for the forest, the king has expired of grief, and Bharat has returned to learn the awful truth, that Sagar's efforts to absolve Kaikeyi resume in earnest.

There is the scene of Dashrath lying in state on a flower-bedecked bier (invoking the now-familiar imagery of the formal obsequies of India's national leaders) as courtiers pay their last respects. Each of the queens comes forward to place a handful of flowers at his feet, and Kaikeyi weeps profusely, wringing her hands in apparently sincere grief. However, she resumes her haughty and obstinate air during her confrontation with Bharat, but his unexpected denunciations gradually weaken her, until, when he renounces his bond to her and leaves vowing never to set foot in her chamber again, she collapses weeping; the camera lingers on her pathetic, crumpled figure in the deserted room.

A significant innovation follows, just after the court scene in which Bharat refuses the throne and presents his plan to journey to the forest to search for Ram. As noted earlier, Tulsi tells us nothing of the individual queens' reactions to these events, noting only that "all the queens were upset" (2.186) and that, shortly later, "they all mounted palanquins and set out" (2.187.8). But in the serial, as the determined Bharat strides from the hall, he encounters a tearful Kaikeyi in the corridor. He coldly addresses her as "Queen Kaikeyi" (having earlier vowed never again to call her "Mother"). She begs to be allowed to accompany him to the forest, to ask Ram's forgiveness for her sins. When he coldly refuses, she weeps piteously. Then Kausalya appears and, touched by Kaikeyi's desperation, takes pity on her former rival and orders Bharat to relent – he of course must bow to the will of Ram's mother. The scene concludes with the powerful image of Kausalya and Kaikeyi weeping in each other's arms (episode 22). Kaikeyi's redemption is well under way.

En route to Chitrakut, the townspeople are shown debating the issue of Kaikeyi's guilt. The last speaker expresses deep sympathy for her, "How she must be repenting now, poor thing!" (episode 23). On first meeting Ram, Kaikeyi breaks down and pleads for forgiveness, saying that she is to blame for everything. Ram replies that what has occurred is due to fate (episode 24). This might appear to be adequate absolution, but the camera's portrait of the queen's remorse – and of her gradual reintegration into the family – continues unabated. During the emotional assembly scene, the camera

336

repeatedly scans the queens' faces as they listen to Bharat, Ram, and Vasistha debate the terms of the exile, until at last, unable to restrain herself, Kaikeyi speaks up – as she never does in Valmiki or Tulsi – to publicly declare her own willingness to withdraw the boons (Ram counters that only the king himself could take or give back boons (episode 24.)

When in due course it is settled that Ram will remain in the forest and Bharat return to the capital to reign as regent, every viewer reared on Valmiki and Tulsi would expect to turn away from Ayodhya once and for all to follow the unfolding adventures of the princes and Sita in the forest. Instead, Sagar cuts back repeatedly to contrast scenes in the palace with the doings of the three principals. These scenes further develop our sympathies for the home-bound family members, especially the women, and in one lengthy and innovative scene Kaikeyi pays a visit to her son's ascetic ashram on the outskirts of the city. Bharat, scribbling royal edicts before Ram's enthroned sandals, first ignores her and then coldly addresses her as "Queen Kaikeyi." When she pleads with him to call her "Mother," he replies that "Queen Kaikeyi killed my mother," and cruelly reviles her. By this point, viewers' sympathies are likely to be with the queen. Telling her son that the comforts of the palace torture her, she begs to be allowed to come live with him, to do penance for her sins. Bharat sternly orders her to return to the city, but allows just the slightest hint that perhaps, by enduring her sentence in the palace, she may eventually be freed of guilt. As a mournful chorus sings of her pain, the queen collapses into a palanquin and is borne back to the city, where the camera follows her as she wanders through the empty corridors of the palace, alternately weeping and laughing – a sort of Hindu Lady Macbeth (episode 26).

All this is innovation, true, but with a traditional basis. Sagar's portrayal of Bharat's rigid and guilt-ridden personality accords well with the image presented in the *Mānas* (a Banarsi friend of mine once called Bharat "Tulsi's 'portrait of an obsession'"); his prolonged treatment of Kaikeyi's redemption through suffering satisfies popular longing to salvage Dashrath's youngest queen. The viewer's curiosity about the domestic aftermath of the banishment is more than satiated, and he is left with a feeling of intimate knowledge of the royal family. Female viewers are presented with a story in which women are more pervasively present and forcefully active than in most written versions. More than ever, this ultimate soap opera emerges as a family saga, in which the members of the sundered royal clan are shown as united in their emotions even though physically apart. Thus it will come as no surprise, in episode 28 (when the princes and Sita are deep in the Dandak forest) to find the camera whisking us back to Ayodhya to focus on the loneliness of Lakshman's wife, Urmila,[12] and later, to show us Kausalya standing at the palace window, visibly greying as she endures her long vigil of awaiting Ram's return.

These scenes reflect Sagar's exploitation of a narrative convention common in modern prose literature, and which developed to its logical conclusion with the advent of film. The oral storyteller generally unfolds his narrative by focusing listeners' attention on a single location and withdrawing to a narrative frame in order to announce the transition to another scene, as when Tulsidas informs us "I've told of Ram's lovely journey to the forest; now hear how Sumantra came back to Ayodhya" (2.142.4). Such shifts are usually kept to a minimum, and it is almost as if the storyteller (and with him the audience) must physically accompany some character – Sumantra on his return to Ayodhyha, Bharat on his journey to Chitrakut, Hanuman on his quest for Sita – in order to move about within the geography of the tale. In contrast, much modern fiction has preferred an invisible narrator who takes the form of an omnipresent eye. But in substituting images for words, film and television provide ultimate license to this eye, and the quick cuts and fades possible in these media all but eliminate any experience of scenic transition – the very abruptness of the change becoming a new convention that is exploited by directors. What this means for narrative is that the storyteller becomes so otiose that he disappears entirely, for the great illusion of the camera is that the viewer himself is the eyewitness narrator. Hence film and television partake of – indeed aim for – the quality of collective fantasies: of dreams that myriads of dreamers can believe that they share.[13] To further this illusion, the camera's eye anticipates and indulges our every curiosity: thus it records Ram's conversation with Sita on their wedding night (episode 11), shows us the thoughts that flash through Dashrath's mind as he lays dying (episode 20), reveals the reaction of Bharat's wife, Madhvi, to his self-imposed exile (episode 26), and so on. This approach stands in sharp contrast to that of a performance genre like *Rāmlīlā*, which (as Richard Schechner has observed) is multi-dimensional, elusive, and can never be experienced in its totality by any one viewer.[14]

The example of Kaikeyi could be supplemented with many others – for instance, with the characterization of Ram's demon adversaries, who are similarly humanized by the voyeuristic eye of the camera, and emerge as complex, tragically-flawed titans, much in contrast to their two-dimensional treatment by Tulsidas, but again, in keeping with a major strand in their folk conceptualization. Such examples help explain how Sagar, like many a *Rāmāyaṇī* before him, successfully sustained his audience's interest, week after week, in a slow-moving story, the plot of which they already knew, by making them look forward to the manner of its telling.

Critical perspectives

I regard the Sagar serial as an independent Ramayan: an original retelling in a new medium that affords distinctive capabilities to a storyteller. Such innovations have occurred before – the *Rāmlīlā* is a good example – and they have not occurred in a vacuum, but have arisen out of existing forms, often through the intervention of patrons concerned to project a particular cultural vision. A similar phenomen is occurring with the twentieth-century medium of video, and it is notable that during roughly the same period that *Ramayan* was being aired in India, audiences in China were viewing a government-sponsored serialization of *Hung-lou meng* (*The Dream of the Red Chamber*), the voluminous novel of aristocratic life under the Ching dynasty. In the west, such projects stand out less strikingly amidst the flood of TV programming, yet Soviet TV's treatment of Tolstoy's *War and Peace*, BBC serializations like *Masterpiece Theatre*, and the ABC mini-series, *Jesus of Nazareth*, all reflect a desire on the part of national élites to translate their cultural classics into the new mass medium.[15] To dismiss such efforts as a pastiche of cultural elements – as when critics label Sagar's work a kitsch blend of Tulsidas, the *Rāmlīlā*, calendar art, and mythological films – is as unsatisfyingly reductionist as viewing the *Mānas* itself, for example, as a blend of Valmiki's plot, the non-dualist philosophical stance of the *Adhyātma rāmāyaṇa*, and the devotional fervor of the *Bhāgavata purāṇa*. These ingredients are all present in the Hindi epic, of course, but its vast appeal derives more from its original exploitation of the new medium of melodious and idiomatic Hindi verse. An effective analysis of Sagar's *Ramayan* must consider not only the various influences reflected in the production, but its distinctive exploitation of the video medium.

In the ongoing debate among intellectuals throughout the world over the value and effects of television, both sides are inclined to stress the revolutionary nature of its impact. Media enthusiasts like Marshall Macluhan and detractors like Neil Postman both posit the transformation of a typographical universe into one dominated by moving images, and either speak glowingly of an "information explosion" and a leap to "electronic literacy," or sound ominous warnings of a "trivialization" of discourse and "passivization" of audiences. English-educated intellectuals in India generally share with their western counterparts an attitude of disdain for the vulgarly accessible mass medium.[16] Yet if one looks at literature on the impact of television, one finds that it is primarily based on the Euro-American experience and may be of questionable relevance to the Indian situation. Having noted some of the continuities the *Ramayan* serial shares with older genres of epic-based performance, I shall now examine some assumptions that seem implicit in the criticisms directed at it within India, with a view to developing a more balanced and culturally relevant assessment of its impact.

Commercialization and commodification

The *Illustrated Weekly of India* began its cover story on *Ramayan* with the charge, "Ramanand Sagar's teleserial is a commercial proposition, the sole purpose of which, despite the director's protestations, is to make money." Terming the series, "a blockbuster like none other on the idiot box, the ultimate grosser," the author suggested that the aesthetic deficiencies of the serial were directly related to its director's avaricious motives (*Illustrated Weekly* 1987: 9). Articles in the English-language press tended to emphasize the commercial success of the production, quoting statistics on the unprecedented revenues it generated. The fact that Sagar and his sons refused to release details of their earnings irritated reporters and led to much speculation on their actual gain, which was estimated at roughly Rs 1 crore (somewhat under US$1 million). The sources of this profit were analyzed in detail: the actual production budget, the sale of the official cassette version both within and outside India, and the franchising of serial-related spin-off products, such as children's toys, comic books, and audio cassettes.[17]

Implicit in much criticism of the selling of the serial was the assumption that it represented an assault on a hitherto pristine and uncommercial tradition – no article that I have seen raised the possibility that the Ramayan had ever been "marketed" before. Yet this epic has clearly been supporting a large (if decentralized) industry on the subcontinent for many centuries. I refer not only to the marketing of printed Ramayan texts during the last 150 years (such as the numerous competing editions of the *Mānas*, each claiming to present the "authentic" version), but to the whole complex of professional and semi-professional performers: expounders and singers, professional *līlā* troupes, and priests and *sadhus* who perform ritual recitations for a fee. The expenditures involved in such performances are often not insignificant – some *Mānas* expounders are lavishly rewarded by their patrons, and the commerce generated by the *Rāmlīlā* (itself a costly enterprise employing large numbers of people) represents an important factor in the economy of Ramnagar – but we need not restrict ourselves to the cold currencies of our age. For, as Pierre Bourdieu reminds us, other forms of wealth must be taken into account in reckoning the "worth" of traditional activities: unquantifiable elements such as social status, prestige, and political influence, that often interact with (are obtained from or translated back into) material wealth (Bourdieu 1977: 171–183).

I venture no judgment as to whether the "marketing" of a story like the Ramayan is "good" or "bad;" I only propose that it is not new and has in fact always been inseparable from the dissemination and performance of the epic. The introductory cantos of the Sanskrit *Rāmāyaṇa* represent the poet Valmiki taking an existing story tradition and transforming it into an elegant poetic composition which is then publicly performed by trained bards, who receive lavish praise and generous gifts for their efforts. Yet we tend to assume that the bards' motives are not "solely" commercial; they are obeying their teacher, praising a king, and sharing a great work of art – Bourdieu might observe that they are generating large amounts of "symbolic capital," and that Ramanand Sagar is doing the same.

But isn't there an essential difference, one may ask, between Lav and Kush's live singing, and rows of shrink-wrapped cassettes with shimmering mylar labels? Walter Benjamin, writing in the 1930s, argued that original works of art possess an "aura" which is dissipated through mechanical reproduction (Benjamin 1955: 223). Others (myself included) have warned that the process of "commodification" inherent in modern consumer societies lessens the participatory experience by turning audiences into passive consumers (Butsch 1985: 65–66; Lutgendorf 1991a). I shall take another look at the question of audience passivity below; here let us note the Sagars' efforts to promote their cassettes (in an ironic twist on Benjamin's notion of "aura") as potent religious artifacts:

> as Sagar points out, no consumer can mistake the pirated version for the original. The originals are beautifully packaged, with almost a religious aura about them. Each tape is surrounded by a rosary, wrapped in a red satin bag .... As Prem Sagar says, ". . . We want people to preserve it. It gives out good vibrations; no one has received it without touching it to their foreheads."
>
> (Melwani 1988)

Such hype is aimed at the middle-class householder (especially the non-resident Indian), who would like to pass on the Ramayan tradition to his Nintendo-playing children, and who hopes that the presence in his home of orange video cassettes with an "almost religious aura" will help effect this. The same consumer is addressed by other companies marketing various reifications of the Ramayan, such as Shree Geeta Press of Chandigarh (not to be confused with the famous Gita Press of Gorakhpur, the name of which it has apparently pirated), which placed a full-page advertisement in the international edition of *India Today* for a Rs 100 edition of the *Mānas*. The ad announced that Tulsidas's epic is both "a scripture, epitomizing the teachings of the Vedas, Smrities, Purans," and also "an art, highly developed to compete with the greatest epic poems of world" (*India Today* March 15, 1986: 22), thus reassuring overseas buyers that the epic of their motherland is not only holy, but also (like athletic equipment and concert pianists) "world class." This too is a kind of "aura," drawing on symbolic capital's new international currency. It is clearly very different from Benjamin's romantic notion of the lingering presence of an individual creative genius, but is it wholly unlike, say, the more impersonal "aura" of authority claimed by Tulsidas for his common-language epic, through the invocation of an immemorial tradition of exalted narrators?

Video-latry

To both Indian and foreign reporters, one of the most striking features of the public response to *Ramayan* was its religious dimension: the ceremonies of worship that developed around the weekly broadcasts and the spontaneous expressions of reverence that greeted the public appearances of the stars.

News stories described the purificatory *pūjā* of television sets, the burning of incense before the screen, and pious fans' prostrations before Arun Govil and Dipika Chikhlia (Ram and Sita). More critical responses, especially in English-language publications, ranged from bemused condescension at the incongruity of "worshipping" an electronic gadget, to disgust at what was seen as an embarrassing cultural anachronism. Arvind N. Das wrote in the *Times of India*: "Through the electronic Ramayana .... the Indian juggernaut is moving at a frenetic pace – backwards" (Das, 1988: 6). In an interview in the *Illustrated Weekly*, one reporter pressed Dipika to evaluate the religious response of viewers:

> *Reporter*: In the mofussil towns, and even in the cities people have a bath and do pooja of their television screens before watching the serial. Do you think this is right?
>
> *Dipika*: There's no right and wrong about it. It's a matter of their belief. We haven't asked them to do it, it's the way they feel.
>
> (*Illustrated Weekly* 1987: 15)

Notable is the reporter's disdain for what she regards as rustic religious customs, now seeping back from provincial towns into "the cities." Such critics are often out of touch with the religious customs of their own urban neighbors, and choose to overlook, for example, the purificatory *pūjā* of motor vehicles, printing presses and other mechanical devices, which is common throughout the country. Equally prevalent is the custom of bracketing religious performances with auspicious rites. When a *kathāvācak* is preparing to expound the Ramayan, care is always given to the seat he is to occupy, which must be purified in order to be worthy of the divine sage, Veda Vyas, who will speak through the storyteller. Similarly the crowns, ornaments, and weapons of *Rāmlīlā* actors are worshipped before the start of the pageant. Since the Ramayan serial became a weekly inhouse *kathā* or *Rāmlīlā* for millions of families, the TV screen has become the new seat of the storyteller and ritual stage for the *līlā*, and its perch in the family sitting room has to be sanctified.

Of course, a more reflective critic might also have noted that backward Indians are not the only people who "worship" TV sets. Behind the modern secular smile of condescension lies a joke at our own expense, for the television set became the central altar of the American home some three decades ago – the main focus of the common room, displacing the hearth/fire altar as the nucleus around which family members gathered for communion and sustenance. It is only a highly compartmentalized notion of religion that blinds us to the ritual dimensions of such activities. Neil Postman's assertion that television is unsuited to religious experience because it is "so saturated with our memories of profane events, so deeply associated with the commercial and entertainment worlds that it is difficult to be recreated as a frame for sacred events" (Postman 1985: 119) suggests the over-facility of the conventional sacred/profane dichotomy; in any case it is clearly inapplicable to the Indian situation. Millions of Hindus did indeed feel a need to sacralize their TV screens each week in order to make them "a frame for sacred events," yet they apparently found no more difficulty in doing this than they do in sacralizing their town squares for *Rāmlīlā* plays each October, their kitchens for monthly *ekādaśī* rites, or piles of cow-dung for *govardhan pūjā*.

And now, the "couch pakora?"

Television, like religion, is frequently assailed by critics as an "opiate" that deadens and desensitizes its devotees; Robert MacNeil called it, "the soma of Aldous Huxley's *Brave New World*" (cited in Postman 1985: 111). Many Indian intellectuals similarly despise the "idiot box" and feel particularly disturbed by the presentation of "fundamentalist" religious material through its hypnotic medium. A critic in the *Times of India* explained the appeal of *Ramayan* – even to those who should have known better – by invoking the tube's power to lull:

> What about the Westernized elite which is not basically religious but nevertheless almost religiously viewed Ramayana in spite of making snide comments about its poor production? The answer . . . is to be found in a complex situation where mass culture, the search for roots, entertainment and education have all got mixed into an addictive and soporific compound which reinforces intellectual passivity. That this compound is available without much effort by the recipient adds to its ethereal charm as the medium itself becomes the message.
>
> (Das 1988: 6)[18]

Such facile analysis, effortlessly (and without citation) incorporating the *mahāvākya* or "great utterance" of the pre-eminent western media pandit of the 1960s, typifies the knee-jerk reaction to the serial of many English-language critics. Yet how applicable is this warmed-over approach to the Indian situation? The technology of mass media may be much the same everywhere, but their utilization and impact depend on specific conditions – even specific "ways of seeing" – which vary in culture-dependent ways. In his perceptive study, *Amusing Ourselves to Death*, Neil Postman bases much of his critique of television on an historical analysis of the impact of literacy and publishing in the United States during the eighteenth and nineteenth centuries, arguing that Americans were the most print-oriented people in the world, and that their cultural emphasis on the printed word influenced all forms of public discourse. His most damning case against TV is that it leads to the trivialization of information and the reduction of all forms of discourse to "entertainment." Yet he is careful to point out that this effect derives in part from the specific circumstances of American television: the fact that it is available 24 hours a day on multiple channels, and is presented mainly in tiny segments jarringly juxtaposed with commercial messages or (in news programs) contrasting bits of information.[19] It is the constant bombardment of decontextualized information through a relentlessly amusing visual format that Postman views as promoting desensitization and passivity, rather than the act of "viewing" itself – for although they lack direct contact with performers, television viewers need not be more "passive" than audiences at other mass events.

For most Indian viewers, the *Ramayan* serial was not simply a program to "see," it was something to *do* – an event to participate in – and this participation was nearly always a group (extended family, neighborhood, village) activity. Audience participation included pre- and post-performance rituals, cheers of "*Rājā Rāmcandra kī jay!*," and distribution of sanctified food. In addition, each episode became a prime subject of conversation throughout the week: was each character portrayed properly? Were the special effects up to standard? How did the screenplay depart from the *Mānas* or the Valmiki *Rāmāyaṇa*? – such matters were endlessly debated, and everyone had an opinion. Moreover, some viewers made their opinions known through a dialog with the storyteller that, in its own way, resembled the dialectic that goes on in *kathā* sessions. Since Sagar's crew often worked on episodes until just before screening time, it was sometimes possible to incorporate audience feedback with little delay. The scene in which Ram and Lakshman are temporarily overpowered by a serpent weapon wielded by Ravan's son Indrajit, and lie helpless and wounded on the battlefield, was regarded by many viewers as a catastrophe comparable to an eclipse of the sun (some devotees took ritual baths, as during an eclipse, for protection during the Lord's period of helplessness). When Sagar chose to extend it for two broadcasts, he was deluged with letters and was forced to make an onscreen apology the following week for this undue extension of a painful and inauspicious scene. His sense of audience expectations was usually more on target, however. One feature article included an account of a day's shooting in which, as Ram completed a poignant speech on how sorely he missed Sita, Sagar, wiping his eyes with a handkerchief, rushed from behind the camera to embrace his actor, exclaiming, "*Vāh, beṭā, vāh!*" ("Superb, son, superb!), while an onlooker chimed in, "The whole country will cry next Sunday" (Vaid-Fera 1987: 13).

Clearly, the impact on Indian culture of the proliferation of television needs to be carefully studied, particularly as programming schedules continue to expand, the bombardment of commercial messages increases, and VCRs provide bored viewers with a wider range of choices. Yet such research must be informed by cultural specifics: by the fact that Indian typographic technology is only a little more than a century old and has never produced the kind of print-saturated culture that developed in the United States; that "oral literacy" (in which people who cannot read and write are familiar with and sometimes creators of sophisticated bodies of literature) remains prevalent; that great religious significance attaches to the act of seeing (*darśan*) and hearing (*śruti*); and that a wide range of oral performance genres continue to flourish. All these factors contribute to creating an environment in which the advent of television may produce less jarring discontinuity and cultural alienation than it has in the United States.

Homogenization, hegemony and the multiform text

The fact that a single version of the Ramayan, accorded high status by virtue of being aired on state-run television, was presented to an audience of unprecedented size was viewed by many critics as the single most ominous aspect of the production, for it was seen as not only threatening the nation's modern "secular" ethos, but as overwhelming and obliterating a vibrant and multivocal cultural tradition. In short, such critics assumed that Sagar's opus was the Ramayan to end all Ramayans. The Hindi critic Sudhish Pachauri wrote: "The Ram story is the people's story. But this folk story has never had a single form nor has everyone recited and understood it in one distinct, regulated context" (*Jansattā*, 1987). While conceding that the Tulsidas version also achieved a normative status in earlier centuries, another critic observed that

> the people . . . added to it their own concerns and gave it their own colors which came out when it passed through the prisms of the many versions of the Ramlila. The text was one, discourse remained many and de-construction retained the possibility of plurality.

But such deconstruction is no longer possible, he continued, because the impact of the Sagar *Ramayan* "has put paid to Ramlilas. Indeed the purveyance of Ramayana through television has destroyed the very concept of *līlā*" (Das 1988: 6).

This grim prognosis for the fate of *Rāmlīlā* plays in post-Sagar India was echoed by other writers, and only the passage of time will permit us to judge its validity. Clearly, standardized and mass-produced recordings of religious performances offer both convenience and technological glamor and have been adopted for a variety of uses; what is less certain is the impact such usage has on genres of live performance. The audio cassettes of the sung rendition of the *Mānas* by the film singer Mukesh were immensely popular in the early 1980s and became the Muzak-of-choice for broadcast at a wide range of religious functions. Yet I found *Mānas* singing to be still alive in Banaras in 1990, coexisting with the booming amplification of Mukesh, and I hesitate to conclude that the presence of electronic media spells the doom of other forms of performance – an assumption often made with reference to American culture (where each new technological advance is characteristically touted as epoch-making) but which may not even hold true there.[20]

345

A sensitive statement of concern over the prospect of cultural homogenization is contained in an essay on the serial by historian Romila Thapar. She is particularly concerned with the fact of state sponsorship of the production, which she sees as raising troubling questions:

> Were we perhaps witnessing an attempt to project what the new culture should be, an attempt to expunge diversities and present a homogenised view of what the Ramayana was and is? . . . . Where culture is taken over by the state as the major patron, there the politics of culture is inevitably heightened. It is therefore often easier for the state as patron to adopt a particular cultural stream as the mainstream: a cultural hegemony which frequently coincides with the culture of the dominant social group in the state.
>
> (Thapar 1989: 72)

In this instance, Thapar sees the dominant group as "the middle class and other aspirants to the same status," and argues that the "received version" (i.e., definitive text) of the Ramayan popular among this group – the *Rāmcaritmānas* – is being projected as an expression of "mainstream national culture." But, she warns, such cultural hegemony "requires the marginalising and ironing out of other cultural expressions" (ibid.: 74). Much of her essay is devoted to tracing the diversity of the Ramayan tradition over the past two millennia, through Buddhist, Jain, and tribal variants, and through individual oral performances, as well as through such influential texts as the epics of Valmiki and Tulsidas. She emphasizes that the changes introduced in the numerous retellings,

> were not simply variations in the story to add flavor to the narrative. They were deliberate attempts at taking up a well-known theme and using it to present a new point of view arising out of ideological and social differences in perspective.
>
> (ibid.: 72)

While conceding that the Doordarshan serial is an effective evocation of "the world of middle class fantasy," she pronounces emphatically that "The TV version is not a folk genre" (apparently the middle class, however large, can never be "the folk"), and she too warns that its popularity may ruin the *Rāmlīlā* (ibid.: 74).

Sagar's *Ramayan* does display what may be termed a mainstream Sanatani iconography and ethos, but this reflects only another step in a long historical process. Tulsi's epic was already an attempt at a grand synthesis of Vaishnava and Shaiva traditions, as well as of orthodox and heterodox currents of devotionalism. Embraced by ever wider audiences, it did indeed largely supplant earlier versions of the story (including that of Valmiki), but itself became the basis for endless reinterpretation, as the patronage of aristocratic and commercial élites led to the creative proliferation of its performance genres. At the same time the tradition acquired greater standardization through the impact of new technologies for the mass reproduction of images, texts, and sounds. A certain homogenization has been one result of this process: visually speaking, the characters and settings of the Sagar serial look much like those of the Amar Chitra Katha comic books, which in turn look like poster and calendar art.[21] Ashish Nandy warns that such standardization "impoverishes all the imagination and fantasy which is associated with the Ramayan," adding, "This serial leaves no scope for fantasy. Every motion is right there. There is no scope for new interpretations" (*Illustrated Weekly* 1987: 14–15). Yet I hope that some of what I have written above may help assuage this fear. As a visual statement, the serial is unavoidably explicit (as the *Rāmlīlā* too is forced to be) about many matters that written texts could treat in more ambiguous terms, and it often attempts to avoid controversy by projecting positive and humanized characters. Yet in so doing it has offered new interpretations which have already become the subject of lively public debate.

Although urban intellectuals now idealize the diversity and creativity of "folk performances," for the most part they neither patronize nor even observe them – they are more likely to watch television or go to the cinema. If they did view local genres in detail, they would find such performances as the celebrated *Rāmlīlā* of Ramnagar (and perhaps even tribal tales and village folksongs) to be bound up in local networks of power and hegemony – to duplicate, in fact, at the local level what the TV version is accused of doing nationally. They would also find such performances, by and large, exceedingly dull, for most folk stagings of the epic are lengthy, slow-moving, highly contextualized, and very demanding of their audiences. The intelligentsia might enjoy an artistic documentary on the Ramnagar *Rāmlīlā*, but an airing of the complete thirty-one day cycle, even if it were it possible (what would one show of a "play" that goes on in many locations simultaneously?), would make even Sagar's sluggish staging look like an action-packed synopsis. Most critics are content to champion "the folk" and their ways from afar, and no longer choose to invest the time and effort needed for immersion in the local "received text," without which, as one Banaras connoisseur playfully remarked to me, "our *Rāmlīlā* is probably the most boring play in the world!" (Singh 1983).

Thapar's view of the TV serialization as a "received text" seems to reflect the Sagar company's own hopes in marketing the cassettes. Ads display the numbered boxes in an impressive array that resembles a set of encyclopedias and beckon to the consumer with a message of reified and enduringly packaged culture: "Treasured for over 10,000 years. Enshrining ideals that are ageless. Teaching lessons that are timeless."[22] In interviews, the producer reminds us that "videocassettes can be kept in your library, like valuable books, to be referred to always" (Melwani 1988: 56–57). Beneath the hype and novelty of the new medium, however, are limitations as well as possibilities. A video *kathā* can be shown to large audiences, true, and has great visual appeal. Yet it is not as "accessible" as may at first appear: it requires costly technology and a steady supply of electricity. The twenty-eight cassettes are heavy, bulky, and fragile. To view a favorite scene may require much fast-forward or rewind searching through a cassette, and in this respect the serial compares unfavorably to a printed text – a pocket edition of the *Mānas* offers the whole epic in a compact format and can be instantly opened to any scene – and still more so to the remembered/memorized version that many still carry "in their throats."[23] The serial makes frequent reference to this text, quoting it in sung excerpts and even sometimes (with charming reflexivity) in speeches – as when Dashrath, assuring Kaikeyi of his faithfulness to his promise, quotes a *Mānas* verse:

> The way of the Raghus has ever endured –
> Give up your breath but not your word.
>
> (2.28.4)[24]

As is the case with *Rāmlīlā* audiences, TV viewers well acquainted with the *Mānas* are able to derive more pleasure from the serial, and there seems no reason to assume that the video and written texts cannot continue to coexist in their respective spheres.

When critics bemoan the serial as a vulgarization of a "literary treasure," they invoke the Ramayan as one of the Great Books in a Mortimer Adler model of human culture: a reified monument to be enshrined on a shelf and periodically cited as a cultural reference point, and perhaps occasionally even "read." They overlook the fact that millions of people recite, sing, enact, and in their own words retell the epic every day, generating a powerful cultural meta-text which functions at every point along a shifting spectrum that outside observers chart with such terms as "folk" and "classical," "élite" and "popular." The Tulsi *Mānas*, for example, was long scorned by Sanskrit pandits as a crude popularization of the elegant classic of Valmiki, concocted to please the sensibilities of illiterates. Yet the same text, patronized by royal dynasties, expounded by scholars, and celebrated in voluminous commentaries, has come increasingly to be viewed as a hoary masterpiece of India's "classical" heritage.

Those who have come to view the Ramayan as a text rather than a tradition are understandably concerned over Sagar's casting of it into a "permanent" visual form.[25] Should their fears prove correct and this effort come to stand, in time, as the definitive and exclusive version of the story, then the making of the serial would indeed represent a sad impoverishment of a multiform tradition. But I still doubt whether the advent of video technology can produce such a rapid sea change in Indian culture. Instead, I suggest that the bulk of the audience will continue to regard the "Sagar Ramayan" – like the "Tulsi Ramayan" and the "Valmiki Ramayan" – as an enthralling but not exclusive rendition of a story which is itself more a medium than a message.

They will continue to argue the production's merits and flaws, its innovations and continuities, and to be aware of numerous variations that find no place even in its protracted screenplay. They will continue, in short, to owe primary allegiance to what A. K. Ramanujan calls the "meta-Ramayan," incorporating the versions of countless tellers but never fully encompassed by any one of them. This meta-Ramayan includes, for example, the story of Ram and Sita's romance in a flower garden (told by Tulsi and Sagar but not by Valmiki), of Shabari's sampling the fruits she offers to Ram, and Hanuman's writing Ram's name on the stones of the monkey-bridge (told by Sagar but not by Tulsi); it also includes the stories of Ahi Ravan, and of the self-immolation (*satī*) of Indrajit's wife, Sulochana (told by none of these three, yet known to every north Indian villager). The tale that contains all these, and more, is alive and well, and unlikely to succumb quickly to the assault of either intellectuals or cameramen. If nothing else, the success of the Sagar serial has once again forcefully demonstrated that the Ramayan remains, throughout much of the subcontinent, a principal medium not only for the expression of individual and collective religious experience, but also for public discourse and social and cultural reflection.

Notes

* This essay was originally written for a conference on "Religion and Media in South Asia," sponsored by the Social Science Research Council and held in Carmel, California in 1989. A longer version of it appeared under the title "Ramayan: The Video!"in *The Drama Review* 34 (2) (summer 1990). The present version also appears in the volume that grew out of the conference, *Media and the Transformation of Religion in South Asia*, ed. Lawrence A. Babb and Susan S. Wadley (Philadelphia: University of Pennsylvania Press, forthcoming), and is reprinted here by kind permission of the editors.

1 *Rāmcaritmānas*, 1.33.6. All references to the epic are to the popular Gita Press version (Poddar 1938; reprinted in numerous editions). Numbers refer to book (*kānd*), stanza (understood as a group of lines ending in a numbered couplet), and individual line within a stanza. When a stanza concludes with more than one couplet, these are indicated with roman letters (for example, 12a, 12b, etc.). Throughout this essay, the term "Ramayan" is used to refer to the overall tradition of stories about Ram. The title of the Sanskrit epic of Valmiki is transliterated *Rāmāyana*, and the Hindi epic of Tulsidas is generally referred to (as in Hindi sources) as "the *Mānas*." Proper nouns from Indic languages are transliterated without diacritics and certain common romanizations are used – for example, "Doordarshan" for *dūrdarśan*.

2 I am grateful to Cynthia Ann Humes, who collected articles on the serial for me (with the help of a newspaper vendor in Mirzapur, Uttar Pradesh) while carrying out research at the Vindhyachal Devi temple in 1987–1988. I am also indebted to Chitranjan Datt of Landour Language School, who assisted me in translating several articles.

3 A film often cited as one of the finest and most popular of the genre was the Marathi-language *Sant Tukaram* (1936). In the 1960s and 1970s the Telugu film industry churned out a steady diet of mythologicals, featuring the star whose

portrayal of epic characters in forty-two musicals (he played Ram in six films, Ravana in three others, and in one – through the miracle of the camera – both roles at once) earned him the leadership of a political party – N. T. Rama Rao.

4 *India Today*'s critic carped that "everything seems to be wrong with *Ramayan* ... [it] has all the finesse of a high school function" (Bhargava 1987: 70). The *Illustrated Weekly* complained that the serial had "destroyed the spirit and the superb literary quality of the original, in its obsession for the megabuck" (*Illustrated Weekly of India* 1987: 9). A critic in *Economic and Political Weekly* termed it, "A poorly acted, still more poorly produced, lurid dramatisation of the epic" (Deshpande 1988: 2215).

5 For example, Pachauri in *Jansattā* (Pachauri 1987); I am grateful to Monika Thiel-Horstmann for alerting me to this article. While condemning the series as a vulgar commercialization likely to inflame communal violence, Pachauri, like many other Hindi critics, devotes much attention to what he sees as misinterpretations of the *Mānas* text – a line of attack used by few English-language writers (perhaps because they have not read Tulsidas?). This criticism does not seem especially well-informed, however; thus, Pachauri mocks the "flower garden" scene of Ram and Sita's first meeting (episode 6), claiming that it shows Ram as "a flirtatious dandy" and is inspired by the love scenes of Bombay films. "Tulsi," he primly asserts, "disposed of Lord Ram's romance in two verses." This is patently untrue – the garden scene in the *Mānas* occupies nearly 100 lines and, precisely because of its romantic content, has become one of the most beloved passages in the epic.

6 Reported in *The Ramayan Phenomenon*, an article apparently reprinted from an unidentified magazine and included in a promotional brochure distributed by Sagar Enterprises.

7 This decision gave rise to a tumultuous controversy over the deletion of Valmiki's Seventh Book, the *Uttarakāṇḍa*, which led to strikes, political agitation, High Court cases, and the eventual commissioning of a sequel series of twenty-six episodes which was aired during 1989. Fascinating though it was, the controversy is beyond the scope of this essay.

8 The renowned early nineteenth-century expounder, Ramgulam Dvivedi, is said to have once discoursed on a single line from Book One for twenty-one days. I myself witnessed a seven evening performance by the Banaras expounder Shrinath Mishra, based on one line from Book Seven (see Lutgendorf 1989, 1991b).

9 He was not the first director of a religious film to assume this responsibility – cf. Cecil B. Demille's opening speech, before a golden curtain, at the start of *The Ten Commandments*.

10 All such details have a long history and reflect an ongoing controversy over the precise nature of Ram's *vānar* allies, who as incarnations of deities in simian guise both are and are not "monkeys."

11 American cinema and television in recent years have favored constant visual stimulation, often at the expense of dialog and extended character development. The trend is especially striking if one compares films of the 1920s and 1930s with those of the past two decades; in the latter, camera angles constantly shift, scenes often last only seconds, and character is sought to be conveyed through a few expressive close-ups and terse exchanges; the style has become such a convention that we may no longer notice it. According to Neil Postman, the average length of time during which a single image remains on the American television screen is only 3.5 seconds (Postman 1985: 86). The commercial success of MTV in recent years, with its numbing flood of decontextualized images, has further upped the ante on visual stimulation throughout the media.

12 Though barely mentioned in the Valmiki and Tulsidas versions, Urmila receives much attention in folk traditions, and her renunciation is often said to exceed that of her husband. Sagar develops this theme through several scenes.

13 They thus disguise their manipulative intent, for (as Susan Sontag has argued) their storytellers hide from us and pretend to impartiality, even while they remain as partisan as other artists, and seek, through carefully ordered images, to influence our thoughts and feelings (Sontag 1973: 22–24).

14 For example, the spectator has to choose whether to be with Sita in the Ashok Grove, or (several miles away) with Ram and Lakshman in the forest of Kishkindha (Schechner 1983: 284). Some might argue that the camera's assumed omniscience lulls the dreamer/viewer into passivity and impoverishes his own imagination. I shall return to this question in my conclusion.

15 An American company plans to create "The New Media Bible," consisting of 225 hours of video (Postman 1985: 96).

16 For example, the *Illustrated Weekly* invariably labels it "the idiot box," though it cannot overlook its appeal even to its own readers, and, under this heading, has for several years been offering color photos of TV starlets, obviously in demand for pin-up purposes.

17 The budget was estimated to have been Rs 4 lakhs per episode, though Sagar claims to have spent most of this on production costs. Video cassettes market within India for about Rs 325 each or Rs 7,000 for the series; the North American distributor, Ramimex International of Jamaica, New York, asks $779.74 for the set. However, while sales of serial-related items were reported to be brisk, the Sagars' profits were reduced by the weak enforcement of Indian copyright laws and the resultant piracy of images, logos, and audio and video tapes. Despite efforts to give a distinctive cachet to the authorized tapes, and a printed warning that "IT IS NOT ONLY A CRIME BUT ALSO A SIN TO PIRATE RAMAYAN CASSETTES," illegal versions lifted directly from the broadcasts began appearing in shops long before the first Sagar cassette was released, and sold for less than a third its price. Thus the Ramayan serial functioned as a kind of cottage industry exploited by numerous petty entrepreneurs – streetcorner video dealers, small-town printers, even jewellery and cosmetic companies that made unauthorized use of serial styles and logos.

18 See also the Hindi article by Satyendra Shrivastav, "Rāmāyaṇ ke nām par afīm" ("Opium in the name of Ramayan"), *Svatantra Bhārat* (August 3, 1988), p. 5.

19 For example, a report on a catastrophic famine is juxtaposed with singing actors munching hamburgers, then immediately followed by an "upbeat" sports story (Postman 1985: chs 6–7).

20 For example, even the slick, packaged culture of commercial rock music coexists with thousands of aspiring neighborhood bands, and new styles continually develop out of the rich matrix of amateur talent.

21 J. S. Hawley reports that Sagar hired some of the Amar Chitra Katha artists as costume and set designers, to achieve a look which would be acceptable to his audience (Hawley 1989).

22 Advertisement for the international edition of the *Ramayan* serial, *c.* June 1988.

23 Hindi speakers declare a memorized text to be *kanthasth* – "situated in the throat."

24 Similarly, when lecturing Ravan, Vibhishan quotes a *Mānas* verse on the dangers of following the advice of sycophants (5.37), prefacing it by stating, "*śāstra* declares" (episode 49).

25 Though it is worth noting that the mere translation to a visual format is not necessarily objected to, but only the "vulgar" middle-class idiom of the production; thus Sunil Bandopadhyay suggests in the *Illustrated Weekly* that Doordarshan redeem itself by giving "a huge amount of money to Satyajit Ray to make an *authentic* version" of the Sanskrit epics (*Illustrated Weekly* 1987: 20; emphasis mine).

Bibliography

Āj (1988) "Alvidā 'dūrdarśan Rāmāyan'" (Farewell to 'Doordarshan Ramayan'", July 31, p. 6.

Bakker, Hans (1986) *Ayodhyā*, Groningen: Egbert Forsten.

Barnouw, Erik and Krishnaswamy, S. (1980) *Indian Film*, New York: Oxford University Press.

Benjamin, Walter (1955) "The Work of Art in the Age of Mechanical Reproduction," in Hannah Arendt (ed.), *Illuminations*, New York: Harcourt, Brace & World.

Bhargava, Simran (1987) "Ramayan: Divine Sensation" *India Today*, April 30, p. 70.

Bourdieu, Pierre (1977) *Outline of a Theory of Practice*, Cambridge: Cambridge University Press.

Butsch, Richard (1985) "The Commercialization of Leisure," in Vincent Mosco and Janet Wasko (eds), *The Critical Communications Review, Vol. III: Popular Culture and Media Events*, Norwood, NJ: Ablex Publishing Company.

Dainik jāgaran (1988a) "Dhārāvāhik Rāmāyan: hiy kī pyās bujhai na bujhāye" ("The Ramayan serial: the heart's thirst is still unsatisfied"), July 3, p. 7.

Dainik jāgaran (1988b) "Landan mem bhī mujhe sab pahcān gae the" ("Even in London everyone recognized me"), June 13.

Dainik jāgaran (1988c) "Rāmāyan dekho, mālpuā pāo" ("Watch Ramayan and get sweets"), June 6, p. 3.

Dainik jāgaran (1988d) "'Rāmāyan' ke mauke par bijlī jāne se upkendra per pathrāv, āgjanī" ("Stoning and arson of substation when power fails during 'Ramayan'"), March 21, p. 3.

Dainik jāgaran (1988e) "Rāmrājyābhisek per 21 man dūdh kī khīr bāntī gayī" ("1,800 pounds of sweets distributed for Ram's enthronement"), August 1, p. 3.

Das, Arvind N. (1988) "Electronic Religiosity: Meaning of Goswami Ramanand Sagar," *Times of India*, August 6, p. 6.

De, Aditi, (1988) "The Man From Malgudi," *Indian Express Magazine*, October 2, p. 5.

Deshpande, G. P. (1988) "The Riddle of the Sagar Ramayana," *Economic and Political Weekly*, October 22, pp. 2215–2216.

Hawley, John Stratton (1989) Personal communication, February 24.

Hein, Norvin (1972) *The Miracle Plays of Mathurā*, New Haven, Conn.: Yale University Press.

Illustrated Weekly of India (1987) "The Ramayan," November 8–14, pp. 8–17.

India Today (1986) "Shree Geeta Press Ramayan" (advertisement), March 15, p. 22.

India Express (1988) "Fanfare marks 'Ramayan' end," February 8.

Jain, Madhu (1988) "Ramayan: The Second Coming," *India Today*, August 3, p. 81.

Jansattā (1988) "Binā 'Rāmāyan' ravivār kt subah sūnī-sūnī sī" ("Sunday morning seems empty without 'Ramayan'"), September 8.

Lutgendorf, Philip (1989) "Ram's Story in Shiva's City," in Sandria Frietag (ed.), *Culture and Power in Banaras*, Berkeley, Calif.: University of California Press.

—— (1991a) "The 'Great Sacrifice' of Ramayana Recitation," in Monika Thiel-Horstmann (ed.), *Contemporary Ramayana Traditions: Written, Oral, Performed*, Wiesbaden: Otto Harrassowitz.

—— (1991b), *The Life of a Text: Performing the Rāmcaritmānas of Tulsidas*, Berkeley, Calif.): University of California Press.

Mazumdar, Debu, (1988) "Mandi House Had Rejected Ramayana," and "Traders' Ultimatum to Punjab Government," *Indian Express*, August 1, p. 5.

Melwani, Lavina (1988) "Ramanand Sagar's Ramayan Serial Re-Ignites Epic's Values," *India Worldwide*, February, pp. 56–57.

Pachauri, Sudhish (1987) "Savāl to rāmkathā ke istemāl kā hai" ("The real question is of the use of the Ram story"), *Jansattā* August 6.

Pfleiderer, Beatrix and Lutze, Lothar (1985) *The Hindi Film: Agent and Re-Agent of Cultural Change*, Delhi: Manohar Books.

Poddar, Hanuman Prasad (ed.) (1938) *Śrī Rāmcaritmānas*, Gorakhpur, UP: Gita Press.

Postman, Neil (1985) *Amusing Ourselves to Death*, New York: Penguin Books.

The Ramayan Phenomenon (1987?) Promotional brochure, Sagar Enterprises, Inc.

Read, Michael R. (1985) "Understanding Oscar: The Academy Awards Telecast as International Media Event," in Vincent Mosco and Janet Wasko (eds), *The Critical Communications Review, Vol. III: Popular Culture and Media Events*, Norwood, NJ: Ablex Publishing Company.

Schechner, Richard (1983) *Performative Circumstances from the Avant-Garde to Ramlila*, Calcutta: Seagull Books.

Schechner, Richard, and Hess, Linda (1977) "The Ramlila of Ramnagar," *Drama Review* 21 (September), pp. 51–82.

Singh, C. P. N. (February, 1984) personal communication.

Shrivastav, Satyendra (1988) "Rāmāyaṇ ke nām par afīm" ("Opium in the name of Ramayan"), *Svantantra Bhārat* (August 3), p. 5.

Sontag, Susan (1973) *On Photography*, New York: Farrar, Straus & Giroux.

Thapar, Romila (1989) "The Ramayana Syndrome," *Seminar 353*, January, pp. 71–75.

Times of India (1988) "Early Diwali," September 8.

Vaid-Fera, Mimi (1987) "Hare Rama! Hare Sagar!," *Imprint*, October, pp. 6–17.

van der Veer, Peter (1988) *Gods on Earth*, London: Athlone Press.

Whaling, Frank (1980) *The Rise of the Religious Significance of Rāma*, Delhi: Motilal Banarsidass.

18

Sacred serials, devotional viewing, and domestic worship

A case-study in the interpretation of two TV versions of *The Mahabharata* in a Hindu family in west London

Marie Gillespie

Field diary: Saturday, November 11, 1990

First visit to the Dhanis, a Hindu family living in Southall, west London to view Peter Brook's televised theatrical production of *The Mahabharata* broadcast on Channel 4.

6:00 p.m.   I arrive at the Dhanis' three-bedroom terraced house in old Southall. Shoes are removed in the hallway. The smell of incense hangs heavily in the air. Mother, father, and seven children (aged from 11 to 21 years old) are seated in the living room. We greet each other from a distance. Malati, a bright-eyed, smiling 14-year-old girl (and an ex-pupil of mine) ushers me to the sofa where I sit cushioned between the younger children and we chat. The parents and older siblings are seated at the far end of the room near the kitchen. They remain silent but observant. The living room is a comfortably furnished through-lounge with TV set in the window bay and a long, tall sideboard decorated with family photos, pictures of Hindu gods draped with tinsel, incense holders, ornaments, and a cassette/record player. A large picture of Krishna hangs on the wall opposite with a formidable presence.

6:30 p.m.   Tea and biscuits are served as we watch *Blind Date* and chat. The older sisters move closer to the screen and while watching stroke the young children's hair or feet in affectionate intimacy. Silence falls as the girl on *Blind Date* is about to choose her partner. From the far corner of the room the mother cries "Number two! number two!" Sure enough the girl chooses boy number two. We all laugh heartily. The ice is broken.

7:00 p.m.   The younger children and I eat dal (lentils) and hot chapattis. There is much hustle and bustle around the house in anticipation of the start

354

of *The Mahabharata* – it will involve 6 hours' viewing so preparations are made.

7:30 p.m. *The Mahabharata* begins. The international casting has the immediate effect of rendering their dearly loved gods unrecognizable. The confusion is expressed in a loud barrage of repartee:

Ranjit: That's Ganesha!

Sefali: No it isn't, be quiet!

Lipi: That's Vishnu!

Malati: Don't be silly, it's Vyasa!

Ranjit: But Vyasa is Vishnu.

Sefali: No he isn't, he's Krishna!

The room is filled with a sea of noise. The children appeal to their mother for help but she could not recognize the gods either. At this point I realize that the mother speaks very little English. The children continue to shout and argue as Brook's production unfolds. I too am confused. Watching TV with a family of nine is a very new experience. I can't concentrate or hear what is being said.

8:00 p.m. The father and eldest son leave the house, proclaiming "It's no good! It doesn't carry the meaning."

We continue watching half-heartedly while chatting. The children tell me stories about the gods in *The Mahabharata*, their special qualities and attributes, especially their love for Lord Krishna. They are devotees of Krishna and reserve a special love and affection for him. They love him especially as a child and they tell me that in every child Krishna can be seen. They tell me that they have already watched most of the seventy-five episodes of *The Ramayana*, the "sister" epic of *The Mahabharata*. This is the most popular of the Hindu scriptures and every Hindu child is familiar with its stories. Several times during the course of our half-hearted viewing the children say "Oh! you should see *Sita's Wedding* [an episode from *The Ramayana*], it's great, it's much better than this." The mother is clearly not enjoying the Brook production. She says she feels ill and lies down on the sofa.

10:00 p.m. Silence prevails as intense viewing begins at the moment in Brook's production where Krishna incites Arjuna to go to war and fight his cousins. At this stage in Brook's production the children become increasingly alarmed. Why is Krishna telling Arjuna to kill his own cousins? Why is he telling them to go to war? They express confusion at this moral paradox and are troubled by not being able to recognize goodness in Krishna. "You don't know who the goodies and the baddies are in this version," said Malati. "Why are we watching this anyway? I mean no one is enjoying it are they?"

said Sefali. Their explicit contempt for and displeasure at Brook's production is apparent.

10:25 p.m. The TV is switched off at this point. There is an instant change of atmosphere, a marked sense of relief. The mother and her eldest two sisters climb the stairs to their domestic shrine in the middle bedroom. They performed a *puja* (a prayer ritual). I hear a horn blowing faintly, bells tinkling, and some quiet chanting. Downstairs the children explain that their mother and sisters are "doing a *puja*." The conversation shifts. It seems strange to me. The girls start telling me how their mother's father was a very holy man and how he read holy books every day to his family. The holy books were very thick and that's why their mother knows so much. There is a lot of talk about just how holy their grandfather was. He could read the holy books like *The Mahabharata* and *The Ramayana* in Sanskrit. They tell me that it is not written in everyone's fate to read the holy books but for those that can and do special blessings are bestowed. Malati says that is why she is studying Hindi at school. One day she will read the holy books. The mother returns from *puja*, smiles and nods in agreement. This is a great thing to do. "Mum says if you understand *The Ramayana* and *The Mahabharata* you can understand life itself," retorts Ranjit with the air of an elderly sage. A calm descends upon the evening.

10:30 p.m. Suddenly Sewanti, the elder sister asked, "Do you want to see *Sita's Wedding*?" The mother looks brighter. I am fearful of overstaying my welcome and aware that *Sita's Wedding* is a 3-hour film. Malati had already explained to me that once a "god film" has been put on it has to be watched until the end. I suggest that perhaps I should return another time. But the children ask me to stay. The mother perks up at the thought of watching *Sita's Wedding* and urges me to stay. Incense is lit.

10:50 p.m. Jubilation as *Sita's Wedding* is placed in the video. "Why didn't we think of this before?" the children cried. The mother sits on the floor with the two youngest children beside her in front of the TV screen. The others on the sofa and armchairs. Their close and intimate affection for each other is touching. Ranjit (11 years old) is larking around. His mother playfully chastises him. She asks him to sit upright, to behave properly in front of the film, and to show respect. He does so and then cuddles up to her. The family sing along to the religious songs. When Krishna appears on screen a salutation is made as in an act of worship at the temple – a joyful atmosphere reigns for the first time in the evening.

Introduction

The Dhanis are a Hindu family living in west London whose religious beliefs and practices, especially their devotion for Krishna, are woven into the fabric of their everyday lives. *The Mahabharata* and its "sister" epic *The Ramayana* are their most important holy books. They are also the foundational myths of Indian culture. However, *The Mahabharata* is not just one text but a constellation of variant interpretations and representations of the foundational Sanskritic texts that span all art forms as well as high, folk, popular, and mass culture.[1] In the fieldnotes above, it is clear that for the Dhani children its religious authority originates in the written text and in the male voice of the grandfather who communicated it to their mother in India. The mother is seen as a repository of the beliefs and knowledge that are considered to be held within it. In turn, she tells some of its many stories orally to her children, in fragments, over a period of years. Its length and expansiveness mean that few Hindus know it in its entirety. Both *The Ramayana* and *The Mahabharata* are percived as the source of their religious beliefs and knowledge and thus as sacred texts. Why then was Brook's production not perceived as sacred? And why was *Sita's Wedding*, in contrast, received as a sacred text and viewed in a devotional manner?

Immediately, several seemingly obvious dichotomies spring to mind: sacred and profane versions; Indian versus European contexts of production and reception; the targeting of middle-class western audiences as opposed to Indian, popular, mass audiences; Brook's orientalist interpretation versus an iconography and narration which are distinctively Indian. All of these in principle seem plausible. However, empirically, answers to these questions only began to emerge in the fieldwork when, whether by chance or by scheduling design, BBC2 began broadcasting Doordarshan's (India's state monopoly channel) ninety-two part TV serial of *The Mahabharata*. This was immediately recognized by the Dhanis as a sacred version of the text and generated what I shall refer to as "devotional viewing."

The Dhanis had already seen most of Doordarshan's *The Ramayana* and were delighted by the arrival of *The Mahabharata* on their screen. These sacred soaps have penetrated Indian popular culture in an unprecedented manner. It is claimed that these are the most popular TV serials in the history of TV.[2] If rating figures are a criterion of popularity, then this seems indisputable. *The Ramayana*, for example, attracted some 650 million viewers in India alone. They are also hugely popular in the Hindu diaspora where the video cassette recorder, satellite, and cable TV have made them accessible on a global scale.[3]

The appearance on British TV screens of two antithetical representations of *The Mahabharata* within weeks of each other provoked the Dhani children into performing a contrastive analysis of the two versions and launched the project of this case-study. Comparing and contrasting two contemporary attempts to represent *The Mahabharata* in a holistic, cohesive way was for them of intrinsic interest in itself. Yet, a more important reason for undertaking this contrastive textual analysis is suggested in the fieldnotes. The social drama of this first evening revolved around first, switching off Brook's production at the moment where Krishna's divinity and moral integrity seem to be thrown into question; second, performing a *puja*, a rite of purification or an intiation into a mode of consciousness which is receptive to the sacred; and third, returning refreshed or restored to view *Sita's Wedding* in a devotional manner, or, in other words, with an observable demeanor of piety and pleasure.

Brook's production was distasteful to the Dhani children. The mother later claimed that "it left a bad taste in my mouth – I had to watch *Sita's Wedding* to get my taste back." The children sought to resolve the contradictions which they perceived in Brook's version, especially the portrayal of Krishna and the ambiguity of good and evil, fate and free will that were suggested to them by the text. They wanted to know why Krishna, a god, had engineered a war by trickery and deceit and incited Arjuna to kill his own cousins. They wanted to be able to explain and defend his actions to themselves, to each other, and to me. Their mother could not, in their eyes, provide satisfactory explanations to these problems. The moral complexitites of *The Mahabharata* troubled and intrigued them and they wanted to know more. This provided a powerful incentive to view Doordarshan's serial.

Empirically, this case-study focuses upon the cultural specificity of what I shall refer to as "devotional viewing," demonstrating how it is integrated into domestic religious rituals and acts of worship. It further examines the generic conventions of "sacred serials" through a contrastive textual analysis of Doordarshan's and Brook's productions of *The Mahabharata*. And it highlights the religious didacticism of this sacred serial and its appropriation by the Dhani family for the joint purposes of pleasurable entertainment and of deepening their religious knowledge and understanding.

The precise connections between the different dimensions of this case-study are not clear-cut. I propose the term *devotional viewing* to refer to a culturally distinctive form of TV consumption which is based upon observations of, and participation in, the life of the Dhani household over a two-year period of fieldwork which was catalyzed by this first evening's viewing. The *contrastive textual analysis* was an activity which we performed collaboratively over several months. We reviewed segments of both versions on video. The pause button allowed us to move freely in, and out, and across these texts in a way that encouraged dialog between ourselves and the texts. The data generated provided the basis for my own further analysis. The *religious world-view* which is articulated, in an increasingly sophisticated manner, by the Dhanis is a result of their developing understanding of Hinduism. However, the elaboration of their religious world-view was assisted by their progressive viewing of the sacred serial, by its didacticism as well as by its serial form. While the didactic nature of viewing constitutes only a part of their religious learning, alongside visits to the temple, it is nevertheless an important and pleasurable part of it. The data upon which this case-study is built are also a product of an ongoing dialog between us and the friendship and mutual affection which developed during the course of the research.

These different dimensions of the case-study – the cultural and domestic context of viewing and of religious worship, contrastive textual analysis, the expression of religious beliefs and principles – comprise distinct analytical registers. No necessary causal connections are posited between them. Thus, for example, the perceived sacredness of the serial does not explain devotional viewing any more than does its serial form, nor indeed does it explain the experience of viewing devotionally for any individual member of the Dhani family. Similarly, although devotional viewing is integrated into domestic worship and religious practices it does not in itself provoke the articulation of the beliefs that constitute their religious world-view, any more than does comparative textual analysis. Rather, these are contingent cultural processes which may occur at any one moment in time as well as across time. Thus both synchronic and diachronic cultural processes can be brought into focus through the case-study.

While the case-study does not claim representative status, it permits analysis of the microprocesses of TV reception in everyday life in the context of broader considerations of how global TV serials are appropriated and interpreted in specific local contexts and how they are implicated in the construction and strengthening of religious beliefs and practices. It highlights how ethnically-specific TV consumption in the British context may simultaneously lock into global networks of TV consumption in the Hindu diaspora. Therefore, the different analytical registers of this ethnographic case-study, together, shed light on local interpretations of a global TV serial and on being Hindu in London.

Several propositions are woven through this essay. First, the juxtaposition of the English and Indian versions of *The Mahabharata* in the domestic context catalyzed contrastive readings of the texts. These readings provide a key with which to unlock the cultural specificity of the interpretive frameworks which the young people in this family draw upon to interpret *The Mahabharata*, and so highlight the nature of devotional viewing.

Second, in responding to *The Mahabharata*, two world-views emerge in the discourses of the young Dhanis: the first may be described as a common-sense world-view, in that it emphasizes the pragmatic rather than the ideal course of action. The other is a religious world-view, informed by Hinduism as a cultural system, which transcends, as well as contradicts, the pragmatic world view. Viewing and discussing *The Mahabharata* contributes directly to their religious world-view which shapes activity in the pragmatic world. The interaction of these distinctive world-views are evidenced in their readings of *The Mahabharata*.

Third, the video cassette recorder and local cable TV have made popular Hindi TV programs and films available to families in Southall on an unprecedented scale. The didactic use of religious films and programs and their integration in acts of religious worship and ritual are contributing to changes in the practices of Hinduism itself. In particular, such uses are

359

facilitating the increasingly central role of domestic as opposed to public worship among Hindus in Southall.

Fourth, for the young people in this family, and in Southall more generally, there is no easy equation between geography, culture, and media. The new TV delivery systems allow Hindus in London to keep in touch with Indian popular culture. TV plays a significant role in re-creating and re-presenting "tradition" among first and second generation Hindus in Southall.[4] But the ideological implications of viewing *The Mahabharata* are a more elusive matter. Already in India, the hugely popular TV serializations of *The Mahabharata* and *The Ramayana* are criticized for playing into the hands of a growing Hindu fundamentalism.[5] And yet their ideological connotations are surely very different in the context of Southall, a Punjabi Sikh town where, in certain quarters, Sikh fundamentalism thrives, where Hindus themselves are a minority, and where Hindi audiovisual media dominate. The complexities of this situation require further analysis. For the moment, suffice it to say that the system of beliefs and values that *The Mahabharata* and *The Ramayana* propagate are to be found reinscribed and reinstated in every contemporary popular Hindi film. So pervasive is their influence that, it is argued, they function as a pan-Indian meta-discourse, an understanding of which is essential to any exploration of contemporary Hindi media.[6]

Finally, while ethnographic methods have long been advocated in media audience research, few studies have taken on board what characterizes ethnography as a method, namely long-term participant observation in a selected field. A more fully ethnographic approach to audience research can deliver the kind of data that would take us beyond the sterile dichotomy often erected between approaches which emphasize "TV doing things to people" and those which consider "people doing things with TV." Conversely, anthropologists who have long ignored everyday uses and interpretations of the media in their studies of contemporary cultures will find, as I have done, that audience research can offer a beautifully oblique strategy that can deliver rich ethnographic data.

The chapter is divided into three parts. The first part describes the cultural and domestic context of viewing and of religious worship. It characterizes devotional viewing as viewing with both piety and pleasure. The second part focuses upon a contrastive textual analysis of Doordarshan's and Brook's versions of *The Mahabharata*. In particular, it examines differences in iconography, narrative structure, and narration. The final part returns us to the questions posed by the first evening's viewing, but empirically focuses upon data gathered toward the end of our viewing of Doordarshan's *The Mahabharata*. It explores the deeper philosophical issues of good and evil, free will and fate, conceptions of time, causality and moral contradiction, which the Dhanis have explored in the process of viewing the serial over a two-year period.

Piety and pleasure: the cultural and domestic context of viewing and religious worship

At the start of fieldwork the Dhani household consisted of nine people – mother and father in their late 40s, five daughters aged between 12 and 23, and two sons aged 11 and 18. They emigrated to Southall from Calcutta in 1978. The father, mother, and two eldest daughters are all employed in low-paid jobs in local catering and cleaning firms.

Their main leisure activity is watching TV. When all the family is together they watch mainly Hindi films, Indian TV serials, and British news. In contrast, viewing with siblings usually means watching British, American, and Australian TV and video films. The children watch popular soaps with their mother, especially *Neighbours* which they view on a daily basis. Such viewing is agonistic in that it invites both intimacy and censure. *Neighbours* provides alternative sets of values and norms of social behavior for the Dhanis to consider, some of which contradict and contravene those established in parental culture. This is particularly true in the areas of kinship duty, courtship and marriage, and social relations within the local "community." Through their viewing of *Neighbours* they participate in a global TV network of youth culture and negotiate with their mother their ideas about changing gender and generational relations. They bring both their religious and pragmatic world-views to bear upon their interpretations of *Neighbours*.[7] In contrast, their viewing of the Indian serial of *The Mahabharata* and religious Hindi films and TV more generally tends to support and sustain a world view consistent with traditional Indian values and norms, and may even strengthen Hinduism, as it does among the Dhanis, or exacerbate Indian nationalism and/ or fundamentalism variously in India and in the Hindu diaspora. However, the Dhani children are increasingly in the position of being able to translate back and forth between these global serials which though generically similar are, culturally, quite different.

At the weekend the Dhanis watch two or three popular Hindi films as well as several "god films." This is a distinctive genre of films sometimes referred to as "mythologicals" or devotional films. They occupy a unique position in the history of Indian cinema. This was the first type of film to be made, and it has continued to exercise an important influence on the development of popular Hindi cinema.[8] These films present episodes and stories from Hindu texts, in particular *The Ramayana* and *The Mahabharata*, and combine entertainment with religious didacticism. They also popularize new deities like the eponymous *Jai Santoshi Maa*. In many Hindu families in Southall, and undoubtedly elsewhere in the Hindu diaspora, viewing devotional films has come to replace the reading of holy books. In some families domestic worship which incorporates viewing has come to substitute for more public acts of worship in the temple. Certainly, in the domestic context, mothers exploit the films for didactic purposes. The values which they supposedly foster are seen as helping to maintain religious traditions and observances in a secular British culture.

The Mahabharata is not simply a written text but an *"Itihasa,"* or fundamental source of knowledge and inspiration for all the arts.[9] Over centuries certain iconographic traditions associated with the representation of the deity been have crystalized and stabilized. This was assisted by the introduction of popular, mass-produced prints which resulted in fixed stereo-typical portrayals of the gods.[10] Such conventional images of the gods adorn Hindu homes in India and in Britain. They are the focus and object of daily acts of devotion and worship. The visual representation of the deity in popular images as well as in religious films and TV serials like *The Mahabharata* play a crucial symbolic role in communicating the character of the gods and the values they embody. Religious films and the sacred serials may be regarded as animated conventional iconography. This highlights the import-ance of understanding religion as both a cultural and a symbolic system – as a source of general yet distinctive conceptions of the world, self, others, and the relations between them, as well as a model of and for reality.[11]

Mrs Dhani is the keenest viewer of religious films in the family. She will often stay up with her children until the early hours of the morning viewing them, especially at the weekend. There is a tone of guilty pleasure in her voice when she admits to having hired four or five videos and watched all of them over the weekend (12–15 hours viewing). Such admissions are accompanied by playful reprimands from her husband and children who complain that she cannot get up in the morning after a heavy session of religious viewing.

Religious films provide her with comfort and solace from life's everyday anxieties. When she or a member of her family is ill or when she is worried she will view them almost compulsively and use them as a focus of her prayers. Devotional viewing is incorporated into religious observances and rituals. For example, at the start of films considered worthy of devotional viewing incense is lit and a salutation to the divinity is made. A *puja* may be performed before or during viewing. Furthermore, once a sacred film or serial is switched on, it must be viewed until the end out of respect – a devotee would not stand up and leave his or her guru in mid-sentence. Food should not be eaten while viewing, except *prasad* or holy food that has been blessed. If, for instance, Krishna appears on screen the mother will encourage the children to sit upright and make a salutation, as in an act of worship at the temple. Thus it can be observed that devotional viewing involves the kinds of taboos and prohibitions that surround sacred objects – in this case the TV set showing a sacred text functions as a type of shrine.

Viewing god films is seen, especially by the mother, as a pleasurable act of devotion in itself. The appearance on screen of cherished gods such as Krishna, in close-up, gazing direct to camera, with eyes seemingly pen-etrating the viewer's inner core, is like a divine apparition. It is as if Krishna were speaking directly to the viewer via the actor and TV. Of course they do not, as some suggest, confuse the actor with Krishna.[12] Such viewing is thought to bring the gods into you and if, after watching, you can bring the gods into your dreams then it is considered to be like a divine visitation where blessings are bestowed and favors may be requested.

I have just described the observable aspects of devotional viewing. However, religious belief and a religious mode of consciousness are pre-requisites to devotional viewing. Entry into a sacred sphere which is set apart from daily life is achieved through various rituals and rites of initiation, purification, and consecration such as are practiced daily in all religions. But viewing with piety does not preclude the pleasures associated with enter-tainment. It is perhaps a unique feature of Hindi religious films and sacred serials that they combine the pleasures of entertainment with a strong religious didacticism.

Clearly, the meanings of texts and of viewing are not pre-given, but are created by viewers, albeit within certain parameters. *The Mahabharata* and *The Ramayana*, like many popular religious films, are important because they are perceived as sacred texts and viewed devotionally. There is an a priori acceptance of their religious and cultural authority which is a product of this family's religious beliefs and world-view as well as of its particular textual representation. These TV programmes are not seen as variants of the Sanskritic texts but as synonymous with them. They are attributed with an "aura of factuality."[13] They are not seen to be myths, epic poems or dramas, but as Sefali says: "I believe that these are not simply stories. I believe they are true stories, history which actually happened." Religious belief precedes religious knowledge.

Competing claims of greater knowledge and understanding of *The Rama-yana* and *The Mahabharata*, and by association of Hinduism, are made by the children. The youngest boy Ranjit, who is 11 years old, whispered to me

> Well, I know most really about the gods because I sleep downstairs with my mother and she always tells me stories before I go to sleep and when she's watching late at night she'll keep waking me up and saying "watch this Ranjit, it's important." So often, I go upstairs and splash my face with cold water and then we sit up until 3 or 4 in the morning with her.

Malati, who is 14, claims a better understanding of the films and of Hinduism, because she does Hindi at school and so has better access to the language. Her ambition is to read *The Mahabharata* in Sanskrit like her grandfather. Sefali, who is 19, claims greater knowledge because she is older and is doing English A-level, and she often relates aspects of *The Mahab-harata* to Shakespearean texts such as *King Lear* and to Greek tragedies such as *Antigone*.

In contrast to *The Ramayana*, few Hindus, young or old, are very familiar with *The Mahabharata* in its entirety due to its length and the complexity of its narrative and moral paradoxes. However, most Hindus are more or less familiar with parts of it, particularly *The Bhagavad Gita*, which begins with the dialog where Krishna incites Arjuna to go to war against his cousins and goes on to expound the essence of Hindu philosophy. It was at this point in our viewing of Brook's production that the TV set was switched off.

Constrastive textual analysis of the sacred soap and TV play

The Mahabharata tells the story of a long and bloody quarrel between two groups of cousins of divine origin: the Pandevas, of whom there were five, and the Kauravas, of whom there were 100. The family quarrel over who will rule the kingdom ends with an earth-shattering war to decide the fate of the earth.

Doordarshan's production is aimed at a mass, national audience, many of whom are illiterate. However, it appeals across class, caste, regional, and even religious boundaries, and it bridges "high" and "low" cultural forms. As a genre it most resembles the continuing serial or soap in its length (approximately 70 hours), its preoccupation with family conflicts and kinship ties, and the intimacy and familiarity with the characters which develops alongside the unfolding narrative.

The sets are majestic and palatial, inhabited by kings and queens, gods and goddesses. We are transported from the heavens to earth, from magnificent palaces to epic battlefields. The costumes and jewellery are opulent, regal, and highly colorful. Special effects are employed to convey the actions or miracles of the gods. At one moment, thousands of arrows are seen darting across the heavens and goddesses magically appear from the sea, while at the next moment we are invited to share in the splendor of the gods in paradise. Dramatic moments in the story are powerfully reinforced by music, song, and special effects. The earth is made to tremble and shake, lightning and thunder split the sky asunder in order to convey the solemnity of a promise or the anger of the gods. In accordance with Hindi film conventions, the narrative moves through successive modes of spectacle, action, emotion, song, and intense dialog in circular rather than linear fashion. As we shall see this has considerable consequences for the representation of Hindi notions of cyclical time.

Brook's TV production is based on his theatrical version of *The Mahabharata*. An international co-production, spearheaded by Channel 4, it was shot on 35 mm film at the Joinville Studios, Paris. The visual style of the film and its modes of realism were thus crucially determined by the studio setting. The sets, which are sparse, bare, and earth-colored, match the costumes which are equally simple and somber. There are no realistic exteriors, no battalions of warriors. Costumes, lamps, weapons, and furnishings were brought from India in order to ensure "close-up" realism. The result is the cinematic equivalent of the stage version.[14] The cast of Brook's production is international and drawn from each of the five continents, in order to emphasize the universal nature of the story and to ensure international appeal.

Brook's version is theatrical, authored, and targeted at a middle-class, educated audience. Although broadcast over six consecutive hours on a Saturday evening, it defies any simple generic classification. If it falls into any generic category, the "single play" tradition of British television would be most appropriate. It is divided into three main parts: the Game of Dice, Exile in the Forest, and The War. I shall now outline key points of difference as articulated by the Dhanis, particularly with reference to the iconographic and narrative features of both texts.

Iconography

The whole dilemma on the first viewing of Brook's version revolved around identifying the characters. The Dhanis were familiar with the basic story-line and the main characters and their attributes, from cartoon strips and from a 3-hour Hindi film of *The Mahabharata*.[15] They felt that if they succeeded in recognizing and naming the characters, they would then be more likely to be able to situate them within the narrative. Viewing became a frantic guessing game, as they had few visual clues to help them. While the dialogs were simple and clear, they demanded a degree of concentration difficult to achieve amidst the noise. After confusion, irritation set in:

Sefali: You can't even recognize Krishna here, normally he's blue.

Malati: Gunga and Bhisma normally wear white because it's a symbol of purity and truth.

Ranjit: All the strong characters are black, like Bhisma and Kunti but Bhisma should look more physically strong.

Sefali: Black seems to symbolize strength.

Ranjit: Duryodhana should wear red, shouldn't he? Red stands for blood, anger and fire.

Certain conventional visual codes had been flouted, such as the use of colors, usually symbolic of certain qualities and associated with particular character attributes. Such color classification and symbolism is to be found in many ancient religions and provides a kind of primordial classification of reality.[16] This was simply the tip of the iceberg. More alarming than the disruption caused by the visual codes was the transgression of deeply-rooted cultural codes, but this only became apparent upon viewing the Indian version. It was not until then that they were able to articulate the difference between these quite distinct iconographic styles.

Sefali: All the gods are born into royal families. In the Indian one you can tell the gods from humans but not in the English one. In the Indian one you can tell who is the king from what he wears, how he talks and behaves, you can tell by his strength. Like the gods, they actually show their strength and also when Krishna appears there's always joyful music. There are other details, like the king will always wear gold and the prince silver.

Sewanti: Like in the Indian one you can tell a baddy because he will be wearing black clothes and the music will have an evil feel to it, but in the English one you can't tell who's who, they've left it all to language, whereas in the Indian one everything contributes to the meaning, the way they speak and how they are spoken to, how they behave, what they wear, their clothes, jewelry, their actions, everything has meaning.

Malati: The respect is missing, like you would never hear Krishna being called by his name like that, it would always be Lord Krishna, you would never hear someone call their elder by their name, you would have to show them respect by using their proper title. Like in the Indian one people show Krishna respect by kneeling and kissing his feet. The way you greet someone, how you sit and talk, all these things are missing. These might seem like little things but they are very important.

The casting, the visual representation of the gods, the flouting of well established iconographic and cultural codes made it difficult for the Dhani family to "read" and therefore enjoy the Brook production. They expressed their distaste at its profanity.

Munni: It doesn't, you know, concern me.

Sewanti: They show the culture as if people lived in the jungle.

Lippi: Some of the actors can't act or speak properly, they've got funny accents.

Sewanti: They've spoilt the picture of the culture, they've done us disservice, really.

Munni: There's no, you know, no feeling in it, you can't feel for the characters.

Malati: They borrowed the story but not the culture, the culture is missing.

Ranjit: Mum says it left a bad taste in her moth and that she had to watch the Indian one to get her taste back.

Sewanti: You see, we can't accept Krishna being shown like he was just anybody. He's not given any dignity.

The lack of distinction between gods and humans is distasteful to them because the gods are not portrayed with due status, dignity, and respect. In contrast, the representation of the gods in the Indian version conforms to traditional iconographic conventions. Consequently, they can be worshipped on the screen, as are the popular images that adorn homes. Devotional viewing may take place at various moments or during segments of the serial, for example, the appearance of one of the gods may precipitate a devotional demeanor. Similarly, the narrative weighting afforded key actions, incidents, promises, and vows, and the narrational strategies of the serial may engender devotional viewing.

Narrative structure and narration

The experience of viewing a 6-hour televised drama is hardly comparable to the weekly viewing (every Saturday afternoon or evening if replayed on video) of a 45-minute episode of a ninety-two part serial. The Indian version is seen to resemble various soap operas. The young Dhanis claim that the Indian version is like a soap because it allows for greater identification with the characters and their dilemmas and a deeper affective engagement with them. In fact Ramanand Sagar, the director of Doordarshan's serial, chose unknown actors to encourage a closer identification with the characters/gods depicted.[17]

Malati: You get to know the characters much better in the Indian one and the funny or special things about them. Like Bhisma, in the Indian one whenever he gets a chance he is eating, he's playful and silly but aggressive when he wants to be.

Sefali: Another thing is that you can identify with the characters better, because it's slower, you get to know the characters you like and dislike, you can put yourself in their shoes, but not with the English one, they all seem far away, distant, but in this one you feel you're in it, you're involved.

The frequent moments of "high" melodrama, often involving the uninhibited expression of heightened emotion, are compared with similar moments in weekly American soaps like *Dallas* and *Dynasty*. Furthermore, they are compared not only in terms of their luxurious settings (the palatial homes in *Dallas* and *Dynasty* and the dazzling opulence of courtly life in *The Mahabharata*), but also in terms of their central preoccupation with good and evil. Other parallels with soaps are made: the complex interweaving of plots; the cliff-hanger endings, the pleasurable anticipation of viewing, intense involvement while viewing, subsequent discussions about what has happened in an episode, the mobilization of knowledge about past events in making sense of the unfolding story, and predictions about what might happen.

The addictive pleasures of the soap format are highlighted with reference to *Neighbours*. However, the Dhani children maintain that most of the trivial subplots in *Neighbours* which arise in one episode are simplisitically resolved in the next episode, on the following day. They contrast this with actions and events in the serialized *Mahabharata*, which may have repercussions over centuries and may contribute to deciding the fate of the world. The serial narration is contrasted with the economy and density of the narration in the English version which condenses and inflates the main narrative events, eliminating the many subplots.

Malati: It's like *Neighbours* because you get hooked on it.

Sefali: The English one has a beginning and an end but the Indian version seems to have no beginning and no end.

The serial narrative of the Indian version is better able to represent epic, cyclical, and mythical notions of time, which constitute the philosophical core of *The Mahabharata*. This enables the Dhani children to mobilize and develop their knowledge about the cyclical patterns of repetition, of birth, destruction, and rebirth in which human beings are caught until they escape by reaching "spiritual union with the gods." *The Mahabharata* as a whole is seen to represent one such cycle of birth, destruction, and rebirth – a game played by the gods in a previous era with continuing and profound significance for Hindus and others in the 1990s. This is contrasted with the linear conception of time in Brook's version.

The role of the narrator also differs between the two versions. In Brook's *The Mahabharata*, the story is narrated by Vyasa and transcribed by Ganesha (the elephant god who is an incarnation of Vishnu). A young Indian boy accompanies Vyasa and Ganesha. The children most closely identify with the boy:

Malati: I think the boy is an example of a human being and he's there to show us what we can gain from watching. The story is being told to the boy by Vyasa and he asks the questions that we would.

Sefali: You see, when the boy asks, "Do I have the same blood, do I come from the gods?," that is how the story starts, that is how the human race came about and we are like the boy, a part of the human race, it is telling us that we are all one.

In the English version we see Vyasa the narrator, whereas in the Indian version the narrator is invisible and given a divine quality. The story is directly narrated by Vishnu who does not appear in person but as a disembodied voice, a shadow emanating from heaven who represents Time:

Sefali: In the Indian one you see the shadow of the world going round, that symbolizes Time and destiny, which goes on and on, because Time waits for no one. It is the shadow that is telling the story. It is Vishnu. Vishnu is Time and Time rules the gods and the universe. Time is eternal.

Malati: When there's something important, like Bhisma's vow, he interrupts the story and explains things because some people might not understand the importance of it. The Indian one explains everything to you. It helps you understand the meaning of the story. The English one doesn't really explain the important things to you.

Sefali: Vishnu is Krishna and he is the only one who can tell the story. Without him there would be no story because Krishna is Vishnu and Vishnu is Time, that's why Krishna's got the Chakkar around his wrist, that's how you always recognize Krishna, by the Chakkar.

The Chakkar is a bracelet, a distinguishing feature of Krishna, symbolizing the circle of Time or eternity. Time is one of the central themes of *The Mahabharata* – although in contrast to the western notion, is not conceived of as linear but as cyclical. The children struggle to understand and express such complex philosophical notions with the help of the narrator. The narrator takes on a much more interventionist and didactic role in the Indian version. Unlike conventional soap operas in the west, this "sacred soap" does not allow the viewer to adopt a shifting point of view. The narrator provides the dominant discourse, guiding and leading the viewer to a "proper" understanding of themes and events. These didactic passages, which explain notions of Time or the interchangeability of the gods, narrated from the heavens, are rewound and reviewed and listened to by the family again and again until they arrive at some understanding of what is being explained.

For the Dhani children, one of the most beneficial features of the Indian version is the presence of subtitles. If something is not understood in Hindi, they can read the subtitles in English. Although the Dhanis' mother-tongue is Bengali, they understand Hindi very well, partly as a result of their long-term exposure to Hindi films. Hindi is also the language of religious worship in the temple. While Bengali is used to discuss the finer points of interpretation with their mother, the young Dhanis will use English among themselves. They learn Sanskrit by memorizing the songs in the Indian version, practice their Hindi by imitating the characters' dialogs, and are able to translate the private world of their religious beliefs and practices into what is for them the more public language of English.

Furthermore, in their eagerness to understand the full intricacies of the story and explore the philosophical depths of *The Mahabharata*, the gaps in their understanding of the TV serials have encouraged them to read various versions of the story in English and in Hindi. The interaction of various kinds of literacies (audiovisual and written), different linguistic registers, and different cultural systems allows the Dhanis to develop and intellectually benefit from their multi-lingualism. It also helps them to integrate their religious world-view into their everyday life more effectively. I also suspect that being able to articulate their religious views in a sophisticated manner in English allows them to feel a greater sense of pride in their religion. The Dhanis would be the first to acknowledge that these cultural and linguistic competences have been developed through their viewing of *The Mahabharata* over a two-year period.

Narrative weighting

One further difference between the two versions is in the dramatic weighting given to events. This has significant consequences for the Dhanis' readings. In general, the children perceive narrative events in the English version as unrealistic, magical, and metaphorical, whereas in the Indian version they are understood morally and literally. The perceived realism of events is a function not only of the different modes of representation employed but also of the religious beliefs they bring to the text and of their conviction that *The Mahabharata* recounts actual historical events. This has profound implications for their engagement in the dramatic process. The weighting given to events and actions, and the moments of tension, dramatic climax, and resolution are entirely different in the two versions. In order to demonstrate this point more fully let us compare how each version deals with two episodes of *The Mahabharata*: Bhisma's Vow, which occurs near the beginning, and Draupadi's Humiliation.

Bhisma's Vow Santanu, the king, is married to Gunga. They are gods who were cursed by Brahma (Gunga's father and The Creator) and sent to earth to suffer as humans. Upon marrying Santanu, Gunga made him promise that he would never question any of her actions. She gives birth to seven sons and each of them she drowns to save them from human suffering. The king is broken-hearted but he cannot ask her why she drowns their sons. On the birth of the eighth son he breaks his promise and saves his child. That child is Bhisma who is witness to the entire story. The children are able to interpret this seeming act of cruelty as being for the greater moral good. Gunga sacrifices her children because she knows they are cursed to suffer as humans. She is seen as possessing greater moral strength than her husband who, cursed to suffer as a human, acts with human frailty.

Years later, Gunga having disappeared and Bhisma become a grown man, King Santanu falls in love with Satiavati and asks her father for her hand. Her father will only agree to their marriage if King Santanu forbids Bhisma

370

to claim his right to the throne, thus allowing Satiavati's son to be the king's successor. The price is too high for the king because he loves and respects his son and rightful heir, Bhisma. But in an act of supreme self-sacrifice and devotion to his father, Bhisma makes a vow, renouncing the throne and promising to remain celibate forever. He hopes to prevent any contest over the throne in future generations. To reward his son for such moral strength, Santanu blesses Bhisma with the power to choose the time of his own death.

The dramatic weighting given to these events in the two versions is entirely different. In the Indian version the moral order is disturbed by Santanu breaking his promise never to question his wife and this is given dramatic effect by the music, acting style, and the narrator's interventions. Moral order is restored when Bhisma makes his vow. It is hard to convey the emotion and awe that this act inspired in the children:

Ranjit: In the English version they make it seem like it's just a little promise but in the Indian version, Bhisma's vow shakes the earth, thunder and lightning open up the skies. No human would be able to make a promise like that just to please his father. I love that bit, it's pure! If he does that for his father, imagine what he would do for his mother!

Lipi: In the English version you don't get all the background so you don't really understand the importance of the vow. If Bhisma had been king, the whole history of the world would have been different. There wouldn't have been a fight for the throne.

Furthermore, in order to underline the significance of this vow, the narrative flow is interrupted by shots of the heavens, accompanied by the narrator's voice saying: "Never has there been such a man." Thereafter follow scenes of intense emotional power, intimate exchanges between father and son revealing the king's guilt for his son's suffering which causes him to die a broken-hearted man. His father's death leaves a void and opens up the further problem of his succession; a theme which dominates the entire narrative. The movement of the narrative, from disruption to resolution to further disruption, is moral in nature. The intense emotional exchange between Bhisma and his father, which powerfully expresses the strength of kinship bonds and duty, has a profound affective impact on the Dhani children. Scenes such as these function as normative guides to conduct in the family and serve to reinforce established values of respect, loyalty, honor, obedience in their own family life.

By contrast, the English version emphasizes narrative events which are not very signficant to them. For example, Brook's production gives enormous weighting to the divine births of the Pandevas and Kauravas. Indeed, the births form the dramatic high point of the first part:

Malati: In the Indian one, Kunti never tells you where she gets her children from, it's taken for granted that the Pandevas are gods, not like in the English one where they had to explain that to English people because they probably wouldn't understand that they are superhuman, so you have to adapt it to them.

Sefali: It's like the idea of Dharma. Every Hindu person will know the importance of this word. It means law and duty. It's, like, the law upon which the order of the world rests, and if you don't get that, you can't understand *The Mahabharata*. It's like the idea of Karma as well. We know something about these ideas but they have to explain it for English people.

In the Indian version, certain cultural knowledge is assumed. In constructing and responding to the narrative, the children are able to draw upon this knowledge while also being able to position themselves as English spectators who need certain "taken for granted" things explained. But it would be a mistake to assume that this knowledge or cultural competence is somehow complete or equally shared and agreed upon among the Dhani children. On the contrary, they constantly battle with each other over differences in comprehension and details of interpretation in a manner similar to the way in which they discuss the intricacies of character and plot in *Neighbours*. Indeed the sanctity of a vow is easily translated into the importance of keeping a promise and used in judging a character's actions in *Neighbours*.

Draupadi's Humiliation   Another episode which was much discussed by the Dhani children was that of Draupadi's humiliation. It raised many questions about traditional gender roles. Draupadi is the wife of the five Pandevas. Yudhishtira, the eldest of the Pandevas, is cajoled into a game of dice with Duryodhana, the eldest of the Kauravas. His weakness for gambling leads him to lose everything the Pandevas possess. He even bets and loses his wife Draupadi. The Kauravas attempt to humiliate her and violate her honor by stripping her of her sari in public. Krishna intervenes and magically bestows upon her a sari of infinite length thus safeguarding her honor. This is a turning-point in *The Mahabharata* since her humiliation requires revenge to be taken by her husbands, and consequently the path to war is set. However, again the lack of narrative significance attributed to this event and the mode of its portrayal in Brook's version appeared inept and even shocking to the Dhani children:

Malati: In the English version when they drag her into the court, she lets everyone know that she shouldn't be seen in public because she has her period. In the Indian version they just hint at it. It's understood because she's wearing yellow clothes

372

and she's segregated – normally she's all dressed up like a queen.

Sefali: In the Indian version . . . the true strength of her character comes out. She questions all the men in the court . . .

Ranjit: And in the English one Bhisma looks at Duryodhana trying to strip her clothes off her. He would never do that.

Malati: They call her a prostitute and insult her really badly but the hurt of all this doesn't come across in the English one.

Sefali: In the Indian one, there's that amazing vision of Krishna. . . . Krishna performs the miracle. They don't show miracles in the English one.

Ranjit: She swears she will get her revenge and after that she keeps the wound alive.

Sefali: It's this incident which really leads to the war.

According to the Dhanis, the deep insult of Draupadi's humiliation, her self-defense, and Krishna's divine intervention in this episode are not given due weight and authority in Brook's version. To them, Draupadi represents a powerful symbol of female strength and authority. In the Indian version she rejects silence and her anger explodes in court. In doing so she raises a whole series of questions concerning her status as woman, as wife, as property, as slave, as subject, and as object – questions which Brook misses.

Critical commentaries on Brook's version which I have come across more recently, highlight Draupadi's humiliation as exemplifying Brook's 'orientalist' mis-interpretation of the epic. For example, one Indian critic, Bharucha, is clearly seething at what he calls Brook's "inter-cultural experiment," his "cultural appropriation" of The Mahabharata:[18]

> not once are we made to feel that Draupadi has been seriously wronged.
> . . . One never really senses the threat of rape in Duhsassana's handling
> of Draupadi. . . . When Draupadi wails, "Where is Dharma?," it seems
> like pointless hysteria, a case of a woman not being able to shut up on
> time.

The coincidence of viewpoint between Indian cultural critics, the Dhanis, and others whom I interviewed in Southall about The Mahabharata would suggest that such negative responses to Brook's "westernized" production are perhaps more widespread than this case-study can convey.[19] The lack of a clearly defined religious framework of reference, the lack of contextualization within the social and ritual processes of Hindu society, and the loss of humanity which Draupadi and Yudishthira undergo are but three of the other criticisms that Bharucha makes and which correspond with those of the

Dhanis. According to both, Brook does not have a sufficient grasp of the religious and philosophical basis of *The Mahabharata* or of Hinduism to convey the dramatic significance of certain events. Cultural codes and conventions which have powerful symbolic meaning are so frequently flouted that the credibility of the production is destroyed.

Articulating a religious world-view through a sacred serial

Talking about the two versions of *The Mahabharata* served as a catalytic agent or tool for the Dhanis which assisted them in exploring, developing, and articulating their religious conceptions of the world. Over a two-year period of viewing, the Dhani children were able to express their religious world-view with increasing and impressive sophistication. Clearly this cannot be explained by their viewing of the sacred serial alone. Not only domestic devotional viewing, but other interactions in the family and, of course, the temple provide the Dhani children with rich and ample opportunities to practice and educate themselves in the tenets of Hinduism. However, the serial form and its didacticism provided one of the most sustained and comprehensive contexts in which to explore and deepen their religious knowledge and beliefs.

We shall now examine the deeper philosophical questions that were raised in our discussions and inspired by our viewing. In particular, we shall now return to the moral paradox that presented itself to the Dhanis upon first viewing Brook's production. The reader will remember that on this evening the TV set was switched off at the point when Krishna persuades Arjuna to go to war, fight, and kill his cousins the Kauravas. Krishna is a god, an incarnation of Vishnu, and yet he engineers deceit and provokes war. In Brook's version of *The Mahabharata* this most important episode was given a mere 5 minutes in a 6-hour production and failed to make Krishna's words and actions comprehensible to them. They could no longer recognize Krishna and this provoked a crisis leading to the performance of a *puja* which allowed them to disengage from this profane rendering and enter into an attitude and a mood more conducive to transforming viewing into a spiritual experience.

Sita's Wedding, like Doordarshan's *The Mahabharata*, allows such a transformation to take place, and we have seen some of the textual features which are relevant to achieving this effect. In *Sita's Wedding*, Krishna is represented as "sweet" and unambiguous. He is portrayed in an almost monotheistic way, demonstrating "goodness" in his every word and deed. His character inspires the greatest love and devotion. Little wonder, therefore, that Krishna as he appears in Brook's version of *The Mahabharata* should so disturb and disarm the Dhani children. At this point in viewing Brook's production, it became very difficult for Malati and her family to continue believing in the divinity of Krishna.

374

Sefali: Why does Krishna persuade Arjuna to go to war if he is a god?

Ranjit: Why didn't he prevent the war from happening?

Malati: He throws away the Chakkar at the battle. He's no longer in control of Time. He lets the war happen.

Ranjit: He shouldn't have done that.

In an attempt to overcome their bewilderment at Krishna's incitement to war, the episode of Doordarshan's version of *The Mahabharata* which covers the battlefield dialog between Krishna and Arjuna was obtained from the video shop and we viewed it several times. A copy of *The Bhagavad Gita* was also borrowed from the local public library. One of the most sacred of Hindu texts, it is said to contain the essence of Hindu wisdom. Through repeated viewings, reading, and dialog the Dhanis learned to rationalize the moral paradox that confronted them and to articulate some of the more profound philosophical themes of *The Mahabharata*. The didacticism of Doordarshan's *Mahabharata* enabled them to learn the discursive register of *The Bhagavad Gita*'s teachings and to take pleasure in explaining its principles to each other and to me:

Malati: *The Gita*, it's strange because it makes you see good in bad and bad in good.

Sefali: That's because everything depends upon Time. In the early stages of Time, human beings lived close to the gods and things were in harmony. But then Time moves on to a stage where humans move away from the gods and then chaos comes. Krishna was born into the Age of Destruction.

Malati: You see, Krishna is starting the war off, he says to Arjuna that he must take the kingdom even though it means killing his own family. But you can't say Krishna is being bad, he's doing the best for mankind in the long run.

Through reviewing various episodes of *The Mahabharata*, an understanding emerges, and it is accepted that, while the actions of the gods may seem immoral in the short term, in the long term, they will be for the good:

Ranjit: If the world doesn't have Yudishthira for king then the world will be bad anyway. Krishna's intentions are good. He knows that you have to go through a bloody war, all because of justice. He does it to fulfil Dharma.

Sefali: You see, humans are ruled by Time and so is the world. Not even the gods can prevent some things happening. The world has to fulfill its own destiny in Time like human beings. That is our fate to be reincarnated until we attain Nirvana.

Thus repeated viewings of *The Mahabharata* enable them to articulate a cosmic view of the world which challenges and negates some of the certainties of their pragmatic everyday world. These distinctive world-views interact, coexist, and even contradict one another. This is evident when the radical nature of the ideas expressed about Time, the ambiguity of good and evil, and the paradoxical actions of the gods are implicitly taken back and *The Mahabharata* is reduced to a battle between "goodies and baddies":

> *Malati*: Krishna has taken sides with the Pandevas because before the battle he sees Duryodhana and says, "What do you want, my army or me?" and Duryodhana replies, "Your army," because he thinks that will help him win the battle. Then he goes to Arjuna and asks, "What do you want, my army or me?" and he replies, "You." The Pandevas brothers are more holy than the Kauravas. They make the right decision. That's why Krishna drives their chariot for them.

This is a consolation. By giving a reason why Krishna protects the Pandavas – they are good, unlike the Kauravas, and are worthy of his protection – the everyday pragmatic world-view rears its head again and the notions of good and bad are reinstated as categories.

> *Sefali*: *The Mahabharata* makes you see life like it's a battle between good and evil that everyone fights . . . a battle for, sort of, justice or Dharma, and when the equilibrium is lost you have chaos, like in *King Lear*.

For the Dhanis, the possibility for human beings in any stage of history to escape chaos by moral action is a necessity for pragmatic, everyday living. Thus, in the short term, through honesty, devotion, and performing one's duty, moral action is possible. However, in the face of eternity, the distinction between good and evil disappears. Indeed the consequences of moral actions can never be presumed:

> *Sefali*: Human beings have a free will, they can choose between different actions. Destiny or fate don't control everything, neither do the gods, people have some freedom to choose their path. But you can't do something good with the hope of getting a reward. You must first know what is right and then do it. But if you do something good you can't be sure the outcome will be good.

> *Ranjit*: We're created by the gods, but in the war if the Kauravas had won it, all the world would have been bad. But when Arjuna

and Krishna won the battle, they gave good people to the
world and even though there are always some bad people in
the world there are always good people to show them the way.
Anyway, [he chuckles] that's what the gods thought!

The application of ideas and beliefs derived from their religious world-
view, and undoubtedly developed and refined by their viewing of *The
Mahabharata*, is evident in many aspects of the children's everyday lives.
The examples in my data are too rich in detail and too numerous to recount
here. Suffice it to say that notions of Time, fate, destiny, enlightenment, self-
knowledge, reincarnation, and salvation are deeply embedded in their consciousness and frame their perceptions of everyday reality. The Dhanis'
responses to *The Mahabharata* have helped to make explicit the connections
and interactions between their beliefs, actions, and value systems. The
integration of religious and common-sense world-views becomes apparent in
the way that notions of Time, in particular the Age of Destruction, are linked
to the contemporary threats of nuclear and ecological disasters:

Sefali:　Time moves in circles and there are times when the world
moves away from god, don't you think it's a bit like that
now? We have the ultimate weapon, like the Pandevas, we
have nuclear weapons. Humans are destroying the environment. Birds and fish are dying because humans don't respect
them. Money is god today. *The Gita* teaches us that our
real wealth is our soul because that is eternal and that if you
act upon knowledge and do good then you can't be destroyed,
ultimately.

Malati:　If you think about it, why do holy men meditate? It's to get
their soul pure, so that the body becomes immaterial. You
have to lose desire and when you get to this state, Krishna
takes your senses, he comes into you and you see through him,
hear through him, everything you touch is through him,
everything. It is then you become harmonious with god –
that's Nirvana.

The high point of the entire ninety-two episodes of *The Mahabharata* came
during the *Bhagavad Gita* sequence, when Krishna shows himself in his
Universal Form. The sheer awe with which this sequence was viewed by the
family was as stunning as the images on the screen. Krishna only reveals
himself to those who are enlightened and when Arjuna, full of self-doubt
before the battle, asks Krishna, "How should I recognize you?" a shaft of
light shoots out from Krishna's hand into Arjuna's eye. A low-angle tracking
shot follows Krishna, surrounded by a golden aura, and, as he moves
gracefully through the air, his figure expands to dominate the screen and his
multifarious incarnations successively appear around him amidst flames and

shafts of water. These images represent to the believing viewer the trans-
migration of souls. Small human bodies float into the mouth of one of
Krishna's incarnations and out of another as if on a waterfall. It represents
for the Dhanis a divine vision. Inside Krishna's mouth one is offered a view
of eternity and the cosmos. It is as if Krishna makes an appearance in the
living room. For the Dhani children, full of awe and wonderment at this
vision, it is like Nirvana on TV. It is devotional viewing at its fullest
intensity.

Acknowledgments

Special thanks to the Dhani family, whose friendship I value much more than
the research, for sharing their lives with me. Many thanks to Dr Gerhardt
Baumann, a dear friend and fellow fieldworker in Southall, for his comments
on earlier drafts of this essay. My thanks to Tom Cheesman for his incisive
insights and criticisms. I am grateful, too, to Professor Adam Kuper whose
comments have improved the exposition of the arguments and for the
encouragement he provided. Thanks should also go to Nick Garnham who,
in a critique of a presentation of an earlier draft, helped me clarify my
arguments. Whatever problems remain are entirely of my own making.

Notes

1 *The Mahabharata*, one of the foundation myths of Indian society, is said to
enshrine the philosophical basis of Hindu religion, culture, and tradition. It is the
longest poem ever written. The first versions, written in Sanskrit, date back to the
fifth and sixth centuries BC, but by the third and fourth centuries AD it began to
take more definitive forms. Variations abound according to regional traditions and
to the interpretations of the writers. *Maha* in Sanskrit means "great" or
"complete." *Bharat* is the name of a legendary character, a family, and a clan.
In a more extended meaning *bharat* means Hindu, and even more generally,
"mankind" or "race." So *Mahabharata* is variously translated as the "The Great
History of Mankind" or as "The Great History of the Indian 'race'." It tells the
story of the long and bloody quarrel between two groups of cousins: the Pandevas,
who were five brothers, and the Kauravas, of whom there were 100. The family
quarrel over who will rule ends with an earth-shattering war, an Armageddon,
where the fate of the world is at stake. For centuries *The Mahabharata* and its
sister epic *The Ramayana* have been communicated in a variety of forms; in
Sanskrit, as well as in folk and classical theater; by village storytellers and mass-
produced cartoon strips. But now it is principally through TV that it is
communicated to people in India and to Indians in the diaspora.
2 Cited in *We Have Ways of Making You Think* (BBC2, 1992), a program about the
propagandistic uses of popular soaps and serials made by governments and
political parties in several countries including India. It highlights the ways in
which the TV serial *The Ramayana* was exploited by the BJP, the Hindu nationalist
party, in India. An unknown actress played the lead female role of Sita and was,
without any previous political experience, elected to parliament following a
populist campaign by the BJP.

3 The popularity of the TV serials broadcast by the government monopoly channel, Doordarshan, is unparalleled. On Sunday mornings all India stops while some 650 million people tune in simultaneously to view these "sacred soaps." The uproar that ensues if a community set breaks down or if viewing is interrupted by a power cut is well documented. Fans of these epic TV serials claim they have enormous social benefits as they encapsulate Hindu religious beliefs and reinforce traditional values while providing popular entertainment for the masses. However, critics claim that they are exacerbating the trends toward religious fundamentalism, intolerance, and ritualism which are seen to characterize religious communities in India today. It is argued that Doordarshan, in broadcasting such religious epics, is contravening the Constitution of India and eroding the basis of the secular state. As ever the dividing line between religion, culture, and politics remains elusive. See P. C. Chatterji, "*The Ramayana* TV Serial and Indian Secularism," *Intermedia* 17 5 (October–November 1989).

4 See Marie Gillespie, "Technology and Tradition: Audio-Visual Culture among South-Asian Families in West London," *Cultural Studies* 3 (2) (May 1989). This work is part of a more extensive study which examines the ways in which young Punjabi Londoners use TV as a resource in negotiating issues of cultural difference and identity. The research involved intensive and extensive fieldwork in Southall, a predominantly Punjabi town in west London and one of the largest "Asian" communities in Europe. Since the first phase of migration from the Punjab in the 1950s Southall has developed into a thriving commercial and cultural center. Its demographic majority are of the Sikh religion, although Muslims, Hindus, and Christians of various denominations are also represented. Rather than being a homogeneous "Asian community," social boundaries are marked by cross-cutting differences in national, regional, religious, caste, and linguistic heritage. For details of this research see my Ph.D thesis, "TV Talk in a London Punjabi Peer Culture" (Department of Human Sciences, Brunel University, Uxbridge, Middlesex, 1992). It is shortly to be published by Routledge, as *TV, Ethnicity and Cultural Change* (forthcoming, 1995).

5 See Vijay Mishra, in D. Williams (ed.) "The Great Indian Epic and Peter Brook," in D. Williams (ed.), *Peter Brook and The Mahabharata: Critical Perspectives* (Routledge, London: 1991), pp. 201–202.

6 Vijay Mishra, "Toward a Theoretical Critique of Bombay Cinema," *Screen* 26 (3–4) (May–August 1985).

7 For a full account see M. Gillespie, "Soap Opera, Gossip and Rumour in a Punjabi Town in West London," in P. Drummond and R. Paterson (eds), *National Identity and Europe: The TV Revolution* (London: British Film Institute, 1993).

8 *Raja Harischandra* (Phalke 1913), the first feature-length Indian film to be made, was based upon episodes from *The Mahabharata* and modeled upon Hollywood's early version of *The Life of Christ*, which Phalke had seen on a trip to the USA.

9 *Itihasa*: literally, "it is what actually was;" history.

10 The visual codes associated with the representation of Hindu deities have developed over centuries. However, the introduction of popular, mass-produced prints has resulted in fixed stereotypical portrayals of the gods. Tapati Guha-Thakurta has traced the changing iconography of popular religious picture production in India. She describes how the introduction of lithography presses and color printing in the domain of artisanal picture production led to the increasing turnover of gaudy chromolithographs of Hindu deities which have

loud flamboyant colours, dazzling costumes and majestic backdrops as their main trademark. These pictures have a rather tenuous basis in realism except in the solidity and roundedness they imparted to all forms. . . . The

379

humanisation and domestication of divinity, theatrical postures and expressions became part of the fixed stereotype of the gods.
(Tapati Guha-Thakurta, "Artisans, Artists and Mass Picture Production
in the Late 19th and Early 20th Century in Calcutta," paper presented
at the South Asia Research Conference, School of Oriental and
African Studies, University of London (summer 1986), p. 11)

11 Geertz defines religion as

(1) a system of symbols which acts to (2) establish powerful and pervasive moods and motivations in men [*sic*] by (3) formulating conceptions of a general order of existence and (4) clothing these conceptions with such an aura of factuality that (5) the moods and motivations seem uniquely realistic.
(Clifford Geertz, "Religion as a Cultural System," in Michael Banton
(ed.), *Anthropological Approaches to the Study of Religion*
(London: Tavistock, 1966), p. 4)

12 See note 2.
13 See Geertz, op. cit.
14 See Channel 4's program, *The Mahabharata: A Viewer's Guide to Peter Brook's Epic Film* (1989). For full production details see Garry O'Connor, *The Mahabharata* (London: Hodder & Stoughton, 1989).
15 Amar Chitra Katha's cartoons of *The Mahabharata*, published in Bombay, number about 200.
16 See, for example, Victor Turner, "Colour Classification in Ndembu Ritual," in Banton (ed.), *Anthropological Approaches to the Study of Religion* (London: Tavistock, 1966).
17 See note 2.
18 Rustom Bharucha, "A View from India," in D. Williams (ed.), *Peter Brook and The Mahabharata*. esp. p. 244.
19 See also Mishra, "The Great Indian Epic"; and in the same volume, Maria Shevtovsa, "Interaction and Interpretation: *The Mahabharata* from a Socio-Cultural Perspective;" and Gautum Dasgupta, "Peter Brook's Orientalism."

Select bibliography

Shari A. Novek

Allen, Jeanne. "Harlequins, Gothics and Soap Operas: Addressing Needs and Masking Fears." *Quarterly Review of Film and Video* 11, 1989, pp. 113–115.

Allen, Robert C. "On Reading Soap Operas: A Semiotic Primer." In E. Ann Kaplan (ed.), *Regarding Television – Critical Approaches: An Anthology*, Frederick, Md.: University Publications of America, 1983, pp. 97–108.

——. *Speaking of Soap Operas*. Chapel Hill, NC: University of North Carolina Press, 1985.

——. *Channels of Discourse, Reassembled: Television and Contemporary Criticism*, 2nd edn. Chapel Hill, NC: University of North Carolina Press and London: Routledge, 1992.

Ang, Ien. *Watching "Dallas:" Soap Opera and the Melodramatic Imagination*. London: Methuen, 1985.

——. "Melodramatic Identifications: Television Fiction and Women's Fantasy." In Mary Ellen Brown (ed.), *Television and Women's Culture: The Politics of the Popular*. London: Sage Publications, 1990, pp. 75–88.

Arai, Yoichi and Kaplan, Frederick I. "Growing Up and the Old Kentucky Home: An Examination in Japanese Popular Culture of Divorce and the Broken Family." *Journal of Popular Culture* 22, 1988, pp. 131–41.

Baehr, Helen and Dyer, Gillian (eds). *Boxed In: Women and Television*. New York: Pandora Press, 1987.

Barbatsis, Gretchen and Guy, Yvette. "Analyzing Meaning in Form: Soap Opera's Compositional Construction of 'Realness.'" *Journal of Broadcasting and Electronic Media* 35, 1991, pp. 59–74.

Brandt, George W. *British Television Drama*. Cambridge: Cambridge University Press, 1981.

Brooks, Peter. *The Melodramatic Imagination*. New York: Columbia University Press, 1985.

Brown, Mary Ellen. "Motley Moments: Soap Operas, Carnival, Gossip and the Power of the Utterance." In Mary Ellen Brown (ed.), *Television and Women's Culture: The Politics of the Popular*. London: Sage Publications, 1990a, pp. 183–198.

——. *Television and Women's Culture: The Politics of the Popular*. London: Sage Publications, 1990b.

——. "Strategies and Tactics: Teenagers' Readings of an Australian Soap Opera." *Women and Language* 14, 1991, pp. 22–28.

Brunsdon, Charlotte. "*Crossroads*: Notes on Soap Opera." *Screen* 22, 1981, pp. 32–37, reprinted in E. Ann Kaplan (ed.), *Regarding Television*. Frederick, Md.: University Publications of America, 1983, pp. 76–83.

Brunsdon, Charlotte and Morley, David. *Everyday Television: "Nationwide."* London: British Film Institute, 1978.

Brunt, Rosalind. "Don't Fade Away." *New Statesman and Society* 2, 1989, pp. 53–54.

Buckingham, David. *Public Secrets: "EastEnders" and Its Audience.* London: British Film Institute, 1987.

Buckman, Peter. *All For Love: A Study in Soap Opera.* London: Secker & Warburg, 1984.

Buerkel-Rothfuss, Nancy L. and Mayes, Sandra. "Soap Opera Viewing: The Cultivation Effect." *Journal of Communication* 31, 1981, pp. 108–115.

Butler, Jeremy. "Notes on the Soap Opera Apparatus: Televisual Style and *As the World Turns.*" *Cinema Journal* 25, 1986, pp. 53–70.

——. "'I'm Not a Doctor, But I Play One on TV': Characters, Actors and Acting in Television Soap Opera," *Cinema Journal* 30, 1991, pp. 75–91.

Cantor, Muriel and Pingree, Suzanne. *The Soap Opera.* Beverly Hills, Calif.: Sage Publications, 1983.

Cassata, Mary. "The More Things Change, the More They Are the Same: An Analysis of Soap Operas from Radio to Television." In Mary Cassata and Thomas Skill (eds), *Life on Daytime Television: Tuning-In American Serial Drama.* Norwood, NJ: Ablex, 1983, pp. 85–100.

Cassata, Mary and Skill, Thomas (eds). *Life on Daytime Television: Tuning-In American Serial Drama.* Norwood, NJ: Ablex, 1983.

Cassata, Mary, Skill, Thomas, and Boadu, Samuel O. "Life and Death in the Daytime Television Serial: A Content Analysis." In Mary Cassata and Thomas Skill (eds), *Life on Daytime Television: Tuning-In American Serial Drama*, Norwood, NJ: Ablex, 1983, pp. 23–36.

Coelho, Luiz A. and Perrone, Charles A. "Teledramas: A New Television Language." *Studies in Latin American Popular Culture* 7, 1988, pp. 89–95.

Compesi, Ronald J. "Gratifications of Daytime Serial Viewers." *Journalism Quarterly* 57, 1989, pp. 155–158.

Coward, Rosalind. "Come Back Miss Ellie." *Critical Quarterly* 28, 1986, pp. 171–178.

Craven, Ian. "Distant Neighbours: Notes on Some Australian Soap Operas." *Australian Studies* 3, 1989, p. 17.

Daniels, Therese, Gerson, Jane, Mercer, Kobena, Medhurst, Andy, Pines, Jim, and Bourne, Stephan. *The Colour Black: Black Images in British Television.* London: British Film Institute, 1990.

Derry, Charles. "Television Soap Operas: Incest, Bigamy, and Fatal Disease." *Journal of the University Film and Video Association* 35, 1983, pp. 4–16.

Docker, John. "Unprecedented in History: Drama and the Dramatic in Television." *Australasian Drama Studies* 1, 1983, pp. 47–61.

Downing, Mildred. "Heroine of the Daytime Serial." *Journal of Communication* 24, 1974, pp. 130–139.

Dyer, Richard. "Television – Quality Pleasures." *New Statesman and Society* 2, 1989, pp. 42–44.

Dyer, Richard, Geraghty, Christine, Jordan, Marion, Lovell, Terry, Paterson, Richard, and Stewart, John. *"Coronation Street."* London: British Film Institute, 1981.

Easthope, Anthony. *What A Man's Gotta Do.* London: Paladin, 1986.

Elsaesser, Thomas. "Tales of Sound and Fury: Observations on the Family Melodrama." In Bill Nichols (ed.), *Movies and Methods, Vol. II.* Berkeley and Los Angeles, Calif.: University of California Press, 1985, pp. 165–189.

Esslin, Martin. "The Art of Television Drama." *Boston Review* 9, 1984, pp. 12–14.

Fachel Leal, Ondina and Oliven, Ruben George. "Class Interpretations of a Soap

Opera Narrative: the Case of the Brazilian *Novela 'Summer Sun.'*" *Theory, Culture and Society* 1, 1988, pp. 81–100.

Feuer, Jane. "Melodrama, Serial Form and Television Today." *Screen* 25, 1984, pp. 4–16.

——. "Narrative Form in American Network Television." In Colin McCabe (ed.), *High Theory/Low Culture*. Manchester: Manchester University Press, 1986, pp. 101–114.

Finch, Mark. "Sex and Address in *Dynasty*." *Screen* 27, 1986, pp. 24–42.

Flitterman, Sandy. "The Real Soap Operas: TV Commercials." In E. Ann Kaplan (ed.), *Regarding Television*. Frederick, Md.: University Publications of America, 1983, pp. 84–96.

Flitterman-Lewis, Sandy. "All's Well That Doesn't End – Soap Opera and the Marriage Motif." *Camera Obscura* 16, 1988, pp. 119–127.

Frentz, Suzanne. "Soap Opera's Heroines: Helen Trent's Legacy." In Pat Browne (ed.), *Heroines of Popular Culture*. Bowling Green, OH: Popular Press, 1987, pp. 149–157.

——. (ed.). *Staying Tuned: Contemporary Soap Opera Criticism*. Bowling Green, OH: Bowling Green State University Press, 1992.

Geraghty, Christine. *Women and Soap Opera: A Study of Prime-Time Soaps*. Cambridge: Polity Press, 1991.

Gledhill, Christine. *Home Is Where the Heart Is*. London: British Film Institute, 1987.

——. "Pleasurable Negotiations." In Deidre Pribram (ed.), *Female Spectators: Looking at Film and Television*. New York: Routledge, 1988, pp. 64–89.

——. "Speculations on the Relationship between Soap Opera and Melodrama." *Quarterly Review of Film and Video* 14, 1992, pp. 103–124.

Goldberg, Adrian. "Beyond the Corner Shop." *New Statesman and Society* 4, 1991, pp. 28–29.

Goodwin, Peter. "The Road from *Coronation Street*." *Sight and Sound* 1, 1991, pp. 26–28.

Greenberg, Bradley S., Neuendorf, Kimberly, Buerkel-Rothfuss, Nancy, and Henderson, Laura. "The Soaps: What's On and Who Cares?" *Journal of Broadcasting* 26, 1982, pp. 519–535.

Gripsrud, Jostein. "Toward a Flexible Methodology in Studying Media Meaning: *Dynasty* in Norway." *Critical Studies in Mass Communication* 7, 1990, pp. 117–128.

Hanke, Robert. "Hegemonic Masculinity in *thirtysomething*." *Critical Studies in Mass Communication* 7, 1990, pp. 231–248.

Harrington, C. Lee and Bielby, Denise D. "The Mythology of Modern Love: Representations of Romance in the 1980s." *Journal of Popular Culture* 24, 1991, pp. 129–144.

Hobson, Dorothy. *"Crossroads:" The Drama of a Soap Opera*. London: Methuen, 1982.

——. "Soap Operas at Work." In Ellen Seiter, Hans Borchers, Gabriele Kreutzner, and Eva-Maria Warth (eds), *Remote Control: Television, Audiences and Cultural Power*. London and New York: Routledge, 1989, pp. 150–167.

Intintoli, Michael James. *Taking Soaps Seriously*. New York: Praeger, 1984.

Irwin, Barbara. "An Oral History of a Piece of Americana: The Soap Opera Experience." *Dissertation Abstracts International* 52, 1991, p. 11A.

Johnson, Randal. "Deus e o Diablo na Terra da Globo (God and the Devil in the Land of Globo): Roque Santeiro and Brazil's 'New' Republic." *Studies in Latin American Popular Culture* 7, 1988, pp. 77–88.

Joyrich, Lynne. "All That Televsion Allows: TV Melodrama, Postmodernism and Consumer Culture." *Camera Obscura* 16, 1988, pp. 129–153.

Kaplan, E. Ann (ed.). *Regarding Television*. Frederick, Md.: University Publications of America, 1983.

Kaplan, Frederick I. "Intimacy and Conformity in American Soap Opera." *Journal of Popular Culture* 9, 1975, pp. 622–625.

Katzman, Natan. "Television Soap Operas: What's Been Going On Anyway?" *Public Opinion Quarterly* 36, 1972, pp. 200–212.

Kielwasser, Alfred P. and Wolf, Michelle A. "The Appeal of Soap Opera: An Analysis of Process and Quality in Dramatic Serial Gratifications." *Journal of Popular Culture* 23, 1989, pp. 111–124.

Kingsley, Hilary. *Soap Box: The Australian Guide to Television Soap Operas*. Sydney: Sun Macmillan, 1989.

Kreizenbeck, Alan. "Soaps: Promiscuity, Adultery and 'New Improved Cheer.'" *Journal of Popular Culture* 17, 1983, pp. 175–181.

Kreutzner, Gabriele and Seiter, Ellen. "Not All 'Soaps' Are Created Equal: Towards a Crosscultural Criticism of Television Serials." *Screen* 32, 1991, pp. 154–172.

LaGuardia, Robert. *"Ma Perkins" to "Mary Hartman": The Illustrated History of Soap Operas*. New York: Ballantine, 1977.

Liebes, Tamar and Katz, Elihu. *The Export of Meaning: Cross Cultural Readings of "Dallas."* Oxford and New York: Oxford University Press, 1990.

Lopate, Carol. "Daytime Television: You'll Never Want to Leave Home." *Radical America* 2, 1977, pp. 33–51.

Lowry, Dennis T. and Towles, David E. "Soap Opera Portrayals of Sex, Contraception, and Sexually Tranmitted Diseases." *Journal of Communication* 39, 1989, pp. 76–83.

McAdow, Ron. "Experience of Soap Opera." *Journal of Popular Culture* 7, 1974, pp. 955–965.

McAnany, Emile G. "The Logic of Cultural Industries in Latin America: The Television Industry in Brazil." In Vincent Mosco and Janet Wasko (eds), *Critical Communications Review*, vol. 2. Norwood, NJ: Ablex, 1984, pp. 185–208.

McLoone, Martin and McMahon, John (eds). *Television and Irish Society*. Dublin: RTE/IFI, 1984.

Mander, Mary. "Dallas: The Mythology of Crime and Moral Occult." *Journal of Popular Culture* 17, 1983, pp. 44–50.

Manus, Willard. "*Lindenstrasse*: The Man Who Brought the Soaps to Germany [Hans W. Geissendorfer]." *Sight and Sound* 58, 1988–89, p. 6.

Matelski, Marilyn J. *The Soap Opera Evolution: America's Enduring Romance with Daytime Drama*. Jefferson, NC: McFarland & Co. Inc., 1988.

Mattelart, A. and Schmucler, H. *Communication and Information Technologies: Freedom of Choice for Latin America?* Norwood, NJ: Ablex, 1985.

Mattelart, Michèle. "Chile: Political Formation and the Reading of Television." *Communication and Class Struggle*, 1, 1979. New York: International General Edition, 1979.

Mattelart, Michèle and Mattelart, Armand. *The Carnival of Images: Brazilian TV Fiction*. New York: Bergin & Garvey, 1990.

Mayne, Judith. "*L.A. Law* and Prime-Time Feminism." *Discourse: Journal for Theoretical Studies in Media Culture* 2, 1988, pp. 30–47.

Miller, Daniel. "The *Young and the Restless* in Trinidad: A Case of the Local and the Global in Mass Consumption." In R. Silverstone and E. Hirsch (eds), *Consuming Technologies*, pp. 163–82. London: Routledge, 1992.

Modleski, Tania. "The Search for Tomorrow in Today's Soap Operas." *Film Quarterly* 33, 1979, pp. 12–21.

——. *Loving With a Vengeance: Mass-Produced Fantasies for Women*. New York: Methuen, 1984; Hamden, Conn.: Archon, 1982.

Moore, Suzanne. "Australian *Neighbours*: A New Utopia." *New Statesman* 116, 1988, p. 5.

Morley, David. *The "Nationwide" Audience: Structure and Decoding*. London: British Film Institute, 1980.

——. *Family Television: Cultural Power and Domestic Leisure*. London: Comedia, 1987.

Morton, Gerald W. and Clements Morton, Claire. "Three Hundred Years of Reruns: Renaissance Plots and Characters in Modern Soap Operas." *Markham Review* 11, 1982, pp. 32–36.

Mulvey, Laura. "Melodrama In and Out of the Home." In Colin McCabe (ed.), *High Theory/Low Culture: Analyzing Popular Television and Film*. New York: St Martin's Press, 1986, pp. 80–100.

Mumford, Laura Stempel. "Plotting Paternity: Looking for Dad on the Daytime Soaps." *Genders* 12 (1991): 45–61.

Neale, Steve. "Melodrama and Tears." *Screen* 27, 1986, pp. 6–22.

Nelson, Jenny L. "Soaps/Sitcoms: Television Genres as Situated Discourse." In John Deely (ed.), *Semiotics 1984*. Lanham, Md.: University Publications of America, 1985, pp. 137–145.

Newcomb, Horace. "A Humanist's View of Daytime Serial Drama." In Mary Cassata and Thomas Skill (eds), *Life on Daytime Television: Tuning-In American Serial Drama*. Norwood, NJ: Ablex, 1983, pp. xxix–xxxv.

Nochimson, Martha. *No End to Her: Soap Opera and the Female Subject*. Berkeley, Calif.: University of California Press, 1992.

Norton, Suzanne Frentz. "Tea Time on the 'Telly': British and Australian Soap Operas." *Journal of Popular Culture* 19, 1985, pp. 3–19.

Nown, Graham (ed.). *"Coronation Street:" 25 Years (1960–1985)*. London: Ward Lock Ltd, 1985.

Oram, James. *"Neighbours:" Behind the Scenes*. Sydney, Auckland, and London: Angus & Robertson, 1988.

Pennacchioni, I. "The Reception of Popular Television in Northeast Brazil." *Media, Culture and Society* 6, 1984, pp. 337–41.

Petro, Patrice. "Criminality or Hysteria? Television and the Law." *Discourse: Journal for Theoretical Studies in Media and Culture* 10, 1988, pp. 48–61.

Phil Redmond's "Brookside:" The Official Companion. London: Weidenfeld & Nicolson, 1987.

Porter, Dennis. "Soap Time: Thoughts on a Commodity Art Form." *College English* 38, 1977, pp. 782–788; reprinted in Horace Newcombe (ed.) *Television: The Critical View*, 3rd edn. New York: Oxford University Press, 1982, pp. 122–131.

Press, Andrea L. "Class, Gender, and the Female Viewer: Women's Responses to *Dynasty*." In Mary Ellen Brown (ed.) *Television and Women's Culture*. Beverly Hills, Calif.: Sage Publications, 1990, pp. 158–182.

——. *Women Watching Television: Gender, Class and Generation in the American Television Experience*. Philadelphia, Pa.: University of Pennsylvania Press, 1991.

Pribram, Deirdre (ed.). *Female Spectators: Looking at Film and Television*. New York: Routledge, 1988.

Rabinovitz, Lauren. "Sit-Coms and Single Moms: Representations of Feminism on American TV." *Cinema Journal* 29, 1984, pp. 2–27.

Radway, Janice A. *Reading the Romance: Women, Patriarchy and Popular Literature*. Chapel Hill, NC: University of North Carolina Press, 1984.

Rafferty, Terrence. "Television: Hot Spots." *Film Comment* 22, 1986, pp. 67–70.

Rodina, Michelle Lynn, Cassata, Mary, and Skill, Thomas. "Placing a 'Lid' on Television Serial Drama: An Analysis of the Lifestyles, Interpersonal Management Skills and Demography of Daytime's Fictional Population." In Mary Cassata and Thomas Skill (eds), *Life on Daytime Television: Tuning-In American Serial Drama*. Norwood, NJ: Ablex, 1983, pp. 3–22.

Rogers, Deborah D. "Guiding Blight: The Soap Opera and the Eighteenth-Century Novel." *The Centennial Review* 34, 1990, pp. 73–91.

——. "Daze of Our Lives: The Soap Opera as Feminine Text." *Journal of American Culture* 14, 1991, pp. 29–41.

Rogers, E. M. and Antola, L. "Telenovelas: A Latin American Success Story." *Journal of Communication* 35, 1985, pp. 24–35.

Rosen, Ruth. "Soap Operas: Search for Yesterday." In Todd Gitlin (ed.), *Watching Television*. New York: Pantheon, 1986, p. 45.

Rosenberg, Howard. "Ten Years After: In A Decade of *Dallas* Clones and 'Infotainment,' Was Anything Real?" *American Film* 15, 1989, p. 18.

Schemering, Christopher. *The Soap Opera Encyclopedia*. New York: Ballantine Books, 1985.

Seiter, Ellen. "The Role of the Woman Reader: Eco's Narrative Theory and Soap Operas." *Tabloid* 6, 1981, pp. 36–43.

——. "Promise and Contradiction: The Daytime Television Serials." *Screen* 23, 1982, pp. 150–163.

——. "Men, Sex, and Money in Recent Family Melodrama." *Journal of the University Film and Video Association* 35, 1983, pp. 17–27.

Shatz, Thomas. "*St. Elsewhere* and the Evolution of the Ensemble Series." In Horace Newcombe (ed.) *Television: The Critical View*, 4th edn. New York: Oxford University Press, 1987, pp. 85–100.

Sheehan, Helen. *Irish Television Drama: A Society and its Stories*. Dublin: Radio Telefís Eireann, 1987.

Sijl, Alessandro. *East of Dallas: The European Challenge to American Television*. London: British Film Institute, 1988.

Skill, Thomas. "Television's Families: Real by Day, Ideal by Night." In Mary Cassata and Thomas Skill (eds), *Life on Daytime Television: Tuning-In American Serial Drama*. Norwood, NJ: Ablex, 1983, pp. 139–146.

Spence, Louise. "Life's Little Problems . . . and Pleasures: An Investigation into the Narrative Structures of *The Young and the Restless*." *Quarterly Review of Film Studies* 9, 1984, pp. 301–308.

——. "Life's Little Problems . . . and Pleasures: Watching Soap Operas." *Dissertation Abstracts International* 51, 1991, p. 2547A.

Spigel, Lynne. "Detours in the Search for Tomorrow: Tania Modleski's *Loving with a Vengeance: Mass-Produced Fantasies for Women*." *Camera Obscura* 13–14, 1985, pp. 215–234.

——. "The Riddle of the Reader in Mass-Produced 'Women's Ficton.'" *Quarterly Review of Film and Video* 11, 1989, pp. 107–112.

——. "Television in the Family Circle: The Popular Reception of a New Medium." In Patricia Mellencamp (ed.) *Logics of Television: Essays in Cultural Criticism*. Bloomington, Ind.: Indiana University Press, 1990, pp. 73–97.

Strantzali, Evangelia Matthildi. "A Sociolinguistic, Conflict and Functional Analysis of Dialogue in the American TV Drama." *Dissertation Abstracts International* 48, 1988, p. 2618A.

Stratton, Jon. "Watching the Detectives: Television Melodrama and Its Genres." *Australasian Drama Studies* 10, (1987): 49–66.

Straubhaar, Joseph D. "The Development of the Telenovela as the Pre-Eminent Form of Popular Culture in Brazil." *Studies in Latin American Popular Culture* 1, 1982, pp. 138–150.

——. "Brazilian Television: The Decline of American Influence." *Communication Research* 11, 1984, pp. 221–40.

——. "The Reflection of the Brazilian Political Opening in the Telenovela (Soap Opera), 1974–1985." *Studies in Latin American Popular Culture* 7, 1988, pp. 59–76.

Tegler, Patricia. "The Daytime Serial: A Bibliography of Scholarly Writings, 1943–1981." *Journal of Popular Culture* 16, 1982; reprinted in Mary Cassata and Thomas Skill (eds), *Life on Daytime Television: Tuning-In American Serial Drama.* Norwood, NJ: Ablex, 1983, pp. 187–196.

Thompson, Douglas C. "Manuel Puig's Boquitas pintadas: 'True Romance' for Our Time." *Critique: Studies in Contemporary Fiction* 23, 1981, pp. 37–44.

Timberg, Bernard. "The Rhetoric of the Camera in Television Soap Opera." In Horace Newcomb (ed.) *Television: The Critical View*, 4th edn. New York: Oxford University Press, 1987, pp. 164–178.

Torres, Sasha. "Melodrama, Masculinity and the Family: *thirtysomething* as Therapy." *Camera Obscura* 19, 1989, pp. 86–106.

Tulloch, John. "Responsible Soap: Discourses of Australian TV Drama." *East–West Film Journal* 1, 1986, pp. 90–108.

Tulloch, John and Moran, Albert. *A Country Practice: "Quality Soap."* Sydney: Currency Press, 1986.

Varis, T. *International Flow of Television Programmes.* Paris: UNESCO, 1985.

Verzea, Ileana. "The Serial Novel and the TV Serial." *Synthesis: Bulletin du Comite National de Litterature Comparee de la Republique Socialiste de Roumanie* 9, 1982, pp. 75–80.

Vink, N. *The Telenovela and Emancipation.* Amsterdam: Royal Tropical Institute, 1988.

Wakefield, Dan. *All Her Children.* New York: Avon Books, 1976.

White, Mimi. "Television: A Narrative – A History." *Cultural Studies* 3, 1989, pp. 282–300.

——. *Tele-Advising: Therapeutic Discourse in American Television.* Chapel Hill, NC and London: University of North Carolina Press, 1992.

Williams, Carol Traynor. *"It's Time For My Story:"* Soap Opera Sources, Structure and Response. Westport, Conn.: Praeger (Media and Society Series), 1992.

Yeager, Gertrude. *"Angel Malo* ('Bad Angel'), a Chilean Telenovela." *Studies in Latin American Popular Culture* 9, 1990, pp. 249–262.

Zimmerman, Patricia R. "Good Girls, Bad Women: The Role of Older Women on *Dynasty.*" *Journal of Film and Video* 37, 1985, pp. 89–92.

INDEX

Aankhen (Eyes) 325
ABC 113, 166–7, 170, 203, 205–8, 234, 250, 339
Abercrombie, Nicholas 123
Abrahamsson, Ulla 52
Academy Awards 326
Active Life of Dolly of the Dallies, The 33
Adler, Mortimer 348
Adler, Renata 56
Adventures of Kathlyn 33
AIDS 200, 202–3, 206–8, 217–18, 224, 228
Aktenzeichen XY Ungelöst 238
Alcott, Louisa May 183
Alexander, Karen 53
All in the Family 110–11
All India Radio 324
All My Children 27, 150, 168, 170, 172–3, 175, 184, 186, 189–92, 201–2, 208
All the Rivers Run 118
Allen, David 133
Allen, Fred 35
Allen, Robert 35–6, 38, 50, 56–7 126, 128, 151, 153, 200, 292, 293, 306
Amado, Jorge 265
Amándote 265–7
Amar Chitra Katha (comic books) 347
American Home Products 36
American New World Entertainment 113–14
American Telephone and Telegraph (AT&T) 34
America's Most Wanted 238
Amerika 27
Amory, Merle 68
Amos 'n' Andy 27, 35, 41

Anderson, Benedict 114
Andy Gump 35
Ang, Ien 9–10, 52, 55–8, 60, 114, 128, 139
Angel Malo (Bad Angel) 263
Angélica, mi vida (Angelica, my love) 267
Angell, Barbara 131–2
Another World 38, 168, 186, 188
Anselmo, René 267
Antenna (Greece) 15
Antenne 2 (France) 115–16, 118
Apple Mary 32
Arabian Nights 29
Archers, The 12
Archie Bunker 110
ARD (Germany) 236, 238, 252–3
Arena (production company) 250
Aristotle 229
Arnheim, Rudolph 58
Arzoo (Desire) 325
As the World Turns 38, 145, 149, 153, 155–6, 158–9, 185, 187, 202–3, 208
Azcárraga Milmo, Emilio 267–8
Azcárraga Vidaurreta, Emilio 267

Back to the Future 40
Baehr, Helen 53, 57
Bal, Mieke 188
Baldwin, Kate 3, 11, 13, 16
Ball, Lucille 54
Bangkok Hilton 111
Banks-Smith, Nancy 107
Bapu, Morari 331
Barrett, Michèle 51
Barrow, Sydney 184
Barthes, Roland 27–9, 154, 191, 242
Baudrillard, Jean 141, 188

388

Bauer, Charita 19
Baywatch 113
BBC (UK) 8, 12, 16, 67, 85, 92, 103, 105–7, 117, 339, 357
Beijing Television Art Center 302
Bell, Bill 228
Ben Casey 250
Benjamin, Walter 309, 340
Bennet Jr, James Gordon 31
Berg, Louis 5
Berlitz 268
Beto Rockefeller 262, 279
Beverly Hills 90210 100, 109, 113
BFI (UK) 8
Bill, The 93
Bing Crosby Productions 250
Black Entertainment Network 15
Blackett-Sample-Hummert (advertising agency) 36
Blast 227–9
Blind Date 354
Bob 40
Bobby Benson 36
Bobo, Jacqueline 59
Boccho, Stephen 250
Bogaty Tozhe Plachut (The Rich Also Cry) 285; *see also Los Ricos También Lloran*
Bold and the Beautiful, The 15, 189
Bolshoi Theater 297
Bomb 227
Bouchers, Hans 57
Bourdieu, Pierre 160
Bourne Identity, The 28
Brand, Falsey 250
Breathed, Berke 40
Breen, Joe 202
Brighter Day, The 38
Broadside 53
Bronner, Dane 187
Brook, Peter 354–5, 357–8, 360, 364–5, 368, 371–4
Brooks, Peter 23, 127, 184, 193, 261, 302
Brookside 21, 66–75, 77–9, 85, 117
Brown, Barry 105–6
Brown, Mary Ellen 57
Brown, Meredith 149
Brown, Ruth 105–7
Brunsdon, Charlotte 10, 56, 136, 234
Buchanan, Pat 206
Buck Rogers 27
Buckingham, David 4, 10, 57, 69, 77, 90

Buniyaad (*Foundation*) 324–6
Buñuel, Luis 152
Burnett, Carol 188
Butcher, Helen 56
Butler, Judith 295

Caballo Viejo (Old Horse) 280
Cage aux Folles, La 110
California Clan (Santa Barbara) 253
Cagney and Lacey 54, 112
Callan, Mark 99
Canby, Vincent 99
Caniff, Milton 32
Capitol 184–5
Capra, Frank 101
Captain Midnight 37
Captain Video 37
Cassetta, Mary 53
Castro, Verónica 268–9, 297–8
Caughie, John 83
CBS 35, 38, 113, 172, 185, 208, 234
CBS Morning Program 185
Chamberlain, Richard 250
Chances 122–5, 128–9, 131, 134–42
Channel 4 (UK) 53, 67–8, 85, 98, 354, 364
Channel Nine (Australia) 113, 123, 134
Channel 13 (Chile) 263
Channel 2 (Australia) 106
Cheers 39, 112
Chicago Evening 33
Chicago Tribune 32–3
Chikhlia, Dipika 325, 342
Ching dynasty 339
Chips 268
Chitrahaar 324, 326
Chopra, Ramchand *see* Sagar, Ramanand
Church of England 108
Cinq, La (France) 117–18
cinq dernières minutes, Les (The Last Five Minutes) 116
Cisneros, Gustavo 268
Cisneros, Ricardo 268
Clive James Show 98
Coca-Cola 213
Colgate 36, 258
Collins, Joan 253
Collins, Michael 103
Collor, Fernando 266
Columbia Pictures 215
Commissaire Moulin 116
Commonwealth Channel Ostankino

One (Russia) 285–6, 289, 293
Communication 54
Comolli, Jean-Louis 152–3
Congress of People's Deputies 285
Connor, Dale 32
Coolangatta Gold 114
Cooper, Jeanne 149, 185, 228
Coral Pictures 13
Cornhill Magazine 30
Coronation Street 8–9, 17, 19, 21, 61, 66–7, 69, 85, 103–4, 117, 129, 164
Corpo e Alma (Body and Soul) 266
Correll, Charles 35
Cosby Show, The 40, 112, 253
Couchman, Peter 131–2, 138
Country Practice, A 103, 111, 118, 125, 128–9, 132–7, 139–42
Cousin, Rolande 115–16, 118
Coward, Rosalind 51, 56
Cowie, Elizabeth 309
Craven, Ian 100–1, 130
Cristal 256, 280
Cristal, Bob 13, 110–12
Crocodile Dundee 99, 106, 108, 113–15
Crofts, Stephen 13, 16, 129–31
Crossroads 8–9, 103–4, 137
Cruz, Celia 269
Cultural Revolution 301, 303–12, 314
Cuna de lobos (Cradle of Wolves) 280
Curran, James 57

Dacheng, Song 313
Dada-didi ki kahaniyan (Grampa and Grandma's Stories) 325
Daily Telegraph 106
Dallas 2–3, 9–10, 13, 17, 39, 55, 60, 62, 91, 99, 102, 116, 118, 124, 134, 139, 164, 173, 213, 215, 217, 220, 234, 236–9, 242, 244–7, 251, 253, 259, 286, 289, 367
Dangerous Women 111
Darling, Ron 188
Das, Arvind N. 342
Davidson, Doug 185
Davis, Jr Sammy 188
Dawson, Peter 67
Days of Our Lives 38, 147–8, 153, 182, 185
Daytime TV 187
de Balzac, Honoré 30
de Certeau, Michel 269
de Girardin, Emile 30–1
de Lauretis, Teresa 309

de Pádua, Guilherme 266
Delaney, Kim 150
Democratic National Convention (1992) 203
Denton, Lisa 158
Denver-Clan (dubbed German version of *Dynasty*) 238
Depression 32, 35
derecho de nacer, El (The right to be born) 278
Derrida, Jacques 138
Derry, Charles 151
Designing Women 54, 253
Desperate Desmond 32
Dhani, Lipi 55, 66, 71
Dhani, Malati 354–6, 363, 365–6, 368–9, 372–7
Dhani, Mrs 362
Dhani, Munni 366
Dhani, Ranjit 355–6, 363, 365–6, 371, 373, 375–6
Dhani, Sefali 355–6, 363, 365–6, 368–9, 372–3, 375–7
Dhani, Sewanti 356, 366–7
Dick, Philip 288
Dick Tracy 32, 34, 37
Dickens, Charles 1, 29
Dickson, Brenda 148–9
Dietrich, Marlene 156
Dighe, Anita 57
Dinas (City) 91
Dirk, Rudolph 32
Doane, Mary Ann 165
Dr Kildare 250
Doctor Who 332
Dohm, Gaby 242
Dolphin Cove 111
Don Tafler International 110
Donovan, Jason 100, 104, 115
Doogie Howser, M.D. 250
Doordarshan (India) 321, 324–6, 328, 346, 357–8, 360, 364, 367, 374–5
Dos mujeres, un camino (Two women, a road) 268–70
Downing, Mildred 53
Drummond, Philip 57
Du, Lao 305
Dumas, Alexandre 31
DuMont network 37
Dutacq, Armand 30–1
Dwyer-Dobbin, Mary Alice 206
Dyer, Gillian 57
Dyer, Richard 8, 56, 148–9, 152, 155

Dynasty 2–3, 13, 39, 91, 99, 124, 134, 164, 213, 215, 220, 223, 234, 236–9, 242, 244–9, 251, 254, 286, 289, 367

E Street 113, 131, 137, 139
EastEnders 4, 8, 16, 21, 66–79, 85, 98, 103–5, 111, 117
Easy Aces 35–6
Eco, Umberto 248
Edge of Night, The 19, 36, 38
Edison Company 33
EINSPLUS (Germany) 253
Ellis, John 147
Elsaesser, Thomas 166, 173
Emery, Lisa 208
En cas de bonheur (In Case of Happiness) 117
Episodes 113
Epstein, Mikhail 297
Erofeev, Viktor 298
Esclava Isaura, La (Isaura, the Slave) 264–5, 280, 283
Estrada, Erik 268
E.T. 115
ET-1 (Greece) 15
Eurocops 238
Evening American 33
Eveready 40
Express 227

Falcon Crest 13, 39, 215
Fallon, Michael 104
Families 103–4
Family Television 10
Fantasy Island 239
Fatal Attraction 115
FCC 267
Feininger, Lyonel 32
Feng, Lei 309–11
Ferrera, Juan 268
Feuer, Jane 39, 56, 244, 251
Fiallo, Delia 267
First Capital 267
First Hundred Years, The 38
First World War 31, 146
Fiske, John 10, 59
Flash Gordon 27, 32, 34
Flitterman-Lewis, Sandy 56–7
Flying Doctors 103, 111
Forsthaus Falkenau 252
Forsyte Saga, The 38, 117
Forsythe, John 247
Foucault, Michel 141, 190

Foster, Harold 32
Fox (production company) 238
Fox-Cat (production company) 234
Francis, Genie 147–8
Freud, Sigmund 159, 187–9, 192, 291, 295
Friedan, Betty 50
Frost, Lindsay 153, 155–9
Fuqua, Joy 22
Fuss, Diana 294

Gallagher, Margaret 52, 57
Galvin, Cathy 99
Gandhi, Mahatma 323
García-Márquez, Gabriel 261
Gay and Lesbian Alliance Against Defamation 207
Gay Switchboard 73
Gaytán, Bibi 268
Geary, Anthony 147–8
Gender and Mass Media 52
General Electric 34
General Foods 36
General Hospital 38, 112–13, 147–8, 166, 168, 170–1, 253
Generations 15
Geraghty, Christine 8, 18, 56, 57, 132, 139
Ghost Writer 40
Giddens, Anthony 230
Gillespie, Marie 16, 84, 119
Gita Press 341
Gledhill, Christine 56–8, 128, 141, 287, 260–1
Gloria's Romance 34
Golden Girls, The 54, 254
Gosden, Freeman 35
Gottlieb, Linda 206
Good Times, Bad Times see *Gute Zeiten, Schlechte Zeiten*
Goodman, Robyn 206
Gorbachev, Mikhail 234
Gordon, Noele 9
Gould, Chester 32
Govil, Arun 325, 331, 342
Grade, Michael 103
Granada Television (UK) 8, 85, 103
Grand Cyrus, Le 29
Grant, Cary 154
Graphic 30
Gray, Ann 55
Gray, Harold 32
Green Hornet, The 34

Greer, Germaine 50, 101, 130
Griffin, Grahame 102
Griffith, David Wark 278
Gross, Larry 199–200
Grossberg, Lawrence 188
Groves, Seli 185
Grundy Organization 13–14, 98, 103, 105, 108, 111, 130
Grupo Bronco 268
Guardian 104, 227–8
Guerra, Blanca 269
Guiding Light 2, 17, 19–20, 36, 38, 167, 178, 184, 188, 253
Guignol, Peggy 192
Guitiérrez, Eduardo 277
Gulf War 99
Gurevitch, Michael 57
Gute Zeiten, Schlechte Zeiten (Good Times, Bad Times) 14, 252

Habermas, Jürgen 125
Hagedorn, Richard 1, 12
Hairbreadth Harry 32
Hall, Deidre 182
Hall, Jerry 98
Hall, Stuart 8
Hallmark Inc. 267
Ham log (*Us*) 324
Hardy, Thomas 29
Health Visitors' Association 68
Hearst, William Randolph 31, 33
Heartbeat 250
Heat 227
Heimat (Homeland) 239
Heimatfilm 239
Herbert, Hugh 104
Hershfield, Harry 32
Herzog, Herta 58, 250
Hill Street Blues 39, 236
Hilmes, Michele 34, 37
HIV 202–3, 208
Hobson, Dorothy 4, 8–10, 54, 56, 58
Hoeppel, Rotraut 239, 249–50
Hogan, Hulk 188
Hogan, Paul 113
Hogan's Alley 32
Hoggart, Richard 8, 82
Holland, Tony 69, 72
Holmes, Ian 103
Holocaust 39
Home and Away 99–100, 103, 107, 113, 138
Honey, I Shrunk the Kids 115

Hood, Stuart 84
hooks, bell 51
Hotel 239
Hughes, Howard 149
Human Rights Commission 138
Humblot, Catherine 118
Hummert, Anne 36
Hummert, Frank 36
Hung-lou meng (The Dream of the Red Chamber) 339
Hurtado, Aida 59
Huxley, Aldous 343

I'll Fly Away 39
Illustrated Weekly of India 339, 342
Independent Broadcasting Association (UK) 103
Independent Television Commission (UK) 78
India Today 327, 329, 332, 341
Instituto Cubano de Radio y Televisíon (ICRT) (Cuba) 264
Insurgent Sociologist 54
Iser, Wolfgang 17, 187
Iskander, Rome 68
Island Son 250
ITV (UK) 85

Jack Armstrong, the All American Boy 27, 36
Jackie 104
Jacob, Carl 218
Jacob, Carol 218
Jagger, Mick 98
Jai Santoshi Maa 323, 361
Jameson, Fredric 177
Janes, Lucy 105
Jansettā 328
Janus, Noreene 53
Jesus of Nazareth 339
JNP (UK) 103
Joinville Studios (Paris) 364
Jordan, Marion 56, 129
journal des débats, Le 30
journal do Brasil, O 266
Judge Parker 32
Just Plain Bill 35–7

Kabelkanal (Germany) 253–4
Kahles, Charles W. 32
Kaplan, E. Ann 49, 52, 56–7
Kate and Allie 54
Katz, Elihu 102

Katzenjammer Kids, The 32
Kauffman, Helen 58
Kazen, Elia 278
KCOP/13 (Los Angeles) 108, 110–11
Keown, Dale 40
Kewang (Yearnings *or* Expectations) 2,
   17–18, 24, 301–3, 305–11, 313–15
Khanna, Padma 335
Khoj 326
Kilborn, Richard 83
Kinder-Kids, The 32
King, Barry 155
King Features Syndicate 33
Kingston, Hilary 126
Kleberg, Madeleine 52
Knots Landing 39, 109–10, 245, 253
Kojak 220
Kopkind, Andrew 297
Kreutzner, Gabriele 57
Krimis 238, 252
Krimmer, Wortham 207
Krishna avatar (Lord Krishna) 325
Krishna Janma (The Birth of Krishna)
   323
Krishnan, Prabha 57
Kristeva, Julia 292, 295
Kuhn, Annette 53, 56
Kuleshov, Lev 160

L'Astrée 29
L.A. Law 27, 236
La Plante, Lynda 54
Lace 39
Ladies World 33
Lahri, Sunil 325
Laibson, Michael 153
Lamb, Tiffany 114
Lampropoulos, Candy 190
Landarzt, Der 252
Lanka Dahan (The Burning of
   Lanka) 323
Lash, Scott 123
Lass of the Lumberlands, A 34
Lattanzi, Matt 114
Lau, Laurence 150
Law and Order 40
Le Pen, Jean-Marie 115–16
Leach, Penelope 285
Leal, Ondina 11
Leavitt, David 202
Lederer, Hanni 187
LeDoux, Harold 32
Leibes, Tamar 102

León, Laura 268
Lesage, Julia 246
Lever Brothers 36, 258
Lewis, Lisa 55
Liddiment, David 103
Liebes, Tamar 57
Lifetime 15
Lindenstrasse, Die 238
Literaturnaia Gazetta 287
Little Nemo in Slumberland 32
Little Orphan Annie 27, 32, 36
Liu, Marc 186
Livingston, Sonia 57
Lone Ranger, The 34
Longhurst, Brian 123
Lopate, Carol 54, 56, 234
Lopez, Ana 23
Lopez-Pumarejo, Tomas 11
Lord and Thomas (advertising agency)
   35
Lorde, Audre 193
Lorenzo James 36–7
Lorimar (production company) 234, 250
Lost in Space 106
Loughton, Roger 103
Love and War 236
Love Boat 239
Love of Life 38
Lovell, Terry 8, 56, 60–1
Loving 15, 184
Lucci, Susan 150
Lucecita 280
Lucille Love, Girl of Mystery 33
Lucky Charms (breakfast cereal) 40
Lumière Brothers (French production
   company) 323
Lutgendorf, Philip 2
Lynch, David 236

Ma Perkins 27, 36–8
McArthur, Colin 82, 85
McCay, Winsor 32
McCormack, Thelma 58
McCormick, Cyrus 33
McCready, John 69
McCrindle, Jean 56
MacDonald, Dwight 4
McDonalds 5, 213
McFarlane, Tod 40
McGoohan, Patrick 110–11
McKenna, Christopher 208
McLachlan, Craig 100
MacLaughlin, Don 145, 149

Macluhan, Marshall 339
McNamara, James 114
MacNeil, Robert 343
Mad Max Beyond Thunderdome 115
Madonna 100
Magnate, El 267
Mahabharata, The 354–65, 367–70, 372–7
Maigret 116
Malone, Michael 205–8
Mambo Kings 269
Mandi House 324–5, 328; *see also* Doordarshan
Mapplethorpe, Robert 307
Marchand, Roland 220
Marcus, Steven 124
Marcus Welby, M.D. 250
MaríElena 267–8
Marienhof 252
Mark Trail 37
Marseillaise, La 152
Marsh, Gwenda 138, 142
Martín-Barbero, Jesús 257, 263
Marx, Karl 214
Mary Noble: Backstage Wife 37
Mary Worth 32
Master of the Game 39
Masterpiece Theatre 17, 40
Matelski, Marilyn 53
Mattelart, Armand 11, 223
Mattelart, Michèle 11, 56
Mayflower Madame 184
Maxon, Rex 32
Mazziotti, Nora 11
Meech, Peter 83
Meibion Glyndwr (Sons of Glyndwr) 89
Melrose Place 39, 113
Méndez, Lucia 267
Menendez: A Murder in Beverly Hills 28
Mercer, Kobena 307
Merck, Mandy 202
Mersey Television (UK) 85
Metz, Lee 190
MGM 250
Midweek 68
Miller, Daniel 16
Miller, Nancy K. 183
Million Dollar Mystery, The 33
Minder 93
Minh-ha, Trinh T. 187
Minogue, Kylie 100, 104, 115–16, 119
Mission: Impossible 114
Modleski, Tania 7, 10, 52, 54–6, 58, 168, 176, 201–2, 234, 247, 311, 313
Mona Lisa 245
Monde, Le 118
Moore, Mary Tyler 54
Morales, Marilyn 190, 192
Moran, Albert 57
Morgan, Debbie 191
Morley, David 10, 84, 234
Moscow Times 286
Moscow Tribune 286
Moskovsky Komsomoletz 286
Motion Picture Story Magazine 146
Moxon, Joseph 29
MTM (production company) 236
MTV 15, 159
Mulvey, Laura 178
Mumford, Laura Stempel 19
Murdoch, Rupert 104
Murphy Brown 54, 253–4
Murray, Les 107
Musil, Robert 187
Mutt and Jeff 35
Myrt and Marge 35
mystères de Paris, Les 27
Mystery 40

Naipaul, V. S. 221
NAMES Project AIDS Memorial Quilt 204, 207
Nandy, Ashish 347
National Enquirer 202–3
National Socialist 240
National Viewers' and Listeners' Association 67
Nationwide 10
Narayan, R. K. 329, 332
Natraj Studios (India) 325
NBC 5, 15, 34–5, 37, 182, 208, 236, 238, 250
NBC Blue Network 35
Neale, Steve 294–5
Neighbours 3, 13–14, 69, 92, 98–119, 125, 128–33, 135–7, 139–42, 361, 368, 372
New Star 302
New York Daily News 32, 111
New York Morning Journal 31–2
New York Times 301
New York World 31
Newcomb, Horace 56
Nintendo 341
No Boundaries 221
Northern Exposure 236, 250

Nukkad (Streetcorner) 324
Number 96 103, 124
Nursing Times 68
NYPD Blue 27, 39

O'Brien, Peter 100, 104
One Life to Live 167, 170, 203, 205–8
Orr, Martha 32
Orr, Peggy 190
Ortiz, Fernando 278
Ortiz, Renato 11
O'Sullivan, Judith 32
Our House 182
Outcault, Richard Felton 31–2
Outland 40
Ovaltine 36

Pachauri, Jagdish 345
Panorama 221
Paradise Beach 113–14
Paterson, Richard 56–7
Pathè (French film company) 28, 33
patria argentina, La 277
Pawar, Lalita 335
PBS 16, 38, 40
Pearl, The 27
Pearson, Tony 69
Penley, Constance 55
People's Liberation Army 309
Perenchio, Jerrold 268
Perez, Daniela 266
Perez, Gloria 266
Perils of Pauline, The 27, 33
Pero sigo siendo el Rey (But I am Still King) 280
Petty, Moira 102
Peyton Place 2
Phalke, Maharashtrian Brahman Dadasaheb 322–3
Phantom Rider, The 27
Phillipe, Ryan 207–9
Phillips, Anne 51
Phillips, Irna 36, 58, 167, 234
Photoplay 146
Picket Fences 39
Pictures of Women collective 53
Pillsbury Company 5, 36
Pilon, Daniel 188
Pingree, Suzanne 215
Pinne, Peter 106, 109, 111, 113
Pitt 40
Pobol y Cwm (People of the Valley) 81–2, 84–8, 90–2, 95–6

Por estas calles (In These Streets) 266
Postman, Neil 335, 342–4
Premiere 40
Press, Andrea 55, 57
presse, La 30
Prime Suspect 54
Prisoner 110
Prisoner: Cell Block H 103, 111
Pro7 (Germany) 252–3
Procter & Gamble 15–16, 36, 38, 146, 215
Professional Teachers Association 67
Protele (Mexican) 267
Proust, Marcel 229
Public Opinion Quarterly 6
Public Secrets 4
Pulitzer, Joseph 31
Punch 227–8

QBVII 39
Quiroz, Maria Teresa 11
QW 207

Radio Caracas TV (Venezuela) 13, 256, 259, 266
Radio Corporation of America (RCA) 34
Radio Marti (Cuba) 264
Radio Research Bureau 58
Radner, Janice 177
Radway, Hilary 51, 168, 175, 177
Railroad Riders 27
Rajah Harishchandra 323
Rakow, Lana 54
Ralston cereal 36
Ram Rajya 323
Ramayana, The, or *Ramayan* 2–3, 17, 321, 323, 326–9, 332, 339, 341–6, 355–7, 360, 363
Raymond, Alex 32
Rear Window 154
Rector, Monica 11
Redmond, Phil 21, 67, 69
Reed, Margaret 185
Renoir, Pierre 152–3
Republican National Convention (1992) 203, 206
Restless Years, The 14
Return to Eden 118
Rich Man, Poor Man 39
Richard, Cliff 104
Richardson, Dorothy 183
Richardson, John H. 40

Richmond Hills 103
Ricoeur, Paul 229–30, 232
Ricos También Lloran, Los (The Rich Also Cry) 17, 280, 283, 285–93, 295, 296, 299
Right to Reply 67
Riordans, The 22, 85
Rise of the Goldbergs, The 35
Roach, John 105
Robbins, Kevin 84, 234
Rocky I–IV 40
Rofel, Lisa 2, 18, 24
Rogers, Everett M. 257
Rogers, Suzanne 185
Rogers, Tristan 113
Rogers, Will 35
Rolling Stone 40
Romance of Helen Trent, The 36
Root, Jane 57
Roots 38
Roque Santiero 23, 276, 280
Roseanne 253–4
Roseanne 112, 253–4
Rovin, Sam 208
Rowbotham, Sheila 50
Royal Family 104, 108
RTL (Germany) 236, 252–3
Rudder, David 218, 220
Runyeon, Frank 148–50, 156–9
Ryan, Meg 153, 155–9
Ryan, Michelle 82
Ryan's Hope 188

S4C (Sianel Pedwar Cymru/Channel 4 Wales) 81, 85
Sagar, Prem 341
Sagar, Ramanand 321, 325–6, 328–9, 331–41, 344–9, 367
St Augustine 229
St. Elsewhere 39, 236
Salvador da Patria, O 257
Sampoorna Ramayana 323, 329
Santa Barbara 101, 116, 118, 253, 286
Saralegui, Cristina 269
Sarris, Andrew 99
SAT1 (Germany) 252
Saturday Review 292
Saunders, John 32
SBS (Australia) 98
SBT (Brazil) 259
Schechner, Richard 338
Schement, Jorge Reina 257
Schlesinger, Philip 84

Schwarzwaldklinik, Die 234–40, 243–6, 249–52, 254
Scoop 104
Scruples 39
Seall, Eric 105
Search for Tomorrow 27, 38, 186
Second World War 216
Secrets of Lake Success, The 208
Seiter, Ellen 56–9
Selig (film company) 33
Selinger, Henry 35
Shan, Tang 311
Shanghai Bund, The 302
Shifu, Yu 307
Shiralee, The 111
Shree Geeta Press 341
Shukla, Ramnarayan 329
Sicher ist Sicher (Secure is Secure) 252
siècle, Le 30
Silj, Alessandro 237–8
Simmel, Georg 214, 231
Simplemente María 265, 267
SIN (Spanish International Network) 267
Sinclair, John 257
Singh, Dara 325
Sinha Moca 253
Sippy, Ramesh 324
Sirk, Douglas 278
Sisters 39
Sita's Wedding 355–8, 374
Skill, Thomas 53
Sky Channel (UK) 113
Slide, Anthony 33
Smith, Julia 67, 69, 72
Smith, Marilyn Crafton 53
Soap 27
Soap Opera Digest 148–9, 151, 157, 185–6, 191, 199, 207
Soap Opera Digest Award Show 203
Soap Opera NOW! 207
Sobchak, Anatoly 291
Spawn 40
Spelling, Aaron 234, 239, 250
Spence, Louise 10
Spielberg, Steven 332
Spigel, Lynn 55
Spindler-Brown, Angela 53
Springfield Story, Die (Guiding Light) 253
Square One 40
Stamp Act of 1712 30
Star Trek 39, 332

Star Trek: Deep Space Nine 39
Star Trek: The Next Generation 39
Star Wars 40
Stella Dallas 36–7
Stern, Lesley 56
Stevens, Greg 138
Steiner, Linda 53
Stewart, James 154
Stewart, John 56
Stratton, Jon 114, 127, 293
Straw, Jack 104
Streep, Meryl 160
Sue, Eugene 30–1
Sullivans, The 103, 111
Superbowl 326
Swan, Michael 185
Swan Lake 297
Swanson, Gillian 56

Tarzan 32
Tasters' Choice coffee 40
Tatort 238
Taylor, Elizabeth 188
Taylor, Rod 113
Teen Beat 289
Tele5 (Germany) 252
Tele Azteca Channel 13 (Mexico) 268
Telemundo (USA) 259, 267, 268
Televisa (Mexico) 2–3, 11, 13, 15, 256–7, 259, 267, 268, 276, 283
Temple, Shirley 156
Terence Higgins Trust 73
Terry and the Pirates 32, 37
TFI (France) 118
Thaper, Romila 346–7
That Obscure Object of Desire 152
Thatcher, Margaret 104
Thompson, Edward P. 8, 82
Thompson, John O. 154–5
Thomson, David 154
Thornbirds, The 118
Till Death Do Us Part 110
Times of India 342–3
Today's Children 5
Tolkien, J. R. R. 288
Tolstoy, Leo 339
Tom Mix 36
Top Models 116
Topacio 256, 265
Townsend, E. W. 32
Treichler, Paula 54
Trenker, Luis 239

Trollope, Anthony 29
Tuchman, Gaye 53, 56
Tulloch, John 57
TV-Globo (Brazil) 3, 11, 13, 15, 256–7, 259, 262, 264–5, 276, 283
TV Guide 147, 149, 185–6
TV-Tupi (Brazil) 262
Twentieth Century Fox 250
24 Horas 268
Twin Peaks 27, 123, 142, 236
Two in Twenty 53

Undersea Kingdom 34
UNESCO 52
Universal 250
University of Birmingham, Centre for Contemporary Cultural Studies 9
Univisión (Mexico) 259, 267–9
Unser Lehrer, Doktor Specht (Our Teacher, Dr Specht) 252
Unsolved Mysteries 238
USA Today 109

Vaid-Fera, Mimi 333
Vale Tudo (Anything Goes) 264
Valentina 268–9
Valles, Awilda 190, 192
van den Haag, Ernest 4
van Zoonen, Liesbet 52, 57
Vanishing, The 110
Variety 108, 110, 115, 256, 258, 267
Vasudev, Kumar 324
Vater Braucht Eine Frau (Father Needs a Wife) 252
Venevisión (Venezuela) 259, 268
Vera Wesskamp 252
Verlorene Sohn, Der (Prodigal Son) 239, 241
Vertigo 154
Vicks 150
Video 9 96
Vidor, King 278
Vikram aur vetal (King Vikram and the Vampire) 325
Village Roadshow *see* Channel Nine
Vink, Nico 23
Voisin, voisine 117
Voisins, Les 115
Vrindavan Studios (India) 326

Wadia, Homi 323
Wall Street 110
Wall Street Journal 109–10

Wallace, Michèle 52
Walton, Jess 185
Wartella, Ellen 54
Warth, Eva-Maria 57
Washington Post 2
Watson, Reg 98, 104, 110, 130
Watt, Ian 125–6
Weaver, Sylvester 37
Westinghouse 34
WGN 35
What Happened to Mary? 33
When Harry Met Sally . . . 159
White, Mimi 151
White, William 34
White-Haired Girl 302
Whitehouse, Mary 67
Who Will Marry Mary? 33
Wild Palms 27, 39
Willeman, Paul 83
Williams, Darnell 191
Williams, Raymond 8, 81–2, 84, 125, 146
Wiltech (razorblades) 332
Windship, Janice 56, 60

Wise Guy 39
Wolfe, Tom 40
Woman 104
Woman to Remember, A 37
Woman's Day 104
Wonder, Stevie 188
WWOR/9 (New York) 108, 111

Xianliang, Zhang 313
Xiaolan, Huang 310

Years of Our Lives 112
Yellow Kid, The 32
Yeltsin, Boris 135, 297
Ying, Mo 311
York, John J. 113
Young and the Restless, The 148–9, 172, 184–5, 188–9, 214–17, 219–22, 224, 226–8, 230
Young Doctors 103, 118

ZDF (Germany) 234, 236–9, 245, 251–3
Zola, Emile 31